The Child and the
ENGLISH
LANGUAGE ARTS

Fifth Edition

The Child and the
ENGLISH
LANGUAGE ARTS

Mildred Donoghue

California State University, Fullerton

 Wm. C. Brown Publishers

Book Team

Editor *Chris Rogers*
Developmental Editor *Sue Pulvermacher-Alt*
Production Coordinator *Carla D. Arnold*
Photo Editor *Carrie Burger*

 Wm. C. Brown Publishers

President *G. Franklin Lewis*
Vice President, Publisher *George Wm. Bergquist*
Vice President, Publisher *Thomas E. Doran*
Vice President, Operations and Production *Beverly Kolz*
National Sales Manager *Virginia S. Moffat*
Advertising Manager *Ann M. Knepper*
Marketing Manager *Kathy Law Laube*
Production Editorial Manager *Colleen A. Yonda*
Production Editorial Manager *Julie A. Kennedy*
Publishing Services Manager *Karen J. Slaght*
Manager of Visuals and Design *Faye M. Schilling*

Part Opening Photographs: Part A, © James L. Shaffer; Part B,
© James L. Shaffer; Part C, © Richard Anderson; Part D, © James
L. Shaffer; and Part E, © Dianne Carter.

Cover photo by Bob Coyle

Cover design by Mary Sailer

To my children,
Kathleen and James,
with their quiet respect for the
English language

Contents

Contents

Preface

The most potent discipline in the entire elementary curriculum is deemed to be the English language arts; it constitutes the foundation for all other subjects commonly taught to children. Certainly no young student can gain appreciably in the mastery of one language art (or skill) without advancing simultaneously in at least two others because they all reinforce and complement one another consistently.

Research justifies such an emphasis on an integrated approach to language arts instruction because none of the arts and skills can realistically be taught or learned in total isolation from the others. After several years of determined effort, however, the critical aspects of such an integrated program still remain threefold. First, there is a professional need for a basic understanding of each individual language art or skill. Second, there is a professional need for resolving the crucial problem of implementation. And lastly, there is a professional need to explain convincingly to parents and other community members what it is we are doing and why. In other words, we must comprehend the parts that make up the whole, but we must also comprehend how to combine all of them effectively as one entity and receive public support for our monumental task. All three critical aspects of an integrated program have been uppermost in my mind during the preparation of this fifth edition.

Major textual changes in this edition include the following. In the Reading section is a new chapter, entitled "Reading and Study Skills," which includes not only study skills per se but also library and locational skills, book utilization skills, organizational skills, and reading flexibility skills. The section on Writing begins with written composition and also covers separately the three major writing tools: handwriting, spelling, and grammar. The final section, entitled "Language Arts for Every Child," stresses the contemporary need for teaching linguistically differing children. And among the appendicies, the list of media resources for elementary school language arts is confined to one hundred entries, all of which have received national or international awards.

Pedagogical aids that are introduced or refined for this edition include short lists of major goals, which open each chapter, and discussion questions, suggested projects, and lists of related and recommended readings from 1984–1989, which conclude each chapter. Continued is the challenging "Discover As You Read This Chapter Whether" section, which begins each chapter with a series of detailed true or false statements that provoke greater student interaction with the text. Continued also are the popular descriptions for building language arts learning centers found in the projects sections of most chapters.

Finally, every portion of the book has been revised substantially in an effort to keep inservice and preservice teachers aware of current and pertinent research findings.

For this edition I have relied on my colleagues and graduate students for criticism and commentary, and I wish to thank them for their efforts. I would also like to thank the reviewers who were involved at each stage in the progress of the manuscript: Louise Giddings, University of South Alabama; Elaine Vilscek, University of Northern Colorado; Emily Johnson, West Georgia College; and Marilyn Yoder, Iowa Wesleyan College.

Although many persons helped during the preparation of this book, I particularly wish to express my appreciation to Chris Rogers, Associate Editor; Sue Pulvermacher-Alt, Developmental Editor, and Carla Arnold, Production Coordinator, who encouraged and supported my writing.

Mildred R. Donoghue

Preface

The Child and the
ENGLISH
LANGUAGE ARTS

Part A Foundations

Chapters

Language and the Child Learner

1

Major Chapter Goals

After studying Chapter 1, the reader will be able to

1. Distinguish among the four major theories concerning language acquisition in children.
2. Explain how to foster language development in prekindergartners as well as in school beginners.
3. List provisions for meeting individual differences among elementary language learners.

Discover As You Read This Chapter Whether*

1. Preschool children learn whatever language is used by their families and playmates.
2. Learning experiences affect only the productive modes of the language arts.
3. Psycholinguists have finally agreed on how young children acquire language.
4. When boys and girls enter kindergarten, their phonological development is complete.
5. Children use syntax (or word order) correctly from the very beginning.
6. Girls and boys must be active participants in the language-learning process.
7. Language acquisition and the thought processes always develop at the same rate.
8. Children's language and thought patterns differ from those of adults.
9. Elementary teachers are especially concerned with the students' concrete operations period described by Piaget.
10. Responsible teachers provide for individual differences in language abilities.

*Answers to these true-or-false statements may be found in Appendix 5.

Small children are not taught a language but learn it by themselves without conscious effort and application. Because they seem to possess an inborn faculty for language generally, the language they learn depends wholly on the language—or languages—to which they are exposed until about the age of puberty.

By the time children are ready for kindergarten, they already have marvelous control over the pronunciation and syntax (word order) of their native American English because they have learned it from their families and playmates. The school then begins to share with home and community the responsibility for the children's language development. Both inside and outside the school environment, the children are continually increasing their command of the language through informal means: conversing; playing; listening to tapes and to adult dialogue; watching films and television; reading signs, magazines, and books; and writing notes and creative pieces. Therefore, and to a greater extent than in any other discipline, the language arts program demands a knowledge of each child's social, emotional, cultural, and intellectual background and development.

Due to the variety of student experiences in any level or grade, an effective program in language learning must focus upon children as individuals. Boys and girls must be involved actively and positively in genuine learning situations that have meaning for them.

As children progress through the grades, they must be permitted greater responsibility in choosing learning experiences because these experiences influence their gradual acquisition of the productive and the receptive modes in the English language arts. The productive or expressive areas stress composition in both oral and written forms. The receptive areas concern reading and listening. Yet all four modes are so intricately interrelated that none of them can be learned in complete isolation from the others, and growth in one area promptly promotes growth in the others.

Language Acquisition

Young children in all cultures appear to master the complex task of acquiring an understanding of the phonology (sound units), morphology (meaning units), syntax, and semantics (variations in meaning) of their native language. This competence enables them to produce an infinite variety of sentences, to understand and make judgments about sentences, and to develop an unconscious awareness of both the limitations and the creative capacity of language. Yet most of this knowledge is acquired early in life (primarily between the ages of two and five) without direct instruction. Psycholinguists are still investigating how children attain this knowledge; thus far there has been no explanation acceptable to everyone.

Since the 1950s, four major theories about language acquisition in children have evolved, according to Menyuk.[1] First to appear in historical order is the *stimulus-response-reward theory* (S-R-R), developed by B. F. Skinner and others, which holds that girls and boys learn their language through imitation of adult models and environmental conditioning. Proponents describe the learning process as a process of forming stimulus-response-reward chains, which come about because of the nature of the environment that provides the language stimuli. Children who produce desired language patterns receive social and material reinforcements as rewards. Opponents contend, however, that (1) children utter certain expressions that they have never heard anyone say (so that their language is hardly a faithful imitation); (2) children's speech is highly resistant to alteration by adult intervention; and (3) the practical task of memorizing all of the possible language structures is virtually impossible. The S-R-R theory is known also as the behaviorist or environmental view.

The second prevalent theory is the *innatist theory.* Its best-known proponent is Noam Chomsky, and it maintains that boys and girls learn their language from within themselves because language is indeed innate; children are preprogrammed genetically to acquire it. Supporters contend that (1) the onset and accomplishment of minimal language development seem unaffected by linguistic or cultural variations; (2) language cannot be taught to nonhuman forms of life, whereas the suppression of language acquisition among humans is almost impossible; and (3) only humans have the necessary physiological and anatomical features to engage in sustained language. Opponents argue that language learning cannot be separated from cognitive development. The innatist theory is also known as the biological, generative, rationalist, or nativistic theory.

Proponents of the *cognitivist theory* believe that language development is dependent on cognition. Children develop knowledge of the world generally (nonlinguistic knowledge) and then "map" this knowledge onto language relations and categories. Any teaching aimed at developing the intellect will simultaneously promote language. Opponents contend, however, that because new knowledge can be generated through talking and writing, language itself affects cognition.

Advocates of the *learnability theory,* which evolved during the 1970s, propose that language acquisition occurs because of the special interaction between the child's cognitive abilities and the learnability of language. Many of the basic beliefs of the advocates are exactly the same as those of cognitivists and innatists. The learnability theory is therefore said to be an attempt to come up with a unified theory of language development.

Language Development

Studies of the stages of language development vary to some extent, depending on the observer and the techniques used. Clear-cut delineations are not possible. Nevertheless, authorities generally agree upon certain age ranges which may indicate progressive stages of speech development in young boys (or girls), as shown in Table 1.1.

The *undifferentiated cry* occurs during the first month of life and appears to be wholly reflexive. It is part of the total bodily response to a new environment. The *differentiated cry,* observed between the second and third months of life, varies with the type of situation or stimulus: thirst, hunger, pressure, or fear. All of the characteristic sounds exercise the speech apparatus.

Table 1.1
Checklist of Language Behavior of a Preschool Boy

Average Age	Question	Average Behavior
3–6 months	What does he do when you talk to him?	He awakens or quiets to the sound of his mother's voice.
	Does he react to your voice even when he cannot see you?	He typically turns eyes and head in the direction of the source of sound.
7–10 months	When he can't see what is happening, what does he do when he hears familiar footsteps . . . the dog barking . . . the telephone ringing . . . candy paper rattling . . . someone's voice . . . his own name?	He turns his head and shoulders toward familiar sounds, even when he cannot see what is happening. Such sounds do not have to be loud to cause him to respond.
11–15 months	Can he point to or find familiar objects or people when he is asked to? *Example:* "Where is Jimmy?" "Find the ball."	He shows his understanding of some words by appropriate behavior; for example, he points to or looks at familiar objects or people, on request.
	Does he respond differently to various sounds?	He jabbers in response to a human voice, is apt to cry when there is thunder, or may frown when he is scolded.
	Does he enjoy listening to some sounds and imitating them?	Imitation indicates that he can hear the sounds and can match them with his own sound production.
1½ years	Can he point to parts of his body when you ask him to? *Example:* "Show me your eyes." "Show me your nose."	Some children begin to identify parts of the body. He should be able to show his nose or eyes.
	How many understandable words does he use— words you are sure *really* mean something?	He should be using a few single words. They are not complete or pronounced perfectly but are clearly meaningful.
2 years	Can he follow simple verbal commands when you are careful not to give him any help, such as looking at the object or pointing in the right direction? *Example:* "Johnny, get your hat and give it to Daddy." "Danny, bring me your ball."	He should be able to follow a few simple commands without visual clues.
	Does he enjoy being read to? Does he point out pictures of familiar objects in a book when asked to? *Example:* "Show me the baby." "Where's the rabbit?"	Most two-year-olds enjoy being read to and shown simple pictures in a book or magazine, and they will point out pictures when you ask them to.
	Does he use the names of familiar people and things such as *Mommy, milk, ball,* and *hat?*	He should be using a variety of everyday words heard in his home and neighborhood.

Table 1.1 (cont.)

Average Age	Question	Average Behavior
	What does he call himself?	He refers to himself by name.
	Is he beginning to show interest in the sound of radio or TV commercials?	Many two-year-olds do show such interest by word or action.
	Is he putting a few words together to make little "sentences"? *Example:* "Go bye-bye car." "Milk all gone."	These "sentences" are not usually complete or grammatically correct.
2½ years	Does he know a few rhymes or songs? Does he enjoy hearing them?	Many children can say or sing short rhymes or songs and enjoy listening to records or to mother singing.
	What does he do when the ice cream man's bell rings (out of his sight), or when a car door or house door closes at a time when someone in the family usually comes home?	If a child has good hearing, and if these are events that bring him pleasure, he usually reacts to the sound by running to look or by telling someone what he hears.
3 years	Can he show that he understands the meaning of some words besides the names of things? *Example:* "Make the car go." "Give me your ball." "Put the block in your pocket." "Find the big doll."	He should be able to understand and use some simple verbs, pronouns, prepositions and adjectives, such as *go, me, in,* and *big.*
	Can he find you when you call him from another room?	He should be able to locate the source of a sound.
	Does he sometimes use complete sentences?	He should be using complete sentences some of the time.
4 years	Can he tell about events that have happened recently?	He should be able to give a connected account of some recent experiences.
	Can he carry out two directions, one after the other? *Example:* "Bobby, find Susie and tell her dinner's ready."	He should be able to carry out a sequence of two simple directions.
5 years	Do neighbors and others outside the family understand most of what he says?	His speech should be intelligible, although some sounds may still be mispronounced.
	Can he carry on a conversation with other children or familiar grown-ups?	Most children of this age can carry on a conversation if the vocabulary is within their experience.
	Does he begin a sentence with "I" instead of "me"; "he" instead of "him"?	He should use some pronouns correctly.
	Is his grammar almost as good as that of his parents?	Most of the time, it should match the patterns of grammar used by the adults of his family and neighborhood.

Source: *Learning to Talk: Speech, Hearing and Language Problems in the Pre-School Child* (Bethesda, Maryland: National Institute of Health, 1977), pp. 22–24.

Babbling appears between the third and sixth months and consists primarily of vocal play in which children produce a great variety of sounds. Children emit sounds which occur in a language other than that of their speech community, numerous sounds that far surpass those prevalent in any one language. In fact, infants of all nations and cultures babble the same sounds and in the same order, following a highly stereotyped pattern. In the case of the congenitally deaf child, speech development terminates with the babbling period because deaf children lose interest in playing with mouth movements and exercising their vocal muscles.

Critical to the process of early language acquisition is the role of adults and siblings. If they focus the infant's attention on sounds produced that are approximations of words, the infant is likely to repeat those sounds again due to the positive reinforcement. By rewarding selective responses, families are apt to motivate infants to produce the phonemes (or the significant speech sounds) comprising the language.

The production of phonemes steadily increases so that a 30-month-old child is using vowels and consonants with a frequency approximating that of an adult. Age three represents the upper-age limit for mastery of most diphthongs (or blends of vowel and semivowel sounds) and of most vowels, as well as of the consonants *m, p, b, w, h, t, d,* and *n.* By age four most of the remaining consonants are being produced correctly, and the child's phonological system closely approximates the model system of the language. Complete mastery, including two- and three-consonant blends, is attained at about eight years for most boys and girls. *Phonological development is not complete when children enter kindergarten.*

While the phonemes are being acquired, the child is combining them appropriately to express words. The age for the appearance of the first word ranges from nine to nineteen months for normal children with the average set at eleven to twelve months.

The child's first words are likely to be *holophrases* (or single words) used to express a more complex idea. They generally take the form of a noun, pronoun, verb, adjective, or adverb. Although anecdotal studies and case histories show that first words are the monosyllabic or reduplicated monosyllabic *mama, daddy,* and *bye,* research indicates that more functional words than these may appear first. For instance, one study of middle-class Hebrew boys revealed that the first words elicited by their mothers in the home were *this, that, here, no,* and *food.*[2] These words, together with gestures, resolve most children's problems by age twelve months. By twenty-four months some boys and girls have a vocabulary of more than 150 words. By forty-eight months many children have a vocabulary of 1,000 words.

In contrast to their gradual mastery of phonology, children use syntax correctly (though incompletely of course) from the very beginning. By age two, and sometimes as early as eighteen months, children begin to string together two or more holophrases and have thereby arrived at the *telegraphic stage.* Their utterances are devoid of function words and resemble messages that adults would send by wire. For instance, "Jimmy truck" could represent "That truck belongs to Jimmy," or "Give me my truck." Meanings will often depend upon the context and intonation of the utterance. All telegraphic speech, however, consists of acceptable grammatical sequences, which are the precursors of the sentence. Normal children will acquire at least a few hundred presentences by the time they reach thirty months of age.

By age three most children are constructing simple affirmative-declarative sentences, putting together a subject and predicate. Gradually their sentences become longer and more complex, due partly to adult expansion and extension of child speech and partly to child induction of the latent structure of language. Boys and girls are apparently able to process the speech they hear and induce from it general rules of structure that they later use in their own speech.

The rule system that children construct makes it possible for them to generate an infinite number and variety of sentences, including many never heard from anyone else. The system is a set of rules for sentence construction, rules that neither the children nor their parents know explicitly. It consists of a series of grammars that have their own phonological, syntactic, and semantic components at each successive stage in the development of language. Girls and boys take all speech, interact with it, and somehow develop the systems that constitute the grammar of their language. Like phonological development, *syntactical development is not complete when children enter kindergarten.*

Research has suggested three guidelines for enriching the language environment in the elementary classrooms, especially in the kindergarten and primary grades, in an effort to foster language development:[3]

Positive Language Classroom Environments

1. *Children are active learners.* Girls and boys are not passive receptors of information who, having once been presented with proper language forms, will promptly and continuously use those forms. Instead, language learning is an interactive process, and children must be regarded as active participants in it. Just as they practice riding a bicycle or walking, children need to practice language skills to perfect them. Boys and girls must never be viewed as small individuals whose speech must be constantly modified or corrected by an all-knowing adult.

2. *Children need accepting atmospheres.* Continued scrutiny of deficiencies in children's speech reduces self-esteem. Consequently, teachers should emphasize the meaning of communicative efforts, rather than the form, and control impulses to correct student errors. They should be attentive listeners and show an interest in what each child is saying. Patience is often required while waiting for child responses. In an accepting atmosphere, teachers accept whatever type of verbal communication the child offers. The boy or girl then finds talking more rewarding because teachers truly attend to what he or she is saying.

Acceptance by classmates and teachers, especially in the primary grades, foster and enrich language development. (© James L. Shaffer.)

3. *Children need child-centered speech from adults.* Rather than reflecting the child's concerns, directiveness in adult speech is apt to reflect the adult's concerns. The wise teacher, however, uses child-centered speech when addressing the child's topic. In this way, he or she conveys respect for the child and also makes it easier for the child to remember what has been said because it is meaningful. There are five techniques available to the teacher when talking with students, especially younger children. The first is *modeling,* which means that adults use grammatically correct speech in order to allow the student to internalize grammatical rules. The second is *expatiation,* whereby the teacher maintains the child's topic but also adds other important information so that new concepts are introduced meaningfully (for example, Child: "It's hot." Teacher: "It's very hot in the summer."). *Open-ended questioning* is another approach; it stimulates thinking and permits the student to respond without the threat of being wrong (for example, Teacher, upon seeing the child put a pie into a toy oven: "How did you make your pie?"). A fourth technique is *expansion,* or corrective feedback, which restates (partially or wholly) the child's incomplete statement and thereby makes it a complete, logical whole (for example, Child: "Basketball." Teacher: "Yes, today we have a new basketball."). All of this occurs without any negative response or any demand that the student repeat the first statement in

a new or better way. The last approach is *recasting,* a form of expansion in which the statement's content is maintained but its grammatical structure is changed (for example, Child: "I like oranges." Teacher: "Oranges taste good, don't they?").

Intellectual Development According to Piaget

Language development is closely related to the development of the thought process, and the world-renowned Swiss psychologist, Jean Piaget, viewed intellectual growth in children as a matter of sequential stages.

These stages in the development of a child's capacity to use increasingly difficult thought operations are clearly defined. They are generally regulated by wide age spans and follow in an ordered sequence. A new stage will not be successfully undertaken until the previous stage has been properly attained. As children modify and add new experiences to those previously absorbed, new abilities evolve from the old. Although the sequence in which the stages appear are the same for all children, such factors as motivation, environment, native intelligence, and diversity of experience may retard or hasten the process of intellectual growth.

The sequence of stages described by Piaget begins with the *sensorimotor period* (birth to age two years). The first stage of interest to elementary teachers, however, is the *preoperational period* (ages two to seven years). This period is divided into the *egocentric* phase, which lasts until about age four, and the *intuitive* phase. In the egocentric or preconceptual phase, symbols are constructed in which boys and girls imitate and represent what they see through language and action. In the intuitive phase, children extend and combine their action-images and correct their intuitive impressions of reality. During the preoperational period girls and boys are continually seeking information, asking questions, and acquiring new concepts. The relationship between language and concepts may be strengthened through puppetry, creative drama, and imaginative play. Additional growth in the ability to relate language symbols and objects may be found in children's initial efforts to draw and make graphic representations.

The next stage of intellectual development is the *concrete operations period* (ages seven to eleven or twelve years), when children lose much of their egocentricity. They become less dependent on either immediate perceptual cues or on actions as their thinking becomes "decentered." In this period boys and girls accept ideas other than their own as they communicate with their peers. They are now able to do mentally what they previously had to act out. Their internalized thinking operations help classifying, ordering in series, numbering, grouping, and subgrouping of action-images. This is a period of avid reading.

The fourth and final stage is generally beyond the immediate concern of most elementary school teachers. It is the *formal operations period* (ages eleven or twelve years to age fifteen years and beyond), when children advance to the solution of complex problems through reasoning. Their thinking is flexible and they perceive many possibilities, including those beyond any actual situation. They are no longer bound to the concrete but can think with symbols.

Several principles from Piaget's theory can provide the bases for the English language curriculum in the elementary school:

1. *Although the acquisition of language is closely related to the growth of the thought process, both competencies do not necessarily develop at the same rate.* A dominant factor in stimulating language growth is a specific set of environmental conditions. Thought processes, on the other hand, develop more slowly and are affected by a much wider (and more accessible) variety of environmental factors. A teacher should provide for children activities that are commensurate with their ability to understand rather than to articulate; otherwise the teacher will be deceived in attributing to the more verbal children mental growth that is beyond their years. The teacher must not assume that because a child can utter the word, he or she knows the concept. Language alone is not the answer. Nor does language training by itself lead to intellectual development.

2. *Children's thought and language patterns differ from those of adults.* A child must attain each level of thought development alone, and the child does so through interaction with his or her world. Although boys and girls may be helped to move to a higher level of thinking through proper experiences, they will not benefit from verbal explanations that are extraneous to their ways of thinking. The imposition of intellectual growth by means of formal instruction is not possible.

3. *Learning is an active process, and children learn best from concrete activities.* In this type of learning, there is intrinsic motivation that stems from children's innate curiosity about their world and the rewards that can be reaped by satisfying that curiosity through knowledge. When learning is physically and mentally active, thought is the internalization of that action.

   Young learners especially must be able to actively manipulate and explore varied materials and equipment in their environment so that they may construct their own knowledge. They are capable of intuitive learning when they have some part in purposeful activities both in and out of the classroom.

4. *Though there is a fixed sequence in development, each child proceeds at his or her own rate.* Knowledge of the developmental stages in children's thinking can help teachers become aware of the limitations as well as the possibilities at each stage. Still, each boy and girl is different and should not be forced to learn material for which he or she is not ready.

   Even though all children are not at the same place at the same time, all of them enjoy the same kinds of materials at the same stage of maturity. Therefore, differences in ability do not constitute a major factor in determining and providing for the listening, reading, and viewing interests of boys and girls. However, there are differences in the rates at which children pass through the various stages and in the number and complexity of book and nonbook materials they choose.

5. *Children learn from social experiences with their peers and with adults.* In addition to learning by interacting with their physical environment, boys and girls learn by sharing experiences and discussing reactions and viewpoints with others. As they grow older, they lose their egocentricity; they have their opinions challenged, they encounter new ideas, and gradually they reshape and reconstruct their knowledge.

Teachers are therefore warned to listen *to* an answer, nor *for* an answer; children's answers can provide excellent information about children's thinking.[4] The unexpected answers can be used advantageously as another starting point. By accepting pupil's egocentric replies, teachers encourage young learners to be intellectually honest rather than to be looking, listening, or waiting for the right answer to be provided.

Providing for Individual Differences

Within every heterogeneous classroom, there are wide variations in the children's physical and emotional health and in their out-of-school experiences. The children are highly individual persons, shaped and influenced by the environment in which they have developed. The teacher's most challenging responsibility is to provide a program that meets children where they are, recognizes their potential, capitalizes upon their strengths, and moves them along at a pace consistent with their ability. The teacher recognizes, for example, individual variations in abilities to understand and speak standard English, to listen attentively, to use appropriate and extensive vocabulary, and to verbalize experiences.

Because children learn at different rates, they require different materials, experiences, and instructional techniques. A single group activity often affects each member differently. The following section describes various types of learners and offers suggestions for adapting instruction and material to their needs.

Some Children	The Teacher
Use patterns of language that represent a dialect unlike the standard English classroom dialect.	Accepts each child's nonstandard dialect for communication purposes. Offers additional instruction in standard English.
Have speech patterns that result in poor communication with teacher or classmates.	Assists each child in the speaker-audience situation. Plans program designed to improve pronunciation and intonation. Uses tape recorder for children to record and play back their own voices in various situations.
Are learning English as a second language, having had little or no practice with the structure, sound system, and vocabulary of the English language.	Supplements the class program with additional instruction and practice in English. (See Chapter Fourteen.)

Some Children	The Teacher
Find their vocabulary inadequate, unfamiliar, or inappropriate in school situations.	Plans activities to develop concepts and related vocabulary. Checks constantly on word meaning. Replaces vulgarisms with acceptable expressions.
Use actions, gestures, facial expressions, and noises rather than words to communicate.	Encourages children to use oral language to make known their wishes and needs or to describe actions, by letting them hear repeatedly what they are expected to say.
Lose interest in sustained "talking" by the teacher or other adults.	Tries to watch his or her own "talking" time. Encourages dialogue with children. Intersperses verbal instruction with gestures, visuals, and realia. Provides children with interesting events to discuss; limits "listening time."
Listen actively when a physical response or game element is present or when there is a visual focal point of attention.	Uses listening games that call for action rather than verbal response. Involves listeners in activities such as refrains, pantomime, and rhythms. Makes provision for interaction (teacher-student, student-student), noting how each child feels and responds.
Find it easier to discuss and evaluate incidents that are presented through dramatization rather than through verbalization.	Allows the children to act out incidents with projective devices that promote free speech. Uses realia, pictures, stories, filmstrips, and firsthand experiences as the basis for conversations and discussions.
Are shy in revealing personal fantasies and the realm of their imagination.	Involves the children in creating additional incidents for familiar story and TV characters or in creating imaginary characters and incidents. Encourages children to select media for interpretation.

Every teacher must provide for the wide variety of individual differences that exist among children—physically, emotionally, and academically. (© James L. Shaffer.)

Some Children	**The Teacher**
Are less confident in school situations than in out-of-school situations.	Builds confidence so that the children can expect positive reactions and rewards from adults when they complete a task, ask questions, or explore ways of finding answers. Communicates to the children, by word or manner, any recognition of their progress, no matter how slight it may be.
Require special support, strengthened by the interest and cooperation of the school and the home.	Reports frequently and formally to the children and their parent(s). Plans regular parent-teacher conferences, providing a translator when necessary, and includes the children on appropriate occasions.

Some Children	**The Teacher**
Have a limited range of the concepts and vocabulary useful in school. Are not accustomed to looking for similarities that help them classify objects.	Checks frequently on each child's understanding of common, everyday words and provides experiences to develop better understanding. Plans activities involving classifying, labeling, and discussing objects. Uses verbal experiences to deepen understandings.
Lack confidence in their ability to learn.	Develops assurance by providing activities, materials, and assignments that promote successful learning.
Learn and work at a slower pace than others in the group. Need to take smaller learning steps.	Adapts instruction to individual and group needs. Introduces new concepts slowly, allowing time for understanding. Allows sufficient work time.
Have limited experience with school-type materials—pictures, books, educational toys, and games. Are insecure in handling and responding to them.	Provides abundance of intellectually stimulating materials and time to peruse and enjoy them. Gives careful direction in the handling and use of those materials.
Lack interest in standards and study. Work without goals or an organized system.	Gives close supervision to development of work-study habits, setting sensible standards and requiring children to meet them.
Are not inclined to review experiences or to see the relationship between what happened today and yesterday.	Increases the number of experiences designed to stimulate recall and to relate the past to the present and the future.
Find it difficult to relate to unfamiliar adults or to confide in them.	Finds opportunities to establish a one-to-one relationship with every child. Comments positively on each child's personal appearance and performance. Encourages each child to talk with him or her about individual interests and problems.

Some Children	The Teacher
Tend to rely on physical skill and courage to bolster self-image and to meet problems.	Shows the children that discussion is a better way of solving problems than name-calling and physical force.
Are limited in ability to draw inferences or to generalize on the basis of related experiences.	Offers activities through which he or she can guide children to arrive at generalizations and draw inferences.
Are happiest and most confident when they are permitted to engage in physical activities.	Provides ample time for physical expression—running, jumping, skipping, dancing, balancing, and playing singing games. Praises gross motor skills.
Can accept responsibility and enjoy the importance of being asked to share in classroom duties.	Rotates duties and assignments. Discusses need for monitors. Stresses individual responsibility for class pride in room appearance.
Are accustomed to considerable freedom of movement and self-determined and self-directed play activities. Are ingenious in devising materials and games.	Praises independence of action and thought. Encourages creative use of time and equipment.
Pursue individual interests of academic value—collecting rocks or reading about dinosaurs.	Challenges children to continue and to extend their interests. Helps them plan ways of sharing their hobbies with the class.
Approach problem solving creatively and use materials and equipment imaginatively.	Praises original ideas and solutions. Provides the materials and equipment with which to work out problems.
Learn rapidly. Read at levels considerably beyond those of the majority of the group.	Provides special activities beyond the usual group assignments. Sees that books and other printed materials cover a sufficiently wide reading range. Offers nonprinted resources.
Can handle abstract ideas. Are able to generalize and hypothesize.	Poses problems, questions, and situations that require children to select, relate, and evaluate ideas and to make generalizations.

Evaluation of Student Progress in Language Development

Three formal instruments for assessing language growth among normal and handicapped children are the *Northwestern Syntax Screening Test,* the *Test of Early Language Development,* and the *Test of Language Development.* All three instruments have received favorable reviews.[5] The first measures the expressive and receptive language skills of children ages three to seven. It is individually administered, considered to be primarily a screening instrument (as stated in its title), and requires approximately fifteen minutes to administer. It is published by the Northwestern University Press (Evanston, Illinois). The second instrument also measures the same expressive and receptive skills but is used with children ages three to eight. Like the first test, it is a screening instrument. It consists of thirty-eight items, uses twelve printed stimulus cards, and requires fifteen to twenty minutes to administer. It is published by PRO-ED (Austin, Texas).

The *Test of Language Development* (also published by PRO-ED of Austin, Texas) comes in two forms: Primary (or TOLD-P) and Intermediate (or TOLD-I). The first form assesses comprehension and expression of spoken language in children ages four through eight; the second assesses them in children ages eight and one-half through twelve. Both are untimed tests, TOLD-P requiring thirty to sixty minutes to administer and TOLD-I requiring thirty to forty-five minutes. Neither form is intended for use with children speaking a non-standard English dialect or with children whose primary language is not English.

Discussion Questions

1. Which theory or theories concerning language acquisition in children do you find professionally acceptable? Why?
2. Describe a supportive classroom atmosphere for language development.
3. Why are social experiences so critical to the intellectual development of children?
4. As an aide or teacher, how can you adapt instruction or materials to students who (a) use gestures or noises to communicate, (b) have a limited range of concepts and vocabulary useful for school, or (c) lack interest in school-type resources?

Suggested Projects

1. Watch an educational television show for young children. Then describe how it promotes language development.
2. Tape some spontaneous conversations in a first-semester kindergarten classroom. Then verify whether either phonological or syntactical development is complete when girls and boys start school.
3. Collect ten narrative replies by children. Then choose the three longest and most detailed replies and describe what type of information they furnish about the thinking abilities of elementary students.
4. Visit a first-grade classroom to see how often the teacher uses modeling, expatiation, expansion, recasting or open-ended questioning when talking to individual children or small groups.

Geller, L. 1985. *Wordplay and Language Learning for Children.* Urbana, IL: National Council of Teachers of English.

Gleason, J., ed. 1985. *The Development of Language.* Columbus, OH: Merrill.

Lee, D. 1986. *Language, Children, and Society: An Introduction to Linguistics and Language Development.* New York: New York University Press.

Lindfors, J. 1987. *Children's Language and Learning.* 2nd ed. Englewood Cliffs, NJ: Prentice Hall.

Plaum, S. 1986. *The Development of Language and Literacy in Young Children.* 3rd ed. Columbus, OH: Merrill.

Rogers, D., Perrin, M., and Waller, C. 1987. "Enhancing the Development of Language and Thought Through Conversations with Young Children," *Journal of Research in Childhood Education, 2*(1), 17–29.

Smith, F. 1988. *Joining the Literacy Club.* Portsmouth, NH: Heinemann.

Szekeres, S., Boom, L., Tittnich, E., and Schonburg, R. 1988. *Facilitating Children's Language.* New York: Haworth Press.

Wells, G. 1986. *The Meaning Makers: Children Learning Language and Using Language to Learn.* Portsmouth, NH: Heinemann.

Zigler, E., and Finn-Stevenson, M. 1987. *Children: Development and Social Issues.* Lexington, MA: Heath.

Recent Related Readings

1. P. Menyuk, *Language Development: Knowledge and Use* (Glenview, Illinois: Scott, Foresman, 1988), pp. 26–44.
2. J. Zonshin, *One-Word Utterances of Hebrew-Speaking Children* (Master's thesis, University of Tel-Aviv, 1974).
3. J. Dumtschin, "Recognize Language Development and Delay in Early Childhood," *Young Children,* 1988, *43*(3), pp. 21–23.
4. A. Bingham-Newman and R. Saunders, "Take a New Look at Your Classroom with Piaget as a Guide," *Young Children,* 1977, *32*(3), pp. 62–72.
5. J. Mitchell, Jr., ed., *The Ninth Mental Measurements Yearbook,* Volume II (Lincoln: University of Nebraska Press, 1985), pp. 1059, 1557, and 1574.

Chapter Notes

Language and the Language Arts Program

2

Major Chapter Goals

After studying Chapter 2, the reader will be able to

1. Describe a modern language arts program and its proposed outcomes.
2. Distinguish among the structure, modes, and functions of the English language.
3. Explain why integrating the language arts is both sensible and significant.

Discover As You Read This Chapter Whether*

1. Most of the languages spoken in the world today are represented in writing.
2. Language keeps changing constantly, and therefore some of the nonstandard forms used today may become acceptable tomorrow.
3. Phonology is concerned with the distinctive sounds that make up a language.
4. Morphology deals with word order and how groups of words are arranged to convey meaning.
5. Some language modes are first learned informally at home.
6. Language and thought can be separated.
7. Comprehension processes are involved in the receptive language modes.
8. The expressive language modes include both oral and written composition.
9. Learning to use more than one function of language should be delayed until Piaget's formal operations period.
10. Unlike reading readiness activities, language readiness activities are not recommended before students begin to use books and writing tools.

*Answers to these true-or-false statements may be found in Appendix 5.

Contemporary American society believes that the goals of education are to prepare all students to function as effective and informed citizens in a democracy, to function efficiently in the world of work, and to realize personal fulfillment.[1] The English language arts curriculum must therefore promote those three goals by communicating clearly a sense of common objectives and values that respect diversity; by featuring a systematic literature program founded on intensive reading, listening, speaking, and writing; and by emphasizing a delight in the heritage and beauty of the English language.

Proposed outcomes of such a language arts curriculum would include the following:

1. Children will have the desire and the ability to listen, read, and view for information and enjoyment.
2. Children will have the desire and ability to read and compose literature in order to clarify and extend personal experiences.
3. Children will have the desire and ability to predict, paraphrase and question ideas they encounter in their spoken and written language.
4. Children will become aware of the literary tradition and its value, purpose, complexity, and relationship to culture.
5. Children will apply knowledge of both spoken and written language in various language situations.
6. Children will use language to discuss language when constructing personal messages and when analyzing the communications of others.
7. Children will express feelings, thoughts, and experiences in both spoken and written language.
8. Children will first organize and later evaluate new ideas and experiences in both spoken and written language.[2]

Such a language arts program (1) is based on balanced instruction that presents listening, speaking, reading, and writing so that they become mutually reinforcing, (2) emphasizes the reading and study of important literary works, and (3) includes classroom activities based on student experiences. Consequently, the English language arts can truly be an integral part of the entire elementary curriculum.

Nature and Structure of Language

A basic understanding of both language structure and the nature of language is important for all classroom teachers so that they may implement some of those language aspects into their lesson planning in the language arts areas, whether for primary children or for intermediate students.

Nature of Language

The English language and all other languages throughout the world share several features in common:

1. *Every language has grammar.* Although the grammar of each language is different, some closely related languages (such as English and Spanish) share

many features that denote meaning or the relationships of elements in sentences. Children who speak two languages often have problems with the differences in the grammars of those languages. Because word order (or syntax) is a vital part of grammar, Spanish-speaking pupils enrolled in an ESL (English as a Second Language) class, for example, will be asking ungrammatical questions should they persist in using the Spanish order when posing questions in English.

2. *Every language is oral.* Scholars have counted about 3,000 spoken languages, although less than half of them have ever been represented in writing. Spoken language is older, is more widespread, and communicates ideas better than written language. Every normal child learns to talk with little or no formal assistance, whereas he or she ordinarily learns to write only with the help of others, and then that writing is a mere representation of earlier speech.

3. *Every language is social.* The form of each language reflects the social needs of the group that employs it. Children may possess the biological capacity for language, but they cannot develop that potential without interaction with others in their society. There is even evidence that language learning is inhibited when social interaction becomes blocked.

4. *Every language is symbolic and arbitrary.* Words (the symbolic aspect of language) permit children to discuss a ride in the space shuttle, even though they have not as yet experienced it directly. Language is a type of code that allows abstract ideas and experiences to be encoded by the speaker, transmitted by speech, and decoded by the hearer. Although words symbolize real objects or events, they themselves are arbitrary. English speakers, for example, call a four-legged animal that gives milk a *cow,* but there is no inherent trait in the animal that demands it be called *cow.* Even onomatopoeic words are arbitrary symbols and do not, therefore, have meaning in themselves; consequently, the dog that says *bow-wow* in the English community barks *wang-wang* in the Chinese community.

5. *Every language changes.* Because it is spoken by living people, language too is alive and therefore changing. New ideas, products, and institutions make the need for such change necessary. Because English and the other languages exist in the oral expression of the persons who use them, some of the nonstandard usage of today may become the accepted usage of tomorrow.

6. *Every language is systematic and describable.* All languages in the world can be described using identical techniques, according to the science of descriptive linguistics. Each is consistent in its structure and not a haphazard collection of symbols and sounds. Most sentences, therefore, although they are created spontaneously, still follow a system of rules of which even the users are often not totally aware. Children learn the system as they learn the language.

7. *Each language is unique and diverse.* In order to comprehend how unique each language is, it is important to recall that the most popular definition of a language is that form understood by members of one *speech community* (such as France) but not by those of another speech community (such as Spain). (Even elementary school children are surprised to learn that there

are reported to be fifty-four distinct linguistic groupings for North American Indians alone!) When groups of persons are socially or geographically separated from one another, their speech reflects changes in grammar, vocabulary, and pronunciation. Such language diversity is ordinarily a cumulative process.

Language Structure

For the most part boys and girls acquire their understanding of the underlying structure of the English language in an informal fashion. However, there are portions of that knowledge that can be and are formally studied in school, such as learning about prefixes and suffixes in the middle and intermediate grades.

The English language is a structure of arbitrary systems relating sounds and meanings. A child or adult is described as "knowing" the language when he or she understands the sounds used, the basic units of meaning, and the rules combining sounds and meanings to form sentences. That person is then said to have command of the phonological, morphological, syntactic, and semantic systems.

Phonology

Each language has its own set of vocal sounds (*phones*). As children grow into productive members of the speech community, they develop only those phones that they find useful in communicating. The study of phones is called *phonetics*.

Of the many phones in the English language, only a relatively small number differ significantly from each other. Those that do differ are called *phonemes,* or minimal contrastive elements. While English is generally said to possess forty-four phonemes, there is actually little agreement as to the number of phonemes in the American English language. The reported totals range from thirty-three to forty-five because there are various classification schemes and because sounds that are significant in one dialect may be less so in another. The study of phonemes, or distinctive sounds that make up a language, is called *phonology.* When phonemes appear in textual matter, the symbol for a phoneme appears between slanted bars: /   /.

There are both segmental phonemes and nonsegmental (or suprasegmental) phonemes. The first group of thirty-two includes consonants, vowels, and semivowels (or phonemes that function either as consonants or as parts of diphthongs such as /w/ and /y/) and constitutes the sequential elements, with some overlapping and gliding of syllables, words, and sentences.

The second group of twelve includes phonemes of stress, pitch, and juncture, which occur simultaneously with the segmental phonemes, or separate them, and which are often considered together under the heading of *intonation.* Combinations of suprasegmental phonemes are responsible for the rhythm and cadence of a language. Their function is similar to that of punctuation in writing.

Stress refers to the relative degree of intensity of loudness of various syllables in a spoken sentence, and there are four stress phonemes that can be quite simply indicated for purposes of discussion: primary (the strongest) stress (/);

secondary stress (\); tertiary stress (∧); and weak (slight) stress (‿). When pronounced alone, one-syllable words usually have the strongest (or primary) stress, for example, *fĕet, ădd, ĭf.* Words of two or more syllables have varying patterns of stress, as in *ínvălìd* or *ìnvălíd* and *mágnèt* or *màgnétîc.* Phrases may vary in stress according to the meaning expressed, as in *lóud speàkĕr* or *lòud speákĕr.* Sentences, too, have varying patterns of stress, depending upon the meaning intended, for example, *Jóhn bought three books; John bóught three books; John bought thrée books;* or *John bought three bóoks.*

Pitch refers to the ups and downs, or tunes, in a stream of speech. Although many changes in pitch do not affect meaning, there are some that do. Differences in pitch distinguish between statements and questions in English. A way of picturing this difference might be as follows: *John bought/three books?* or *John/bought three\books.* A statement has a falling pitch contour; a question has a rising pitch contour. There are four significant pitch phonemes in English, designated as low, normal, high, and highest and numbered lowest to highest from one to four. The basic pitch of a person's voice, regardless of whether the person is a man or woman, is marked as pitch two.

The term *juncture* refers to the ways a speaker of English makes the transition from one phoneme to the next. There are four juncture phonemes, and all are relevant to the teaching of spelling. Open or internal juncture (+) is the vocal signal that usually divides words from each other; it is the slight retarding of the flow of sound that distinguishes *ice cream* and *I scream.* The three terminal junctures are the vocal signals that generally divide sequences of words into constructions: (a) falling, or fade-fall terminal (↘), ordinarily ends statements, commands, and some questions; (b) rising, or fade-rise terminal (↗), usually ends questions that are intended to express surprise, doubt, regret, or other emotion; and (c) sustained, or level terminal (→), marks the divisions between certain constructions within a sentence.

When students listen carefully to someone speaking his or her native language, they will notice that although the speaker always uses certain phonemes in certain places, the same phoneme is not always pronounced in exactly the same way each time. The speaker's various pronunciations of the same phoneme, however, are of a kind that indicate clearly to someone familiar with the language which phoneme is being used. Most native speakers do not realize that they make these differences in sounds, and a student of the language is free to use any one of the pronunciations in such cases. Such variations are *allophones,* two or more forms of the same phoneme.

While children are acquiring the phonemes of a language, they must also learn that phonemes go together in a predetermined order. Only certain orders are allowed, and there are rules that determine whether a phoneme can appear at the beginning, in the middle, or at the end of a word. Therefore, in English, for example, PWLODB is not a word because it does not follow the phonological rule concerned with sequencing.

Morphology

When children and adults speak, they utter a sequence of individually meaningless phonemes as well as a sequence of meaningful morphemes. The sentence *The cat chased the birds* consists of vowels and consonants (segmental phonemes) spoken at varied *pitches* with different degrees of *stress*. It is simultaneously a string of the following *morphemes:* (the), {cat}, {chase}, {-d}, {the}, {bird}, {z}.

Morphemes are larger building stones that cannot be defined as precisely as phonemes. Whereas phonemes only distinguish between meanings without adding to or changing them, *morphemes* are units of discourse that carry meaning. In the words *big* and *bag,* for example, there is a contrast in sounds by which one word is distinguished from the other, but the sounds responsible for the distinction do not in themselves carry any meaning and are therefore phonemes. In the words *bag* and *bags,* however, the sound that has been added causes a change in meaning, and such a sound is termed a morpheme. One morpheme may contain one phoneme or several phonemes. Linguists write the symbol for a morpheme between braces: { }.

Morphemes are the smallest units of speech that have identifiable meanings of their own. They are not necessarily identical with syllables or words. The major morpheme classes in English are *bases* and *affixes*. Most bases (or roots) stand alone as words and so are described as *free* morphemes. Affixes never stand alone; they are always attached to bases, either before them as prefixes or after them as suffixes, and so are called *bound* morphemes. The study of morphemes or units of meaning is known as *morphology*.

Affixes are either derivational or inflectional. All prefixes are derivational affixes, but suffixes may be either derivational or inflectional. In English no new inflectional affixes have been added for 700 years, although derivational affixes are added routinely as needed, such as the recent prefixes {*mini*}, {*midi*}, and {*maxi*}.

Inflectional suffixes never change the word's part of speech, but derivational suffixes usually do. For example, the inflectional suffix -s, added to the noun *friend,* creates *friends,* which is still a noun with the added meaning "plural." However, the derivational suffix -ly changes the noun *friend* to the adjective *friendly.*

Just as each language has a separate set of phonological rules, so each language has a distinct set of morphological rules that children (and nonnative speakers) must learn if they are to combine morphemes into suitable words. Too, just as phonemes have allophones, morphemes have *allomorphs,* or positional variants. For example, the prefixal morpheme *in* has four allomorphs: *in-* (inactive), *il-* (illogical), *im-* (immodest), and *ir* (irrelevant).

Syntax

Morphemes cannot be arranged one after another in any elective order. Instead, for each language there are combinations in which morphemes can be put together in an utterance. Such combinations are known as constructions, and *syntax* is the study of these constructions. Syntax deals with word order and how words or groups of words are arranged to convey meaning. For example, the words *the* and *cat* can be grouped together in the construction, *the cat,* but not *cat the.* As mentioned earlier, most syntactic structures are used by even the youngest children who must learn to follow a finite set of rules determining how grammatical sentences may be formed in the native language.

The largest English construction is the *sentence*. Children should therefore have considerable experience in changing sentences about, in modifying and rearranging the information that sentences provide, and in exploring relationships among the various kinds of sentences. During the elementary years, basic sentence patterns can be taught inductively and largely without emphasis on terminology.

All theories of grammar recognize that English sentence patterns have two main parts: the subject and predicate (according to traditional grammar) or the noun phrase and the verb phrase (according to transformational grammar). Although linguists do not agree as to the number of patterns to be considered basic, the following five sentence patterns are the ones most generally used in the elementary school, with the first two types accounting for 85 percent of the sentences found in the speech uttered by children:

Pattern I. N^1 V. Noun (or pronoun) and (intransitive) verb.
　　　Example: *Birds sang.*
　　　　Subject/predicate
Pattern II. N^1 V N^2. Noun (or pronoun), (transitive) verb, and noun (or pronoun).
　　　Example: *Mother bought cookies.*
　　　　Subject/predicate/object
　　　(Can be transformed to passive voice.)
Pattern III. N^1 L V N^1. Noun (or pronoun), linking verb, and noun (or pronoun).
　　　Example: *Father is a teacher.*
　　　　Subject/predicate/predicate noun
　　　(Can be an equation pattern because nouns or pronouns can exchange places.)
Pattern IV. N^1 L V Aj. Noun (or pronoun), linking verb, and adjective.
　　　Example: *Summer is hot.*
　　　　Subject/predicate/predicate adjective
Pattern V. N^1 B V Av (of place). Noun (or pronoun), verb "to be," and adverbial (of place).
　　　Example: *Tom was here.*
　　　　She is on the swing.
　　　　Subject/predicate/predicate adverbial
(Adverbial can be a single word or phrase.)[3]

The study of word meanings or the role of language in human life is called *semantics*. It explains how language is used to express feelings and thoughts, to transmit information, to control behavior, to persuade, and to create and express social cohesion.[4]

Semantics

Because semantics deals with word meanings, children must learn about concrete concepts (such as the difference between *horse* and *dog*) as well as about the more difficult abstract concepts (such as *color*). They must become familiar with spatial relationships (*behind, here*) and with opposites (*hot* and *cold*).

However, semantics also deals with the attitudes that people have toward particular words and expressions. It thus covers both the denotation and the connotation of certain vocabulary. *Denotation* refers to the literal, objective meaning of a word; *connotation* concerns the personal, subjective meaning that a word possesses for one individual. Little wonder that the identical word may have a variety of associations for various children or adults when words are so often learned in different settings.

Children today must understand certain concepts about language content primarily because they are constantly exposed to the pervasive effects of the mass media. They must comprehend propaganda and persuasion techniques. They must learn to distinguish between what is actually reported, what is inferred from the report, and what judgment has been formed. They must realize the importance of context and how words or sentences lifted out of context can distort meaning. They must understand that the attitudes of writers and speakers can frequently be discerned by studying the words they use. Magazine and newspaper advertisements are readily accessible sources that children can use for examining and analyzing how language may be manipulated.

Categorizing Language

It is important to the language arts program for teachers to realize that two ways in which language may be categorized are by modes or by functions.

By Modes

The four modes of language are *listening, speaking, reading,* and *writing,* and so the language arts have traditionally been defined as the study of those four. Considered by some as the fifth mode is thinking; however, because it permeates all four modes, it should hardly be considered separately.

The primary, or oral, language modes are listening and speaking, and they are first learned, informally at least, in the home before the children enter school. The secondary, or written, language modes are reading and writing, long considered to be the domain of the school. All four modes, however, should receive due attention in the modern elementary classroom.

Listening and reading are deemed to be *receptive language* modes because students comprehend or receive messages orally (through listening) or in printed form (through reading). *Expressive language* modes are speaking and writing because students produce or express messages orally (through speech) or in written form (through composition). Receptive language modes therefore concern comprehension processes; and expressive languages modes concern composing processes.

Even though each language mode is often studied separately (and listed thus on children's report cards), it is rarely used alone. Instead, nearly every language arts activity demands more than one language mode; generally three or even all four are involved.

A second and newer way to categorize language is by function, and *pragmatics* is the formal study of when and how language is used when communicating with others. After all, in any meaningful communication between a reader and a writer, or a listener and a speaker, the reader and the listener must be aware of both the actual words and the expressions, as well as of the social function of what has been written or said.

Although numerous frameworks for categorizing language by function have been created, one of the best-received is by Halliday, who believes that a child acquiring language "learns how to mean."[5] Part of that acquisition concerns mastery of seven universal functions of language:

1. *Instrumental language* used to satisfy needs. "I want. . . ."
2. *Regulatory language* used to control the behavior of others. "Go away."
3. *Interactional language* employed during social activities or for the purpose of getting along with others. "Let's play together."
4. *Personal language* used to express private opinions or to allow a child to tell about himself/herself. "I want to be a pilot."
5. *Imaginative language* employed for creating a fantasy or a make-believe world. "Once upon a time. . . ."
6. *Heuristic language* used to seek information and ask questions. "Why do. . . ?"
7. *Informative language* employed to inform others. "I've got something to tell you"[6]

Elementary students need opportunities to use each of the seven functions; research has shown that primary children particularly use interactional language (or language for social purposes) most often but rarely use heuristic language (or language to seek information).[7] A teacher should consequently plan realistic communication episodes that incorporate one or more language functions because some may not occur spontaneously in student speech and writing.

A second popular framework, initially published in England by Tough after being empirically tested in a classroom environment, has been modified by Shafer, Staab, and Smith for American classrooms and appears in Table 2.1.[8] Any of its five functions can be used within either an imaginary or a real setting, and no distinction has been made between the two.

Integrating the Language Arts

An understanding and an acceptance of how language functions constitute the basis for integrating the language arts. Because language in the world outside school is largely instrumental and used in meaningful contexts that help persons comprehend the world, children are capable and experienced language learners by the time they enter school.[9]

Language learning is indeed a flexible and broad process not amenable to narrow curriculum structuring. Nevertheless, in many schools separate time blocks are given to spelling, handwriting, reading, oral language, literature, written

Table 2.1
Five Functions of Language with Subfunctions and Examples

Function 1: Asserting and Maintaining Social Needs

Subfunction	Examples
1. Asserting personal rights or needs	a. I want some juice. b. Give it to me, it's mine. c. I'm first 'cuz I'm the oldest. d. I hit him because he hit me first. e. I need a blue crayon.
2. Asserting negative expressions: criticizing, arguing, threatening, and giving negative opinions	a. You're talking too much. b. I told you to quit it. c. Stop it or I'll tell. d. That looks dumb.
3. Asserting positive expressions:	a. Yes, I think so too. b. I like your building. c. It tastes good to me.
4. Requesting an opinion	a. Do you like this?
5. Incidental expressions	a. Oh, gee. b. Good grief.

Function 2: Controlling

Subfunction	Examples
1. Controlling actions of self and others	a. Turn it around (to self). b. Get one egg. c. Give me the blue one. d. Put your name at the top, and I'll give it to the teacher.
2. Requesting directions	a. How do you do this? b. Where shall I put this?
3. Requesting another's attention	a. Watch this. b. Look here.

Function 3: Informing

Subfunction	Examples
1. Commenting on past or present events: labeling, noting details, noting specific incidents, or noting sequence (includes statements made in both first and third person)	a. That's a car. b. It's blue and white. c. I (the boy) have (has) some paint. d. I put the red on before the yellow.
2. Comparing	a. The first bus is longer than the second.
3. Making generalizations based on specific events and details	a. My brother is sick today. b. The cars were in an accident.
4. Requesting information	a. What color is this? b. Is this one longer?

Table 2.1 (cont.)

Function 4: Forecasting and Reasoning

Subfunction	Examples
1. Noting or speculating about cause/ effect relationships	a. The bridge fell because the logs were too heavy. b. You won't be able to carry that bag, it's too heavy. c. If you want the bottle to float, you'll have to put the cap on.
2. Speculating about an event	a. It might rain tomorrow. b. That probably won't work.
3. Noting or speculating about an event followed by its solution (includes drawing conclusions)	a. You're too tall, so you'll have to bend over. b. We better not run away from home, we might get hungry.
4. Requesting a reason	a. Why can't I go? b. Why does this happen?

Function 5: Projecting

Subfunction	Examples
1. Projecting into the feelings and reactions of others	a. He's feeling sad. b. He's probably mad about it.
2. Projecting into the experiences of others	a. I wouldn't like to live in the zoo like tigers. b. That boy's parents are fighting, and he is caught in the middle.

Source: From *Language Functions and School Success* by Robert E. Shafer, Claire Staab, and Karen Smith. Copyright © 1983 by Scott, Foresman and Company. Reprinted by permission.

composition, creative drama, and the other remaining areas of the language curriculum—despite the fact that even beginning teachers quickly realize the interrelatedness of the language arts. They see how spelling scores improve when the words come from vocabulary introduced during reading assignments, how drama sessions are more easily motivated when they follow the telling or reading aloud of a well-regarded piece of literature, and how handwriting lessons are considerably more effective when they contain words the children can read by themselves.

Integrated language arts demand a careful selection of materials, curriculum, and teaching techniques.[10] Materials should be authentic and brought in from the real world. Language modes should be combined because separations that seem logical to adults do not make sense to children and do not help them learn the skills that must eventually be mastered. Finally teaching techniques should encourage imitation of written and spoken models, and should provide opportunities for oral communication that is a purposeful exchange of ideas and that represents genuine oral interaction. Such instruction should stress project teaching in which students learn through integrated, sustained work that produces tangible results, not unlike what adults do in the outside world. Projects offer a background for expansion of grammatical structures and vocabulary, and they help children use language to fulfill specific goals.

Teachers should be aware of three principles that guide integration.[11] First, the goal of elementary language arts is broad communication effectiveness; children need significant and applicable language attitudes, processes, skills, and knowledge as they go on learning for a lifetime. Second, language learning is optimal when it occurs in meaningful situations; children learn language best as they use it in cognitive contexts, social contexts, and expressive contexts. And third, the intrinsic interrelationships among the various modes of communication are maximized when language is integrated throughout teaching; they are diminished when it is not.

One of the latest efforts at integration aimed at improving literacy development in the schools is the *Whole Language* program, which is based on the following ideas: (a) language use always occurs in situations; (b) situations are crucial to meaning growth; (c) language is for accomplishing purposes; (d) written language is language, so what is true for language is generally also true for written language; (e) the cuing systems of language (phonology, morphology, syntax, semantics, pragmatics, and spelling or orthography) are always present simultaneously and interact in any event of language in use.[12] The major assumption of Whole Language is that acquiring language through genuine use (and not through practice exercises) is the best way to help children learn reading and writing, as well as the best way to help children learn in general. Both oral and written language are seen as natural in the sense that when either is used with beginners, language is learned "incidentally." Reading and writing instruction in Whole Language classrooms utilizes complete and "real" texts (including newspapers, juvenile trade books, cake-mix directions, etc.) in communicative situations rather than in isolated language drills. Students in Whole Language classrooms are encouraged to experiment with writing and reading strategies in order to communicate with classmates, teachers, and other adults. One large urban system that implemented the program in September 1984 is the Denver Public Schools.

Developing Language Readiness

An important segment of any language arts curriculum, whether it be integrated or not, is language readiness. Activities promoting such readiness cannot be differentiated from other language learning experiences except that they represent experiences that should take place before boys and girls begin the routine use of readers and textbooks. The following major types of beginning activities are described in order to help kindergarten and first-grade teachers with their entering students.

Listening to enjoyable stories, whether they are told or read, helps this beginning student develop language readiness. (© James L. Shaffer.)

Because a language is a system of arbitrary verbal symbols, children cannot listen, speak, read, or write successfully until they have acquired a large number of those symbols and their corresponding concepts. Therefore, children need extensive firsthand experiences with places (such as the zoo, the airport, and the supermarket) and with concrete objects (such as a flower, an umbrella, or an aquarium) in order to attain a functioning vocabulary. They also need experiences that will help them learn the meanings of some abstract concepts (such as kindness, fairness, and responsibility). The development of vocabulary is a prerequisite to language fluency.

Firsthand Experiences

Videos, motion pictures, and filmstrips effectively develop concepts, foster literary appreciation, and teach language patterns. Such (secondhand) filmed experiences, however, must be followed by a related verbalization if maximum benefits are to be obtained. (Selected titles are provided in Appendix 1.)

Use of Videos and Filmstrips

Imaginative Experiences

Looking for forms in the clouds and listening for messages in the wind or rain are all experiences that stimulate the imagination. Such activities offer occasions to use the descriptive words and figurative speech that help children enjoy poetic literature and increase their language power.

Sensory Experiences

The experiences of smelling, seeing, touching, tasting, and hearing are related to firsthand experiences but imply greater refinement. Pupils need to learn to identify numerous objects by shape, texture, or sound. Appropriate experiences include making and classifying collections, playing identification games when blindfolded, and participating in tasting parties. As the children learn to use their senses, they extend their vocabularies and store up percepts that will help them in their reading and writing.

Picture Interpretation

Children can tell a story illustrated by a single picture, "read" a story from a wordless picture book or a sequence of pictures, and sort and classify pictures according to various topics or word elements. They can illustrate concepts with pictures and play matching games with pictures. Picture dictionaries help teach early work-study habits. And it is possible for the teacher to stimulate concept development through the use of pictures collected from magazines, discarded textbooks, and used workbooks.

Story Listening

Listening to well-selected stories gives children opportunities to learn listening and comprehension skills and to become acquainted with the various qualities of literature that make it enjoyable. Probably nothing has more effect on the development of the desire to learn to read than listening to appealing stories.

Early Handwriting

Children's first writing experiences may be the drawing of their initials in manuscript capitals on booklets related to unit activities. When they are ready to learn to write their full names, they should be taught to use both uppercase and lowercase letters so that there is no problem of relearning writing habits later. Next, the more advanced students can learn to make signs as part of their unit work.

Telling Original Stories

The early retelling by children of stories they have heard aids them in learning to relate events in sequence. Experience-chart planning and picture-interpretation projects also add to creative skills. The first expression usually consists of recounting personal experiences, and some beginners never progress any further. Others can compose an entire original story several sentences long. Young children who can express their ideas with some degree of sensitivity and imagination are well along the road to language fluency.

Dictated Stories

It is only a short step from telling personal experience stories and original stories to dictating them for the teacher to record. As boys and girls dictate and watch the teacher write the dictation, they learn page orientation and gradually attain a sight vocabulary. With guidance, children generalize that certain letters and letter combinations stand for specific sounds that occur in words. Each child's dictated stories contain his or her own vocabulary and are as long or as short as attention span and ability permit them to be. Because the work is so completely individualized, one immature student can enjoy participation in the activity without learning to read a single word, whereas another may advance to the second- or third-grade reading level. Dictated stories lead toward experiences in writing one's own stories and in reading books, so they are important milestones in a coordinated language arts curriculum.

Resources that are available can be classified into three language instruction categories: concept development, literary appreciation, and auditory discrimination. (Selected titles are provided in Appendix 1.)

Use of Cassettes and Recordings

Singing games such as "London Bridge" and "Looby-Loo" teach articulation and the rhythm of the language.

Musical Games

The children whose home backgrounds cause them to use words habitually in patterns that are considered nonstandard will be handicapped in speaking, reading, and writing in many situations. Most commercial word and sentence games provide practice in standard English usage, which will help these students.

Word Games

Programs, such as "Mister Rogers' Neighborhood" and "Sesame Street," promote language development among many young viewers. Children may watch them on the classroom set or at home. Research has shown that viewers of such shows make significant gains over nonviewers in the reading skills the programs are designed to teach and that the programs are an effective instructional supplement for target-age students in the bottom half of their class who are just beginning to experience reading difficulty.[13]

Use of Educational Television

These charts may be employed for constructing group experience stories, recording plans, displaying information, and a number of other purposes. Through their use, children learn page orientation, sequential organization, initial sight vocabulary, and various language functions.

Experience Charts

It is essential that the daily schedule provide some periods when girls and boys work quietly on individual projects and other periods when they can learn the give-and-take of lively, polite conversation. A short session for sharing out-of-school experiences may stimulate conversation, especially if the class is broken into small cooperative learning groups for the activity so that simple social responsibilities and courtesies may be taught. Classroom snack times also offer occasions for teaching and learning language usage.

Conversation Periods

In these activities children step into other people's shoes and portray others' personalities. In learning to identify with others they learn to think creatively, to use common courtesies, and (in dramatic play) to use the mechanics of oral communication to express themselves in clear and colorful ways.

Dramatic Play and Pantomime

Working with puzzles helps this young child develop eye-hand coordination and habits of concentration, both important aspects of language readiness. (© Richard Anderson.)

Puppets and Paper Dolls

Classrooms often display puppets, but paper dolls are not frequently utilized in teaching. Children love to work with both, however, and through such experiences, they grow in eye-hand coordination. Puppets and paper dolls have the advantage of permitting shy students to hide behind their characters, thereby making it easier for boys and girls to speak freely.

Puzzles

Jigsaw puzzles that have large pieces provide purposeful practice in differentiating shapes and sizes. They develop eye-hand coordination and habits of concentration.

Poetry Experiences

Young children readily appreciate the poet's ability to paint word pictures and to express various moods. They quickly learn to sense the rhythm and listen for rhyming sounds. Repetitive phrases aid them in hearing varied speech sounds, and nonsense verse leads them into their own efforts at creative expression. Poems can help the students see themselves, develop a healthy sense of humor, and even increase their ease in communication situations.

Discussion Questions

1. Do you agree that none of the four language modes can be used alone in a language arts activity? Defend your position.
2. Which of the major types of beginning language activities would you use with less advantaged first graders who are enrolled in a school district noted for its limited financial resources?

3. Why is a systematic literature program gaining an increasingly significant role in the current language arts curriculum?
4. Why do modern media demand a greater understanding of semantics, even among young children?
5. Why is there such resistance among many parents and administrators, and even among some teachers, to all proposals concerning the integration of language arts? Is it all a matter of tradition?

Suggested Projects

1. Determine how many morphemes are contained in the first paragraph of today's lead story on the front page of the local newspaper. Which ones are free morphemes, and which are bound?
2. Prepare for the grade of your choice a list of ten goals that would be appropriate for the language arts program of a nearby school.
3. On a sheet of graph paper, draw and label a classroom arrangement conducive to the development of language readiness in kindergarten. Then, on the other side of the sheet, briefly list other items that would further stimulate such development in that environment.
4. Role-play a third-grade teacher who justifies the forthcoming integration of the language arts in his or her classroom before a group of doubtful, even hostile, parents.

Recent Related Readings

Barbour, N., Webster, T., and Drosdesk, S. 1987. "Sand: A Resource for the Language Arts," *Young Children, 42*(2), pp. 20–25.
Bromley, K. 1988. *Language Arts: Exploring Connections.* Boston: Allyn and Bacon.
Clarke, M. 1987. "Don't Blame the System: Constraints on 'Whole Language' Reform," *Language Arts, 64*, pp. 384–396.
Cox, C. 1988. *Teaching Language Arts.* Boston: Allyn and Bacon.
Finegan, E. and Besnier, N. 1989. *Language: Its Structure and Use.* New York: Harcourt.
Loughlin, C., and Davis, M. 1987. *Supporting Literacy: Developing Effective Learning Environments.* New York: Teachers College Press.
Monson, D., Taylor, B., and Dykstra, R. 1988. *Language Arts.* Glenview, IL: Scott, Foresman.
Schwartz, J. 1988. *Encouraging Early Literacy.* Portsmouth, NH: Heinemann.
Shapiro, J., and Doiron, R. 1987. "Literacy Environments: Bridging the Gap between Home and School," *Childhood Education, 63,* pp. 263–269.
Temple, C., and Gillet, J., *Language Arts—Learning Processes and Teaching Practices.* Glenview, IL: Scott, Foresman.

Chapter Notes

1. California State Department of Education, *English Language Arts Framework* (Sacramento: Author, 1987), p. v.
2. *Ibid.,* pp. 1–2.
3. C. Eisenhardt, *Applying Linguistics in the Teaching of Reading* (Columbus, Ohio: Merrill, 1972), pp. 96–98.
4. California State Department of Education, *English Language Framework for California Public Schools* (Sacramento: Author, 1976), p. 48.

5. M. Halliday, *Learning How to Mean—Explorations in the Development of Language* (London: Edward Arnold, 1975), pp. 19–21.

6. *Ibid.*

7. G. Pinnell, "Language in Primary Classrooms," *Theory Into Practice,* 1975, *14,* pp. 318–327.

8. J. Tough, *Focus on Meaning: Talking to Some Purpose with Young Children* (London: Allen & Unwin, 1973); and R. Shafer, C. Staab, and K. Smith, *Language Functions and School Success* (Glenview, Illinois: Scott, Foresman, 1983), pp. 40–43.

9. J. Yatvin, "Integrating the Language Arts," in *Language Arts Instruction and the Beginning Teacher,* C. Personke and D. Johnson, eds. (Englewood Cliffs, New Jersey: Prentice Hall, 1987), p. 2.

10. *Ibid.,* pp. 7–10.

11. B. Busching and S. Lundsteen, "Curriculum Models for Integrating the Language Arts," in *Integrating the Language Arts in the Elementary School,* B. Busching and J. Schwartz, eds. (Urbana, Illinois: National Council of Teachers of English, 1983), pp. 9–15.

12. B. Altwerger, C. Edelsky, and B. Flores, "Whole Language: What's New?" *The Reading Teacher,* 1987, *41,* pp. 144–154.

13. J. Cooney, *Children's Television Workshop: Progress Report.* (ERIC Document Reproduction Service No. ED 095 892).

Part B Oral Language

Chapters

Listening 3

Major Chapter Goals

After studying Chapter 3, the reader will be able to
1. Understand how the basic mode of listening relates to the other language arts.
2. Describe a dozen factors that affect the listening ability of children.
3. Outline some instructional activities for promoting each of the major kinds of listening.

Discover As You Read This Chapter Whether*

1. According to federal legislation, listening is a basic skill.
2. Everyone who can hear knows how to listen.
3. Elementary school children spend nearly one-third of their daily classroom activity time in listening.
4. Incidental approaches to teaching listening have proved just as effective as structured lessons.
5. There is as yet no developmental sequence of listening skills.
6. Teachers readily accept children with hearing aids.
7. Attentive listening is more concentrated than critical listening.
8. The greatest part of the school day is spent on attentive listening rather than on either appreciative or critical listening.
9. Primary children are incapable of critical listening.
10. A good listening test uses stimulus materials that are spoken.

*Answers to these true-or-false statements may be found in Appendix 5.

In 1987 the first issue of the *Journal of the International Listening Association* appeared. The Association itself was created in 1980, representing an important step toward the development of research and resource materials on listening. Two years earlier another crucial step was taken when the United States Office of Education added listening to the list of basic skills under a new Title II (of the Elementary and Secondary Education Act) passed by Congress as Public Law 95–561 (20 USC 2881). It seems almost ironic that the first language skill to appear chronologically and the oldest language art on record has finally been recognized and made legitimate.

Although reading and writing are the more recently developed of the communication skills in human societies, they have been more readily accepted as proper subjects of school instruction than have the older skills of listening and speaking. Since the establishment of compulsory education in many countries in the nineteenth century, elementary schools have traditionally been concerned with providing training in the skills of literacy and, to some extent, of speaking. Any listening skills that the pupils acquired came incidentally in the course of studying other subjects or were learned indirectly at home.

Today, however, given the new emphasis on basic skills in public education, federal legislation and the efforts of the International Listening Association (ILA) should lead to more student and teacher time being devoted to listening lessons. By 1985 there were already thirty-three states reporting some move toward the teaching of listening, according to a survey conducted by the Speech Communication Association.[1]

Questions Teachers Often Ask About the Listening Program

What Is Listening?

There is apparently no one definition of listening that is widely accepted by educators and researchers at present. Lundsteen has defined listening simply as that process by which spoken language is converted to meaning in the mind.[2] Linguistically, it is a learned receptive skill. Because verbal communication is carried on primarily so that others may comprehend the information transmitted and react accordingly, listening implies comprehension of the material heard. It is a personal, often private absorption of ideas and attitudes expressed through oral language. It differs from hearing, which does not involve interpretation.

Why Is Listening Important?

Listening is not only the first language skill for most persons, but it is generally also basic to success in all other areas of the language arts. Progress in reading, speaking, and writing is directly governed by listening ability. It is quantitatively the most important of the four modes because nearly half of the adult's working day and more than half of the child's classroom activity time are spent in listening. Listening is also a critical part of today's culture in the United States where approximately 75 percent of the people reside in urban areas, causing person-to-person relationships to typify modern lives. Moreover, the knowledge explosion since the mid century has demanded the processing of greater amounts of information through listening.

Listening constitutes the mainstay of several recreational and educational media. According to the latest census, for instance, each child and adult in this country has more than one radio available to him or her and, in 98 percent of the households, the use of one or more television sets as well. Cassette tapes are heard at home, in the classroom, and in many automobiles, and videotape rentals (and sales) have been soaring during the past few years.

Many reasoning-thinking skills are practiced in a listening-speaking environment before those skills are taught in a reading situation. For this reason, listening skills occupy a prominent position in reading instruction. A major means of learning and recall, particularly for poor readers, listening is essential to success in the phonetic analysis of words and the ability to discriminate among sounds and identify initial and final sounds.

During the early school years, most instruction takes place through oral language. Even after a child begins reading, listening remains the more effective tool for gaining information until the sixth- or seventh-grade level. It directs attention to details and their synthesis.

Listening is a basis for the good human relationships that are considered to be among the most important educational goals. It influences value formation. It results in greater emotional responses and changes in attitude than other language arts. Finally, according to the Florida State Department of Education, listening constitutes the threefold problem of today's generation that must decide what to listen to, how to strengthen listening ability, and how to listen appreciatively and critically.

Can Listening Be Taught?

Because hundreds of studies have concluded that listening skills can be taught, teachers are assured that they are not wasting time when planning and presenting structured lessons in listening. They should be aware that such directed lessons make boys and girls more conscious of good listening habits than do incidental approaches.

Lessons that demand active verbal responses on the part of the children both during and after listening increase listening comprehension. Such comprehension is also improved through listening to literature or participating in lessons primarily directed toward increasing reading comprehension.

Incidentally, the grade level of the students does not matter insofar as listening instruction goes. From kindergartners to college freshmen, all students who receive such instruction (in contrast to those who do not) evidence significant improvement in listening ability.

How Is Listening Related to the Other Language Arts?

Not only does language processing include the major skills of transmission and reception, but language in all its facets is an integrated phenomenon.[3] Because effects in one of language's subsystems will later show up in the others, improving listening is likely to affect other language arts.

The relationship between the receptive skill of *listening and the expressive skill of writing* was explored in research on children with normal hearing and on those with impaired hearing. Children able to hear were found to use more complex types of language structure and more concise composition, thereby reflecting a higher degree of maturity in writing expression than that of children who were deaf or who had partial hearing. Comprehension of meaning in writing depends on the base of comprehension in listening. Furthermore, while composing ideas in written form, some children speak and listen internally as they record.

Research has established a positive statistical correlation between *listening and speaking.* Not only are speech patterns learned largely through listening to other persons speak, but in turn, the growth of the listener function in an individual probably plays an important role in the ultimate development of his or her skill as a speaker in being able to order verbal behavior. (No wonder the child born into a large, overcrowded, noisy household often learns "practiced inattention.")

An interesting dimension in the listening-speaking relationship is distortion, which can occur while boys and girls are listening to spoken messages.[4] Four distortions that create differences between messages sent and messages delivered are (1) attitude cutoff, which stops information at the oral source; (2) motive attribution, which tries to attribute a motive to the speaker; (3) organizational mix-up, which sometimes occurs during message organization; and (4) self-preoccupation by listeners so intent on formulating responses that they cannot attend fully to the messages being sent. Briefly then, although the message should be the same for speaker and listener alike, differences in communication may and often do occur.

Both *listening and reading* are phases of language serving as major avenues for the acquisition of information. Both are a complex of related skill components, and the same postulated higher mental processes seem to underlie the two of them (although the evidence indicates that each receptive skill may contain verbal factors individually unique). Both flourish in a relaxed environment where the ideas and vocabulary are at least partially familiar to the receivers. And both use signals such as intonation and pauses in oral language and their corresponding punctuation marks in written language.

In listening, however, the rate is determined by the speaker; the ideas are usually presented only once; the listener loses a portion of the content whenever his or her attention lapses; and the listener's evaluation of that content is often influenced by the speaker's use of gestures or voice inflections. Communication through reading, on the other hand, is less personal and may include visual aids. The reader proceeds at his or her own rate and may reread the material as often as needed to gain the information. Also, printed ideas are more likely to be expressed in well-organized fashion.

Because listening and reading are receptive skills, early researchers assumed that they are highly interdependent. More recently, however, research findings have been mixed.[5] On the one hand, Lemons and Moore taught listening skills to black, inner-city fourth graders and found the children made significant improvements on the Metropolitan Achievement Test in reading skills, in contrast to pupils in the control group not exposed to such instruction in listening skills. Another group of fourth graders, as studied by Hoffman, was also given training in listening comprehension and made significant gains in reading comprehension in contrast to a control group in the same grade not provided with such training. Finally, Tinzmann and Thompson compared listening and reading cloze procedures and found that, among the third through sixth graders in their study, fourteen of the sixteen correlations between all variables were significant, suggesting that scores on student oral language ability tests can predict reading ability.

On the other hand, Haugh studied the relationship between listening comprehension and reading comprehension among first graders and found a correlation of only .317. Hildyard's comparison of third- and fifth-grade readers' and listeners' comprehension of a narrative text demonstrated that readers and listeners adopt different, not similar, strategies when comprehending narrative material. Readers studied paid more attention to what was "said," and listeners paid more attention to what was "meant." In their review of some thirty-one studies comparing reading comprehension and listening comprehension at various grade levels, Sticht and others found that in grades one through six, most comparisons favored the listening comprehension mode, but the advantage shifted to the reading comprehension mode from grades seven to twelve.

In view of the conflicting evidence, one recent recommendation (labeled only as "pretty sure") stated that at almost any age level, students will benefit from direct efforts to improve comprehension abilities, although much transfer from listening to reading cannot be expected.[6] Nevertheless, after pupils become mature readers (at grade eight or above), cross-modal transfer is possible, and what benefits reading comprehension will likely benefit listening comprehension, and vice versa.

A sequential program in listening skills is as important as a sequential program in reading skills. Because most children are not accomplished listeners, a developmental listening improvement program is needed in many schools. However, there is as yet no published research outlining a special developmental sequence of listening skills.[7] Still, one hierarchy has been compiled, based on theories of the development of auditory abilities, and it covers both sighted as well as visually handicapped children.[8] It includes sections on auditory discrimination skills, listening comprehension skills, and environmental skills, the last being those skills involved in the identification and interpretation of sounds from the environment (excluding verbal sounds) that play an important role in the orientation and mobility skills of visually handicapped (VH) persons. In this hierarchy, discrepancies in the time when certain skills are apt to occur in sighted and visually handicapped persons are indicated by (VH*).

Discrimination skills for pupils in kindergarten through third grade include recognizing the differences in initial consonants, final consonants, and medial sounds auditorily; recognizing the discrete words within a sentence as well as the sequence of words within a sentence; learning that sounds differ in intensity (VH*), pitch (VH*), pattern, and duration; identifying the accented words within a sentence, the number of syllables within a word, and the accented syllable within a word; changing the accent from one syllable to another; discriminating among

Is There a Learning Hierarchy of Listening Skills?

the temporal order of sounds within words; recognizing the initial and final consonant sounds, the short vowel and long vowel sounds, and rhyming words; and recognizing and discriminating among word endings.

Comprehension skills for pupils in kindergarten through third grade include using new words learned by listening, using context to predict words in a sentence, associating spoken words with pictures or miniature objects (VH*), associating auditory cues with motor responses, recognizing verbal absurdities, sequencing details correctly, identifying the main ideas of a simple story, relating new information to past experiences, listening for specific information, and following travel directions (VH*).

Comprehension skills for children in grades four through six include distinguishing between true and false statements and between relevant and irrelevant statements; generalizing from details and drawing inferences and conclusions; following the directions in making things; recognizing associations and relationships; interpreting the feelings of the characters; comparing and contrasting; and evaluating critically.

Environmental skills for pupils in kindergarten through third grade are (1) learning that sounds differ in intensity (VH*), pitch (VH*), pattern and duration; and (2) learning the concept of distance in relation to sound localization and movement (VH*). Skills for children in grades four through six include (1) identifying sounds in the environment at particular times of the day and evaluating them in terms of orientation and mobility (VH*); and (2) promoting growth of echo perception and spatial orientation (VH*).

Table 3.1 covers the developmental sequence or hierarchy of listening skills for elementary students.

Which Factors Influence Listening?

There are at least a dozen factors that affect the learning processes generally and the teaching of listening particularly. Conversely, some of them could also be listed as possible causes for specific listening deficiencies.

The first and most obvious is *hearing sense*. The human ear is said to be able to detect sounds in the range of 20–20,000 cycles per second, or Hertz (Hz), the standardized international unit for measuring frequency. During the hearing process, the ear receives and modifies speech sounds, the range being 250–3000 Hz. Approximately 5 to 10 percent of the school population is deemed to be hearing-impaired.

A second factor is the *involvement level required of the listeners*. This has generally been described as an enhancing factor because child listeners must actively process the information heard and can be neither bored nor discouraged. However, it may become an inhibiting factor if the speaker's voice is monotonous or if the aural message relates to topics arousing negative reactions, such as fear of nuclear war, for example.

Another factor is the *family*. Children in small families generally obtain higher listening scores than those in large families. Pupils coming from smaller, television-viewing families are better listeners than those of larger, television-viewing families.

Table 3.1
A Hierarchy of Listening Skills

Environmental Skills

Kindergarten–Grade Three
Learns that sounds differ in intensity (VH*).
Learns that sounds differ in pitch (VH*).
Learns that sounds differ in pattern.
Learns that sounds differ in duration (the length of time they can be heard).
Learns the concept distance in relation to sound localization and movement (VH).

Grade Four–Grade Six
Identifies sounds in the environment at certain times of day and evaluates them in terms of orientation and mobility (VH).
Promotes growth of echo perception and spatial orientation (VH).

Discrimination Skills

Kindergarten–Grade Three
Learns that sounds differ in intensity (VH*).
Learns that sounds differ in pitch (VH*).
Learns that sounds differ in pattern.
Learns that sounds differ in duration.
Recognizes differences in word sounds.
Recognizes differences in initial consonants (*cat-mat*) auditorily.
Recognizes differences in final consonants (*mat-map*) auditorily.
Recognizes differences in medial sounds (*map-mop*) auditorily.
Recognizes discrete words within a sentence.
Recognizes sequence of words within a sentence.
Identifies accented words within a sentence.
Identifies number of syllables within a word.
Identifies accented syllable within a word.
Changes accent from one syllable to another.
Recognizes initial and final consonant sounds.
Recognizes short vowel sounds.
Recognizes long vowel sounds.
Recognizes rhyming words.
Recognizes and discriminates word endings (*s, ing, er*).
Discriminates temporal order of sounds within words.

Comprehension Skills

Kindergarten–Grade Three
Recognizes verbal absurdities.
Associates spoken words with pictures or miniature objects (VH*).
Associates auditory cues with motor responses.
Uses new words learned by listening.
Uses context to predict words in a sentence.
Relates new information to past experiences.
Identifies the main ideas of a simple story.
Sequences details correctly.
Listens for specific information.
Follows travel directions (VH*).

Grade Four–Grade Six
Follows directions in making things.
Recognizes relationships and associations.
Draws inferences and conclusions.
Interprets feelings of characters.
Generalizes from details.
Distinguishes true and false statements.
Distinguishes between relevant and irrelevant statements.
Compares and contrasts.
Evaluates critically.

Source: Abridged from S. S. Weaver and W. L. Rutherford, "A Hierarchy of Listening Skills," *Elementary English*, 1974, *51*, pp. 1149–1150. Reprinted with permission of National Council of Teachers of English.

Although evidence concerning the possibility of a relationship between listening and family size is not yet conclusive, it has been speculated that the heightened noise and confusion in a large group leads to the development of a protective insulation, or a nonlistening attitude, that children transfer to the classroom. Socially and economically, good listeners tend to come from middle- and upper-middle-class homes, whereas poor listeners come from lower- and lower-middle-class homes. Middle children (those who have older *and* younger brothers and sisters) are no better listeners than the oldest or the youngest children in the family. More good listeners than poor listeners, however, are first-born or only children.

In the area of *personality and social development,* good listeners are better adjusted than poor listeners. They are indicated to be more participating, ready to try new things, and more emotionally stable and free from nervous symptoms. They are chosen significantly more often than poor listeners as work partners and play companions. Their teachers also seem to be aware of the differences for they rate poor listeners as lower in such traits as willingness to work, vigor, ability to get a task done, cheerfulness, and participation in class and playground activities. Emotional and social adjustment is therefore vital.

Listening achievement increases with *chronological age and grade level.* This factor holds true even when the rate of presentation is increased and speech is compressed. Older, intermediate-grade boys and girls always comprehend more by listening than do their younger, primary-age friends who, in turn, surpass kindergarten and preschool pupils.

A sixth factor is a *structured program.* As mentioned earlier, listening skill and listening performance can be and have been improved by instruction. Even at the first-grade level, children profit from a structured listening program.

Another factor is *thinking skills.* Many of the operations involved in listening are mental operations, with listening said to involve facets of thinking and reasoning of a high order. Although the relationship between listening and thinking has not yet been firmly determined by researchers, there are those who already believe that poor listeners may have thinking problems. Thinking skills allow students to index, make comparisons, note sequence, react by forming sensory images, draw inferences, abstract main ideas, categorize, recognize relationships, and use appreciation.

The extent to which meaning is associated depends initially on the listeners' *experiential background.* Words are more easily apprehended when they form a part of predictable and meaningful speech. Children who come to school with a broad background of experiences can apprehend each word to which they listen and therefore enjoy listening to their teachers and peers.

A ninth factor concerns the *physical condition of the listeners.* Boys and girls who are hungry or tired are not physiologically able to attend to the listening tasks effectively.

Once the listening pupil has identified a sound or recognized a sound sequence as a familiar word, the *presentation variables of mode and rate* must be considered. Primary children listening to a story-telling program across three modes of presentation, for instance, had their highest comprehension performance for videotape and lowest for audio cassette.[9] Also, comprehension has generally increased as the rate of presentation increases, and most spoken language can be comprehended satisfactorily at rates twice that of normal talk of 120 words per minute. Although research studies are conflicting in this area, other studies do support slower rates of presentation for the verbally disadvantaged, the auditorily handicapped, and young children generally.[10]

Recognition of voices is the eleventh factor. The differentiation that is made between the voices of other persons depends on the period during which the threshold becomes lower and lower and allows the hearer to be increasingly confident in his or her recognition of the speaker. Children find it easiest to listen to a single voice. They can also comprehend a conversation or recitation that involves several voices, but in one setting. They do not perceive, however, a situation in which several persons are talking without being in the same place, or a situation in which voices are added from the outside either to comment on a scene or to produce some psychological or moral effect.

Finally children have the best opportunity to improve their listening ability in a *supportive classroom environment*. Such an environment is flexible. Children learn to communicate best when they have the chance to practice in small groups first, and later in increasingly larger groups. Furniture that allows freedom of movement from one type of organization to another is desirable.

Such an environment has opportunities for interaction. When listeners are active in the communication process, their level of personal involvement reaches its highest peak. The amount of interaction possible often depends on the group structure, whereas only minimum response is possible in a whole-class discussion with a questioning teacher and answering children, maximum interaction can occur when children work in pairs or cooperative learning groups. Pupils need practice in communicating in groups of various sizes and for many purposes.

Such an environment stimulates speaking and listening. Children will communicate about those activities and objects that they encounter in their classroom. When the room has ample materials and interest centers, pupils are stimulated to improve the quality and increase the quantity of their oral language.

Such an environment is relatively quiet. One study of 40 five- and six-year-olds showed that even young children with normal hearing have significantly more difficulty in comprehending speech against a background of noise than do young adults.[11] In fact, the range of speech discrimination in noise scores for the boys and girls indicated great variability in their ability to handle even low levels of noise of competing messages. The researchers concluded that the open-plan classroom should be questioned from an acoustical viewpoint because it generally provides poorer signal-to-noise ratios than does the self-contained classroom.

How Can the Teacher Help the Hearing-Impaired Listen Better?

The elementary teacher today will generally enroll two or more children with reduced hearing each year. Because the teacher is concerned with developing listening skill in hearing-impaired pupils, he or she will make sure to

1. *Seat them carefully.* Place them from six to ten feet from the area where teaching is centered. Permit them to move their seats if the teaching center moves to another part of the room. Permit them to turn around to hear their classmates speak. Make sure that each pupil's better ear is toward the source of significant sounds and not toward the windows or hallway.
2. *Speak properly.* Avoid using loud tones, exaggerated mouth movements, or too many gestures. Avoid talking when walking about the room or when facing the chalkboard. Avoid placing hands or books in front of the face while speaking. Avoid using homophones (such as *road-rode*), which look alike on the lips. Use clear enunciation. Check frequently and informally to make sure that the handicapped children comprehend the discussion.
3. *Assist them casually.* Write new words on the chalkboard because names of people and places are difficult for them to understand. Ask other children to help them get the correct assignment. Provide special help in such language activities as spelling and reading in which sounds have unusual importance. Explain special events such as field trips well in advance. Repeat instructions as often as needed.
4. *Watch their physical condition.* Prevent further hearing loss by noting respiratory infections and other ailments. Prevent undue fatigue from the strain of seeing and listening intently by providing alternating periods of physical activity and inactivity in the day's planning.
5. *Encourage participation.* Allow extracurricular activities, especially vocal music. Help them discover abilities and talents by guiding them to activities in which they can achieve their share of success.

Finally, teachers should personally avoid stereotypical images of hearing-impaired pupils. Results from a recent survey in northern Illinois of 104 elementary teachers who had pupils with hearing aids supported the conclusion that such images do exist.[12] Asked to list all traits that may be used to describe elementary school age children with hearing aids, the teachers noted undesirable traits to desirable ones by a ratio of 3.5 to 1. The data support the claim that elementary classroom teachers need greater understanding of the child who has a hearing aid; the largest number of responses was grouped in terms of emotional implications rather than educational ones. Teachers were apparently projecting their own feelings rather than listing attributes of the children.

Instructional Activities

Like all language skills, listening demands responsible and systematic teaching and practice. Without the guidance of a teacher and the reinforcement of parents, children are unlikely to attain the facility required by the impact of listening competence upon contemporary society.

This child is engaged in appreciative listening for enjoyment and creative response. (© James L. Shaffer.)

Although listening is a receptive language art, it is also an active process, entailing thinking and interpretation on the part of the listeners. They question, accept, reject, enjoy, or dislike some, if not all, of what they hear. At the same time, they are called upon to recall what they have heard or read earlier in the same area in order to evaluate more accurately the present information.

Although as many as twenty-five kinds of listening have been identified (ranging from accurate and active to responsible and selective), basically there are only three types of listening: appreciative, attentive, and critical. They differ primarily in the degree of concentration demanded, with appreciative listeners being considerably less tense than critical listeners. It must be pointed out, however, that all listening demands interpretation and consequently some degree of concentration. Listening is not merely hearing; therefore, when two or more distractions are present, during a radio broadcast for example, children only *hear* the presentation on the radio. They cannot *listen* to it until the number of distractions is reduced and they give conscious attention to the performer or performance. Listening is more than a physiological reaction, and it demands more than passive participation.

Appreciative listening is the ability to listen for enjoyment and creative response. It is less concentrated than either attentive or critical listening, and the hearer is therefore more relaxed. Children may listen to tapes and records, to radio and television programs, and to concerts. They may listen to shadow plays, puppet shows, roll movies, sound filmstrips, and readers theater. They may also simply listen to enjoy pleasant sounds, indoors or outdoors, such as a cricket's chirp or a canary's song.

Appreciative Listening

Boys and girls may fingerpaint or draw designs to music or use chalk or clay to express ideas inspired by a recording of Tchaikovsky's *Nutcracker Suite;* Dvořák's *Slavonic Dances;* Grieg's *Peer Gynt Suite;* Rossini's *William Tell Overture;* or Gershwin's *Rhapsody in Blue.*

They can paint their responses to poetry they have heard, including Silverstein's "Smart" and "Hug O'War," Viorst's "Since Hanna Moved Away" and "Mother Doesn't Want a Dog," Prelutsky's "Nature Is" and "The Four Seasons," and Livingston's "Lazy Witch" and "History."

Children can divide themselves into small literary committees, each selecting one of its members to read aloud to the others. The child's audience listens, with books closed, to poems rich in imagery or to poems that evoke excitement, contentment, or drowsiness. Sometimes the reader selects stories that have a dominant mood such as three of those for older pupils by Hans Christian Andersen; the audience can sense sadness-triumph-surprise for "The Ugly Duckling," sadness-pity for "The Little Match Girl," and exaggeration-arrogance of "The Princess and the Pea."

Choral speaking provides for participation as well as for appreciative listening. At times as many as six to ten pupils can recite while the rest of the class listens. Suggestions for simple choral activities are given in Chapter 13.

Watching performances of a children's theater group also involves appreciative listening. The theater provides enjoyment and expression, allowing the young audience to identify with the onstage characters and actions. Listeners are sometimes subtly exposed to learning about cultures of other lands as well.

Story telling also offers children the opportunity to learn to listen appreciatively to their teacher, a media center specialist, or their peers. Children can tell round-robin chain stories in which each participant carries on from where the preceding speaker stopped or they can tell, extemporaneously, an original ending to a classic story that they have heard.

Kindergartners and early primary pupils are generally interested in finger plays, which are excellent devices to foster appreciative listening. Sometimes a child can even be encouraged to develop his or her own finger play to share with classmates. Younger children also often enjoy interpreting music with simple rhythm instruments. Older pupils can select background music for an original class story or a poem from a favorite anthology.

Finally, children may compile a picture book of sounds with separate sections devoted to sounds at home, sounds of the city (or country), sounds in the classroom, and sounds on the playground. Younger pupils may wish to include only pictures; older children can write an accompanying text.

Attentive Listening

Attentive listening demands that the attention of the listener be focused on one person or on one electronic medium so that the listener can purposefully respond either orally or in written fashion. It may or may not involve a two-way conversation or discussion, for in some cases it is strictly a one-way communication process. The listener, however, must think carefully about the telephone conversation, radio broadcast, recording, telecast, play, lecture, or classroom announcement.

When students listen for directions regarding an assignment, they are engaged in attentive listening. (© James L. Shaffer.)

Attentive listening concerns the ability to respond to directions and explanations. In the primary grades children may be sent on errands throughout the building after they have received exact directions about how to get to the custodian's and the principal's offices or how to locate the sixth-grade classroom. They should have many opportunities to recall the directions given for their safety regarding standards for fire drills and playground behavior. They can explain to newcomers how to handle a particular classroom routine that requires three or four steps in sequence; for instance, how to care for paintbrushes, how to line up for morning recess, or how to be a book monitor. Individual pupils can give directions for reaching their nearest public library, and the class can later evaluate the clarity of these directions. In the intermediate grades, one group of pupils may explain the steps in a science experiment while a second group follows the directions as stated and a third group evaluates both procedures. In another instance, the teacher can read the instructions for using a word processor and let the children retell the steps in order.

This kind of listening, which occupies a greater part of the school day than either appreciative or critical listening, also includes the ability to recognize and respond to grapheme-phoneme relationships, rhyming, onomatopoeia and alliteration, and gross sounds (by identifying, duplicating, or classifying them). It involves as well the ability to retell in sequence what has been heard; to recognize specific details in a story told on tape; and to note similes, metaphors, and other figurative language in poems read orally. Therefore primary children can, for example, do the following attentive listening activities:

1. Sit quietly outdoors and name the sounds around them.
2. Classify sounds according to intensity and pitch or by the specific object with which each is linked.

3. Choose pairs of rhyming words out of three- and four-word series of mixed words.
4. Supply single words to complete rhyming couplets.
5. Name three other words that begin with the same initial consonant blend as the chalkboard word that the teacher has just pronounced.

Fourth, fifth, and sixth graders develop attentive listening habits when they are given an opportunity, for example, to

1. Answer specific questions about an article on Australia, which the teacher has just read aloud.
2. Note the visual imagery after listening to Thurman's *Flashlight and Other Poems* (Atheneum, 1976).
3. Identify the triple blends (such as *scr* and *spl*) in lists of words that have been taped.
4. Listen to two stories and then compare and contrast them.
5. Discuss the alliterative unit in tongue twisters recited by their classmates.

This type of listening is labeled as purposeful listening by Devine, who also considers it highly teachable.[13] It is one segment of the curricula from which students may profit promptly by acquiring those listening skills most necessary for success in school.

Critical Listening

Critical listening is the most complex kind of listening to teach or to learn. At the same time it is a matter of grave significance under the First Amendment, which guarantees freedom of speech to all, regardless of ethical or educational backgrounds. It is a judgmental process as well as an analytical one.

Implied in critical listening is the use of a highly conscious standard or criterion for evaluating spoken material while comprehending it. It is this advanced degree of evaluation or reflection about what is heard that is crucial and intricate. A continuum of the goals or skills involved in lessons in critical listening in the elementary school should include teaching the children how to do the following:

1. Distinguish fact from fantasy, according to explicit criteria.
2. Distinguish relevant statements from irrelevant ones and evaluate them.
3. Distinguish well-supported statements from opinion or judgment and evaluate them.
4. Evaluate the qualifications of a speaker.
5. Detect and evaluate the bias, emotional slant, or lack of objectivity of a speaker.
6. Recognize and evaluate the effects of devices the speaker may use to influence the listener, such as propaganda, voice intonation, or music.
7. Evaluate the validity and adequacy of the central theme or point of view of a performer or performance.

Primary children are capable of critical listening. For example, a day after telling the class the story of "The Three Bears," the teacher can read them Graves' *The Wright Brothers* (Putnam, 1973) and then ask them to give evidence of why yesterday's tale was fantasy or make-believe and why today's story is real. Another day, the teacher can pose a series of questions, some of which are meaningful and some of which are not. The child responding must determine in each instance whether the question is nonsense (Why is the grass red?) or whether the question is reasonable (If chickens are birds, why can't they fly?).

Intermediate pupils can listen to recordings of talks or conversations by unidentified persons and then decide whether the speakers showed prejudice or used loaded words during the presentations. On another occasion, they can listen to a selection containing instructions for making paper snowflakes, for instance, which contain some extraneous information; after omitting all irrelevant data, the class must then make the snowflakes. Sample textbook exercises in critical and other listening skills for intermediate students are shown in Figure 3.1.

That both late primary and intermediate pupils can be helped to develop critical listening has been substantiated by research in Maryland involving 200 children, ages eight to ten.[14] The boys and girls, both white and black, were given lessons to help them become aware of propaganda employed by commercial advertisers in their television programs. It was concluded that children can be made conscious of commercial propaganda emanating from television. Furthermore, they can successfully transfer their new critical listening skill to other disciplines as they begin to recognize propaganda in reading, in conversations with teachers and peers, and in newspaper and magazine advertising.

Learning activities that promote each of the three basic types of listening are listed in Table 3.2. The suggested grade level for each instructional activity also is included.

A Strategies Approach

In addition to having the opportunity to participate in instructional activities (which are often group lessons), students also need to acquire strategies they can use individually while listening so that the messages they receive are clearer and more readily recalled. Such a strategies approach is especially useful for promoting attentive listening but can also be used during critical listening and, to some extent, during attentive listening sessions as well. The following six strategies were developed by Tompkins, Friend, and Smith for elementary students to learn and use:[15]

1. *Imagery,* or Making a Picture in Your Mind. When the information being presented has numerous visual details, images, or descriptions, the listening students can draw a mental picture to help them remember that message.

Table 3.2
Sample Instructional Activities in Elementary School Listening

Type of Listening	Grade Level	Learning Activity or Teaching Procedure
Appreciative	K, 1, 2	The teacher will play a musical selection via record, piano, or cassette while the children listen. The children will then respond by describing how the music makes them feel (sad, happy) through pictures or words.
Appreciative	3–4	The children will listen to the story the teacher has chosen to read or tell. They will then be able to state whether the story has made them angry, unhappy, or delighted.
Appreciative	5–6	The teacher will read Carl Sandburg's "Chicago," which denotes approval, joy, and ambition.
Attentive	K, 1, 2	The teacher will choose to tell any story that has a definite beginning, middle, and end; then prepare pictures illustrating actions in each part of the story. Later, the children will arrange four or five pictures in sequence.
Attentive	3–4	The teacher will read or tell a story to the class and then ask five questions concerning what happened in the story.
Attentive	5–6	The teacher will read orally the instructions for making a paper-mâché animal. After listening to the instructions, the children will outline the steps involved and then make the animal.
Critical	K, 1, 2	The teacher will read a story with conversation or action that reveals feelings. The children will evaluate orally the conversation or action of the story characters in order to determine feelings.
Critical	3–4	A student is assigned to speak on "Pollution of the Streams and Rivers in Our State." Classmates listen to the speech and criticize it for substantiating facts and qualified opinions.
Critical	5–6	The teacher will locate newspaper advertisements for a particular product, and the pupils will be able to identify orally examples of such well-known propaganda techniques as plain folks, glittering generalities, testimonials, and band wagon.

Critical Listening

A **fact** is a statement about something that has really happened or is true. It can be proved. An **opinion** is one person's idea about something or someone. Opinions cannot be proved.

Every speaker uses a mixture of facts and opinions. A good listener must be alert to separate them. Watch out especially for overgeneralization.

A **generalization** is a statement of fact based on details. For example, imagine that fifteen out of twenty students in your class say that the Ferris wheel is their favorite ride. You could generalize that most of the class likes the Ferris wheel best. An **overgeneralization** is a statement that is too broad to be true. If you said that the favorite ride of *all* students is the Ferris wheel, that would be an overgeneralization. To spot overgeneralizations, listen for words such as *everyone, always, never, every, nobody, everybody, all the time,* and *no one.*

Exercises   Using Listening Skills

A. In pairs, act out the following situations. Discuss the communication barriers that you notice between the characters.

1. A student comes home from school two hours late and meets a parent at the door.
2. A brother and sister both believe it is the other's turn to do the dishes.
3. One student has lost another student's book. The second student did not even know the first had borrowed the book.

B. With a partner, make up a commercial to sell a product. Present your commercial for the class. The class should do the following:

1. Point out facts that were presented in the commercial.
2. Identify opinions.
3. Identify any generalizations and overgeneralizations.

Source: Pg. 257, *McDougal, Littell English, Gold Level,* Copyright © 1987 by McDougal, Littell & Company, Box 1667, Evanston, Illinois 60204.

Figure 3.1. Exercises in Critical Listening and Other Listening Skills.

2. *Categorization,* or Putting Information into Groups. When the major topic the children are listening to has several separate subheadings of information, comparisons, or contrasts, they should group or *cluster* in a diagram those related subtopics through a series of rays emanating from the nucleous word or topic. An example of a cluster diagram is shown in Figure 3.2.
3. *Questioning.* This two-part process concerns questioning the speaker in order to aid comprehension and questioning oneself in an effort to determine understanding.
4. *Organization,* or Discovering the Plan. Informational speech uses such common organizational patterns as comparison and contrast, problem and solution, cause and effect, description, and time or sequence. Signal words that often reveal organizational patterns include *first, second, third, next,* and *finally.*

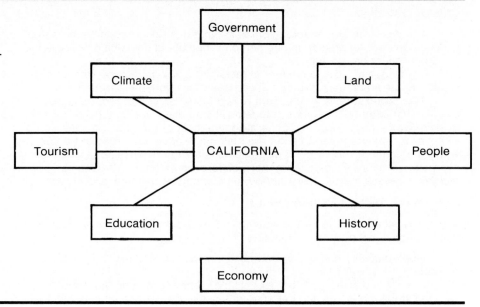

Figure 3.2. Cluster Diagram Prepared on the Topic of California by a Fifth Grade Class.

5. *Note-Taking,* or Getting Down Important Information. Crucial to this strategy is the ability to match the purpose for listening to the kinds of notes that must be made. Notes taken during a sixth-grade-class science experiment, for example, will differ widely from those taken as telephone messages for other members of the student's household.

6. *Attention-Directing,* or Getting Cues from the Speaker. Speakers often use either or both verbal and visual cues to convey information. Verbal cues cover pitch (with speakers lowering or raising their voices for emphasis), speed (with speakers slowing their voices down to stress certain points), and repetition (with speakers reiterating significant information, sometimes more than twice). Visual cues include facial expressions, gestures, and the writing of critical facts on the chalkboard or transparency.

Learning Games in Listening

Some of the skills essential to the development of good listening among girls and boys can be reviewed through a variety of purposeful games. All of the games outlined in Figure 3.3 are instructional group games that can be adapted by the teacher to meet the needs of a particular classroom of children. Few of the ten games described in the figure require special materials or much advance preparation, which should make them especially useful.

Figure 3.3. Ten Learning Games in Listening.

Airplanes Fly

1. The teacher is the first leader, and the players are seated (or standing) far enough apart to move their arms freely.
2. The teacher describes a flying object or animal, and if the statement is true (e.g., "Airplanes fly"), the players wave their arms. Should the statement be false (e.g., "The chalkboard flies"), players must keep their arms still.
3. Any player who moves his or her arms when the statement made by the teacher-leader is false is dropped from the game.
4. The player who remains in the game the longest wins the first round and becomes the next leader.
5. Variations: (a) Fish Swim, (b) Frogs Jump, and (c) Dogs Run.

Bouncing Ball

1. The children are seated with their eyes closed.
2. The teacher, as "It," bounces a rubber ball or tennis ball a number of times at random.
3. The players listen and count the number of bounces silently.
4. "It" calls on one player who responds, "You bounced the ball . . . times." If the player's response is correct, he or she is allowed to have the next turn to be "It." If the player's response is incorrect, another player has a turn to give the proper number of bounces.
5. The winner of Bouncing Ball is the player who is "It" the longest.
6. Variation: The ball may be bounced three times, and then after a pause, and then bounced four times more. The player responds, "You bounced the ball three and four times," or "Three and four are seven."

Cross Out Relay

1. Before the game, the teacher writes on the left half of the chalkboard fifty or more numerals with which the class is familiar, presenting them in a mixed or inconsecutive order. Then on the right half of the board, the teacher repeats the process, using the same numerals but in a different mixed order.
2. Two teams are chosen and stand facing the class, *not* the numbered board. The player on each team who is nearest to the board receives a piece of chalk.
3. The teacher calls out one number at a time, and a player from each team must quickly cross out that numeral on the board and pass the chalk to the next player.
4. Any player who does not cross out the proper numeral must return to the board, erase his or her mistake, and rewrite the numeral.
5. The team that has the smaller amount of numerals left after a designated time is declared the winner of the Cross Out Relay.

I Am Packing a Bag

1. The children are seated at their tables or desks.
2. The first child chosen as "It" says, "I am packing a bag and will put something in it that begins with . . . (and names a single consonant sound) *b*."
3. Then all the other players who can supply a needed word raise their hands.
4. "It" calls on one player who correctly says "book," "bear," or "bicycle." That second player now becomes "It" and chooses the next and different sound.
5. Suggestions: (a) A large paper bag or book bag makes an effective prop for "It"; (b) With older children, this game may be played with teams and scoring of points as each player says a different word with the same initial sound; (c) Initial blends may be used on occasion.

Figure 3.3. (cont.)

1. The teacher reads or tells a story. It may be an original tale, an old folk tale, or a simple anecdote. 2. Each player is then assigned to be a character or object in the story. 3. The teacher now retells the whole story, except that this time each player must jump up (or stand up, in a crowded classroom) every time his or her character or object is mentioned. 4. The players with superior listening skills are all declared the winners. 5. Variation: As the players jump up, each must make a sound characteristic of his or her own role.	**Jump Up**
1. The children are seated at their desks or at their tables. 2. With a drumstick, the teacher beats out on a drum or tabletop the exact number of syllables found in a child's name. 3. The players listen for the number of syllables in their first name, and later in their first and last names. 4. When a child believes that his or her name has been tapped out, the child stands and claps as many times as there are syllables in his or her name. 5. All players who succeed in recognizing the number of syllables in their names in any one round are declared the winners of that round. 6. Suggestions: (a) The teacher may select a child to beat the drumstick; (b) Older children may sound out the names of songs or the first lines of familiar poems or song lyrics.	**Rat-A-Tat-Tat**
1. The teacher is Sally (or Sam) during the first round and stands in front of the room. The children stand at their seats. 2. When Sally precedes a command with "Sally says" (e.g., Sally says "Touch your toes"), each player performs the command with Sally. If Sally does not precede a command with "Sally says," the players must ignore the command, no matter what Sally does, or be dropped from the round. 3. A child who is out of the first round sits down and the last child standing becomes Sally (or Sam) during the second round. 4. Suggestions: (a) Sally (or Sam) should work quickly and always perform her (or his) own command, (b) Actions and clothes can be stressed as well as parts of the body.	**Sally Says**
1. The teacher needs pictures of foods available at the market. 2. One player is chosen as "It"; the other players sit in a large circle with no empty chairs and hold up pictures that are visible to "It." 3. "It" walks around the circle saying, "I went to the market and in my shopping cart I put some . . . and some . . . (etc.)," naming different foods that he or she sees pictured. The players holding those pictures leave their chairs and follow "It" around the circle. 4. When "It" decides to stop shopping, he or she says, "My shopping cart fell over." Then "It" and the players following "It" must find empty seats. 5. The player left standing becomes "It" for the next round of Shopping Cart.	**Shopping Cart**

Figure 3.3. (cont.)

1. The players are seated in a circle. 2. The teacher holds a large, brightly colored ball of rewound yarn with knots (tied earlier at intervals of two to three feet) and begins to Spin A Yarn, or tell a tall tale. She/He unwinds the ball slowly while talking but stops abruptly when the first knot is reached. 3. The player seated at the teacher's right receives the ball and continues to Spin A Yarn—talking and unwinding—until the second knot is reached. 4. Players take turns, and the tale continues until the ball of yarn is completely unwound and the final knot reached. 5. All players who picked up the yarn (story and ball) deftly are deemed good listeners and therefore winners of Spin A Yarn.	**Spin A Yarn**
1. The children are seated at their desks or tables. 2. The teacher as the first "Director" chooses one volunteer player to follow directions that are given all at once and that demand the performance of several actions within the classroom. For instance, the teacher may say, "Walk to the chalkboard. Draw a circle. Then draw a square inside the circle. Write the word *dog* inside the square. Run to your seat and sit down." 3. If the player successfully follows all the directions, he or she becomes the second Director. 4. The Director who retains the post the longest wins the Utellem game. 5. Suggestions: (a) The directions must be given slowly and clearly; (b) The teacher may need to help the succeeding Directors decide whether the directions have been followed properly; (c) The directions may relate to some current classroom unit such as New York Geography, and the Director could say, "Draw a map of New York. Locate Albany. Locate Buffalo. Label the Hudson River."	**Utellem**

A listening test should possess the following features: (a) Stimulus materials should be taped (audio or video) and always spoken. They should never be literary passages read aloud by a narrator on a tape or by the teacher. (b) Stimulus materials should demand a simple and minimal response. Both messages and questions should be on tape, and test items should not be obstructed by difficult or lengthy reading matter. (c) Stimulus materials should be short, ranging from thirty seconds to three minutes. (d) Stimulus materials should be interesting and taken from real-life occurrences that are meaningful to the students. (e) Vocabulary used in stimulus materials should be controlled. Otherwise the instrument more aptly tests general verbal knowledge.[16]

One or more of the foregoing features is present in both of the commercially available listening tests listed below and published in the United States for the purpose of yielding evaluative judgments concerning skills in children (in some or all of the elementary grades).[17] Although each is considered appropriate for

Evaluation of Student and Teacher Progress

the target population, reviewers have often warned that listening tests, especially for younger children, frequently fail to discriminate between reading readiness indicators and indicators of proficiency in receptive communication.[18]

Signals Listening Tests (1982 edition). For grades three and five. Published by Project SPOKE, Norton, Massachusetts. Time of test: thirty-five minutes. Specimen set available.

Stanford Achievement Test: Listening Comprehension Tests (1982 edition). For three primary levels and two intermediate levels. Published by Psychological Corporation, Cleveland, Ohio. Time of test: twenty-five to thirty-five minutes for the primary levels; thirty-five minutes for intermediate levels.

Informal Evaluation

Formal tests are hardly a substitute for informal tests, and in the evaluation of listening, both kinds of measuring devices should be developed and used. Informal techniques are more appropriate for specific classroom situations in order to evaluate objectives established for individual programs.

The alert teacher will discover numerous opportunities to determine the extent of listening progress displayed in her or his classroom as the children plan units of work, make announcements, present reports, or read stories aloud. The teacher can evaluate the listening skills of cooperative learning groups by asking: Can the pupils follow directions? Can they identify main ideas, supporting details, or a sequence of events? Can they distinguish between fancy and realism, between opinion and fact, between statements and questions? Have they been developing a meaningful listening vocabulary? Do they listen attentively and courteously? Can they make critical or value judgments about what is heard? Do they listen for enjoyment and aesthetic appreciation? Can they identify with a character and his or her problems?

As children mature and learn, they become more aware of the characteristics of good listeners and of their own strengths and weaknesses relative to those standards. Fourth, fifth, and sixth graders are better qualified to listen than six-year-olds and are also more capable of evaluating their own listening according to a checklist such as that shown in Figure 3.4.

The teacher's role in informally evaluating listening in the classroom is not complete until the teacher has evaluated his or her own listening abilities and program as outlined in Figure 3.5. Realizing that listening *can* be taught, the teacher plans carefully and then displays the same unfailing interest and courtesy in listening to the oral contributions of the pupils that they are expected to show to him or her and to each other. Children who observe their teacher sorting papers or taking roll while they are talking to him or her can hardly be expected to develop into attentive listeners.

Figure 3.4 Listening Checklist for an Intermediate Student.

Intermediate Student's Self-Evaluation Checklist in Listening

Physical Aids	Always	Sometimes	Never
1. Do I clear my desk of all unnecessary articles?			
2. Do I have everything out of my hands except when writing?			
3. Do I watch the speaker for helpful facial expressions and gestures?			
4. Do I make sure that I am not a distraction?			

Attitude			
5. Do I practice all rules of courtesy?			
6. Do I shut out all distractions?			
7. Do I listen with an open mind?			
8. Do I withhold final evaluation until comprehension is complete?			
9. Do I actively engage in listening?			

Content			
10. Do I understand the purposes and goals for this listening experience?			
11. Do I understand the kind of listening to use for this listening experience?			
12. Do I screen the material for what I need?			
13. Do I concentrate on what the speaker is saying?			
14. Do I listen for main ideas first and details second?			
15. Do I take notes when they will be of use to me?			
16. Do I use past knowledge to give meaning to the current listening experience?			
17. Do I ask questions at the appropriate time?			

Figure 3.5. Listening Checklist for a Classroom Teacher.

Classroom Teacher's Self-Evaluation Checklist in Listening

	Always	Sometimes	Never
1. Do I pursue a program in which listening skills are consistently developed?	_____	_____	_____
2. Do I prepare for the listening activities to be presented?	_____	_____	_____
3. Do I initiate activities to which the children want to listen?	_____	_____	_____
4. Do I create an emotional climate for good listening?	_____	_____	_____
5. Do I create a physical climate for good listening?	_____	_____	_____
6. Do I realize that the attention span of children is limited?	_____	_____	_____
7. Do I realize that the concentration span of children is limited?	_____	_____	_____
8. Do I help the children develop an appreciation and awareness of sounds?	_____	_____	_____
9. Do I help the children establish purposes for each listening activity?	_____	_____	_____
10. Do I listen to each child during the school day?	_____	_____	_____
11. Do I encourage the children to listen to each other?	_____	_____	_____
12. Do I use changes in pitch, loudness, and rate in my classroom voice?	_____	_____	_____
13. Do I secure the attention of the group before beginning to speak?	_____	_____	_____
14. Do I give attention to unfamiliar vocabulary?	_____	_____	_____
15. Do I help children recall related experiences that may aid their understanding?	_____	_____	_____
16. Do I pose questions that promote careful listening?	_____	_____	_____
17. Do I try not to repeat my presentations or directions?	_____	_____	_____
18. Do I express appreciation for what each child says?	_____	_____	_____
19. Do I promote good listening by not talking too much myself?	_____	_____	_____
20. Do I make myself available for listening and teach listening in every subject area?	_____	_____	_____

1. What is the difference between hearing and listening?
2. Why is the teaching of listening so often neglected?
3. Why is listening more important today than ever before?
4. Which factors that affect listening fall within the domain of the teacher?
5. How can elementary teachers improve the listening ability of those children who have hearing impairments?
6. How could a school evaluate the basic skill of listening? Would a letter grade ever be justified?
7. Should all types of listening receive equal attention by the classroom teacher? Why or why not?

1. Plan for intermediate pupils a listening lesson that involves critical listening.
2. Try to arrange an experiment involving the physical conditions in one elementary classroom and their effect on children's listening.
3. Read aloud a short, little-known poem to a group of third graders and ask the children to guess the title or to make up a title. Encourage them to give reasons for the choice they make.
4. Ask a group of fourth graders to list all of the sounds they hear in ten minutes. Later have them tell which sounds they enjoyed hearing and why.
5. Develop six learning experiences in attentive listening and six more in appreciative listening for a grade level of your choice.
6. Spend one hour each in the kindergarten, second-grade, and fifth-grade classrooms. Record the amount of time the students spent listening and the amount of time the teacher listened. Do older children have as many opportunities to listen as younger pupils do?
7. Examine two current language text series for one intermediate grade level to see how listening skills are being presented. Compare, for example, the material in the Scott, Foresman series with that of the McGraw-Hill series. Which do you prefer and why?
8. Set up the learning center for listening shown in Figure 3.6.

Figure 3.6. Language Arts Learning Center: Listening.

TYPE OF CENTER: **Listening** TIME: 10 minutes
GRADE LEVEL: 1 NUMBER OF STUDENTS: Varies

INSTRUCTIONAL
OBJECTIVE: The students should be able to identify a sequence of sounds by listening carefully to a prepared tape.

MATERIALS: Tape recorder, tape of sounds, pictures of objects, two small boxes, paper, pencil, a folder for worksheets.

DIRECTIONS:
Teacher: Instruct children on how to use the tape recorder. (If listening headset centers are used, direct the children to put on earphones, then turn on the tape recorder.)

Student:
1. Follow the directions on the tape.
2. Turn the tape on. The tape will say the following: Listen carefully to the following instructions. Take a worksheet from the blue box. It is numbered one through nine. As you hear the following sounds, write the letter that goes with the picture of the object that made the sound you hear. Take your time.
3. There will be thirty seconds between each sound. Each sound will be repeated again very quickly.
4. Now check your answers with the cards in the yellow box.
5. When you are finished, please turn off the recorder and put your answers in the folder.

KEY
Order of Sounds
1. whistle   4. water running   7. bell
2. door slamming   5. car motor   8. paper tearing
3. change jingling 6. phone ringing   9. shoe shuffling

EVALUATION: Have the students exchange papers with a classmate and check their answers.

Source: From PATHWAYS TO IMAGINATION by Angela S. Reeke and James L. Laffey, © 1979 by Scott, Foresman & Company. Reprinted by permission.

Burns, J., and Richgels, D., "A Critical Evaluation of Listening Tests," *Academic Therapy, 24*, pp. 153–162.

Choate, J., and Rakes, T. 1987. "The Structured Listening Activity: A Model for Improving Listening Comprehension," *The Reading Teacher, 41*, pp. 194–201.

Feitelson, D., Kita, B., and Goldstein, Z. 1986. "Effects of Listening to Series Stories on First Graders; Comprehension and Use of Language," *Research in the Teaching of English, 20*, pp. 339–356.

Hobbs, C. 1986. "Helping Your Student to Listen Better," *Learning, 14*(8), pp. 66–67.

Leverentz, F., and Garman, D. 1987. "What Was That You Said?" *Instructor, 96*(8), pp. 66, 68, 70.

Oregon Department of Education. 1987. *Oral Communication.* (English Language Arts Concept Paper No. 1). Salem, OR: Author.

Paley, V. 1986. "On Listening to What the Children Said," *Harvard Educational Review, 56*, pp. 122–131.

Strother, D. 1987. "On Listening," *Phi Delta Kappan, 68*, pp. 625–628.

Winn, D. 1988. "Developing Listening Skills as a Part of the Curriculum," *The Reading Teacher, 42*, pp. 144–146.

"Your Attention, Please," 1986. *Changing Times, 40*, pp. 127–129.

1. D. VanRheenen et al., "State Practices of Speaking and Listening Assessment: A National Survey, 1985." Paper presented at the annual convention of the Speech Communication Association, Denver, 1985.

2. S. W. Lundsteen, *Listening: Its Impact at All Levels on Reading and the Other Language Arts* (Urbana, Illinois: National Council of Teachers of English, 1979), p. 1.

3. P. D. Pearson and L. Fielding, "Research Update: Listening Comprehension," *Language Arts,* 1982, *59,* p. 624.

4. J. D. Stammer, "Target: The Basics of Listening," *Language Arts,* 1977, *54,* pp. 661–664.

5. R. L. Lemons and S. C. Moore, "The Effects of Training in Listening on the Development of Reading Skills," *Reading Improvement,* 1982, *19,* pp. 212–216; S. M. Hoffman, *The Effect of a Listening Skills Program on the Reading Comprehension of Fourth Grade Students* (Unpublished doctoral dissertation, Walden University, 1978); M. B. Tinzmann and G. R. Thompson, *A Comparison of Listening and Reading Cloze Procedures and a Standardized Reading Achievement Test,* ERIC Document Reproduction Service No. ED 162 249 (1977); E. K. Haugh, *Reading Versus Listening: Modes of Presentation of a First Grade Reading Test,* ERIC Document Reproduction Service No. ED 172 157 (1979); A. Hildyard, *On the Bias of Oral and Written Language in the Drawing of Inferences on Text* (Ontario: Ontario Institute for Studies in Education, 1978); and T. G. Sticht et al., *Auding and Reading: A Developmental Model,* ERIC Document Reproduction Service No. ED 097 641 (1974).

6. Pearson and Fielding, *Research Update,* p. 625.

7. J. M. Kean, "Listening," in *Encyclopedia of Educational Research,* H. Mitzel, ed. (New York: Macmillan, 1982), p. 1102.

8. S. S. Weaver and W. L. Rutherford, "A Hierarchy of Listening Skills," *Elementary English,* 1974, *51,* pp. 1146–1150.

9. H. S. Wetstone and Z. B. Friedlander, "The Effect of Live TV and Audio Story Narration on Primary Grade Children's Listening Comprehension," *Journal of Educational Research,* 1974, *68,* pp. 32–35.

10. M. Martin, "Listening in Review," in *Classroom-Relevant Research in the Language Arts,* H. G. Shane and J. Walden, eds. (Washington, D.C.: Association for Supervision and Curriculum Development, 1978); and M. Berry and R. Erickson, "Speaking Rate: Effects on Children's Comprehension of Normal Speech," *Journal of Speech and Hearing Research,* 1973, *16,* pp. 367–374.

11. G. Larson and B. Petersen, "Does Noise Limit the Learning of Young Listeners?" *Elementary School Journal,* 1978, *78,* pp. 264–265.

12. C. G. Fisher and K. Brooks, "Teachers' Stereotypes of Children Who Wear Hearing Aids," *Language, Speech, and Hearing Services in Schools,* 1981, *12,* pp. 139–144.

13. T. G. Devine, *Listening Skills Schoolwide: Activities and Programs* (Urbana, Illinois: National Council of Teachers of English, 1982), p. 19.

14. J. E. Cook, "A Study in Critical Listening Using Eight- to Ten-Year-Olds in an Analysis of Commercial Propaganda Emanating from Television," *Dissertation Abstracts International,* 1973, *33,* pp. 3146A–3147A.

15. G. Tompkins, M. Friend, and P. Smith, "Listening Strategies for the Language Arts," in *Language Arts Instruction and the Beginning Teacher: A Practical Guide,* C. Personke and D. Johnson, eds. (Englewood Cliffs, New Jersey: Prentice Hall, 1987), pp. 30–41.

16. P. Backlund et al., "Recommendations for Assessing Speaking and Listening Skills," *Communication Education,* 1982, *31,* pp. 9–17.

17. J. Mitchell, Jr., ed., *The Ninth Mental Measurements Yearbook,* Volume II (Lincoln: University of Nebraska Press, 1985), pp. 1379, 1452.

18. D. L. Rubin et al., "Review and Critique of Procedures for Assessing Speaking and Listening Skills among Preschool through Grade Twelve Students," *Communication Education,* 1982, *31,* pp. 285–304.

Speaking 4

Major Chapter Goals

After studying Chapter 4, the reader will be able to

1. Describe the significance of nine speech arts commonly taught to children.
2. Outline the skills in the communicative development program, which the classroom teacher can present.
3. Recognize communicative disorders that teachers should refer to speech-language clinicians.

Discover As You Read This Chapter Whether*

1. Oral langauge proficiency is a predictor of school readiness.
2. Elementary school girls are linguistically superior to boys at comparable ages.
3. Children's speech characteristics do not affect the expectations that teachers have of elementary pupils.
4. Sharing time is a legitimate form of informal reporting.
5. Discussions are concerned with problem solving and critical thinking skills.
6. Interviewing is a speech art in which kindergartners can participate.
7. Lessons involving marionettes are appropriate for elementary school language arts programs.
8. Communicative disorders are more prevalent among girls than among boys.
9. The largest proportion of articulation problems occurs among children in grades one through three.
10. About 1 percent of school age children suffer from stuttering.

*Answers to these true-or-false statements may be found in Appendix 5.

The child's control of the features of language proceeds along a continuum of mastering the highly predictable and productive features toward mastering less common forms with limited distribution. Speech skills necessary for effective oral communication must therefore be taught through a developmental process, with learning opportunities offered in varied areas of the curriculum.

Most of what children know of language when they enter school has been learned by accident because effective oral communication is not inherent. Consequently, speech habits formed in the preschool years will vary greatly with the individual child, and teachers who are cognizant of the variations will modify their programs to meet student needs.

Even though most elementary teachers are aware that competence in spoken language constitutes the basis for competence in reading and in written composition, kindergarten and first grade teachers particularly should scan the results of one study in Texas of seventy-four five- and six-year-old preschoolers.[1] Conclusions of standardized tests individually administered to the group of white, black, Mexican-American, and Asian children showed that it is *intelligence and not oral language proficiency that is a predictor of school readiness.*

Other investigations among pupils from kindergarten through grade seven have shown that children in each succeeding year speak more words, produce more communication units, and increase the average number of words in those units. The fastest spurts in development of oral expression appear to occur between kindergarten and the end of first grade and between the end of fifth grade and the end of seventh grade.

These studies in speech found no evidence of linguistic superiority of girls over boys at comparable ages. (Possibly changes in social, cultural, and educational environments have reduced differential behavior of the sexes.) There is, however, a frequently recurring pattern of boys at the extreme ends of a number of measures: boys in the high-ability group surpass the girls in the same group, whereas the boys in the low-ability group are the least proficient of all pupils observed.

Whether these children are academically advantaged or not, their language patterns are largely established by the time they reach school age. Still, every person who has contact with the children from the day they enter kindergarten influences their speaking patterns.

In turn, the children's patterns and other speech characteristics affect the expectations that teachers hold for elementary students. Investigations have found that such teachers of both majority and minority children tend to evaluate student speech samples in terms of two relatively global dimensions. One is confidence-eagerness and is found to be related to a child's fluency, lack of hesitations, and tendency to participate actively in a linguistic interview. The second can be labeled ethnicity-nonstandardness and is a reflection primarily of the degree of nonstandard English found in a child's speech.

Consequently, all teachers enrolling pupils whose native language or non-standard English dialect is unfamiliar to the school must be certain that their own attitudes affect the children's progress in the classroom environment positively. They must recall that all dialects are fully formed language systems. They must also recognize that the speech education program developed and maintained by the school needs the active support of the home and the community.

Such a comprehensive speech curriculum should incorporate three major components:

> *Speech arts for all children,* planned by the classroom teacher in every grade in order to present applications of specific skills.
>
> *Communicative development for all children,* planned by the classroom teacher in every grade in order to implement specific lessons in articulation and other skills.
>
> *Communicative remediation for deviations or disorders for the few handicapped children* in every grade who suffer from mild deviations or more pronounced articulation disorders, stuttering, voice disturbances, or delayed speech development. These boys and girls require the services of a clinician who in turn relies on the follow-up support of the classroom teacher. In districts that do not employ speech-language clinicians, the teacher has sole responsibility for communicative remediation.

To create an effective oral language program, the teacher must consider several notable factors. First, since students learn to speak by speaking, *the environment of the classroom* should resemble that of a communication center and allow children to translate their thoughts into words for questioning, comparing, contrasting, reporting, evaluating, and summarizing. Yet that center cannot deteriorate into a classroom of unorganized confusion in which students ignore the social amenities needed for interaction. Second, *the role of the teacher* must be that of listener, facilitator, and participant in learning. Third, *the role of the student* must be an active role, whether it be in small groups, in whole-class groups, or with a partner. Fourth, skills and activities using *the components of oral language* should be those emphasizing vocabulary, syntax, fluency, intonation, and articulation. Finally, language is *a communication tool* and therefore should be used for re-presenting the meaning of experiences.[2]

The teacher must also learn to recognize the child in the classroom who has language deficiencies. Such a student

1. Has difficulty learning new vocabulary and, instead, uses the same words over and over again.
2. Is confused by multiple meanings of words and, instead, uses one meaning of a word in all circumstances, appropriate or not.
3. Exhibits poor understanding of word definitions or explanations of similarities and differences.

4. Has difficulty thinking of an appropriate word when speaking, showing "word-finding" problems to the point of appearing to stutter.
5. Has poor quality of verbal expression, using vague terms and "talking around" a subject.
6. Does not use verbal information to make inferences or to draw appropriate conclusions.
7. Exhibits grammatical errors in oral or written language.
8. Displays defective interpretation of and response to social situations, with an inability to process rapid conversation and frequent topic shifts.[3]

Speech Arts

Learning to communicate through speech demands frequent opportunities for oral language skills. Through the speech arts program, favorable attitudes may be established by the students toward good speech and toward themselves as speakers. Desirable social relationships may be fostered to meet the needs of individuals and groups. Progressive speech development may be stressed through a variety of beginning and advanced kinds of speaking situations. Pleasant voices may be encouraged in order to promote an effective and natural manner. Practical standards of speech may be determined and maintained mutually by the children and their teacher.

The speech arts primarily include giving talks, conversing, discussing, debating, following parliamentary procedure, interviewing, developing social courtesies, participating in readers theater, and using puppets, as well as engaging in choral speaking, story telling, and creative drama. The last three arts listed are discussed in Chapters 5 and 13. The other nine speech arts are in Table 4.1, which includes instructional activities that involve each of them.

Talks

Oral language ability is viewed by some as the most important domain of the language arts. School settings being rarely conducive to talk, however, it is up to the teacher to transform the classroom atmosphere by simulating a variety of settings with a variety of audiences with different genuine purposes and subjects available for potential talkers. If the teacher can accomplish this task, most of the effort to motivate talkers will be unnecessary because the environment itself will stimulate speech.

Talks center around one of five basic purposes: to inform, to move to mental and sometimes physical action, to inquire, to enjoy (which is the most wide-ranging category), or to conjoin (which is made up of language used to maintain cultural and social rituals or relationships).[4] Although several kinds of talks are included in this segment of the language arts, the majority of them fall under either of two categories: reporting or announcing-explaining-directing.

Reporting

In the lower grades there is *informal reporting*. The teacher begins by sharing with the class some anecdotes, incidents, and descriptions from his or her own life in order to extend the children's experiences. The teacher than encourages the boys and girls to report on news that they think important by helping them

Table 4.1
Sample Instructional Activities in Elementary School Speech Arts

Kind of Speech Art	Grade Level	Learning Activity or Teaching Strategy
Conversing	K–6	Six students participate in a (directed) conversation about children's television shows available on Saturday mornings.
Debating	5–6	Two boys and two girls debate the proposition that no four-legged pets should be allowed in apartments.
Discussing	3–6	All the children engage in a round-table discussion about the responsibilities involved in being left alone at home.
Following parliamentary procedure	5–6	All the students are involved in various committees that must report back to the class regarding the year-end picnic at a nearby park.
Giving directions	1–3	The child has just encountered someone from an unidentified flying object that landed on the school playground and must direct this being to the principal's office.
Interviewing	4–6	Two students interview a neighborhood woman who weaves small rugs and sells them to a New York gift shop.
Making announcements	4–5	Two Girl Scouts announce, completely but concisely, a forthcoming event: the annual cookie sale.
Making introductions	2–6	Michael picks a friend to be the New Boy in the Class. Then "during recess" he first introduces himself to him and later introduces the boy to other classmates.
Participating in readers theater	3–6	One group of students adapts a script from the Aesop fable "The Miller, His Son, and the Donkey." Later, in front of an audience, other students use that script in reading their roles.
Reporting	1–3	The child informally reports to the class what the members of his or her family do and do not like to eat.
Telephoning	5–6	Using a coin telephone, the child receives from the information operator the telephone number of a local television station showing a favorite series that has just been cancelled for next season.
Using puppets	K–3	Three children use hand puppets to stage a play describing the downfall of Foolish Freddy who refused to brush his teeth.

When a student plans a report carefully, it can provoke audience interest and reaction. (© James L. Shaffer.)

understand which incidents are appropriate for sharing with the class and which are better suited for relating to him or her alone. After listening attentively to the reports the students share with their classmates, and assisting with sequence, relevancy, and length, the teacher asks the listeners for constructive comments or questions. Also, the teacher compliments each speaker on some aspect of his or her report, calling attention to choice descriptive or action words, sentence patterns, or speech skills. The teacher explains the cues Who? Where? What? Why? When? How? and lists them on a chart. Sometimes informal reactions to particular films or television programs can be elicited as the teacher points out qualities that make certain productions worthwhile.

In turn, the children begin to develop a sensitivity to suitable topics for informal reporting and to gain confidence in their ability to share ideas with others. In their role as listeners, they pay close attention and ask questions truly related to the reports presented. In their role as reporters, they try to remember to speak audibly, to look at their audience, to use an opening sentence that is an attention-getter, and to keep to the topic.

Informal reporting or so-called Sharing Time in the primary classroom, is of special interest for three reasons.[5] First, it may be the only official classroom time when out-of-school experiences are acceptable topics in school. Second, it is often the only time that children can speak on elective topics that do not have to meet specific criteria of relevance to previous discussions. Finally, this time is a context for the production of the most universal kind of text—the narrative.

Recent studies in Massachusetts and California revealed the four categories of responses that teachers can make to many Sharing Time narratives.[6]

Two at the appreciation end show the teacher's clear understanding of the story or provoke an extended collaboration between a questioning teacher and a reporting child that results in a more complete story. One at the negative end concerns cases that confuse the teacher and therefore provoke her/his inability to keep track of the story as the child relates it, possibly due to problems of relationships based on the child's words. The other, and even closer to the negative end, is a response by the teacher that moves the topic to one the teacher either values more or understands better.

Because some children are less self-conscious when they *show and tell* about an object, especially one that bears a personal significance for its owner, their oral reports are likely to be longer, livelier, and less rambling. Young pupils find it easier to share facts and experiences while they are showing objects that can be held in the hand and admired by the class—an arrowhead, a toy, or a seashell. Teachers may choose to vary this type of activity in several ways, but the basic experience remains valuable for developing body control, a sense of audience, and an ability to elaborate on a topic the speaker knows well.

A recent study of show-and-tell conditions in the kindergarten concluded that a more informal setting and a decrease in the status differential between children and teachers result in increased participation on the part of the boys and girls.[7] There is also an increase in the amount of responsibility on the part of the children for structuring the flow of sharing time.

Planned or *formal reporting* is common in the intermediate grades where students are taught to organize, outline, and use reference materials. Besides being a good listening exercise for the audience, such reporting provides an opportunity to build on skills in the selection and collection of material and the organization and presentation of the report. The children can be shown how to delimit the scope of their talks and how to choose pertinent material quickly by using the index and by scanning and skimming. They can learn to take notes relevant to the major ideas, to keep a record of the books used, and to organize their material into a logical order by making an outline of the main points to be stressed. Finally, class members can be shown how to give reports extemporaneously without obvious reference to their papers. Some children may wish to use visual aids to enhance their presentations.

Topics for talks may be assigned by the teacher or determined by the children in cooperation with their teacher. The range of topics suitable for reporting include weather reports, school news, committee reports, and student council reports. Special subject reports for social studies, science, or current events could focus on the sport of hang gliding, on plants and music, on drinking water from the sea, or on the black widow spider.

The skills and abilities necessary for making announcements and for giving directions and explanations are similar to those in reporting. The verbal message should be brief, exact, and complete, answering the questions Who? What? When? Where? and sometimes How? and Why? It should be arranged in suitable order and presented enthusiastically so that listeners will become convinced that the matter is worthy of their time and attention.

Announcing-Explaining-Directing

Announcements may be made about the safety patrol, community events, ball games, scout meetings, lost-and-found articles, and exhibitions. In schools that have public-address systems, the students can make announcements about the PTA meeting. In classrooms they can use puppets to announce a forthcoming classroom drama. Boys and girls can listen to commercial television or radio and list the many kinds of announcements heard in one hour. Their teacher can invite a local anchorperson to talk to the class about his or her job and the preparations necessary before going on the air. The teacher and the children can tape a series of announcements and then play back the material in order to evaluate it in terms of sufficiency and relevancy of information.

Explanations may be offered about a variety of topics ranging from the operation of a battery-operated toy to the passage of ships through a canal. Children may give *directions* for playing handball, for building bird houses, for setting up experiments, and for planting radish seeds. Sometimes, however, talks giving directions are really *speeches of demonstration,* useful for elementary school classes because there is a visible crutch to supply meaning to the listeners if and when the speaker stops momentarily. Because demonstrations involve processes, they reinforce the need for orderly sequence. Boys and girls often use them in social studies or science. Sample exercises in giving directions, as provided in current language arts text series, are shown in Figure 4.1.

Evaluation of Talks

The teacher can evaluate the class progress in giving talks by asking these questions about the students:

- Are they becoming better able to discriminate between significant and insignificant information in planning their talks?
- Are they describing details more accurately?
- Are they developing the habit of observing sequence?
- Are they learning to face an audience with reasonable confidence and to speak up clearly?
- Are they incorporating properly the use of visuals in their presentations?

Conversation and Dialogue

In some of the current language arts texts for both primary and intermediate grades, *conversation* is included as a speech activity. Conversation is an informal and spontaneous experience in which the stress is primarily on the development of social skills. It contributes to the child's ability to make friends, to acquire self-confidence, and to speak easily and well. Conversation may be stimulated by sharing such uncommon experiences as hiking in the mountains, riding in the desert, visiting a national park, and exploring a cave. It also develops from ordinary activities that children can recall, including washing the dog, shopping for new clothes, watching a ball game, and playing a musical instrument.

To encourage conversation the teacher again has the responsibility of creating the proper environment. It must be invigorating and ever-changing. At the same time, however, the teacher must also provide a relaxed classroom atmosphere with wholesome teacher-student and student-student relationships that make every child feel secure and accepted.

Speaking and Listening

Figure 4.1. Exercises in Giving Directions.

Giving Directions

People often ask you how to do something. A friend might ask how to do a math problem or how to get to the bus station. Usually, you give directions orally.

When you give directions aloud, the listener has to remember and understand them. He or she will not be able to look at written instructions. Think about the directions before you speak. Explain them as clearly as you can. Let the listener ask questions. Be patient. Use these guides.

Guides for Giving Directions
1. Speak clearly.
2. Choose words that give exact information.
3. Give all the steps in the correct order.
4. Invite your listeners to ask questions.

Exercises: Giving Directions Aloud

A. First, draw a simple design. Use only circles, squares, triangles, and lines in the design. Do not show the design to anyone.

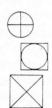

Next, choose a partner. Give the partner directions for drawing your design. Tell the person exactly what to do.

Now compare your design with what your partner drew. How much are they alike? Did you give good directions?

B. Choose a partner. Take turns explaining to each other how to get from school to your house. When it's your turn, listen carefully to your partner's directions. Ask questions if you need to. Then repeat the directions.

Source: Pg. 242, *McDougal, Littell English, Aqua Level.* Copyright © 1987 by McDougal, Littell & Company, Box 1667, Evanston, Illinois 60204.

Social conversations can take place during free periods or during ongoing activities in the classroom or on the playground. A small group of children may assemble around a learning center or bulletin board indoors or in the swings area or on the softball diamond outdoors. Their informal sharing of reactions in a small group makes it possible for children to respond freely, each in his or her own way. Even timid pupils are encouraged to enter into a small circle of participants.

When there are only two pupils instead of several, such a language experience can be termed a *dialogue*. Dialogue offers a combination of human closeness and immediacy of feedback that is appealing to girls and boys. Informal kinds of dialogue activity include the preparation by two pupils of a project, research assignment, or skit. More formal activity can develop questioning skills or inferences, as in the following examples:

1. The first child has a specific sense experience that he must then narrate to his partner. She in turn must select the correct olfactory, visual, auditory, or tactile cue from a group of three or four such cues. She questions carefully.
2. The first child is shown how to make or do something; for example, fit a part into a machine. In the meantime, the second child has been given the necessary materials for the project. Now the first child must explain to her partner how to complete or do the job with the materials provided.[8]

One research study about children's conversation examined the verbal interactions among boys and girls assigned to multiage rather than single-age classrooms.[9] It was concluded that conversation is affected by the number of ages in that one classroom. When *three* ages are combined, the older children tend to dominate the conversation directed to other boys and girls in the classroom, whether the ages of the children are three-four-five, six-seven-eight, or nine-ten-eleven. Although interaction within each age group is high, interaction between groups is low, and only the pupils of the middle age tend to interact randomly across age groups. On the other hand, in multiage classrooms composed of children from *two* age groups (six-seven, eight-nine, nine-ten), children from each of the two-age groups initiate conversation randomly across groups. In summary, then, grouping children of different ages together in one class can result in verbal interaction across age groups, but it is not likely to occur if children of three ages are grouped together.

Evaluation of Conversations

After some conversational experiences, the children, with the help of their teacher, could ask themselves the following:

- Was our subject an interesting one? Did we keep to the subject?
- Were we careful listeners? How did we show we were interested in our classmates' ideas?
- Did everyone in our group have a turn to talk? If someone didn't have a turn, how can we invite him or her to talk the next time?
- Could we hear each speaker?
- Did someone use an "unusual" word in today's conversation?
- Because conversations often include something that is said only for fun, was anything said that made us smile or laugh?

Discussion

Like conversation, discussion uses oral language in a small-group setting. Unlike conversation, however, its purpose concerns problem solving, critical thinking, and decision making. Sticking to the topic is a critical quality of a good discussion for the goal is to reach a conclusion. Conversations, on the other hand, generally meander from topic to topic, rarely probing for any final resolution. Cooperative learning groups must therefore promote discussion, not conversation.

The kinds of topics most appropriate for beginning discussion call for listing or enumeration ("How many ways does an animal get food?" or "How can you tell what will cost a dollar and what will cost a dime?"), which in turn leads to comparison topics by making the category either one of similarities or one of differences ("In what ways are cars and airplanes alike?" or "What are the differences between dogs and cats?"). A third kind of topic calls for chronology—planning an action or telling how something is made ("How can John get his bicycle back?" "How will we raise money to buy a record player for the classroom?"or "How should we go about building a miniature mission?").

One practical aspect for promoting good discussions involves seating arrangements. Greater and more effective interaction is promoted by face-to-face grouping patterns. There are both single-circle and double-circle arrangements. The *large single circle* of participants guided by a teacher or student leader often promotes one, two, or more *small single-circle spin-off groups*. These small groups meet for special interests or needs and later share their results with the large parent group. The *double-circle* or fishbowl arrangement involves an outer circle of listeners and an inner circle of talkers.

Other forms of discussion procedure include the round-table discussion, the panel discussion, and the buzz group. The *round-table discussion* generally involves between three and eight students. There is a moderator who guides the group, introduces the members, presents the problem (e.g., Eliminating Playground Litter), and keeps the discussion moving. It can be used in the middle and upper grades by having one group discuss a problem before the rest of the class or by dividing the class into several small discussion groups that function without an audience.

The *panel discussion* is much like the round-table discussion, but there are also some important differences. First, the procedure is more formal, usually opening with a short statement by each discussant. Second, there is a greater responsibility on the part of the panel members to prepare themselves, for each panelist is considered to be a knowledgeable "expert" on the topic (e.g., Nominating and Electing the Vice-President of the United States). Finally, panels are more audience-oriented than round tables, with some provision being made for questions from, or participation by, the observers at the end of the panel's presentation.

Buzz groups can occur when a whole class is divided into small groups for a limited time and purpose. They solicit suggestions, reactions, or comments to problems informally. There may or may not be leaders designated and conclusions reached. Still they are helpful in clarifying ideas and getting students to participate who might otherwise be reluctant or fearful. Because such brainstorming can readily get out of hand, however, standards must be established or reviewed before each buzz session.

Group discussion demands a wide range of language skills, and teachers cannot take for granted that students will learn those important skills without specific efforts to develop them in school environments. At all levels of education, beginning in kindergarten, group discussion should be the expected language activity.[10] These skills need to be developed in every child because they are actually practiced in the social world.

Evaluation of Discussion

Following a discussion the teacher and class might find it useful to evaluate the participants and the leader separately:

Rating Scale

Did the discussion leader—

1. State the problem or question correctly and in a manner that the class members could understand?

2. Summarize important points brought out along the way?

3. Skillfully keep the discussion progressing?

4. Give a good summary and conclusion at the end of the discussion session?

Did each participant—

1. Understand the problem and keep in mind the purpose of the discussion?

2. Contribute his or her share of information and consider contrary ideas?

3. Listen attentively and critically?

4. Have an acceptable attitude toward suggestions?

The children could also evaluate their own roles by silently asking themselves the following:

- Did I participate at all today?
- Did I participate too much?
- How did I treat my classmates whose ideas differed from mine?
- Did I encourage someone who is very shy to add his or her ideas to the discussion? How?
- Was I able to ask questions that helped others think?
- Did I make my point promptly?

Debating

Debating has been successfully used with intermediate children who have been given opportunities to develop reasoning skills. It provides them with basic experience in democratic procedure and teaches them that more than one solution of an issue may be both possible and sound.

A debate is the presentation of arguments between two teams (often consisting of two members each) who represent positions in opposition to each other on a single subject or *proposition*. That issue or proposition is stated briefly and affirmatively; for example, Only sixth graders can be officers in the Student Council. The affirmative team supports the proposition, and the negative team attacks it.

Beginning-level exercises for this area of speech arts would include expansions of decision-making assignments, such as having each child name something appropriate to wear in certain situations and then offer reasons for that selection.[11] Intermediate-level exercises would involve more advance preparation and could include, for example, having boys or girls give accounts of historical events together with explanations of why those events occurred. Advanced-level exercises demand the presentation of one viewpoint with adequate organization of that position, such as having each student gather facts about a family vacation choice and then give a speech on whether or not it is indeed an ideal selection.

In a classic debate, the constructive speeches by both sides appear first, followed by the rebuttal speeches by both sides, which attack the opposing arguments. The order for four debaters, for example, would be as follows:

1. First affirmative—constructive speech
2. First negative—constructive speech
3. Second affirmative—constructive speech
4. Second negative—constructive speech
5. First negative—rebuttal speech
6. First affirmative—rebuttal speech
7. Second negative—rebuttal speech
8. Second affirmative—rebuttal speech

In this manner the affirmative team speaks first and last, and each debater presents one constructive speech, prepared in advance, as well as one rebuttal speech. The latter is more of an impromptu address, in which the speaker differs with the arguments and information of the opposing side while defending the arguments and information of his or her side.

The debate has a chairperson to introduce the topic and the team members to the audience, a timekeeper (elementary debates average thirty minutes), and judges to determine which side debated better and so won the debate. Often the judges include all the members of the class who are not debating.

Elementary school debates can be informally evaluated by asking the following:

Evaluation of Debating

- Was the proposition a significant issue?
- Were the constructive speeches carefully prepared?
- Could all the speakers be heard?
- Was sufficient time available for the contest?
- Was the judgment fairly determined?

Following Parliamentary Procedure

Parliamentary procedure is used universally wherever organized groups exist in order to help them carry on activities in an efficient and democratic manner. Like several other speech activities, parliamentary procedure is learned best by participation, and the elementary school is an ideal place to begin to practice the proper way to conduct a meeting. Activities that call for group decisions and require a presiding officer should be conducted within the framework of parliamentary procedure. Adaptation and informal use of many of the procedures in

Robert's Rules of Order Newly Revised can be appreciated by pupils as early as the fifth grade, and some can be taught or incorporated as early as third grade. Even a first grader can be taught to raise his or her hand and not speak until recognized by the teacher.

In every grade the parliamentarian is the classroom teacher. Both the children and the parliamentarian must become familiar with five segments of procedure: *motions* ("I move that our class visit the Museum of Natural History to see the dinosaur exhibit."); *resolutions* ("Resolved that we thank the room parents for the Halloween party they gave us."); *amendments* ("I move to amend the motion about visiting the Museum of Natural History by adding the words 'on Saturday, March 14.' "); referral to *committees* of problem topics that arise during a class meeting ("I move to refer the motion about visiting the Museum of Natural History to a committee of three students appointed by our chairperson. I believe the committee should tell us its recommendation by Friday afternoon."); and *voting* on either an idea or a motion ("Would someone make a motion about how many classes we should invite to see our Thanksgiving program?"). The sixth segment of parliamentary procedure—*the table of precedence of motions*—need only be understood in the elementary school by the parliamentarian.[12]

When an intermediate teacher believes that students are ready to be organized as a club, he or she may act as chairperson until the club or class president has been elected. The president then asks for nominations for the remaining officers. After nominations have been closed, voting is done by raising hands or marking ballots. Later, after several meetings have been held, the officers and the other students in the room will probably conclude that much time could be saved if standard parliamentary procedures were used in conducting the meetings. It is then that the teacher quietly introduces some of these rules of order:

- Calling the meeting to order: "The meeting of the _____ class (or club) will please come to order."
- Reading of the minutes: "Will the secretary please read the minutes of the last meeting?"
- Approving or correcting the minutes: "Are there any corrections or additions?"
- Announcing the result: "The minutes are approved as read." (or) "The minutes are approved as corrected."
- Asking for reports of committees: "We will now have a report of the _____ committee."
- Approving reports of committees: "Is there any discussion of the report?" and "The report is accepted."
- Asking for announcements: "Are there any announcements to be made at this time?"
- Asking about unfinished business: "Is there any unfinished business?"
- Asking about new business: "Is there any new business to be brought up?"

- Turning the program over to the program chairperson: "I shall now turn the meeting over to the program chairperson."
- Ending the meeting: "If there is no further business, the meeting stands adjourned." Usually the chairperson ends the meeting but during the meeting any member can make a motion to adjourn at any time (provided the motion does not interrupt another speaker). Once the motion has been seconded, the chairperson immediately calls for a vote.

The teacher-parliamentarian will note the students' gradual development in the areas of social skills and speech skills. Critical points from both of these skills are incorporated into the criteria that children typically formulate—with the help of their teacher—for evaluating club meetings:

Evaluation of Club Meetings

- Are we following the rules of parliamentary procedure?
- Are the meetings worthwhile?
- Are members courteous to one another? Do they show respect to the officers?
- Do members use well-planned sentences when presenting items of business? Do they speak convincingly?
- Are the club activities run by a minority or by a majority of the members?

Children watch interviews on television news programs and are therefore familiar with the techniques used. The ability to conduct interviews can thus become a speech activity readily presented to boys and girls from their kindergarten year through the sixth grade.

Interviewing

There is both informal and formal interviewing, with the latter involving preplanning and the formulation of questions in advance by the group or the individual child. The presentation, for example, of a shy kindergartner who brought some wooden animals to show her classmates during the sharing period would probably become more lucid if her classmates *informally interviewed* her. They could ask casually, one at a time, about the cost, origin, and production of the animals. On the other hand, the anticipated visit by a room mother familiar with the Chinese New Year would prompt a different and more formal type of questioning. In the lower grades, children could work as a whole class, developing a list of questions on the chalkboard with the help of their teacher. In the intermediate grades, students could divide up into groups and write their own questions to ask the resource visitor. The *formal interview* involving about ten to twelve questions and answers would later be conducted respectfully, and the information collected would be shared by all participants.

Younger boys and girls can also use dramatic play for interviews between child and parent, child and teacher, and child and school principal. Later, after they have all interviewed each other, primary pupils can go out in small teams with a list of prepared questions to use in interviewing the media specialist, the cafeteria manager, the custodian, and other school workers. Their teacher may wish to help them develop another set of questions before inviting a police officer, fire fighter, or other community worker to visit the classroom for an interview. Slowly, the teacher and the children will begin to use the tape recorder as they conduct interviews.

Older classes can set up interviewing criteria and techniques and list these on charts. The students can interview foreign exchange students as well as parents or teachers who have recently visited other countries. Some of them can interview classroom committees that are preparing to report on a science project, or they can role-play in social studies imaginary interviews between such personages as Sacagawea and Meriwether Lewis or William Clark. They can interview the principal for the school paper or dramatize a "Meet the Press" type of interview. A few more intrepid students may even elect to work in small groups or individually outside the school, conducting interviews with residents familiar with the history of the town, area, or county. Information gathered through such oral history projects, whether by tape recorder or written reports, can later be published in a school or community newspaper. Incidentally, for self-evaluation of interviewing techniques, the tape-recorder is a useful tool.

Several observations have been made regarding the effects of recent interviewing programs conducted in several Georgia schools in both the primary and middle grades.[13] First, bringing outside guests (such as motorcycle officers and airline pilots) into the classroom increases interest in listening, speaking, writing, and reading. It releases a drive to communicate as children assume language roles all too often allowed only to adults. Second, students enjoy being in control as active participants, and in some instances, they are able to abandon earlier images of themselves as school failures. Third, interviewing unifies the communicative process as listening and speaking leads naturally to writing and then to reading. Finally, when children become interested in their topics, they write more and use more sophisticated and specialized vocabulary.

Evaluation of Interviewing

After a practice or actual interview conducted in class, the teacher and children should ask each other the following:

- Did the interviewer maintain a natural, easy posture?
- Was his or her voice audible?
- Did the interviewer get the information he or she wanted?
- Was the interviewer courteous?
- Did the interviewee help the interviewer?
- Was the interviewee in a hurry?
- Was the interview concluded properly?

Developing Social Courtesies

The fundamentals of social conventions should be initially presented in the primary grades and then amplified in the intermediate grades. Telephone etiquette, informal introductions, proper table manners, and politeness toward others should be stressed early in the child's school life. Because most social conventions are accompanied by polite speech, teaching the proper conduct in a variety of situations is one responsibility of the language arts program.

Merely knowing what they are to do without experiencing a sufficient number of occasions to practice the social behaviors tends to make students self-conscious rather than secure. Consequently, opportunities to let the children use the newly learned courtesies must be furnished routinely. Confidence and social understandings grow best through realistic social experiences throughout the school year at every grade level.

The critical factor in the program is the teacher because courtesy is indeed contagious. The climate that the teacher creates in the classroom must be accepting and encouraging, helping the students learn the pleasant and polite thing to do. Social behavior is learned chiefly by imitation. Knowledge about everyday courtesies contributes to the children's sense of security and orderliness.

It is hoped that planned lessons about correct social behavior and thoughtfulness toward others will elicit the following generalizations:

- Social courtesies are genuine expressions of respect and regard for other persons.
- Basic good manners provide the individual with poise and personal satisfaction.
- The customs of good manners vary from place to place and change from time to time.
- Basic good manners depend on honesty, tact, and common sense.

Social Skills and Attitudes

Included in this segment of speech activities is the development of courtesy in the classroom, courtesy in the school, and courtesy in the community. The first involves accepting personal responsibility for the completion of certain tasks and showing consideration for fellow members by adjusting one's personal desires for the common good. It also suggests ways of working together, solving group problems, and being a proper host or guest.

The second category—courtesy in the school—teaches consideration for the rights and property of others on the playground and in the halls, auditorium, and media center. It stresses thoughtfulness of others and respect toward teachers, aides, administrators, and other staff personnel. It shows students how to be well mannered during assembly programs and lunch periods.

Courtesy in the community—the final group of social skills and attitudes—emphasizes awareness that good manners should be used wherever one happens to be. It teaches children to avoid conduct that might attract unfavorable attention to themselves when they are in the synagogue or church, in the neighborhood theater, in a public restaurant, or at the local supermarket.

Numerous occasions arising naturally both inside and outside the school demand the proper use of social skills by the young child: introducing a parent to the teacher during the first parent conference of the semester, acting as room host for an open house, winning a school award and accepting congratulations quietly, apologizing to the school secretary/nurse for being late in returning a medical slip, thanking neighbors while collecting papers during a Scout drive, taking a telephone message for another family member, meeting a distant cousin who has just arrived from Australia, and telephoning a friend about a homework assignment. In each of these instances, the child presumably reacts with a suitable degree of poise and courtesy.

Introductions

Of the two areas of social courtesies that are especially studied in the elementary school, the first is making and acknowledging introductions. Boys and girls learn to introduce themselves to a new person or a new group by giving their names and stating something about themselves. When they are introducing a newcomer to others, they should remember to say something interesting about the new person or suggest a topic of conversation.

Children learn to handle introductions through role-playing sessions, especially if both correct and exaggeratedly incorrect procedures can be observed. Tape recordings of such activities may also prove helpful for later evaluation of the greetings and conversational topics selected. Because it is not sufficient for the pupils merely to memorize the correct wording and manner for making and acknowledging introductions, they should be allowed ample practice time before the class to demonstrate such situations as the following:

- How Ken introduces his friend, Paul Stern, to Jim Clay (a classmate), to Dr. Jack Collins (his uncle), and to Ann Parks (his sister).
- How Karen introduces her friend, Patty Wong, to Donna Green (a classmate), to Ms. Colleen Henderson (her aunt), and to Andy Fox (her cousin).
- How Joanne introduces her mother, Mrs. Johnson, to Mr. Harry Miles (the principal), to Mrs. Janet Cohen (her teacher), and to Jeff Jordan (her girlfriend's brother).

Older children can discuss practical criteria for making and receiving introductions. They can also prepare a chart illustrating proper techniques or complete sample textbook exercises in introductions as shown in Figure 4.2.

Telephoning

The second area of social courtesies suitable for study by young children is the use of the telephone. Conversing by telephone has become increasingly important in daily living, with the United States ranking first among the countries of the world served by telephone. There are approximately 165 million telephones in the country today. Although the public makes three kinds of telephone calls—local, long distance, and overseas—over 90 percent of the calls in the United States are local calls, which children can receive and place routinely. Students should therefore learn how to make and answer a telephone call, how to take messages, and why it is important to speak clearly and courteously.

To become familiar with the proper way of using the telephone, older children can be introduced to the teletrainer distributed at no cost by most local telephone companies. The teletrainer is a relatively simple device, usually consisting of two telephones attached by approximately 25 feet of cord to an amplifying unit. The cord allows the phones to be passed around the room, and

Speaking and Listening

Figure 4.2. Exercises in Making Introductions.

Making Introductions

You can help others get acquainted. It is fun to introduce one person to another. Once they meet, the people may become friends.

A good introduction gives both people information about each other. You tell each person's name. You also tell something about each person. Use sentences correctly as you give quick, clear information. For example, you could say, "Martin, this is my cousin Tom. He likes baseball, and he is a good skater. Tom, meet my friend Martin. He has that great baseball card collection I was telling you about."

If you are introducing someone your age to an adult, tell the adult the younger person's name first. Follow this example:

"Aunt Martha, I'd like you to meet my friend Amy. She's a pitcher on my softball team. Amy, meet my favorite relative, Aunt Martha. She's visiting us for the week."

Whenever you make introductions, follow these guides.

> **Guides for Introducing People to Each Other**
> 1. Say each name clearly.
> 2. Tell something about each person you introduce.
> 3. Help the people begin their conversation.

Exercises: Introducing Friends

A. Form groups of three. Take turns introducing each other. Follow the Guides above.

B. Form groups of three. Take turns pretending that you are introducing your friend to someone famous.

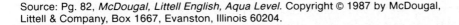

Source: Pg. 82, *McDougal, Littell English, Aqua Level.* Copyright © 1987 by McDougal, Littell & Company, Box 1667, Evanston, Illinois 60204.

because there are two phones, a typical conversation can take place. The amplifier permits the class to hear the conversation. The teacher has the added advantage of being able to control volume of voice with a special switch on the back of the amplifying unit, as well as being able to control telephone rings, busy signals, and dial tone. The students who are speaking on either of the two telephones can hear themselves over the amplifier as well as through their individual phone units as they act out situations involving social, business, or emergency reasons for telephoning. They may call to obtain a dental appointment, to order ice cream for a class party, to wish their grandmother a happy birthday, to report a fire, or to obtain the new number of a former classmate who recently moved.

Primary children can learn to name the parts of the telephone and to recognize the dial tone, the busy signal, and the ordinary ringing sound. They can practice taking messages, learning to listen carefully for details, and repeating the message before writing it down. They can be made aware that there are various instrument models. Their teacher can help them develop an illustrated chart on telephone courtesy.

Older students can become proficient in using a telephone directory, including the classified section. They can determine the area codes of nearby towns, as well as those of the major metropolitan centers such as Chicago (312), San Francisco (415), New York (212 and 718), Boston (617), New Orleans (504), and Los Angeles (213 and 818). They can prepare a class directory of pupils' names and telephone numbers. They can learn the proper way to handle wrong numbers that have been dialed by mistake either by themselves or by someone else. They can practice making long-distance calls, either by dialing direct or with operator assistance, to places within the United States or to foreign countries. Their teacher may plan a field trip to the local telephone building or invite a resource person from the telephone company to visit the class.

Intermediate grade pupils may wish to research and discuss such questions as (a) Do all telephones need wires? (b) How does the weather affect the work of the telephone repairperson? (c) Why is the telegraph still used when it is so convenient to make a telephone call? (d) How would a picture phone (a telephone with a TV screen) operate? (e) How does the transmission of sound in a string-and-can telephone differ from the transmission of electricity in a real telephone? (f) How have computers affected telephone service? (g) Is it merely an inconvenience to be without a telephone?

Finally, older and younger boys and girls alike must be reminded not to reveal to a stranger on the telephone that they are home alone. Any and all information concerning their parents' whereabouts should also not be mentioned. Any child who is in doubt as to how much to tell on the telephone should remember to ask only for the stranger's name, telephone number, and brief message.

| Evaluation of Telephone Conversation | Student participation in evaluating how others use the telephone is probably the most effective way to promote good telephone usage. Among the more important criteria to be considered in rating a telephone conversation are these: |

- Did both parties listen as well as talk?
- Was identification of the caller made early in the conversation?
- Was the purpose of the call achieved to the satisfaction of both parties?
- Was the conversation courteous?
- Was the message clear?
- Did both parties use pleasant speaking tones?
- Was the call concluded politely and promptly?

Readers theater is a form of oral reading in which two to twelve students present works of literature in front of an audience. It involves no memorization and only minimal use of scenery and costumes; readers usually work from copies of printed scripts and sit atop stools of various heights. Physical movement is only suggested, and the mood is projected by means of voices, facial expressions, and restrained gestures. Suitable for readers theater are excerpts from fiction prose, nonfiction prose, or poetry read in their original form or adapted by the children themselves.

Participating in Readers Theater

The most important role is that of the narrator who speaks directly to the audience and sets the scene. He or she describes the situation, theme, action, and characters to further the comprehension of the literary work.

The instructional potential of this speech art includes expansion of social awareness; cooperative work in heterogeneous groups; development of new concepts, information and vocabulary; stimulation and preparation for writing; and encouragement of below-average readers in the middle and upper grades by its lure of performance.[14]

Step-wise, readers theater first requires the children to choose their character parts and to rehearse individually. Next there are informal practice sessions. Finally the production is staged in front of an audience or else presented on videotape or on a regular tape recording. For elementary school students, ten to thirty minutes of playing time are most effective.

For teachers who are newcomers to this exciting combination of creative drama, reading, and literature, there is a Readers Theater Script Service in San Diego, California, which supplies both early elementary and advanced elementary packets containing cast scripts, director's prompt books, and other materials and information. The Service is part of the Institute for Readers Theater established in 1973.

One means of assessing the readers theater experience is the rating scale shown in Figure 4.3. With it the teacher can judge each student's response and progress.

Evaluation of Participation in Readers Theater

Using Puppets

Acting through the medium of dolls is termed puppetry, and it has existed as an entertaining and educative medium since the days of ancient China and Egypt. When the dolls are operated by strings, they are called marionettes and are suitable for manipulation by adolescents or adults. When they are worked directly by hand, the dolls are appropriate for manipulation by children and are called puppets. Elementary school language arts programs should be concerned with lessons involving puppets only.

At any grade level, beginning puppetry should revolve around the fun of using the puppets, and a wise teacher keeps a supply of inexpensive puppets available for this purpose. Later, after the children have become acquainted with puppetry and have learned to enjoy manipulating the figures, the teacher can assist them in making their own puppets. Even kindergarten children are capable of making and manipulating simple stick and hand puppets.

Figure 4.3. Rating Scale of Pupil Progress in Readers Theater Participation.

Rating Scale of Pupil Response to the Readers Theatre Project

Directions: Rate each item on the basis of 4 points for outstanding quality or performance, 3 points for better than average, 2 points for average, 1 point for inferior, and 0 for unsatisfactory. Encircle the appropriate number to indicate your rating, and enter the total of these numbers at the bottom of the sheet.

1. How would you rate this pupil's enthusiasm for the project?   0 1 2 3 4

2. To what extent did this pupil seem eager to seek out and read material for possible use in the project?   0 1 2 3 4

3. To what extent did this pupil seem eager to read a part in the group script?   0 1 2 3 4

4. To what extent did this pupil contribute ideas for the creation and staging of the script?   0 1 2 3 4

5. How would you rate this pupil's receptiveness to ideas generated by his or her classmates?   0 1 2 3 4

6. How would you judge this pupil's interest in listening to the readings delivered by his or her fellow classmates?   0 1 2 3 4

7. How would you evaluate this pupil's comprehension of the literature used in the project?   0 1 2 3 4

8. To what extent did this pupil appreciate the literature used in the project?   0 1 2 3 4

9. To what extent did this pupil respond to the voice, diction, and interpretive reading exercises?   0 1 2 3 4

10. To what extent did this pupil exhibit improvement in his or her oral reading skills?   0 1 2 3 4

Total of encircled numbers: _____

Reprinted from Shirlee Sloyer, READERS THEATRE, National Council of Teachers of English, 1982, p. 65. Used with permission.

The teacher should realize that puppetry is especially helpful for both shy and aggressive pupils because puppeteers are generally hidden from their audience and so lose themselves in their characterizations. The attention of the audience is channeled away from the puppeteers to the puppets they are operating. In this fashion, the timid children lose some of their self-consciousness, and the highly extroverted pupils become more restrained. Children suffering from such speech handicaps as defective articulation, stuttering, or loudness also benefit from repeated roles as puppeteers. They are motivated to practice correct speech patterns so that their puppets' conversations can be understood.

A new technique for using puppets is called *interaction puppetry* and helps children acquire problem-solving skills.[15] They learn to explore alternative solutions, identify consequences of interpersonal behaviors, develop causal thinking, and become sensitive to personal and interpersonal experiences and problems. Interaction puppetry involves one adult puppeteer behind the stage, who manipulates the puppets and brings them to life, and one adult facilitator, who sits in front of the stage and promotes the child-puppet interaction. The boys and girls comment on what is happening, and the puppets agree or disagree with the pupil responses. The adult facilitator maintains control and helps the children express their ideas.

When designing an interactional puppet skit, there are four guidelines that are both important and interrelated. First, there must be developed a "puppet family" with several puppets that have definite but different personalities (e.g., one puppet that is sad, lonely, and very frightened; another that is an aggressive extrovert). Second, a problem must be identified, such as hitting or rejection. Third, there must be a worthwhile storyline that is brief, uncomplicated, and significant. Finally, there needs to be a clarification of the types of problem-solving responses desired from the audience. A few of the numerous possible themes for interaction puppetry would include emotional development, racism, conflict, cooperation, body awareness, sensory development, and friendship.

In preparing to give a show, it is first necessary to select a story that is suitable for the age of the puppeteers and their audience. The story should have numerous short lines, with no more than three characters performing simultaneously. It must be fast-moving to sustain the attention of the viewers.

Steps in Classroom Puppetry

Next, the class must choose puppets that can best tell the story and begin to imagine how each puppet should look and act. Although some groups will wish to make puppets of their own at this point, others may still prefer to use puppets from the teacher's supply or to bring puppets that have been made at camp, Scout meetings, or summer recreational centers.

Then the boys and girls should discuss the dialogue and try out various tonal qualities in order to match the voices with the characters. With children who are timid or inexperienced, this step will take a longer period of time than with fluent and resourceful pupils. Written scripts, however, are not necessary.

Fourth, the puppeteers should set up the stage and manipulate the puppets. They must decide how to hold the figures and how to enter or exit from the stage. They must realize that puppets are like human actors and have to show feelings, move, and speak so that they can be heard and understood.[16] The puppeteers should be reminded that there are various ways of holding puppets and that each should use the way that works best for him or her; there is no one best approach. Manipulating puppets is not easy, and the job becomes even more challenging when lines are added to the actions.

The class is now ready to present the puppet show for a useful experience in creative action. Background scenery may be screened through the opaque projector. Sound effects, miniature portable properties, and music may also be added for variation and interest.

Finally the children and their teacher evaluate the performance. Suggestions for improving the manipulation of the puppets and the voices of the puppeteers are in order.

Suggested Stories for Puppetry

Because there should not be too many characters in a puppet show staged by or for elementary-school pupils, the teacher may wish to encourage the class to write its own script. If the children should choose to do that, they have to realize that (1) all action must take place in the present; (2) each section must arise naturally from the preceding section; (3) the plot has to be brief and simple with a definite beginning, middle, and end; and (4) the characters must be faced with a problem whose solution brings conflict to the action of the play.

Sometimes, however, the teacher may find that the boys and girls prefer to adapt a literary story they have heard or read. Folk tales such as "The Story of the Three Little Pigs," "Snow White and the Seven Dwarfs," "Henny Penny," "Tom Tit Tot," "The Bremen Town Musicians," "The Three Billy Goats Gruff," "Jack and the Beanstalk," and "The Pancake" have simple plots that can be easily adapted for puppetry.

Other stories that lend themselves to interpretation include Kipling's *The Elephant's Child* (Harcourt, 1983), Travers' *Mary Poppins in Cherry Tree Lane* (Harcourt, 1982), Lionni's *Alexander and the Wind-Up Mouse* (Pantheon, 1969), Potter's *The Tale of Peter Rabbit and Other Stories* (Knopf, 1982), Milne's *Winnie-the-Pooh* (Dutton, 1974), and Andersen's *The Princess and the Pea* (Holiday, 1982) and *The Emperor's New Clothes* (Harper, 1982).

Puppets that Children Can Make

Young children are capable of constructing a large variety of puppets, and simple directions for making puppets can be found in books by Frieda Gates (1981), Robyn and Lauren Supraner (1981), Laura Ross (1978), Shari Lewis (1977), Lis Paludan (1975), and David Currell (1975). There are four major groups of puppets that boys and girls can create.

The *push,* or *table, puppets* are the easiest of all to operate and are recommended especially for early puppet dramatization. These small figures stand on their own. When a child wants such a puppet to perform in a moment of play, he or she will lift it by its head or push it along to its next position. This frees the puppeteer to concentrate on his or her oral expression. Children can readily use watercolors or construction paper to transform into a stationary puppet such a commonplace item as a bottle, can, block of wood, paper cone, water glass, balloon, or cup. They may also bring from home two-dimensional plastic manlike or animalistic figures to help in the development of stories about favorite poems or folk tales.

Another group includes the familiar *hand puppets,* which fit somewhat like gloves. The most common variety is worked by two fingers and the thumb. The pointer finger is projected into the neck, and the fourth and little fingers remain in the palm of the hand. The heads of hand puppets may be made from a wide selection of commonplace and inexpensive materials such as fruits and vegetables, stuffed socks, rubber or styrofoam balls, stuffed napkins, paper-mâché, or small boxes. After the head is finished, the operator's hand is covered with a piece of colored fabric about the size of a man's handerchief; then rubber bands are slipped over the fingers to help define the arms, and the head is put into position.

Probably the simplest type of hand puppet, from the standpoint of materials and construction, is the paper-bag puppet. A sturdy bag such as a lunch sack is placed flat on the desk and colored with crayons. When it is time for a performance, the bag is slipped over the entire hand without making allowance for puppet arms. The children must remember, however, that the mouth opening always falls on the fold of the bag so that the underside of the flap is the inside of the mouth. For the advanced type of paper-bag puppet, the head is stuffed with torn newspapers or paper toweling to create a three-dimensional effect.

Another kind of hand puppet is the finger puppet, which usually slips over an individual finger. Properly cut, a finger puppet can also slip up onto the second knuckles of two fingers so that the puppet walks. Finger puppets can be made from rolled cylinders of construction paper, from toilet-paper rolls, or even from mittens. Face and body features can be added with crayons, marking pens, or other materials.

A third and large category of puppets is composed of the *stick puppets,* which consist of pictures, drawings, objects, or push puppets attached to sticks. Each is animated by moving the stick up and down or from side to side. Types of sticks include tongue depressors, yardsticks, pencils, broomsticks, dowel sticks, and narrow plywood. Hand-puppet heads may also be mounted on sticks for quick puppetry.

When a stick puppet has two sticks instead of the usual one, it is known technically as a rod puppet. The second stick or rod is attached to a jointed arm or head. Operators of such puppets must be capable of using both their hands skillfully while simultaneously delivering their lines. Consequently, rod puppeteers are generally fifth or sixth graders.

The fourth and final group of puppets useful in the elementary curriculum comprises *shadow puppets.* An extension of rod puppets, they are distinct, flat figures that have been cut from cardboard, stiff cellophane, or tagboard and painted. They are manipulated on long rods by the players who animate them against a tightly drawn translucent screen lit from behind. The lights must be placed between the screen and the operators, and the puppets are pressed against that screen by two wire rods in order to produce well-defined shadows. Jerking or twisting the rods sets the puppets into motion.

Fifth graders in one suburban Chicago school became involved in the writing, figure-making, and staging of this type of puppet show during their "Folk Tales from Other Lands Through Shadow Theater."[17] Their teacher reported that shadow puppets enrich the reading program, provoke an interest in story telling and creative drama, and sharpen research skills as the boys and girls become involved in preparing authentic scripts for these translucent silhouettes.

Although facial expressions are obviously invisible on shadow puppets, they are critical to push, hand, and stick puppets. The teacher must therefore impress upon the students the importance of building character into the faces of the puppets they construct and decorate. Incidentally, the teacher should also stress the importance of saving all remnant pieces of items that could be used in future puppet-making projects. Such leftover bits can go into a large cardboard box for the production of so-called "junk-box puppets."

Puppet Stages

The stage and the staging for a puppet show should be as uncomplicated as possible. Elaborate preparations are beyond the scope of young children, but there is a variety of temporary stages that the pupils can make quickly.

At least four temporary stages are readily and inexpensively assembled. The first is a *table stage*. A rectangular table is placed on its side with the top part facing the audience, a large piece of cloth is strung as a curtain around the sides and front of the stage, and the puppeteers crouch behind the curtain in order to operate the puppets from below. If two tables are available, one can be turned on its side on top of the other. Then the front and sides of the bottom table can be wrapped with butcher paper or with cloth to hide the puppeteers from the audience. A bookcase or portable chalkboard properly covered also provides a good stage surface.

The second type of temporary stage is a *box stage*. A large cardboard appliance box or shipping container is used and the upper half of its front is cut back so that the puppeteers can enter from the rear. The box is then painted and some type of anchor applied to prevent the box from tipping over. Should a smaller grocery carton be available, the back of the carton is completely removed and the front is cut to give the effect of a curtain drape. After the box has been painted, a table is covered with a sheet or blanket, and the back edge of the carton is placed along the back edge of the table. The puppeteers then kneel behind the table and are hidden from view. Even a shoe box can become the stage for puppets of suitable size.

The *doorway stage* is a third kind of temporary stage. A single drape, sheet, or blanket is fastened to a rod or rope or is thumbtacked across an open doorway so that it reaches the floor. It is attached at a point one inch above the heads of the puppeteers so that the players can remain completely hidden, even when they stretch their arms to show their puppets. When a pair of drapes or sheets can be found, the shorter one is hung so that it falls from the top of the doorway and leaves a twenty-to-thirty-inch opening, and the second one is hung down to the floor. The puppeteers reach up to work the figures in the opening.

A fourth stage is a *chair stage*. A board may be placed across the top of two chairs placed back to back and a cloth, sheet or blanket draped over the board. Should a large upholstered chair be available, the puppeteer can kneel on its seat and manipulate the puppets so that they are visible to an audience facing the back of the chair.

Besides temporary stages, there are also more permanent puppet stages that take longer to construct and are more costly to assemble. Among them are wooden stages and screen stages, the latter using three-fold screens. Sometimes room parents or school parent-teacher groups will furnish such stages for classroom puppetry.

Properties for both the permanent and temporary stages, however, should be few and restricted to essentials, with all other items painted on the inside of the stage or on the backdrop. The scenery should be suggestive rather than realistic, with careful attention paid to the matter of size in relation to the height of the puppets. It is paramount that the figures, and not the background, dominate any puppet stage.

The teacher can readily evaluate the progress of the boys and girls in using puppets by asking the following:

- Do the children show increasing ability in handling puppets?
- Are their overall speech patterns becoming consistent in speaking for a particular puppet?
- Can they make up adventures for an inanimate figure?
- Does the use of puppets stimulate interest in developing sentence sequence?
- Are there increasing variety and quality in creative puppet dialogue?
- Are the children whose speech sounds are sometimes defective, distorted, or omitted gaining incentive to improve their speech?

Evaluation of Puppetry

The American Speech-Language-Hearing Association has recommended that comprehensive speech-language programs be organized along a continuum. This continuum has at one end a communicative development component, has in the middle a communicative deviations component, and has at the other end a communicative disorders component. It recognizes the wide range of needs among children and attempts to accommodate each of them.

Formerly known as "speech improvement," the communicative development component is a preventive program. It recognizes that the development of verbal-auditory skills is basic to the academic achievement of all boys and girls. Such development is consequently a major objective of the language arts curriculum. In light of current educational philosophy and budgets, it is apparent that the classroom teacher is responsible for attaining that objective, although school clinicians or university clinical instructors in speech-language pathology can serve as consultants in designing and implementing a language development program.[18]

Communicative Development

The fact that children come to school knowing, with varying degrees of effectiveness, how to speak should not mislead the teacher into believing that no instruction is needed. As a matter of fact, it is only through the disciplined correlation of the factors of language, thought, voice, and action that effective oral communication can be achieved.

Because the development of speech depends on physical and psychological development, it is to be hoped that each child will have normal organs of speech and hearing as well as the security of a psychologically comfortable environment. When some students lack these assets, it becomes the teacher's responsibility to assist the children in making the adjustments necessary for effective speech.

Through such various speech arts as were presented earlier in this chapter, children learn the values of pleasant, audible speech; clear articulation; attentive, discriminating listening; and the correct use of stress, phrasing, and intonation. The program of speech in action, however, may not provide sufficient instruction and practice in proper posture, breathing habits, and control of the speech organs. Nor may it pinpoint minor speech faults that must be corrected. Specific instruction in speech skills, therefore, is critical and constitutes that integral part of the language arts curriculum that is known as communicative development. It is concerned with building positive attitudes and attempts to meet the speaking needs of all children in the classroom.

Such a program does not require the services of a speech-language clinician but can be implemented successfully by the classroom teacher. It can incorporate commercially available communicative development stories and picture cards, and it can involve fifteen-minute daily lessons in the early grades. A sample kindergarten plan covering the *k* sound, for instance, could run as follows:

The teacher says

1. Let me see how sharp your ears are. Do you think you all know the crowing sound of *k* now? We'll see. I'm going to say two words, like *key/tea*. Where did you hear the crowing sound of *k?* In the first *key* or in the second *tea?* Now here are some more pairs of words. Tell me where the *k* is. Is it in the first or second word? Listen to both words and then answer "first" or "second" —*call/tall, tan/can, pearl/curl, cop/top.*
2. Here are some words with *k* at the end. Listen to both words and then answer "first" or "second" . . . *sick/sit, back/bat, like/light, lock/lot, oat/oak.* (The teacher should exaggerate the sounds, but no more than necessary.)
3. Who likes riddles? I'm thinking of something beginning with *k*
   . . . and it's yellow and I like to eat it on the cob (*corn*).
   . . . and it's soft and furry, and it says "Meow" (*kitty* or *cat*).
   . . . and it's a long orange vegetable. Rabbits like it too (*carrot*).
   . . . and we ride in it and get driven to many places (*car*).
   . . . and soup comes in it and all kinds of other foods too (*can*).

4. I'm thinking of something with a *k* in the middle
   . . . and it's something that lives at the zoo, climbs trees, and does very funny tricks (*monkey*).
   . . . and it's something I have on my coat that I put paper or money or important things into (*pocket*).
   . . . and it's orange and I make a jack-o'-lantern out of it at Halloween (*pumpkin*).
   . . . and it's something I eat for Thanksgiving dinner (*turkey*).
5. I'm thinking of something with a *k* at the end
   . . . and it's white and we drink it (*milk*).
   . . . and it's the sound a clock makes (*ticktock*).
   . . . and it's the thing we wash our hands in (*sink*).
   . . . and it's what you put on your foot before you put on your shoe (*sock*).
   . . . and it's what I am if I have to stay in bed and can't go to school (*sick*).
6. Who wants to make some riddles for us to guess? (The children will not be able to do this if they are left entirely on their own. However, if the teacher gives them one of the picture cards containing a *k* sound and lets them describe the picture, it should go fairly well.)

A new dimension of interest in communicative development lessons such as this one has resulted from research studies showing significant relationships both between defective articulation and auditory discrimination and between reading retardation and auditory discrimination.

The Sounds of English: Some Problems

The sound system of English can create problems in the sequence of speech development in children with respect to six areas. The first of these is *reversals* because a child may say *alunimum* for *aluminum* due to immaturity, inadequate learning, or cerebral damage; some of the words commonly reversed appear in Table 4.2. Another problem area is *consonant blends* because either the nervous system or the muscular system of the child may not be sufficiently mature to master two or three consonants bound together such as *str*. In this instance teachers must monitor the words introduced to pupils in the early stages of reading because a student's failure to read a word aloud correctly may be an articulation difficulty and not a reading error.[19] Even though the ability to discriminate among sounds develops at various rates in various people, an eight-year-old child who says *wabbit* for *rabbit* is showing vestiges of *baby talk,* which is a third area of difficulty.

Then there is *voice pitch,* which is related to general body tension, inadequate loudness, outdoor yelling, heredity of vocal apparatus, or a change of voice. There is also *voice loudness,* which may involve discriminational, psychological, physical, or environmental causative factors. The final problem area is *mispronunciations,* which may be resolved, in part at least, by the teacher's model pronunciation of all words and especially of those found in Table 4.2.

Table 4.2
The One Hundred Most Frequently Mispronounced of the Commonly
Used Words

1. aluminum	35. gather	69. recognize
2. American	36. genuine	70. regularly
3. apron	37. geography	71. rinse
4. arctic	38. get	72. roof
5. asked	39. government	73. room
6. athlete	40. height	74. sandwich
7. battery	41. hundred	75. secretary
8. because	42. iron	76. sink
9. booths	43. Italian	77. smile
10. bury	44. keg	78. soot
11. bushel	45. larynx	79. spoil
12. can't	46. length	80. squash
13. catch	47. library	81. statistics
14. cavalry	48. Massachusetts	82. such
15. cement	49. material	83. sure
16. child	50. men	84. surprise
17. children	51. Michigan	85. ten
18. chimney	52. milk	86. tired
19. column	53. nuclear	87. tournament
20. could you	54. onion	88. towel
21. cushion	55. orange	89. tower
22. dandelion	56. our	90. veteran
23. davenport	57. particularly	91. vision
24. deaf	58. party	92. vowel
25. Detroit	59. peony	93. wash
26. diphtheria	60. percolate	94. wheelbarrow
27. eggs	61. perspiration	95. where
28. escape	62. picture	96. wiener
29. film	63. police	97. wouldn't
30. finally	64. power	98. wrestle
31. fire	65. pumpkin	99. years
32. fish	66. push	100. your
33. fists	67. put	
34. flower	68. radish	

Source: A. W. Huckleberry and E. S. Strother, SPEECH EDUCATION FOR THE ELEMENTARY TEACHER (Boston: Allyn & Bacon, Inc., 1973), p. 307.

Testing and Recording Speaking Patterns

In order to plan lessons well and to use time wisely, the teacher must be cognizant of the specific speech faults that prevail among some boys and girls. The teacher can observe during several short periods of class activity the habitual patterns employed by those pupils and then record these impressions quickly and accurately with *yes* or *no* answers on individual profile sheets. Taping the activities may sometimes help the teacher form conclusions in doubtful cases. Such profile sheets can be used later for referrals to speech-language clinicians or for consultations with parents, administrators, or other teachers. A typical profile sheet is shown in Figure 4.4.

Profile of General Speech Faults

Child's Name _____ Date _____

1. Articulation and Pronunciation
   a. Does the child distort sounds? _____
   b. Does the child substitute one sound for another? _____
   c. Does the child omit sounds? _____
   d. Does the child mispronounce? _____

2. Voice
   a. Is the child's voice loud? _____
   b. Is the child's voice nasal? _____
   c. Is the child's voice hoarse? _____
   d. Is the child's voice monotonous? _____
   e. Is the child's voice inaudible? _____
   f. Is the pitch abnormally high? _____
   g. Is the pitch abnormally low? _____

3. Rate and Fluency
   a. Is the child's speech too rapid? _____
   b. Is the child's speech too slow? _____
   c. Is the child's phrasing poor? _____
   d. Is the child's speech hesitant? _____
   e. Is the child's vocabulary limited? _____
   f. Is the child able to organize his or her thoughts? _____

4. Attitude toward Speaking Situations _____
   a. Does the child enjoy speaking situations? _____
   b. Does the child apparently avoid speaking situations? _____
   c. Is the child reluctant to speak in group situations? _____
   d. Does the child participate actively? _____

Figure 4.4. Sample Profile Sheet for Recording General Speech Faults of Elementary Students.

Skills

When a school program begins with the kindergarten classes and is subsequently developed throughout the grades, the students, upon completion of the sixth grade, have the ability to *modulate their voices* to reflect feeling, mood, and meaning. They can *speak in clear and pleasing tones,* giving attention to intonation and tonal quality. They are able to *use their teeth, lips, and tongues to give precise enunciation* to beginning sounds, middle sounds, and ending sounds. Finally they can *pace their speech* in order to obtain and maintain sustained listening.

Ability to Modulate the Voice

In both the primary and the intermediate grades, the ability to modulate the voice may be developed and improved through a variety of learning experiences. Younger children can dramatize stories in which the characters feel strong emotions, such as the animals in *The Three Little Pigs, The Three Billy Goats Gruff,* and *The Three Bears,* or in which a variety of voices is demanded, such as *Jack and the Beanstalk* and *Hansel and Gretel.* They can listen to poems such as Stevenson's "The Wind" and discuss how the refrain should sound.

Their teacher can exhibit visuals of active children and allow each pupil to select one picture as a basis for an impromptu oral composition. The teacher may also display chalkboard sentences that express happiness, surprise, or fear (such as "What a good time we had!" and "Stay away from the fire!") and encourage the pupils to practice saying these sentences aloud, preferably using a tape recorder. Sometimes the teacher may read or tell a story to the class and then have the children evaluate his or her reading or telling in terms of feeling, mood, and meaning.

Older students can participate in choral speaking of longer poems such as McCord's "At the Garden Gate" and Prelutsky's "The Grobbles." Their teacher can have them recite or read statements that can show both annoyance and pleasure, such as "Who left this box here?" and "Is this for me?" Also, the teacher can encourage the children to suggest words that describe a pleasant voice, such as one that is soft or musical, as well as words that characterize an unpleasant voice, such as one that is gruff or whining. Finally, the teacher and the students can prepare and tell two brief stories, each ending with the same sentence but showing a different feeling; for example, "He dropped the letter into the fire."

Ability to Speak in Clear and Pleasing Tones

Young children can develop and improve the ability to speak clearly in pleasing tones through dramatic play activities planned in conjunction with a unit on the home. They can recite or read sentences such as "It is snowing" and "Come here" with various inflections. They may listen to tapes or records of appropriate stories and orchestral selections for changes in volume and pitch.

A primary teacher can read poems to the class and discuss how intonation must change with meaning. The teacher may encourage the children to read chorally "The Three Little Kittens" as he or she points out the sounds that help make the Mother Goose rhyme a favorite with listeners. Also, the teacher can introduce the class to various kinds of bells and let the students imitate the bells for the purpose of distinguishing among the tone and the pitch of the telephone, the doorbell, and the smoke alarm.

Children in the intermediate grades can help list criteria for pleasing speech such as "Speak slowly" and "Use the lips and tongue to make clear speech sounds." They can use a teletrainer kit described earlier in this chapter and then chart standards for pleasant telephone conversations.

Their teacher can help the class participate in the oral reading of poems from books such as Smaridge's *Only Silly People Waste* (Abingdon, 1976), listening for distinct beginnings and endings of words. The teacher can ask each child to present a one-minute talk on a topic such as "Noise Pollution in the School" or to spin a one-minute tale from a beginning phrase such as "One dark and rainy night . . ." Finally, the teacher and the students can discuss how pitch and stress are used during telecasts or broadcasts of sports events or news reports of tragedies.

To practice proper articulation, boys and girls in kindergarten and the primary grades can recite those nursery rhymes, including "Sing a Song of Sixpence" and "Baa, Baa, Black Sheep," that feature the consonant sounds of *s, b,* and *p.* They can hold a piece of tissue paper before their mouths, trying to keep it vibrating as long as possible while they sound out certain consonant digraphs such as *sh* and *th.* The children can create and recite sentences with alliteration, such as "Paul Pipwick prefers pumpkin pie," or sentences that contain tongue twisters, such as "Many mothers make money mending mittens." Finally, with the help of their teacher, they can compile a list of word pairs that begin or end with the following letters: *d* and *t, p* and *b,* or *th* and *t.*

Ability to Use Teeth, Lips, and Tongue for Proper Articulation

Students in the intermediate grades should continue to do oral exercises with rhyming words and tongue twisters. They can divide polysyllabic words, learning to enunciate distinctly the sequence of sounds in words like *chronological* and *arithmetical.* They can listen for the often-forgotten syllable in words like *family, geography,* or *poem.* Lastly, they can compile lists of words using the consonant sounds of *l, r,* and *z,* and the digraph *ch.*

While young children are hearing and reciting tongue twisters, they can be shown how the difficulties in pronouncing and understanding the sayings increase with the tempo of the recitation. They can listen to poems with definite rhythms, such as Lindsay's "The Mysterious Cat," and discuss how rhythm affects pace. They can discover by rereading some of the sections in their basals how oral pacing is related to the subject matter of a narrative.

Ability to Pace Speech

Older boys and girls can contrast two poems such as Stevenson's "Windy Nights" and Moore's "Snowy Morning" in order to establish the relationship between mood and pacing. They can make announcements over the public address system and later play back their presentations so that they may evaluate the pace they exhibited. Finally, the class can take turns giving directions relevant to artificial respiration or other first aid, for example, in order to demonstrate the importance of clarity and variety of pace in instances of emergency instructions.

Self-evaluation by the teacher and by the child by means of a checklist (Figures 4.5 and 4.6) has proved worthwhile, although the teacher can also occasionally appraise the speech of each pupil from time to time (Figure 4.7). A comparison of the teacher's rating with the student's appraisal often leads to a better understanding of exhibited weaknesses and strengths, especially when the suggestions are specific enough to point the way to growth. Generalities such as *interesting* or *good* offer little practical assistance. Records of evaluations should be kept up to date on individual cards or in separate folders in order to provide a basis for diagnosis.

Figure 4.5. Sample Checklist for Teacher's Self-Evaluation in Speech.

Classroom Teacher's Self-Evaluation Checklist of His or Her Role in Speech

	Always	Sometimes	Never
1. Do I provide a good speech example?	_____	_____	_____
2. Do the children in my class feel socially and emotionally secure when they talk to each other and to me?	_____	_____	_____
3. Do I keep records of my children in order to chart development in speech over a period of time?	_____	_____	_____
4. Do I maintain separate standards for each group of children in recognition of the differences in readiness to learn?	_____	_____	_____
5. Do I provide ample time for the children to hear the correct production of sounds in a variety of activities?	_____	_____	_____
6. Do the parents know that I am working on improving children's speech, and do they understand and approve of the methods I use?	_____	_____	_____
7. Do I consciously integrate speech activities with the rest of the school program?	_____	_____	_____
8. Do I encourage the whole group to participate in the communicative development activity so that no one is singled out for individual correction?	_____	_____	_____
9. Do I give praise for good speech by the children?	_____	_____	_____
10. Do I promptly refer children with communicative disorders to the speech-language clinician and do I then follow his or her recommendations closely?	_____	_____	_____

Intermediate Student's Self-Evaluation Checklist in Speech

	Yes	No
1. Is my voice pleasant to hear?	_____	_____
2. Is my voice too loud or too soft?	_____	_____
3. Is my voice too high or too low?	_____	_____
4. Do I use a variety of inflections?	_____	_____
5. Do I speak too slowly or too fast?	_____	_____
6. Do I speak distinctly?	_____	_____
7. Do I use a varied vocabulary?	_____	_____
8. Do I use appropriate language for each speaking situation?	_____	_____
9. Do I explain myself well so that others can understand my ideas?	_____	_____
10. Do I remember to wait for my turn to speak?	_____	_____

Figure 4.6. Sample Checklist for Student's Self-Evaluation in Speech.

Classroom Teacher's Evaluation of Student Speech

Student's Name _____ **Date** _____

(The teacher should check the vocal difficulties below each speech technique that is rated *average* or *unsatisfactory*.)

Tempo   Very Good _____ Average _____ Unsatisfactory _____

_____ Too fast

_____ Too slow

_____ Unvarying, monotonous

_____ Poor phrasing; irregular rhythm of speaking

_____ Hesitations

Loudness   Very Good _____ Average _____ Unsatisfactory _____

_____ Too loud

_____ Too weak

_____ Lack of variety

_____ Force overused as a form of emphasis

Figure 4.7. Sample Form for Teacher's Evaluation of Student Speech.

Figure 4.7. (cont.)

Pitch Very Good _____ Average _____ Unsatisfactory _____

_____ General level too high

_____ General level too low

_____ Lack of variety

_____ Fixed pattern monotonously repeated

_____ Lack of relationship between pitch changes and meaning

_____ Exaggerated pitch changes

Quality Very Good _____ Average _____ Unsatisfactory _____

_____ Nasal

_____ Hoarse

_____ Breathy

_____ Throaty and guttural

_____ Strained and harsh

_____ Flat

_____ Thin and weak

Articulation Very Good _____ Average _____ Unsatisfactory _____

Consonants: _____ Slurred over or omitted

_____ Specific sounds defective

Vowels: _____ Improperly formed

_____ General diction careless or slovenly

Assessment of students through observations by classroom teachers is one of the recommendations made to the Massachusetts Department of Education concerning a rating scale to assess speaking skills.[20] Teachers should observe students at least twice in a given period (such as a semester or a year). For the sake of reliability checks, students should be rated at least once by two teachers or at two separate times by the same teacher. A second recommendation concerns the principal features of the rating scale and states that these features should represent lists of delivery skills, language skills, organization skills, and skills of purpose. The third important recommendation relates to the type of situations in which such student assessment should occur. Rather than contrived situations that isolate assessment from regular classroom activities, naturalistic situations should be employed which ask the student to demand and provide straightforward information; to use survival words for coping with emergency situations; to question others' opinions; or to describe objects, experiences, and events.

There are two commercial tests published in the United States for the purpose of assessing speaking skills in children, and both meet the significant criterion of individual administration.[21] The first is *Circus Say and Tell,* published by Addison-Wesley (Reading, MA) for children in preschool through grade three; for Part I, the child describes objects, and for Parts II and III, the child responds verbally to pictures. The second is *Language Facility Test,* published by Allington Corporation (Alexandria, VA) for normal children ages three to fifteen; the child is asked to tell a story about each picture presented to him or her.

A recent review of the major sources of prevalence data on communicative disorders in the United States revealed that a national study of nearly 40,000 public school students in grades one through twelve showed the presence of articulation errors, voice problems, and stuttering in 5.7 percent of the children, as evaluated by trained examiners.[22] In each of the three categories, the prevalence was higher among males than among females. One state (New Mexico) published the results of its own survey and identified almost 8 percent of its school-age population as being speech-impaired, and that figure did not include bilingual children. Neither of these percentages includes incidence of communicative disorders among the learning disabled, physically handicapped, emotionally disturbed, or mentally retarded, which would surely raise the percentages considerably. Although estimates do vary, the largest single group of handicapped children in the nation's schools, claims the United States Office of Education, are those with speech disorders.

Communicative Remediation for Handicapped Children

According to Van Riper and Emerick, speech is abnormal when it deviates so far from the speech of other people that it calls attention to itself, interferes with communication, or causes the speaker or his/her listeners to be distressed.[23] Briefly, it is conspicuous, unintelligible, or unpleasant.

Teachers should be aware of criteria that have been developed for evaluating the level of an individual's communication skill based on social acceptability:

1. Does the individual function with adequate linguistic skill in his or her own speech community? (If the answer is yes, then go on to evaluative question 2.)
2. Does the individual function with adequate linguistic skill outside his or her own speech community? (Again, if the answer is yes, go on to evaluative question 3.)
3. Are there any minor differences in the speech patterns of the individual that contribute to social differences, which in turn lead to social devaluation or reduction of status? (If the answer is no, the individual's communication can be rated as adequate or possibly superior.)[24]

Should a child be unable to function linguistically in his or her own community, the chances are slight that he or she will be able to do so outside that community, such as in a school situation. Consequently, it is important that elementary teachers are able to identify speech disorders and refer speech-handicapped children.

Studies have shown that the percentage of accurate referrals tends to rise as the severity of the disorder increases. Teachers are most accurate in referring stutterers because interruptions in speech fluency and the accompanying mannerisms tend to interfere with the communication process to a greater extent than do most other speech disorders. Teachers are least accurate in referring children with voice disorders because such disorders often do not affect speech intelligibility. At least one survey reported that overall, teachers are uncertain about the particular handicaps that speech-language clinicians handle.[25] In fact, only 58 percent of those responding felt certain they could recognize a speech- or language-defective child in their own classrooms.

Yet elementary teachers can be taught to identify speech-defective pupils if they are given training in the use of pragmatic criteria.[26] Such useful referral criteria include linguistic nonfluency, revisions, delays before responding, nonspecific vocabulary, inappropriate responses, poor topic maintenance, and the need for repetition (although the last criterion may indicate a hearing problem).

Teachers must also have a tolerant attitude toward the speech-defective children in their classrooms. If they say nothing, they are indicating that the children's speech is not noticeably objectionable. This creates the most favorable environment for the speech-handicapped pupils whose peers then accept them readily. On the other hand, the teacher who demands unusually high standards of speech behavior, with little tolerance for individual deficiencies, tends to generate reduced acceptance of the speech-defective children by their classmates.

The matter of teacher attitude toward the speech-impaired child as well as toward the speech-language clinician and toward the speech and language program was recently explored in a study of 147 teachers.[27] It was concluded that classroom teachers have a more positive attitude toward the clinician and the speech and language program than they do toward the afflicted child. Furthermore, such demographic variables as teachers' age, sex, academic degree, or teaching experience have no significant correlation with the attitude expressed.

In a school district with an adequate number of speech-language clinicians, the elementary teacher can and should work closely with them in helping speech-handicapped children gain intelligible speech. He or she can help these pupils develop a sense of carry-over in their speech correction activities from the speech class to the regular classroom and can quietly urge the children to focus attention daily on the sound or sounds the therapist is presenting. Through conferences with clinicians, the teacher can provide information regarding the strengths and weaknesses of the children referred from his or her classroom. Finally, the teacher can report to the clinician any progress the children are making, and together they can plan an approach for speech reeducation, which will provide maximum success for the pupils.

In school districts with relatively few speech-language clinicians, the classroom teacher includes communicative remediation in lesson plans by employing one of these practices:

1. A weekly speech-period plan that sets aside a specific period every week for concentration on the skills of speech, or

2. An adaptive instruction plan that schedules remedial speech lessons during periods when other pupils are engaged in reasonably self-directed study

The elementary teacher will ordinarily encounter one or more of the four common groups of speech deficits in the classroom: disorders of articulation, voice disturbances, stuttering, and disordered or delayed language. The teacher will want to do whatever possible to help the pupils with speech problems by assisting those with minor cases and referring those with more serious disorders to speech-language clinicians. Some children will, of course, have deficiencies in more than one dimension of speech.

Speech surveys in the public schools have indicated that most children with speech problems fall into the category of speech disorders classified as problems of articulation. As many as 80 percent of all speech problems found in the elementary classroom will concern those pupils who cannot make certain phonetic sounds either within blends with other phonetic sounds or in isolation. The largest proportion of these problems occurs in the population of grades one through three, even though, by the age of five, 75 percent of the males and females produce all sounds correctly. By fifth grade, most children have acquired articulatory proficiency, according to the results of a five-year longitudinal study of the spontaneous development of such proficiency in 60 boys and girls who had misarticulated at least one phoneme in the first grade.[28] Forty-seven of the sixty children developed adequate articulation with no speech intervention, suggesting that a substantial amount of phonological maturation does occur without the intervention of speech services. For the remaining thirteen children, however, school speech pathology services were desirable.

Disorders of Articulation

Children who have difficulty with articulation are not able to produce consistently and effortlessly the accepted sound patterns of speech. Instead, they may form some sounds poorly (making distortion errors), leave some sounds out completely (making omission errors), or exchange one sound for another (making substitution errors) as they find that there are some sounds, such as *s, r, th, l,* and *z,* that seem to be harder to learn than others. Of the three categories, the predominant type of misarticulation—at least among primary children—is simple substitution.

Articulation disorders may be classified as either *phonetic errors* (resulting from organic malformations or malfunctions) or *phonemic errors,* sometimes called functional errors, for which no neurological or physiological basis seems to exist. Both types of disorders are associated with certain factors, including general language deficits, low intelligence, socioeconomic status (with interdental lisping, for example, tending to come from high socioeconomic levels but omission-type errors occurring more frequently among low socioeconomic levels), hearing loss, structural abnormalities, auditory discrimination and auditory memory, and reduced motor ability.

This student has an articulation disorder and is receiving special help from a speech language clinician. (© Jon Jacobson.)

Representative tests of phoneme production that can determine which children need to attend a school speech clinic include the following:

> *Arizona Articulation Proficiency Scale* (Western Psychological Services, Los Angeles)
> *Compton Phonological Assessment* (Carousel House, San Francisco)
> *Fisher-Logemann Test of Articulation Competence* (Houghton-Mifflin, Boston)
> *Goldman and Fristoe's Test of Articulation* (American Guidance Service, Circle Pines, MN) in filmstrip format[29]

Finally, the United States Department of Health and Human Services offers these suggestions to the teachers and parents of children with disorders of articulation:

1. Let speech be fun by letting the children know that you like to hear them talk and that you like to talk to them by playing games with sounds and words, and by telling them stories and reading aloud to them.
2. Build up their feelings of success about speech by letting them use the few words or phrases that they have been practicing at times when the words are easy for them and by praising them for trying to talk.

3. Help them to learn new speech skills through imitation and ear training by choosing sounds or words that fit in with daily activities, and by showing them how those sounds are made.

Teachers and parents alike should recall one important finding of a fifteen-year followup report of children with speech-language disorders: overall, those subjects initially diagnosed as primarily articulation-disordered appear to have the best prognosis for correction of the problem.[30]

Voice Disturbances

Speech is made up of tones and noises, and in articulation, noises are added and tones modified. Sometimes, however, the tones themselves may be defective, varying too far from the norm to be acceptable. There may be impairment of the tones, partial loss, or (rarely) complete loss. One report based on data from several surveys estimates that 1–2 percent of the children in the six- to fourteen-year age range have voice problems, although an earlier figure covering grades one through twelve was 3 percent.[31] There is an age-related prevalence for vocal disorders, ranging from as high as 5.6 percent among first graders to a low of 1.0 percent among high school seniors.

Common types of voice disturbances include inadequate or inappropriate loudness, faulty pitch range, defects of quality (such as hoarseness among younger children), and voice "breaks." These are usually caused by poor physical health, hearing loss, physical anomalies (including the common cold), glandular disturbance (especially of the thyroid gland), poor habits of vocalization, personality disturbances, pubertal changes (usually beginning at age twelve), poor habits of vocalization, inappropriate nasal resonance, or imitation of poor models.

The United States Department of Health and Human Services suggests that parents and teachers of children with disorders of voice (a) refer children for medical examinations; (b) help them relax by easing tensions and pressures in the environment; (c) give them a chance to talk without interruption so that they need not strain their voices; (d) help the children find a pitch level that is comfortable for them, changing the pitch of their own adult voices if necessary (because the children may imitate them); and (e) discuss "voice rests" with a clinician (because the children's problems may be serious enough to require a period of silence).

Stuttering

A frequent abnormal disruption in the relative continuity or fluency of speech is known as *stuttering*. It is marked with repetitions and prolongations of syllables and sounds and by hesitancies in the utterance of syllables, sounds, and words. Sometimes there are interjections of unneeded sounds as well as associated lip, eye, or head movements. About 1–2 percent of Americans suffer from stuttering or stammering.

The ability to produce fluent speech is a skill that develops as children grow. All girls and boys, especially under the age of seven, are occasionally disfluent as they start to put words and sentences together. Several developmental areas must reach a certain stage of competence before fluent speech is possible: motor coordination and timing, linguistic knowledge, cognitive knowledge, and emotional maturity.

Although much about stuttering is yet to be documented, there are a few generalizations about this speech defect that are widely accepted. First, whole-word repetitions are the most common normal disfluencies and occur most often at the beginnings of sentences. Second, stuttering is more prevalent among boys than among girls (with an average ratio of three or four to one), endures longer among boys than among girls, and tends to be more severe among boys than among girls; but both boys and girls show fewer repetitions as they get older. Third, stuttering is more apt to begin when the child is in the preschool, kindergarten, or primary grades because about 75 percent of stutterers first experience the speech disruption between the ages of three and seven. Fourth, two warning signs that the child is developing a stutter are part-word repetitions and prolongation of sounds. Fifth, many students in kindergarten and first grade who appear to be potential stutterers with hesitant, repetitious speech, never actually become stutterers because they are exhibiting only normal disfluencies. Sixth and last, contrary to popular belief, stutterers are no more anxious or tense than the general public, and no one stutters all the time. Stutterers may be fluent when talking to themselves, to animals, or to those in a lower status position (such as younger children). They also do as well as other students in choral speaking or group singing situations.

While theories regarding the causes of stuttering are diverse and numerous, Eisenson and Ogilvie present three current points of view.[32] One school believes that stuttering is a constitutional problem with physical reasons predisposing certain individuals to stammering. Proponents of a second viewpoint consider stuttering as essentially a learned form of behavior that can befall anyone. The third and older position is that stuttering is mainly a manifestation of an underlying neurotic personality. Incidentally, in addition to the three viewpoints just listed, there are at least two others that explain stuttering as having not one but multiple origins.

Though many people have feelings of pity and embarrassment toward stutterers, current trends in mainstreaming handicapped children may have some positive effects on changing attitudes. One study showed that elementary school boys did not differentiate (in ranking social position) between classmates who stuttered and those who were fluent speakers.[33] The pupils were aware of the defect but simply evaluated stutterers as poorer speakers than peers who did not stutter.

In an effort to help enhance children's speech fluency, the classroom teacher should attempt to

1. Slow the rate of speech and the conversational pace when talking with disfluent children.
2. Simplify grammar and vocabulary and use shorter sentences.
3. Reduce use of direct questions.
4. Model social amenities for children.
5. Try to respond to the meaning of children's speech.
6. Eliminate interruptions.

7. Discourage evaluations of children's verbal performance either by children or by teachers.
8. Let speakers finish talking.
9. Allow plenty of time for all activities.
10. Avoid requests for verbal performance.
11. Keep the daily schedule as predictable as possible.
12. Eliminate teasing, bullying, and other excitable situations that may be frightening, tiring, or frustrating.
13. Build children's sense of self-esteem.[34]

Teachers and parents alike should realize that even though about 50 percent of childhood stutterers recover on their own, the remainder do require treatment. The most successful therapy for such children is called "fluency building" and is done under the direction of a speech-language clinician.

Delayed Language Development

Among some children there is an orderly sequence in learning the language code, but language development is not appropriate to the chronological age of the user. These boys and girls know the rules consistent with their level of development. They are learning the grammar in proper sequence, for example, but they are doing so at a slower pace than other children in their age group. They use the proper inflections for regular plurals and regular past tense verbs, for instance, but they overgeneralize those endings to other plurals and verbs. They can also use the simple affirmative-declarative sentences with some transformations but are incapable of the advanced degree of embeddings and coordination that they should be using. Although these children seem to comprehend and engage in social conversations, their deficiencies become more obvious in their written language and in their reading comprehension. They have difficulty understanding instructional language, and they become generally retarded in educational achievement.

In most districts the classroom teacher of nonexceptional children will have in his or her class one or two children who suffer from delayed language development. To assist these children, it has been recommended that teachers continue to

1. Be sensitive to individual needs, providing a program that is relevant to current social, economic, and cultural patterns of speech-retarded children.
2. Create a pleasant and stimulating atmosphere in which learning can occur.
3. Offer an individually determined curriculum, incorporating the children's weaknesses and strengths.
4. Encourage the children to want to talk and to talk more clearly.
5. Teach them new sounds and then put the new sounds together to make whole words.

Incidentally, it has been observed that the chief cause of speech delay is mental retardation and that direct teaching is critically important to such speech-impaired children.

Figure 4.8. Language
Arts Learning Center:
Oral Language.

Type of Center:	**Oral Language**
Grade Level:	4–6 (adaptable)
Time:	Varies
Number of Students:	3–4

Instructional Objective:	The child will be able to tell a story about an object selected from the box.
Materials:	Any box will do. It can be covered, and the directions can be written on the inside of the lid.
Directions:	1. Take an object from the "Story Box." 2. Tell a story about this object.
Suggested Ideas:	Some of the objects that could be placed in the box include: a ruler, a hat, an umbrella, a toy car, a shoe, a bird nest, a lantern, a calendar, a stuffed animal, etc.
Evaluation:	The children will work in small groups of three or four at a time. They will evaluate each other's stories. The teacher should preface this activity with a discussion of points to remember in telling an interesting story.

Source: From PATHWAYS TO IMAGINATION by Angela S. Reeke and James L. Laffey.
Copyright © 1979 by Scott, Foresman and Company. Reprinted by permission.

**Evaluation of
Student
Progress**

In the critical field of speech arts, evaluative techniques vary among the numerous facets of the skill. As a consequence, methods of evaluation have been described at the conclusion of the discussion of each facet. The reader may wish to review these techniques briefly at this point.

**Discussion
Questions**

1. Sharing time should be a significant kind of informal reporting. What guidelines might help the primary teacher who uses this activity?
2. What advantages does readers theater have over ordinary story dramatization in the classroom? Are there any disadvantages?
3. Why is puppetry enjoyed by so many children?

4. How would you propose to resolve some of the problems created by the sound system of English during communicative development in children?
5. In schools where there are no speech-language clinicians, what specifically can the classroom teacher do to help boys and girls who stutter?

Suggested Projects

1. Begin a card file of common situations that involve speech arts. Arrange cards by major headings such as Interviewing.
2. Examine some of the free materials available for school use from the telephone company. Plan a lesson incorporating their use.
3. Rewrite some of *Robert's Rules of Order Newly Revised* and then plan a beginning lesson in parliamentary procedure for fifth graders.
4. Make a puppet that a third grader could construct and manipulate as well as an adult does. Then assemble a temporary stage and demonstrate how that puppet moves and talks.
5. Interview the speech-language clinician in a local school. Discover what types of communicative deviations or disorders are being encountered and what types of remedial procedures are proving successful.
6. Set up the learning center on speaking shown in Figure 4.8.

Recent Related Readings

Bauer, C. 1987. *Presenting Readers' Theater.* New York: H. W. Wilson.
Cooper, P. 1988. *Speech Communications for the Classroom Teacher,* 3rd ed. Scottsdale, AZ: Gorsuch Scarisbrick.
Galvin, K., Cooper, P., and Gordon, J. 1988. *The Basics of Speech.* Lincolnwood, IL: National Textbook.
Garrard, K. 1987. "Helping Young Children Develop Mature Speech Patterns," *Young Children, 42*(3), pp. 16–21.
Hunt, T., and Renfro, N. 1987. *Celebrating Holidays Through Puppetry.* Austin, TX: Renfro Studies.
Integrating Speaking Skills into the Curriculum (Special Issue). 1986. *The Leaflet, 85*(1).
O'Keefe, V. 1986. *Affecting Critical Thinking Through Speech.* Urbana, IL: ERIC Clearinghouse on Reading and Communication Skills.
Oken-Wright, P. 1988. "Show-and-Tell Grows Up," *Young Children 43*(2), pp. 52–59.
Schwartz, S., and Miller, J. 1987. *The Language of Toys: Teaching Communication Skills to Special Needs Children.* Kensington, MD: Woodbine House.
Thompson, M., et al. 1987. *Language Assessment of Hearing-Impaired School Age Children.* Seattle: University of Washington Press.

Chapter Notes

1. R. Gray et al., "Is Proficiency in Oral Language a Predictor of Academic Success?" *Elementary School Journal,* 1980, *80,* pp. 261–268.
2. California State Department of Education, *English Language Framework for California Public Schools* (Sacramento: Author, 1976), pp. 23–24.
3. T. Zirkelbach and K. Blakesley, "The Language Deficient Child in the Classroom," *Academic Therapy,* 1985, *20,* pp. 605–612.
4. M. L. Klein, "Designing a Talk Environment for the Classroom," *Language Arts,* 1979, *56,* pp. 650–651.

5. C. Cazden, "Research Currents: What Is Sharing Time For?" *Language Arts,* 1985, *62,* pp. 182–183.

6. Ibid., pp. 183–186.

7. P. Lazarus and S. Homer, *Sharing Time in the Kindergarten: A Study of the Relationship between Structures and Content.* ERIC Document Reproduction Service No. ED 194 930 (1980).

8. M. L. Klein, *Talk in the Language Arts Classroom* (Urbana, Illinois: National Council of Teachers of English, 1977), pp. 41–44.

9. J. Way, "Verbal Interaction in Multiage Classrooms," *Elementary School Journal,* 1979, *79,* pp. 178–186.

10. G. S. Pinnell, "Communication in Small Group Settings," *Theory Into Practice,* 1984, *23,* p. 254.

11. M. Willbrand and R. D. Rieke, *Teaching Oral Communication in Elementary Schools* (New York: Macmillan, 1983), pp. 162–166.

12. A. W. Huckleberry and E. S. Strother, *Speech Education for the Elementary Teacher* (Boston: Allyn & Bacon, 1973), pp. 228–229.

13. S. Haley-James and C. D. Hobson, "Interviewing: A Means of Encouraging the Drive to Communicate," *Language Arts,* 1980, *57,* pp. 497–502.

14. B. Busching, "Readers Theater: An Education for Language and Life," *Language Arts,* 1981, *58,* pp. 332–335.

15. C. A. Smith, "Puppetry and Problem-Solving Skills," *Young Children,* 1979, *34*(3), pp. 4–11.

16. N. McCaslin, *Puppet Fun* (New York: David McKay, 1977), p. 19.

17. N. Nirgiotis, "Shadow Theater," *Childhood Education,* 1983, *59,* pp. 316–320.

18. M. Pickering and P. Kaelber, "The Speech-Language Pathologist and the Classroom Teacher: A Team Approach to Language Development," *Language, Speech, and Hearing Services in Schools,* 1978, *9,* pp. 43–49.

19. R. Allen, K. Brown, and J. Yatvin, *Learning and Language Through Communication* (Belmont, California: Wadsworth, 1986), p. 40.

20. P. Backlund et al., "Recommendations for Assessing Speaking and Listening Skills," *Communication Education,* 1982, *31,* pp. 12–14.

21. D. Rubin and N. Mead, *Large Scale Assessment of Oral Communication Skills: Kindergarten Through Grade 12* (Annandale, Virginia: Speech Communication Association, 1984), pp. 33–34, 60–61.

22. J. Eisenson and M. Ogilvie, *Communicative Disorders in Children* (New York: Macmillan, 1983), pp. 16–17.

23. C. Van Riper and L. Emerick, *Speech Correction: An Introduction to Speech Pathology and Audiology,* 7th ed. (Englewood Cliffs, New Jersey: Prentice-Hall, 1984), p. 34.

24. M. C. Bryne and C. S. Shervanian, *Introduction to Communicative Disorders* (New York: Harper, 1977), p. 5.

25. G. M. Clausen and N. Kopatic, "Teacher Attitudes and Knowledge of Remedial Speech Programs," *Language, Speech, and Hearing Services in Schools,* 1975, *6,* pp. 206–210.

26. J. Damico and J. W. Oller, Jr., "Pragmatic Versus Morphological-Syntactic Criteria for Language Referral," *Language, Speech, and Hearing Services in Schools,* 1980, *11,* pp. 85–94.

27. L. Signoretti and M. Oratio, "A Multivariate Analysis of Teachers' Attitudes toward Public School Speech Pathology Services," *Language, Speech, and Hearing Services in Schools,* 1981, *12,* pp. 178–187.

28. R. C. Bradley and R. J. Stoudt, Jr., "A Five-Year Longitudinal Study of Development of Articulation Proficiency in Elementary School Children," *Language, Speech, and Hearing Services in Schools,* 1977, *8,* pp. 176–180.

29. Eisenson and Ogilvie, *Communicative Disorders,* pp. 285–287.

30. R. King et al., "In Retrospect: A Fifteen Year Follow-up Report of Speech-Language Disordered Children," *Language Speech, and Hearing Services in Schools,* 1982, *13,* pp. 24–32.

31. Eisenson and Ogilvie, *Communicative Disorders,* p. 337.

32. Ibid., pp. 383–395.

33. C. L. Woods, "Social Position and Speaking Competence of Stuttering and Normally Fluent Boys," *Journal of Speech and Hearing Research,* 1974, *17,* pp. 740–747.

34. S. Gottwald, P. Goldbach, and A. Isack, "Stuttering," *Young Children,* 1985, *41*(1), pp. 12–13.

Children's Drama 5

Major Chapter Goals

After studying Chapter 5, the reader will be able to
1. Outline the distinctions between children's theater and creative drama.
2. Describe the five major groups of activities constituting creative drama.
3. Explain why children should first dramatically interpret some stories before attempting improvisation.

Discover As You Read This Chapter Whether*

1. Children's theater is concerned chiefly with the audience.
2. Creative drama is product oriented.
3. The children's theater movement has reached a standstill in the United States.
4. Most children enjoy creative drama but do not benefit otherwise from their participation.
5. Dramatic play should be an insignificant area of today's preschool/kindergarten curriculum.
6. Pantomime is not participant centered.
7. Role playing always concerns a group situation.
8. Sociodrama increases skill in communication.
9. Interpretation involves going beyond a basic story in order to expand upon its theme.
10. The discussion and resolution of inferential questions about a particular story must precede any improvisation of that story.

*Answers to these true-or-false statements may be found in Appendix 5.

Children's drama in the United States is a twentieth-century educational endeavor. It encompasses two aspects: children's theater and creative drama. *Children's theater* is formal, product oriented, and concerned primarily with the audience; *creative drama* is informal, process oriented, and concerned chiefly with the players. Although its performances are occasionally staged in a school auditorium, children's theater is neither the curriculum responsibility nor the language art that creative drama is.

No conflict prevails between the two areas of children's drama; both are art forms when given the proper guidance (creative drama) or direction (children's theater). Experiences in creative drama build appreciation for formal plays because the pupils learn about play construction as they work out their own plays with the assistance of an adult familiar with formal drama. On the other hand, children's theater provides standards for pupils' work in creative drama by helping the children visualize and be objective.

Although creative drama is a relatively young art form, it shares several characteristics with its parent. First, both are ephemeral and transitory, which sets them apart significantly from the literary and visual arts; both are also concerned with the present. Second, their form and content focus on human action and interaction, with live actors communicating to a present audience. Third, they mirror the times, each production relating to the society in which it is staged. Fourth, they involve communication in an intense and direct way as the participants attempt to make sense of a certain event by presenting it to others. Fifth, theater and creative drama are giant metaphors for life itself; for example, a performer does not *pretend* to be someone else but (for a few minutes, at least) actually *is* that other someone. Sixth, both art forms are ensemble arts with group members working cooperatively because each realizes that the success of the entire production depends to some extent on how the group members gel. Finally, theater and creative drama are combinations of a variety of art forms.[1]

Statement of Purposes

The objectives of drama and theater for students are sevenfold:

1. The students will develop the "self," learning to discover themselves, express themselves, and accept themselves. They will become increasingly aware of and learn to trust their sensations, feelings, fantasies, memories, attitudes, thoughts, and values as they seek to give these entities coherent expression in theatrical form.
2. The students will communicate effectively in seeking to express something that has value and meaning to others. Because theater is a cooperative act in every phase, they will learn how to articulate their intentions with increasing clarity in many verbal and nonverbal ways and to receive with sensitivity what others have to express.
3. The students will solve problems inventively in both real and imagined situations, discovering or creating patterns of relationships among people and ideas in fantasy and fact. Whether they deal with imaginary people or real people, they will learn how to play many roles, to try on or simulate a broad range of life experiences, and to evaluate the results.

4. The students will learn from society, past and present, including the rich contributions of the multiethnic and multicultural groups that make up the American heritage.
5. The students will use critical and creative skills. The rigors of the discipline will help them develop skills they can apply to any area of chosen study.
6. The students will be awakened to theater as an art form. They will become more discerning, perceptive, and responsive theatergoers and viewers of other theatrical media (film and television).
7. The students will approach other art forms with insight. Theater has processes and concepts necessarily related to those of the other arts, and it incorporates aspects of all of them.[2]

Children's Theater

Children's theater is the drama *for* children, and the audience is the first consideration. Regardless of whether the play is being acted by adolescents or adults (or both), or whether the players are amateurs or professionals, the value of the experience to the actors must be secondary to what the experience means to the boys and girls who see the play because the success of the project is judged by the cultural value and enjoyment that it gives to the child audience.

Children's theater is based on the traditional theater concept. Concerned with a polished production involving a stage, it does not, in this respect, differ from theater for adults. Lines written by professional playwrights are memorized, action is directed, and scenery and costumes are used. The director attempts to offer a finished product for public entertainment and engages the best actors available, for the goal in this area of children's drama is perfection.

Beginning with the establishment of the first significant children's theater in the United States, which was founded in a New York settlement house in 1903, the children's theater movement has always been guided by worthy objectives. During the movement's first decades of existence, the theater projects, as conceived and administered primarily by social workers, boosted social welfare purposes such as cultural integration and teaching English as a second language. Then, as the movement spread under the auspices of community-oriented organizations, universities, and professional companies, its direction changed to an emphasis on theater as an aesthetic device. Currently, the American children's theater promotes the development in boys and girls of a high standard of taste, provides them with the joy of seeing good stories come alive on a stage, and helps them grow in the understanding and appreciation of life values from the human experiences seen on the stage.

Children's theater is growing rapidly.[3] There are more companies of higher quality, more scripts of greater richness, and a growing national and international network of individuals in the field. Most important of all, the expanded audiences are finding a healthy emphasis on professionalism.

The national organization for the children's theater movement is presently the Children's Theatre Association of America (CTAA), formed in 1944 as a division of the American Theatre Association in order to encourage experience in live theater for all children everywhere; to promote in all communities children's theater activities conducted by educational, community, and private groups; and to encourage high standards in all types of children's theater activity throughout America.[4] Its current membership of some two thousand adults is drawn from all kinds of professional and amateur groups because agencies producing theatricals for children may be either community, educational, or professional organizations.

Community groups, which often present their plays in municipal auditoriums, have such varied sponsors as city recreation departments, the Junior League, and civic theaters in cities such as Seattle, Nashville, Palo Alto, and Midland, Texas. *Educational institutions* (public and private) include universities, colleges, and high schools that offer plays in their own auditoriums and theaters. University activity today is centered at Northwestern, Minnesota, Kansas, UCLA, Florida State, Denver, and Washington. There are also some *professional studios and touring companies* that produce several plays a year. The commercial companies include The Children's Theatre Company and School (Minneapolis), The Traveling Playhouse, The Paper Bag Players, The Mask, and the Honolulu Theatre for Youth. The noncommercial theaters for children are either attached to museums or to adult regional companies. Incidentally, ticket prices vary considerably from theater to theater, ranging in price recently from free to six dollars for children and adults alike.

The most successful plays staged by these various groups for child audiences are those that maintain

1. *Respect*—for the child's sense of wonder, naive emotionality, and physical/ psychological weaknesses.
2. *Entertainment*—comprising nonverbal communication, repetition, direct address, slapstick, childish behavior in adults, romanticism, physical pleasures, suspense, and the antagonist's realization of defeat.
3. *Contemporaneity*—because children lack historical perspective and become most involved in a play when they sense its relevance to them.
4. *Action*—because theater is what is done and what is seen, not what is said: "Show it, don't tell it."
5. *Unity of organization*—or a careful adherence to whatever dramatic element it is that serves to organize and unify a particular script, such as a basic story line.
6. *Variety and rhythm*—because children have short attention spans, they like a rhythm of short and long scenes, talk and action, humor and seriousness, calm and tension.[5]

Consequently, those who present plays for young audiences must not only know theater but must also know how children think, what children think about, and how children feel.[6]

There can be no doubt that the creative drama program in the elementary school has benefitted considerably from the growth in children's theater. Half of a century ago, only a few pioneers bothered with play production for boys and girls, but today several hundred producers (including more than fifty professional companies) devote their time and energy to the development in children of an artistic appreciation for drama.

Incidentally, there is a technique known as readers theater that is sometimes mistakenly described as a form of children's drama. It is in reality a speech art and another form of oral reading done by a group. Scripts are used, and literature ranging from short stories to poetry to plays is shared by the readers with their listeners. Unlike children's theater, readers theater is not a polished, organized production. And unlike creative drama, readers theater is not spontaneous. This speech art was discussed in Chapter 5.

Creative Drama

Creative drama is drama *with* children. Originated by a group of students who are guided (not directed) by a teacher, it is always played with spontaneous dialogue and action and is sometimes termed "informal drama," "playmaking," "developmental drama," "educational drama," or "creative play acting." Participation is all-important because creative drama is not for the talented few, and the experience of the child who lacks ability is often as meaningful and as enjoyable as that of the child with marked dramatic talent. It may be created from an everyday experience, a story, a poem, a special event or holiday, or from an object or an idea. Although it frequently develops from literature or the social studies, creative drama is not confined to a certain subject or time schedule but may be employed in any area of the curriculum where it can be used effectively for the sake of the pupils' social and emotional development.

According to the CTAA, participation in creative drama has the potential to promote a positive self-concept, social awareness, a clarification of values and attitudes, empathy, and an understanding of the art of theater; and to develop problem-solving skills, language and communication abilities, and creativity.

Studies have shown that problem-solving ability, personality or attitude, reading achievement, and oral language growth can all be altered positively through creative dramatic activities.[7]

In an integrated school, for example, primary pupils who engaged in an eleven-week dramatic play program (developed to teach social studies) showed significant improvement in problem-solving skills and in the acceptance of social responsibility. Third graders who participated in a fifteen-week program of creative drama improved in both personal and social adjustment, with the boys making even greater gains than the girls. In two Newark (NJ) schools, black and Hispanic students in grades four through six who participated in a one-year improvisational dramatics program (known as Arts Alternatives) improved their attitudes toward themselves, toward others, and toward their own capability as learners; according to researchers, that improvement could have been easily linked to school achievement because the participants also gained in reading achievement on the Comprehensive Test of Basic Skills.

Other gains in reading achievement occurred on the Lee-Clark Reading Readiness Test, after children's literature had been dramatized for twelve weeks with kindergarten children, and on the Metropolitan Readiness Test, when the drama treatment group of kindergarten students scored significantly higher than the control group after a six-week program. Dramatics have been found to be more effective than traditional basal reader workbooks in developing comprehension skills among black second graders and more significantly effective than either discussion or drawing in promoting those same skills in kindergarten through second grade. Self-directive dramatization from basal and supplementary readers, from science and social studies texts, and from library browsing books promoted reading achievement and self-concept during a fifteen-week program involving primary and intermediate students of both low and high socioeconomic status.

Oral language was also positively affected by creative drama lessons in many elementary grades. For example, kindergartners improved in verbal fluency, flexibility, and originality after a five-week program. Training in sociodrama was found to have a significant effect on fluency after a six-week kindergarten program. During a twelve-week program for language-disordered children in the primary grades, creative drama contributed significantly to language growth; and first and second graders with speech problems benefitted when creative drama was used for eighteen weeks to improve articulation. Fourth and fifth graders who had twenty creative drama sessions increased significantly their total verbal output, total clause output, and total T-unit (one main clause with all subordinate clauses attached) output. Finally, even second language facility was improved when primary Southeast Asian immigrant children with limited English proficiency used drama to make significant gains (over the control group) in the number of words spoken and the length of the utterances during an eight-week program. And Mexican-American children also used creative drama to improve their English skills during a ten-week program involving second, sixth, and seventh graders.

Teachers of the ever-increasing number of emotionally disturbed children can freely use creative drama too. Gillies found that it (1) helps build the troubled children's sense of respect for their own ideas and consequently for themselves; (2) offers them a chance to become aware of and understand their feelings; (3) provides them with the social contacts often eliminated from their daily lives; (4) helps them experience firmness and inner control, so often lacking, in an enjoyable way; and (5) provides an opportunity for the children to be heard alone as well as in a group situation.[8]

That creative drama can bring teachers in contact with insightful clues as to the basis of pupils' emotional illness is readily understood. After all, this form of children's drama is a much more natural form of expression for all young students than is formal drama because it results from their own thoughts and feelings. All children in the group are encouraged to volunteer for all the parts, acting and (with the exception of pantomime) talking as they believe the characters they are portraying would act and talk. Pupils begin to realize that what they say and do is important to other people. They acquire the habit of thinking about what they are saying, rather than memorizing a recitation, because the play is not rehearsed but develops with each presentation. The importance of creative drama, therefore, lies not in the product but in the process, and no school experience (in the estimation of many teachers) gives children a better opportunity to be creative than does playmaking. Still, most schools continue to view creative drama as strictly a peripheral activity, as exemplified in a recent Wisconsin study of one hundred elementary classroom teachers: Although 90 percent believed that children can learn language arts skills through drama, only 56 percent considered creative drama a basic subject in the curriculum.[9]

McCaslin, however, reiterates the many values that prevail in creative playing and contends that these exist in some measure for all participants, regardless of age, circumstances, or previous experience.[10] Consequently, the teacher need not assign different values to various age levels in the elementary school, but she or he should accept the following ten basic values that exist at all levels (although they may vary somewhat in degree): an opportunity for independent thinking, an opportunity to develop the imagination, an opportunity for cooperative learning, an opportunity to build social awareness, a healthy release of emotion, an experience with good literature, an introduction to the theater arts, better habits of speech, recreation, and the freedom for the group to develop its own ideas.

Not all of the above values will appear at once because the total creative process is slow. Consequently, Morgan and Saxton have developed "a taxonomy of personal engagement," which is concerned with the cumulative levels of dramatic activity and which is based in part on the well-known Bloom's Taxonomy developed more than three decades ago.[11] The taxonomy of personal engagement, as shown in Figure 5.1, translates the affective taxonomy to accommodate the cognitive objectives of drama.

---

1. INTEREST

Those components without which drama cannot take place
1.1 Attending:
Because of the process nature of drama, physical presence is imperative.
1.2 Looking:
Evidenced by making and maintaining eye contact.
1.3 Listening:
Evidenced by congruent, appropriate, supportive verbal response.
1.4 Reacting:
Evidenced by congruent, appropriate, supportive nonverbal response.

2. ENGAGING

The active identification with imagined roles and situations
2.1 Acquiescence in being involved:
Evidenced by participation in a congruent, appropriate, and supportive manner.
2.2 Willingness to engage:
Agreement to operate "as if"; the willing suspension of disbelief.
2.3 Relating:
Agreement to accept others, places, and objects into the imagined world.
2.4 Identifying:
Agreement to endow the role with self, summoning past experience to the demands of the present dramatic situation.
2.5 Evaluating:
Satisfaction in the experience.

Figure 5.1. A Taxonomy (of personal engagement) for Creative Drama.

Figure 5.1. (cont.)

3. COMMITTING

The acceptance of personal engagement and responsibility to the work and the group; the initial action of empathy

3.1 Accepting limits:
Acquiescence to the drama framework, bound by the limits of the role and the situation.

3.2 Accepting responsibility:
Recognition of the transfer of power to the role, with the attendant freedom to disagree or change directions by perceiving consequences and implications.

3.3 Empathizing:
Emergence of creative ideas expressed through the attitudes and concerns of the role.

4. INTERNALIZING

The intimate interplay between personal feeling and thought and empathetic feeling and thought

4.1 Organizing, selecting, ordering according to priorities, and refining values, feelings, concerns, beliefs, attitudes, and expectations; submitting them to and making them congruent with the role.

5. DEMONSTRATING

Contextual selection for clarity of communication, not consciously to create theater, but to meet the requirements of the task

5.1 Communicating:
Listening, observing, judging effect, predicting other points of view; expression of thought and feeling, particular to the role.

5.2 Experimenting:
Experimentation with expression (voice, gesture, props, etc.) to discover that which is most effective.

5.3 Adapting:
Readiness to consider other ideas; readiness to negotiate experience outside self; readiness to negotiate experience to the needs of the situation commensurate with the role.

5.4 Analyzing:
Willingness to analyze feeling through defending a point of view.

5.5 Reflecting:
Willingness to operate in the reflective mode through spoken or written work, through graphics, physical action, or inner reflection.

6. EVALUATING

The conscious working in the art form

6.1 Dramatizing:
Selection of appropriate theatrical elements to enhance thought and feeling.

6.2 Symbolizing:
Development of symbolic expression to convey significant meaning.

6.3 Monitoring:
Detached observation, valuation, and employment of the effect of action.

6.4 Recreating:
Evidenced by the infusion of the technical past by the feeling present.

6.5 Evaluating:
Satisfaction in the shared significant experience.

N. Morgan and J. Saxton, "Working with Drama: A Different Order of Experience," *Theory into Practice,* 1985, *24*(3), 213. Copyright 1985, College of Education, Ohio State University.

It must be stressed that, regardless of which level the boys and girls have reached, creative drama remains participant centered, and the only audience, as a rule, is the part of the group not playing at the moment. Still, it is vital that there be onlookers (especially with older children) because they assist in evaluating the production while they themselves are developing an appreciation for drama. Should the creative thinking of the pupils result in a particularly good play, it may sometimes be shared with another group of children or with the parents. Such a sharing is not considered a performance, however, but rather an informal demonstration incidental to the creative experience. The players, nevertheless, are generally so fluent that should the audience be unaware that the dialogue is being improvised, they might readily believe that the play has a written script.

Elementary teachers skilled in playmaking establish a physical setting and an emotional tone in the classroom that stimulate creative drama. Although they do not talk much themselves, they draw out the pupils' ideas through subtle questioning and courteous consideration of all responses. They quietly stress the importance of sense memory (or improvisations based on the five senses) and emotion memory (or improvisations based on feelings). They place emphasis on spontaneity, encouraging the children to create in their own way and to believe in themselves and their abilities. These teachers provide enrichment, as the need arises, with materials and properties, factual information, stories and verse, and audiovisual aids that help develop depth and understanding. At times when children appear unable to make suggestions necessary for the improvement of a play, thoughtful questions from teachers will elicit creative thinking among the group members.

Children up to the age of approximately eleven or twelve years should participate in creative drama exclusively, according to the CTAA Committee on Basic Concepts. Only when pupils are older and have had a background in creative drama and only after they have formed the habit of thinking through their speeches can they be counted on for a much greater degree of naturalness in children's theater roles. Pupils who are enrolled in a school that offers them a program in creative drama, beginning in kindergarten, will enjoy during their elementary school years these five major groups of activities:

1. Dramatic play: nonsocial and social
2. Pantomime
3. Role-playing
4. Story dramatization: interpretation
5. Story dramatization: improvisation

Dramatic Play   Much of the knowledge children absorb is best acquired by exploration in the real world where they may freely and actively construct their vision of reality, rather than be passively instructed about it. Happily, therefore, one of the most spontaneous interests of young children is dramatic play. It involves neither plot nor sequence, just conversation and action. In their dramatic play, children reenact their own experiences, imitate the activities of adults, animals, and inanimate objects, and live in an imaginary world. They are the father, teacher, truck driver, mother, doctor, nurse, fire fighter, and scores of other characters in the home, school and community. During the play period, girls and boys move about freely, choosing their own activities, materials, equipment, and companions, as long as their selections do not interfere with the welfare of the classroom.

What the children do in this initial kind of creative drama is wholly exploratory and experimental. Although they lack the background to bring full knowledge to the situation, they are capable of conceiving ideas, planning their own dramatizations, and performing with the "dress-up" materials, playhouse, boxes, planks, or other properties that will help them produce something that provides them at least with gratification. Sometimes they may shift swiftly from one character to another, playing each role for only a few minutes. In other cases, they may continue the same role for days or weeks, becoming the person, animal, or object with which they have an impulse to identify. Children may play the part of a barking dog, a galloping pony, or a soaring airplane. Dramatic play concerns being rather than playing and incorporates feeling with action. It is fragmentary and fun.

There is no definite beginning, middle, or end. Dramatic play may start anywhere and may conclude abruptly, especially in its early stages, when a child says, "I'm finished."

Sociodramatic Play   A child can engage in dramatic play by himself or herself, with a single friend, or in a group, but this division into several steps (starting with solitary play and culminating in group play) is not a mutually exclusive one. Instead, children's forms of dramatic play are constantly shifting. When involved in play with others or *sociodramatic play,* boys and girls act out complex social situations that concern the reconciliation of players with differing needs, backgrounds, and views. The golden age of sociodramatic play develops between ages four and seven, although the beginnings of such play can occur in much younger children.

Both Smilansky and Christie have listed the following elements as essential to sociodramatic play: persistence (of at least ten minutes for a single play episode); make-believe in regard to objects; make-believe in regard to actions and situations; imitative role play; verbal communication, covering both metacommunications (or exchanges about the play episode) and pretend communications (or exchanges within the episode); and interaction.[12]

For children who are already engaging in an advanced form of sociodramatic play, teacher intervention is not needed and may even disrupt the play. However, should it be noted that the play of the older kindergarten or first-grade children lacks some of the six essential elements, teachers may wish to use either outside intervention (by remaining outside the play episode and only offering special comments to encourage particular behaviors) or inside intervention (by joining the play and demonstrating behaviors previously lacking in the episode). The teacher will most often be called upon to interfere in the play of children from low socioeconomic backgrounds or the play of children with emotional problems. Cultural differences, too, may create differences in play behavior.

The teacher should also be aware that as children mature, the character of their dramatic play changes. Older children demand a higher degree of organization than younger children before beginning to play, as they assume roles and divide responsibilities. Older children also have a desire for some properties that are real, whereas younger children are able to participate in dramatic play in which all the properties they use exist only in their imaginations. As children mature, a distinction between "work" and "play" develops: work involving the constructing, gathering, or arranging of materials for dramatic play; and play concerning the use of those materials for dramatizing an idea or a situation. Consequently, the intervals between play periods obviously lengthen as the children create the properties they need. Finally, the amount of time that is devoted to dramatic play and the place of dramatic play in the daily schedule will differ according to the maturity of the children.

Play is the child's vehicle of growth, and teachers who have successfully guided dramatic play have discovered factors that contribute to stimulating play in the kindergarten and early grades. There must be adequate space to promote free expression and numerous kinds of properties to encourage participation. Proper stimuli from both firsthand and vicarious experiences are needed before young children can play creatively. Development of the children's own ideas, not those imposed by the teacher, is always an encouraging factor. Sufficient time for children to employ previous learnings and to explore additional ones is an especially significant matter in the early grades. Participation by the children in all phases of the play, from problem solving to honest evaluation, furthers creative expression. Finally, there is no unnecessary interference or criticism on the part of the teacher.

Conditions and Developmental Steps

After its beginning weeks in any classroom, according to the Shaftels, dramatic play usually encompasses the following steps:

1. There is an environment arranged by the teacher.
2. The boys and girls explore that environment and are permitted to manipulate and discuss all the materials and tools that it contains.
3. A story may be heard or read to further stimulate interest in the selected area and to provide data.
4. The boys and girls elect to play a part of the story or improvise their own situation.
5. The first play is unguided but carefully observed by the teacher.
6. A sharing period follows the play to clarify dissatisfactions and unexpressed needs.
7. There is a planning period for problem solving and work assignments.
8. Play proceeds on a higher level due to enriched experience.[13]

Pantomime

The art of acting without words, *pantomime* is often considered the most satisfying way of starting work in creative drama. It is by nature kinesthetic and uses both sides of the brain simultaneously. Most children are natural mimes and easily become comfortable using this art form when given a little direction and structure. Teachers like it because the length of any activity is highly flexible (from a few seconds to an hour), because few if any materials are necessary, and because any space may be used creatively.

Pantomime can help children become prepared for story dramatization by letting them become accustomed to transmitting ideas, emotions, and actions to the audience through the medium of body movement, facial expression, and posture. Confidence gained through success in pantomime quietly prepares the way for subsequent success in handling dialogue.

Because mime is done silently, all the students in the class can participate differently, and simultaneously at times, without disturbing anyone. Perhaps this is why children enjoy it, even those who are shy and generally find oral activities distressing. It offers each child an opportunity to develop physical freedom and a feeling of self-worth without the additional problem of dialogue.

Pantomime stimulates the imagination and sharpens observations and perceptions because participants must recall how actions are performed and what objects are truly like. Children learn to use all parts of the body to express a single action. To indicate drowsiness, for example, they can rub their eyes, stretch their arms, droop their shoulders, cover a yawn, or sit down wearily.

Children must realize that during a pantomime performance every action takes place in total silence. They can be reminded that although it is permissable to move one's lips as if talking, the lips must not form actual words. This basic tenet of pantomime is a difficult one for most boys and girls to follow.

Although properties are generally not allowed, a chair or table may occasionally be permitted. Should the performers be holding an imaginary object, they should practice with actual objects first. In that way, during the actual pantomime, they will remember to leave space between the fingers just as if the object were actually in the hand.

The mark of an effective pantomime is that it is clearly presented so that it becomes easy to identify. Sometimes children get the mistaken impression that a pantomime has been well performed if the class is unable to decipher the activity shown. The contrary is true.

Consequently, as the pupils become more adept at their presentations, it is a wise policy for the teacher to encourage them to prepare their pantomimes in advance. They must think through their movements and not rely on impromptu actions. Although it is hardly necessary that all the movements to be used in a prepared pantomime be written down, it is still helpful if the teacher knows in advance just which pantomimes will be presented. Children may sometimes have to be cautioned about using good taste in their performance.

All of the pantomime exercises during the introductory period involve gross actions only. What is being portrayed should be easily recognized by one and all.

If drama is new to both the primary teacher and the class, one starting point is a simple exercise executed in the form of a charade. The teacher asks, "If right at this moment you could do the one thing you enjoy doing most of all in the world, what would it be?"; then as children raise their hands, the teacher adds, "Don't tell us what it is; show us!" Each child then pantomimes an activity that he or she especially enjoys, such as playing ball, helping to sail a boat, running with a dog, or riding a bicycle.

Should the group be timid or afraid of ridicule, the teacher should first set the mood verbally ("It is a snowy day") and then establish a feeling of confidence by doing the first large-movement pantomime. The teacher then asks the children to guess the situation, giving them the opportunity later to present their own interpretations of the same situation. Finally they are ready to enact some familiar actions for their classmates to decipher.

Besides charade-like exercises and guessing games like "Secret" or "Who Am I?", riddles and Mother Goose rhymes are other ways to introduce pantomime to young children. One rhyme that works well is:

One, two, buckle my shoe;
Three, four, shut the door;
Five, six, pick up sticks . . .

The teacher quickly recites the rhyme, demonstrating the actions that might accompany each part. Then he or she asks the children to present their interpretations individually as the rest of the class recites the rhyme. In a few instances, the children merely imitate the teacher's actions, but in other cases, the pupils create and express their own ideas.

In teaching pantomime to intermediate-grade boys and girls who have never engaged in such dramatic activities before, the teacher must always assume the lead and give an informal demonstration. The teacher can pantomime, for example, the humorous efforts to retrieve a pencil that has rolled under a heavy piece of furniture in the corner of the room. This demonstration will generally elicit other amusing pantomimes by the more extroverted pupils. Their demonstrations will, in turn, probably provoke pantomimes by shyer students.

Suggested exercises that may be effective for freeing inexperienced or withdrawn pupils to perform in front of some of their peers include the following pantomimes:

- Pretend to eat a melting ice cream cone, a sour pickle, a freshly toasted marshmallow.
- Pretend to nail two boards together, put on a pullover sweater, brush your teeth.
- Pretend that you are walking on hot sand, through fallen leaves, through very deep snow.
- Pretend to throw a baseball, a basketball, a football.

Short individual pantomimes are an early stage in the art of acting without words and should provoke prompt recognition by the audience.
(© James L. Shaffer.)

Developmental Stages

True pantomiming concerns more than mere mute action; it expresses vividly the participant's feelings and thoughts as well. Consequently, once children have learned to react to the typical large-movement pantomimes that make suitable class beginnings, it is time for pantomimes that focus on emotional attitudes, sensory awareness, and occasional conflicts or problems.

The first group of these should be *short individual pantomimes* that will allow each member of the class to perform at least once during the lesson. Whole-class attention, however, is not necessary as the boy or girl pretends to be

- Biting into a sour apple,
- Drinking cocoa that is too hot,
- Hiking up a rocky hill,
- Walking on an icy sidewalk, or
- Picking up a crying baby.

After children have had some experience performing and watching brief pantomimes, they will be encouraged to select topics for *lengthy individual pantomimes*. At this stage, they may either develop their own themes or choose to mime situations like these:

- Seeing a kindergartner who is mistreating a small cat that does not belong to her, becoming very angry, running between the girl and the cat, rescuing the frightened kitten, and finally scolding the thoughtless child
- Walking down the street on the way home from school, noticing a three-year-old boy dart into the street after a ball just as a truck comes rapidly around the corner toward him, and reacting properly

- Receiving a letter from a favorite aunt with an invitation to take a trip to Florida to visit Disney World, thinking about what fun it will be, and hurrying to tell a parent the good news

A third stage in pantomime activities is reached when children choose partners and perform *double pantomimes* such as the following:

- A barber cutting the hair of a wiggling boy
- A Boy Scout walking an elderly person across the street
- A beginning driver backing out of the garage with a nervous friend

A variation of the double pantomime is the *mirror pantomime* in which two players must harmonize their movements so as to give the impression of one person looking at his or her reflection in a full-length mirror. All actions are done in unison as the players face each other (and appear sideways to the audience). They should be of approximately the same size, though they need not be dressed alike. They should use broad gestures that are clearly visible to the audience, and they should make all movements with moderate speed.

After some practice with double pantomimes, the children may wish to attempt team or *group pantomimes* with character analysis and finer movements. Demanding the cooperation of several children, group pantomimes are especially suited for those pupils who are still hesitant about giving individual performances but who nevertheless enjoy pantomime. Groups in the primary or middle grades may decide to do individual themes or variations on the same theme. They may even wish to perform a *narrative pantomime* in sequence from a complete book such as

> *Ants Have Pets* by K. Darling (Garrard, 1977)
> *The Bakers* by J. Adkins (Scribners, 1975)
> *Cosmo's Restaurant* by H. Sobol (Macmillan, 1978)
> *A Day in the Life of a Veterinarian* by W. Jaspersohn (Little, 1978)
> *No Bath Tonight* by J. Yolen (Crowell, 1978)
> *Octopus* by E. Shaw (Harper, 1971)
> *Pete's House* by H. Sobol (Macmillan, 1978)
> *Skunk for a Day* by R. Caras (Windmill, 1976)
> *The Web in the Grass* by B. Freschet (Scribners, 1972)

Material suitable for group pantomime in the intermediate grades includes many of the fables, folktales, legends, and fantasy stories to which the pupils have been introduced during their literature periods. Readily found in several anthologies are stories that can be pantomimed such as "Pecos Bill and His Bouncing Bride," "The Mad Hatter's Tea Party," "The Crow and the Pitcher," and "The Milkmaid and Her Pail." Narrative pantomimes may also be developed from such complete books as

> *And Then What Happened, Paul Revere?* by J. Fritz (Coward, 1973)
> *Doctor in the Zoo* by B. Buchenholz (Viking, 1974)
> *How a House Happens* by J. Adkins (Walker, 1972)
> *Julie of the Wolves* by J. George (Harper, 1972)

The Long Ago Lake by M. Wilkins (Scribner, 1978)
Lumberjack by W. Kurelek (Houghton, 1974)
Thor Heyerdahl and the Reed Boat "Ra" by B. Murphy and N. Baker
   (Lippincott, 1974)
Wolf Run by J. Houston (Harcourt, 1971)
Wrapped for Eternity by M. Pace (McGraw, 1974)

One successful group pantomime consists of having one fluent student read aloud a lively story while a selected cast simultaneously pantomimes the action. Other kinds of group pantomimes include *sequence games* and *add-on pantomimes*. For the first, pantomime activities are pictured or written on cards, with cues, and the cards are given out at random to the children. Each player's pantomime is then interpreted correctly before the next player in sequence can perform. Sequence games may tell a simple story or describe an activity that follows a step-by-step procedure (such as following a recipe or performing a task). Add-on pantomimes are played similarly with each player's nonverbal message being understood before the next performer can begin. However, in this activity, each child must first invent a pantomime to fit the topic (such as making breakfast or building a clock) and then perform it at the proper time during the sequence.

Role-Playing

Like pantomime and both kinds of dramatic play, role-playing is participant centered and encourages spontaneous actions. However, role-playing *always* concerns a group situation in which a problem in human relations is enacted and reenacted until alternative solutions have been elicited. Observers evaluate the variables involved as well as the possible solutions. The purpose of role-playing is educative and preventive rather than therapeutic. It helps students understand both current events and historical incidents.

Children often learn to resolve problems in real life by working them out successfully in role-playing situations. They find that by exchanging roles, they gain a better understanding of the dilemmas that others face. They learn to develop awareness of their own feelings and to release those feelings safely. They acquire new ways of handling acceptance and rejection, criticism and praise, failure and success, and such confusing predicaments as sibling rivalry, parent-child conflicts, social isolation, and integrity in friendship relations.

Current topics of special interest to the intermediate-grade students include dealing with someone who harasses them, calling on a shut-in (adult or child), reporting observed misconduct by a classmate to an authority figure, declining or accepting an invitation from a peer in culturally appropriate fashion, dealing with peer pressure (particularly with regard to alcohol or drugs), and handling difficult communication situations with parents.

One specialized kind of role-playing is *sociodrama*, which has been defined as decision making in a social crisis involving a conflict of values. Should a controversial issue such as racial tensions, for example, exist in the school or community, and should the children be mature enough to understand some of their own anxieties, elementary classroom teachers may wish to use sociodrama. They may also choose to schedule some sociodrama sessions during the presentation of certain social studies units if the children are intermediate students and have had earlier experiences with structured dramatic play.

Sociodrama and role-playing alike increase skill in communication. Role-playing, however, is the more useful method of helping pupils resolve the many routine problems that arise daily. A quarrel develops on the playground, for instance, because there is a shortage of equipment. The teacher arranges an enactment by getting the attention of all the children, discussing the setting of the "play" situation, and choosing the participants: Sean has the role of an aggressive child who will not share the equipment, Heather plays a polite child who wishes to use the equipment but will not fight to get it, and Brian plays a shy pupil who is disturbed by the quarrel.

It is helpful when the situations chosen represent the problems of the group, and the members want to explore them. Situations in which the pupils feel misunderstood, those in which they have difficulty in making up their minds about what is right to do or say, or those that make them unhappy are all suitable for role-playing. There should never be a feeling that there is only one right way of behaving in a given situation. Instead, the same situation may be replayed several times so that the children can reexamine the facts and reach solutions that are personally satisfying. Thus participants and audience alike find new ways of behaving that will broaden any skills they may already possess in dealing with personal problems. The teacher's role is to remain nonjudgmental about students' solutions and efforts, and to emphasize the use of role-play character names instead of real names.

Whether situation role-playing is done with students working in pairs or in small groups, teachers should take sufficient time to clarify the various roles and explain the situation—not the solution—before they ask for volunteers for the various roles. (If there are no volunteers, they should select those pupils who are neither shy nor readily upset.) Next, they can arrange the details of the situation, discuss the physical setting, and prepare the nonparticipants for their role as observers. Promptly after the first unrehearsed enactment, teachers and children should discuss the presentation and summarize how the problem was resolved. Then the first actors may be replaced by new ones who have different ideas of how the roles should be played, and again the enactment should be evaluated and modifications suggested. Sometimes a third version may ensue.

One of the most effective stimulants for decision making through role-playing is the unfinished problem story that presents an unresolved conflict or dilemma that demands alternative solutions. Some teachers choose to use the more than sixty such stories written by the Shaftels concerning areas such as moral development, citizenship, interpersonal and intergroup relations, and self-acceptance.[14] Other teachers elect to produce their own stories, believing that they know best their own students' maturity level and interests as well as the attitudes and values to be explored with the individual group. Under the circumstances, these teacher-authors also understand more clearly the numbers and types of character parts to be included in the unfinished story.

In an effort to aid beginning teachers in the upper elementary grades who are interested in role-playing sessions, the Fairfield (Connecticut) schools have developed a checklist for guiding teachers during such sessions involving problem stories.[15]

Classroom Teachers' Checklist for Guiding Role-Playing

Part A

1. Define the problem (Recall).

   After reading the story, allow time for the children to reflect and to make voluntary comments. Then ask: What is happening here? Should the children still seem to be having difficulty in moving into the situation, ask further recall questions: Who is involved? How are they affected by this situation? How is Chief Character feeling? Why is he or she feeling this way? How are Other Characters feeling? Why?

2. Delineate alternatives (Projection).

   Ask: What do you think will (*not* should) happen now?

   Invite ideas from the children.

   Both antisocial and socially sanctioned solutions will generally be mentioned.

   If only one kind of solution is offered, however, ask: Is this the only way in which such a situation usually ends? Then if still no other solution is proposed, proceed into role-playing.

3. Explore alternatives.

   If the group has offered both negative and positive proposals for solving the story dilemma, begin with a consideration of the antisocial or impulsive solutions first.

   a. Negative solutions

      (1) Choose one negative solution and hold a brief discussion.

      (2) Choose a volunteer to role-play the proposal. Ask the volunteer: Whom will you need to help you? Then assist him or her in selecting other volunteer role-players.

      (3) Set the stage for the role-playing session by asking: Where is this happening? What time of year (or day) is it? What is each of you doing?

      (4) Prepare the audience. If beginners, ask the group to evaluate, as they watch, how realistic the role-playing is by pondering: Could this really occur? Are the persons behaving as they would in real life?

      If the class is experienced in role-playing, divide the members into observer groups and ask Group I to observe for true-to-life behavior, Group II to observe how individual players feel, and Group III to consider next steps for solving the dilemma.

      (5) Start the role-playing and continue it only until the acting has clearly delineated the proposed solution.

      (6) Start the discussion by asking: What has been happening? How does Chief Character feel? Why does he or she behave in that way? What will happen next?

   b. Interim

      Decide whether it is worthwhile to continue further enactment exploring the negative solution or to go on to explore proposals offering alternative courses of behavior. Should time allow for elaborated role-playing, consult Part B.

   c. Positive solutions

      (1) Choose one positive solution and hold a brief discussion.

      (2) Proceed as outlined under 3a—sections (2) to (6).

4. Make a decision.
   a. If the group has reached some definite understanding of the alternatives explored and of the consequences that may ensue, ask: Which one of the solutions to this problem do you believe to be the best? Why? For whom is it best? Who will benefit from the solution and who will suffer? If you were (One Story Character), how would you decide? If you were (Another Story Character), how would you decide?
   b. Ask: At which point in the story could a choice have been made that would have precipitated an acceptable solution?

Part B
1. Add extra steps to role-playing when time allows.
   For occasions when the group may be guided into role-playing with some depth, up to three additional steps may be added to the process.
   a. Extend exploration of the consequences of the proposed solution to the dilemma by suggesting another scene to be enacted. This second scene should logically be an aftermath of the proposed behavior.
   b. Reverse the roles of the chief characters in the problem story. (In order to convince an individual who is unaware of the effect of his or her behavior upon others, it is often impressive to put this individual into the position of the person most seriously affected by that behavior.)
   c. Seek out the implications of the proposed alternative by means of analogy. Apply the principle suggested by the alternative to other situations outside the story.

Story Dramatization: Interpretation

Constituting the most popular means for pupils and their teachers to get behind the printed word, *story dramatization* helps develop a new dimension in understanding literature.

Children who are younger or less experienced in creative drama generally want to do stories already familiar to them and only gradually abandon stereotypes and conventions for more original creations. Briefly, this illustrates the sequence of *interpretation* and *improvisation*. In planning story dramatization with students, the teacher begins with an interpretation of the story or an accurate re-creation of the author's intent and statement. Then as the pupils mature and become more knowledgeable in dramatization, the teacher can proceed to improvisation, which involves going beyond the basic story in an attempt to extend or expand on the thematic material.

Finally, teachers interested in story dramatization should be aware of a study recently completed at Auburn University that investigated the effects of adult intervention and story familiarity on children's ability to use creative drama for story comprehension.[16] It concluded that students who have experience reenacting stories recall more than those who merely discuss those stories and that an adult who is nondirective is beneficial for children when they are acting out a familiar story.

Developmental Steps

When the class has shown readiness for story dramatization *the teacher tells or reads a well-structured story* that possesses most or all of the following characteristics:

1. Brevity—as in one of Kipling's *Just So Stories* (Rand, 1982)
2. A simple, strong, dramatic conflict—as in Seuss' *The 500 Hats of Bartholomew Cubbins* (Vanguard, 1938)
3. One setting—as in Slobodkina's *Caps for Sale* (Scholastic, 1976)
4. Natural, interesting characters—as in Brown's *Stone Soup* (Scribners, 1986)
5. A simple plot that hinges on action—as in the Grimm Brothers' *The Shoemaker and the Elves* (Scribners, 1960)
6. Dialogue that furthers the action—as in Galdone's *The Three Little Pigs* (Houghton, 1972)
7. A strong climax and a quick, definite ending—as in Jacobs' *The Three Wishes* (McGraw, 1961)

Before reading or telling the intended story, the teacher becomes so familiar with it that he or she can reflect upon the thoughts, movements, appearances, and feelings of the characters in order to make these figures real. The teacher attempts to establish one version to which the pupils can repeatedly return in the dramatization. During the recitation, the teacher watches for external clues from the children that may indicate their interest and involvement. It is vital that all or most of the children like the narrative that will be dramatized. The teacher may be certain that they will enjoy a story if it appeals to their emotions.

The teacher's own viewpoint about the story is also important. The teacher can hardly guide children to create successful dialogue and action from literary selections concerned with values or characterizations that he or she personally finds unacceptable.

Once a story has been told, *the teacher poses questions to stimulate discussion of sequences, characters,* and *setting.* The children must be able to bring out in their dramatization the essential elements of the story just read. So the teacher asks the pupils carefully framed questions to point up the key actions and lines that will move the play along. In some instances more than one discussion period may be necessary to stimulate thoughts about the story plot and people; it is wise not to pose more than five specific questions during a single discussion.

After they have carefully analyzed the story, *the children determine the characterization and the scenes.* Whether the story requires one scene or several, the pupils will find that the playing proceeds more smoothly if they decide in advance the number of scenes and the characters who appear in each scene and if they plot all these details on the chalkboard. A sample textbook exercise in story dramatization is shown in Figure 5.2.

Characterization being principally a matter of imagination, the teacher should always stress developing a character from within. Boys and girls should try first to understand how the other person thinks and feels before they attempt to act like the person. In one New York classroom, for example, there is a "Magic Stage," a special space reserved for creative drama activities. Once children step

Use English in Drama

Figure 5.2. Exercise in Story Dramatization.

There are many ways to tell a story. A story may be written or spoken aloud. A story may also be told as a drama or a play.

Exercise: Presenting a Play

Work with a group of friends to give a play. Choose a story that you would like to act out. It may be a story from your reading book, a fairy tale, or a tall tale. Then look at these four important parts of a play. Follow the suggestions.

Story Work together to plan the play from the story. Decide what the characters will say. You may want to write what everyone says.

Actors Decide who will play each character.

Costumes If you need costumes, you can make them from paper or old clothes.

Setting The setting is the place where the play happens. Make a big picture of the setting. Hang it on the wall behind the actors. You may need some furniture, dishes, or other things the characters use.

Practice your play. The actors should think about how their characters would look, talk, move, and feel. Each actor should learn the part he or she is playing. Speak clearly so that everyone can hear.

When your play is ready, perform it for the class.

Source: Pg. 124, *McDougal, Littell English, Brown Level.* Copyright © 1987 by McDougal, Littell & Company, Box 1667, Evanston, Illinois 60204.

onto this stage, they are encouraged to be the characters they have chosen to portray by acting like them with both their bodies and their minds. To help the boys and girls keep clear about the characters and their goals and obstacles in the story, the teacher and the class play a game called Circle of Characters, in which they take turns asking the characters on the Magic Stage various questions to help them establish who they are: Where do you live? What is your favorite color? What hobby do you have? Which animals do you like? Which foods do you prefer to eat? What is your favorite sport? What do you like to do best? How old are you? Who is your best friend?

As they follow the general outline of the story, *the children create the dialogue and the dramatization.* Due mainly to the discussion periods held earlier, the students can generally speak all or nearly all of the key lines. They can also add other phrases to make the play their own and to round out the characterizations. For the first performance, the teacher designates a space within the room as a stage or playing area and chooses five or six confident volunteers. This group is then permitted time for a brief planning conference away from the rest of the class so that each member will know exactly what to do and say.

During story dramatization the students are asked to be the characters they have selected to portray by acting like them with both their minds and their bodies. (© James L. Shaffer.)

Now the play is ready to start; it must move along without interruption because, to the children, this step is the most important of all. The teacher should try to limit performances in the lower grades to five minutes; in the middle and intermediate grades, to fifteen minutes.

As soon as the performance is done, *the class promptly evaluates the presentation.* Such appraisal under the positive guidance of the teacher is vital training for all age levels, beginning in the second grade. It starts with an acknowledgement of strengths: What did you see that you liked? What was good (about Cinderella's step-sisters)? Once accustomed to looking for what is good or for what they liked, the children can soon reach the second level of discussion: How can we make that scene more real (or more powerful, more exciting)? What shall we change or add the next time we play it?

Throughout the discussion, the students should examine the action and consider the voice and diction of the actors. They can study the characterizations, carefully using the character names, not the player names, in order to be more objective in their criticism. They can ask each other these questions:

- Was the play just like the story we heard?
- Were the characters the way we imagined them to be?
- What did we like about the opening scene?
- What did we like best about the performance?
- How could we improve the play the next time we act it out?

Slowly the class can be led through creative group appraisal to realize that although first dramatic efforts may appear uneven, story dramatization slowly improves. Therefore, every sincere attempt of each child is acceptable and praiseworthy, and every child has the right to reject or modify proposed changes in the roles undertaken.

Finally, *the children reenact the dramatization,* incorporating the constructive criticisms just discussed. Properties are still kept simple and at a minimum. Eventually several casts are drawn up, with every child playing at least one part. Variations in actions and dialogue are anticipated (and appreciated) during each performance.

All of the traditional folk tales listed here have proved suitable for informal dramatization and can be adapted to various age groups. Readily located in most standard anthologies of children's literature, they include the following:

Suggested Stories

"Briar Rose"
"Cinderella"
"Hansel and Gretel"
"Jack and the Beanstalk"
"Little Red Riding Hood"
"Puss in Boots"
"The Gingerbread Boy"
"The Three Bears"
"The Three Billy Goats Gruff"

Those same anthologies are also apt to include some stories in verse form that children and teachers may enjoy dramatizing:

Browning's "The Pied Piper of Hamelin"
Field's "The Duel"
Follen's "Three Little Kittens"
Moore's "A Visit from St. Nicholas"

Stories in prose form that invite dramatization by elementary school children, in addition to the folk tales listed earlier, include the following:

Balet's *Fence, a Mexican Tale* (Delacorte, 1969)
Fleischman's *The Hey Hey Man* (Little, 1979)
Freeman's *Corduroy* (Viking, 1968)

Fritz's *What's the Big Idea, Ben Franklin?* (Coward, 1976)
Grahame's *The Reluctant Dragon* (Holiday, 1953)
Heller's *Lily at the Table* (Macmillan, 1979)
Hodges' *The Wave* (Houghton, 1964)
L'Engle's *A Wrinkle in Time* (Farrar, 1962)
Paterson's *The Great Gilly Hopkins* (Harper, 1978)
Piper's *The Little Engine That Could* (Platt, 1954)
Sawyer's *Journey Cake, Ho!* (Viking, 1953)

Story Dramatization: Improvisation

Improvisation involves going beyond the basic literary material. The children are compelled to extrapolate and enrich the material by drawing from within themselves. Their thoughts, emotions, and conclusions are based on, but not truly found in, the poem or story in question.

This type of story dramatization encompasses many of the same developmental steps that were discussed earlier for the interpretation category. The major difference lies in the sort of questions that the teacher must write. Unlike the literal variety demanding strict recall, which is a significant part of interpretation, questions that are developed in preparation for an improvisation session are inferential. They require original, creative thinking because they are open-ended.

For example, as a prelude to improvisation, a teacher who had told the familiar myth of King Midas to a class that had been interpreting stories for months might pose such questions as the following:

1. Why do you believe the king was so greedy? What might have caused him to be that way?
2. Why was his daughter so sweet, despite the fact that she had been raised alone in the castle with her father as an example?
3. How did the king react to other people? (Remember that the story did not show him interacting with others.) How did he treat his servants? The townspeople?
4. In what other ways might he have resolved his problem?[17]

Other, more general questions could be asked regarding the physical, social, and psychological facets of additional characters in the story.

What the teacher must emphasize to the class is that there is no one right answer to an inferential question and that all responses are valuable. Children will then be encouraged to offer a variety of opinions and insights before any improvisation session begins.

Only after the children have had sufficient time to ponder carefully both the questions and the answers can they proceed to the final three developmental steps previously explored under Story Dramatization: Interpretation. They create the dramatization complete with dialogue and that event in turn provokes an evaluation session and a subsequent reenactment of the improvisation.

Appraisal of the growth of the child in this area of the English language arts can be made on an informal and individual basis through observing to what extent he or she fulfills the following:

Evaluation of Student Progress

- Does the child participate freely and wholeheartedly in imaginative play-making?
- Does the child find enjoyment and satisfaction as a member of the audience at informal creative drama activities or at formal children's theater productions?
- Does the child control situations by words rather than by physical force?
- Is the child developing the nonverbal elements of communication such as body language?
- Is the child able to interact comfortably with others?
- Does the child recall a series of episodes in sequence and distinguish between central ideas and subordinating details?
- Is the child's vocabulary expanding properly?
- Is the child able to organize stories, verse, and other media for dramatic expression?
- Has the child developed physical coordination and good posture habits?
- Have the child's voice quality and projection improved?
- Has the child increased in self-confidence and self-direction, whether working alone or before an audience?
- Has the child formed the habit of original flexible thinking?
- Has the child's problem-solving ability expanded?
- Has the child developed a respect for the creative forms that he or she has experienced and for the creative efforts that fellow classmates have demonstrated?

Discussion Questions

1. As a beginning teacher, how would you explain your creative drama program to a group of stolid parents?
2. How can a teacher interest fifth graders into doing pantomime or story dramatization if they have never attempted either one before?
3. Listening is said to improve after creative drama sessions. How can you explain this improvement?
4. Should a teacher assign a letter grade to the young performer in creative drama? If not, how can the teacher better evaluate the child's participation in this critical area?

Suggested Projects

1. Write an unfinished problem story that could serve as the basis of a role-playing session in the fourth grade.
2. Observe a group of pupils in kindergarten or first grade who are engaged in dramatic play. What values are apparent in this type of creative drama?

Figure 5.3. Language Arts Learning Center: Creative Drama.

TYPE OF CENTER: **Creative Dramatics**
GRADE LEVEL: 2-4

TIME: 10-15 minutes
NUMBER OF STUDENTS: 3-5

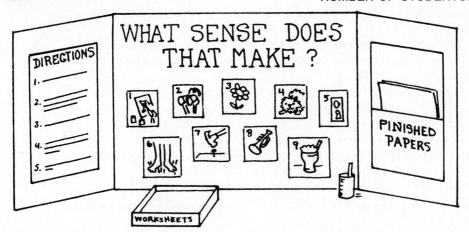

INSTRUCTIONAL OBJECTIVE: The students will become aware of the functions of the five senses through the use of pantomime.

MATERIALS: Three sides of a cardboard box, contact paper, a large manila folder for finished papers, worksheets, various pictures showing objects having to do with the use of the five senses.

DIRECTIONS:
1. Take a piece of paper and a pencil.
2. Look at the pictures on the center. Decide what you would do with the objects in the pictures if you had them, and use the words *see, smell, taste, hear, touch.*
3. Write your answers on the worksheet.
4. Think how you could pantomime several of the items so the class could guess what you are doing. You may act them out when told to.
5. Put your finished paper in the *Finished Papers* folder.

SUGGESTED IDEAS: Pictures could include flowers; types of food; someone playing a musical instrument; someone hammering a nail; a keyhole; someone looking through a pair of binoculars; a furry animal; someone walking with bare feet on a green lawn or a thick rug; someone painting or drawing a picture, making a clay bowl, weaving a pattern, sewing. Every other day, change the pictures to add to the variety and to interest the children.

EVALUATION: Look over the ideas given by the students on the worksheet. Set aside a period at a convenient time to permit students to dramatize a given item.

Source: From PATHWAYS TO IMAGINATION by Angela S. Reeke and James L. Laffey.
Copyright © 1979 by Scott, Foresman and Company. Reprinted by permission.

3. List the organizations in your community that are currently sponsoring children's theater productions. Visit one of their performances and assess its reception by a young audience.
4. Plan a beginning pantomime lesson for primary pupils.
5. Examine one of the standard anthologies of poetry for children, such as the Opies' *The Oxford Book of Children's Verse* (Oxford, 1984). List several ballads and story poems that pupils might enjoy dramatizing.
6. Set up the learning center on creative drama shown in Figure 5.3.

Recent Related Readings

Bontempo, B., and Iannone, R. 1988. "Creative Drama, a Special Kind of Learning," *Teaching Pre K–8, 18,* pp. 57–59.

Cottrell, J. 1987. *Creative Drama in the Classroom: Grades 4–6.* Lincolnwood, IL: National Textbook.

Dodge, M., and Frost, J. 1986. "Children's Dramatic Play: Influence of Thematic and Nonthematic Settings," *Childhood Education, 62,* pp. 166–170.

Erickson, K. 1988. "Building Castles in the Classroom," *Language Arts, 65,* pp. 14–19.

Fox, M. 1987. *Teaching Drama to Young Children.* Portsmouth, NH: Heinemann.

Harp, B. 1988. "When the Principal Asks, 'Is All That Drama Taking Valuable Time Away from Reading?' " *The Reading Teacher, 41,* pp. 938–940.

McCaslin, N. 1987. *Creative Drama in the Primary Grades.* White Plains, NY: Longman.

Morgan, N., and Saxton, J. 1988. "Enriching Language Through Drama," *Language Arts, 65,* pp. 34–40.

San Jose, C. 1988. "Story Drama in the Content Areas," *Language Arts, 65,* pp. 26–33.

Scher, A., and Verrall, C. 1987. *Another 100 Plus Ideas for Drama.* Portsmouth, NH: Heinemann.

Chapter Notes

1. H. S. Rosenberg, *Creative Drama and Imagination* (New York: Holt, 1987), pp. 79–84.
2. California State Department of Education, *Drama/Theatre Framework for California Public Schools* (Sacramento: Author, 1974), pp. 6–7.
3. J. R. Wills, "Who Are You? A Question for Children's Theatre?", *Children's Theatre Review,* 1985, *34*(3), p. 4.
4. *Children's Theatre Review,* 1981, *30*(2), p. 2.
5. M. Goldberg, *Children's Theatre: A Philosophy and a Method* (Englewood Cliffs, New Jersey: Prentice Hall, 1974), pp. 127–135.
6. Wills, "Who Are You?", p. 3.
7. K. Vitz, "A Review of Empirical Research in Drama and Language," *Children's Theatre Review,* 1983, *32*(4), pp. 17–25; A. Gourgey, J. Bosseau, and J. Delgado, "The Impact of an Improvisational Dramatics Program on Student Attitudes and Achievement," *Children's Theatre Review,* 1985, *34*(3), pp. 9–14; E. Hartshown and J. C. Brantley, "Effects of Dramatic Play on Classroom Problem-Solving Ability," *Journal of Educational Research,* 1973, *66,* pp. 243–46; E. C. Irwin, "The Effect of a Program of Creative Dramatics upon Personality as Measured by the California Test of Personality, Sociograms, Teacher Ratings, and Grades," *Dissertation Abstracts,* 1963, *24,* p. 2188; J. W. Stewig and L. Young, "An Exploration of the Relation Between Creative Drama and Language Growth," *Children's Theatre Review,* 1978, *27*(2),

pp. 10–11; J. W. Stewig and J. A. McKee, "Drama and Language Growth: A Replication Study," *Children's Theatre Review,* 1980, *29*(3), pp. 10, 14; and L. Carlton and R. H. Moore, *Reading, Self-Directive Dramatization and Self-Concept* (Columbus, Ohio: Merrill, 1968).

8. E. Gillies, *Creative Dramatics for All Children* (Washington, D.C.: Association for Childhood Education International, 1973), p. 48.

9. J. W. Stewig, "Teacher's Perceptions of Creative Drama in the Elementary Classroom," *Children's Theatre Review,* 1983, *33*(2), pp. 27–29.

10. N. McCaslin, *Creative Drama in the Classroom* (New York: Longman, 1984), pp. 15–21.

11. N. Morgan and J. Saxton, "Working with Drama: A Different Order of Experience," *Theory Into Practice,* 1985, *24,* pp. 213–214.

12. J. F. Christie, "Sociodramatic Play Training," *Young Children,* 1982, *37*(4), pp. 27–28; and S. Smilansky, *The Effects of Socio-Dramatic Play on Disadvantaged Preschool Children* (New York: Wiley, 1968).

13. F. R. Shaftel and G. Shaftel, *Role Playing in the Curriculum,* 2nd ed. (Englewood Cliffs, New Jersey: Prentice Hall, 1982), p. 89.

14. *Ibid.*, pp. 153–316.

15. Abridged from J. Strauss and R. DuFour, "Discovering Who I Am: A Humanities Course for Sixth Grade Students," *Elementary English,* 1970, *47,* pp. 100–103.

16. P. Williamson and S. Silvern, "Eliciting Creative Dramatic Play," *Childhood Education,* 1986, *63,* pp. 2–5.

17. Adapted from J. W. Stewig, *Informal Drama in the Elementary Language Arts Program* (New York: Teachers College Press, 1983), p. 11.

Part C Writing

Chapters

Written Composition 6

Major Chapter Goals

After studying Chapter 6, the reader will be able to

1. Understand the factors that affect both the teaching of writing and children's writing performance.
2. Describe the writing process as well as the other major area in the composition curriculum (content).
3. List numerous stimulating topics or situations that motivate written composition among elementary students.

Discover As You Read This Chapter Whether*

1. American students are generally proficient writers.
2. Writing and thinking are deeply intertwined.
3. Well-developed oral language has little or no effect on written composition.
4. Children taught by teachers who themselves practice and enjoy writing will adopt much the same attitudes.
5. The prewriting stage of the writing process can readily be omitted for most elementary students.
6. Children should start proofreading their own written work as early as the fifth grade.
7. Student interest in writing peaks at grade four.
8. Peer-group conferences about writing concern the content of the compositions.
9. Teacher-student conferences about writing assignments should be scheduled monthly for most girls and boys.
10. Holistic scoring of compositions involves correcting errors and writing comments.

*Answers to these true-or-false statements may be found in Appendix 5.

As late as 1986 the Executive Director of the National Assessment of Educational Progress (NAEP) proclaimed that "the nation's elementary and secondary students still do not write well."[1] The NAEP report compiled in the mid-1980s and concerned with the writing achievement of nearly 55,000 students (in grades 4, 8, and 11 enrolled in both public and private schools across the nation) concluded that most students, majority and minority alike, are unable to write adequately except in response to the simplest of tasks.[2] Although performance improves from grade 4 to grade 8, American students in general can write at only a minimal level and cannot express themselves well enough to ensure that their writing will accomplish the intended purpose.

Although most of the students surveyed during the NAEP study seem to recognize that writing can serve a variety of useful purposes (both personal and social), they do not appear enthusiastic about writing. Their attitudes toward writing show a steady deterioration across the grades, with a high of 57 percent being recorded by fourth graders who "like to write" and regard themselves as "good writers."

Finally, the major conclusion drawn from this NAEP report is that students at all grade levels are deficient in higher-order thinking skills. Because writing and thinking are so deeply intertwined, appropriate writing assignments can provide an ideal way to increase students' experiences with such types of thinking.

Factors Affecting Writing Performance and the Teaching of Writing

Many factors affect children's writing and the teaching of written composition.[3] Research studies have established the positive importance of the following factors concerned with child writers:

1. *Intellectual capacity.* Pupils who are superior in verbal ability are also superior in composition writing, producing more words per minute and per paper. IQ scores are significantly related to writing accomplishments. In a heterogeneous sample of three hundred children, ages 7.0 to 9.11, the able group showed an advantage of nearly three years in written language development.
2. *Reading achievement.* Children who read well also write well, whereas those who read poorly write poorly too. In low-income, urban neighborhoods even first graders reveal a high correlation between reading and written composition, whereas sixth graders who rank illiterate or primitive in writing read below their chronological age. Finally, as the students' level of reading comprehension increases, so does the number of compound and complex sentences they can write.
3. *Grade level/chronological age.* Advances in grade and age correlate positively with increasing length of written sentences and of T-units (i.e., terminable units—main clauses together with all phrases and clauses syntactically related). On the other hand, the difference between the performance of the low-achieving groups and the national performance in expressive writing increases at each successive age level.

4. *Sex.* Girls write more than boys. On measures of complexity, boys and girls score at generally the same levels. On most measures of quantity, however, girls score significantly higher than boys. Girls also tend to write compositions that are judged to be of high quality.

   Seven-year-old boys write more about the so-called secondary territory or the metropolitan areas beyond the home and school, whereas seven-year-old girls write more about the primary territory related to the home and school. Girls stress more prethinking and organizational qualities and feelings in characterizations than do boys. Primary boys are more concerned than primary girls with the importance of spacing, formation of letters, and neatness.

5. *Oral language proficiency.* Children who are rated above average in their use of oral language are also rated above average in writing. Those below average in oral expression rate the same in written language.

6. *Parents' level of education.* Students whose parents have a post-high-school education have substantially higher averages of writing achievement than do those whose parents have only graduated from high school, and in turn, children of high school graduates are better writers than are children whose parents have not graduated from high school.

7. *Reading materials in the home.* Students from homes with more reading and reference materials have substantially higher averages of writing achievement than do students who have few such materials available. The five types of such materials include books, magazines, newspapers, a dictionary, and an encyclopedia.

8. *Television viewing.* Zero to two hours a day of television viewing is positively related to writing achievement, but there are noticeable declines in writing achievement when viewing is increased to three to five hours a day. Even greater decreases in achievement occur when viewing is increased to six hours or more per day.

9. *Homework.* Students who receive homework assignments and do them tend to have higher writing achievement levels than those who do not have assigned homework or who do not complete that assigned homework. The best fourth-grade writers, for example, reported one to two hours of homework daily.

Research findings have also established the significance or nonimportance of the following factors concerned with the teaching of writing:

1. *Grammar study.* The teaching of formal grammar, when not directly related with the writing process, has little or no effect on the writing ability of boys and girls. This holds true whether the system taught is traditional, structural, or transformational grammar. In programs where an excessive amount of time has been spent on the study of grammar independently of written composition, the quality of student writing may even decline. Grammar is best taught when a specific need for it becomes apparent in student compositions.

2. *Quantity of writing.* In and of itself, the mere act of writing will not necessarily improve the overall quality of student composition. Consequently, a mere increase in the number of opportunities or assignments without a corresponding increase in instruction does not result in a significant improvement in children's writing.

3. *Free writing.* Research provides little evidence to show that free writing (in which children choose their own topics, write what they want, submit it to peer review, and then revise) is effective. It may be useful as a means of generating ideas, but by itself, it does not go much beyond that. Even a steady diet of free writing (completed daily or several times a week) does not accomplish what its advocates would have teachers believe.

4. *Use of models of excellence.* The study of model pieces of writing is one of the oldest tools in the writing teacher's planning, having been traced back to ancient Greece. Older students are asked to read and analyze various kinds of good or even great writing in order to be able to imitate the techniques involved. Unfortunately, available research shows that the study of models has little impact on writing improvement.

5. *Relationship between writing and reading.* Despite considerable research in this area, the nature of the relationship is still unclear.[4] This is true because the experimental studies have provided little information about what girls and boys learn from their reading that influences their writing, or what they learn from their writing that influences their reading.

Writing instruction is not a substitute for reading instruction and is best undertaken for its original purpose.[5] Conversely, using reading instruction to improve writing is also not effective.

Eckhoff, however, did find that the writing of the second graders she studied contained features of their reading texts.[6] Children reading in a basal text that closely matched the style and complexity of literary prose wrote sentences using complex verb forms, infinitive and participial phrases, and subordinate clauses. Their classmates who read in a basal text with a simplified style wrote generally in the same, less elaborate style. It would appear that the practice of many publishers of using simplified sentence structures in their reading texts in the hope of easing the learning-to-read process has had a negative effect on children's writing.

Finally, good readers and poor readers alike enjoy reading a story significantly more than they enjoy writing about it, and there appears to be no evidence that integrating reading and writing enhances enjoyment of the reading.

Briefly, while a central issue in the study of literacy is the nature of the relationship between writing and reading, that relationship remains somewhat mysterious due to the many unanswered questions about writing and reading.[7]

6. *Use of scales.* Scales, or sets of criteria, are given to students who then apply them to their own writing or to the writing of others. In experiments beginning with sixth graders attending inner-city schools, the children were asked

to examine pieces of writing in terms of a set of questions about the extent to which the writing showed particular characteristics. In some instances the questions were also directed at finding ways to improve the particular piece of writing under examination. Eventually it was found that engaging young writers actively in the use of various scale components, which were applied either to their own or to others' writing, results both in more effective revisions and superior first drafts.

7. *Classroom environment.* Results of writing done in informal settings demonstrate that children do not need supervision in order to write. Informal environments also seem to favor boys because they write more than girls do in such environments, whether the writing is assigned or unassigned. Formal environments, on the other hand, seem to be more favorable to girls because they write to greater length and more often than boys do in these kinds of settings, whether the writing is assigned or not.

8. *Teacher attitude.* If teachers have a phobia about writing, it will be passed on to the students. On the other hand, if teachers routinely compose with the class, using such media as an overhead projector or experience-chart paper, the children will see that their teachers actually write. Briefly, if teachers want each student to write, then they themselves must write.

9. *Structured literature programs.* The type of program described in Chapter 13 provides a balance between fiction and nonfiction, between prose and poetry, and between the traditional and the modern. The ability of children to write often depends on their ability to hear and read good books. They and their teacher should set aside time to share favorite volumes with each other.

10. *Sentence combining.* This is a technique for combining short, choppy sentences into longer, carefully constructed sentences. Sentence-combining exercises, whether oral or written, have proved to be effective in promoting the sentence-writing maturity of children. Sample exercises can be found in Chapter 9.

The curriculum for written composition in the elementary grades is concerned with two major areas. First and foremost is the *content, or ideas,* that the children wish to relate. Second, is the *writing process,* needed for the communication of the content. Both areas are expedited when teachers underscore their planning with the principles discussed in this section.

Generalizations and Guidelines for the Teaching of Written Composition

1. *The child must recognize the significance of writing, in his or her own life and in the lives of others.* Through daily contact with labels, direction sheets, maps, menus, coupons, charts, bulletin boards, and newspapers, pupils can be taught to sense the importance of writing—in the home, school, and community. Studies of such famous writings as historical documents of the past and present offer another dimension to older children's recognition of the role of written composition in society.

2. *The child must realize that writing serves several functions.* The four functions inferred by a two-year ethnographic study of one elementary classroom in a midwestern suburb are writing to participate in community, writing to know oneself and others, writing to occupy free time, and writing to demonstrate academic competence.[8]

3. *The child must have a variety of experiences and interests about which to write.* Firsthand happenings at home or at school, on the playground or at a nearby park, on a study trip or at a club meeting, are all useful means of input. So are vicarious experiences through the media of selected books, magazines, videos, or television programs. Finally, hobbies and sports, from stamp collecting to soccer, furnish material for written compositions too. Input, however, can and must be continued during the year through the ongoing classroom activities and learning centers provided by the teacher in such areas as science, social studies, literature, and health.

4. *The child must communicate orally before he or she can be expressive in written form.* Speaking and listening habits profoundly influence pupils' abilities to write. Until they can express themselves clearly through oral means, they are generally not ready to compose their thoughts in written form. This is true of both school beginners and upper primary children.

   Suggested activities for developing oral communication skills include puppetry, story dramatization, reporting, dramatic play, interviewing, and discussion.

5. *The child must enjoy a satisfying and supportive classroom environment.* In a pressure-free atmosphere students believe that their values, encounters, and feelings are important enough to share with each other. If they are thereby encouraged to talk freely about these experiences and beliefs, they are more apt to be able to use their oral contributions as a basis for their writing.

6. *The child must hear and read literature in order to write well.* Next to direct experience, the reading children do is usually their most important source of new words and ideas. Because carefully chosen literature presented effectively can do much to stimulate good writing, a teacher should plan many types of literary experiences, including storytelling and choral speaking. Scheduled browsing in the school media center or classroom library is also helpful.

   There are specific ways in which the writing ability of students will be enhanced when the teacher reads aloud from quality literary works every day for at least twenty minutes.[9] First, their vocabularies will increase both in comprehension and in word count. Second, their abilities to distinguish among subtle differences in word meaning will improve. Third, their sentence structures will become more effective and more complex. Fourth, they will gain a sense of writing form and organization; for example, their compositions will have proper introductions and conclusions. Fifth, they will gain a reason or rationale for writing after hearing the rhythm of standard speech and the pattern of literary prose.

7. *The child must have a teacher who enjoys and practices writing.* A teacher who fears writing or dislikes it will convey that fear or dislike, just as a teacher who only writes comments on children's work or in reports to parents will demonstrate that writing is solely for administrative and classroom use.

   Negatively stated, this is what Smith terms the Grand Myth about Who Can Teach Writing: People who do not themselves practice and enjoy writing can teach boys and girls how to write.[10] In reality, boys and girls taught by a teacher who sees writing as a tedious chore with minimal applications will adopt exactly the same attitude.

8. *The child must understand that the writing process actually consists of four major stages: Prewriting, drafting, revising and editing, and publication (sharing).* The stages should not be thought of as necessarily linear or sequential in nature, nor should every writing assignment demand attention at each of the four stages. Furthermore, the amount of attention given to each stage will vary from student to student. Nevertheless, a major goal of a writing program must be to acquaint children with the stages that experienced writers routinely go through as they draft and refine their work.

9. *The child must realize that a writer always communicates with someone when he or she writes.* The subject or subjects being addressed by a writer comprise "the audience." Writing attitude as well as writing style and language are all dependent on the nature of that audience. Elementary school boys and girls usually move from inner-person or self-as-audience to an unknown audience (that may be geographically many miles away or, at least, that may be unknown to the writer).

10. *The child must have broad-based experiences in which writing is integrated across the curriculum.* They need frequent opportunities to engage in extended writing about the material they are studying. Research infers that better learning occurs when students *use* writing to think about what they are learning in their various classes.

11. *The child must appreciate that vocabulary is a major element contributing to effective writing.* Students can be taught to refer to a variety of sources in which they can locate the words they need, including appropriately graded dictionaries, word boxes, basal readers, spelling books, and special chalkboard or chart lists. To improve their written communication, they must also learn to select expressive words, employ synonyms and antonyms, and become acquainted with a beginning thesaurus.

12. *The child must be aware that writing occurs in various forms or domains.* Until recently the widespread practice has been for teachers in the elementary school to concentrate on creative writing (mainly imaginative, narrative writing). Traditionally, however, there have been at least three domains in the writing curriculum: descriptive, narrative, and expository.

    For more than a decade now, the Los Angeles Unified School District has recommended four domains in its composition program: sensory/descriptive, imaginative/narrative, practical/informative, and analytical/expository. The recommendation has been based on the fact that because some students do better in one domain than in another, the curriculum should be balanced to offer equal opportunity for all. Also, the recommendation has been based on the fact that although the domains are not totally separate, each has a place in writing and thinking development, and all are necessary for competent writing.

The easiest of the four is sensory/descriptive writing because it deals with the concrete. The second domain concerns telling a story—sometimes imaginary, sometimes real—but the intent of the imaginative/narrative domain is to tell what happens. The third domain of practical/informative writing demands that the writer present information without much explanation or analysis. The most difficult and the most abstract is the fourth domain of analytical/expository writing in which the intent is to persuade, influence, and explain while telling how and why.

13. *Children must become actively involved in evaluating their own writing.* Through writing conferences with their teacher, students acquire the ability to revise occasionally and to edit routinely. They keep papers in individual folders for periodic review and for noting the progress made.

14. *Children must be encouraged but not forced to share their writing with others.* Because writing implies communication, compositions may be read aloud in the classroom or posted in the halls. They may be delivered to parents or published in local newspapers or in national journals. On the other hand, compositions may be quietly placed in children's language folders or the teacher's file and never displayed at all. Even though the teacher can and should guide pupils to share their writing with peers and parents, it is the children themselves who must finally choose to accept or decline publication of their written compositions.

For students who are eager to share their writing with a wide audience, there are more than a dozen national children's magazines, ranging alphabetically from *Cricket to Stone Soup,* that publish the creative efforts of elementary school pupils. Competition is keen and delays in notification of the acceptance or rejection of submitted material are common. Still, each of the magazines accepts two or more of the following: poems, riddles, book reviews, jokes, letters, stories, puzzles, recipes, photographs, comic strips, drawings, and articles. All work must be original and accompanied in most instances by a signed statement to that effect. Occasionally a magazine will pay a small sum for work accepted.

Major Areas of the Curriculum in Written Composition

There are two major areas in the written composition curriculum, the foremost of which is *content,* or substance. Despite the current emphasis on the *writing process,* wise teachers realize the paramount significance of the fresh viewpoint or novel description contained in student writing. They rank the writing process as important but subordinate because it is only the catalyst needed to express content fluently and accurately.

Most students, whether they are beginning or advanced writers, will need some **Content or Ideas** assistance in working with the ideas that they wish to communicate. Because the substance of all written expression consists of ideas, the ability to work with them effectively is fundamental. Because ideas may be handled in a variety of ways, writers may employ any one of five interrelated kinds of thinking-writing operations as shown below:

A. *Reflecting on the world:* As child writers represent accurately what they have seen, heard, or read.

1. Describing characteristics of objects, persons, or materials
2. Reporting on an event
3. Telling how something is done
4. Retelling in other words something read or heard
5. Summarizing briefly key events or points

B. *Relating phenomena existing in the world:* As child writers identify relationships among instances or items.

1. Comparing similarities among items
2. Contrasting differences among items
3. Classifying common properties of items
4. Analyzing qualitatively which items are higher or lower, larger or smaller
5. Analyzing sequentially which items come first, second, and so forth
6. Explaining why something happened

C. *Projecting hypotheses, theories, and designs:* As child writers suggest ideas that appear possible but go beyond current data.

1. Hypothesizing or making predictions
2. Generalizing or theorizing
3. Designing or planning systems

D. *Personalizing:* As child writers express their own opinions or beliefs.

1. Expressing feelings
2. Expressing preferences
3. Expressing opinions
4. Expressing judgments

E. *Inventing:* As child writers must go beyond actual occurrences to create people, situations, and conversations.

1. Creating descriptions
2. Creating dialogue
3. Creating characters
4. Creating plot[11]

If teaching children to write is basically teaching them to think—reflect, relate, project, personalize, and invent—then there will be instances when "writing lessons" may not involve writing at all but may consist primarily of oral-thinking activities. Students will hypothesize, judge, retell, describe, or summarize orally

When the teacher shares her favorite book with the class, whether it is poetry or prose, children will respond creatively to this prewriting strategy. (© James L. Shaffer.)

before attempting to express themselves on paper. Furthermore, because thinking has many dimensions and is hardly a single-faceted cognitive operation, school writing programs must include more than just stories and poems. Opinions, reports, short descriptive paragraphs, and analyses should also be among the writing assignments. Classroom writing activity must therefore be conceived broadly and must encompass thinking as a developmental process, which becomes increasingly more complex and difficult as the writers mature and move upward through the grades.[12]

Writing Process

Elementary schoolteachers guide students through four distinct stages of writing, sequentially labelled *prewriting, drafting, revising and editing,* and *publication,* or *sharing.* The amount of attention and time spent on any given stage will vary from child to child depending on many factors, including the purpose of the writing assignment. Purpose includes the audience, the literary type or form, the format of the final product, the topic itself, and the amount of time available for the particular assignment. Determining the purpose must precede the prewriting activities.

Prewriting

Prewriting has been defined as any activity, exercise, or experience that motivates the girl or boy to write, that focuses a writer's attention upon a certain subject, or that generates ideas and materials for writing.[13] Its goal is simply to move the writer from mere mental consideration of a topic to the physical activity of writing about that topic. Younger or less experienced writers are in even greater need of this stage than older, sophisticated ones.

Guidelines for prewriting developed at Auburn University during a summer seminar suggested that the teacher should

1. Set aside enough *time* to allow for reflection prior to putting thoughts on paper.
2. Provide an *environment* conducive to thinking or writing and a *stimulus* that is meaningful to the class.
3. Communicate exactly the *expectations* and *purposes* for the composition, including some attention to the matter of audience.
4. Use *discussion* or *questioning* in an effort to encourage reflection and visualization.
5. Promote *organization of ideas* by jotting down critical phrases or words.[14]

Numerous kinds of prewriting strategies are both possible and useful, as well as being readily adapted to varied levels of writing experience. Included are brainstorming (during which all contributions are listed on the chalkboard), examining photographs, posters, or pictures; becoming involved in story dramatization (whether interpretation or improvisation); listening to stories, story records, or tapes; studying common objects such as forks or sweet potatoes; painting or crayoning pictures of one's thoughts; going on walking or field trips; using puppets or watching puppet theater productions; taking opinion surveys among family members or classmates; viewing films or filmstrips; examining globes or collages; enjoying hands-on and taste-on experiences with such items as fabrics and foods, for example; and clustering (involving a key word written on the chalkboard that elicits from the students other associated words).

Prewriting activities include observing, thinking, reading, remembering, and discussing. Any and all of these must be appropriate to the student's interests and age. That is the crucial factor because prewriting itself constitutes the critical stage in the writing process, often comprising about 80 percent of the writing period.[15] Coverage of this important stage in one language arts series is shown in Figure 6.1, which also displays one example of a clustering chart.

Drafting

The teacher's principal responsibilities during the drafting stage are to be sure that the classroom atmosphere is conducive to writing and that he or she is generally available for reassurance, assistance, or occasional prodding. The child writers must be comfortable in supportive surroundings and should see their own teacher occupied with writing tasks from time to time.

Boys and girls need not restrict their working tools to pencils but may freely use pens, felt markers, finger paints, typewriters, chalk, or water colors. Nor do they need to write in solitary confinement. After all, if well-paid adult writers in advertising agencies or on newspaper staffs can compose together, so children can write productively in pairs, in small groups, or at times even in large groups.

In a similar vein, just as some adult writers prefer to dictate their compositions, there may be boys and girls (especially young children) who need secretaries to whom they can dictate their expressions. Such personal scribes can be found among intermediate-grade students, volunteer adults (including retirees

Figure 6.1. Exercises Useful During Prewriting.

Prewrite: Finding Ideas

Focus
Good ideas for writing can be found in many ways.

Have you found that the hardest part of writing is getting started? Unless a topic is assigned by your teacher, do you just sit with a blank sheet of paper and wait for an idea to pop into your head? There is a better way to begin. The following methods may help you think of interesting ideas.

Journal Writing Write your ideas, thoughts, feelings, and experiences in a notebook. Write about everyday happenings as well as special moments in your life. Write in your journal often. It will be a good source for writing ideas.

Brainstorming Begin by thinking about one general idea. Then think of as many related ideas as possible. Jot down anything that comes to mind. Below is a **clustering chart** that one student made while she brainstormed. You might make a clustering chart like this one.

Discussion and Interviews Listen carefully to what other people say. Their stories and experiences might provide interesting ideas to write about.

Reading and Researching Flip through books, newspapers, and magazines. You will find an endless variety of topics. Encyclopedias and other resource books are also good sources of information. Save ideas in a writing folder or journal.

Observing Look at what goes on around you. Take notes on anything you see or hear that makes you curious or that you just find interesting.

Questioning Jot down a few questions and answer them. Question anything you would like to know more about. Questions might be about real or imaginary situations.

What people do I admire? Why?
What would a city be like without cars?
What would happen if people could become invisible whenever they
    wanted?

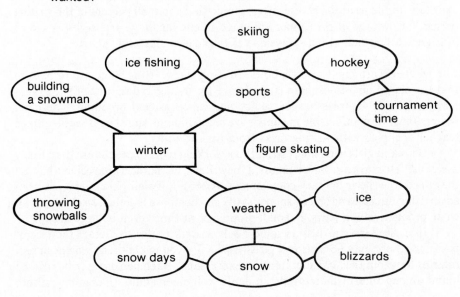

Exercises: Discovering Topics

Figure 6.1. (cont.)

A. Brainstorming Write down the first person, place, and thing that comes to mind. Then think of as many related ideas as you can for each. You may work alone or with a partner or group. Follow the example of the clustering chart given. Save your ideas in a writing folder.

B. Journal Writing Begin a writer's journal. Write down one funny, eerie, or exciting experience that happened to you in the last year. Think of as many details as possible about the experience. Or, simply write in your journal every day for one week. Record your thoughts, feelings, ideas, and experiences. Some entries might be a few sentences. Others might be several paragraphs. Look over your journal at the end of the week. What ideas for topics do you find?

Source: Pg. 102, *McDougal, Littell English, Gold Level.* Copyright © 1987 by McDougal, Littell & Company, Box 1667, Evanston, Illinois 60204.

---

or grandparents), or even the classroom teacher. Also handy are the more impersonal tape recorders that will also allow the student to concentrate on the content of the composition rather than the mechanics, during this phase of the writing process. In classrooms that have computers with word processing programs the teacher can take the children's dictation on the word processor, or the students can draft their own compositions on that processor.

An effective writing program encourages students to develop fluency, to write for an audience, and to identify a specific purpose for each piece of writing.[16] When students are fluent writers, they have much to say, and the words flow easily from the mind to the paper. A teacher can help boys and girls develop fluency by using such strategies as having them keep journals, logs, or diaries; by having them dictate ideas and stories to a student recorder; by using a kitchen timer and having children write as much as they can before the bell rings; or by making lists of familiar objects.

Student writing for an audience can at times be egocentric, and the child may choose to write for only himself/herself in ways not fully understandable to others. Students gradually begin to realize, however, that an audience demands that writers communicate ideas in more controlled forms than those used in egocentric writing. Therefore, writers must always attempt to envision their audience and recall whether they are writing to friends, family members, business concerns, or government agencies. A few may even eventually learn to write to a broader, unknown audience (such as the readers of a juvenile magazine) and will consequently have to adjust their writing accordingly. Activities that may help students learn to accommodate their writing abilities to various audiences include writing for specific and varied purposes (e.g., get-well wishes, complaints, or ordering of merchandise), writing the same message in four ways for four audiences, or writing about a real or imagined school event twice (once for children in kindergarten through second grade and once for pupils in grades five through six).

There is a variety of purposes that motivate composition, including writing to explain, to record, to persuade, to complain, to entertain, to inform, or to comfort. As mentioned earlier, purpose is one matter that should be decided early in the writing process because it serves as an underlying guide and is often related to the type of audience that will read that particular piece of writing. Activities that help writers improve their composing for a purpose include writing on the same topic with different objectives in mind, discussing models of various purposes in writing, compiling lists of goals for writing, and identifying author purposes in what is read. More sophisticated writers may even attempt to parody a piece of writing to indicate a change in purpose.

Among the stumbling blocks in the drafting process are loss of momentum, loss of focus, lack of information, and difficulty in getting started. Teachers should also realize that the goal of the drafting stage is not an error-free paper.

Revising and Editing

At almost any time during the writing process the student writer makes overt contact with an audience. That reader response (whether in the form of a statement, question, or suggestion) is essential in helping the student see his or her work through the eyes of others. It triggers the next stage of revising and editing.

A true revision has been defined as that step during which a writer "rethinks" or "resees" a composition many times while writing and rereading it, with emphasis on how effectively the written material projects her or his intent to the audience.[17] The student must therefore consider such matters as clarity, word choice, transitional words or phrases, organization, supporting evidence or information, concrete examples, and qualifying or sensory details.

Especially valuable in the revision process is the use of peers who provide student writers with reactions to early drafts. Their comments help writers clarify ideas and aims and eliminate mechanical errors. The commentators themselves also benefit by gaining a better understanding of the writing process.

Whereas revision concerns a reexamination of the content of the composition, editing demands a correction or refinement of that composition and is more complicated than revision. Editing can be divided into the following categories of concern: the conventions of writing (discussed later in this chapter); diction or appropriate word choices; syntax (discussed in Chapter 2); accuracy of text in the areas of quotations, dates, and tables; proper manuscript form in the areas of margins and headings; and proofreading so that what appears on the page is exactly what the student writer intended to be there.

Publication or Sharing

Publication or sharing is an essential component of the writing process. It helps children become aware of the significance of their work and also aids them in establishing a value for that written work. Otherwise, students may believe that what they write is only something that fulfills a teacher-made assignment and is not a piece of writing with an important message for an equally important audience.

Children may use practical pieces of writing (such as business letters) in actual transactions with others; they can adapt narratives for dramatizing, or they can read their work aloud to a small group or an entire class. There can be school displays of successful writing, or superior writing can be recognized through writing contests, awards, or assembly programs.

Publication of student work can be done through PTA newsletters; school newspapers; bulletin boards; books for a classroom, school, or public library; student pages in local newspapers; broadcasts over the public address system; and juvenile magazines. A composition can be considered to be for publication when the purpose for writing is the production of a composition to be read by others.

Occasionally, of course, a piece of writing may be put away for personal use by its owner or even discarded. However, a student must never be allowed to forget that what he or she writes is appreciated and is useful.

Lessons involving the writing of poetry by children do not always fit neatly into the stages of the writing process described earlier. Instead, one successful lesson plan in this area breaks down the presentation into five steps: **Writing Poetry**

1. The teacher gives a short *introduction* or conceptual overview of the lesson.
2. The teacher provides *examples,* stressing that all have been written by other boys and girls of the same age. This boosts the confidence of young would-be poets. Because examples tend to have a powerful modeling effect, the teacher must present poetry with a broad spectrum of qualities, including sound, imagination, feeling, and imagery. Unless a variety is presented to them, the children will promptly write poems showing only the single quality exhibited in the poem(s) that the teacher introduced.
3. *Discussion* follows so that everyone understands exactly what is happening and what he or she is to do. The teacher must remind the class of two critical guidelines: There is to be no rhyming, and there is to be no concern with spelling or handwriting. All questions are answered and comments encouraged.
4. The *work session* now begins. The children start to write either alone or in teams. They are given plenty of personal space to minimize problems of privacy and copying. The teacher provides as much personal attention as he or she can because often even a small amount of such interest is sufficient as a strong incentive to create. Dictation is a good technique to use with boys and girls who may have an unusually difficult time expressing themselves with a pencil, pen, or crayon. The teacher writes as the child talks. Sometimes collective dictation is encouraging also and can be done at the chalkboard or on the tape recorder, word processor, or typewriter.
5. *Presentation* by the teacher of student poetry is the final step. It takes place promptly (after a work session of twenty to thirty minutes) because an audience reinforces writer efforts and delights beginning poets. The teacher (not the child writer) should read aloud the new poetry because students sometimes have trouble reading their own handwriting and therefore are apt

to mumble. Furthermore, teachers can edit the poems as they read them, cutting out possible obscenities and choosing one particularly appealing portion while explaining its appeal. Should some students prove reluctant to have their poems read aloud, the teacher can either omit the poet names or allow the students to develop humorous pseudonyms.[18]

Another five-step approach, but this time generally restricted to the writing of the five-line cinquains, runs as follows:

1. The teacher chooses a *general topic* that allows flexibility and with which everyone is familiar; e.g., Foods I Love to Eat. Cinquain poems usually describe something, but they may also tell a story.
2. There is individual *brainstorming* as students list words or phrases about the chosen topic. The teacher moves about the class, reassuring and encouraging. After three to five minutes, sample words may be shared with the group.
3. There is the *selection of one of the words* or *phrases* elicited during the previous step.
4. There is additional student *brainstorming,* again with considerable teacher encouragement and again for only a short time.
5. A cinquain *poem is written.* Upon all the words that have been brainstormed, a simple five-line form is imposed, generally with two syllables in the first line, four in the second, six in the third, eight in the fourth, and two in the fifth. The poem need not rhyme. Nor do all the brainstormed words have to be used, although some words may be repeated, added, or reordered. However, the formula is: first line contains a one-word title or subject, second line describes the title or subject, third line expresses action, fourth line expresses feelings or observations, and fifth line describes or renames the subject.

Older children prefer working in groups of three to four, discovering quickly that cinquains almost write themselves. Younger children, on the other hand, respond more positively when allowed two or three sessions in which to complete their cinquains. It is believed that these five-step brainstorming cinquain sessions can launch a flexible though controlled approach to poetry writing.[19]

Skills with the Conventions of Writing

The conventions of writing (or mechanics of writing) include spelling, handwriting, capitalization and punctuation, paragraphing and sentence sense, and usage. A national survey in the form of questionnaires distributed to 1,000 fourth-grade teachers revealed that 96.5 percent of them "have students do punctuation and capitalization exercises" either "almost always" or "frequently."[20] It would appear, therefore, that teachers do indeed consider some conventions of writing as important.

However, mastery of the conventions or mechanics takes place more readily and efficiently, not through the form of completed workbook pages or other prepared exercises, but rather through the context of regular writing. The best motivator appears to be need; consequently certain skills are learned or improved more effectively at particular stages of the writing process. Handwriting, for example, often improves abruptly during the drafting phase, and spelling, capitalization, and punctuation generally dominate the revising and editing phase.

In the early grades, most editing is done in conference with the teacher. Because many beginning compositions are relatively brief, a great deal can be accomplished in a short period. By the third grade students are capable of greater self-reliance and can be introduced systematically to techniques of editing that they can gradually apply on their own. By the fourth grade, many children can function as independent editors, provided that they have had a lengthy introduction to corrective procedures. Some groups even adopt a few professional proofreading marks:

∧	Insert a word, punctuation mark, or sentence.	Christmas is here∧
≡	Capitalize.	He is <u>mr</u>. Mason.
/	Don't capitalize.	She moved to the /State of Washington.
ℐ	Delete a word, punctuation mark, or sentence.	I can <del>can</del> go home.
¶	Start a new paragraph.	. . . my aunt. ¶The horse ran away . . .

Child writers should compose knowing that their work may possibly need editing. If they write on every other line and leave broad margins, they may later insert, delete, or correct material without problems of space. To help them identify choppy sentences or letters and words omitted unintentionally, they can read their poems or reports aloud to classmates or to a tape recorder. Such listening, or oral proofreading, aids self-editing. Many omissions of the subject, the verb *be,* tense markers, articles, expletives, and capital letters can be detected and corrected, and most extraneous and redundant words can be deleted.

Mechanical skills are never introduced all at once or taught in isolation. Neither are they stressed to the point that they curb the creativity of students and cause a loss of interest in writing. Nevertheless, mechanical skills are considered a legitimate extension of the written form of speech, and children can gradually become self-confident editors.

Spelling

While writing, each child needs to know what to do independently upon discovering a word that he or she cannot spell. To avoid breaking the writer's train of thought or interrupting work with other boys and girls, the teacher may advise the student with a spelling problem to leave a space on his or her paper temporarily (writing in only the initial letter or syllable of the troublesome word). The teacher can then help the pupil later. Or better yet, the teacher may do the following:

1. Encourage invented spelling among beginning writers.
2. Place topic words on reference charts for copying as needed. Most classrooms have various kinds of classification charts showing word lists that grow out of the units of study.

3. Compile a chalkboard list of class-dictated words to be used when needed.
4. Obtain appropriate dictionaries, preferably one for each student. Such books should list single-entry words in alphabetical order and supply some classification pages.
5. Encourage children to consult a familiar basal or storybook that contains the word they need to spell.
6. Promote the construction of individual notebooks, dictionaries, or word boxes.
7. Allow the experienced writer with a spelling problem to receive aid from a classmate.

Handwriting

Related to spelling is handwriting, for each depends on the other for communication. When letters are correctly proportioned and words are properly spaced, the composition is more readily understood.

The real issue is not the form of the handwriting but its legibility. Although the primary pupil ordinarily uses traditional manuscript, or printing, and although the intermediate pupil employs traditional cursive writing or the typewriter, each boy or girl should be encouraged to compose in whichever form he or she chooses to use. Nevertheless, because some types of writing always require the use of printing, the teacher will wish to help every child develop or maintain skill in that form of penmanship.

Capitalization and Punctuation

Children tend to use too many capital letters rather than too few and are much more likely to omit a punctuation mark than to use a particular mark incorrectly.

Primary and intermediate students alike possess individual writing needs, and it is these needs that should determine what is taught in the areas of punctuation and capitalization at each level of development. Most teachers, and particularly those concerned with the writing process, prefer to provide explanations that have a functional base. At times the specific demands of a small group of children permit specialized drills tailored to the temporary needs. Then the teacher may choose to employ an opaque projector or the chalkboard to promote group discussion and correction of an unidentified paper, with special attention to the elements of capitalization and punctuation.

Elementary school children are able to understand that punctuation marks help translate speech into writing. And the teacher can point out how, through the use of punctuation, a writer can convey meaning to readers without benefit of the help a speaker has—gesture, pitch, stress, juncture, and facial expression.

Paragraphing and Sentence Sense

Children can be helped early to understand and to write good sentences. Even in the beginning primary years when students are dictating stories, they can gradually discover that a sentence may tell something, ask a question, express strong feeling, or give a command. As their sentence skill develops, they can move from the one-sentence composition to the two- and three-sentence compositions. Finally, children learn that a group of sentences (or occasionally even one long sentence) telling about one idea or one topic is called a paragraph.

Before students can write a competent paragraph, they must first be able to classify and group ideas. Next they must understand and ably choose one main idea that is stated in a topic sentence and that unifies the paragraph. Then they must support that main idea with all necessary details and facts. Last, the writers must place the main idea and all supporting details in a logical sequence.

Beginning in grade four, students can write *narrative paragraphs* (following chronological order and using exact verbs) and *descriptive paragraphs* (arranging details effectively).

Boys and girls need practice with sentence-combining activities to illustrate sentence variety and construction. Such practice may help them eliminate the run-on sentence, the choppy sentence, and the excessive use of the *and* connective. It may also encourage sentences using the basic transformations. The values of sentence manipulation or combination in the realm of written composition are discussed in Chapter 9. The average elementary school boy or girl will probably need to be knowledgeable with only a few aspects of usage during the writing process. These would include subject-verb agreement, use of negative forms, use of appropriate participle forms, use of possessives, and use of past and future forms of verbs.

Usage

Researchers have found that children clearly do not leap at the opportunity to do creative writing. On the whole, they enjoy reading a story significantly more than they enjoy writing about it, regardless of whether the writing task is creative or noncreative, assigned by the teacher or self-selected. Furthermore, better readers do not respond any more positively to the writing task than do the poorer readers.

School Stimuli for Writing

The problem of motivating written composition remains acute. Today's children are more accustomed to electronic devices that stress the spoken word over the written word. Still, writing in the elementary grades can be spurred on through a variety of stimuli, and recent research among some 13,000 students in ten states shows that student interest in writing becomes a critical factor beginning in the intermediate grades.[21] Exactly why such interest peaks in grade four and falls so rapidly is not at all apparent, but the decline is very clear. Teachers in those grades must therefore make special efforts to capture student excitement about writing and remain alert to the issue of overall student interest in writing-related topics.

Some seventy stimulating topics or situations are explored in this section, with additional activities described briefly in Table 6.1. Most of them can be adapted easily to a grade level other than that mentioned in the text or table.

Table 6.1
Instructional Activities in Elementary School Written Composition

Instructional Objective	Grade Level	Learning Activity or Teaching Strategy
Understand the relationship between speech and writing.	K	Class cooperatively dictates to the teacher the directions for responding properly to a fire drill.
	1	The teacher brings in a hand eggbeater and a sponge for squeezing water into a tin pie pan. Then he or she asks the children to dictate what the eggbeater and the sponge may be saying as they are being used.
Comprehend the relative permanence of writing.	1	Children individually prepare picture scrapbooks to share with classmates. They paint, draw, or cut out pictures and then paste them on heavier paper. Finally they label the pictures.
Understand that people write to influence the behavior or convictions of others.	4	Each child writes a pro or con argument on littering.
	5	Each child designs a food advertisement for a billboard.
	6	The debate teams write out their opinions and facts before the oral presentation. Resolved: Christmas has become too commercial.
Understand that people write to record information clearly and accurately.	2	Upon returning from a field trip to the science museum, each child writes a description of his or her favorite item and reads it aloud to a small group. The group must guess the identity of the object; whoever guesses correctly becomes the next reader.
	3	Each child keeps an individual journal for two weeks. At the end of each day the child writes one or two sentences about the day's happenings.
	4	Students record observations of the behavior of mealworms as seen under a microscope.
	5	Each student prepares a brief bibliography on American presidents. Bibliographies are exchanged, and the receivers must check the library shelves to determine accuracy of the documentation.
	6	Class makes a time line tracing the development of the growth of democracy from ancient times to 1776.

Table 6.1 (cont.)

Instructional Objective	Grade Level	Learning Activity or Teaching Strategy
Understand that people write to respond to a verbal or written stimulus.	2	Children examine mail catalogs and complete enclosed forms correctly, pretending to be ordering merchandise.
	3	Children write friendly letters to the room parents after the Valentine's Day party.
	4	Children individually write a definition of a common object (such as a balloon) by naming and classifying it properly and by giving one identifying characteristic.
	5	Each student chooses a topic sentence about a special interest, sport, or hobby and proceeds to write a paragraph using details to expand that sentence.
	6	Class lists several transitional words and phrases that keep time order straight in a paragraph or story and that keep the relationships clear between ideas (e.g., *if, when, then, while, because, first*).
Apply mechanical skills (i.e., punctuation, capitalization, spelling, and handwriting) to all writing.	1	Children take turns erasing capitalization errors and correcting the errors with colored chalk in a dictated experience-chart story written on the chalkboard.
	2	The teacher displays one concrete item and has each child write a sentence about it. The sentences are collected and read aloud to the class (with the owners' permission), and the class must decide which are complete sentences.
	3	Some children are chosen to be question marks; others, exclamation marks; and the rest are periods. The teacher reads aloud a class summary of a field trip, which includes all three marks. After a question, the question marks stand up, and so on.
	4	For a science experiment, children are given written instructions that have no periods. The class places periods in the correct places.
	5	Each child writes a paragraph summary about a film the class recently viewed, purposely misspelling five words. The children exchange papers, and each then proofreads the new paragraph carefully for proper spelling.

Table 6.1 (cont.)

Instructional Objective	Grade Level	Learning Activity or Teaching Strategy
	6	Portions of editorials that the pupils have written are projected on a screen (with owners' names deleted). The class must evaluate the handwriting—slant, size, shape, spacing, and alignment.
Organize expository writing logically and clearly.	6	Children bring to class copies of their favorite comic strips and list details that happen in each frame.
Understand that people write to express their ideas, opinions, and insights, both for themselves and for others.	1	Class cooperatively writes "Fun at a Picnic" (via the teacher and the chalkboard) just to a certain point, at which time the children individually conclude the story.
	2	Children are given a worksheet entitled "This Is How I Feel." The children individually write a sentence or two about what makes them glad and what makes them sad. On the back, they choose one other emotion to discuss in writing.
	3	Children are given the middle sentence of a story. They must write one sentence that shows what may have happened before and one sentence that shows what may have happened after.
	4	Children write a legend about an event or a figure in state or local history.
	5	Class writes three original sentences containing metaphors and copies them on the chalkboard, underlining the words that constitute the metaphor in each. Then each child writes a poem in metaphoric language.
	6	Each student personifies (or gives human qualities to) an inanimate object such as a baseball, a pencil, an apple, or a paper clip, and writes a story about it. Example: My Life as a Stepladder.

Patriotic Holiday   During the early part of October, the boys and girls in the fourth grade each chose to *keep a personal journal* (as might have been written by Columbus in the final days of his first voyage to the New World) or to *keep a logbook* of the *Niña,* the *Pinta,* or the *Santa Maria* (as written by the first mate of each vessel during the fall of 1492). The final entry in either the journal or the logbook was dated October 12.

Over several days, the second-grade teacher sometimes read and sometimes recited numerous poems about mail carriers, fire fighters, and other community workers. After discussing the poems with their teacher, the children decided to *write riddles* about the community helpers that had been described. The riddles were later placed in a folder on the library table for all to read and attempt to solve.

Poetry Presented by the Teacher

The sixth-grade teacher distributed some reproductions of famous paintings on four-by-six-inch postcards. She encouraged children to look at the reproductions carefully and to keep a favorite. The students later studied the lives of the artists of their favorite paintings before *preparing biographical sketches* to read to their classmates.

Art Reproductions

In the midst of their unit on Japan, the fourth-grade class became interested in *writing haiku and tanka.* After the initial drafts had been completed, large sheets of wrapping paper were spread around the room, and the nine-year-olds copied their poems with large vigorous strokes of their paintbrushes or thick-tipped felt pens. Both haiku and tanka are Japanese verse forms concerned with nature or seasons. The first consists of seventeen syllables arranged in three lines: 5–7–5; the second contains thirty-one syllables arranged in five lines: 5–7–5–7–5. Each contains a single clear image.

Social Studies Unit

When two second graders reported during the same week that their pet cats had had litters, they and their classmates decided to *write a classified ad* of twelve words or less in which they would try to find good homes for the new kittens. The ad was later posted—in excellent manuscript—on the news board at the local market.

Free Kittens

The first graders enjoyed watching the "Mister Rogers' Neighborhood" program. After several weeks of such viewing, the students were able to *write short reviews* of the program, advising their family members as to whether or not some of them would enjoy watching the show at home.

Telecasts

The sixth-grade class was responsible for writing, duplicating, and distributing the *Commonwealth Register* each month. Some of the boys and girls especially enjoyed *writing editorials* on such diverse topics as dress codes, longer lunch hours, and student government.

School Newspaper

Fourth graders took a short trip to collect (with permission) items from a nearby field such as leaves, twigs, rocks, worms, feathers, insects, and bits of wood. They brought their collections back to the classroom and chose the most interesting specimens for further examination. Each child was then asked to *write a description* of a favorite (unnamed) specimen. Later, papers were exchanged, and sketches were drawn in accordance with the written description. Finally, comparisons were made among the items, the written descriptions, and the sketches.

Nature Specimens

Puppet Theater

The third graders first constructed hand puppets based on the tale of *The Three Billy Goats Gruff.* Then they built a puppet theater out of a bicycle carton. Later they *wrote scripts* and decided to tape them. Thus the puppet operators could concentrate on manipulating the puppets while the tape recording supplied the voices.

Geometric Shapes

During their review of geometric shapes, which the class had studied, each fourth grader chose two shapes and then wrote sentences or very short stories to go around each shape appropriately. They liked to *do concrete or shape writing.*
Example:

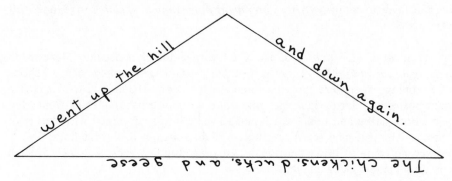

Filmstrip

After the second graders had seen the nonverbal filmstrip *Pancakes for Breakfast* (Weston Woods), they wanted to make a filmstrip of their own from sheets of wrapping paper. Later, although they kept their filmstrip silent, they chose to *write appropriate captions* for each picture frame.

School Camp

The sixth graders at Warrenton Elementary spent five days camping in the mountains with their teachers. Because five pupils in the grade had been unable to attend the activities, the teachers asked the campers to *write a summary* of the week's experiences to share with their parents as well as with their absent classmates.

Interclass Debate

The fifth graders in Room 15 were getting ready for a debate on the United Nations with their peers in Room 16. In order to be able to verify statements made by their team during the debate, the pupils in Room 15 *prepared a bibliography* listing all books (and the significant page numbers).

Library Media Center Budget

The gifted sixth graders had read and discussed several novels. When they learned that the school board had found it necessary to reduce the budget for the book collection at the media center, they decided to *write individual full-length books.* The writing process ran from November to April. The rest of the spring was devoted to copying the texts on unlined, margined paper with blue or black ink and to binding the books with the help of the art teacher. Most of the children wrote fiction. All of the books were placed in the library media center and permitted to circulate.

The fifth graders were provided with cameras and film. They took photographs of flowers, friends, trees, the kindergarten swing set, and the school building. Later each *wrote a lengthy poetic composition made up of several couplets* describing the subject of the picture or an impression or reaction to that subject.

Cameras

The sixth graders had glued to small individual cardboard sheets various objects such as steel wool, velvet, cotton balls, nylon, sandpaper, bits of fur, redwood bark fragments, long nails, and a sponge. The sheets were then placed into a large covered box that had a slot on top. After the children had carefully handled each object without seeing it, they proceeded to *write jingles* consisting of a succession of sounds or a repeated phrase.

Buried Treasure

As the night for group parent conferences approached, the kindergarten children painted pictures about springtime. They then *dictated labels* for their paintings, which were put on display both in the corridor and in the classroom.

Parents' Night

The third graders had been invited to perform some of the classroom experiments they had done with magnets at the school science fair. To assure a successful learning experience, their teacher urged that any student or group of students that had volunteered to do an experiment at the fair should *write down the steps of the selected experiment.*

Science Fair

Fourth graders became concerned with consumer education. Each child brought in one colorful label from a grocery item and *wrote a short television commercial* describing the product honestly. The most successful thirty-second commercials proved humorous.

Grocery Labels

After several weeks of construction work, the first graders were ready to participate in dramatic play concerning transportation. Still they needed such captions as Hangar and Garage to place on their sets. With the help of their teacher, they were able to *dictate and copy signs* that aided their activity.

Dramatic Play

The fifth- and sixth-grade pupils were eligible to join the Safety Patrol, whose members served as crossing guards for the children coming to and leaving school. The patrol meetings were held once a week, and their adviser selected a different secretary each month to *write up the club minutes.*

School Club

When the kindergarten class learned that an unnamed nine-year-old kangaroo had hopped away from the local children's zoo, each child wished to draw the kangaroo and then *dictate a name (for him or her) and one sentence* telling why the animal had decided to run away.

Escape of Wild Animal

Various kinds of playground balls, used during outdoor recess periods, kept disappearing from the second-grade classroom. In order to *make a written report* on the situation, the students got busy *gathering data from verbal sources* in small and large groups, hoping to resolve their common problem.

Burning Issues

Mother's Day/ Father's Day Gift	In preparation for the annual May or June festivity, each fifth grader hilariously *wrote one unique recipe*. The collection of recipes was then reproduced and stapled together so that each student presented one parent with a Crazy Culinary Cookbook. One fifth grader began his Fillet of Sole recipe as follows: Take one rubber boot, three buckets of fresh rain water. . . .
Foreign Exchange Student	Attending the local high school one year was an exchange student from Scotland. The sixth-grade teacher invited him to her classroom, and the young man enjoyed talking to the boys and girls. He arranged to get names of children in Scotland who wished to correspond with their peers in the United States. The sixth graders were soon busy, as they started to *write friendly letters* to their foreign pen pals and to exchange inexpensive souvenirs.
Class Walk	In a school located close to a lake, the first-grade teacher suggested one morning that the children put on their coats and walk over to see the waves on the lake. The lake was especially choppy that day, and the pupils commented excitedly about the waves. Back in the classroom, the teacher asked each child to write one sentence describing how the waves made him or her feel. The papers were collected and assembled into group *free verse*.
Special School Event	The fourth-grade teacher had been placed in charge of faculty participation in the forthcoming school carnival. He invited his students to publicize the carnival by creating comic-strip advertisements for distribution around the school. Committees were chosen, and each included at least one artist, one idea person, and one student who could *write comic strip dialogue*.
Student Birthdays	About one week before any member of the third-grade class celebrated a birthday, classmates prepared interview questions about the celebrant's family, pets, toys, favorite sports, or hobbies. Later, each student had to *write up the interview* that took place on the festive occasion. Children whose birthdays occurred in the summer or on weekends were allowed to choose alternate days for their interviews.
Nonsense Titles	The teacher posted on the chalk tray a variety of nonsense titles, including "How to Catch a Snapperdinck" and "The Day I Met a Rhinoraffoose." Each second grader selected one such caption to illustrate. Later the children were able to *write original fanciful stories* about their drawings and captions. Children who preferred to develop their own titles rather than use the teacher's stock were encouraged to do so.
Flannelboard Figures	Each reading group in the second grade chose its favorite basal story. The children then made felt figures of all the characters in that story. Finally they decided to *write new story endings* and present them on the flannelboard to the other groups.

Fifth graders were permitted to *write original realistic stories for younger readers.* Working individually or in pairs, they had to be careful to choose subjects that would interest six-year-olds, and they had to develop a beginning-level vocabulary list. After the best stories—as rated by the class—had been carefully printed, the pages were stapled and the books delivered to the first-grade pupils.

Books for Beginning Readers

The second graders had visited the zoo on Monday. On Tuesday some children expressed a desire to learn more about the little-known animals they had seen, such as the llama. Other pupils wondered how the big bears, lions, and elephants were captured and brought to the zoo. The teacher encouraged each child or group of children to use the school media center in order to *make a report, gathering data from nonverbal sources,* about the animals in which there was special interest.

Study Trip

The sixth graders brought to class various items they had made at home, ranging from vases and pot holders to kites and model airplanes. As these objects began to collect on the display table, the class nicknamed them their Make-It Collection. Each pupil was able to *write an explanation* giving the steps for making or assembling his or her item.

Homemade Objects

For securing the largest number of PTA members, the fifth-grade class earned a new wall map of the United States. Each child chose one state for an in-depth study and began to *write business letters for information* to the major chambers of commerce in that state. The replies, accompanied by some free materials, arrived within two months.

New Wall Map

After school one day the teacher pasted large paper footprints on the floor and the walls of the classroom. The next morning the first graders were delighted to *dictate an experience chart story* about their strange visitors.

Mysterious Footprints

When school opened in the fall, the fifth graders each brought some snapshots from home showing summer outdoor activities in which they had participated. After some discussion, the class voted to *write limericks.* Jeff's humorous verse began: There was a tall boy at the park, Who regarded softball as a lark. . . .

Snapshots from Home

Sixth graders were shown pictures of a star-nosed mole, a flamingo, some jellyfish, a pelican, a gar fish, and a gnu. Then each pupil was encouraged to *write appropriate similies and metaphors* involving these animals.

Pictures of Unusual Animals

Second graders discussed the significance of numbers in everyday life. They noted that four, for example, is the number of walls in a room, the number of seasons, the number of petals on the dogwood flower, and the number of directions on the compass. Then each boy and girl chose one number and prepared to *write a quatrain* about the number.

Numbers

Story-Box Slips

In the fifth grade there were three story boxes. In the first were some slips with the names of the seasons; in the second, slips with the names of places; and in the third, slips with the names of actions. Each student drew one slip from each box (e.g., *summer, Pacific Ocean, sailing*) and then proceeded to *write a personal expository paragraph* incorporating the words on the three slips. The children stapled or pinned the story-box slips to their completed paragraphs.

Open House

The kindergarten class planned to bake cookies to serve to visitors for open house festivities. After each child had participated in purchasing, measuring, mixing, or shaping the ingredients, the group *dictated the recipe* for the teacher to post on a chart near the serving table. The cafeteria was happy to cooperate in the venture by handling the oven chores.

Clay Figures

Fifth graders created three-dimensional figures of fabulous beasts and monsters. They provided these nightmarish figures with original names. Then they began to *write character sketches* or stories about the creatures.

Wrapped Secrets

Students in the third grade each brought from home an inexpensive, inanimate, but carefully wrapped personal possession. The packages (with the owners' initials carefully hidden) were prominently displayed on the library table for most of the morning. Just before the noon recess, every child was allowed to *write a detailed guess* about the contents of a package other than his or her own.

Weather Conditions

The winter that their state was experiencing record snowstorms, the sixth graders became interested in meteorology. They studied about the weather and *kept weather logs* for two weeks. Each daily log consisted of two sections: one for observations and one for actual weather measurements (temperature, humidity, barometric pressure, wind, and precipitation).

High School Sports

Some of the boys and girls in the third-and-fourth-grade-combination class had brothers on the high school football team. The class was invited to see the game one Friday evening. The following Monday, the children decided to *write new cheers* for the team.

Christmas/ Hanukkah Gifts

During December, when the newspapers were filled with advertisements of gift items for boys and girls, the fifth-grade teacher collected many pages of such advertisements. Each child chose one or two pages and *wrote a math story problem* involving some of the games, clothes, books, or other gift items. The following day the problems were exchanged and solved.

Party Invitation

Veronica, whose family had recently arrived in Newton, invited all the girls in her first-grade class to a Halloween party. However, none of them was familiar with the new area where Veronica lived, so the teacher worked with the girls to help them *write down the directions* to Veronica's house.

As a result of their unit on sound, the fifth-grade class became interested in sound effects developed by radio stations. After each student who wanted to *write a radio commercial* about his or her favorite food had completed the assignment, the convincing—and sometimes comical—commercials were taped and appropriate sound effects added.

Science Unit

The first-grade teacher placed a silver gravy boat on his desk one morning as he told the children his favorite poem about three wishes and read them an abbreviated version of "Aladdin and His Wonderful Lamp." Each student was then allowed to rub the "magic lamp" three times before drawing his or her wishes. Later the teacher stopped at each table so that each child could *individually dictate a story* about his or her picture.

Magic Object

When the district nurse visited the fifth grade, she reviewed the importance of good nutrition and the daily need for the basic food groups. Then she suggested that each student *complete a chart* of the kinds of food he or she should eat for balanced breakfasts, lunches, and dinners for one week.

Nurse's Visit

Each month the PTA program chairperson selected a different grade to supply the entertainment for the all-school meeting. When it came time for the second graders to perform, their teacher suggested they *write invitations* to each of their families to attend the Thanksgiving songfest they had planned.

Assembly Program

During National Safety Week, the boys and girls in the third grade decided to *make a list* of all the precautions each was taking regarding pedestrian safety. The lists were later discussed informally with the school crossing guard.

Community Campaign

A professional music instructor visited the school where some of his students were enrolled, and presented two violin concerts in the auditorium. The first-grade teacher whose class had attended the morning performance encouraged her pupils to *write notes of appreciation* to the school visitor to let him know how much they had enjoyed the concert.

Visitor

The sixth-grade students (some individually, some in small committees) created montages by first collecting images found in magazines, postcards, calenders, and newspapers. Then they pasted them on cardboard and gave each montage a theme such as "Patriotism." Later, the children decided to *write dramatic paragraphs* about their montages.

Montages

The third graders acquired some rabbits, mice, and goldfish. On a lined sheet of writing paper, the teacher wrote the first two entries of a journal about the animals and pinned it to the bulletin board. Then each child was encouraged to keep a *written observational record* of the activities of his or her favorite animal at school or of a pet at home.

Nature Study

Prose Read Aloud by the Teacher	To launch a unit on myth writing, the teacher read aloud to her fifth-grade class from Farmer's *Beginnings: Creation Myths of the World* (Atheneum, 1979). The adventures of Prometheus, Pandora, and other gods were used to encourage each boy and girl to *write an original myth* that offered a convincing explanation of a natural phenomenon to a primitive group of people.
Newspaper Headlines	The sixth-grade teacher cut out intriguing headlines from daily newspapers and pasted each on a sheet of lined writing paper. The papers were turned face-down on the teacher's desk and each student chose one sheet on which to *write a news story* that fit the headline. (On another occasion the teacher provided the original newspaper articles so that the children could compare their stories with the published accounts.)
Book Jackets	The fifth-grade teacher removed all blurbs from the many colorful book jackets pinned on the bulletin board with the caption "What's It All About?" Because he had succeeded in selecting book titles that were unfamiliar to a majority of the pupils, the short *book review* each student prepared (based on his or her favorite book jacket) proved enjoyable to read as well as to write.
Cartoon Characters	The first-grade class had seen the cartoon characters in the primary filmstrip unit "Safety Every Day" (Scholastic) and had discussed various safety precautions. Their teacher then offered them some short jingles about traffic safety and asked the boys and girls whether these reminded them in any way of Mother Goose rhymes. With her encouragement, the children began to *write contemporary nursery rhymes* about safety involving familiar characters. One result began: "Jack and Jill stepped off the curb."
School-Made Products	The first-grade class was planning to make gingerbread men in conjunction with their economics unit. The pupils wanted to try to sell some of their products in order to raise money for the class library. They chose to cooperatively *dictate an announcement* about the gingerbread sale that could be read in other primary classrooms.
Community Sports	The YMCA had arranged to hold swimming classes for both beginners and advanced students of elementary-school age. As teachers discussed the formation of the classes with the children, they urged the boys and girls to talk over the matter at home. Three days later, each interested child was given time to *complete an application* for admission to the swimming class.
Sick Classmate	When six-year-old Stephanie got the mumps, her classmates told their teacher that they wished to *dictate a get-well message* to their friend. The group letter was accompanied by many funny pictures the children had drawn to cheer up Stephanie.

Intermediate children enjoy listening to some of the music written by George Gershwin, Ferde Grofé, Peter Tchaikovsky, and others. Against such a background, they can *write, collectively or individually, an original ballad* based on a current event. Any incident having dramatic, relevant, and contemporary interest can be fashioned into a ballad whose lines are organized into a quatrain, or into a quatrain plus a refrain.

Recorded or Taped Music

The fourth graders listened intently to their principal after she had stopped by one morning to review appropriate behavior on the school bus. She encouraged them to *take notes* during her visit so that the whole class might later recall the important points of the discussion.

Principal's Visit

Primary children made animals from discarded gift boxes and scrap materials, including yarn, velvet, feathers, colored cord, and egg cartons. The following day each student was asked to *write an original definition* of his or her "wild thing." Some even wished to *develop new name words* for their creations.

Wild Things

After a week-long study of NASA and its many programs and centers, fifth graders *wrote unrhymed verse* about the many sensory images each could experience as a future member of a space shuttle crew.

Space Shuttle

In keeping with the light-hearted mood of the day, third graders *wrote ads* (for posting on the bulletin board) concerning the sale of useless or unusual objects found at home or in the garage.

April Fools' Day

The fifth graders had learned "Godfrey Gordon Gustavus Gore" in a cumulative arrangement. Later, following a prolonged discussion, the children were eager to *write three-line tercets* about other problem children who also had names that rhymed with their owners' conditions. Examples: Kate who was always late; Murray who was forever in a hurry.

Choral Speaking

On January 17 (Benjamin Franklin's birthday), the sixth graders decided to *write proverbs* much like those contained in *Poor Richard's Almanac*. Some even chose to paint or otherwise illustrate their maxims. One child drew a boy and his dog clinging frantically to a rope as they recalled "When you come to the end of your rope, make a knot and hang on."

Birthdays of Famous Americans

The fourth graders watched an animated film called *A Crack in the Pavement* (Film Fair), whose sound track contains no narration. Then they were divided into committees in order to *write a film narrative*. The short film was subsequently rerun several times until each committee's composition had been read aloud as an accompaniment.

Film

Puzzle Pieces

When a second-grade teacher lost some of the pieces from his 500-piece jigsaw puzzle, he brought the remaining pieces to school. After he had distributed them among the pupils, the boys and girls arranged the pieces face down on manila paper and pasted the odd shapes into pictures. Those who wished to do so could *dictate couplets* about their pictures into the tape recorder.

Samples of Children's Writing

Compositions written by pupils aged five to twelve encompass a multitude of forms, ranging from the long-established prosaic paragraph to the relatively new, seven-lined diamond-shaped poem known as diamanté. Such written products may be quite brief, consisting of merely seventeen syllables of imagery in nature, for example, in the form of haiku poetry. On the other hand, they may become fairly lengthy, expanding to several pages of expository prose relating to a plant-growth experiment. Some written communications may follow a predesigned structure; others may be arranged freely and extemporaneously.

In all instances, however, what truly matters is that the composition represents a boy's or girl's approach to life—straightforward, honest, inquisitive, observant. It is a reflection of the discoveries that a child makes in his or her day-to-day progress. Essentially, it displays the child's awareness and thinking skills. Each composition included in this section meets these standards.[22]

Sally

Sally was picking flowers. It started to rain. She started going into the tent. Then it started getting sunny again so she took a nap. Then she ran and skipped and walked.

Renee
Written in Kindergarten

Skidder

This is a John Deere 540-A skidder. It weighs about thirty tons and is about ten or eleven feet tall. It lifts with a hydraulic blade. This skidder has a winch line on it. It winches about four-foot logs. There are 440, 540, 640, and 740 John Deere skidders. Sometimes they fill the tires of a skidder with water for extra weight.

Jim
Written in Grade 4

Who Am I?

I have many things I want to say
But
No one will listen.

I have many things I want to do
But
No one will let me.

I have many places I want to go
But
No one will take me.

And the things I write are corrected
But
No one reads them.

Jody
Age 8

My name is Don M. I live on a small dairy farm. It's a lot of work.

We milk the cows twice a day and have to make sure they have hay and water all the time. A cow drinks about 35 gallons of water a day. That's a lot. It's my responsibility to make sure their water tub stays filled. They drink out of an old bathtub. I fill it twice a day or three times when it's hot.

There should always be hay in the feeder, so the cows can eat it whenever they want. A cow has to spend a lot of time eating and chewing. First, she eats very fast, getting as much hay down her as she can. That hay goes into her first stomach or rumen. Then she lays down and just like a burp, a wad of food comes back up to her mouth so she can chew it. This is called chewing the cud or ruminating. A cow spends about eight hours a day just chewing her cud. A cow has four stomachs in all. She needs her complex stomach system in order to digest grass and hay and get food value out of them. Her fourth stomach is like ours, the other three are extra, just for digesting this roughage.

Don
Age 11

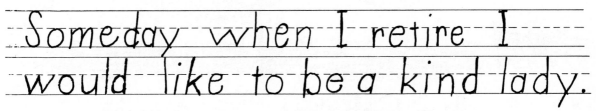

Brenda
Written in Grade 1

Fish

Fish	swim	and
bob	and	eat
food	and	swim
so	gracefully	and
have	a	stroke
like	a	butterfly
when	I	
watch	them	in my
	fish	tank.

Greg
Written in Grade 4

Diamanté

Predator
Strategic, unpredictable
Hunting, stalking, attacking
Lions, Sarengeti dogs, gazelles, zebra
Fleeing, warning, eating
Careful, alert
Prey

Paul
Written in Grade 4

The Cat and The Mouse

The Cat and the Mouse

It was a stormy day. It was lightning outside. It was raining outside. The cat and the mouse were outside. The cat saw the mouse. The mouse was drowning. The mouse said, "Help! Help!" The cat picked the mouse up. He took him onto some dry land. The cat was getting ready to eat the mouse. The mouse got away. He looked at the cat and said, "Thank you but I don't like you chasing me or eating me."

Daren
Written in Grade 1

"A Thought"

To all the people in the world,
Remember this thought,
That everyone serves a purpose.
So find your own,
And be happy.

Blake
Age 12

Where the Witches Sleep

If I knew where the witches slept, I'd go there every day
I'd have to be in a place very far away
I'd hide behind a big black pot and there I'd quietly lie
I'd wait for the witches to arrive from their nightly fly
I'd tiptoe down the dark dank cave and then I'd secretly pry
into their magic book of spells, of spider's legs and flies
Lizard's gizzards and all that gook, just waiting to be boiled and cooked
Imaginary, yet it's true but you really must construe
When I get very angry and am feeling very rotten, I stir up a pot of frog leg
stew, and my troubles are forgotten.

Kim
Written in Grade 6

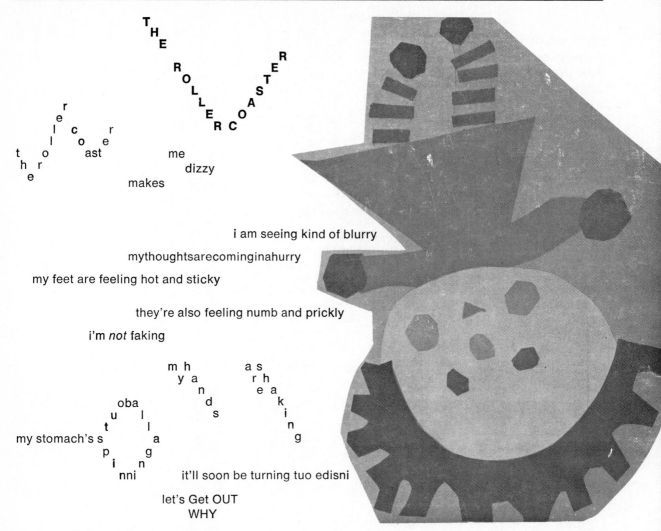

THE
R
O
L
L E R C O A S T E
R

r
e r
l c o e
t o ast   me
h r   dizzy
e
makes

        i am seeing kind of blurry

   mythoughtsarecominginahurry

my feet are feeling hot and sticky

    they're also feeling numb and prickly

  i'm *not* faking

          m h   a s
         y a   r h
           n   e a
   oba   d   k
    u   l   s   i
   t   l   n
my stomach's s   a   g
    p   g
    i n
     nni   it'll soon be turning tuo edisni

    let's Get OUT
    WHY

  BeCause I'm

    S c A r E d !

Janine
Written in Grade 6

My Lost Tooth
By Cheryl's Class

I was happy when I came to school this morning. Nothing was wrong. My tooth was loose. I went to the cafeteria to eat my lunch. I was happy. Nothing was wrong. I hoped my tooth would come out. I took one bite of a potato chip, and my tooth went clear up into my mouth. It was just hanging there. It was just hanging by one little edge. I pulled it clear out. I was happy! I could take it home so I could put it under my pillow. I hoped I would get some money from the fairy. Susie told me to hold it in my hand real tight. My tooth was in a paper napkin. Then I accidentally dropped it into the big trash can with my milk carton. It dropped so fast I couldn't catch it! I went to Mr. Hunt, our principal. I was almost starting to cry. Mr. Hunt tried to look for it. He looked in a napkin, but it wasn't there. He looked in everything. My tooth wasn't there. I came to the room to tell my teacher. I was crying! I told her that I lost my tooth. We wrote this letter to the fairy.

Dear Fairy,
    I lost my tooth. I accidentally dropped it in the trash can with my milk carton. It was a big trash can in the Orangethorpe School cafeteria. Please forgive me, and please give me some money!

Love,
Cheryl

P.S. The children in Room 25 helped me write this letter. Mr. Hunt, our principal, helped me look for the tooth. We couldn't find it.

The Sad Worm

The sad worm is trying to climb up the tree to get the apple, but he couldn't climb up the tree.

It is a sunny day and the sad worm is trying to get in his hole, but he can't find it.

The sad worm climbs up the tree and finds his hole in the tree, then he changes into being happy.

John Wilde

There was a young Frenchman
   of Cault
Who had but one little fault;
   He liked to rob banks
   To steal all their francs,
Until one day he got locked in
   a vault.

Paul
Written in Grade 6

Cat

Quiet, gentle

Rolling, playing, climbing

Yarn, mice, shoes, bones

Running, digging, jumping

Noisy, rough

Dog

Lori
Written in Grade 6

There was a young man from
   Orum
Who bought some new pants
   and he wore 'em.
He stooped and he sneezed;
He wiggled his knees;
And he knew right where he
   had tore 'em.

Jeff
Written in Grade 6

"Quack" went the duck in the spring———.

"Ee-ah" went the donkey in the spring———.

"Oink" went the pig in the spring———.

An-i-mals feel like singing in the spring.

Quack, oink, ee-ah; quack, oink, ee-ah.

Leland
Written in Grade 1

Round is the center of a flower
so the petals will stay on.

Carol
Written in Grade 1

City

Fast, busy

Rushing, moving, hurrying

Streets, buildings, trees, fields

Yielding, rolling, harvesting

Quiet, free

Country

Martin
Written in Grade 6

Turtle

Below the shell and
Above the plastron,
A little creature lurks.

Ben
Written in Grade 4

Dear Elders,

Please try to listen to what I have to say. Let me, please, tell you of my opinion. You may speak out when I am done; and if you listen and you think my opinions are valid, you may think differently than you do now.

The clothes I wear are different from yours. But is my outward appearance that important? Won't you look further? My hair is long, hanging loose; sometimes it's messy after I've played too hard and my cheeks are flushed, but need that close up our relationship? Sometimes I think differently than you—is that why I'm the foolish younger generation?

Sincerely,

Melinda
Written in Grade 6

Bam, Bam, Bam

Bam, bam, bam
Goes the steel wrecking ball;
Slam, slam, slam
Against a concrete wall.

It's raining bricks and wood
In my neighborhood;
Zam goes a chimney,
Zowie goes a door.

Bam, bam, bam
Goes the steel wrecking ball,
Changing it all,
Changing it all.

Eugene
Written in Grade 4

Why the Platypus Is So Mixed Up

When God was done creating the world, he had some leftover parts. He had a giant chimney, the skin of a beaver, the bill of a duck, and two pairs of geese feet.

Well, he thought and planned and pondered and finally thought of something to do with the giant chimney. He would stick it down in the United States and call it Chimney Rock!

Now he had gotten rid of the chimney, but what about the other things? Well, God thought and thought and at last came up with something. He would make it into an animal! It would be a little bit strange but so what?

So he mixed them together and came up with the duck-billed platypus. Poor creature!

Carol
Written in Grade 5

The Boston Massacre

No one person knows the boy's name, except he worked for a barber on King Street. King Street was the site of a mad massacre in 1770. The boy yelled at a guard and got quite personal, too. The guard smashed the butt of his rifle on the boy's head.

News spread fast through taverns and shops and warehouses. Soon men were prowling corridors and streets, both British and colonial. The mobs met at King Street and threw things at the guard. There were about one hundred men yelling at one guard. The colonists rushed into the porch of the customs house. The guard held them back with his bayonet. The frightened soldier yelled for help and got it from the 29th Regiment.

They warned the colonists to stay back or they would fire. The colonists dared them and threw things at them. They hit a soldier with a heavy stick. Montgomery accidentally pulled the trigger and shot Crispus Atucks.

In the excitement the other soldiers fired and people ran everywhere, leaving three dead and eleven injured. Jake was in the crowd and so were Paul and the twenty-two other men.

Written in Grade 5: Excerpt from James's 62-page Historical Fiction Book

The teacher-student conference is a critical part of the modern writing program in the elementary school. (© James L. Shaffer.)

Evaluation of Student Progress

The teacher's use of the technique of rewarding student writers by personal interest in their ideas rather than by close grading of their compositions has proven to be a positive factor influencing beginning writers. In addition to that kind of *ungraded appraisal,* many school districts (and some state education departments as well) also demand *graded appraisal* as evidence that their students are literate.

Ungraded Appraisal

In many contemporary schools teachers have ceased to function as chief evaluators of children's writing. Instead, the program is structured so that girls and boys gradually begin to operate as their own editors (in the area of mechanical skills) and as their own revisionists (in the area of content). By the intermediate grades, most of the students can handle these responsibilities independently. As early as second grade, there can also be peer group conferences, during which classmates listen to the content and then ask questions to help the writer define the direction of text revisions.

Figure 6.2. Self-Check Writing List for Children.

Checking My Writing

1) Is it clear?
   Does my writing make sense to me?
   Will others understand it?
   Do all sentences and words make sense?

2) Is it suitable?
   Who will my audience be?
   Did I write in a way that they will understand?
   Did I choose the best words?

3) Is it complete?
   Does my topic sentence say everything it needs to?
   Does it say too much?
   Have I said all I need to say about my subject in order for the audience to understand and enjoy it?

4) Is it well-designed?
   Do all of my sentences deal with the main idea?
   Are there any unnecssary sentences or words?
   Are my sentences in proper order?

Source: COMPOSITION IN THE LANGUAGE ARTS, GRADES 1–8: AN INSTRUCTIONAL FRAMEWORK, Wisconsin Department of Public Instruction, 1976, p. 38.

By and large the teacher in each classroom serves as a supportive resource person who helps the students acquire the specific language skills as well as the technical skills they will need to serve as their own editors. The teacher also introduces the writers to a self-check list, similar to the one shown in Figure 6.2, or helps them develop such a list cooperatively.

The foundation of any program in which students learn to revise their own work is the teacher-student conference. It is regularly scheduled about once each week. Each child keeps a writing folder of all work in progress (and may even choose to designate some papers as first drafts and others as final drafts) and brings this folder to the conference. The teacher works on the child's own level by attempting to identify the child's composition weaknesses in much the same fashion as he or she tries to diagnose the child's reading difficulties. With one child, it may be difficulty in sequencing. With another, it may be paragraph unity. The teacher also helps every student develop an individualized editing guide, which is posted on the inside of the writing folder to aid in proofreading.

When receiving a child's piece of writing during a conference, the teacher can help the student value and assess her or his work by asking five kinds of questions.[23] *Opening questions* help the child realize that the adult wants to know more about the piece, *following questions* reflect what the child has already said and are filled with redundancies of earlier statements made by the young writer, and *development questions* help the teacher observe development in three categories—use of information, process, and standards. *Basic structure questions* force the child to concentrate on major relationships in information, helping him or her understand the main idea; and *process questions* assist the child in learning to speak about the writing process itself.

Because the aim of the conference is primarily to foster a desire in the child to tell the teacher about the subject of the composition, the teacher must never imply greater knowledge of the topic but practice patience and listen attentively. Furthermore, if the student is involved in individual conferences beginning in the primary grades and is led to discover strengths and deficits in his or her communication, that student will also use the writing process more effectively and become a stronger writer. Consequently, both major areas of the composition curriculum benefit.

Probably the strongest advocate of the teacher-student writing conference is Donald Graves of the University of New Hampshire, who began his work on the composing process of elementary school children during the 1970s.[24] The following are some of the more common questions asked about the conduct of such conferences together with abbreviated versions of Graves's replies:

1. *How do I find time to do conferences?*
   ___ As writers learn to accept more responsibility, two or three ten-minute conferences every two weeks will suffice. At first, however, the teacher may confer with boys and girls according to this sample timetable:
   a. First ten minutes: children who need immediate help. Teacher in a "roving" type conference moves among six or seven children whose writing folders were reviewed the night before.
   b. Next 15 minutes: children who are regularly scheduled and meet the same day each week. They bring their folders to discuss their writing progress.
   c. Last 12 minutes: individual conferences with four or five children at critical stages of their writing pieces *or* one clinic group of five children needing to learn a common convention of writing.
2. *What are the other children doing during conference time?*
   ___ In some classrooms, the other children are writing. In other classrooms, the boys and girls are working at learning centers or are occupied with their workblocks of reading/math/science/writing. Routine classroom procedures must be established quickly in order to limit conference interruptions.
3. *What is the easiest way to keep conference records?*
   ___ Records must be kept simple or else they will not be used. A notebook can be maintained with each child's name on a tab for easy reference. Each lined page covers an entry showing the following: the date, the title of the writing, the skill shown, a brief rating, and a short note. At first, no more than fifteen seconds are required per entry; later, more elaborate records may be kept.

4. *How can I tell whether I am improving in my conference conduct?*
   ___ Keep your perspective on the entire writing program, and keep tape-recorded samples of your conferences both with children who do well and with those who are struggling. Videotape recordings may also help self-assessment.
5. *What is the best way to start conferences?*
   ___ Concentrate on one thing—the child's information.
6. *How do I shorten conferences?*
   ___ Teach only one thing; overteaching leaves the child more confused at the end of the conference than he or she was at the start. When children speak first, much time is saved.
7. *How do I do less talking and allow the children to do more?*
   ___ Do not feel the pressure of time; just wait. Expect the boys and girls to talk first.
8. *What do I do when the piece has major problems and the boy or girl believes that it is good just the way it is?*
   ___ Ask the child why he or she thinks that it is worthwhile; children should be asked to tell the teacher why a piece is good far more frequently than is the actual practice. Should there be problems of meaning with the piece, choose a section that demonstrates a skill the child can handle or an area the child knows well.
9. *How can skills or conventions of writing be taught in conference? Why not teach them in group settings instead?*
   ___ Skills last longest when presented within the context of the child's own paper. However, some skills can be taught in a group setting after the teacher has reviewed writing folders and discovered that several children need to discuss quotation marks, for example.

Incidentally, one survey of elementary-school writing classes in three Western countries concluded that the most important difference among them lay in the methods the teachers used to give children feedback about writing efforts.[25] Teachers in the United States seemed prone to think that evaluating children's work and having the children make corrections somehow inhibits their creativity, but teachers in England and Canada had no compunctions about making evaluations. In both of these countries, in open settings, there was individual conferencing during which the children read their compositions aloud so that they could discover for themselves areas for improvement. The teacher would ask each pupil, "How can you make me understand better what you mean?" Subsequently, when the child would offer solutions, the teacher would either accept them or respond with more guiding questions.

Graded Appraisal

Because the teacher-student conference is still relatively uncommon in the area of composition evaluation, many educators believe that teachers have the responsibility for *scoring* children's writing. Two principal methods currently used are holistic scoring and primary trait scoring.

Holistic scoring is based on the idea that the whole composition is greater than its components, that all components should be judged simultaneously, and that the overall effectiveness of a piece of writing depends upon its communication value. It involves reading and scoring a paper on the total effect of the first impression. Instead of evaluating student writing with a red pencil in hand, the teacher responds to the entire piece with one score, and that is the only mark he or she puts on the paper. Usually the scale goes from one to four, from one to six, or from one to nine. A sample four-point scale could run as follows:

1. Needs intensive help.
2. Shows below grade-level competency.
3. Shows grade-level competency.
4. Shows high competency.

This type of holistic judgment grading is probably the one most used in schools today and has been described as general impression marking and rated as the simplest of the procedures in holistic evaluation.[26] It demands neither a detailed discussion of features nor a summing of scores given to separate features.

Although holistic scores come from the general impression of the evaluator, they do not evolve from casual judgments; they come from *rubrics,* specific scoring guides devised for each writing assignment to set the standard by which every paper will be evaluated. Although holistic scoring does not provide for the correction of errors or the writing of comments to boys and girls about their work, its use of rubrics and scales does give young writers more information than the oft-given grade of "average".

Primary trait scoring, or the primary trait system (PTS) is designed to assess the ability of students to write for precisely defined purposes. The student is given a specific objective or primary trait for writing, such as "Write a narrative paragraph about a sad experience that you have had, and arrange the events in sequence so that the reader can easily follow their order." A complete scoring guide, including category points (usually from one to four, indicating from Inadequate or Minimal to Competent or Highly Skilled) with exact definitions for each category, is used to measure student success in attaining the primary trait.

Primary trait scoring provides an analysis focusing on one trait that is crucial to a given kind of writing. Holistic scoring, on the other hand, gives an overall impression of the quality of the writing as an integrated whole. General feedback to students and teachers is given with holistic scoring. Specific feedback is provided by primary trait scoring. Both methods take one to two minutes per paper.

Finally, in addition to completing holistic scoring or PTS, teachers sometimes may be asked to examine (or administer) *nationally standardized instruments* for written language. Certain achievement batteries such as the *Comprehensive Tests of Basic Skills* (published by CTB/McGraw-Hill, Monterey,

CA) and the *Stanford Achievement Test* (published by the Psychological Corporation, Cleveland, OH) include sections for language expression. Both were revised in the early 1980s and have received good reviews critically.[27] The *Stanford,* however, also has a new optional writing assessment (beginning in grade 3.5) that requires student writing samples in response to four passages, each of which is later rated on five criteria: general merit, quality and quantity of ideas, organization, wording, and syntactic status.

One instrument strictly concerned with writing composition is the *Test of Written Language* (published by PRO-ED, Austin, TX) for grades three through twelve, which provides six subtest scores (in the areas of vocabulary, thematic maturity, spelling, word usage, style, and handwriting) plus a written language quotient (based on four or six subtests, depending on age of student). Revised in 1983, the test takes forty minutes to administer. Although group administration is acceptable, individual administration is preferred. It has earned good reviews for being structurally sound and instructionally relevant in the area of written language.[28]

Discussion Questions

1. How could it prove helpful to the composition curriculum to have the students guided by teachers who are writers themselves?
2. Which of the guidelines for the teaching of written composition would you emphasize in the primary grades? In the intermediate grades?
3. Why is teaching children to write another way of teaching them to think?
4. Would you rank the four stages of the writing process as being of equal importance? Support your position.
5. How should teachers evaluate children's written expression?

Suggested Projects

1. Encourage a five-year-old to dictate a report of a personal experience to you; then share that report with your peers.
2. Collect several compositions written by different children in a particular grade or age bracket. Note the variations in content.
3. Plan a middle-grade bulletin board that will encourage self-editing of written work.
4. Examine three national children's magazines that publish original prose or poetry by elementary school boys and girls.
5. If poetry is talking to oneself, share a collection of unrhymed poetry with intermediate children in order to show them that their own writing need not rhyme to be poetry.
6. Begin a picture file that will aid your composition program. On the back of each picture, place a typed label describing how you would introduce or use that picture with young writers.
7. Set up the learning center on written composition shown in Figure 6.3.

Figure 6.3. Language Arts Learning Center: Written Composition.

TYPE OF CENTER: **Creative Writing**   TIME: 20-30 minutes
GRADE LEVEL: 2-3   NUMBER OF STUDENTS: 2

INSTRUCTIONAL OBJECTIVE: Children will use their imaginations and write down what they think the animals might be thinking or saying.

MATERIALS: Supply of pictures of animals so that they can be changed, paper and pencil, a folder for finished papers.

DIRECTIONS:
1. Think about each of these animals and what they might say about the world today and how human beings treat them.
2. Using your imagination, write your ideas on the paper.
3. Proofread what you have written.
4. When you have finished your paper, place it in the folder on the back of the learning center.

EVALUATION: The teacher will read the papers looking for originality; later the students will read their own papers aloud to the class, or mount them on a bulletin board.

Source: From PATHWAYS TO IMAGINATION by Angela S. Reeke and James L. Laffey, © 1979 by Scott, Foresman and Company. Reprinted by permission.

Recent Related Readings

Beutler, S. 1988. "Using Writing to Learn about Astronomy," *The Reading Teacher, 41*, pp. 412–417.

Euretig, M. 1987. "Brainstorming: A Prewriting Technique," *Writing Teacher, 1* (2), pp. 31–34.

Jalongo, M., and Zeigler, S. 1987. "Writing in the Kindergarten and First Grade," *Childhood Education, 64*, pp. 97–104.

Kostelny, S. 1987. "Development of Beginning Writing Skills Through a Total School Program," *The Reading Teacher, 41*, pp. 156–159.

Newkirk, T., and Atwell, N., eds. 1988. *Understanding Writing*, 2nd ed. Portsmouth, NH: Heinemann.

Parry, J., and Hornsby, D. 1988. *Write On: A Conference Approach to Writing*. Portsmouth, NH: Heinemann.

Shanahan, T. 1988. "The Reading-Writing Relationship: Seven Instructional Principles." *The Reading Teacher, 41,* pp. 636–647.

Staton, J. 1988. "Dialogue Journals," *Language Arts, 65,* pp. 198–201.

Temple, C., et al. 1988. *The Beginnings of Writing,* 2nd ed. Boston: Allyn and Bacon.

Within, D. 1988. " 'Good, Now Try Some Sentences!': A Fluent Writer Enters First Grade," *Educational Horizons, 66,* pp. 122–125.

Chapter Notes

1. A. Lapointe, "Students' Writing Skills Found Distressingly Poor by NAEP," *Education Week,* 1986, 5.

2. A. Applebee, J. Langer, and I. Mullis, *The Writing Report Card* (Princeton, New Jersey: Educational Testing Service, 1986).

3. G. Hillocks, Jr., *Research on Written Composition* (Urbana, Illinois: ERIC Clearinghouse on Reading and Communication Skills, 1986); California State Department of Education, *Handbook for Planning an Effective Writing Program* (Sacramento: Author, 1986); Applebee, Langer, and Mullis, *The Writing Report Card;* A. Humes, "Putting Writing Research into Practice," *Elementary School Journal,* 1983, *84,* pp. 3–17; J. Chall and V. Jacobs, "Writing and Reading in the Elementary Grades: Developmental Trends among Low SES Children," *Language Arts,* 1983, *60,* pp. 617–626; E. Jane Porter, "Research Report," *Language Arts,* 1975, *52,* pp. 1019–1026; D. Graves, "An Examination of the Writing Process of Seven Year Old Children," *Research in the Teaching of English,* 1975, *9,* pp. 227–241; E. McDaniel and T. Pietras, "Conventional Test Scores and Creative Writing among Disadvantaged Pupils." *Research in the Teaching of English,* 1970, *4,* pp. 181–186; L. Golub and W. Frederick, "An Analysis of Children's Writing under Different Stimulus Conditions," *Research in the Teaching of English,* 1970, *4,* pp. 168–180; B. Miller and J. Ney, "The Effect of Systematic Oral Exercises on the Writing of Fourth Grade Students," *Research in the Teaching of English,* 1968, *2,* pp. 44–61; P. Shapiro and B. Shapiro, "Two Methods of Teaching Poetry Writing in the Fourth Grade," *Elementary English,* 1971, *48,* pp. 225–228; and S. Zeman, "Reading Comprehension and Writing of Second and Third Graders," *The Reading Teacher,* 1969, *23,* pp. 144–150.

4. A. Jaggar, D. Carrara, and S. Weiss, "Research Currents: The Influence of Reading on Children's Narrative Writing (and Vice Versa)," *Language Arts,* 1986, *63,* p. 298.

5. S. Stotsky, "Research on Reading/Writing Relationships: A Synthesis and Suggested Directions," *Language Arts,* 1983, *60,* pp. 627–643.

6. B. Eckhoff, "How Basal Reading Texts Affect Children's Writing," 1986, ERIC Document Reproduction Service No. ED 276 969.

7. M. Wilson, "A Review of Recent Research on the Integration of Reading and Writing," *The Reading Teacher,* 1981, *34,* pp. 896–901.

8. S. Florio and C. Clark, "The Functions of Writing in an Elementary Classroom," *Research in the Teaching of English,* 1982, *16,* pp. 115–130.

9. C. Gay, "Reading Aloud and Learning to Write," *Elementary School Journal,* 1976, *77,* pp. 87–93.

10. F. Smith, "Myths about Writing," *Language Arts,* 1981, *58,* p. 797.

11. D. Hennings and B. Grant, *Written Expression in the Language Arts* (New York: Teachers College Press, 1981), pp. 13–15.

12. *Ibid.,* p. 41.

13. California State Department of Education, *Handbook,* p. 11.

14. N. Andreasen et al., "The Child and the Composing Process," *Elementary School Journal,* 1980, *80,* p. 251.

15. B. Faust, "Writing as Process in the Language Arts," in *Language Arts Instruction and the Beginning Teacher*, C. Personke and D. Johnson, eds. (Englewood Cliffs, New Jersey: Prentice-Hall, 1987), p. 67.

16. California State Department of Education, *Handbook,* pp. 14–16.

17. *Ibid.,* p. 18.

18. D. Greenberg, *Teaching Poetry to Children* (Portland, Oregon: Continuing Education Publications, 1978), pp. 13–15.

19. L. Markham, "Writing Cinquains: Start with a Word or Two," *Language Arts,* 1983, *60,* pp. 350–354.

20. W. Petty and P. Finn, "Classroom Teachers' Reports on Teaching Written Composition," in *Perspectives on Writing in Grades 1–8,* S. Haley-James, ed. (Urbana, Illinois: National Council of Teachers of English, 1981), p. 23.

21. T. Hogan, "Students' Interests in Writing Activities," *Research in the Teaching of English,* 1980, *14,* pp. 119–126.

22. Examples are taken from *Writings* (Irvine, California: Irvine Unified School District, 1981), pp. 72, 86; L. Jenkins, ed., *Reading, Writing and Arithmetic* (Corvalis, Oregon: Oregon State University, 1980), pp. 35, 40, 47; R. Atkinson and K. Hearn, eds., *How the Poet Got the Word* (Dover, Delaware: Delaware State Arts Council, 1978), pp. 7, 8; N. Welbourn et al., eds., *Let the Children Speak* (Washington, D.C.: Teacher Corps, U.S. Office of Education, 1976); and *Impressions,* Vols. 26–28 (San Diego, California: San Diego City Schools).

23. C. Vukelich and L. Leverson, "Text Revisions: Helping Children Modify the Content of Their Writing," *Childhood Education,* 1987, *63,* pp. 258–259.

24. D. Graves, *Writing: Teachers & Children at Work* (Exeter, New Hampshire: Heinemann Educational Books, 1983), pp. 141–148; and "Donald Graves on Teaching Writing," *Writing Teacher,* 1987, *1*(1) pp. 3–43.

25. L. E. Williams, "Methods of Teaching Composition in Open Classes—England, Canada, and the United States," *Innovator,* 1978, *9,* pp. 1–3.

26. C. Cooper, "Holistic Evaluation of Writing," in *Evaluating Writing,* C. Cooper and L. Odell, eds. (Urbana, Illinois: National Council of Teachers of English, 1977), pp. 11–12.

27. J. Mitchell, Jr., ed., *The Ninth Mental Measurements Yearbook,* Volumes I–II (Lincoln: University of Nebraska Press, 1985), pp. 257, 1172.

28. *Ibid.,* p. 1602.

The First Writing Tool— Handwriting 7

Major Chapter Goals

After studying Chapter 7, the reader will be able to
1. Explain the goals of handwriting instruction and the need for writing readiness.
2. Outline the differences between traditional manuscript (or printing) and cursive handwriting.
3. Describe some alternative forms of handwriting, including typewriting.

Discover As You Read This Chapter Whether*

1. Legibility is a more important goal than fluency in teaching handwriting.
2. As a technique for introducing beginners to handwriting, tracing is superior to copying.
3. Writing readiness is an important area of a successful handwriting program.
4. Hand preference is usually stable after the age of five.
5. It has been proven that beginners who use special primary pencils and primary paper improve the quality of their handwriting.
6. Traditional cursive writing is easier and faster than traditional printing.
7. Italic handwriting is now being taught to children.
8. The keyboards of a typewriter and a microcomputer are almost identical.
9. Left-handed students should be separated from right-handed children for handwriting instruction.
10. Most elementary schools today do not issue a handwriting grade on the report card.

*Answers to these true-or-false statements may be found in Appendix 5.

Handwriting instruction has changed very little during most of the century, according to a survey of sixty years of handwriting research and practice.[1] After that lengthy period of time, there is still no widespread acceptance of what constitutes legible writing or how that writing should be evaluated. Furthermore, a society that types public documents and puts word processors in the hands of clerical workers as soon as possible shows little regard for the beautifully penned script that was once the mark of an educated human being.

It is this preference for electronically processed print over penned script that is currently influencing handwriting instruction. Such instruction is unpopular with teachers and students alike and is often regarded as wasting valuable class time.[2] Although all agree on the need to teach handwriting, many admit that it is the most poorly taught segment of the elementary curriculum, especially in the intermediate grades.

Nevertheless, handwriting continues to maintain its important role in the integrated program of language arts. It extends into all written work and merits attention throughout the school day. Although separate handwriting periods are necessary, even instruction and practice provided during these periods can involve children in practical writing situations related to reading, spelling, and social studies assignments.

Writing concerns language. Because studies have shown positive correlations among abilities in the various language arts, the best instructional program teaches all of the language arts in a communication framework while still recognizing the need for directed teaching of specific skills such as handwriting.

The primary goal in teaching handwriting is legibility. The first essential is correct letter formation, and the second is proper spacing of letters and words. Size, within certain limitations, may be still another consideration. Legibility has sometimes been defined as the ease with which something can be read.

There are several significant aspects in teaching legibility.[3] The first is practice, according to research studies. Another is the amount of emphasis placed on good handwriting by the teacher because students strive harder to improve the quality of their work when their teacher stresses the importance of legible handwriting. Finally, children cannot be led to believe that neatness and legibility are synonomous, although some adults tend to overemphasize neatness for all writing tasks. Instead, boys and girls should understand from the start that the degree of neatness demanded for a specific piece of writing is related to the intended audience and purpose.

The secondary goal in teaching handwriting is fluency (without loss of legibility). Although it is not a factor in the early grades, beginning at grade three there is a consistent increase in the fluency or speed of writing among both printers and cursive writers. The rate at which one is able to produce letters and words is important for note taking, summarizing, and drafting original material.

Early in their schooling, children realize the difference in legibility when they write for their own use or under the pressure of speed and when they write for others or without pressure of time. In the fourth, fifth, and sixth grades, girls write more rapidly than boys, but left-handed and right-handed writers show no significant difference in writing fluency.

Fluency is important, and teachers must be aware of the problems facing a child who is unable to vary his or her writing speed comfortably. The stress on speed is directed toward the goal that writers must be able to compose in thought units rather than word by word, or worse yet, letter by letter.[4] Fluency appears to be a more difficult problem for many children than the actual formation of letters.[5] Occasional speed drills will assist students in increasing fluency and will also aid the teacher in determining areas of deficiency.

Handwriting is an individual production influenced by physical, mental, and emotional factors. The development of handwriting skill is closely related to the total growth and development of the student. Teachers who recognize that children's growth patterns are not identical will not insist that every child meet the same standard of achievement. Instead, each student will be encouraged to develop his or her own optimum rate of writing and level of writing pressure. These teachers will allow an individual show of readiness to precede each step in the writing process and will encourage handwriting practices adjusted to individual differences in motor control.

Because the motor control that plays such a large part in learning to write legibly is not highly correlated with intelligence or scholastic achievement, high skill in handwriting may be possible for many children who do not have widespread academic success. It can help them maintain a positive self-image.

Handwriting lessons for both slow and fast learners in the intermediate grades should stress individualized practice on only those few letters that remain troublesome.

Handwriting is primarily a tool of communication. It is a means to an end and an individual tool. Consequently, from the beginning of instruction the students must write material that is meaningful to them. Children who write for a valid reason and not just as a mechanical task (and even copying from the chalkboard or book can be made purposeful) accept the importance of handwriting. They recognize that if their writing is so illegible that what they have written cannot be read, their attempts at communication have failed.

Correct posture, correct hand movement, and proper position of writing paper and handwriting tools must be developed by each child. Good posture and position in writing influence how well children write.

The table or desk should be a height comfortable for the student and have a writing surface that is smooth and flat. It should be positioned so that the light falls over the child's left shoulder if he or she is right-handed or over the right shoulder if the writer is left-handed. The child should face the table or desk squarely, leaning slightly forward. Both arms should rest on the writing surface. Elbows, however, should be off the table or desk to permit free arm movement.

Proper positioning of the writing paper is another important factor. For manuscript writing, the right-handed student places the paper squarely in front of him or her, with the left or writing edge of the paper even with the midsection of the body. The left-handed child tilts the paper up and toward the right so that the lower-right corner is slightly to the left of the body's midsection. During cursive writing, the right-handed student tilts the paper toward the left so that the lower edge of the writing surface and the lower edge of the paper form a 30-degree angle. The left-handed writer, however, tilts the paper toward the right (about 35 to 45 degrees) so that the lower-right corner of the paper points either toward the body's midsection or to the right of the midsection. Whatever the handedness, the nonwriting hand should be on the paper, shifting it to keep the total writing area visible to the student.

Well-planned lessons develop proficiency in handwriting. Since handwriting is definitely a skill, it improves with proper systematic instruction. Most schools teaching handwriting offer it on a whole-class basis daily in grades one to four but after that less frequently. Class periods average ten to twenty minutes at all grade levels, with shorter planned lessons being more effective than longer unplanned periods. In England, for example, research has revealed limited handwriting activity as reported by 936 schools sampled for their six- and nine-year-old students.[6] In most schools with both age groups, class-based work occupied at best thirty minutes a week, and only 20 percent of the students were encouraged to practice handwriting during their free time, again with a limit of thirty minutes per week. Twelve percent of the younger children and 21 percent of the older ones had *no* time allocated for handwriting.

Copying is superior to tracing as a technique for introducing beginners to handwriting.[7] Kindergartners, for example, who did not copy letters but used faded tracing dots that outlined letter shapes did not learn to write those letters. After all, copying is a cognitive task and it has been shown that what children learn is not a motor pattern but a set of rules that enables them to copy from a model. Indeed, copying may be effective because, when reproducing letters, the boys and girls are actively engaged in developing and applying rules that govern letter production. Such rule-based instruction improves performance on target letters and also permits transfer of learning to new letters. The key to that transfer has proved to be a demonstration of rules. However, because independent copying practice results in no transfer, teachers must provide prompt feedback on the learners' writing movements or on the products. Incidentally, fifth-grade teachers should be aware of a recent study concluding that although the ability of children to copy seems to develop continuously during the first four years of school (grades one through four), their chances to improve the copying function as a psychomotor skill by training are diminished by age ten.[8]

Research in handwriting has revealed that the most effective instructional strategies use direct instruction, provide guided practice, identify the objective of the activity, and reduce the learning to manageable steps through task analysis.[9] Handwriting has been successfully taught through computers, educational television, and animated flip-books. Other more experimental but equally useful methods include hand-eye coordination training, motor and perceptual tasks, verbalization of handwriting rules, and the use of the videotape recorder. When having videotapes of the handwriting act modeled properly for both the left-handed and the right-handed students, the close-up views have proved far superior to the view ordinarily provided to the young writers in the classroom. According to Furner, children learn better from an active model than they do when they see only still pictures of the process.[10] Although there are only three major systems for teaching handwriting, the *El-Hi Textbooks and Serials in Print, 1985* (published by Bowker of New York), contains sixty-three entries under the heading "Handwriting," so obviously there are more than three publishers whose materials fit into one of the following categories:

1. Ball and stick traditional manuscript or printing followed by traditional cursive.
2. Continuous stroke manuscript followed by cursive.
3. Italic (unconnected) followed by cursive (connected) italic.

Teachers must be aware that effective model handwriting programs all provide opportunities for students to verbalize the rules of letter formation and to evaluate their own progress. They also combine visual and verbal feedback with reinforcement or rewriting.[11]

Handwriting readiness, like reading readiness, has come into vogue during the past fifteen years. Although handwriting is being taught to young children today in more and more kindergarten and early childhood programs, some boys and girls are being pushed into handwriting before they have acquired adequate prehandwriting skills. Consequently, handwriting causes discouragement among them. And according to the Oregon Department of Education, this often overlooked readiness issue may be the major reason some students find learning handwriting so difficult.[12]

Writing Readiness

Many years ago Maria Montessori stated, after extensive experimental work with young children, that learning to write demands both intelligence and an efficient motor mechanism. Children can acquire mental readiness through experiences that value handwriting and promote interest in learning to write. They attain motor readiness through activities that enable them to learn to hold the writing tools and to perform the simple movements required.

Specifically, six prerequisite skill areas for handwriting have recently been identified.[13] *The first is small muscle development and coordination.* When girls and boys start school, they use their arm and leg muscles fairly well, but skill in the use of wrist and finger muscles comes slowly. Before they can develop skill in writing, they must be able to hold the chalk, crayon, or pencil without noticeable strain and able to make the finger muscles respond so that they can copy simple geometric or letterlike characters. If children lack the ability to control those muscles in a manner necessary to produce legible handwriting, or if they overexert themselves in order to attain the muscular coordination needed for writing, they may develop an antagonistic attitude toward all writing. Forcing children to write before they are physically ready may cause long-term or even permanent problems with their handwriting.

Activities that enhance small muscle development include many manipulative tasks such as working with jigsaw puzzles and snap beads or playing with blocks and doll furniture. Day-to-day experiences including zipping, buttoning, tying, and sewing also promote coordination. Too, the art curriculum enhances

Handwriting readiness is just as important for young children as reading readiness. (© Jean-Claude Lejeune.)

muscle development with painting, coloring, drawing, sketching, and tearing or folding paper. A child who can cut easily with small scissors is displaying readiness for handwriting instruction.

The second series of handwriting skills consists of hand-eye coordination tasks. These are plainly related to small muscle development skills, and therefore many of the activities just mentioned also promote hand-eye coordination, often referred to as visual-tactual integration. Playing the piano, stringing beads, pushing buttons, working puzzles, typing, and balancing blocks all require precise hand motions. Numerous paper-oriented tasks such as pasting and finger painting refine coordination. Even large muscle activities such as jumping rope or climbing a ladder are helpful for hand-eye precision.

Children who consistently construct tall buildings out of blocks without knocking them down, follow mazes without touching exterior lines, or hammer nails straight into wood are revealing readiness for handwriting lessons.

An ability to hold writing tools properly is the third prerequisite skill area. Young children need to manipulate tools at the water table and at the sand table as part of their early childhood curriculum. Gardening, with its rakes and hoes; cooking, with its spatulas and spoons; and painting, with its sponges and brushes—all provide experiences with utensils and tools.

Every child who is learning to write cursively will profit from the individualized attention, which the teacher provides. (© Jean-Claude Lejeune.)

There is an apparent hierarchy of difficulty in using writing tools. When young children are given a choice of four tools with which to write their names—a pencil, a felt-tip marker, a crayon, and some chalk—they overwhelmingly prefer the marker as the easiest tool to use followed by chalk, crayon, and pencil, in that order. There is, incidentally, no advantage to the oversized pencils used by young children in some classrooms. Actually, some boys and girls write better with standard (adult) pencils from the start rather than with beginning pencils, which have exceedingly soft lead and no erasers. Some research has even indicated that the use of the beginner's pencil should be terminated in the lower grades.[14]

Teachers can readily determine whether children are holding a pencil properly. The first indicator is the depth of impression on the page caused by the amount of pressure used. If the writing paper has holes in it or is covered by strokes that are too light, the child is using improper pressure and may become a slow writer. The other indicator of correct pencil usage is the ease with which the tool can be removed from the writer's hand as he or she is writing. Children who are experiencing stress will grip the pencil too tightly and may be unable to write for a reasonable period of time.

If young children have not firmly determined a hand preference by the time they begin school, teachers should encourage them to participate in activities leading to left-handedness if they are left-eyed or in activities leading to right-handedness if they are right-eyed. Numerous instances of mixed laterality (especially involving the eye and hand) have been associated with reading and learning disabilities as well as with autonomic disturbances. In a follow-up study of children over three years of age, it was reported that hand preference usually seems stable after the age of five (as does foot and eye preference).[15]

A fourth prerequisite skill area is the ability to form basic strokes. Circles and straight lines should be made smoothly in the appropriate direction and with clean intersections. Such strokes should evolve through time and through activities such as stirring, drawing, painting, sand play, and water play.

Until circles and straight lines occur naturally in a child's drawings of houses, flowers, people, and trucks, the boy or girl is not ready for formal handwriting instruction. Even then the transition from drawing to handwriting may be a slow process involving basic strokes in both artistic and written form.

Letter perception is the fifth prerequisite skill area. Attention to perception in a handwriting program develops better writers than a conventional program because handwriting is more than a physical activity. Because children should observe the finished product (letter or word) as well as the model formational act, left-handers should have left-handed models for aid, and right-handed pupils should have right-handed ones. They must all be able to notice likenesses and differences among the forms and able to provide accurate verbal step-by-step descriptions of the productions of the same forms.

In the initial stages of handwriting, reversals may often occur. When a child reverses a *b, d, s,* or uppercase *N,* for example, the teacher must help by pointing out the differences in direction and by providing practice in dealing properly with the confusing symbols. Reversals generally disappear as children mature.

The importance of adult modeling of correct letter formation cannot be overstressed. Boys and girls must virtually perceive the way the alphabet letters are formed. The more often they see their teacher write on paper (and not merely on the chalkboard) the better. Equally critical is self-correction of initial attempts at handwriting as an aid in the letter perception. Incorrect habits are difficult to break later.

The sixth and final prehandwriting skill is actually an entire set of skills concerned with the orientation to printed language. One of these is an interest in writing and a desire to write. As the children observe the teacher writing in a meaningful way, their desire to do the writing themselves begins to grow. They soon sense a personal need to communicate in writing and enjoy learning to write their names. As the children watch, the teacher writes their dictated captions for pictures and experience charts as well as their dictated messages to absent classmates. The teacher also involves the children in discussions of personal experiences that culminate in party invitations, thank-you notes, and weight-and-height records.

Another skill is an understanding of the concept of left-to-right progression. Before starting to write, children need to know the meaning of the terms *left* and *right*. Although some girls and boys begin school with an understanding of the differences between the terms, others must gradually begin to comprehend them through teacher-planned psychomotor activities such as Looby-Loo and the Hokey-Pokey. Additional activities recommended to help children master the bodily concept of left-right orientation demand

1. Creating a dramatic play setting for fire fighting and then providing the boys and girls with toy fire engines to move from the fire station at the left to the "fire" area at the right.
2. Drawing green "go" and red "stop" signs on the chalkboard and then providing the children with colored chalk to draw the left-to-right horizontal lines between the signs. Later, a simulation game can be played with toy cars being "driven" along the lines from "go" to "stop."

Another skill is language maturity. When girls and boys verbalize satisfactorily, their oral experiences provide meaningful vocabularies for the first writing experiences. They enjoy listening to stories as well as composing and sending written messages. They should have many opportunities to dictate stories, poems, reports, plans, ideas, and funny or frightening incidents. When writing for the students, the teacher is not only introducing them to writing and reading, but she or he is also helping to bridge a gap between oral and written language. Children need to write through the teacher about themselves and their friends.

Traditional Manuscript Handwriting or Printing

Manuscript writing is a twentieth-century development. It was invented by a British elementary school teacher named Margaret Wise whose classic text, *On the Technique of Manuscript Writing,* was published in 1924. The style was soon adopted by hundreds of American public schools. Today it is part of the curriculum in many primary grades throughout the country because it is consistent with the motor and perceptual development of young children.[16]

Manuscript handwriting (printing) has several advantages. It is written with only three basic strokes and so is similar to the kind of drawing with which the students are familiar. Because it can be written with little physical strain, it allows the children to rest between strokes if necessary. Because each letter is separate, even a child with poor muscular control can produce readable results. It demands few eye movements, making it easier on the eyes of all young children and especially on those with visual difficulties. It is less tiring and, therefore, can be employed for longer periods of time. It can be written rapidly without loss of legibility. Furthermore, studies have shown that learning to print creates ease and allows the children to produce better writing.[17]

Because manuscript writing resembles the print found in many primary reading materials, it aids beginning reading and composition. Only one alphabet needs to be mastered, and Piaget's work suggests that the preoperational child (usually from two to seven years of age) will learn to write and read better and faster when a single alphabet is used. Because the student writes more, and therefore comes into contact with more words, manuscript writing improves spelling. It increases the quantity of written composition. Because it promotes proofreading, printing also improves the quality of composition work because many spelling errors are actually handwriting illegibilities.

Children exposed to printing in the early grades become better cursive writers than those who never received manuscript lessons. Those with legible manuscript are more apt to write legibly when they switch to cursive, and legibility is an important consideration for young pupils. Unlike adults who can "fill-in" illegibilities, primary children are relatively unacquainted with written language and so lack the ability to "fill in." Their first writing experience should be based on a legible script that encourages them to read their own writing.

Finally, printing can be learned easily by those who are non-English speaking, learning disabled, or physically handicapped. It is as useful with illiterate adults as it is with illiterate children. It has even been recommended that manuscript handwriting replace cursive handwriting as the style used by teachers for all classroom work because it is so legible.

Chalkboard Writing

Chalkboard writing gives young children an opportunity to use their large muscles. They can also write on a broad surface without the restriction they find in writing on paper.

As several children show numerous signs of writing readiness, the teacher gathers them into a group. The children are taught to face the chalkboard, standing comfortably to enable a good arm movement and adequate visualizing of letters and words. They are shown how to hold a half-length piece of chalk about one inch from the writing end (between the thumb and first and second fingers). They are told to hold the elbow close to the body.

The section of chalkboard used should hang low enough to permit children to write at or near eye level. Guidelines may be permanently ruled on the board to help children gauge the size, shape, spacing, and linear evenness of their writing.

When a group of children is ready for its first writing experience, the teacher plans instruction at a time when the members are not fatigued. Each pupil is carefully supervised so that correct habits are established and focus is centered on proper letter formation.

Paper Writing

Following the experience of writing at the chalkboard, writing activities using crayons or paint and brushes on unlined newsprint, tag board, or manila paper are the next step. The teacher may guide the making of simple figures that use the basic strokes, emphasizing large, free movements, left-to-right direction, and a feeling of form and space.

When beginning writers are ready to use lined paper, teachers should recall that studies have shown that although using lined paper increased legibility over unlined paper, there was no difference between wide-ruled and narrow-ruled paper in terms of legibility. However, an additional study concerned with first graders found more accurate letter strokes using wide-lined paper, so it appears reasonable to use that type of paper when children are being introduced to printing.[18] Second graders who are still printing do not, however, need the wide-lined paper.[19]

When beginning writers are ready to use pencils, teachers should recall that children appear to write well with standard adult pencils, felt-tip pens, and ballpoint pens; they do not write better when using the beginner's oversized pencils. Children enjoy the variety of writing tools available to them, and they should be encouraged to experiment. Anything that adds to the interest and enthusiasm of girls and boys as they learn this new handwriting skill should be encouraged.[20]

Once children have learned how to write the manuscript alphabet, the first writing they wish to complete is that of their names. The purpose is significant and readily achieved. They repeat the writing often, whenever they must sign drawings or paintings, label personal possessions, or mark worksheets. Many teachers prepare individual name cards in manuscript writing so that each child has a guide to keep on his or her desk or table for reference at all times.

Guiding Rules

When introducing the manuscript alphabet shown in Figure 7.1, the lowercase and uppercase (or capital) letters should be presented together, one or two letters at a time. Letters that are similar should be introduced together, such as *o* and *c, v* and *w,* and *m* and *n.*

The letters of the manuscript alphabet vary widely in difficulty. The ten easiest letters for first-grade children are *l, o, L, O, H, D, i, v, I,* and *X;* the most difficult letters are *q, g, p, y, j, m, k, U, a* and *G.* Uppercase letters are usually easier than lowercase letters for pupils to write.

The classroom teacher should model through chalkboard, chart, and paper writing six areas of the manuscript style:

Alignment

All letters must rest on the baseline. There should also be an evenness of the letters along their tops with letters of the same size having even heights.

Size and Proportion

Maximum letters extend the full space from the baseline to headline and include all uppercase letters and the "tall" lowercase letters. All other lowercase letters (except *t*) extend from the baseline to the midline. The lowercase *t,* the only intermediate letter in manuscript writing, extends from the baseline to halfway between the midline and the headline.

Spacing

The most difficult element in manuscript writing for many children is spacing. Pupils should space words four fingers apart for chalkboard writing, two fingers for newsprint, and one finger for first attempts on ruled paper. The width of an *o* is proper spacing when the size of writing has been reduced. Circular letters (such as *a, b,* and *d*) are placed closely together, but vertical letters (such as *i* and *l*) are placed farther apart.

Figure 7.1.
Manuscript
Handwriting Alphabet.

Letter Formation

Because this is the core of the writing program, beginning writers are more concerned with letter formation than with any other aspect of legibility.

All letters are made with circles and straight lines. Vertical lines of a letter are formed before the horizontal lines, and movements go from left to right. All vertical and all slant lines start at the top. Strokes within a letter are made separately and touch each other.

Circles or parts of circles made counterclockwise begin at the two o'clock position and proceed to the left. Circles or parts of circles made clockwise, however, begin at the ten o'clock position and proceed to the right.

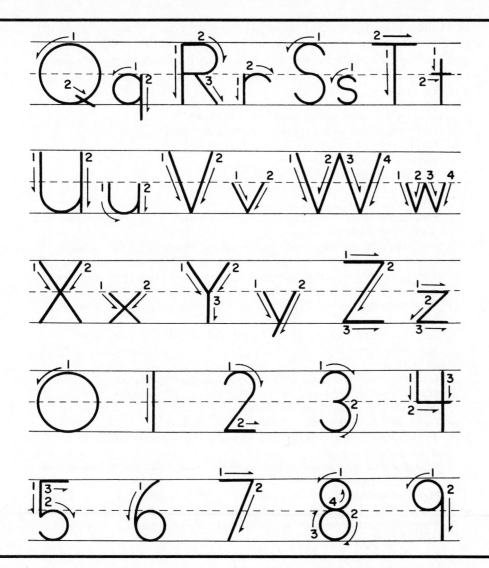

There should be no slant because manuscript letters are vertical.

Slant

The evenness, smoothness, and thickness of the pencil or pen line are important. Sometimes the writing instrument is held improperly and a heavy line results. Sometimes the line is too light because the instrument itself is too hard or too fine.

Line Quality

Some children learn best when information is introduced through a single modality or when one modality is dominant. They can be labeled auditory learners, visual learners, or kinesthetic learners. A handwriting curriculum that relies on each of the three educationally relevant modalities would include the following list of objectives:

1. Auditory (with oral directions, letter name, or strokes)
   a. Told letter names, writes uppercase manuscript letters
   b. Told letter names, writes lowercase manuscript letters
   c. Given letter sound, writes letter
   d. Told letter names, says letter strokes
   e. Told numeral names, writes numerals *1–30*
   f. Told number names, writes number words *one–ten*
   g. Presented with oral directions, writes uppercase manuscript letters grouped by similarity of strokes
   h. Presented with oral directions, writes lowercase letters grouped by similarity of strokes
   i. Told names of punctuation marks, writes punctuation marks: period, comma, question mark, exclamation mark, quotation marks
   j. Told letter names, writes without reversal letters that are often reversed: *b-d, p-g-q*
   k. Told words, writes without reversal words that are often reversed: *on-no, was-saw*
2. Visual (with model)
   a. Presented with letter models, writes uppercase manuscript letters
   b. Presented with letter models, writes lowercase manuscript letters
   c. Presented with numeral models, writes numerals *1–30*
   d. Presented with models, writes number words *one–ten*
   e. Presented with letter models, writes without reversal letters that are often reversed: *b-d, p-g-q*
   f. Presented with word models, writes without reversal words that are often reversed: *on-no, was-saw*
   g. Presented with letter models, writes uppercase letters grouped by similarity of strokes
   h. Presented with letter models, writes lowercase letters grouped by similarity of strokes
   i. Presented with models, writes punctuation marks: period, comma, question mark, exclamation mark, quotation marks
3. Kinesthetic (tracing, motioning, chalkboard)
   a. Presented with example, traces or motions in air uppercase letters grouped by similarity of strokes
   b. Presented with example, traces or motions in air lowercase letters grouped by similarity of strokes
   c. Presented with example, traces or motions in air numerals[21]

**Functional Use of
Manuscript Skills**

In a modern handwriting program the teacher should develop many purposes for which the pupils need to write. Instruction in manuscript writing must not become an exercise period set aside for meaningless drill.

Primary pupils can be encouraged to label exhibits and displays in the classroom. With ballpoint or marking pens, even first graders can make posters and flashcards. They can then prepare picture captions, keep weather reports, and send notes to parents about school activities. Children can write verses, invitations, stories, letters of thanks, and messages for greeting cards. On the chalkboard they can copy the daily program and other announcements, including classroom news.

Teachers must realize that instruction in printing can eventually accomplish ten goals for children: ability in visual discrimination, awareness that words are composed of letters, awareness that letters stand for sounds, understanding of *same* and *different* applied to letters, knowledge of letter names, understanding of the left-to-right orientation of print, understanding of "beginning of a word," understanding of "beginning sound," awareness that the writing (spelling) of a word is related to its pronunciation, and knowledge of some letter-sound correspondences.[22]

Traditional Cursive Handwriting

Cursive handwriting is usually introduced in late second grade or third grade with grade three being by far the more popular throughout the United States. Research has shown that although the time of transition does not affect grade-to-grade progress, it is a factor influencing children's handwriting performance: Late transition is associated with rapid writing; early transition is associated with legible handwriting. Some research also supports the idea that second and third graders make a smoother transition than do fourth graders or older children. Finally, poor printers do not necessarily become poor writers.

Cursive (or running) writing is not faster, easier, or more legible. And because the adult world generally accepts printing, it is tradition, not research, that demands the transition from printing to cursive handwriting.[23]

The cursive style involves four performance tasks. First, children must learn to habitually turn the paper in front of them. Second, they must keep the nonwriting hand out of the way, at the top of the sheet, for easy paper shifting. Third, they must slant their writing. Finally, they must learn to slide their pens or pencils laterally to join the cursive letters.

Readiness

Students arrive at the threshold of advanced writing readiness at varying times. Because neither chronological age nor grade placement is a reliable index, a teacher must adapt instruction and plan flexibly.

A group can be successfully introduced to the cursive style when most of its members are

1. Children who want to write in the cursive style.
2. Children who are unconsciously starting to join manuscript letters.
3. Children who can write all the manuscript letters from memory and do it well.
4. Children who can copy a selection in manuscript at a rate varying from twenty to forty-five letters per minute.

5. Children who are able to reduce the size of their manuscript letters.
6. Children who have attained adequate physical development so that there is muscular coordination of the arm, head, and fingers.
7. Children who can read writing. A definite relationship exists between the ability to read print and to read cursive writing. Pupils who have developed adequate skill in reading manuscript style will require little instructional emphasis on reading cursive style. Those who have experienced difficulty in learning to read print will need more attention. One answer may be to postpone the addition of cursive writing until enough growth has occurred in reading manuscript. Another solution is to precede the introduction of cursive writing with the reading of material written cursively.

Finally, one word of caution from recent research findings: It is possible that teachers should move all the students to cursive handwriting at the same time because the delayed children could lose motivation and self-esteem while not receiving adequate handwriting lessons.[24]

Comparison to Printing

The outstanding difference between traditional cursive and manuscript writing is sliding laterally to join letters. Cursive writers lift their pens and pencils from the paper upon completion of each word. Printers lift their writing tools after each letter.

The basic shapes used in cursive writing are slant strokes, connecting strokes, and ovals. In manuscript writing, they are circles and straight lines.

The letters *i* and *j* are dotted and the letter *t* is crossed after the complete word has been written in cursive style. In printing, the dotting and crossing occur immediately after the letters are formed.

The uppercase letters in the cursive alphabet always differ considerably from the lowercase letters. However, nearly one-third of the manuscript alphabet is much the same for uppercase and lowercase letters—*c, o, p, s, v, w, x, z.*

In cursive writing, the spacing between letters is controlled by the slant and manner of making connective strokes. In printing it is determined by the shapes of the letters. Cursive letters shown in Figure 7.2 differ from book print, but manuscript letters closely resemble such print.

Guiding Rules

The classroom teachers should model through paper, chalkboard, or chart writing six areas of the cursive style.

Alignment

Every letter rests on a baseline, whether the line is visible or not.

Size and Proportion

All twenty-six uppercase letters are of maximum height. All lowerloop letters (whether uppercase or lowercase) take a full descender space below the baseline. All upperloop letters extend a full space from the baseline to the headline.

Slant

The downstrokes or slant strokes of the letters slant uniformly and in the same direction. Cursive writing, which has a consistent forward slant, is easier to read than writing that slants too much or is irregular. A slant between 60 and 70 degrees is regarded as the most acceptable.

Figure 7.2. Cursive Handwriting Alphabet.

Aa Bb Cc

Dd Ee Ff

Gg Hh Ii

Jj Kk Ll

Mm Nn Oo

Pp Qq Rr

Figure 7.2. (cont.)

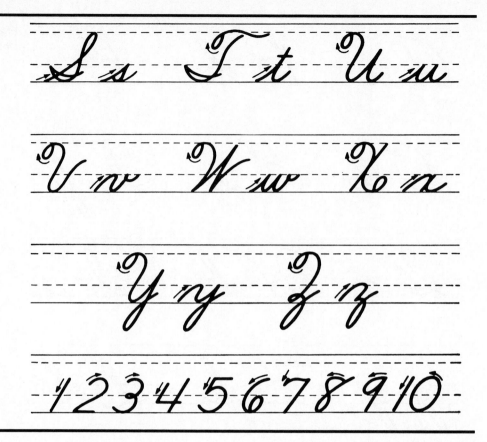

Spacing

Between each letter there is an even distribution of sufficient blank space. Between each word there is the space of one letter.

Letter Formation

All the cursive letters are comprised of overcurves and undercurves. They originate from the oval and are combined with slant strokes of other curves. There are *loop letters* (such as *j* and *p*) whose up-strokes must curve and whose downstrokes must be straight. There are *retraced letters* (such as *m* and *n*) that must not become loops. There are *rounded turn letters* (such as *x*, *y*, and *z*) that must not be pointed. There are *closed letters* (such as *a* and *d*) that must not overlap.

When either the undercurve or the overcurve is made hastily, however, it tends to become merely a straight stroke and difficult to read. When the undercurve becomes straight, *e* becomes *i*, and the *r* and *s* become overcurves. When the overcurve is made straight:

a becomes u   n becomes u
d becomes il   o becomes u
g becomes y or ij   v becomes u
m becomes w   y becomes ij

Figure 7.3. The Most Difficult Cursive Letters and Numerals Constitute Half of All the Handwriting Illegibilities.

	Right	Wrong		Right	Wrong
a like o	*a*	*o*	n like u	*n*	*u*
a like u	*a*	*u*	o like a	*o*	*a*
a like ci	*a*	*a*	r like i	*r*	*i*
b like li	*b*	*b*	r like n	*r*	*n*
d like cl	*d*	*d*	t like l	*t*	*t*
e closed	*e*	*e*	t with cross above	*t*	*t*
h like li	*h*	*h*	5 like 3	*5*	*5*
i like e with no dot	*i*	*e*	6 like 0	*6*	*6*
m like w	*m*	*w*	7 like 9	*7*	*7*

Source: Adapted from California State Series *Handwriting Made Easy*, Part III. Sacramento: State Board of Education, 1963.

Some problem areas are shown in Figure 7.3.

The most difficult letter is the letter *r*. Its malformations account for more than 10 percent of all illegibilities. Other cursive letters that pupils often malform are *h, i, k, p,* and *z*.

Joining

Joining the cursive letters is as important as forming the letters. The four letters that give the most trouble in joining are *b, o, v,* and *w,* for they connect the next letter at the top and not on the line. These difficult combinations of overcurves and undercurves are shown in Figure 7.4.

By the sixth grade, the teacher may introduce joinings of uppercase to lowercase letters. There are seventeen uppercase letters that have a natural joining finish and so must be taught as joinable capitals. The remaining letters—*D, F, L, O, P, Q, T, V* and *W*—do not readily permit joining.

Functional Use of Cursive Skills

Repetitive drill can quickly dull children's desires to improve their handwriting techniques. Therefore wise teachers build a program that encourages all students to write primarily to communicate ideas and feelings.

Middle- and upper-grade children can use cursive handwriting for preparing stories, poetry, book reports, and invitations. They can take notes, make outlines, keep vocabulary lists, and plan the school newspaper. They can keep

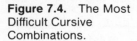

Figure 7.4. The Most Difficult Cursive Combinations.

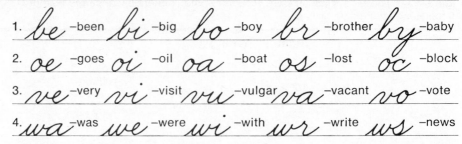

1. *be* –been *bi* –big *bo* –boy *br* –brother *by* –baby
2. *oe* –goes *oi* –oil *oa* –boat *os* –lost *oc* –block
3. *ve* –very *vi* –visit *vu* –vulgar *va* –vacant *vo* –vote
4. *wa* –was *we* –were *wi* –with *wr* –write *ws* –news

minutes of club meetings or compile a class directory. Students can write letters to government offices or to private firms asking for information or arranging study trips. They can write up interviews with resource speakers or class visitors. Through routine but significant assignments, children are made aware of the many purposes for acquiring cursive skills.

Alternative Forms of Handwriting

For teachers who do not wish to present the traditional handwriting forms to their classes, there are now available some alternate forms of the Roman alphabet for beginning writers.

D'Nealian Handwriting

Developed by teacher–principal Donald Neal Thurber, this alternative form was introduced nationally in 1978. In the D'Nealian method, children begin by printing in slanted script that resembles cursive writing. They learn to make twenty-one of the lowercase manuscript letters with a continuous stroke, retracing at times as they would in traditional cursive. The five exceptions requiring special introductory lessons are the dotted letters *i* and *j* and the crossed letters *f, t,* and *x*.

Since children slant the manuscript forms from the very start, no new alignment procedures are needed for transition to cursive. With the exception of *f, r, s, v,* and *z,* manuscript letters become cursive letters as soon as the children add simple joining strokes. Whether cursive or manuscript, however, all uppercase letters are delayed until all the lowercase letters of the same style have been mastered. Transition to cursive can occur as early as late first grade or early second grade. D'Nealian handwriting has proved to be equally useful for mainstream, average, and above-average children. Transfer students familiar with traditional manuscript are said to "shift unconsciously" into the D'Nealian models after sufficient exposure to the new style. Sample alphabets are shown in Figure 7.5.

Italic Handwriting

An alternative of special interest to educators concerned with teaching children two systems of handwriting is italic handwriting because boys and girls need to learn only one system. Developed in Italy during the Renaissance, it presents a modified single form approach that is neither manuscript nor cursive. The shapes of the letters (both uppercase and lowercase) resemble the shapes of printed letters.

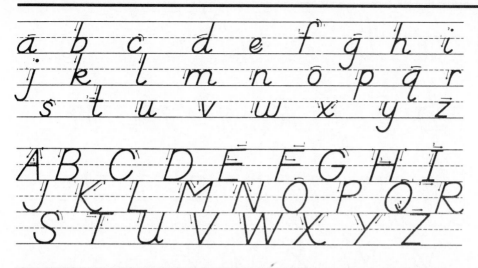

Figure 7.5a. One Alternative Form of Handwriting: D'Nealian™ Manuscript Alphabet

D'Nealian™ Cursive Alphabet

Figure 7.5b. D'Nealian™ Cursive Alphabet

D'Nealian™ Numbers

Figure 7.6. Another Alternative Form of Handwriting: Basic Italic.

Source: Reprinted from HANDWRITING RESOURCE BOOK, GRADES 1–7, Ministry of Education, Province of British Columbia, Canada, 1981, p. 53. Used with permission.

Whereas traditional lowercase manuscript letters are called ball-and-stick letters because they are based on circle shapes (and straight lines), lowercase italic letters are based on egg shapes (and slanted lines). The system is therefore sometimes referred to as egg-and-stick printing.

Once the children have mastered the techniques of producing individual letters, they can give their handwriting cursive (running) flow by adding entry and exit strokes (called joins) and by learning how to space the resulting words.

Italic handwriting has earned the approval of public school officials in Oregon and other states and in at least one Canadian province (British Columbia), where it is referred to as loop-free cursive. Sample alphabets are shown in Figure 7.6.

Research

Few studies have been published regarding D'Nealian and italic handwriters because these alternate forms of handwriting have only recently been widely disseminated.

Teachers—and concerned parents—interested in possible difficulties that children trained in the D'Nealian method might encounter when making the transition to cursive should be relieved with the findings of two studies.[25] In the first, students in the first grade produced initial cursive letters of similar quality, whether they had learned to print using D'Nealian or the traditional manuscript approach. In the second, children in the D'Nealian group reversed fewer cursive letters than writers in the traditional manuscript group, although their work was not considered as legible.

In another study, the efforts of primary-grade children who had been taught italic writing were compared with the efforts of their primary peer group that had been taught the traditional manuscript writing followed by the traditional cursive approach.[26] After three years, and on a speed test at the end of the third grade, the italic group produced more letters during a two-minute time span than did the comparison group. Furthermore, in the area of legibility, the italic group deviated only one half as much from their letter models as did the comparison group.

Typewriting Skill

Once children have reasonably learned the handwriting skill, they are ready to acquire an addition to handwriting by learning how to typewrite. The teaching of typing skills to elementary age students has been revitalized with the introduction of microcomputers into American society at large.

The keyboard of the microcomputer and the keyboard of a typewriter are almost identical, except for a few function keys (such as CONTROL), so the ability to use a typewriter is a definite advantage when working with computers. Children can then focus their cognitive energies on conceptual matters rather than on the mechanics of punching keys. In fact, a major obstacle to using word processors for teaching composition is the students' inability to type. However, children must receive formal typing instruction and learn the correct methods from the very beginning, because typewriting is a skill.

Learning how to use the keyboard is an early step toward computer literacy even among kindergarten children who can receive assistance from an older student. (© Jean-Claude Lejeune.)

Typing and the Language Arts

Typewriting has recently been proven to improve reading, composition, punctuation, spelling, and grammar among children six to twelve years old.[27] Earlier, learning-disabled students between seven and ten years of age who used typewriters showed significant gains in reading ability over their peers who had completed exercises using handwriting.[28] Researchers have explained the gains—and the advantages of typing—by stressing that the task of typing is easier than handwriting at the beginning stages because the child merely has to point; also, typing is more responsive and less threatening than handwriting and therefore promotes more positive attitudes about learning to write and to read.

Consequently, according to Balajthy, typing should be used as one method for the teaching of language skills.[29] To develop touch-typing ability, typing drills are necessary, as is an emphasis on such positive typing habits as a proper posture (in order to avoid muscle fatigue during lengthy keyboard sessions) and the avoidance of looking at the keys. Children should begin with the "home keys" (A, S, D, F, and J, K, L, semicolon), practice until finger placement is well established, and then move on to the other keys, one by one. Typing of isolated words can start once the students have mastered the home keys, using words composed of those seven letters. The four vowel letters found in the top line of the keyboard should be taught after the "home keys" (which include the fifth vowel) so that many words can be typed by the girls and boys.

When all the letters have been mastered, students can start to use the keyboard for many communication activities. Compositions written in class or at home, for example, can be typed and later photocopied and placed in a class book. Spelling lists can also be typed for future review. Articles can be prepared for the school paper. The important goal is to move the students from an emphasis on motor tasks concerned with finger movements to a stress on meaningful language use during class assignments and during the completion of written personal interests.

Teaching Typing Skills

The teaching of typing is a highly structured series of lessons, particularly in the early stages in which properly sequenced drill and practice activities are essential. Teachers must be both capable and willing to devote the time to teach students patiently.

Beginning instruction is most efficiently handled on a large-group or whole-class basis. In most elementary schools, only one or two microcomputers are available in each classroom, and typing instruction is better done outside the regular classroom in an area with many typing stations. However, a limited amount of practice can be completed on the classroom micros because typing on computer keyboards is not as noisy as on standard typewriters.

Other suggestions for typing instruction include the following:

1. Recording oral presentations of typing drills on cassette for future use.
2. Using vocabulary and spelling words for targets during drills.
3. Ordering printed cardboard keyboards for practice drills.
4. Grading student typing work separately for accuracy and speed in order to give better feedback to the typists.[30]

The teacher may also wish to examine one of the typewriting textbooks especially designed for elementary students. A sample lesson from one of these is found in Figure 7.7.

Providing for Children with Special Needs

Indirectly related to the whole area of self-evaluation, motivation, and pupil interest is individualized learning. Although whole-class instruction still prevails in the majority of schools, efforts have been begun to meet individual differences in handwriting needs. Individualization is most effective before the students' handwriting habits have been fairly well established—probably before the fourth grade. Sample lessons promoting individualized learning in handwriting are listed in Figure 7.8.

Every teacher must view a handwriting program in terms of satisfying individual pupils with varying needs. Most of them must be grouped together temporarily to overcome a common deficit. A few other students will require instruction for longer periods of time. Chiefly these are children with learning disabilities and left-handed writers.

Figure 7.7. Sample
Typewriting Lesson for
the Elementary School.

LESSON 7

The Full Alphabet

Hooray, hooray, you finish the alphabet
today.
　　There are only three letters left to
learn—"C," "X," and "Z."
　　They are all in the bottom row.
　　Be sure that you learn to hit them only
with the proper finger, as shown in the
chart.
　　Remember—do not look at the keys
when you type; look only at the chart.

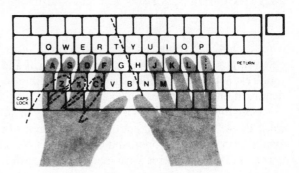

Now, without looking at the keys, copy the following exercise.

DCDCDCDCDCDCDCDCDCDC
SXSXSXSXSXSXSXSXSXSX
AZAZAZAZAZAZAZAZAZAZ

CLO CLO CLO CLO CLO CLO
FGHJ FGHJ FGHJ FGHJ FGHJ

LOSW LOSW LOSW LOSW LOSW
PAQ PAQ PAQ PAQ PAQ PAQ

EXY EXY EXY EXY EXY EXY
ZKM ZKM ZKM ZKM ZKM ZKM

JIR JIR JIR JIR JIR JIR
FTY FTY FTY FTY FTY FTY

HEW HEW HEW HEW HEW HEW
ZJ: ZJ: ZJ: ZJ: ZJ: ZJ:

IT IT IT IT IT IT IT IT
OF OF OF OF OF OF OF OF

QUH QUH QUH QUH QUH QUH
SEL SEL SEL SEL SEL SEL

SXJM SXJM SXJM SXJM
FVRH FVRH FVRH FVRH

READ READ READ READ
NOW NOW NOW NOW NOW

COP COP COP COP COP
XKN XKN XKN XKN XKN

HYZ HYZ HYZ HYZ HYZ
BVD BVD BVD BVD BVD

Type your own name five times.

This is a great day.
We are now using all the letter keys.

Sample Creative Lessons in Handwriting

1. Children each bring in five handwritten envelopes that came through the mail to their home. They practice writing the addresses on sheets of paper or at the chalkboard. Later, each receives five blank business-sized envelopes with address lines on which to write the final copies. Older children should be able to match the cursive or manuscript style used on the original cancelled envelopes. Younger students should bring in only envelopes using printed letters. (This activity adapts readily to typing practice.)
2. Boys and girls can write with finger paints or with oil paints and brushes on large sheets of butcher paper. Although this exercise is especially valuable during introductory lessons in manuscript or cursive, it also continues as a helpful review activity done periodically after writing skills have been learned.
3. Intermediate writers can take turns leading a small-group handwriting lesson and using an overhead projector. Under the supervision of the teacher, they do their cursive lettering on clear plastic sheets or on the plastic roll provided with some machines. Because the overhead can be used in a lighted room, the other children in the group can follow the leader easily, practicing difficult letter combinations or words targeted for improvement. Peer tutoring can be a motivational change from adult instruction.
4. Girls and boys each bring in a short favorite recipe for the Class Cookbook. The teacher checks each one for accuracy before the children begin to practice copying their contribution in printing, cursive, or typewriter writing. Sufficient copies of each recipe are later run off so that the class can assemble and decorate individual booklets.

Figure 7.8.
Handwriting Lessons.

Children With Learning Disabilities

Problem areas in handwriting have been identified as visual-perception input, visual-spatial relationships, visual-motor ability, and short-term visual recall.[31] For a learning-disabled child, there may be a deficit in one while the other areas are developing normally. For example, a learning-disabled student can have good short-term visual recall and still have inadequate visual-spatial relationships. A checklist of possible handwriting difficulties for a learning-disabled child is shown in Figure 7.9.

Visual-perception input means the ability to perceive a configuration. Boys and girls who perceive a shape incorrectly focus the motor response incorrectly, and thus their writing consists of twisted letters, inconsistently reversed letters, and letters slanted diagonally toward the line. Remediation for visual-perception-input difficulty starts with the use of cardboard form boards to help the children visually recognize like and unlike shapes. They are given one of the boards and a variety of cutout shapes and parquetry blocks to place on that board. Later, they can sort the blocks and shapes into piles together with shaped templates.

Figure 7.9. Teacher's Checklist of Major Areas of Handwriting Difficulty.

A handwriting sample should be obtained by having the child copy at least three lines of writing either from the board or from another paper. The example to be copied from should not exceed 18 letters or spaces per line. The child should be instructed to copy the example exactly.

If these things are observed	the child experiences difficulty in:			
	visual-perception input	visual-spatial relationships	visual-motor ability	visual recall
Parts of letters not connected	x			
Shape of letters distorted	x			
Reversed letters*	x			
Upside down letters*	x			
Twisted letters*	x			
Unequal spacing of letters		x		
Unequal size of letters		x		
Letters not on the line		x		
Heavy use of the pencil			x	
Light use of the pencil			x	
Tense grip while writing			x	
Pencil held in fist grip			x	
Wavering lines			x	
Deterioration of letter shape as repeated across line			x	
Letters copied out of sequence				x
Letters omitted or words omitted				x

*These must be constant and not just an occasional learning error.

Source: Reprinted from CORRECTING HANDWRITING PROBLEMS, Lexington Public Schools, Lexington, Massachusetts, 1974, p. 18. Used with permission.

Along with this exercise, the boys and girls also match shapes to form designs or pictures. Finally, they advance to learning the actual letter shapes visually and kinesthetically by using sandpaper, clay or playdough, crayons, tagboard, and writing paper.

Visual-spatial relationships develop from the ability of children to relate themselves to space and then to relate two objects in space to each other. Students with a weakness in this area of handwriting have difficulty placing letters on the line, organizing the letters on the paper, and positioning the spaces correctly. They often produce a disproportion in the sizes of their letters. Remediation in the visual-spatial area demands that heavy dark lines or colored lines be drawn or printed on writing paper to visually accentuate the spatial orientation of the letters. Another technique is to color the three writing spaces blue, green, and brown and then to designate the letters as being "placed in the sky," "placed on the grass," or "placed under the ground." Later, such lines are gradually lightened until boys and girls can properly place the letters without guide lines.

Children experiencing difficulty in *visual-motor ability* produce lines of writing that are either very light or very heavy. They will often take an unusually long time to form one letter or to complete one writing lesson. Although they have been taught how to hold a pencil properly, they either hold it so tensely that they make holes in the paper or so lightly that their letters are barely visible. Such students will try to make many erasures because they realize that they are not making the letter shapes properly. Remediation begins at the chalkboard: A pupil is given a piece of chalk in each hand and told to draw parallel lines, then large squares, and finally large circles with both hands while simultaneously saying the directions of the movements being made. Then the child gradually traces pictures, traces letters, and finally writes letters with crayons.

Because the fourth area involves visual imagery, a problem in *short-term visual recall* occurs when children have difficulty transferring letters or words from one paper to another or from the chalkboard to their papers. Letters or words may be omitted or letters may be copied out of sequence. Remediation requires teaching visual sequencing by matching a group of manipulative objects with a row of pictures of the same objects. The same process can also be used with parquetry blocks. To help children copy items in proper sequence, a cardboard strip (the width of three writing spaces) can be used when copying from another sheet of paper. The cardboard strip is drawn along the line of print that is being copied, exposing only one letter at a time. Gradually, more letters can be uncovered at once until the strip becomes unnecessary.

When teaching cursive handwriting to learning-disabled children, it has been recommended that one lowercase letter be taught during a fifteen-minute period each day. The two easiest letters are *i* and *t*, with the next easiest being *b, e, f, g, j, k, l, p, r, s, u,* and *w.* By writing words like *ill* and *bit,* the teacher can illustrate words that are somewhat alike in both cursive and manuscript writing.

Left-Handed Children

The one form of individual differences that appears most often during hand-writing instruction is left-handedness. About one in ten children is left-handed, with boys slightly in the majority.[32] Although some research states that left-handed writers produce less legible writing, other studies report no real difference and point to instructional strategies as accounting for differences in legibility.

Teachers must realize that, even though evidence for a genetic base for handedness remains positive, no direct link has been established. The development of preferred handedness can also be affected by such factors as cultural and social pressures, family preference, educational practices, specific brain damage, and the prevalence of certain types of devices more suitable for one hand than the other. Even today many European schools demand that all students learn to write with the right hand.

Consistency in the use of one writing hand is important from the beginning. If either the left or right hand is used without strain, teachers and parents can encourage use of that hand. Children who shift readily from one hand to the other, however, should be encouraged to use the right hand. Teachers must always remember that the brain determines the hand that is used, and it is not wise to change the handedness of girls and boys. To do so may lead to psychomotor confusion, learning difficulties, delayed manual skill, and impaired confidence.

Teachers should realize that left-handed persons seem to be endowed with a negative genetic package, according to research completed recently at Harvard University by Geschwind and Behan.[33] Questionnaires answered by 500 strong left-handers and 900 right-handers showed that left-handers had about ten times the rate of learning disabilities and nearly three times the rate of autoimmune diseases (such as multiple sclerosis and myasthenia gravis) as right-handers. Furthermore, compared to the relatives of the right-handed samples, even relatives of left-handers had three times the rate of learning disabilities and autoimmune diseases! Lipson therefore recommends a friendly interview with each parent of a left-handed child in order to fill in missing answers concerning the student's medical history.[34]

Kindergarten and first-grade teachers should carefully administer individual measures of handedness and eyedness to assess child preferences. Such informal tests involve familiar materials adapted to the age and development of the children. Teachers should repeat each stage of a test a sufficient number of times to detect the dominant hand or eye. They must remember never to hand the materials to the students during the dominant hand tests.

Dominant Hand Tests

Sorting Colored Cards

The teacher cuts assorted colored papers about the size of playing cards and shuffles them. He or she places a pile (of at least twenty) of these cards where the child can reach them and then tells the child to get the cards and sort them according to colors. The teacher observes which hand the pupil uses in picking up the cards and in sorting them.

On the table are the large pieces of a sturdy puzzle, preferably a wooden one. The child is asked to assemble the puzzle.

Putting a Puzzle Together

A hand puppet sleeve is placed on the table and the child is asked to participate in puppet play. The teacher observes to see on which hand the student puts the puppet.

Playing with a Hand Puppet

The child picks up a ball and then bounces it ten times, catching it on each re-bounce. Since only one hand can be used, the pupil's preference is easy to note.

Bouncing a Ball

The teacher observes the child during snack time, at the lunch table, or in a dramatic play situation in which the child must use a spoon. The dominant hand is quickly discovered.

Holding a Spoon

The teacher padlocks a cupboard in the classroom and places the key on the desk. The child is asked to take the key, unlock the padlock, and bring one object from the cupboard. He or she is observed unlocking the padlock and picking up the object.

Unlocking a Cupboard

On the table are an old magazine and a small pair of right-handed scissors. The child is asked to cut out a picture. A repeat test with the other hand will show whether or not there is a preferred hand. The left-handed child will have more difficulty than the right-handed one.

Cutting Pictures

Dominant Eye Tests

In the center of a card or sheet of stiff paper, the teacher cuts a hole about one inch in diameter. The student holds the card in both hands with arms extended and is asked to sight (with both eyes open) a distant object through the hole. Then one eye is covered. If the child can still see the object, the dominant or preferred eye is the uncovered eye. If he or she cannot see the object, it is apparent that the dominant eye is covered. The teacher should have the child try the test from various positions because one trial may not be sufficient.

Hole-in-Card Test

The student sights a distant object with both eyes open and then points fingers at the object. Then she or he closes (or covers) the left eye, and if the fingers are still in line with the object, the child is right-eyed. When she or he closes (or covers) the right eye, the child is left-eyed if the fingers are still in line with the object.

Aiming Test

On the table is a long mailing tube and an object the student has not seen before in the classroom. Asked to look at the object through the tube and describe it, he or she will use the preferred eye to sight the object.

Simple Tube Test

Advanced Tube Test	Holding a long mailing tube about six inches from both eyes, the pupil looks through it at a distant object in the room. Both eyes remain open. The right eye is now covered, and if the child continues to see the object, she or he is left-eyed. Then the left eye is covered, and if the student continues to see the object, he or she is right-eyed.

Guiding Left-Handed Writers

With proper instruction of left-handed and right-handed children, no significant difference will appear in handwriting performance. Each teacher should guide left-handed writers to

1. Learn first the four manuscript letters that begin with a stroke to the left, because these develop muscular control most readily: *a, d, g,* and *o.* Then, develop coordination in the forward motion from left to right by practicing the manuscript letters *b, e, f, i, l, r, t, u,* and *w.*
2. Realize that they can use the manuscript style indefinitely if they find that it is easier to write.
3. Use a writing tool that does not smudge, such as a ball-point pen with an extended tip.
4. Hold back about one and one-half inches on the writing tool so that they can see over or around the writing hand. (A thin strip of masking tape can be put around the instrument at the point where it should be held.) They should grasp the tool lightly.
5. Sit at the left half of the writing surface, which should be slightly lower than that for right-handed children to aid in seeing what is being written.
6. Use pushing strokes rather than pulling strokes.
7. Use the chalkboard often. Left-handed writers are especially comfortable if they can stand at the right end of the chalkboard. However, they need two spaces—one in which to stand and one in which to write.

Left-handed students should be separated for instructional purposes from right-handed students. This is important because they will write in reverse if they interpret directions as demonstrated by a right-handed teacher in the routine teaching strategy. By producing such mirror writing, they are correctly interpreting only visual directions or directions given to the right-handed students. The teacher should group left-handers together for instruction so that these children can help one another with paper position and letter formation. It is important that left-handed students have opportunities to observe other left-handed writers. It has been recommended also that if the classroom teacher cannot model left-handed techniques, he or she should invite a parent, an aide, or another teacher to do so.[35]

Evaluation of Student Progress

Throughout the literature, it is stressed that a crucial component of any handwriting program is the self-evaluation of letter formation, which places the responsibility for any needed changes on the *student.* Nevertheless, approximately 70 percent of the schools actually assess handwriting—and issue report card

Group discussion of the qualities of good handwriting may precede individual goal-setting by the students. (© James L. Shaffer.)

grades—on the basis of *teacher* observation. Because a child may repeat the same mistakes over and over again until poor-quality handwriting becomes a habit, the teacher must be a good evaluator of learner achievement in handwriting.

Presumably, such evaluation occurs individually or on a small-group basis. The teacher who understands that growth patterns naturally vary will not insist that every child in the grade meet identical standards of handwriting achievement. Some students who make appreciable progress during the year still will not write as well as others who have average ability for the grade. To force such slow learners to meet a kind of standardized norm is unfair and promotes apathy. Children who exhibit very little improvement, as well as those who show unusual growth, may be progressing consistently with their rate of overall development.

Because the aims of the handwriting program are legibility and fluency, evaluation of each child's progress demands that these two factors be measured objectively. The only form of rating that has meaning for the young writer occurs when he or she and the teacher set up goals for the improvement of personal writing skill. Studies have shown that students have difficulty judging the quality of their work, and especially so if they are poor handwriters; thus class or group discussion on the qualities of good writing may precede the time for personal conferences and goal setting. Evaluation then becomes an ongoing technique as well as a long-term device to measure growth.

Children and teachers are only occasionally concerned with the secondary goal of a handwriting program, which is the rate of writing. In those instances where speed has become an issue, it can be easily measured by having the students write a familiar passage for a specific number of minutes. Because speed

Figure 7.10.
Handwriting Checklist
for Self-Evaluation.

Manuscript (Or Cursive)
Handwriting Check List

Element	Child Rating	Teacher Verification
Alignment	_____	_____
Letter Formation	_____	_____
Line Quality	_____	_____
Size and Proportion	_____	_____
Slant	_____	_____
Spacing	_____	_____

is generally expressed in letters per minute, it can be readily determined by dividing the total number of letters written by the number of minutes allowed. The average speed for manuscript writing in the second grade, for example, is about thirty letters per minute, whereas the standard speed for cursive writing in the fifth grade is about sixty letters per minute. Beginners in either style write more slowly, of course, than advanced pupils.

The following is a possible guide in determining speed attainments in cursive writing by grade level.[36]

Grade	Letters Per Minute	Letters Per Line
2	30	14–16
3	40	16–20
4	50	20–22
5	60	22–25
6	67	25–28

Legibility

Legibility in handwriting involves alignment, letter formation, line quality, size and proportion, slant, and spacing. These elements, listed in Figure 7.10, may be informally measured in manuscript and cursive writing in several ways. Evaluation and correction of cursive handwriting problems in particular are shown in Figures 7.11 and 7.12, respectively.

Alignment

The evenness of the letters along the baseline and along the tops of the letters should be compared. All letters of the same size should be of an even height. The child can draw a light line horizontally along the tops of all the maximum letters, another line along the tops of all minimum letters, and finally a third line along the tops of the intermediate letters and compare the results. Then, with a ruler, he or she can draw a line touching the base of as many of the letters as possible, and determine if this line is the same as the baseline.

Figure 7.11.
Evaluation Sheet of
Student Cursive
Handwriting.

	O.K.	Needs Review
1. Performance observation.		
a. pen or pencil is held properly	☐	☐
b. paper is positioned at a "normal" slant	☐	☐
c. writing posture is acceptable	☐	☐
d. writing speed is acceptable	☐	☐
2. Correct letter formation.		
a. closed letters are closed	☐	☐
b. looped letters are looped	☐	☐
c. stick letters are not loops	☐	☐
d. i's and j's are dotted directly above	☐	☐
e. x's and t's are crossed accurately	☐	☐
f. m's and n's have the correct number of humps	☐	☐
g. all lowercase letters begin on the line (unless they follow b, o, v, or w)	☐	☐
h. b, o, v, and w end above the line	☐	☐
i. all lowercase letters end on the line	☐	☐
j. v's and u's are clearly differentiated	☐	☐
k. connecting strokes of v and y are clearly not ry and ry	☐	☐
l. uppercase letters are correctly or acceptably formed	☐	☐
m. numbers are correctly formed	☐	☐
3. Fluency.		
a. writing is smooth, not choppy	☐	☐
b. pencil pressure appears even	☐	☐
c. words appear to be written as complete units	☐	☐
d. letter connection is smooth	☐	☐
4. Letter size, slant, and spacing.		
a. lowercase letters are uniform size	☐	☐
b. uppercase letters are clearly larger than lowercase letters	☐	☐
c. uppercase letters are uniform in size	☐	☐
d. tail lengths are consistent and do not interfere with letters on the line below	☐	☐
e. tall letters are a consistent height and are clearly taller than other letters	☐	☐
f. writing is not too small or too large	☐	☐
g. slant of letters is acceptable	☐	☐
h. slant of letters is consistent	☐	☐
i. spacing of letters and words is consistent	☐	☐

Figure 7.11. (cont.)

5. Student attitude toward writing
   a. student's opinion of his writing skills ☐ ☐
   b. "writing is hard" ☐ ☐
   c. writes too slowly ☐ ☐
   d. feels good about writing ☐ ☐
6. Overall teacher evaluation.

Teacher Recommendation:

☐ You appear to write smoothly and easily. Your letters are formed correctly. Letter size, slant, and spacing are good. Your writing is neat and legible. It is *not* necessary for you to complete the handwriting exercises.

☐ You appear to write smoothly and easily. You have developed your own writing style which is acceptable, neat and legible. It is *not* necessary for you to complete the handwriting exercises.

☐ You appear to write smoothly and easily. However, your letter formation, neatness, and legibility need some work. Please complete the handwriting exercises.

☐ Writing seems to be difficult for you. You need practice in handwriting skills. Please complete the handwriting exercises.

Reprinted by permission from Lynne R. Ruedy, "Handwriting Instruction," ACADEMIC THERAPY, Vol. 18, 1983, Novato, California, Academic Therapy Publications, pp. 427–428.

Figure 7.12. Correction of Common Cursive Handwriting Problems.

Handwriting is so small that it cannot be read easily.	*in adult proportion*	• Use ruled paper on which a midline appears or rule a midline on standard writing paper. Explain that minimum letters touch the midline. • Practice large writing at the chalkboard. • Give correct models of words, have the student copy them, then evaluate for size. • Identify the problem so that the student is aware of what must be corrected.
When two maximum undercurves are joined (*ll*, *fl*,), letter formation suffers.	*parallel*	• Emphasize that the basic undercurve stroke must be made correctly. • Make a wide undercurve to allow room for the loop that follows. • Make slant strokes parallel to each other.
The height of the lowercase letters is not consistent.	*Write freely*	• Use paper that has a midline and a descender space, or rule a midline on standard paper. • Have the student identify maximum, intermediate, and minimum letters. • Evaluate writing for alignment by drawing a horizontal line across the tops of the letters that are supposed to be of the same size. • Shift paper as the writing progresses.

Figure 7.12. (cont.)

The maximum letters (*b, f, h, k, l*) are made without loops.	*little*	• Demonstrate and explain proper formation of undercurve that begins loop of letter. • Demonstrate and explain proper formation of the slant stroke. • Point out that the top of the letters is rounded and determines the width of the loops.
The slant of the writing is irregular.	*flight*	• Check for correct paper position. • Pull strokes in the proper direction. • Shift paper as writing progresses. • Shift hand to the right as writing progresses. • Evaluate slant by drawing lines through letters to show the angle at which they are made.
When an undercurve joins an overcurve (*in, um,*) the letters are poorly written.	*instrument*	• Show how the undercurve to overcurve is a smooth, flowing stroke. • Explain that the undercurve ending continues up and then quickly overcurves into the downward slant stroke.
The quality of the writing changes within a single word.	*laboratory*	• Shift both the paper and the hand as the writing progresses. The paper moves toward the student, and the hand moves away. • Write in the same area of the paper, roughly a six-inch-diameter circle that is located at the midpoint of the body about ten inches from the edge of the desk. • Do not reach out to write or write very close to the body.
The letters *a, d, g, o, q* are not closed.	*break amount*	• Stress proper beginning strokes. • Write correctly formed model letters on the student's paper, explaining the strokes while the student watches.
Nonlooped letters such as *t, p, i, u, w* are looped and become difficult to read.	*little*	• Demonstrate that there is a pause at the top of these letters. • Encourage the student to write slower because speed causes the loops in the letters. • Pause before making the slant stroke in the letters *a, d, g, i, j, p, q, t, u, w,* and *y*. • Emphasize the retrace in these strokes.
Checkstroke joinings (for example, *br, we*) are poorly made.	*break weather*	• Demonstrate the letters *b, v, o,* and *w* and explain the strokes as you form them. • Use the auditory stroke description "retrace and swing right" as students practice *b, v, o, w*. • Demonstrate correct joinings in which the first letter has a checkstroke. • Point out the letter forms that change when they are preceded by a checkstroke: *br, os*.

Figure 7.12.   (cont.)

Handwriting is so slow that there is no smoothness in the individual letters.	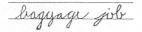	• Encourage students to write letters with smooth and complete motions. • Engage in relaxation exercises before practicing writing. Excessive muscle tension is the cause of slow writing. • Emphasize rhythm rather than alignment or slant. These qualities can be developed later.
Joinings involving overcurves (such as *ga, jo*) are not well made.	*baggage job*	• Show how all overcurve connections cross at the baseline, not above or below it. • Make the overcurve motion continuous. Do not change its direction in mid-stroke. • Check letter formation.

Reprinted by Thomas M. Wasylyk and Michael Milone, Jr., CORRECTIVE TECHNIQUES IN HANDWRITING: CURSIVE, Zaner-Bloser Educational Publishers, Honesdale, PA., Professional Pamphlet Series #12, 1980. Used with permission.

Letter Formation

Manuscript writing consists of horizontal, vertical, and slanted lines and circles and parts of circles. Correct letter models placed adjacent to the child's writing will aid evaluation.

Cursive writing involves two basic motions: the slant and the oval. Because every cursive letter uses either or both motions, the child's letter formations may be evaluated by placing correct letter models near the writing paper. Incidentally, transparent overlays can be used to measure the range of deviations in handwritten letters from given model letters.

Line Quality

Letter line quality is described as the evenness, smoothness, and thickness of the pencil or pen line. Some lines may be too light, some too heavy, and others of varying quality. Light lines may result from writing instruments that are too fine or too hard. Heavy lines occur when the child bears down too heavily on the paper or grips the writing instrument too tightly. Varying line quality results from inconsistent pressure, which in turn is due to fatigue or overly rapid writing.

Size and Proportion

Proportion refers to the height of letters in relation to each other and to the writing space. For manuscript and cursive writing, lines may be drawn along the tops of letters to see whether they are uniformly written, as suggested in the particular handwriting program. In manuscript, are the uppercase letters and the tall lowercase letters a full space high? Do all other letters except the lowercase *t* extend from the baseline only to the midline?

In cursive, there are two proportions used (primary and adult) with the change from primary to adult proportion usually occurring at the fifth-grade level. In primary proportion, are the minimum letters one-half the size of maximum letters? Are the intermediate letters midway between minimum and maximum letters in size? Do the uppercase letters, the maximum letters, and the lowercase *b, f, h, k,* and *l* touch the headlines?

There should be no slant in manuscript writing because letters are vertical. Vertical quality may be evaluated by drawing light lines through the vertical strokes of the letters.

All cursive letters slant whether they are lowercase or uppercase. Regularity of slant is readily determined by drawing straight lines through the slant strokes of the letters. If the lines are at different angles, the slant is irregular; if the lines are parallel, the slant is uniform and the writing legible. If lines are parallel but the slant is too extreme or too little, the writer must change the tilt of the paper.

Spacing between letters, words, and sentences should be uniform. In manuscript, is the widest space between the straight-line letters? Is the second widest space between a circle and a straight-line letter? Is the least amount of space between two circle letters? Does the spacing between words equal one lowercase *o?* Does spacing between sentences, for margins, and for indentations equal lowercase *o*'s? Is spacing consistent throughout the writing?

In cursive, is there enough spacing between letters within a word so that each letter appears legible by itself? Does spacing between sentences equal one uppercase *O?* Does spacing between paragraphs equal two uppercase *O's?* Is spacing consistent throughout the writing?

Evaluation of each child's handwriting progress should occur regularly through teacher-student conferencing. Teachers may wish to keep a small box of four-by-six-inch file cards, listing each student's strengths and deficits in the handwriting area. Such a box, incidentally, is also valuable during parent conferences because handwriting is regarded by many parents of elementary school children as a critical skill and a primary tool of communicating and recording information and thoughts.

Conferencing involves using an individual chart, folder, or scale:

1. In their notebooks, the students keep a chart that has been adapted to one writing skill. They can use it to indicate progressive levels of achievement and to determine a new target goal. The *individual chart* can be marked off in monthly columns.
2. The students file one handwritten or typed composition in their folders weekly, dating each paper. If the folders are begun at the start of the school year, the children can detect their own progress and note areas for improvement. The *individual folder* may include papers from other curricular areas such as social studies. Again, the teacher and students can use the folders in setting up goals.
3. The children can make handwriting scales from specimens of their own writing. They begin by collecting several of their papers over a period of some three or four weeks and then (a) cut a few lines at random from each paper; (b) date each sample and arrange them all in order of quality (not date); and (c) paste them on a large sheet of paper, putting the best specimen at the top. Such an *individual scale* should be made each semester for a better indication of growth.

School and Commercial Handwriting Scales

It has been suggested that one teacher or a group of teachers can collect many samples of handwriting for a specific grade level and then divide them into various categories of global legibility (ranging from excellent to poor). For each category, one or two samples can be mounted as models for comparison purposes. Then for each level, a range of elements (including alignment, slant, and spacing) may be illustrated. If a value from five to one is assigned for each element, the total score for an overall rating is readily determined. These samples can be collected on a school-wide or district basis.

The use of commercial scales is not especially helpful to the classroom teacher (except sometimes in the area of assigning grades) for several reasons. The reliability of the scales is either not given or only moderate. All material used for writing is copied or memorized by the writer. There is no assurance that the range of the handwriting quality of a given population of children has been explored. The scales predominantly measure only cursive writing. Right-handed writing is mixed with left-handed writing in a single scale. Finally, teachers are generally either unfamiliar with the scales or inconsistent in using them, although once they become adept at using scales to rate handwriting samples, they can soon rate samples without even using the scales.

Discussion Questions

1. How can you determine when a young child is ready to learn handwriting?
2. If handwriting is primarily a tool of communication, how can you justify teaching children one of the alternative forms as their only system of handwriting?
3. What specific practices would you use to teach a left-handed pupil to write?
4. Should all students be able to type in today's computer age? If so, should typewriting instruction be mandated in every elementary school? Would it be feasible?

Suggested Projects

1. Examine some of the more commonly used resources that accompany any one commercial system of handwriting. Then, if possible, compare several systems (including Zaner-Bloser, D'Nealian, and Palmer), noting similarities and differences in philosophy, equipment used, and evaluative techniques.
2. Administer to a five- or six-year-old child one informal test for handedness and one for eyedness. Report your results to your peers.
3. Plan an introductory lesson in traditional cursive writing for a group of third-grade boys and girls.
4. Evaluate your own handwriting, whether it be manuscript or cursive. Could it serve as a model for young learners?
5. Collect handwriting samples from five elementary school children. Then confer (or describe how you would confer) with each in order to help the student improve his or her printing or cursive handwriting.
6. Set up the learning center on handwriting shown in Figure 7.13.

Figure 7.13. Language Arts Learning Center: Handwriting.

TYPE OF CENTER:	**Handwriting—Manuscript**	TIME: 15–20 minutes
GRADE LEVEL:	2	NUMBER OF STUDENTS: 2–4

INSTRUCTIONAL OBJECTIVE:
The students will become more familiar with the alphabet through writing practice.

MATERIALS:
Cardboard for three-sided fold-out, *finished papers* folder, large envelope for letter cards, tag paper for letter cards (cut three-by-three-inch cards and print one letter on each card), paper and pencils.

DIRECTIONS:
1. Take a worksheet and write your name on it.
2. Pick a card from the envelope.
3. Write the letter you see on the card.
4. On that same line, write a word that begins with the letter that follows the letter you write. Look at the example. If you wrote **b,** write a word that begins with **c.**
5. Pick another card and write the letter on that card.
6. On that same line, write a word that begins with the following letter.
7. Do this same task with each card you choose.
8. Put your finished paper in the *finished papers* folder.
9. Put all of the cards back in the envelope for someone else to use.

Note: A tape recorder could be used to give oral directions for retarded readers. Thus, the student will associate the printed directions with the identical oral directions.

SUGGESTED IDEAS:
This activity could be adapted to cursive writing for grades three to five.

EVALUATION:
The teacher checks all completed work. Incorrect responses, spelling errors, or poor writing skills indicate that the student needs assistance to achieve better results.

Source: From PATHWAYS TO IMAGINATION by Angela S. Reeke and James L. Laffey,
© 1979 by Scott, Foresman & Company. Reprinted by permission.

Recent Related Readings

Alston, J., and Taylor, J. 1987. *Handwriting: Theory, Research, and Implications for Practice.* New York: Nichols.

Barbe, W., et al., eds. 1984. *Handwriting: Basic Skills for Effective Communication.* Columbus, OH: Zaner-Bloser.

Binderup, D. 1988. "Computer Keyboard Savvy," *Instructor, 97*(8), pp. 31–33.

Bing, S. 1988. "Handwriting: Remediate or Circumvent," *Academic Therapy, 23,* pp. 509–514.

Duvall, B. 1986. *Kindergarten Performance for Reading and Matching Four Styles of Handwriting.* Arlington, VA: ERIC Document Reproduction Service (CS 209 466).

Getman, G. 1985. "Hand-Eye Coordinations," *Academic Therapy, 20,* pp. 262–275.

Manning, M. 1988. "Handwriting Instruction," *Childhood Education, 65,* pp. 112–114.

Smith, P. 1987. "Handwriting in the United Kingdom," *The Reading Teacher, 41,* pp. 27–31.

Stowitscheck, J., et al. 1987. " 'I'd Rather Do It Myself': Self-Evaluation and Correction of Handwriting," *Education and Treatment of Children, 10,* pp. 209–224.

Williams, B. 1988. "Preparing Teachers to Teach Keyboarding to Elementary Students," *Business Education Forum, 42,* pp. 27–29.

Chapter Notes

1. V. Froese, "Handwriting: Practice, Pragmatism, and Progress," in *Research in the Language Arts,* V. Froese and S. B. Straw, eds. (Baltimore: University Park Press, 1981), p. 227.
2. S. Graham and L. Miller, "Handwriting Research and Practice: A Unified Approach," *Focus on Exceptional Children,* 1980, *13,* pp. 1–15.
3. M. Peck, E. Askov, and S. Fairchild, "Another Decade of Research in Handwriting: Progress and Prospect in the 1970's," *Journal of Educational Research,* 1980, *73,* pp. 283–298; M. Milone, Jr. and T. Wasylyk, "Handwriting in Special Education," *Teaching Exceptional Children,* 1981, *14*(2), pp. 58–61; and K. Koenke, "ERIC/RCS—Handwriting Instruction: What Do We Know?", *The Reading Teacher,* 1986, *40,* pp. 214–217.
4. D. Graves, *Writing: Teachers & Children at Work* (Portsmouth, New Hampshire: Heinemann, 1983).
5. J. Phelps et al., "The Children's Handwriting Scale: A New Diagnostic Tool," *Journal of Educational Research,* 1985, *79,* pp. 46–50.
6. Sir A. Bullock, *A Language for Life* (London: Her Majesty's Stationery Office, 1975).
7. E. Askov and M. Peck, "Handwriting," in *Encyclopedia of Educational Research,* 5th ed., H. Mitzel, J. Best, and W. Rabinowitz, eds. (New York: Macmillan/The Free Press, 1982), pp. 764–769; and U. Kirk, "Learning to Copy Letters: A Cognitive Rule-Governed Task," *Elementary School Journal,* 1980, *81,* p. 29.
8. N. Søvik, "Developmental Trends of Visual Feedback Control and Learning Children's Copying and Tracking Skills," *Journal of Experimental Education,* 1980/81, *49,* p. 116.
9. Oregon Department of Education, *English Language Arts Concept Paper: Handwriting* (Eugene: Author, 1987), p. 6.
10. B. Furner, *Handwriting Instruction for a High-Tech Society: Will Handwriting Be Necessary?* ERIC Document Reproduction Service No. ED 257 119, 1985.
11. *Ibid.*

12. Oregon Department of Education, *English Language Arts,* p. 6.
13. L. L. Lamme, "Handwriting in an Early Childhood Curriculum," *Young Children,* 1979, *35*(1), p. 20.
14. M. Peck, E. Askov, and S. Fairchild, "Another Decade of Research in Handwriting."
15. C. Sinclair, "Dominance Patterns of Young Children: A Follow-Up Study," *Perceptual and Motor Skills,* 1971, *32,* p. 142.
16. W. Barbe, M. Milone, Jr., and T. Waslyk, "Manuscript is the 'Write' Start," *Academic Therapy,* 1983, *18,* p. 400.
17. K. Koenke, "ERIC/RCS: Handwriting Instruction."
18. Oregon Department of Education, *English Language Arts,* p. 5.
19. J. Trap-Porter, M. Gladden, D. Hill, and J. Cooper, "Space Size and Accuracy of Second and Third Grade Students' Cursive Handwriting," *Journal of Educational Research,* 1983, *76* pp. 231–233.
20. M. Klein, *The Development of Writing in Children: Pre-K through Grade 8* (Englewood Cliffs, New Jersey: Prentice-Hall, 1985); and R. E. Coles and Y. Goodman, "Do We Really Need Those Oversized Pencils to Write With?" *Theory Into Practice,* 1980, *19,* pp. 194–195.
21. Adapted from W. Barbe and M. Milone, Jr., *Teaching Handwriting through Modality Strengths* (Columbus, Ohio: Zaner-Bloser, 1980).
22. D. Durkin, *Teaching Young Children to Read,* 4th ed. (Boston: Allyn & Bacon, 1987), p. 227.
23. K. Koenke, "ERIC/RCS: Handwriting Instruction."
24. D. Armitage and H. Ratzlaff, "The Noncorrelation of Printing and Writing Skills," *Journal of Educational Research,* 1985, *78,* pp. 174–177.
25. K. Koenke, "ERIC/RCS: Handwriting Instruction."
26. C. Lehman, *Handwriting Models for Schools* (Portland, Oregon: The Alcuin Press, 1976).
27. D. Kaake, "Teaching Elementary Age Children Touch Typing as an Aid to Language Arts Instruction," *The Reading Teacher,* 1983, *36,* pp. 640–644.
28. D. Campbell, "Typewriting Contrasted with Handwriting: A Circumvention Study of Learning-Disabled Children," *The Journal of Special Education,* 1973, *7,* pp. 155–167.
29. E. Balajthy, *Microcomputers in Reading and Language Arts* (Englewood Cliffs, New Jersey: Prentice-Hall, 1986), p. 198.
30. *Ibid,* p. 203.
31. *Correcting Handwriting Problems: Integration of Children with Special Needs in a Regular Classroom* (Lexington, Massachusetts: Public Schools, 1974), pp. 6–17.
32. S. Graham and L. Miller, "Handwriting Research and Practice."
33. N. Geschwind and P. Beham, *Left-Handedness: Association with Immune Disease, Migraine, and Developmental Disorder. Proceedings of the National Academy of Sciences, USA,* 1982, pp. 5097–5100.
34. A. M. Lipson, "Left-Handed Connections," *Academic Therapy,* 1984, *20,* p. 186.
35. S. Graham and L. Miller, "Handwriting Research and Practice."
36. W. Barbe, *Evaluating Handwriting: Cursive* (Columbus, Ohio: Zaner-Bloser, 1977).

The Second Writing Tool— Spelling **8**

Major Chapter Goals

After studying Chapter 8, the reader will be able to

1. Describe the stages of spelling development.
2. Incorporate research-based practices and modern guidelines into the classroom spelling program.
3. Understand how to teach spelling by grouping or by using an individualized approach.

Discover As You Read This Chapter Whether*

1. Learning to spell is a task of rote memorization.
2. Making children write a word repeatedly assures learning the correct spelling of that word.
3. There is an apparent analogy between learning to speak and learning to spell.
4. The first stage of spelling development is called the precommunicative stage and occurs in early kindergarten or grade one.
5. Upper primary children switch from invented spelling to standard spelling without appreciable difficulty.
6. Spelling words should initially be presented in sentences, not in lists.
7. English spelling is highly irregular.
8. Spelling is best taught in conjunction with functional writing.
9. An individualized approach to spelling instruction is inappropriate.
10. Surveys of published spelling series for the elementary grades have raised serious doubts about the usefulness of such programs.

*Answers to these true-or-false statements may be found in Appendix 5.

For many decades it was believed that the spelling system of English was purely alphabetic and irregular and that students had to learn to spell most words by serial memory alone. During the past twenty years, however, research in cognitive and developmental psychology and in linguistics has proved that English spelling can be taught systematically and that its mastery is central to the meaning and acquisition of both writing and reading skills.[1] The English orthography, or writing system, is a highly regular but complex system that represents both speech and linguistic information at the levels of meaning, sound, and syntax.

With the publication of recent research studies, learning to spell is now regarded as a developmental process, not as a low-order task of rote memorization. Consequently, the widely held practice of making children write a word again and again is invalid as a technique for learning the correct spelling of that word.

Learning to spell involves considerable cognitive activity and a high degree of linguistic competence. Most children are not formally taught much of the information about English spelling but must abstract generalizations about the patterns underlying words and do so through exposure to print at home and during formal reading and writing lessons.

Long before boys and girls start school, they acquire the fundamentals of language and even learn to use a grammar to put words together to form sentences. Language development, therefore, proceeds from the simple to the complex. So too does spelling development; maturing children gradually progress toward a greater understanding of English orthography.

During recent years, work with preschoolers, kindergartners, and early primary pupils has shown that there is an apparent analogy between learning to spell and learning to speak.[2] Children learning to talk constantly mispronounce words, omit words, or improperly order words. Nobody actually teaches them to speak. Instead, they learn about their language as they listen and talk and are actively involved in the speech environment. They appear able to identify, classify, and apply concepts about the "rules" of oral language.

In a similar way, boys and girls learn to spell by writing (and later, by reading). Beginning writers quickly realize, however, that the twenty-six letters of the English alphabet are not enough to spell all the words they wish to write because English has more than twenty-six phonemes. Upon making this discovery, the children either ask parents, teachers, or other adults how to spell the missing sounds, or they invent their own nonstandard spelling. They appear able to identify and classify the sounds they hear and do not use graphemes frivolously. Of course they misspell many words when they first write, but given enough opportunities over a prolonged period of time, they will learn to spell. If young children are corrected constantly as they try to talk, they will soon hesitate to speak for fear of correction. Likewise, if they are corrected constantly as they try to spell, they will become thwarted for fear of correction.

Language acquisition is a creative feat, and all children are creative when it comes to learning their own language. This additional aspect of language processing—*invented spelling*—is not confined to just a few boys and girls. As linguists now recognize, children are generally able to spell on their own. The teacher or other adult, however, must give the children the idea that they *can* spell. He or she must also recognize "correctness" (by taking cues from the children and from a few phonetic perceptions—not from standard spelling) and must learn to respond to nonstandard spelling appropriately.

The particular circumstances of the first writing will vary with the child, depending on his or her own timing and the situation in which the need arises. What remains constant is the expectation that children will figure it out for themselves when the time comes. The activity must develop as an expressive one and must not degenerate into a form of exercise. The function of the teacher should be to give boys and girls access to spelling but not require it of them. How much writing they will eventually produce, if any, depends on their interest.

An analogy to painting and drawing is useful. A teacher of young children makes paints, brushes, and paper available to them and encourages them. The teacher still leaves it up to the children, however, to decide when, how, and what they will paint. Early spelling should be treated in much the same way. If a teacher encourages spelling once it starts, welcomes and values the spelling, and transmits a feeling to the children that they are doing something exciting and useful, some children will go ahead and make progress.

Cramer describes how one teacher helped a first grader approximate the spelling of a word needed for a written composition.[3] The child, Jenny, thought she was not able to spell *hospital*. The teacher, Mrs. Nicholas, told Jenny to spell

The Second Writing Tool—Spelling 251

it as well as she could, writing as much of the word as possible. When Jenny insisted that she didn't know any part of the word, the teacher-pupil dialogue proceeded in this manner:

> *Mrs. Nicholas:* Yes, you do, Jenny. How do you think *hospital* begins? (*Mrs. Nicholas pronounced* hospital *distinctly, emphasizing the first part slightly. She avoided distorting the pronunciation.*)
>
> *Jenny (tentatively):* h–s.
>
> *Mrs. Nicholas:* Good! Write down the *hs*. What do you hear next in *hospital*? (*Again Mrs. Nicholas pronounced* hospital *distinctly, but this time she emphasized the second part slightly.*)
>
> *Jenny (still tentatively):* p–t.
>
> *Mrs. Nicholas:* Very good! Write down the *pt*. Now, what do you hear last in *hospital*? (*While pronouncing the word* hospital *for the last time, Mrs. Nicholas emphasized the last part slightly.*)
>
> *Jenny (with some assurance):* l.
>
> *Mrs. Nicholas:* Yes, Jenny, *h–s–p–t–l* is a fine way to spell *hospital*. There is another way to spell the word, but for now, I want you to spell all words you don't know just as we did *hospital*.

Children gradually internalize information about underlying rules that characterize the English orthography, and then they construct and apply those tentative rules in their writing. As they gain more experience with language, children revise their rule systems. They progress through several stages when learning to spell.

Stages of Spelling Development

Boys and girls do not proceed as spellers randomly or by rote. Nor do they all learn spelling in exactly the same way. Still, researchers have found that strategies of learning to spell progress in about the same sequence for all children. Observed in the early writing of young pupils are these spelling strategies:

1. The use of single letters to represent the sound of the full letter name (*hol* for *hole,* and *ppl* for *people*).
2. The omission of nasal sounds before consonants (*plat* for *plant* and *sic* for *sink*).
3. The use of *t* to render /t/ in the past tense form of certain verbs (*likt* for *liked* and *lookt* for *looked*).
4. The omission of the vowel when the syllable has a vowel-like consonant such as *l, m, n,* and *r* (*brd* for *bird* and *opn* for *open*).
5. The use of *d* to render the flap phoneme for *t* between vowels (*prede* for *pretty* and *bodm* for *bottom*).
6. The use of a rather advanced set of linguistic rules for deciding which vowel letter to use when children have not yet learned the spelling of the short vowel sounds (*fel* for *feel* and *fill*).
7. The substitution of *chr* and *jr* for *tr* and *dr* (*chran* for *train* and *jragin* for *dragon*).

8. The occasional use of letters according to their full pronounced names (*yl* for *while* and *r* for *are*).

Stages of spelling evolve systematically, regardless of the geographical location of the children or the instruction they receive. The various stages seem to form a sequence for spelling development, and students do not fluctuate radically between stages or pass backwards from time to time. Five spelling stages used by young children as they move toward correctly spelled words are described as precommunicative, semiphonetic, phonetic, transitional, and correct.[4]

The first is called the *precommunicative stage* and occurs in early kindergarten (for children with previous exposure to print) or grade one (for those with no such earlier exposure). Girls and boys try to approximate writing by random use of symbols from the alphabet, which they are able to produce from recall. Examples of precommunicative or preliterate spellings include IMMMPMPT and BDRNMPM, both of which could only be "read back" by the spellers themselves. The implicit understanding revealed during this stage is that speech can be recorded by graphic symbols. Students may also lack knowledge of the entire alphabet, the distinction between lowercase and uppercase letters, and the left-to-right direction of English spelling.

The *semiphonetic stage* is the second to emerge. Children do not represent essential sound features of words, although they do use letters to represent some speech sounds they hear. They sometimes spell a word with the correct beginning or ending consonant sound and generally use one-, two-, and three-letter representations of complete and separate words. Examples of semiphonetic spellings include MSR for *monster*, DG for *dog*, and P for *pie*, revealing that vowels are often omitted. The implicit understandings shown during this stage are that specific letters stand for specific speech sounds and that speech is made up of discreet words.

The third stage is the *phonetic stage* in which the essential phonetic elements of words are represented even though the letters used may be wrong. Although phonetic spelling does not resemble standard spelling, it is readable to most first-grade teachers and to the writers themselves. Examples of phonetic spellings are PPL for *people* and PRD for *purred*. A major difference between the semiphonetic and phonetic stages is revealed in the spelling of *chirp:* semiphonetically, it is spelled CHP, but phonetically, it is CHRP. The implicit understandings shown at this time are that every sound feature of a word can be represented by one letter or a combination of letters and that the graphic form of a word contains every speech sound in the same order in which those sounds are heard when the word is spoken. Students may be introduced (through writing) to word families, spelling patterns, and word structures.

Children in the *transitional stage* produce words that look like English words even though the spelling is sometimes nonstandard. Generally, in the last half of the first grade or early in the second grade, boys and girls understand many of the orthographic rules of English, even if they do not always apply them precisely. Vowels appear in every syllable and inflectional endings are spelled uniformly.

Phonological, or surface level, information is used, and silent letters are not represented. Children intersperse standard spelling with nonstandard phonetic spelling. Examples of transitional spellings include *com* for *come, eagel* for *eagle,* and *chrip* for *chirp.* The implicit understandings displayed at this stage are (a) there are numerous ways to spell many of the identical speech sounds, (b) every word has a standard spelling that is used in print, (c) many words are not spelled entirely phonetically, and (d) words must be spelled in such a way that everyone can read them readily.

The fifth and final stage is the *correct stage,* during which boys and girls spell words using standard orthography. They finally realize that words are units of sound *and* units of meaning. The developmentally correct spellers have been described as understanding the English spelling system and its basic rules; having mastery of accurate spelling of affixes, contractions, and compound words; knowing how to distinguish honomyns; generally using double consonants and silent letters correctly; having mastery of many irregular spellings; slowly recognizing word origins and using this information to make meaningful associations; thinking of alternative spellings and visualizing words in their mind when spelling new words; and accumulating a large body of known spellings.[5]

Pupils should be introduced to formal spelling instruction early if they advance to the correct stage prior to second grade.[6] Such instruction, however, should be delayed for those older children who are slower to notice orthographic rules. Until they are well into the stages of phonetic and transitional spelling, students cannot be successfully introduced to formal spelling lessons.

It is important to note at this point that none of the children studied by the various researchers have had any difficulty in switching to standard spelling. If spelling is regarded as being based on a set of implicit rules about sound-to-symbol correspondence and morphological principles, then the developing child can be described as modifying those rules easily as he or she acquires new information about standard spelling. Kindergartners, for example, often spell one word several ways in the same story, attacking each word as a new problem. Nevertheless, as they develop and learn the standard orthography for a word, they will spontaneously substitute it for their own. The key to the transition appears to be *exposure*—to extensive writing experiences; to systematic reading instruction, including the acquisition of sight vocabulary; and to an audience willing to read what others have written, provided that indeed it can be read.

Kindergarten, first-grade, and second-grade teachers can help beginning spellers in many ways. They can read to children. They can encourage creative writing, deemphasizing standard spelling and responding appropriately to non-standard spelling. They can immerse students in a language environment (especially through the language experience approach described in Chapter 10). They can not only allow but actively help boys and girls learn the alphabet. They can avoid the instruction, "sound it out." Finally, they can encourage children to compare and to categorize words in various ways.

As students gain more experience with written language, they develop a more integrated view of orthography. They begin to interpret it at the meaning, or lexical, level once they have moved beyond the level of phoneme-grapheme correspondence to a more abstract level. One study of readers in grades four to six concluded that poor readers used only a limited number of strategies in both spelling and reading regular and irregular words.[7] They sounded words out when reading and spelled words the way they sound when completing writing tasks. Good readers, however, used a combination of strategies in both spelling and reading assignments. Finally, although both good and poor readers could pronounce all the words they misspelled, the poor readers were more apt than the good readers to omit a silent letter from words such as *sword* and *doubt*.

Another study concluded that at about age ten, children's use of the so-called analogy strategy appears to grow as their bank of visual word forms increases.[8] Instead of decoding an unfamiliar word, students search for a known word and then pronounce or spell the unfamiliar word by analogy to it.

A third study which was concerned with twelve-year-olds in three South London schools concluded that good readers and spellers had the fewest errors in spelling both real and nonsense words because they appeared to use a combination of strategies, including semantic or structural analogies.[9] Good readers who spelled badly were weak in relating print to sound and were apparently unable to move beyond phonology. The researcher concluded that spelling instruction based only on phoneme-grapheme relationships is incomplete because English orthography reflects knowledge both on the level of sound *and* on the level of meaning.

That conclusion may explain why, according to an older study of twenty-one classrooms in Delaware, the language-experience approach to reading (which combines language skills and is described in Chapter 10) produces significantly better spellers than the basal-reader approach (also described in Chapter 10).[10] Although the students and their teachers were matched evenly, the children in the basal-reader classes found the phonologically irregular words of American English orthography somewhat more difficult to spell than the phonologically regular words, whereas the language-experience classes did not. The latter integrated writing, listening, and speaking in a broad-based reading program, and its members maintained their spelling superiority throughout their elementary school years.

Finally, studies of older students who are poor spellers have concluded that their teachers must provide directed activities in grouping words of similar patterns (such as *explain* and *explanation*). After gaining a meaning-based understanding of English spelling, students can then begin making proper generalizations, which they can apply in their own writing tasks. They can also benefit from a study of some of the more common Latin and Greek roots and combining forms, because learning word origins and learning their relationships to other words derived from the same roots often lead to growth in correct spelling.

Teaching Spelling: Modern Guidelines

Children affect their spelling skills every time they write or otherwise interact with written language, so no commercial spelling program used alone can guarantee spelling achievement. Students learn to spell by spelling and must not be restricted in their progress to those words and generalizations introduced during formal lessons.

Adults concerned with curriculum development in spelling should bear in mind seven principles or guidelines for teaching English spelling today. First, *learning to spell is more an active conceptual process than it is a memorization process*. As discussed earlier, there are underlying cognitive processes in learning to spell that are developmental in nature. As children progress through school, their ability to spell becomes more and more related to their understanding of the structural and semantic relationships of words. As they interact with language both in and out of school, they develop more sophisticated understandings of spelling. In their study of other curricular subjects, they prove to themselves the interrelationships of word components. Thus learning to spell is not an abstract process but a concrete one.

Second, *spelling must be presented in the context of purposeful writing experiences and overall language learning*. It demands knowledge of varied aspects of language—semantics, morphology, and phonology. Because students learn language by actively exploring their linguistic environment, spelling instruction must build upon their curiosity about language by encouraging boys and girls to discover how the writing system operates. It should also provide numerous opportunities for them to practice their findings in new situations.

Integrated with all areas of the curriculum, writing should be a natural part of the daily classroom routine because frequent use of spelling knowledge while writing actually encourages spelling competence.[12]

Third, *children must understand that learning to spell has certain unique aspects*. Spelling has the special function of representing language graphically through handwriting or typewriting. It forms a link between verbal and written forms of language expression. It is a multisensory process involving visual, auditory, oral, and haptical (muscular) abilities. Even though most children are able to use all these sensory modes in learning to spell, they hardly use them all to the same degree or in the same manner. Slower learners, for example, admit that the most effective way for them to learn to spell involves pronunciation of the words by students and teacher. For other pupils, the visual processes represent the chief means by which spelling is mastered. And though spelling ability is generally not truly dependent on haptical experiences, nevertheless haptical memory (so fundamental to typewriting) aids in the act of spelling when combined with the other types of recollections of words. All four mechanisms come into play in the study of each spelling word, as outlined in Figure 8.1.

Furthermore, boys and girls who are learning to spell must actually begin to understand the entire framework of orthography. They will not and should not move one precise in-depth step at a time, going from letters and sounds to syllables, and finally to words. Instead, every learner will follow his or her own logic in moving from one aspect of English orthography to another while attempting simultaneously to keep in mind the total framework.

How to Study a Spelling Word

Figure 8.1. How to Study a Spelling Word.

1. Say the word. Listen to the sounds in it.

2. Look at the word. Notice which letters are used to stand for the sounds in the word.

3. Write the word. Say the word to yourself as you write it. Do not look at the copy.

4. **Proof the word. Check the word against the copy to see whether it is spelled correctly.**

5. Identify the error. Determine which part of the word, if any, has been misspelled.

6. Restudy the word. Study again any word you have misspelled, repeating the steps from the beginning.

Fourth, *children seldom make random errors in spelling, so teachers can use error pattern analysis in formulating spelling strategies.* For example, one study of pupils in grades one through four in various Michigan schools showed only three types of errors in spelling vowels: (1) the use of a letter-name strategy (as in *gat* for *gate*), which accounted for 68 percent of all errors; (2) the addition of an incorrect vowel after a correct vowel (as in *hait* for *hat*), which accounted for 25 percent of errors; and (3) the incorrect substitution of one short vowel for another (as in *spick* for *speck*), which accounted for 7 percent of all errors.[13] The researchers stress that teachers must not become upset when children repeatedly make the same type of errors; those errors are not necessarily caused by "not listening" or "not trying." Instead, they may be due to the length of the children's overall development and exposure to words. Recurring errors do not indicate that children will not or cannot spell correctly at a later time.

By examining children's spelling errors, the teacher can derive hypotheses about each pupil's learning strategies and plan instruction accordingly. Error pattern analysis is a way of regarding the learner and the errors he or she makes during the learning process. Steps that the teacher can take in a diagnostic-prescriptive approach to spelling using such error pattern analysis include the following: (1) collect samples of student writing; (2) place student's misspellings (preferably about twenty-five errors) and the dictionary's correct spellings side by side; (3) surmise the erroneous strategy in conference with the student and record it; (4) suggest a correction strategy and record it; and (5) place correction strategies for all observed problems in order and then determine through teacher-student conference which areas are most in need of improvement.[14]

Fifth, *the goals of a modern spelling program must focus on the purposes of learning strategies to improve spelling.*[15] These strategies include the following: (1) students should attempt to spell every word they want to write, and they should learn to rely on a variety of strategies; (2) students should learn the most frequent 4000 to 5000 common words, which means that there must be some formal instruction in the total program; (3) students should become aware of the words they can and cannot spell so that this patterned behavior evolves in later years into automatic proofreading; (4) students should know and use several resources to check words, including the dictionary, the thesaurus, electronic aids such as computer spelling verifiers, and special works such as a synonym finder.

Sixth, *spelling growth depends on continuous evaluation.* Learning occurs whenever there is feedback on one's actions or efforts. Growth in spelling ability, therefore, only develops through observing and proofreading and through an analysis of errors made. A crucial part of spelling instruction, according to Hodges, is an ability to distinguish incorrect spellings from correct ones and then to correct both the mistakes and their causes.[16] Such instruction must provide students and teachers with many opportunities to evaluate pupil progress toward a total understanding of English orthography.

Seventh and last, *English spelling is actually quite regular but in ways that may have never occurred to most learners.* It is clear that to spell English successfully, one must have a high degree of sensitivity to both the phonological and the morphological structures of words. Students must be permitted to discover the relationships between those structures and English spelling by using materials that have been carefully prepared or properly selected by their teacher.

Good spellers, children and adults alike, recognize that related words are spelled alike even though they are pronounced differently. Such spellers seem to rely on an underlying picture of the words that is independent of the words' varying pronunciations. They internalize the underlying relationships among words. When good spellers encounter a troublesome word, they automatically utilize the idea that although related words may vary a good deal in their pronunciation, their spelling usually remains the same. Once the connection is clear between the new troublesome word and other related words, correct spelling becomes automatic.

To help children develop the habit of seeking such connections, the linguistically oriented teacher may use one of these exercises:[17]

1. Give the children Column A of words with a /ə/ vowel omitted. Ask them to think of related words that give distinct clues to the spelling (Column B). (The clues turn out to be the same ones that preschoolers use in their invented spelling.)

A	B
pres __ dent	preside
janit __ r	janitorial
maj __ r	majority
comp __ rable	compare
ind __ stry	industrial

2. Give the children only Column B from Exercise 1 and ask them to think of other forms of the words. See if they notice how vowel sounds shift around.

3. Help the children guess the proper consonant when two or more seem possible. In Column C, the spelling is ambiguous. In Column D, the related word gives the key to the correct choice.

C	D
gradual (d, j)	grade
nation (t, sh)	native
medicine (c, s)	medical
racial (t, c, sh)	race
criticize (c, s)	critical

4. Help the children observe silent consonants by giving them Column E and asking them to think of related words in which the silent consonants are pronounced (Column F).

E	F
bomb	bombard
soften	soft
muscle	muscular
sign	signal
condemn	condemnation

5. Give the children only Column F and ask them to think of related words in which the underlined consonants become silent.
6. Give the children only Column E and ask them to name the silent consonants.
7. Help the children learn consonant alternations that occur in the pronunciation of words and that are reflected in the orthography too. Because the t–c alternation is fairly common, give the children Column G and ask them to determine the missing consonants in Column H.

G	H
pirate	pira __ y
democratic	democra __ y
present	presen __ e
resident	residen __ e
lunatic	luna __ y

Spelling is not a popular subject, according to research recently completed in grades one through six with 120 children, all of whom were Caucasian with English as their first language.[18] Most of them believed that spelling is important but they ranked it lowest among six curricular areas. Additional negative emotions were revealed when, as early as first grade, 82 percent of the students had a concept of "the bad speller." Although three-quarters of the first graders had a favorable image of themselves as spellers, this proportion declined from second grade on, with the criterion for the depression being "by my test results."

Teaching Spelling: Recommended Practices

Perhaps this distaste for spelling instruction would diminish if teachers used more research-based instructional procedures. Unfortunately, most prefer to use spelling strategies based on tradition and not on empirical evidence. At least one study of nearly 1300 elementary teachers in Iowa confirmed the fact that teachers seldom use research-based practices when planning formal spelling lessons.[19]

Summarized below are empirically-based procedures that should be incorporated into school-based spelling instruction in an effort to improve spelling achievement both formally and informally and thereby also improve student attitudes.[20]

1. The single most important factor in learning to spell is the self-corrected test procedure: The child corrects his or her own test under the teacher's direction.
2. The spelling words of highest frequency in child and adult writing should be the ones studied by elementary students.
3. The child's attention should be directed to each word as a total word and not as a word broken down into syllables.
4. The use of a pretest is a must because the test-study-test method is superior to the study-test method for most spellers.
5. Spelling lessons should run between twelve and fifteen minutes per period, five days a week.
6. Presenting spelling words in list form, initially, is a more successful method than presenting them in sentences or paragraph form.
7. Children need not learn the meanings of the majority of their words in order to learn to spell those words correctly.
8. Spelling lists composed of words from various curricular areas are of little value in increasing spelling ability.
9. Most attempts to teach spelling by phonic rules are questionable, due to the nature of the English language.
10. The major contribution of spelling games is the stimulation of student interest, which by itself is crucial to spelling improvement.
11. Spelling should be taught in conjunction with writing because frequent opportunity to use spelling words contributes greatly to the growth and maintenance of spelling ability.
12. Each student should be taught an efficient technique for studying unknown spelling words (such as the procedure already described in Figure 8.1).

Teaching Spelling: Using a Group or Individualized Approach

In order to plan an effective spelling program, the teacher must understand the importance of phonological and morphological relationships, as well as the significance of oral and written language. Furthermore, the teacher must know the backgrounds, needs, and potential of the children and recall that spelling is a developmental process.

As to the optimum grade for beginning formal spelling instruction, research studies are not in agreement.[21] One national survey of nearly 3000 children in twenty-two states in grades three through eight showed that after grade four, no spelling instruction is almost as effective as formal instruction. These findings were in general agreement with another survey of more than 2000 children in grades two through six, which concluded that many pupils had achieved a "skill in spelling" as early as the third or fourth grade and that tracking them through the sequences of the available spelling programs may not be a worthwhile utilization of their time or energy.

On the other hand, arguing for a delay in formal spelling instruction are researchers involved in a Michigan study of approximately 200 children in grades one through four. They believe that formal instruction may not be appropriate until children have had ample time to develop an understanding of word-attack principles. They state that it is more important to give students a chance to explore words in their writing and their reading rather than to have them write lists of spelling words.

In either instance, teachers should recognize that just as there is an "instructional level" in reading for individual children, there is also one in spelling.[22] This spelling instructional level is generally described in quantitative terms, or *power dimension* (percentage of correct spellings, such as 50 percent to 89 percent, at a grade or difficulty level). For example, if a fifth grader at the start of the school year achieves above 50 percent accuracy on a spelling inventory of fifth-grade words (developed at the school or on a district level), he or she can be properly placed in a fifth-grade spelling curriculum. On the other hand, a spelling score below 50 percent on a fifth-grade inventory could indicate that the child is not ready for a fifth-grade spelling book but should be taught at a lower spelling level, probably fourth grade.

Besides the power dimension, there is a second factor, and that concerns the *quality of children's spelling errors* and what relationship exists between them and spelling power. One recent study of 252 children in grades two through five in three elementary schools located in a Chicago suburb proved that at each grade level, there was a strong correlation between the spelling power of the students and the quality of the misspellings they produced.[23] It suggests not only that low-accuracy spellers (e.g., those below 40 percent) have more grade-level words to learn in a school year but also that these students are deficient in the very orthographic knowledge that underlies the ability to learn any new spelling words. The researchers recommend that conscientious teachers *group students according to spelling ability,* use multilevel spelling materials, and attend more closely to the qualitative distinctions in children's spelling efforts.

As for teachers who no longer group students in reading but prefer to use a strictly *individualized approach,* they may wish to adopt a similar strategy for spelling instruction. Examples of creative and individualized lessons in spelling may be found in Figure 8.2.

As to optimum sources for spelling words useful for study by children involved in either an individualized or group approach, there are currently three sources mentioned.[24] The first is *student writing.* At least one study of spellers in grades two through six showed that fifth graders, for example, are spelling

Figure 8.2. Lessons in Individualized Spelling.

Sample Creative Lessons in Spelling

1. Boys and girls write their initials on a sheet of paper. They then list correctly foods or activities whose names begin with one or more of the initials. They can refer to a cookbook, a dictionary, a newspaper, or the yellow pages of the local telephone book. Example: Jennifer T. Donaldson might list *jumping, jam, tomatoes, tickling, doughnuts, dancing.*

2. Children with handy access to a standard or picture dictionary can write correctly words that have developed from the names of animals. Examples: *dog—doghouse, horse—horseback, man— manhole.* Some boys and girls may choose to write words centered about one animal only. Others may prefer to incorporate two or three animals, wild or domestic.

3. Upper primary children can each receive a dittoed worksheet on which have been sketched seasonal items. Each leaf or pumpkin (fall), snowflake or fir tree (winter), or tulip or umbrella (spring), for example, contains space for writing in one Study Word. Later, after the words have been checked, the child may color in the items appropriately. If any word has been misspelled, however, the child must first write the word correctly before he or she can color in the sketch. The pupil should be cautioned to color lightly so that the words may remain visible. For less confusion, all sketches on any one sheet should be of the same item.

4. Intermediate girls and boys with easy access to a dictionary can review simple geometric shapes. The teacher lists on the chalkboard the names of several shapes, including *circle, square, rectangle, triangle, oval, sphere,* and *cube.* At their desks the children prepare on their papers several columns, each headed with one of the shapes the teacher has listed. Then, each pupil writes the names of items in the classroom, the home, or the neighborhood that resemble those shapes. Examples: *cube—ottoman, oval—mirror, rectangle—bicycle pedal.* The children use their dictionaries to proofread their choices.

incorrectly many high-frequency words.[25] It is therefore recommended that students maintain their spelling dictionaries based on the misspelled words in their daily journals and other written work. Teachers can then use those misspelled words to individualize word lists for students.

The personal spelling dictionary can simply be a loose-leaf notebook, with alphabetical dividers, in which students record words they need to know how to spell in the course of all of their writing experiences in school. The same notebook can be used year after year because the pages can be changed and updated as necessary. Once a class has been introduced to individualized spelling dictionaries, it is important to get children into the habit of using their dictionaries whenever they are involved with writing activities in any area of the curriculum.

The single most critical factor in learning to spell is the self-corrected test procedure during which the child corrects his own test under the teacher's direction. (© Richard Anderson.)

As a pupil is writing and needs to use a word he or she cannot spell, the pupil can ask the teacher or look up the word in a pubished dictionary. The child then promptly records it in his or her spelling notebook. Should the child need to use that word again later and is still unsure of the correct spelling, he or she need only refer back to the personal dictionary.

The second source for spelling words is *frequency vocabulary lists*. There are both graded lists by V. Thomas (1979, 1974), for example, and ungraded lists by such authorities as J. Fitzgerald (1951), and H. Kučera and W. Francis (1967). Teachers in a single school can choose the 3000–4000 high-frequency words basic to any spelling program from one or more of those lists and track individual students.

The third source is the revised *New Iowa Spelling Scale*, published by the University of Iowa. It lists 5507 words by the percentage of students in grades two through eight who spelled the words correctly. Teachers can develop word lists for pupils at a particular grade or ability level by using the available percentages. Data for the Scale were gathered from some 30,000 students per grade in 645 school systems in all types of cities and in most states throughout the country.

Finally, elementary teachers who are considering the possibility of using commercial spelling series as sources for spelling words should be aware of the results of three surveys of published spelling programs for children. All raised serious doubts concerning the feasibility of using such programs. The first survey examined seven elementary series published between 1971 and 1978, and found that most programs do not require children to perform realistic spelling assignments.[26] Instead, they ask pupils to do various copying tasks, which is an unrealistic practice in contemporary society where students must generate their own spelling in response to an internal or external need. The purpose of modern spelling instruction, after all, is the development of independent spelling ability.

The second study examined eleven spelling series published since 1976 and found that no one series was consistent *across* grade levels in the numbers of high-frequency words (based on a standard measure of word frequency) found at each level.[27] Nor was there consistency *within* grade levels. It would appear, therefore, that a school would have to purchase several series simultaneously in order to provide students with lists of appropriate words at each grade level.

The third and last survey of more than 2000 children in grades two through six revealed that many pupils already know how to spell a substantial number of the words included in the spelling textbook program at each grade level.[28] Furthermore, the average child in this suburban sample also seemed to be able to spell a substantial number of words designated for the level one grade *above* his or her present grade placement. The researcher concluded that qualitative differences exist in spelling which may require a greater degree of individualization than that located in the neatly compartmentalized study procedures available in many pubished programs.

A final warning about published spelling series is issued by Gentry who has been concerned about publishers with "research-based" materials.[29] In examining two series with a 1986 copyright, he found that although both contained lengthy bibliographies of research articles, Series B incorporated 31 percent of its research base from the 1980s and 24 percent of it from the 1950s and 1960s; Series A actually incorporated only 4 percent of its research base from the 1980s and 40 percent of it from the 1950s and 1960s. The latter series was interpreted as not providing the teachers with the best in current research-supported practices and strategies. Gentry stressed that the research base for any spelling series must be up-to-date and comprehensive, that materials with no research base should be rejected entirely, and that those with outdated research should be suspect.

Because children learn to spell through constant and enriching interaction with written language through daily writing and reading, teachers must plan a variety of activities that enhance student awareness of words and word formations. The twenty exercises described in this section focus attention on the spelling process and stress correct rather than incorrect spellings. Some are especially appropriate for younger or slower spellers, whereas others may meet the needs of most spellers throughout the elementary grades.

Two children work together with one box of magnetic letters. The first child uses the letters to spell one of the Study Words. The second child then removes one or more of the letters, and the partner must state what is missing and replace the letters in the correct order. They continue to take turns.

Simple pictures of Study Words are drawn on the chalkboard or on worksheets. Children write the correct word under each picture.

The teacher prepares a chart with twenty-six pockets, one for each letter of the alphabet. Then individual cards of Study Words are placed in the pocket, according to the first letter of the word. Students may remove the cards, examine them, and return them to the chart. Sometimes the chart may hold all the cards for a week or month.

The teacher and children gather together all the materials needed for finger painting. Then, instead of painting shapes or pictures, the children write their Study Words in paint. Most children will require more than one sheet of paper.

Children draw pictures of Study Words on construction-paper cutouts of fish. The fish are then placed in a bowl with paper clips attached to them. The students "catch" the fish with a magnet at the end of a short fishing pole. They then write on the chalkboard or on paper the words pictured on the fish that they caught.

Students spell Study Words with alphabet macaroni and then glue them on black construction paper. For a colorful variation, the macaroni can be dyed earlier (using food coloring and rubbing alcohol) and allowed to dry for five to ten minutes.

Each child writes the more difficult Study Words, using glue on construction paper. Then the words are sprinkled with sand or glitter or covered carefully with yarn.

Each student receives one sheet of plain white paper and one sheet of one-inch-squared graph paper. First, the child writes one letter of a Study Word in each of the squares. Second, he or she cuts the squares apart, mixes them up, and rearranges them in correct order. Third, the reassembled letters are pasted in proper sequence on the plain paper. The child continues studying each word, following the three steps.

Instructional Activities

Being Magnetic

Drawing Charades

Examining Pocket Words

Finger Writing

Fishing

Fixing Macaroni Words

Glueing It

Graphing It

Having a Cross Word

Children connect words to form an original crossword puzzle. Partners who are working with similar Study Words can then number the words across and down, write clues, and exchange their puzzles. They may use graph paper and produce a puzzle like this:

				1 b				
		2 m	a	y	3 b	e		
		e			o			
4 b	e	e			5 y	a	r	n
		6 t	a	g	s			

Making Clay Tablets

Like the ancient Sumerians, the children spread ordinary modeling clay out into "sheets" about one half inch thick. Then each child inscribes Study Words in clay, using an opened paper clip or a pencil.

Pasting Spots

Each child makes a large heavy cardboard giraffe and paints it yellow. Then the pupil cuts out a quantity of wide circles from brown construction paper to simulate spots. As Study Words are learned correctly, the child writes the word on one circle and pastes it on the giraffe. If the teacher can provide a grooved piece of wood (or some other device) to help the giraffe stand up, the spelling spots can be more prominently displayed.

Preparing Anagrams

The teacher or children make cutout letters of the alphabet, with several lowercase and several uppercase forms of each one. The letters are placed in a box on a corner table. During free time, one pupil or two partners may go to the table to form various Study Words. Either the teacher or partner can check the correct spellings, using a nearby dictionary if necessary.

Putting Black on White

Children use a white crayon to write their Study Words on a piece of manila construction paper. Later they paint over the paper with a wash of thin black paint. Their spelling words will then magically appear.

Solving a Rebus

On the chalkboard or worksheets, there are sentences for completion that use picture cues for Study Words, such as, *I found some eggs in the* _____ .

The teacher prepares a paragraph that includes many or all of the Study Words. Then the teacher copies it on the chalkboard or on worksheets, purposely leaving no space between words but punctuating and capitalizing the sentences properly. The children must draw lines between the connected words to make sense out of the paragraph.

Spacing Out

Children listen to a taped spelling lesson lasting fifteen to twenty minutes. Then they participate in a five-minute discussion period, during which their teacher answers any questions regarding the taped lesson.

Talking about Taped Lessons

A student writes one Study Word vertically, either on the chalkboard or on writing paper. He or she then tries to use each letter of that word in a new word and may even attempt to form the new words into a sentence or question like this:

Towering a Word

*C*an
T*O*m
*R*un
to*D*ay

The child writes all of the Study Words on a sturdy piece of paper and then turns it over. On the back he or she draws curved lines to make it look like a jigsaw puzzle. Finally, the student cuts the paper apart and tries to reassemble it by using the letters of the words as clues.

Using a Jigsaw

The child writes the Study Words on small rectangles of colored construction paper. He or she then uses these as flash cards, working with a partner. When the words have been mastered, the child may paste the flash cards in a special notebook or on an individual chart.

Using Tiny Flash Cards

Children can write jingles using one or more Study Words in rhyme. Sometimes they learn not only to spell the designated words but other words in the same phonogram (or graphemic base) as well; for example:

Writing Jingles

My sister has a puppy,
I have a little frog.
I'd rather have my clean pet
Than her dirty dog.

The value of word games in the teaching of spelling lies both in the enjoyment they provide for children and in their potential for promoting experimentation and inquiry.[30] Games can be planned for individual players, pairs of students, or teams made up of small groups of children. Because spelling is relevant to writing, spelling games should involve written work and should never consist exclusively of oral exercises. They should stress correct spellings and avoid incorrect ones as much as possible. Experienced teachers who realize that learning games such as those outlined in Figure 8.3 are intended as supplements to, not substitutions for, a spelling program are equally aware that such games encourage children to form concepts about the written code.

Learning Games in Spelling

Figure 8.3. Fourteen Learning Games in Spelling.

Add-On	1. A scorekeeper is selected. Teams are chosen and assigned chalkboard space far apart from each other.
	2. The teacher pronounces a Study Word and has the first member on each team go to the board and write the first letter of the word. As soon as the player is finished, he or she hands the chalk to the second member of the team, urging this player to "add-on."
	3. The second member then writes the second letter, and the round continues until one team completes the word.
	4. The team finishing first in each round scores one point. Points are subtracted, however, for any illegible or incorrect letters.
	5. The team with the most points wins Add-On.
Countdown	1. The teacher prepares to dictate Study Words. A scorekeeper is selected. Teams are chosen and are assigned chalkboard space far apart from each other.
	2. The first player on each team stands at the board, listening to the word the teacher reads. The player then tries to complete writing that word by the time the teacher finishes a "countdown" from ten to one. The teacher can either count softly or indicate the count with his or her fingers.
	3. Each team scores a point every time a player completes writing the dictated word correctly by the time the teacher counts down to one.
	4. Individual winners are all the players who beat the countdown. The winning team or teams of Countdown are those with the most points.
Detectives	1. The players are divided into two-partner teams that are given dictionaries, pencils, and paper.
	2. One partner on each team writes the alphabet on the left side of the paper, skipping one line after each letter. Then both players or Detectives search for objects in the classroom and write each item down opposite its corresponding letter (e.g., A<art, B<book, C<chalk), consulting the dictionary as needed.
	3. Although most of the searching can be done with players at their desks, a team may search more actively if it can do so without disturbing the other Detectives.
	4. When time is called, the teacher writes the alphabet letters vertically on the chalkboard, and each team copies its own list next to the proper letters. Teams may use different colors of chalk for easy tallying.
	5. The team with the longest list of correct words wins Detectives.

Figure 8.3. (cont.)

1. Three players stand at their desks, each holding an eraser and a piece of chalk. A fourth student is chosen as scorekeeper. 2. The teacher writes on the board a list of Study Words, for example, *now, prow, sow, cow, how, chow.* 3. When the teacher asks, "Who can find, erase, and rewrite the word *sow?*", the first player to walk to the board, complete the chore successfully, and return to his or her desk scores one point. 4. The round continues until all the words have been erased at least once. The winner of Erase and Spell is the player with the most points. 5. Variation: The teacher may give a brief definition instead, e.g., "Who can find, erase, and rewrite the word that means a pig?"	**Erase and Spell**
1. One student writes a Study Word on the chalkboard. 2. The next student in turn writes a word that begins with the last letter of the first word. 3. The game continues until one player cannot Hook-On a new word. 4. Partners or teams can play.	**Hook-On**
1. The teacher writes on the board a Study Word, omitting the vowels of the word (e.g., *m ssp ll*). 2. At their seats, the players write the word completely and correctly (i.e., *misspell*) on paper. 3. The teacher selects a player to write his or her answer on the board. If the player's response is correct, he or she may then put a vowel-less word on the board for the rest of the class to solve. If the player's response is incorrect, another player has a turn. 4. The winners of Leave-Out are all the players who solved the incomplete words correctly either at the board or at their seats.	**Leave-Out**
1. The teacher writes on the chalkboard identical lists of words and each word has one missing letter. There are as many words in each list as there are players on the team assigned to that list. 2. At a signal the first player on each team goes to the board and writes in the missing letter in one word on the team's list. As soon as the first player finishes, the second player on the same team attempts to complete a different word. 3. The first team to complete all its words correctly wins Missing Relay.	**Missing Relay**
1. Study Words are written on separate slips of paper, which are then folded and placed in a box. 2. One at a time, the players pull out a slip but do not look at the word. Each player hands the slip to the teacher or to "It," who pronounces the word for the player to write on the chalkboard. 3. If the word is spelled correctly, the teacher or "It" keeps the slip. If the word has been misspelled, the player keeps the slip for future study. 4. Players who have no slips at the end of the round are the winners of Pull and Spell.	**Pull and Spell**

Figure 8.3. (cont.)

Roots	1. Divided into two-partner teams, each team receives a dictionary, a pencil, and a large card with a derived word printed on it (e.g., *fearless, enjoyment, handful*). Each card bears a different word, which also appears on the chalkboard.
	2. Each team determines what portion of its word is the root word and then consults the dictionary in order to compile a list of other words also derived from the same root. The list is written on the back of the word card.
	3. When time is called, Partner One writes the team list on the chalkboard under the word originally printed on the team card. Partner Two proofreads the team list.
	4. The team with the longest correct list wins Roots.
	5. Individuals or larger teams can play.
Spelling Bingo	1. Each player folds a sheet of paper into sixteen squares.
	2. The teacher writes on the chalkboard sixteen words. The players copy the words on their papers, putting only one into a square and determining the locations by themselves.
	3. The teacher erases the board and proceeds to call out the words, one at a time. The players put dry beans or discs on the appropriate squares.
	4. When a player has a row or diagonal filled, he or she calls out, "Spelling Bingo!" and reads the words aloud. The player then writes the four words on the board while his or her classmates and teacher help check the bingo.
Supernatural	1. Each player is given a dictionary, a pencil, and some paper.
	2. He or she must search the dictionary for ten minutes for all the words that have five syllables (just as *Supernatural* does) and then write them down.
	3. When time is called, each player copies his or her list on the chalkboard for everyone to proofread.
	4. The player with the longest list of correct words wins Supernatural.
	5. Variation: Younger players may prefer Super, which requires words of only two syllables.
Touchdown	1. The teacher draws on the chalkboard a large diagram of a football field, indicating the goal lines and the 10–50-yard lines.
	2. Two teams are chosen (Teams A and B) that in turn each select a team captain. The captains determine which goalpost each team will defend and choose a team color. A scorekeeper is selected to continually note the teams' positions on the field with chalks representing team colors.
	3. On the chalkboard, outside the diagram but near the goalpost it is defending, each team is assigned space in which to write the words the teacher will dictate.
	4. The teacher begins the game by reading one Study Word at a time to Team A, whose players in turn write the words in the space allocated. Each word correctly spelled advances the team ten yards, as duly noted by the scorekeeper. If no misspellings occur, a touchdown is scored by Team A after ten words or one hundred yards

Figure 8.3. (cont.)

5. However, if Team A misspells a word on its own 30-yard line, for example, Team B has its turn and can score a touchdown by running only thirty yards or spelling three words correctly. Should Team A misspell a word on Team B's 30-yard line, then Team B can score a touchdown by running seventy yards or spelling seven words correctly.
6. The team with the most touchdowns within a designated period of time wins Touchdown.

Treasure Hunt

1. Teams are chosen, and on the chalkboard, the teacher writes a different word at the end of each team's column. All words, however, contain the same number of letters.
2. At a signal, the first player on each team goes to the board and writes one word that uses letters from the team's assigned word. For example, from *tamer,* the player could write *am, tame, ram, mar, ear, me,* or *mat.*
3. After the first player returns to his or her desk, the second player goes to the board and writes a different word from the same team word.
4. The round continues until time is called. The winner of Treasure Hunt is the team with the longest list of correct words. The teacher or designated Student Hunter proofreads the lists.

Write or Wrong

1. Two teams are established (Teams A and B), and their players prepare individual name tags, which are collected facedown and separated into two piles.
2. The teacher calls out a spelling word. Players on both teams write the word on paper at their seats.
3. The teacher selects a name tag from Team A's pile and calls upon the owner to copy his or her word on the board for the class to see. If the player can do so correctly, Team A gets a point; if the player fails, a tag from Team B is picked.
4. With each new word during Write or Wrong, all tags are returned to their proper pile so that every player has an equal opportunity to be chosen for any one word.

Evaluation of Student Progress

Teacher Evaluation of Students

Evaluation in spelling goes on informally and continually in written composition assignments and instructional spelling sessions. It occurs, too, more formally and less frequently during periodic tests.

Wise teachers provide for both weekly and monthly testing of the child's mastery of his or her word list. Such testing, particularly when followed by brief teacher-student conferences, can contribute to a growing sense of spelling achievement. Every child is encouraged to reflect upon personal growth as the teacher reviews his or her spelling record. Such individual guidance is essential to effective teaching and learning of spelling.

Appraisal of the overall growth of the class in spelling should also be made periodically, though on an informal basis, by observing the following:

- Can the students use correct spelling in their writing assignments?
- Do they locate their own misspelled words?
- Are the students consulting dictionaries or individual word lists?
- Is each student increasing his or her spelling proficiency?

The teacher may also wish to assess class progress in spelling more formally on a monthly or semester basis by designing a test that follows a format developed by the California State Department of Education.[31] It simulates actual written production but involves multiple choice items. It assumes that spelling ability is a result of both word memory and strategies for predicting the spellings of unknown words.

Children choose from a list of possible letter options the one that correctly completes the spelling of a partly spelled word, and then they write the word on the paper. Some examples follow:[32]

Predictable Words   Grade 3   I like to climb tr _____ s.

(a) ee
(b) ie
(c) ea
(d) ei

Grade 6   I enjoyed the dis _____ ussion after the movie.

(a) k
(b) c
(c) ck
(d) g

Words with Suffixes   Grade 3   I gave both bab _____ their toys.

(a) ys
(b) ees
(c) eys
(d) ies

Grade 6   We will go swim _____ every day.

(a) ing
(b) ming
(c) eing
(d) in

Grade 3   I only hit him _____ nce.   Demons

    (a) ou
    (b) o
    (c) wu •••••••••••••••••••••••
    (d) wo

Grade 6   The fire swept thr _____ the woods.

    (a) ioux
    (b) ue
    (c) oo •••••••••••••••••••••••
    (d) ough

Grade 3   _____ not very hot today.   Homophones

    (a) Its
    (b) It's •••••••••••••••••••••••

Grade 6   The boys could _____ strange noises in the cave.

    (a) here
    (b) hear •••••••••••••••••••••••

Infrequently teachers are asked to administer formal standardized tests that are purported to inform teachers, administrators, parents, and school boards where some students stand in relation to other students in the local school system and across the county, state, or nation.

Standardized Spelling Tests

    Rated as recommended are those spelling tests found as subtests of such reputable and standardized achievement test batteries as the *Iowa Tests of Basic Skills* (from the Riverside Publishing Company, Chicago, IL) and the *Metropolitan Achievement Tests* (from the Psychological Corporation, Cleveland, OH). Also earning good reviews is a separate spelling evaluation instrument called *Test of Written Spelling* (published by PRO-ED of Austin, TX) which is norm-referenced and uses the dictation format.[33] It takes twenty-five minutes to administer and can be given on either an individualized or a group basis. Standardized achievement tests, however, do not constitute the best means of evaluating spelling instruction because they cannot measure the growth that has taken place in a particular situation by a particular student.

Students can participate in the process of evaluating their spelling growth in several ways. First, they can correct their own spelling tests. This useful procedure is made even more effective when the children *hear* the teacher read the correct spelling while they *see* each word spelled correctly on a specially prepared overlay.

Self-Evaluation by Students

The Second Writing Tool—Spelling   273

Figure 8.4. Self-Evaluation Progress Chart, Form A.

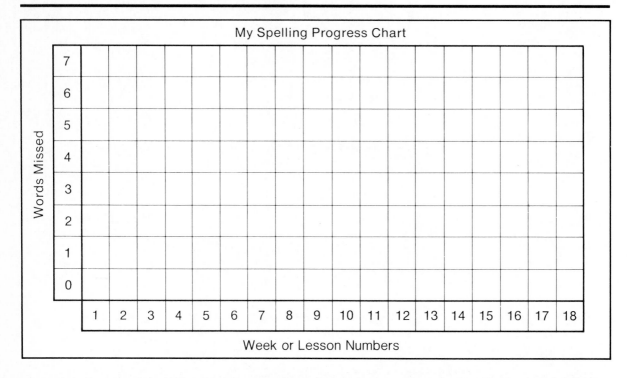

Secondly, students can keep individual progress charts. They can note either the number of words missed, as shown in Figure 8.4, or the number of words correctly spelled (multiplied by a given number to provide a point score), as shown in Figure 8.5. In either case, dots are entered on the simple graphs and connected periodically.

Finally, children can maintain lists of words that they continue to misspell during composition work or in other subject areas. Such a Personal Spelling Demons list for an intermediate student might contain the following words:

money	cousin	business	vegetable
forty	knowledge	review	argument
courtesy	difference	valuable	naturally
often	seize	height	whose
although	anxious	separate	amateur
changeable	occasion	against	mischievous
ninety	persuade	necessary	trouble
straight	receive	calendar	sandwich
hospital	acquaintance	disappear	plaid
absence	sincere	familiar	misspell

Figure 8.5. Self-Evaluation Progress Chart, Form B.

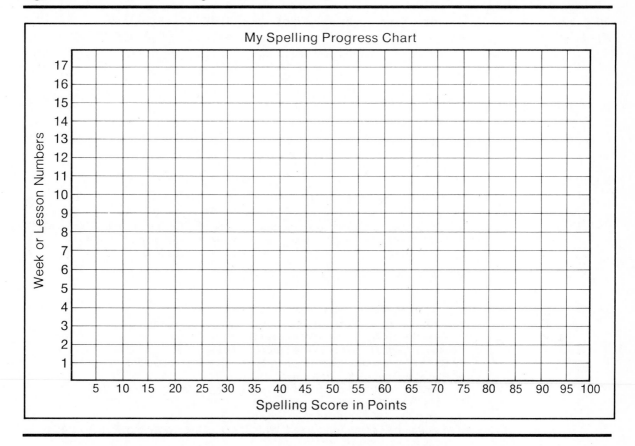

1. If spelling plays a relatively minor role in the total program of most elementary schools, why has it maintained a certain permanence in the curriculum?
2. Would intermediate units about English words and their spellings improve spelling achievement in grades four through six? Why or why not?
3. How can parents promote spelling growth in their child(ren)?
4. In the contemporary elementary classroom, how should student progress in spelling be determined?
5. Do you believe that if there is a strong relationship between spelling and reading, then spelling lists should consist exclusively of words introduced during reading lessons? Why or why not?
6. Why do so many teachers refuse to incorporate research-based recommendations into their instructional spelling program?

Discussion Questions

The Second Writing Tool—Spelling

Figure 8.6. Language Arts Learning Center: Spelling.

TYPE OF CENTER: **Spelling—Prefixes and Suffixes**   TIME: 10-15 minutes
GRADE LEVEL: 4-5   NUMBER OF STUDENTS: 2

INSTRUCTIONAL
OBJECTIVE: The students will practice working with prefixes and suffixes to expand words.

MATERIALS: Four sets of cards containing words that use prefixes (pocket 1) and other words that use suffixes (pocket 3), paper, pencils, activity sheets, an envelope for completed work.

Example: act   en

DIRECTIONS:
1. Take a worksheet and pencil.
2. Take the set of cards out of pocket 1. Look at the cards.
3. Take the prefix cards out of pocket 2.
4. Match the prefix cards to the cards in pocket 1.
5. Say the new words to yourself. Write them on the worksheet.
6. Place the cards off to the side.
7. Take the cards out of pocket 3. Look at the cards.
8. Take the suffix cards out of pocket 4.
9. Match the suffix cards to the cards in pocket 4.
10. Say the new words to yourself. Write them on the worksheet. Put the cards back into the correct pockets.
11. Complete the exercise at the bottom of the activity sheet.
12. When you finish, place the worksheet in the envelope provided.

Suggested Projects

1. Collect samples of primary children's writing and analyze their invented spellings. At which stage of development does each student appear to be?
2. Make a chart that shows How to Study a Word. It could be displayed permanently in the classroom.
3. Obtain some first drafts of compositions written by fourth graders and list the words most frequently misspelled in them. What can you conclude about the more common types of spelling errors?
4. Use one of the learning games described in this chapter with a group of third-grade students. Then report to your peers about the group's reactions.

Pocket 1 Use words such as:

lease	tract	human	dress
way	marine	set	come
correct	appear	bend	able
tend	fit	claim	paid
visible	act	fresh	mount
miss	complete	pack	

Pocket 2 Prefixes to use:

re-	in-	en-
sub-	un-	ex-
be-	dis-	
pre-	de-	

Pocket 3 Use words such as:

add	work	create
power	grace	envy
long	move	entertain
kind	govern	short
fear	loud	slow
call	dark	rapid

Pocket 4 Suffixes to use:

able	ing	ful
ed	less	ly
ness	est	
er	ment	

Worksheet: (Leave the top half of sheet blank for students to write words.) Using these root words, make as many words as you can by adding prefixes, suffixes, or both.

turn	heart	some	strong	avoid
use	water	visible	fury	adjust
cover	ball	self	chant	best

EVALUATION: The teacher will collect a number of papers. Have the students check their own work as you and a group go over the words written. A scoring procedure could be determined by the students and teacher (e.g., one point per word made).

Source: From PATHWAYS TO IMAGINATION by Angela S. Reeke and James L. Laffey, © 1979 by Scott, Foresman and Company. Reprinted by permission.

5. Investigate some of the alternative forms to traditional orthography, such as those designed by Sir James Pitman, John Culkin, and George Bernard Shaw. Do you believe that one of these forms would help resolve the spelling problems of some children?

6. Examine two current editions of commercial spelling programs for level five and compare the kinds of activities suggested for children of high ability and for those of low ability. Determine why such programs do not meet the individual spelling needs of most children.

7. Set up the learning center on spelling shown in Figure 8.6.

Recent Related Readings

Bean, W., and Bouffler, C. 1988. *Spell by Writing.* Portsmouth, NH: Heinemann.

Cummings, D. 1988. *American English Spelling.* Baltimore, MD: Johns Hopkins University Press.

Ehri, L., and Wilce, L. 1987. "Does Learning to Spell Help Beginners Learn to Read Words?" *Reading Research Quarterly, 22,* pp. 47–65.

Gable, R., Hendrickson, J., and Meeks, J. 1988. "Assessing Spelling Errors of Special Needs Students," *The Reading Teacher, 42,* pp. 112–117.

Harp, B. 1988. "When the Principal Asks: 'Why Are Your Kids Giving Each Other Spelling Tests?' " *The Reading Teacher, 41,* pp. 702–704.

Hendrickson, H. 1988. "Spelling: A Visual Skill," *Academic Therapy, 23,* 389–395.

Hoffman, S., and Knipping, N. 1988. "Spelling Revisited," *Childhood Education, 64,* pp. 284–287.

Isaacson, A., Rowland, T., and Kelley, P. 1987. "A Fingerspelling Approach to Spelling," *Academic Therapy, 23,* pp. 89–96.

Quinn, C. 1988. "Sight Word Spelling Tricks." *Academic Therapy, 23,* pp. 287–291.

Stewig, J. 1987. "Students' Spelling Errors," *The Clearing House, 61*(1), pp. 34–37.

Chapter Notes

1. E. Henderson and S. Templeton, "A Developmental Perspective of Formal Spelling Instruction through Alphabet, Pattern, and Meaning," *Elementary School Journal,* 1986, *86,* pp. 305–316.

2. E. Henderson, *Learning to Read and Spell* (De Kalb, Illinois: Northern Illinois University Press, 1981); E. Henderson and J. Beers, *Developmental and Cognitive Aspects of Learning to Spell* (Newark, Delaware: International Reading Association, 1980); J. Zutell, "Spelling Strategies of Primary School Children and Their Relationships to Piaget's Concept of Decentration," *Research in the Teaching of English,* 1979, *13,* pp. 69–80; R. Hodges, *Learning to Spell* (Urbana, Illinois: National Council of Teachers of English, 1981); and R. Gentry, "Learning to Spell Developmentally," *The Reading Teacher,* 1981, *34,* pp. 378–383.

3. R. Cramer, *Children's Writing and Language Growth* (Columbus, Ohio: Charles E. Merrill, 1978), p. 105.

4. Gentry, "Learning to Spell,"; and R. Gentry, "Early Spelling Strategies," *Elementary School Journal,* 1978, *79,* pp. 90–92.

5. R. Gentry, *Spel . . . Is A Four-Letter Word* (Portsmouth, New Hampshire: Heinemann, 1987), pp. 24–25.

6. Gentry, *Learning to Spell,* p. 380.

7. R. Barron, "Visual and Phonological Strategies in Reading and Spelling," in *Cognitive Processes in Learning to Spell,* U. Frith, ed. (London, England: Academic Press, 1980), pp. 195–213.

8. G. Marsh, M. Friedman, V. Welch, and P. Desberg, "The Development of Strategies in Spelling," in *Cognitive Processes in Learning to Spell,* U. Frith, ed. (London, England: Academic Press, 1980), pp. 339–353.

9. U. Frith, "Unexpected Spelling Problems," in *Cognitive Processes in Learning to Spell,* U. Frith, ed. (London, England: Academic Press, 1980), pp. 495–515.

10. R. Cramer, "An Investigation of First Grade Spelling Achievement," *Elementary English,* 1970, *47,* pp. 230–237.

11. K. Anderson, "The Development of Spelling Ability and Linguistic Strategies," *The Reading Teacher,* 1985, *39,* pp. 140–147.

12. E. Lutz, "ERIC/RCS Report: Invented Spelling and Spelling Development," *Language Arts*, 1986, *63*, p. 744.
13. J. Beers, C. Beers, and K. Grant, "The Logic Behind Children's Spelling," *Elementary School Journal*, 1977, *77*, pp. 238–242.
14. L. Ganschow, "Discovering Children's Learning Strategies for Spelling through Error Pattern Analysis," *The Reading Teacher*, 1981, *34*, p. 680.
15. Oregon Department of Education, *English Language Arts Concept Paper #3: Spelling* (Salem, Oregon: Author, 1987), pp. 3–4.
16. R. Hodges, "The Language Base of Spelling," in *Research in the Language Arts*, V. Froese and S. B. Straw, eds. (Baltimore: University Park Press, 1981), p. 222.
17. C. Chomsky, "Reading, Writing, and Phonology," *Harvard Educational Review*, 1970, *40*, pp. 287–309.
18. J. Downing, J. DeStefano, G. Rich, and A. Bell, "Children's Views of Spelling," *Elementary School Journal*, 1984, *85*, pp. 186–198.
19. R. Fitzsimmons and B. Loomer, *Spelling: Learning and Instruction* (Des Moines, Iowa: Iowa State Department of Public Instruction, 1978), pp. 75–78.
20. *Ibid.*, pp. 24–61.
21. Beers, Beers, and Grant, "The Logic," p. 242; D. Hammill, S. Larsen, and G. McNutt, "The Effects of Spelling Instruction: A Preliminary Study," *Elementary School Journal*, 1977, *78*, pp. 67–72; and G. Manolakes, "The Teaching of Spelling: A Pilot Study," *Elementary English*, 1975, *52*, p. 246.
22. D. Morris, L. Nelson, and J. Perney, "Exploring the Concept of 'Spelling Instructional Level' through the Analysis of Error-Types." *Elementary School Journal*, 1986, *87*, p. 182.
23. *Ibid.*, p. 196.
24. P. DiStefano and P. Hagerty, "An Analysis of High Frequency Words Found in Commercial Spelling Series and Misspelled in Students' Writing," *Journal of Educational Research*, 1983, *76*, p. 185.
25. *Ibid.*, p. 184.
26. B. Cronnell and A. Humes, "Elementary Spelling: What's Really Taught," *Elementary School Journal*, 1980, *81*, pp. 59–64.
27. DiStefano and Hagerty, "An Analysis of High Frequency Words," p. 184.
28. Manolakes, "The Teaching of Spelling," p. 244.
29. R. Gentry, "Guidelines for Evaluating a Spelling Series: A Look at the Research Base," *Spelling Progress Quarterly*, 1988, *4*(1), pp. 1, 3.
30. Hodges, *Learning to Spell*, p. 15.
31. California Assessment Program, *Survey of Basic Skills, Grade 3: Rationale and Content* (Sacramento: California State Department of Education, 1980); and California Assessment Program, *Survey of Basic Skills, Grade 6: Rationale and Content* (Sacramento: California State Department of Education, 1982).
32. *Ibid., Grade 3*, pp. 23–24; and *Grade 6*, pp. 46–48.
33. J. Mitchell, Jr., ed., *The Ninth Mental Measurements Yearbook*, Volume II (Lincoln: University of Nebraska Press, 1985), p. 1279.

The Third Writing Tool— Grammar 9

Major Chapter Goals

After studying Chapter 9, the reader will be able to

1. Understand the continuing debate over the teaching of grammar to children.
2. Describe the major kinds of grammar presented in elementary classrooms today.
3. Explain the significance of developing skills in sentence combination.

Discover As You Read This Chapter Whether*

1. Grammar is a controversial area in the language arts curriculum today.
2. There is no one common definition of the word grammar.
3. Kindergartners demonstrate their knowledge of grammar without ever studying it formally.
4. Grammar instruction generally promotes language development.
5. Activities in sentence combination have no effect on receptive or productive language growth.
6. For elementary school children, informal instruction in grammar has only negative results.
7. Among the major kinds of English grammar presented in elementary classrooms is structural grammar.
8. Traditional grammar is concerned with how people do talk and not how they should talk.
9. The newest major kind of English grammar is transformational grammar.
10. Basic sentences in transformational grammar are known as *kernels*.

*Answers to these true-or-false statements may be found in Appendix 5.

The basis of grammar-related language study should be the revision of selected pieces of student writing in view of the audience for that writing. (© James L. Shaffer.)

Grammar is receiving more and more attention in many schools today, due in part to the back-to-basics movement. If students supposedly can neither read nor write as well as they should or as well as their predecessors did, the general public remains convinced that studying grammar will help alleviate the situation.

On the other hand, in the summer of 1986, the National Council of Teachers of English resolved that the use of isolated grammar and usage exercises is a deterrent to the improvement of students' speaking and writing and that in order to better both of those skills, class time must be devoted to more opportunities for meaningful oral and written language.[1] It even urged the discontinuance of testing practices that promote the teaching of grammar over English language arts instruction.

The Continuing Debate Over Grammar

The teaching of grammar therefore remains a major, if controversial, area of the language arts curriculum. There are several aspects to the debate.

The first involves *definitions* and stems from the fact that the very term *grammar* has different meanings for various groups or individuals. Although some writers provide five or more varied interpretations, the following are the three most common definitions of the term:

1. Grammar is a written description and explanation of how language is produced. It is a study of systems and includes the labeling of parts of speech, the labeling of certain types of phrases and clauses, and the labeling of various types of sentences.

Grammar instruction using workbook exercise drills concerned with sentence combination can significantly affect both productive and receptive language growth and development.
(© James L. Shaffer.)

2. Grammar is a set of abstract rules of communication by which even young children (who are normal) comprehend and produce sentences. It is the underlying structure of language that humans use intuitively. Thus, five-year-olds entering school already know English grammar, according to Sanborn, and they know it thoroughly and unconsciously to the level that most high school texts try to teach.[2] Already they have nearly total competence to express meanings they apprehend. Their built-in grammar is such that the primary teacher can informally use vocabulary such as *verb* and *noun* to give the students names for discussing what they already know.

3. Grammar is usage of so-called language etiquette. It is a description of those sounds, units of meaning, and constructions that are preferred and socially prestigious, in contrast to those that are not. To some advocates of this interpretation, grammar even includes writing conventions or mechanics such as punctuation and capitalization.

A second aspect of the ongoing debate over grammar centers on the *values* of such formal instruction. For many years educators argued that the separate study of grammar presented a positive effect on the overall study of language. However, it is now known, after numerous research findings, that studying grammar formally makes few, if any, contributions to the growth of reading or listening skills, to achievement in second languages, or to expansion of productive language generally or written composition particularly. Briefly, grammar instruction by itself has little or no value in promoting or enhancing language development.[3] In fact, taught in certain ways (such as marking every error), grammar instruction has actually proved to have a detrimental effect on student writing.[4]

The one exception appears to be the combining of sentences, both in reading and in writing. During the past twenty years studies with students as young as second graders have shown that activities in sentence combining significantly affect both productive and receptive language growth and development, and may facilitate cognitive growth as well.[5] One form that such activities can assume is the type of workbook exercise drills exemplified later in this chapter, which focus on sentence building. Another form is the revision of selected pieces of student writing, either during private conferencing or during anonymous class display on overhead transparencies for positive peer analysis. Incidentally, such revision of writing in view of the audience for that writing should be the very basis of grammar-related language study, according to Haley-James.[6] A third form of beneficial activities is sentence combination drills found in some language arts textbooks, as shown in Figure 9.1.

The third conflict in the grammar debate relates to the *type of instruction*. The consensus appears to be that formal instruction in grammar only has a negative effect on elementary children, primarily because time devoted to such instruction could be put to better use in helping boys and girls listen, read, speak, and write with greater effectiveness. *Informal* instruction, on the other hand, is useful and even necessary to help pupils perform competently in language by understanding grammatical vocabulary and concepts.

Consequently, it is the teacher who must acquire a knowledge of formal grammar[7] in order to present some of its varied aspects informally to the students at opportune times. This casual strategy is referred to by Kean as teaching grammar from the student's perspective.[8] The teacher must know when to intervene to help children correct their own grammar, and he or she must also make decisions about how, where, and when to help boys and girls improve immature syntax. Those interventions and decisions are best made when the teacher understands the processes by which new sentences may be formed as well as the structure of existing sentences. Instructional activities described later in this chapter typify some of the informal strategies that teachers can adapt for use with small groups of learners or with individual students.

A fourth part of the continuing debate over the teaching of grammar concerns *content* (terminology, elements, and emphases). The three systems most often presented in the elementary classrooms today are traditional grammar, structural grammar, and transformational grammar. Some of their terminologies and elements are similar, but their emphases differ. Each system is discussed later in this chapter.

Some school districts select one grammar over the others, and some elementary language textbook series are equally dedicated. Other districts and texts prefer to present an eclectic grammar that combines elements freely from all three types. They believe that the way to assist students in using language more effectively is not necessarily through a study of any one theory of the nature of

Figure 9.1. Exercises in Sentence Combination.

Combining Sentences by Adding Words

Focus

Sometimes you can combine two sentences by adding a word from the second sentence to the first sentence.

Sometimes two sentences that work well together can be joined into one sentence. The new sentence may express an idea more clearly and smoothly than two separate sentences do. Read these sentences.

Jean bought a notebook. It was purple.

The only word in the second sentence that adds any information is *purple. Purple* can become part of the first sentence.

Jean bought a **purple** notebook.

Read these sentences. Notice how the important word from the second sentence has become part of the first sentence.

Alex studied for the test. *He studied* hard.
Alex studied **hard** for the test.

Lydia rubbed her fingers. *They were* chilled.
Lydia rubbed her **chilled** fingers.

In each example, only the important word in the second sentence was added to the first sentence. The words in italics were left out.

Sometimes you can combine words from more than two sentences. The sentences must all work together. One sentence must tell the main idea. Each of the other sentences must add one important word to the main idea.

A koala clung to a branch. *The koala was* sleeping. *The branch was* sturdy.
A **sleeping** koala clung to a **sturdy** branch.

Exercises: Combining Sentences by Adding Words

A. Combine each set of sentences into one sentence. Leave out the words in italics. Write the new sentence on your paper.

1. The lemon is a fruit. *The fruit is* sour.
2. Al slid down the hill. *Al slid* quickly.
3. The Mustangs tried to win the championship game. *The Mustangs tried* hard.
4. Cut the tomato into slices. *Cut it* carefully.
5. Detective Johnson thoughtfully studied the clues. *The clues were* strange.
6. Ellen spotted the dog. *It was* lost.
7. Mr. Ogami drew a face on the paper I turned in yesterday. *The face was* smiling.
8. Lola and Molly waded in the stream. *The stream was* bubbling. *The stream was* little.
9. Julius unfolded the letter. *The letter was* important. *He unfolded it* slowly.
10. Rosa took off her jacket. *Her jacket was* new. *Her jacket was* corduroy.

B. Combine the sentences in each group. Add important words from the second and third sentences to the first. Write the new sentence on your paper.

1. Dad chopped the celery. He did it quickly. The celery was fresh and crisp.
2. Rosa's hat drooped in the rain. The hat was straw. The rain was heavy.
3. The horses raced through the streets. The horses were frightened. The streets were dark.
4. The car left a spot on the garage floor. It was a large spot. It was a greasy spot.
5. Three coins were inside the box. The coins were silver. The box was locked.

Source: Pgs. 251–252, *McDougal, Littell English, Silver Level.* Copyright © 1987 by McDougal, Littell & Company, Box 1667, Evanston, Illinois 60204.

English grammar. Instead, they believe that there are significant components to be derived from all three grammars. Consequently, these generalizations are worthy of a place in the elementary curriculum:

- The emphasis in grammar instruction should be on how language operates to convey meaning.
- The study of basic sentence patterns should be central to the beginning study of grammar because it can help students become more conscious of the subject-predicate relationship and the rhythm of the sentence. Work with the complete subject and the complete predicate should be introduced when treating basic relationships within the sentence.
- The study of sentences should include the four major word classes (i.e., nouns, verbs, adjectives, and adverbs) and their inflection as well as the most useful classes of structure words (or connectors) and their use.
- The basic sentence patterns may be compounded, subordinated, and transformed. Work in grammar should therefore give much practice in compounding, subordinating, and modifying. It should also include substituting structures within the basic sentence patterns and transforming the patterns themselves.
- Grammatically essential sentence elements tend to be fixed, and grammatically less essential elements tend to be movable. All children should have considerable experience in changing sentences about and in rearranging and changing the information conveyed by the sentences.[9]

Major Kinds of English Grammar

English grammar, as it is known today, did not exist until the seventeenth century. Although grammar was an important part of the school curriculum before that time, the grammar taught in the schools was Latin, not English. English was, after all, only the language of the common folk.

Currently there are three separate and undiluted grammars prominently presented in elementary classrooms in the United States. A fourth kind, the so-called *eclectic grammar,* draws from all three and presumably uses the best elements of each. It is as yet uncharted, however, and varies from district to district and from publishing house to publishing house.

Traditional Grammar

Because Latin was for centuries considered by scholars to be the perfect language, traditional grammar is a classification of English based partly on resemblances, real and supposed, to Latin. Originating in England during the seventeenth and eighteenth centuries, it was written by grammarians whose goal was to prescribe usage, establishing "rules" for speakers and writers to follow.

Refined in this century, traditional grammar accurately emphasizes the subject-predicate nature of the English sentence and the fact that function within the sentence is the ultimate determinant of word classification. It is primarily interested in syntax, and it is always presented to pupils through the deductive method.

Traditional grammar, however, makes little attempt to discover how people learn languages. It fails to distinguish adequately between content words and function words in English sentences. It demands memorization of eight parts of speech (nouns, verbs, adjectives, adverbs, pronouns, prepositions, conjunctions, and interjections) whose inconclusive definitions often mix levels (e.g., the definition of a noun tells what it is, but the definition of an adjective tells what it does). Traditional grammar uses a form of diagramming that does not help many children see clearly the basic building blocks of each sentence. It fails to describe its operations with any consistency. It deals with exceptions, making the pupil unaware of the major grammatical patterns in the language. Finally, it tends to ignore English as a spoken language. Many, but not all, traditional grammarians are *prescriptive,* operating from the false assumption that there is a standard English grammar that is changeless and permanent, and that the school's task is to develop competence in understanding the elements of that grammar.

Traditional grammar is concerned with the knowledge of eight parts of speech. It mandates the ability to define and recognize structural elements of sentences (such as subjects, predicates, complements, and modifiers of all types). It classifies sentences both by purpose (declarative, interrogative, and exclamatory) and by form (simple, compound, complex, and compound-complex). It considers the word as the most important element of communication. And because *traditional grammar deals primarily with the written forms of language,* it tends to explain only what happens when language is used formally by educated people.

Even with good teaching, traditional grammar suffers from the efforts of early scholars to fit English (a Germanic language) into the preferred Latin mold. One major example concerns *verbs.* The six tenses of traditional grammar tally exactly with the Latin. Yet English can be regarded as having only two true tenses (the simple past and the simple present) that are usually represented by single words spelled differently. Tense in English verbs is more often a matter of inflection, rather than time, because other elements in the construction may show time functions too. Latin, on the other hand, expresses time only by variations in the forms of the root word. Little wonder that the attempts to fit English into Latin patterns have resulted in confusion.

What needs to be reiterated at this point is that if many schools insist on teaching certain concepts of traditional grammar (such as identification of parts of speech), they cannot defend those practices as a means of improving the quality of children's writing.[10] This at least is according to numerous research findings over the past twenty years.

Structural Grammar

Developed in the United States in the 1930s by Leonard Bloomfield and others, structural grammar began as a study of the structure of English. Instead of prescribing how people *should talk* (as traditional grammar does), it is descriptive and concerned with how people *do talk* today. It analyzes the living spoken language to ascertain the basic structure of English sentences, the intonation patterns signaling meaning, and the words that operate as signs to indicate parts of speech. Supporters of this system believe that grammar is essentially a description of speech sounds and of sound combinations, and that language goes from form to meaning. They also find that any structure generally accepted by a given speech community is correct for that community; there is no "ideal" language.

The structuralists have developed a technique for classifying words into parts of speech, sometimes referred to as the slot-and-substitution method. The best way to understand this technique is to look at a few examples:

- A noun is a word such as *bicycle* in *The (bicycle) is old.*
- A verb is a word such as *see* in *I (see) the bus.*
- An adjective is a word such as *sad* in *She is very (sad).*
- An adverb is a word such as *quickly* in *The robber ran (quickly).*

Sometimes called Class I, Class II, Class III, and Class IV, there are four *word-form classes* among the words with lexical meaning (i.e., nouns, verbs, adjectives, and adverbs). All other words are called structure words, of which there are fifteen to seventeen groups, depending on the structuralist. The English language is broken into four subdivisions:

1. *Intonation* or melody, whose elements are levels of pitch, degrees of stress, and junctures, as discussed in Chapter 2.
2. *Sentence patterns,* especially including the five basic types outlined in Chapter 2. Examples of each type were Pattern I—*Birds sang;* Pattern II—*Mother bought cookies;* Pattern III—*Father is a teacher;* Pattern IV—*Summer is hot;* and Pattern V—*Tom was here.* Once the children have mastered these basic patterns they are ready for practice in expanding sentence patterns. They can use *compounding* (or adding subjects, predicates, and objects), *modification* (or adding adjectives, adverbs, determiners, intensifiers, prepositional phrases, participial phrases, and dependent clauses), and *subordination* (with relative clauses modifying noun headwords, or with clause modifiers after the noun headword). Examples of these three techniques include, respectively: (a) *Birds and bees fly;* (b) *The three tall boys were brothers;* and (c) *The girl who was in my class went to Japan.*
3. *Structure words,* or function words, primarily show the grammatical and syntactical relationships within sentence patterns. They number about 300, and are used with greater frequency than all other words in the language. Relatively lacking in meaning or content, they are often the most difficult for pupils to learn in reading. Although they are never taught in isolation, the most important structure words include articles, possessive pronouns, conjunctions, prepositions, and forms of *be, do,* and *have.*
4. *Word-form changes* have two main divisions. There are the inflectional suffixes (such as plural endings and possessives) of the four word-form classes, and there are also the derivational prefixes (such as *dis* and *sub*) and suffixes (such as *able* and *ness*) that modify word meanings or convert words from one class to another.[11]

In structural grammar the study of syntax essentially becomes a problem of determining the regularities in the arrangements of form-classes. Constructions have no specific content but comprise a series of "slots" into which particular kinds of material, including form-classes, can be fitted. Each slot must contain a specific kind of material because, if it does not, the result either belongs to another construction or is not accepted as meaningful by the speakers of the language. A sample construction can be diagrammed as follows:

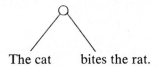

The cat   bites the rat.

Here the little circle represents the construction, and the lines running from it lead to the *constituents* of the construction. There are both immediate constituents and ultimate constituents. In this example the major subwholes, or largest parts of the construction, are the immediate constituents (or ICs for short): *The cat* and *bites the rat*. The ultimate constituents which are its individual morphemes, are [The], [cat], [bite], [-s], [the], [rat].

The structuralists stress oral communication and believe that written language is only a repetition of spoken language. Their goal is to describe and catalog all the observable features of language.

Transformational Grammar

Developed in the United States during the 1950s by Noam Chomsky, the third major kind of grammar is generally known as *transformational grammar*. Like structural grammar, it provides patterns for the analysis of existing sentences; however, it also has rules for producing new sentences. Its proponents assert that, if preschool children with limited experience can generate thousands of new sentences based on the early sentence structures they have learned, there must be an underlying process that can be explained and taught. Consequently, whereas the structuralists are concerned only with the surface level of language structure, the transformationalists are interested in both the *surface structure* (human speech) and the *deep structure* (ideas, thoughts, meaning) underlying actual speech performance. Due to this dedication to the processes by which deep structure is transformed into surface structure, the grammar is therefore called transformational. An example follows:

Surface structure = *They are teaching fellows.*
Deep structure (first meaning) = Those fellows are fellows who teach.
Deep structure (second meaning) = Some people are teaching some fellows.

The term "transformational" also refers to the division of American English sentences into two classifications: basic sentences or *kernels* (with subjects and predicates) and their variations or *transforms*. The formula for a basic sentence may be written as follows: S ⟶ NP + VP (a sentence consists of a noun phrase plus a verb phrase). It can also be diagrammed as follows:

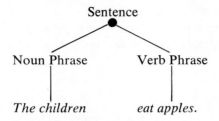

There are four or more basic types of kernels or kernel sentences, depending on the linguist questioned. Each such sentence is affirmative (not negative), and each is a statement (not a question). Each kernel is in the active voice and always begins with the subject. Finally, a kernel contains only a single predication, and that follows the subject. Essential to the basic kernel are the terms *noun phrase* and *verb phrase*.

Four groups of words or kinds of words function as a subject in a kernel: (a) determiner (or article) + common noun (*The boy* walked the dog); (b) proper noun (*Mr. Black* is a teacher); (c) personal pronoun (*They* ran home); and (d) indefinite pronoun (*Everyone* seemed hungry). Each of these subjects is called a *noun phrase,* even though it may be a single word. A noun phrase is the name for a structure but not for a word class, *noun* being an example of a word class.

In a kernel the first word of the predicate is usually a verb or a form of the word *be—am, is are, was,* or *were.* The word *be* and its forms do not behave the way verbs do, so *be* is not called a verb but is considered in a class by itself. Every predicate of a kernel must contain either a form of *be* or a verb. If it contains a form of *be,* something else must follow, as in *He is a sailor.* If the predicate contains a verb, the verb may be or may not be followed by something else, as in *They look sick.* Verbs may also be followed by other words such as adverbials.

The verb phrase has been clearly marked in the following sentences:

The girl *works quickly.*
The girl *is working quickly.*
The girl *has been working quickly.*

A variety and a flexibility of material may appear within a verb phrase.

All English verbs in the present tense have two forms: the simple form (*see, walk*) that goes with the plural subject, and the *s* form (*sees, walks*) that goes with the singular subject. Verbs, however, are not considered singular or plural but merely correspond in form to the requirements of the subject. In transformational grammar there are only two tenses—the past and the present—which are always shown by the first word in the predicate and which are not the same as time.

Any sentence that is not a kernel is a transform or transformation, and most sentences that people use are transformations. The base of any transformation is the kernel (or kernels) out of which it is formed. There are both single-base and double-base transformations.

Transforms

Single-base transformations concern one kernel sentence. Among the most common are the *interrogative,* the *negative,* the *passive,* the *command,* the *expletive* (or "there" transform), and the *indirect object* transformations. One of the simplest is the *yes-no transform.* In order to form a yes or no question, elements are transposed and the final punctuation in written language is changed:

> The girl is pretty. (kernel)
> Is the girl pretty? (transform)

Double-base transformations involve the combination of two or more kernels into a single, more complex sentence. The two most common types are *coordinating transforms* and the more numerous *subordinating transforms.* In the latter group the most frequently used is the *relative clause.* Always beginning with a relative pronoun or relative adverb, it actually replaces the subject of the inserted or embedded kernel:

> My friend has a brown dog. (kernel)
> The brown dog can do tricks. (kernel)
> My friend has a brown dog that can do tricks. (transform)

Exercises A through F are inductive exercises (designed for students in the middle grades) that involve either single-base (Exercises A-B) or double-base (Exercises C-F) transformations.[12] In them the symbol $\Rightarrow$ indicates that this is a transformation rule and is read as "is rewritten as." Furthermore, in each exercise there is a valuable segment entitled Application, which demands that students create their own sentences by employing the specific transformation under scrutiny. Exercises C through F are especially important for young writers because they concern sentence combining, a research-proven technique for positively affecting children's written composition skills.

GIVEN:
1. The dog is in the yard. ⇒ The dog is not in the yard.
2. His father owns a car. ⇒ His father does not own a car.

MATERIAL:
1. The bird was in a bush. ⇒
2. I am a new student. ⇒
3. A freeple is a furple. ⇒
4. A snirkle uggled a smiffle. ⇒
5. A green dog bit a pink postman. ⇒

Exercise A
The Negative Transformation

DIRECTIONS:
Change the sentences in MATERIAL so that *not* will be in each.

CONCLUSION:
1. Where is *not* added in sentences like nos. 1–3?
2. What other changes must be made in sentences like nos. 4–5?

APPLICATION:
Make up four sentences using the word *not*. Two of the four sentences should include the word *did*. Now write these four sentences without the *not*.

GIVEN:
1. The boy is my friend. ⇒ Is the boy my friend?
2. I can go. ⇒ Can I go?
3. Mary has left. ⇒ Has Mary left?

MATERIAL:
1. The orange bat is my friend. ⇒
2. Pete was a little grey squirrel. ⇒
3. Louise has hit the fat cat. ⇒
4. Some of the boys will leave. ⇒
5. The group of children can stay. ⇒

Exercise B
Yes/No—The Question Forming Transformation

DIRECTIONS:
Change each of the above sentences in MATERIAL to questions that a listener can answer with either "yes" or "no."

CONCLUSION:
1. What did you do to the word order when you made questions out of the sentences?
2. What kind of word now comes first after you have a question?

APPLICATION:
1. Make up three sentences like those in MATERIAL.
2. Change them into questions which can be answered with "yes" or "no."

GIVEN:
1. a) Children
      play.
   b) Children
      work.
   } ⇒ Children play
      and work.

2. a) Children
      play.
   b) Children
      work.
   } ⇒ Either children
      play or children
      work.

MATERIAL:
1. a) I like cake.
   b) I like ice cream.
   } ⇒
2. a) The boys have a hot rod.
   b) The boys have a club.
   } ⇒
3. a) You leave.
   b) You stay.
   } ⇒

Exercise C

*The Coordination
Transformation*

DIRECTIONS:
Join sentences "a" and "b" in each group in MATERIAL.

CONCLUSION:
How did you know which sentence group to use "either-or" with?

APPLICATION:
Write a short paragraph using "and" and "either-or" in the writing.

GIVEN:
   a) I didn't
      go to
      school
      today.
   b) I had a
      cold.
   } ⇒ I didn't go to
      school today
      because I had a
      cold.

MATERIAL:
1. a) I got my lessons finished.
   b) I worked hard.
   } ⇒
2. a) Joe had a stomach ache.
   b) He gobbled his supper.
   } ⇒
3. a) We stayed indoors
      today.
   b) The weather was terrible.
   } ⇒

Exercise D

*The Subordination
Transformation*

DIRECTIONS:
Add 'because' to the front of each 'b' sentence in MATERIAL. Now put this with sentence 'a' to form a new sentence like that produced in GIVEN.

_____
_____
_____
_____
_____
_____
_____

CONCLUSION
Can 'because' + sentence 'b' be added to either front or back of sentence 'a'? _____

Exercise E
The Relative Clause Transformation

GIVEN:
1. The boy hit the ball.
2. The boy is my friend.
} ⇒ The boy who is my friend hit the ball.

MATERIAL:
1. The girl was very noisy.
2. The girl had long pigtails. } ⇒
3. The lady quickly left the room.
4. The lady was the oldest. } ⇒

DIRECTIONS:
1. In sentence no. 2 in MATERIAL change *the girl* to *who*. Now place sentence no. 2 between *girl* and *was* in sentence no. 1. Write the new sentence.
2. In sentence no. 4 change *the lady* to *who*. Now place sentence no. 4 between *lady* and *quickly* in sentence no. 3. Write the new sentence.

CONCLUSION:
What can you do with two sentences that have the same first part?

APPLICATION:
Make up three sentences that look like the two you made in DIRECTIONS.

Exercise F
The Combination of More Than One Sentence

GIVEN:
1. The dress is a color.
2. The dress is blue.
3. The color is pretty.
} ⇒ The blue dress is a pretty color.

MATERIAL:
1. The buffalo charged the Indian.
2. The buffalo is old.
3. The Indian is brave.
} ⇒

DIRECTIONS:
Combine the above three sentences in MATERIAL so that they are one. The meaning of the new sentence should be the same as the three separate sentences.

_____
_____
_____
_____

CONCLUSION:
1. Two of the sentences are "put" inside the third. Which two are put inside the third? How?

_____
_____
_____
_____

2. How did you decide which two to put in the other?

_____

_____

APPLICATION:

Below are a number of sentence combinations. Combine the two or three sentences in each group and produce one:

1. a) The car hit the fence.
   b) The car was for racing.
   c) The fence was old.

   _____

   _____

   _____

2. a) The fans clapped their hands.
   b) The fans were eager.
   c) Their hands were cold.

   _____

   _____

   _____

3. a) The judge waved the flag.
   b) The judge was uneasy.
   c) The flag was checkered.

   _____

   _____

   _____

Instructional Activities

Informal instructional activities have proved useful in promoting effective language performance because they introduce or review grammatical concepts and vocabulary. Sample activities are described in this section by grade level.[13]

Grade One and Grade Two

1. Children take everything out of their desks and classify the items by separating them into piles on top of the desks. A discussion follows regarding the classifications the students have chosen (such as colors, shapes, or sizes). In classrooms without desks, the teacher fills a large sack with numerous items and then asks one child to classify the items. Later the teacher writes the child's classification on the board before putting the items back into the sack and asking if another child can classify them in a different way.

2. Each group of children receives individual word cards that make up a possible sentence. Then the members come to the front of the room and arrange themselves into a sentence. (Examples: [a] [Mary] [little] [had] [lamb] and [to] [her] [day] [He] [one] [followed] [school].)

3. Children are shown pictures of objects with two definite parts that can be easily named; for example, frying pan (handle and pan), and book (pages and covers). Then they are given sentences written on slips of paper that must be cut apart into the subject and the predicate. (Example: [The lions] [run fast].)

Grade Three

1. The teacher prepares sets of subject cards and sets of predicate cards. Then each child chooses one card from each set and reads aloud his or her complete sentence. The student may also be asked to identify the subject or the predicate. (Humorous sentences may result in some instances; for example, The boy barked.)

2. Children bring magazine or newspaper pictures from home or draw some pictures in class. Then each child tells which nouns depicted in his or her picture are singular and which are plural. Some pictures may even be arranged on the bulletin board according to the two classifications.

3. Students divide into cooperative learning groups to develop three declarative sentences relevant to a science or social studies unit. These are written on the chalkboard. Then the groups are dismissed, and each child changes the declarative sentences of his or her group into three interrogative sentences and writes them down on a workpaper.

Grade Four

1. Children choose the appropriate noun-verb agreement in each pair of sentences. (Example: *Seals eat fish. Seals eats fish.*)

2. Students collect several newspaper headlines using the noun-verb sentence pattern. They then identify the nouns and verbs in the collected headlines.

3. Children classify the following adjectives into three columns headed Color, Size, and Number: *green, fat, yellow, three, small, twelve, blue, tiny, large, six, short, white, slim, fifteen, slender, brown, dozen, red, tall, thin, purple, black, blond, little, thousand, huge, orange, gigantic, seventy, tan, pink.*

Grade Five

1. Children circle the verbs in a set of sentences prepared by the teacher. (Example: *The rabbit ran fast.*)

2. Students match the words from a column of common nouns with corresponding words from a column of proper nouns and make a statement about the difference between each. (Example: A *city* is any city. *Chicago* is a certain city.)

3. Children list as many activities as possible by fitting verbs in the blank(s) of a set of sentences prepared by the teacher. (Example: *People ___ their homes.*)

Grade Six

1. Every child writes a simple five-line free verse by using one noun (the subject) in the first line, two adjectives in the second line, three verbs in the third, an adverb in the fourth, and the subject and an adjective modifying it in the fifth line:

Ghosts,
Scary, wispy
Glide, float, drift
Slowly,
Pale ghosts.

2. Every child makes up ten jumbled sentences. Then each exchanges sentences with a partner who must rearrange every sentence into meaningful order. (Limits restricting the number of words per sentence are suggested.)
3. Children classify the following words into groups and then make a generalization about each group: *Monday, Baltimore, Thursday, Easter, March, New Year's, Michigan, Christmas, Thanksgiving, September, Idaho, January, Minneapolis, Wyoming, May, Friday, Florida, Alaska, Pittsburgh, Veterans Day, Atlanta, Boston.*

Evaluation of Student Progress

Some well-rated, standardized, achievement test batteries include sections entitled usage, usage and structure, or usage and grammar.[14]

In view of the recognized research-based significance of sentence combination and recognition, however, the classroom teacher may prefer to develop an evaluative instrument that follows a format used recently by the California State Department of Education.[15] It simulates actual written production but involves multiple choice items. Children choose from a list of possible options. The following are examples of exercises that are basically types of progressive and regressive closure tasks.

Sentence Recognition

Supplying Subjects: Grade Three

The teacher says: Fill in the bubble next to the words that are needed to form a complete sentence.

_____ _____ peanut shells at the people.

○ Have thrown
○ Monkeys threw
○ Were throwing
○ To throw

Grade Six

The teacher says: Fill in the bubble next to all of the words that will form one complete sentence.

_____ woke up the neighbors.

○ Every day
○ In the morning
○ His dog
○ Near the fence

Supplying Predicates: Grade Three

The teacher says: Fill in the bubble next to the words that are needed to form a complete sentence.

Sometimes Dan _____ _____ _____ .

○ down the street
○ in the class
○ runs to school
○ to the teacher

Supplying Predicates: Grade Six

The teacher says: Fill in the bubble next to all of the words that will form one complete sentence.

The school carnival _____

- ○ next week
- ○ is coming
- ○ lots of fun
- ○ games and prizes

Sentence Combination— Grade Six

Simple Sentences with Modification

The teacher says: Fill in the bubble next to the sentence that combines the numbered sentences in the best way.

1. Roller skating is a sport.
2. Roller skating is challenging.
3. Roller skating is growing in popularity.
4. Roller skating is played indoors and out.

- ○ Roller skating is a sport, and it is growing in popularity, and it is played indoors and out, and it is challenging.
- ○ Roller skating, a challenging sport growing in popularity, is played indoors and out.
- ○ A challenging sport, roller skating, it is played indoors and out and is growing in popularity.

Compound Sentences and Sentence Parts

The teacher says: Fill in the bubble next to the sentence that combines the numbered sentences in the best way.

1. John is going golfing.
2. James is going golfing.
3. Grace is going bowling.
4. Joyce is going bowling.

- ○ John is going golfing, and James is going golfing, and Grace is going bowling, and Joyce is going bowling.
- ○ John and James are going golfing, but Grace and Joyce are going bowling.
- ○ John is going golfing, James is going golfing, Grace is going bowling, and Joyce is going bowling.

Complex Sentences

The teacher says: Fill in the bubble next to the sentence that combines the numbered sentences in the best way.

1. Ladybugs are beetles.
2. Ladybugs are small.
3. They feed on insects.

- ○ Ladybugs are small beetles that feed on insects.
- ○ Ladybugs are beetles, and they are small, and they feed on insects.
- ○ Ladybugs feed on insects, and they are beetles, and they are small.

The teacher says: Fill in the bubble next to the word that completes the sentence correctly.

Juan has _____ a story about horses.

○ wrote
○ write
○ written
○ writed

The teacher says: Fill in the bubble next to the word that completes the sentence correctly.

Jack _____ his lunch.

○ brung
○ brought
○ brang
○ bringed

The teacher says: Fill in the bubble next to the word that completes the sentence correctly.

_____ went for a ride.

○ Us
○ Him
○ Her
○ We

The teacher says: Fill in the bubble next to the word that completes the sentence correctly.

Send the equipment to Doug and _____ .

○ she
○ me
○ I
○ they

The teacher says: Fill in the bubble next to the word that completes the sentence correctly.

Every day, Martin _____ to school.

○ have walked
○ walks
○ walk
○ were walking

Subject-Verb Agreement: Grade Six

The teacher says: Fill in the bubble next to the words that complete the sentence correctly.

The cats _____ together.

○ was playing
○ plays
○ were playing
○ is playing

Noun Determiners: Grade Three

The teacher says: Fill in the bubble next to the word that completes the sentence correctly.

_____ children broke the toy.

○ This
○ One
○ That
○ Those

Noun Determiners: Grade Six

The teacher says: Fill in the bubble next to the word that completes the sentence correctly.

_____ students are in the marching band.

○ This
○ Them
○ That
○ Those

Discussion Questions

1. Why should the teaching of grammar create almost as much controversy among members of the general public as the teaching of reading?
2. Do you find any similarities among the three major systems of grammar today? What differences exist among them?
3. If instruction in grammatical concepts is preferably conducted on an informal basis, how do you propose to evaluate the girls and boys for their achievement in that area?
4. Were you to be assigned to a school that is planning to introduce transformational grammar next semester, how would you prepare the parents for that grammar in an effort to solicit their support?

Suggested Projects

1. Examine one primary-level book and one intermediate-level book in a single, current language arts text series for their coverage of a grammatical system. Evaluate the content and quality of activities outlined.
2. Survey four teachers in a nearby elementary school to determine whether each presents grammatical concepts to children and how. Be sure that at least one is a primary teacher.

3. Design a learning game for the purpose of reviewing one grammatical concept (e.g., subject-predicate relationships). Try it with a group of children and then refine it.
4. Ask some secondary school English teachers in your local district their viewpoints as to what kind of grammar and how much grammar should be introduced in the elementary school.
5. Examine Maestro's *Busy Day: A Book of Action Words* (Crown, 1978) and then plan an informal instructional activity around that book.
6. Set up the learning center on sentence building shown in Figure 9.2.

Figure 9.2. Language Arts Learning Center: Grammar.

TYPE OF CENTER:	**Functional English—** **Transforming Sentences**	TIME: 30 minutes
GRADE LEVEL:	5–7	NUMBER OF STUDENTS: 4

INSTRUCTIONAL OBJECTIVE:	The students will be able to write better sentences by combining, expanding, and rearranging them.
MATERIALS:	A large box labeled "Magic Generator," smaller flat boxes for "in" and "out" papers, a flag calling for HELP, an "Out of Order" sign, worksheets, paper and pencil.
DIRECTIONS:	This machine changes sentences to make them more interesting. Today the machine is out of order. It needs help to get the work done. Please help!

1. Each student is to select one worksheet from the "in" box.
2. Take a pencil and paper.
3. Write your name and the date at the top of the paper.
4. Follow the directions on the worksheet.
5. You may work with one or two other students on this activity, but each student must hand in a completed exercise.
6. When you have completed the worksheet, return it to the "in" box and put the paper you wrote in the "out" box.

It was nice of you to help. Thank you!

Figure 9.2. (cont.)

Worksheets for Sentence Generating Center

I. Directions: Rewrite each of the following sentences as questions.
  1. The snow storm has lasted the entire day.
  2. The workers built a new fence around the old ball park.
  3. Our cat has chased the ball of yarn.
  4. Eddie mowed the lawn this morning.
  5. The girls have beaten the boys in checkers.
  6. You had read this before.

II. Directions: Write these sentences, adding an adjective (a descriptive word) in each blank space.
  1. My _____ sisters helped.
  2. My _____ brother wrote _____ songs.
  3. The _____ boy threw the _____ magazine away.
  4. A _____ boy wrote a _____ story.
  5. A _____ crowd followed the _____ actors.
  6. The _____ prince visited his _____ classmates.
  7. The _____ mayor greeted the _____ visitors.
  8. Two _____ girls picked the _____ papers off the _____ table.
  9. The _____ world wants _____ peace.
  10. _____ Sue had a _____ dream.

III. Directions: Write ten new sentences by adding words to each part of these sentences. Expand the noun part, then the verb part.
  1. Men work.
  2. Don laughed.
  3. Feet stamped.
  4. Beets grew.
  5. Snow fell.
  6. Bells tinkle.
  7. Bill told a joke.
  8. We called the girls.
  9. Ellen likes tomatoes.
  10. Rain hit the roof.

IV. Directions: Combine each pair of sentences to make one longer, more interesting sentence. Use such connecting words as *but, or, while, so,* or *and.*
  1. Ann will speak. She will take notes.
  2. The cab driver pulled over to the curb. He turned off the motor.
  3. The motor boat raced across the lake. The swimmer raced across the lake.
  4. Sally will sing. She will hum.
  5. Joey must return early. He will not be allowed to go again.
  6. The gardener cut the flowers. He did not water the plants.
  7. The tugboats tooted. The ship tooted back.
  8. The rain stopped. The wind kept howling.
  9. The little boy coughed. He almost choked.
  10. Mrs. Hill spoke. Mr. Hill spoke at the same time.

EVALUATION: The teacher will check the work. Later the class can review papers in small groups.

Source: From PATHWAYS TO IMAGINATION by Angela S. Reeke and James L. Laffey. Copyright © 1979 by Scott, Foresman and Company. Reprinted by permission.

Applebee, A., Langer, J., and Mullis, I. 1987. *Grammar, Punctuation, and Spelling.* Princeton, NJ: Educational Testing Service.

Baugh, L. S. 1985. *Essentials of English Grammar.* Lincolnwood, IL: National Textbook.

Elkins, R. E. 1986. "The Effect of Computer-Assisted Practice on English Grammar and Mechanics Achievement of Third Grade Students," *Dissertation Abstracts International, 47,* 03A. (University Microfilms No. 86–13, 041).

Neville, D., and Searls, E. 1985. "The Effect of Sentence-Combining and Kernel-Identification Training on the Syntactic Component of Reading Comprehension," *Research in the Teaching of English, 19,* pp. 37–61.

Oregon Department of Education. 1987. *English Language Arts Concept Paper # 6: Grammar,* Salem, OR: Author.

Prokopiw, E. 1987. "Making Connections: That's What They're Called," *Language Arts, 64,* pp. 139–140.

Reutzel, D. 1986. "The Reading Basal: A Sentence Combining Composing Book," *The Reading Teacher, 40,* pp. 194–199.

Searls, E., and Neville, D. 1988. "An Exploratory Review of Sentence-Combining Research Related to Reading," *Journal of Research and Development in Education, 21*(3), pp. 1–15.

Strong, W. 1986. *Creative Approaches to Sentence Combining.* Urbana, IL: ERIC Clearinghouse on Reading and Communication Skills.

Willows, D., and Ryan, E. 1986. "The Development of Grammatical Sensitivity and Its Relationship to Early Reading Achievement," *Reading Research Quarterly, 21,* pp. 253–266.

Recent Related Readings

1. National Council of Teachers of English, *Resolution on the Study of Grammar* (Urbana, Illinois: Author, August 1986).
2. J. Sanborn, "Grammar: Good Wine Before Its Time," *English Journal,* 1986, *75*(3), pp. 72–80.
3. S. Straw, "Grammar and Teaching of Writing: Analysis Versus Synthesis," in *Research in the Language Arts,* V. Froese and S. Straw, eds. (Baltimore: University Park Press, 1981), p. 150.
4. G. Hillocks, Jr., *Research on Written Composition: New Directions for Teaching* (Urbana, Illinois: ERIC Clearinghouse on Reading and Communication Skills, 1986), p. 248.
5. *Ibid.,* pp. 142–143.
6. S. Haley-James, "Twentieth Century Perspectives on Writing in Grades One through Eight," in *Perspectives on Writing in Grades 1–8,* S. Haley-James, ed. (Urbana, Illinois: National Council of Teachers of English, 1981), p. 17.
7. C. Weaver, *Grammar for Teachers* (Urbana, Illinois: National Council of Teachers of English, 1979), pp. 83, 86, 90.
8. J. Kean, "Grammar: A Perspective," in *Research in the Language Arts,* V. Froese and S. Straw, eds. (Baltimore: University Park Press, 1981), p. 169.
9. California State Department of Education, *English Language Framework for California Public Schools* (Sacramento: Author, 1976), p. 45.
10. Hillocks, *Research on Written Composition,* p. 138.
11. C. LeFevre, "A Concise Structural Grammar," *Education,* 1965, *86,* pp. 131–137.

Chapter Notes

12. Klein, *Teaching Sentence Structure,* pp. 32–33, 36–37, 40–41, 48–51, 56–57.
13. Bloomington Public Schools, *Language Arts Curriculum Guide K–6* (Bloomington, Minnesota: Author, 1971).
14. J. Mitchell, Jr., ed., *The Ninth Mental Measurements Yearbook,* Volume I (Lincoln: University of Nebraska Press, 1985).
15. California Assessment Program, *Survey of Basic Skills, Grade 3: Rationale and Content* (Sacramento: California State Department of Education, 1980), p. 20; and California Assessment Program, *Survey of Basic Skills, Grade 6: Rationale and Content* (Sacramento: California State Department of Education, 1982), pp. 36–39.
16. *Ibid., Grade 3,* pp. 17–18; and *Grade 6,* pp. 42–43.

Part D Reading

Chapters

The Process of Reading 10

Major Chapter Goals

After studying Chapter 10, the reader will be able to

1. Understand the basal reader approach and its widespread, continued popularity in this country.
2. Outline the major word-recognition skills.
3. Explain the critical relationships of reading comprehension to questioning and to prior knowledge.

Discover As You Read This Chapter Whether*

1. There is a strong relationship between reading and the other language arts.
2. No matter how well a child reads orally, reading does not take place unless there is comprehension of the written material.
3. It has finally been recognized that there is one best way to teach reading to children.
4. Today most girls and boys are ready to read earlier than were their counterparts a few decades ago.
5. Teachers' evaluative judgments about the reading readiness of beginning students have been discredited.
6. The basal reader is used daily in about half of all elementary classrooms.
7. The language-experience approach has proved successful with beginning readers in the kindergarten and primary grades.
8. The individualized reading approach is actually a recreational reading program.
9. It is strongly urged that phonics instruction be continued throughout the elementary grades.
10. Questioning by teachers and students promotes reading comprehension.

*Answers to these true-or-false statements may be found in Appendix 5.

An effective reading program in today's elementary school is based on understanding what reading is, why it should be taught, and what the levels of reading competence are. One popular definition of reading is that it is the process of constructing meaning from written texts.[1] During that process there is an interaction between the reader's experiential background, the reader's language ability, and the printed message. Learning to read is a complex skill that depends on many factors including cognition, motivation, visual perception, the reader's self-image, the teacher's effectiveness, and the caliber of the reading selection.

Reading is taught because it is a direct link between individuals and ideas. It remains one of the best means of retrieving data and thoughts because it can transmit ideas across cultures and across generations. Those who read are said to have access to all of the accumulated knowledge of civilization. They are better able to think critically about a subject, they can fulfill personal interests and needs, and they can, in the long run, contribute to the well-being of society.

The essential skill in reading is getting meaning from a printed or written message, states Carroll, who then delineates the components of that skill as follows:[2]

1. The child must know the language that he or she is going to learn to read.
2. The child must learn to dissect spoken words into component sounds.
3. The child must learn to recognize and discriminate the letters of the alphabet in their various forms (uppercase, lowercase, printed, and cursive).
4. The child must learn the left-to-right principle by which words are spelled and put in order in continuous text.
5. The child must learn that there are patterns of highly probable correspondence between letters and sounds. He or she must learn those patterns that will help him or her recognize words familiar from the spoken language or that will help him or her determine the pronunciation of unfamiliar words.
6. The child must learn to recognize printed words from whatever cues he or she can use—total configuration, letters composing the words, sounds represented by those letters, or meanings suggested by context.
7. The child must learn that printed words are signals for spoken ones and that they have meanings analogous to those of spoken words. As he or she decodes a printed message into its spoken equivalent, the child must be able to apprehend the meaning of the total message in the same way that the meaning of the corresponding spoken message is apprehended.
8. The child must learn to reason and reflect upon whatever he or she reads, within the limits of personal talent and experience.

It is important not only to understand the components of reading skill but also to understand the nature of reading. Three major positions exist regarding the reading process.[3] The first contends that *all reading (beginning or skilled) is holistic* and the reader constructs the text meaning by making predictions, sampling some material for confirmation or rejection of those predictions, and then making new ones; reading then is a process whose focus is the communication of meaning. The second position is that *all reading consists of separate but interrelated subskills,* much like the process of walking, and mastery and integration of the individual skills into a smooth uninterrupted whole marks the advanced reader. The third position which combined the other two makes a distinction between beginning readers and skilled or advanced readers: *Skilled reading is holistic but early reading consists of subskills.*

Although researchers as yet have not resolved the preceeding dilemma, they have determined, according to the Commission on Reading of the National Academy of Education, that becoming a skilled reader demands several different requirements of the students.[4] They must, for example, bet able to draw on their store of knowledge both from everyday life and from school studies when they interpret a text since skilled reading is a *constructive* process. Then they must master basic word identification skills to the point of automaticity because skilled reading is *fluent.* They must also learn to adjust their reading according to their familiarity with the topic and their purpose for reading about it since skilled reading is *strategic.* As it is also *motivated,* students must learn to sustain their attention and realize that printed matter can be both informative and interesting. Finally, since skilled reading is a *lifelong* pursuit, students must accept the fact that reading demands constant practice and refinement.

If then the reading program demands three interrelated and continuous levels of competence (learning to read, reading to learn, and reading for life), there must be several different goals of reading.[5] To acquire the *academic goal,* the student learns to read in order to attain standard spelling, pronunciation, punctuation, handwriting, and interpretation—all of which in turn promote common moral and cultural values transmitted by written material. To achieve the *utilitarian* goal, the student learns to read in order to function efficiently in society and acquires "real-world survival skills" during the instructional program. To attain the *romantic goal,* the student reads to develop understanding of himself or herself and others (with stress on the quality of personal response to a text) during an instructional program that emphasizes literature appreciation, language experience, and value clarification. To achieve the *cognitive-developmental goal,* the student reads to integrate individual development with that of society, including the ability to solve new problems at a personal or societal level. And to reach the *emancipatory goal,* which assumes that society employs education to maintain class distinctions, the student must be placed in an instructional program that eliminates socioeconomic discrimination and that is consistent with the romantic goal of reading.

Principles of Teaching Reading

Generalizations about the teaching of reading, drawn both from research and from classroom observation of actual practices, have recently been compiled in an effort to guide all individuals in planning an effective reading program.[6] The first principle stresses that *reading is a complex act with many factors that must be considered.* The second and third principles state that *reading is the interpretation of the meaning of printed symbols* and that *reading involves constructing the meaning of a written passage.* All the varied aspects of the reading

These primary students know already that reading is enjoyable and entertaining, especially when shared with a friend. (© James L. Shaffer.)

process should be understood by the teacher, who must also realize that reading does not occur without comprehension of the written passage, no matter how well the child reads orally.

Principles four and five emphasize that *there is no one correct way to teach reading* and that *learning to read is a continuing process.* Not only do children learn to read over a period of several years as more sophisticated skills are introduced to them gradually, but adolescents and adults also continue to improve their reading ability even after their formal education stops. Such continuity serves to illustrate the need for teachers to be acquainted with a variety of reading methods so that they may be able to help each classroom learner succeed at assigned reading tasks. The student must be given instruction at his or her own level of accomplishment.

The sixth and seventh generalizations stress that *students should be taught word recognition skills that will allow them to unlock the pronunciations and meanings of unfamiliar words independently,* and that *the teacher should diagnose each student's reading ability and use the diagnosis as a basis for planning instruction.* No one can memorize all the words that appear in print. Children must therefore be instructed in such techniques as phonetic and structural analyses so that they may figure out new words for themselves when helpful peers or adults are not around. Still, they acquire those techniques, as well as the techniques related to comprehension, at individual rates, so the teacher must be continually aware of each student's performance as class lessons are prepared.

The eighth and ninth principles state that *reading and the other language arts are closely interrelated* and that *reading is an integral part of all content area instruction within the educational program.* A review of the results of eighty-nine correlational studies, for instance, shows a particularly strong relationship between written expressive language and reading, which may offer support to those who advocate teaching reading through a combined reading and writing approach.[7]

The tenth and eleventh generalizations emphasize that *the student needs to see why reading is important* and that *enjoyment of reading should be considered of prime importance.* Reading is both entertaining and informative. Teachers can convince young readers of the many benefits of reading by introducing a variety of appropriate materials that meet numerous interest and ability levels.

The final group of principles point out that *reading should be taught in a way that allows each child to experience success,* that *readiness for reading should be considered at all levels of instruction,* and that *encouragement of self-direction and self-monitoring of reading is important.* Success promotes success, and good readers eventually direct their own reading. Nevertheless, reading readiness cannot be restricted to the early primary grades but must be considered whenever instruction in any reading skill takes place, regardless of the grade level.

There are two basic methods for determining reading readiness among beginning students.[8] The first is observation of individual children, using a checklist of characteristics known to have significance in reading success. Teacher judgments have long been recognized as potent evaluative instruments. A sample comprehensive checklist is found in Figure 10.1.

Beginning Reading Readiness

Not all of the items will of course apply to any one child. However, the kindergarten or primary teacher will be better able to help boys and girls make a good start in reading if he or she observes the behavior of children related to the overlapping areas of their physical, social or emotional, and psychological readiness. When the teacher rates any pupil on a majority of the checklist items in the "Usually" or "Sometimes" column, then that boy or girl is more apt to encounter success as a beginning reader than a peer with lower ratings.

The second method of assessing reading readiness is administration of standardized readiness tests. Two group tools that have earned favorable reviews are

1. *Metropolitan Readiness Test, Fourth Edition* (Psychological Corporation, Cleveland, OH). Available in two forms, Level 1 for first-half kindergarten entrants covers auditory memory, rhyming, visual skills, and language skills; it is administered in seven sessions for a total of 105 minutes. Level 2 for second-half kindergarten entrants and first-grade entrants covers auditory skills, visual skills, and language skills; it is administered in five sessions for a total of 110 minutes. A specimen set is available.

Figure 10.1. Teacher Checklist for Assessing Beginning Reading Readiness Among Young Children.

			Child's Name _____			
			Birthdate _____			

CHECKLIST FOR BEGINNING READING READINESS

Category	Item	No.	Usually	Some-times	Seldom	Never
A. Physical Readiness	I. General Health					
	1. Does the child appear well rested?	1.				
	2. Does the child seem well nourished?	2.				
	3. Does the child have sufficient energy to participate in class activity?	3.				
	4. Do his or her teeth and gums appear healthy?	4.				
	II. Eyes					
	5. Can the child see without squinting?	5.				
	6. Can the child see without rubbing his or her eyes?	6.				
	7. Does the child hold materials within normal range?	7.				
	8. Does his or her color recognition appear to be within normal range?	8.				
	III. Ears					
	9. Is it apparent through his or her responses that the child is able to hear what is said in class?	9.				
	10. Does the child respond to a low-voice test at 20 feet?	10.				
	11. Does the child respond to a whisper test at 15 inches?	11.				
	12. Can the child respond without visual contact?	12.				
	IV. Speech					
	13. Can the child talk without stuttering?	13.				
	14. Can the child talk without lisping?	14.				
	15. Does the child speak without gross errors in pronunciation?	15.				
	16. Is his or her voice pleasant, clear, and readily audible?	16.				

Figure 10.1. (cont.)

Category	Item	No.	Usually	Some-times	Seldom	Never
A. Physical Readiness (cont.)	V. Coordination					
	17. Can the child button and unbutton his or her clothes?	17.				
	18. Can the child bounce and catch a ball?	18.				
	19. Can the child control a writing instrument?	19.				
	20. Does the child consistently use one hand without vacillating from the left hand to the right hand?	20.				
	21. Can the child copy three distinct geometric shapes?	21.				
	22. Can the child distinguish between objects of various sizes?	22.				
	23. Can the child pick one specific shape out of a mixed group of shapes?	23.				
	24. Can the child trace a line going from left to right?	24.				
	25. Can the child draw a recognizable human?	25.				
	26. Can the child walk up and down the stairs?	26.				
	27. Can the child walk on a straight line?	27.				
	28. Can the child walk well on a balance beam?	28.				
	29. Can the child hop on the right foot and on the left?	29.				
	30. Can the child jump rope five times in succession?	30.				
	Subtotal A.					
B. Social/ Emotional Readiness	VI. Social Readiness					
	31. Does the child assert himself or herself?	31.				
	32. Does the child meet new peers comfortably?	32.				
	33. Does the child meet new adults comfortably?	33.				
	34. Does the child seem comfortable in the environment?	34.				
	35. Does the child appear to deal confidently with others and with the environment?	35.				
	36. Does the child seek involvement with peers?	36.				
	37. Does the child assume a share of group responsibility?	37.				
	38. Does the child actively participate in group play?	38.				

Figure 10.1. (cont.)

Category	Item	No.	Usually	Some-times	Seldom	Never
B. Social/ Emotional Readiness (cont.)	VI. Social Readiness—contd.					
	39. Can the child be a follower as well as a leader?	39.				
	40. Does the child listen while others speak?	40.				
	41. Does the child comply with the teacher's requests?	41.				
	42. Does the child share materials?	42.				
	43. Does the child respect the rights and materials of other children?	43.				
	44. Does the child offer help to other children?	44.				
	45. Does the child await his or her turn when playing?	45.				
	46. Does the child await his or her turn for help from the teacher?	46.				
	47. Does the child share the teacher's attention with peers?	47.				
	48. Does the child take care of his or her own clothes and materials?	48.				
	49. Can the child take care of personal physical needs?	49.				
	50. Is the child self-directed?	50.				
	51. Can the child work independently?	51.				
	52. Does the child see a task through to completion?	52.				
	VII. Emotional Readiness					
	53. Does the child express feelings verbally?	53.				
	54. Does the child seem happy?	54.				
	55. Is the child able to cope with success?	55.				
	56. Is the child able to cope with failure?	56.				
	57. Does the child accept routines?	57.				
	58. Can the child accept changes in routines?	58.				
	59. Can the child resolve personal problems?	59.				
	60. Does the child seek help when it is needed?	60.				
	61. Does the child attempt new tasks?	61.				
	62. Does the child show curiosity about the environment?	62.				
	63. Does the child show pride in his or her work?	63.				
	64. Can the child comfortably leave the person who brings him or her to school?	64.				
	Subtotal B.					

Figure 10.1. (cont.)

Category	Item	No.	Usually	Some- times	Seldom	Never
C. Psychological Readiness	VIII. Awareness of Reading 65. Does the child appear interested in books and reading?	65.				
	66. Does the child ask the meanings of words or signs?	66.				
	67. Is the child interested in the shapes and sizes of unusual words?	67.				
	68. Does the child recognize common words in the environment; e.g., ''stop'' signs?	68.				
	IX. Mental Maturity 69. Can the child give reasons for his or her opinions about personal work or that of others?	69.				
	70. Can the child make or draw something to illustrate an idea as well as most of his or her peers?	70.				
	71. Is the memory span sufficient to allow memorization of a short poem, song, or commercial slogan?	71.				
	72. Can the child tell a story or relate an experience without confusing the sequence of events?	72.				
	73. Can the child listen or work for five minutes without becoming restless?	73.				
	X. Mental Habits 74. Does the child look at a succession of items from left to right?	74.				
	75. Does the child exhibit creative imagination when describing a given picture?	75.				
	76. Does the child understand that conversation may be presented in written form?	76.				
	77. Can the child predict possible outcomes for a story?	77.				
	78. Can the child add a logical conclusion to an open-ended sentence; i.e., ''I am happy when . . . ?''	78.				
	79. Is the child aware of the consequences of his or her actions?	79.				
	80. Will the child alter his or her behavior in view of the consequences?	80.				
	81. Can the child recall the central thought of a story?	81.				
	82. Can the child recall the important parts of a story?	82.				

Figure 10.1. (cont.)

Category	Item	No.	Usually	Some-times	Seldom	Never
C. Psychological Readiness (cont.)	XI. Language Patterns 83. Does the child constructively contribute to class discussions and conversations?	83.				
	84. Is the child effective in expressing personal needs in large and small groups?	84.				
	85. Is the child effective in expressing personal needs on a one-to-one basis?	85.				
	86. Is his or her speaking and listening vocabulary part of the vocabulary used in preprimers?	86.				
	87. Does the child understand words dealing with the concepts of spatial relationships, directionality, and size?	87.				
	88. Does the child listen to a story with evidence of enjoyment?	88.				
	89. Is the child able to express an experience through dramatic play?	89.				
	90. Is his or her dominant language English?	90.				
	Subtotal C.					
	TOTAL					

2. *CTBS/S Readiness Test* (CTB/McGraw-Hill, Monterey, CA). Level A is for kindergarten through early first grade, and it covers eight tests: letter forms, letter names, listening for information, letter sounds, visual discrimination, auditory discrimination, language, and math. It is administered for a total of 159–216 minutes, divided over several sessions. Level B is available for posttesting. A specimen set is available.[9]

Because readiness test predictions are more likely to be valid for good students than for poor ones, the best determiner of any child's readiness for reading consists of a combination of teacher observation (as noted on a checklist) and the pupil score on a standardized readiness test.

Due to the interrelated factors affecting reading readiness, it is no longer possible to name a specific mental or chronological age as a guarantee of success in reading. Children today have greater exposure to mass media than their counterparts a few decades ago, and therefore, they have a higher readiness level at an earlier age. Results of evaluations of "Sesame Street," for example, show that young regular viewers (ages three to five) have a greater mastery of a wide range of visual and auditory perceptual skills of readiness than children who are not regular viewers.[10] These patterns hold true for all groups of children, regardless of socioeconomic status, mental ability, geographic location, sex, or age.

The Kindergarten Reading Program

Furthermore, many more young boys and girls are attending day-care centers, Head Start programs, and nursery schools than ever before as the number of single-parent families remains high and even continues to rise in some communities. It is not uncommon for such parents to demand at least a semblance of structured academics in which children develop and are taught the skills that had once been exclusively emphasized in kindergarten. Nevertheless, teachers and school administrators alike must never lose sight of the fact that girls and boys who are least ready for systematic reading lessons are the very children who need early opportunities to begin to write and need numerous experiences with printed and oral language.[11]

Consequently, reading instruction in the kindergarten should be sufficiently flexible so that it may be adapted for use at each child's level of development. A responsible teacher will attempt to help the kindergartner progress toward the next level of ability while simultaneously respecting the pupil's need to function confidently at his or her present level. The teacher will limit the size of any instructional group in order to provide for every child's maximum progress, and the teacher will delay beginning reading activities until the child is mature enough to learn to read without difficulty or unnecessary pressure.

In other words, a kindergarten reading program that is developmentally appropriate is guided by the realization that young children

1. Learn through experiences that meet *all* their developmental needs.
2. Learn through self-selected activities as they participate at a variety of interesting centers (including block play, math, science, listening, writing, reading, art, construction, music, manipulatives, and sociodramatic play).
3. Must be encouraged to discuss their experiences with other students and adults in the classroom.
4. Must be involved in a variety of psychomotor experiences (including movement, rhythm, music, small and large motor manipulatives, and outdoor activities).
5. Must be provided with many opportunities to interact with meaningful printed contexts (including participating in shared book experiences, developing key word vocabulary lists, making language-experience books, reading classroom labels, listening to stories, and using print in the various learning centers or stations).[12]

One successful approach to a kindergarten reading program involves the sharing of books by children in a pleasant and stimulating environment. (© Jean-Claude Lejeune.)

A flexible reading program in kindergarten will therefore include three stages—with individual pupils working in various levels of the stages during any part of the reading process because the stages have not been designed as a step-by-step formula:[13]

Stage I: Reading development, during which readiness for reading can be determined. Activities suggested may be used in a total group situation, in small groups, or with individual boys or girls; they are not in sequential order nor do they demand any specific period of time. Should a child show little understanding or interest, the following skill activities should be postponed and more informal activities continued: motor development, identification of self and surroundings, hand-eye coordination, sequencing of events, visual discrimination, visual memory, language usage, auditory discrimination, and listening skills.

Stage II: Initial stage in learning to read. Skill activities include using spoken context, listening for initial sounds, distinguishing letter forms, associating letter sounds and forms, and developing a recognition vocabulary.

Stage III: Stages of progress in fundamental reading attitudes, habits, and skills. Skill activities include word recognition (both sight vocabulary and work attack), recognition of punctuation marks, ability to read for deeper meaning, adaptation of reading method to purpose and content (silent reading and oral reading), and ability to study independently.

Some children may complete Stage III during the kindergarten year, whereas others will progress only as far as Stage I or Stage II. There should be some interaction among the stages because reading readiness activities are continued throughout all levels of learning to read. Nevertheless, it is strongly recommended that the child experience success in the elements of Stage II before attempting Stage III.

One successful approach to the kindergarten reading program involves sharing books with the children. When they listen to and discuss books every day, children generate positive attitudes toward reading and develop familiarity with book language and book characteristics. Such sharing can include poetry charts, song charts, and so-called Big Books that are oversized editions of popular picture books useful for group experiences. Children can cluster around the Big Book as the teacher leads them through the story and encourages them to make predictions based on what they see and hear. When the teacher has finished, the group "reads" the story aloud in unison, although at this stage the children probably cannot recognize individual words. Then after becoming familiar with each Big Book in group fashion, girls and boys like to explore regular-sized versions of the same books either independently or with peers. They become aware of print and of the concept that reading is getting meaning from print.

Predictable books or patterned books with their repetitive semantic patterns or rhythmic syntactic patterns encourage even the slowest children to look forward to reading periods. Five major groups of such structured language books include the following:

1. Books with repetitive patterns in which one particular phrase or sentence is repeated at various intervals during the story; for example, Martin's *Brown Bear, Brown Bear* (Holt, 1983).
2. Books with repetitive-cumulative patterns in which a word, phrase, or sentence is repeated in each sequential episode, thereby adding a new word, phrase, or sentence to the sequence; for example, Guilfoile's *Nobody Listens to Andrew* (Follett, 1957).
3. Books with rhyming patterns, many of which have the rhyme combined with repetition and cumulative-repetition; for example, Emberley's *Drummer Hoff* (Prentice, 1967).
4. Books with predictable plots in which episodes occur in such a way as to enable the listener or reader to predict future events; for example, Burningham's *Mr. Gumpy's Outing* (Holt, 1971).
5. Books with patterns based on familiar cultural categories (including months of the year, days of the week, seasons, colors, cardinal and ordinal numbers, and the alphabet); for example, Keats's *Over in the Meadow* (Four Winds, 1972) and Baskin's *Hosie's Alphabet* (Viking, 1972).

Another use of patterned books is as a resource for written composition—because the children's reliance on a predictable pattern gives them confidence in their abilities to express themselves in writing. Patterns serve as frameworks and models for student expression. Once young children have worked with patterns in their math lessons, they become adept at identifying patterns in their picture books and later at incorporating them into language activities.

Incidentally, the Commission on Reading favors a balanced kindergarten program in language and reading, as based on the best current evidence.[14] Such a program includes both informal and formal approaches with systematic instruction that is free from undue pressure.

Major Instructional Strategies

This section discusses at some length the three major systematic procedures that elementary school teachers presently employ to teach and develop the skills and abilities needed to guide each learner to mature reading. Some teachers prefer an eclectic approach, borrowing a few of the features from each of the major strategies and combining them confidently to meet the needs of one classroom of girls and boys. Others prefer to use programmed instruction (which teaches in small, sequential steps called frames and does not require direct teacher supervision) or computer approaches. The latter includes both computer-assisted instruction (CAI) with its drill-and-practice and tutorial types and computer-managed instruction (CMI) with its assistance to teachers regarding student performance and learning assignments. Both the CAI and CMI are sometimes available in a single coordinated package.

The Basal Reader Approach

The basal reader is not just one book but represents an entire package of books and supplementary materials used to teach reading. This package (and every major publisher has one) is composed of a series of fifteen to sixteen pupil books that range in size and difficulty from preprimers to sixth-, seventh-, or eighth-grade readers. It also includes teacher manuals that correspond to the pupil books, text-related workbooks, a management component or testing program, and supplementary materials such as tapes, flash cards, paperback enrichment books, and kits of readiness or audiovisual resources. No wonder most researchers affirm that the basal reader approach is used in one form or another in 75–90 percent of elementary classrooms on any given day, and that basal programs account for the major part of students' and teachers' time during the reading period.

In comparison to those of earlier decades, features of contemporary basal series reveal better ethnic balance; better male and female balance; inclusion of the handicapped; inclusion of senior citizens; deletion of violence; better balance of urban, suburban, or rural settings; better balance of geographic areas; vigorous graphic arts components; improved literary quality; a more balanced selection of literary genres; sections devoted to glossary study; and (in the teachers' manuals) developmental lesson plans. Because so many of the basal series appear to be nearly identical on the surface, it is suggested that teachers who are asked to examine several programs and then recommend one for their grade level or school use the checklist in Appendix 4 in order to determine significant differences among series and thereby locate the one that best fits their needs.

The typical procedure for teaching a lesson in the basal reader is the Directed Reading Activity (DRA), which generally consists of four to five specific subsections:

1. Motivation, introduction of new vocabulary or concepts.
2. Guided silent reading and sometimes oral reading for definite purposes.
3. Skill-building activities usually focused on decoding or comprehension skills.
4. Follow-up practice, often through workbook exercises.
5. Supplementary or enrichment activities, sometimes in materials furnished by the publisher and often relating the story to art, music, or creative writing.

A viable alternative to the DRA is the DRTA, or Directed Reading-Thinking Activity. It demands that pupils become actively involved in the reading process by asking questions about the story, by processing the information as they read the story, and by receiving feedback about their original questions. Its primary goal is to develop critical readers. Major differences between the DRA and the DRTA run as follows:

1. The DRA is "materials oriented" and "teacher-manual oriented" with specific guidelines, questions, and instructional materials. The DRTA has fewer explicit guidelines, giving the teacher considerable flexibility as well as sole responsibility for the development of the lesson. It can be used in teaching any of the other elementary school curricular areas that demand reading, unlike the DRA which is primarily concerned with basal reader programs.
2. The teacher's role in the DRA is to ask the boys and girls to supply answers to questions found in the manual, and most of such questions are at the literal level of comprehension, which requires convergent thinking. In the DRTA, however, the teacher asks questions that require a higher level of thinking, known as divergent thinking. By so doing, he or she promotes comprehension skills that make reading a dynamic activity that goes beyond responding to factual questions.
3. In the DRA, new vocabulary is introduced before the children open their books. In the DRTA there is no preteaching of vocabulary. Instead, the girl or boy must make use of decoding skills to unlock new words as these appear in the story selection, just as she or he would do during similar situations outside of reading class.
4. In the DRA, the manual details which comprehension skills will be taught and when they will be presented. In the DRTA, however, there is no such prescription, and therefore, the teacher must develop the art of good questioning as well as the ability to accept alternative answers to certain questions.[15]

Briefly, for the beginning teacher concerned with attempting to meet the needs of all the children in his or her classroom every day, the basal reader approach offers several advantages. There is a gradual introduction of word analysis skills and of vocabulary. Skills are presented in sequential order and continued through all the levels. There are ready-made tests and seatwork. Finally, the organization is both horizontal (coordination of materials) and vertical (social organization, comprehension, word analysis skills, and vocabulary).

After inexperienced teachers have worked with the basals and learned the skills sequences, they are better able to organize their own resources and thereby grow in their confidence to handle a reading program competently.

The Language-Experience Approach

Sometimes used in conjunction with the basal reader approach, the language-experience approach (LEA) is founded on the theory that reading and comprehending written language is an extension of listening to and understanding spoken language. The experiences of the children form the basis for reading materials and so the approach is consistent with schema theory described later in this chapter. Boys and girls first dictate to the teacher (in groups or individually) and later themselves write stories about field trips, school activities, and personal experiences outside of school. These stories and other student-produced materials become the texts for learning to read. Many are in the form of charts.

The rationale for this approach has been stated as follows:

- I can think about what I have experienced and imagined.
- I can talk about what I think about.
- What I can talk about, I can express in some other form.
- Anything I can record, I can recall through speaking or reading.
- I can read what I can write by myself and what other people write for me to read.[16]

One popular way the approach can begin occurs after the class has participated in a positive, common experience and has discussed it thoroughly. When it is ready to compose an experience story, the teacher asks for suggestions for a story title, recording the final group choice on a transparency or chalkboard. Each child then offers a detail to the story, which the teacher also records and reads aloud. When all contributions have been given, the teacher reads the entire story to the class, quietly emphasizing left-to-right progression. Finally the class is asked to read the story aloud with the teacher. On the second day, the class is divided into three or four groups, each of which works separately with the teacher who again rereads the story aloud, using a master chart prepared from yesterday's initial effort.

Slowly, students begin to write their own experience stories, sometimes in small groups and sometimes individually, choosing at times to illustrate them. The teacher also develops "word banks" for each child, made up of vocabulary cards of the words used in the group or individual stories.

The main advantage of the language-experience approach is its stress on reading as one part of the communication or language arts process. It also uses the interests and language of the students as the avenue for teaching reading, which makes it especially successful. Still another advantage is its low cost; there are no expensive materials required. Finally, skills are presented to the child as they are needed and applied in contextual reading, not in isolation.

On the other hand, the approach has certain limitations. There is no printed scope and sequence of skills to develop, which may create a haphazard method of reading instruction. There is a lack of both vocabulary control in general and the systematic repetition of new words in particular. There is an unusually high expenditure of teacher time on preparing charts and worksheets concerned with past experiences as well as on planning activities to stimulate future experience stories. Students are apt to become bored with rereading the same stories and other passages again and again, and they may even memorize some of the sentences rather than actually read them.

Briefly, the language-experience approach can be used at any elementary grade level by seasoned teachers interested in integrating their writing and reading programs. It has been well received as an appropriate way to present reading to those kindergartners who display many signs of readiness. It has also proved successful with beginning readers in the primary grades and with remedial readers in the intermediate grades, principally due to the vocabulary and interest levels of the materials. Finally, the language-experience approach has been especially beneficial to students who speak English as a second language (ESL) or who speak a nonstandard English dialect. Sample charts developed by children (with their teacher's guidance) in a beginning ESL class are shown in Figure 10.2.

The Individualized Reading Approach

In this approach the teacher introduces skills as they are needed in reading. The core of the individualized reading approach is the child-teacher conference (held at least once a week), which is generally based on the books that pupils have selected for their own reading. Although steps are sometimes skipped, a suggested format for such conferences covers approximately fifteen minutes (the usual amount of time planned):

1. Greet the child and converse with him or her briefly about a matter of personal interest, such as soccer. (½–1 minute)
2. Ask the child what he or she has read since the last conference and what is being presently read, inviting a brief account of the reading matter. (1–2 minutes)
3. Have the child read a passage aloud from the book he or she is presently reading, noting vocal fluency as well as the level of difficulty of the material. Offer positive feedback. (2 minutes)
4. Check up on a skill reviewed or introduced at the last conference and correct the assignment made (see step 6). Offer praise for any gains made. (2 minutes)
5. Review or introduce a new skill. (3 minutes)
6. Give a follow-up assignment to be checked at the next conference session. (1 minute)
7. Help the child set goals for completion by the next conference, telling him or her when that conference will be and which skills will be practiced. (1 minute)

Figure 10.2. Sample Language-Experience Charts Developed in Beginning ESL Classes by Teachers and Children.

In Our Room

There are 18 boys in our room.

There are 14 girls in our room.

There are 10 goldfish in our room.

There are 2 teachers in our room.

On Mondays

We stand outdoors by the flagpole on Mondays.

We salute the flag.

We sing songs.

We hear speakers.

8. If a new book must be chosen shortly, offer several suggestions and describe each book briefly. (1 minute)
9. Compliment the child on progress already made and then dismiss her or him. (½ minute)
10. Complete your records of items covered during the conference before motioning to the next child to come to your desk. (1 minute)[17]

Two types of recordkeeping have been suggested: children's reading logs and teacher's observational forms.[18] Both kinds are shown in Figures 10.3 and 10.4.

| | My Name _____ Date ____ |
| 1. Copy the title of what you read here _____ |
| _____ |
| 2. Did you like what you read? |
| GREAT!!!   O.K.   NO |
| 3. How did you share or celebrate? _____ |

Figure 10.3a.
Children's Reading
Log (grades K–1).

Reading Log

NAME _____

Figure 10.3b.
Children's Reading
Log (grades 2 and up).

	Copy title here:	Copy author(s) here:	Why did you read this book?	What do you think about this book?	Will you have a conference with the teacher?
1.					
2.					
3.					

Source: Lyndon W. Searfoss/John E. Readence, HELPING CHILDREN LEARN TO READ, © 1985, pp. 127–128. Reprinted by permission of Prentice-Hall, Inc., Englewood Cliffs, New Jersey.

The individualized reading approach is not a recreational reading program, although both foster independent reading. Recreational reading programs are intended only to help pupils understand that reading can indeed be an enjoyable experience. They lack child-teacher conferences, plans for keeping records of pupil progress, book-sharing sessions, and skills-instruction components.

The need for the individualized approach clearly exists for three reasons. First, individualized reading does not depend on basals but involves a variety of materials and can even occur in the absence of the teacher. It therefore simulates closely the type of reading method that literate adults use, and it helps students transfer school learning outside of the classroom. Furthermore, it places a heavy emphasis on the personal enjoyment and satisfaction to be gained through reading,

Figure 10.4.
Teacher's Recording
Form for Individualized
Reading Conferences.

Record Form
Individualized Reading Conference

Child's Name _____ Date _____
Title and Author _____
_____

_____ Fiction   _____ Nonfiction

1. Reason child gave for choosing reading material _____
_____

2. Comprehension of   Good   OK   Poor   Can't Tell

   Central thought or theme   ____   ____   ____   ____
   Plot (if story)   ____   ____   ____   ____
   Details   ____   ____   ____   ____
   Sequence   ____   ____   ____   ____

3. Critical thinking-through

   Relate to other reading   ____   ____   ____   ____
   Inferences, predictions   ____   ____   ____   ____
   Evaluating accuracy   ____   ____   ____   ____
   Personal opinions   ____   ____   ____   ____

4. Did child seek help with words or ideas that were confusing?

                          _____ Yes   _____ No

   (List words, ideas)

5. What will the child do with what has been read? (report, sharing activity)

6. What will the child read next?

7. Estimate the child's overall reaction.

      5   4   3   2   1
   GREAT!   OK   UNINTERESTED

   Estimated time for conference: _____ min.

   Other notes:

Source: Lyndon W. Searfoss/John E. Readence, HELPING CHILDREN LEARN TO READ,
© 1985, p. 129. Reprinted by permission of Prentice-Hall, Inc., Englewood Cliffs, New
Jersey.

thereby establishing lifelong reading habits. Finally, the approach helps the classroom teacher meet the problem of differing reading abilities, which exists at every grade level. Because the differences actually increase as children grow older, the range of ability in the sixth grade has been predicted to be a little more than seven years!

Other advantages of this approach include (1) the development of a healthy rapport between child and teacher as instruction is adjusted to the specific needs

The individualized reading approach demands a wide variety of materials and so simulates the type of reading method that literate adults use. (© James L. Shaffer.)

of each learner and (2) the equally important reduction of comparison and competition among readers. Small groups can be formed as needed for specific purposes when several children encounter similar and temporary difficulties in one area, such as contextual analysis. The key words to this approach are self-motivation, self-selection, and self-pacing.

However, those same key words also relate to a major limitation of the individualized reading approach: a well-stocked library. Besides the books in the media center, the classroom library should always have at least one hundred carefully selected books that cover a wide range of reading abilities and that are changed monthly. Such a collection is both difficult to house in a convenient spot and expensive to gather. Furthermore, it leads to a second important disadvantage of this approach: the time-consuming effort by the teacher to be knowledgeable about the broad array of reading materials that can then be promoted to allow for the most beneficial conferences. Children can be encouraged to read on a variety of subject matter only if materials are available locally on those same subjects and written on reading levels suitable for elementary school boys and girls.

Other weaknesses of the individualized reading approach include the heavy record-keeping burden on the teacher; the stressful requirement that he or she provide a mini-reading program for each pupil; the difficulty of interpreting the reading program to the parents, who are generally much more familiar with and accustomed to the basal readers; and the danger of insufficient skill development due to poor management of time. Finally, some girls and boys may lack the self-discipline needed to profit from the individualized reading approach, which of course becomes increasingly difficult to implement as the range of reading abilities, the size of the class, and the number of remedial readers get larger.

Figure 10.5. Sample Weekly Reading Schedule: First Grade, Second Semester.

	Monday	Tuesday	Wednesday	Thursday	Friday
Sample Weekly Schedule—First Grade Reading Period 9:00–10:30 A.M.					
Above-average Group	Individualized Reading Four Individual Reading Conferences Informal Sharing of Reading Material with One or Two Classmates	Basal Reader Lesson with Most of Its Traditional Steps	Basal Reader Lesson with Most of Its Traditional Steps	Individualized Reading Four Individual Reading Conferences Research Group from Science on Topic "Baby Animals"	Individualized Reading Three Individual Reading Conferences Research Group from Science on Topic "Baby Animals"
Average Group	Basal Reader Lesson with Most of Its Traditional Steps	Individualized Reading Five Individual Reading Conferences Informal Sharing of Reading Material with One or Two Classmates	Basal Reader Lesson Presentation of New Vocabulary Guided Silent Reading	Basal Reader Lesson Purposeful Oral Reading Skill Development Enriching Experiences Workbook	Individualized Reading Five Individual Reading Conferences Research Group from Science on Topic "Baby Animals"
Below-average Group	Basal Reader Lesson Development of Experiential Background Presentation of New Vocabulary Guided Silent Reading	Basal Reader Lesson Oral Reading Skill Development Workbook	Basal Reader Lesson Development of Experiential Background Presentation of New Vocabulary Oral Reading	Basal Reader Lesson Skill Development Enriching Experiences Workbook	Individualized Reading Four Individual Reading Conferences Research Group from Science on Topic "Baby Animals"

Source: TEACHING ELEMENTARY READING TODAY by Wilma H. Miller, copyright © 1984 by Holt, Rinehart and Winston, Inc., reprinted with permission of the publisher.

Briefly, the teacher introducing the individualized reading approach to the grade level (or to the school) might consider doing so under a compromise arrangement that also involves basal reader lessons, workbook exercises, and the development of those library media center research skills to be discussed in Chapter 12. Such a program could include most of the advantages of individualized reading without all of the difficulties. Consequently, a sample weekly schedule for a first-grade, second-semester reading program, as based on the use of three flexible reading achievement groups, is shown in Figure 10.5.

Departments of education in some states (such as California) and some school districts (such as West Des Moines, Iowa) are presently advocating a literature-based program, arguing that if the end of any English language arts program is to develop a thinking, literate society, then the means to that end must lie in devising for students meaningful encounters with effective sources of human expression. [19] It is claimed that such a literature-based curriculum will give students three crucial approaches to finding out for themselves through literature the meaning of human experience: (1) an in-depth study of core literary works, offering students in any district a common cultural background; (2) the reading of extended works that capture children's individual interests and encourage them to explore new avenues independently; and (3) recreational-motivational reading that is based on the natural curiosity of students and that provokes them to read for pleasure.

One school district in Iowa is already implementing such a possible alternative to the traditional basal program.[20] It has kept its basal series but has scaled back classroom use of that series to no more than 50 percent of the allocated reading time. It has developed a trade book program, which includes multiple copies of selected books of literature and skeleton teaching guides for each of the grade levels; books chosen relate to social studies, to science areas, and to such themes as "Heroes and Heroines." It gives daily priority time to independent reading and builds classroom libraries to support that emphasis. Finally, it has incorporated writing time daily into the reading block. Incidently, a key element has wisely been a strong communication program aimed at keeping parents informed both before and during the program's implementation.

Forthcoming Instructional Strategy: A Literature-Based Program

Fluent, capable readers do not pause to identify every single word as they read. Instead, according to Goodman, mature readers merely sample enough of the printed cues to permit them to make and to confirm guesses about words and meanings.[21] Nevertheless, all readers—children and adults alike—at times encounter words they do not promptly recognize. When this occurs, the readers can resort to employing one or more of the following word-attack skills to help them decode the unknown word(s):

Word Recognition Skills

1. Using the dictionary
2. Using context clues
3. Using structural analysis
4. Using phonic analysis

Throughout the elementary school instruction in these skills, however, it must be emphasized that the ultimate goal is to have the boy or girl eventually learn to identify words instantly as wholes. Once the words have become his or her *sight words,* the child no longer must analyze them by using one or more of the skills listed above. Therefore, the underlying need for *developing sight vocabulary* is crucial and basic.

Developing Sight Vocabulary

A large sight vocabulary is important for several reasons. First, it allows the reader to attend to the meaning of the written passage, and comprehension is a critical area. Second, it permits the use of the valuable word-attack skill involving context clues because many unfamiliar words can be indentified by close consideration of the words around them (provided of course that the surrounding words can all be smoothly read). Thirdly, it encourages the development of another important word-identification skill—phonic analysis—because children who know several sight words that begin with the same letter, for example, can then use those words as a basis for learning a generalization about sound-letter correspondences. Fourth, many of the most frequently used words in the English language are phonically irregular, even though they appear in many beginning reading programs and must therefore be recognized on sight as whole configurations. Finally, acquiring at least a beginning sight vocabulary at the very start of reading instruction gives boys and girls greater success in reading and consequently a more positive attitude toward the entire reading program.

Such a beginning sight vocabulary should be based on five criteria: (1) high frequency (*to, and*), (2) children's interests (*Megan, truck*), (3) familiarity (*house, jump*), (4) low phonic regularity (*where, said*), and (5) lack of visual meaning (*because, could*). Word length is not a criterion; short words are not always easier for students to learn than longer ones. Recent research shows no degree of observable relation between word length and word recognition.[22]

Sight words should be introduced gradually, reviewed often, and always presented in a meaningful context. Although some authorities support the so-called key word approach of having the students themselves choose the words they would like to learn, a more sensible solution is to incorporate that idea with teacher selection of words from varied lists, which are described in Chapter 11. One of those compilations of high-frequency sight words is Edward Fry's New Instant Words, as shown in Figure 10.6. The first one hundred New Instant Words (and their common variants) make up half of all written material in English, and the total 300 (and their variants) comprise 65 percent of any such writing sample.

Although many good commercial materials are available for developing sight vocabulary, the following are samples of teacher-developed activities that offer individualized practice:

1. *Build-a-Train*. Engines and railway cards are cut from oaktag sheets. Each piece has one word printed on it. Boys and girls who pronounce the words correctly build a train that becomes longer and longer. The goal can be to see who are the best train builders.

2. *Classification*. On individual cards are printed in color two (or more) words that constitute categories, such as *farm* or *house*. These cards are placed in an envelope along with many other cards on which are printed in black such words as *roof, barn, cows,* and *kitchen*. The latter group must be categorized under the two words printed in color. If the teacher numbers the back of each word card, the exercise can be self-correcting.

Figure 10.6. Fry's New Instant Word List.

The Instant Words
First hundred

First 25 Group 1a	Second 25 Group 1b	Third 25 Group 1c	Fourth 25 Group 1d
the	or	will	number
of	one	up	no
and	had	other	way
a	by	about	could
to	word	out	people
in	but	many	my
is	not	then	than
you	what	them	first
that	all	these	water
it	were	so	been
he	we	some	call
was	when	her	who
for	your	would	oil
on	can	make	now
are	said	like	find
as	there	him	long
with	use	into	down
his	an	time	day
they	each	has	did
I	which	look	get
at	she	two	come
be	do	more	made
this	how	write	may
have	their	go	part
from	if	see	over

Common suffixes: *s, ing, ed*

The Instant Words
Second hundred

First 25 Group 2a	Second 25 Group 2b	Third 25 Group 2c	Fourth 25 Group 2d
new	great	put	kind
sound	where	end	hand
take	help	does	picture
only	through	another	again
little	much	well	change
work	before	large	off
know	line	must	play
place	right	big	spell
year	too	even	air
live	mean	such	away
me	old	because	animal
back	any	turn	house
give	same	here	point
most	tell	why	page
very	boy	ask	letter

The Instant Words
Second hundred (cont.)

First 25 Group 2a	Second 25 Group 2b	Third 25 Group 2c	Fourth 25 Group 2d
after	follow	went	mother
thing	came	men	answer
our	want	read	found
just	show	need	study
name	also	land	still
good	around	different	learn
sentence	form	home	should
man	three	us	America
think	small	move	world
say	set	try	high

Common suffixes: *s, ing, ed, er, ly, est*

The Instant Words
Third hundred

First 25 Group 3a	Second 25 Group 3b	Third 25 Group 3c	Fourth 25 Group 3d
every	left	until	idea
near	don't	children	enough
add	few	side	eat
food	while	feet	face
between	along	car	watch
own	might	mile	far
below	close	night	Indian
country	something	walk	real
plant	seem	white	almost
last	next	sea	let
school	hard	began	above
father	open	grow	girl
keep	example	took	sometimes
tree	begin	river	mountain
never	life	four	cut
start	always	carry	young
city	those	state	talk
earth	both	once	soon
eye	paper	book	list
light	together	hear	song
thought	got	stop	leave
head	group	without	family
under	often	second	body
story	run	late	music
saw	important	miss	color

Common suffixes: *s, ing, ed, er, ly, est*

Source: Reprinted with permission of Edward Fry and the International Reading Association.

3. *Color Match.* On pieces of oaktag are printed words pertaining to various colors. Clothespins of different colors are placed in an accompanying envelope. The participant must attach the properly colored clothespins to the word cards. If the teacher colors the back of each word card with the color printed on the front, the exercise can be self-correcting.

4. *Flashcard Group.* Every member of the reading group is given a small pile of cards, each approximately 1½-by-2½ inches. As a reader encounters an unfamiliar word, he or she must write it on a card. Then several times a week, the children are permitted to meet in groups of three to quiz each other on their cards. Generally at least one of the three children will know the new word. However, there may be times when the teacher or a paraprofessional may be called on to supply help.

5. *Nouns in Color.* On a sheet of oaktag are printed nouns associated with specific colors (e.g., *snow, grass*). Then in an attached envelope are placed small cards of different colors. The participant matches the colored cards with the nouns. If the teacher uses an identification scheme on the backs of the colored cards, the exercise can be self-correcting.

6. *Picture Checkerboard.* The teacher writes sixteen nouns on the chalkboard in numbered order. The children first fold a sheet of drawing paper into sixteen squares and number them correspondingly. Then they draw pictures of the nouns on the numbered squares. Finally the boys and girls exchange and correct their papers.

7. *Picture Dictionary Match.* The teacher obtains a small, inexpensive picture dictionary (available in most supermarkets). From it pictures are cut and pasted in a row on a card measuring nine-by-twelve inches. Under each picture is drawn a space box measuring ½-by-1½ inches. Small word cards are prepared and placed in an envelope, which remains attached to the large picture card. If the teacher numbers the pictures and the backs of the word cards, the exercise can be self-correcting.

8. *Picture Riddle Match.* Children cut pictures out of old magazines and place them in envelopes, five per envelope. Then the teacher writes a riddle about one of the pictures in each envelope and places the riddle in that same envelope. The child is allowed to choose one envelope, examine the pictures, read the riddle, and select the picture that answers the riddle. If the teacher can devise a marking scheme appropriate to the age level of the children, the exercise can be self-correcting.

9. *Word Authors.* Words are printed on the corners of cards with four cards to a set. For example, a set consists of four animal words, four color words, and so forth. A deck of cards generally consists of ten to twelve sets. Each participant is dealt four cards. One child begins the activity by calling for a word, and if he or she gets that word, the child may continue to call for more words until a set is complete. When the opponent states that he or she does not have the word card demanded, the first child draws from the deck that is face down on the table. The winner of the exercise is the child who acquires the most sets. Two to four children may participate at a time.

10. *Word File Pictures.* At the top of each card is printed the name of an object, and at the bottom is placed a picture or drawing illustrating that noun. On the back of the card, however, is printed only the noun. The child reads the words from the backs of the cards and then checks himself or herself by examining the pictures on the front sides.[23]

In a school that provides *tachistoscopes* (devices that allow the presentation of visual material for brief intervals of time), teachers can use them to expose words rapidly for sight-word recognition practice. Children thus become accustomed to the idea of identifying the word instantly and not sounding it out. Tachistoscopes range in complexity from simple handmade cardboard devices to elaborate laboratory instruments.

A recent review of research on methods of teaching sight words concluded that no one method alone was best for every child.[24] Still, it was recommended that words be presented in context rather than in isolation because reading is a language process for obtaining meaning.

Using the Dictionary

Dictionaries can help readers determine pronunciations, derivations, and meanings of unfamiliar words. Should the children have some idea of how a word is spelled, dictionaries can also help with correct spelling. Incidentally, in matters of pronunciation, it should be pointed out that children must be urged to use the other three word-attack skills before turning to the dictionary because (a) readers do not always have a dictionary readily available, and (b) using a dictionary may disrupt interest in the reading passage and thereby hinder comprehension.

Further discussion of dictionary use and skills can be found in Chapter 11 together with twenty-five activities promoting increased understanding and familiarity with this important tool for greater word identification ability.

Using Context Clues

Context clues are meaning clues contained in the passage that surrounds the unknown word. They may appear in the same sentence or in preceding or following sentences. Common types of context clues found in the same sentence are:

1. Definition; for instance, *Lava, which is melted rock, flowed down the mountainside.*
2. Restatement; for instance, *The hardware store sold me some rope made from jute—a tropical plant.*
3. Example; for instance, *The stage manager rented properties such as tables, chairs, and dishes for the play.*

Sample textbook exercises covering these three types can be found in Figure 10.7.

Research tells us that poor readers can use context clues as effectively as good readers. Because learning from context is not affected by reading ability, both good and poor readers increase their scores on vocabulary tests when provided with the words in context. Moreover, simply practicing the art of reading promotes student ability to use context clues.[25] When boys and girls are given sufficient time to read and thereby be exposed to numerous words, they expand their sight vocabulary, which in turn raises their comprehension ability and helps them make improved use of context clues.

Figure 10.7. Exercises in Using Context Clues.

Using Context Clues: Definition, Restatement, and Example

Focus

Context clues can help you learn the meaning of an unfamiliar word in a sentence. A context clue may define, restate, or give an example of an unfamiliar word.

When a writer knows that a certain word will be new to many readers, he or she may use a **context clue.** *Context* means the words or sentences around a particular word.

Definition or Restatement

The writer may give a **definition** of the word or **restate** the unfamiliar word in a different way. Read these sentences.

> She saw a colony of *gannets*—large, white sea birds—perched on the rocks. (definition)

> The balloonists *ascended,* or went up, more slowly than they came down. (restatement)

Example

Sometimes the writer helps the reader understand a new word by giving an example. When you read, check to see if an unfamiliar word is explained by one or more examples somewhere else in the sentence. Read this sentence.

> *Implements,* such as screwdrivers and pliers, are handy to have around the house. (example)

This context tells you that screwdrivers and pliers are examples of *implements.* This helps you understand the meaning of *implements.*

6

Certain key words and punctuation marks signal that a writer is giving a context clue.

Key Words Signaling Definition or Restatement:

which is	or	also known as
that is	in other words	also called

Punctuation Marks Signaling Definition or Restatement:

dashes, commas, and parentheses

Key Words Signaling an Example:

and other	for example	for instance
like	especially	such as

Figure 10.7. (cont.)

Exercises: Mastering Context Clues

A. Use the context clues in these sentences to write definitions for the words in italics. Check your definitions in a dictionary.

1. I enjoy Japanese food—*sukiyaki,* for example.
2. Samantha is a *philatelist.* In other words, she is a person who collects stamps.
3. Old pottery, like *majolica,* is hard to find.
4. Stay away from *toxic* plants such as poison ivy.
5. Diana can do a *half gainer* and other difficult dives.

B. Write what each word in italics means. Then write what key words or punctuation marks helped you tell the word's meaning.

1. Dexter worked with a *farrier,* a blacksmith, to shoe the horses.
2. A *vista*—a distant view—of pine forests and lakes opened before us.
3. Julio asked the grocer for *plátanos* (bananas).
4. Stock up on *gherkins* and other kinds of pickles.
5. I used an *adz,* which is a flat-bladed ax.

Source: Pgs. 6–7. *McDougal, Littell English, Silver Level.* Copyright © 1987 by McDougal, Littell & Company, Box 1667, Evanston, Illinois 60204.

Although there are many good commercial materials available for promoting the use of context clues, the following is a sample of teacher-developed activities that offer individualized practice:

1. Present sentences in which a phonics clue is provided to aid in eliciting the missing word. Readers are told to think of words that fit the blanks appropriately, such as in the following examples:
   a. Sean said that he would th _____ the softball to me.
   b. The kitten dr _____ all the milk in the saucer.
   c. Mother was going to pl _____ vegetables in the garden.
2. Present sentences in which words are completely missing. Readers are told to examine the sentences and determine which words fit the blanks most appropriately, such as in the following examples:
   a. The day was bright, warm, and _____ . (*sunny, dark, cloudy*)
   b. The general had to _____ whether the army should _____ the fort against attack. (*defend, decide*)
   c. The robbers took all the _____ in the bank. (*money, letters, papers*)
3. Present sentences that contain unusual words whose meanings can be determined by using contextual clues. Readers are told to examine the sentences carefully before deciding on the answers, such as in the following examples:
   a. Father will *deflate* the tire by opening the valve. *Deflate* means (a) let air out, (b) put air in, (c) turn over, or (d) damage.

b. The old steamer trunk was *capacious* enough to hold all of Tim's clothes.
   Capacious means (a) colorful, (b) small, (c) large, or (d) plentiful.
   c. My brother works in a brick *edifice* that covers an entire city block.
   Edifice means (a) building, (b) hut, (c) ship, or (d) service station.
4. Employ cloze exercises to encourage readers to look for clues in surrounding sentences (or even in the entire paragraph), as well as in the sentence in which the unfamiliar word first appears. A good way to work on promoting context-clue use is for the teacher to develop a cloze passage in which words have been systematically omitted and replaced with blanks of uniform size. Sometimes the teacher may delete only certain types of words (such as nouns or adjectives), rather than deleting words randomly. The passage is reproduced on a worksheet, chalkboard, or transparency so that the class can discuss reasons for the words selected to be inserted in the blanks. All synonyms should be accepted as well as any nonsynonyms for which students can offer reasonable bases.[26]

Teachers are reminded that all of the above exercises must be accompanied or followed by discussion, questioning, or modeling of which words should be in the blanks (or otherwise chosen). Without such teacher assistance, students will not gain much in their ability to use context clues effectively.

Further discussion about using context clues can be found in Chapter 11.

Using Structural Analysis

A word-recognition skill that uses word parts to determine the meaning and pronunciation of unfamiliar words is termed *structural analysis*. Its subskills include the use of (a) roots or base words, (b) prefixes and suffixes (known together as affixes) (c) compound words, (d) contractions, and (e) syllabication and accent. Structural analysis becomes a worthwhile technique in the upper primary and intermediate grades because the meanings of affixes, in particular, can help readers add many new words to their vocabulary. As early as second grade for instance, boys and girls can be introduced to several structural generalizations for changing base words before adding a suffix. Often such generalizations are derived inductively by the pupils through carefully planned lessons. Structural analysis rather than phonic analysis should be used by readers when attacking unknown words because it deals with units larger than single graphemes. Further discussion of the mastery of roots and of affixes can be found in Chapter 11.

Compound words are made up of two (or sometimes three) words that have been joined together to form a new word; for example, *snowman*. The new word may be one (a) whose meaning is the sum of its parts, such as *houseboat;* (b) whose meaning is related to but not totally represented by the sum of its parts, such as *shipyard;* or (c) whose meaning is not literally related to the sum of its parts, such as *moonstruck,* or whose parts result in multiple meanings, such as *doghouse*.[27]

As early as first grade, children can be introduced to compound words and learn to divide such words between the smaller words that compose them. They can even discuss the reasons for combining certain small words, such as *cow* and *boy, fire* and *man, play* and *house,* and *police* and *woman*.

Also introduced in the first grade, or at least by the second grade, are contractions. They should be presented by sight at first because beginning readers are generally unable to determine what part of the word has been left out when the contraction was formed. Later students can be taught that a contraction is a word composed of two (or more) words in which one or more letters have been left out and replaced by an apostrophe. Common contractions that should be presented to children along with their meanings include:

can't=cannot	they'll=they will
couldn't=could not	they're=they are
didn't=did not	they've=they have
don't=do not	wasn't=was not
hadn't=had not	we're=we are
hasn't=has not	weren't=were not
he'll=he will	we've=we have
he's=he is	won't=will not
I'll=I will	wouldn't=would not
I'm=I am	you'll=you will
I've=I have	you're=you are
isn't=is not	you've=you have
let's=let us	
she'll=she will	
she's=she is	
shouldn't=should not	

Syllabication and accent are also often introduced in the primary grades, with syllabication being presented in second grade and stress or accenting in the third grade. The teaching of accent is actually built on the skills of syllabication because accent has much to do with the vowel sound heard in a syllable.

A letter or group of letters that forms a pronunciation unit is termed a *syllable,* and every syllable contains a vowel sound. It is important not to confuse sounds and letters because some words (such as *weave*) have several vowel letters but only one vowel sound, and therefore only one syllable.

There are both open syllables (which end in vowel sounds) and closed syllables (which end in consonant sounds). There are also accented syllables (which are given greater stress) and unaccented ones (which are given little stress).

Some useful generalizations about syllabication and accent are as follows:

1. Prefixes and suffixes generally form separate syllables.
2. Usually the first syllable of a two-syllable word is accented.
3. Affixes are usually not accented.
4. When two consonants are located between two vowels, the word is divided between the two consonants; e.g., *mon/key.*
5. A compound word is divided between the two words that form the compound as well as between syllables within the component parts; e.g., *thun/der/storm.*

6. When there are two of the same consonant letters within a word, the syllable before the double consonants is generally accented; e.g., *but/ter.*
7. When one consonant is located between two vowels, the first syllable usually ends with the vowel and the second syllable usually begins with the second consonant. Therefore, the vowel in the first syllable is long and the syllable is said to be open; e.g., *ti/ger.*

Incidentally, readiness for learning syllabication involves the ability to hear syllables as pronunciation units. Consequently, even first graders can listen to words and clap for every syllable they hear.

Some supplementary instructional activities for correcting deficiencies in structural analysis include the following, which can be used with individual pupils or even small groups of children:

1. *Roots and Affixes*
   a. A list of words containing common prefixes is distributed to the readers, who must identify the root or base in each word by underlining it.
   b. A list of words containing common suffixes is distributed to the readers, who must identify the suffixes.
   c. A list of words containing common prefixes is distributed to the readers, who must identify the prefixes.
   d. A list of words containing common suffixes is distributed to the readers, who must identify the root or base in each word by underlining it.
   e. Readers are given lists of words and must write a given prefix before each word and tell the meanings of the new words.
   f. Readers are given lists of words with prefixes and must write each word without the prefix and tell how the meaning has changed.
   g. Readers are given lists of words containing suffixes and must use each root word in a sentence.
   h. Readers are given lists of unfamiliar words. They must separate the suffix from each word that contains a suffix and correctly pronounce both the suffix and the root word.
   i. Readers are given lists of unfamiliar words with a known prefix, and they must find the meanings of the new words.
   j. Readers are given lists of words with definitions after each word. They are also given lists of suffixes and must add one of the suffixes to each word so that the newly formed word complies with its definition.
2. *Compound Words*
   a. Two columns of words are distributed to the readers, who then develop compound words by matching the words in the first column with the words in the second column.
   b. Readers are given lists of compound words, and next to each long word they must write the two short words that make up the compound.

c. Lists of compound words are distributed to the readers, who must draw a line between the two short words that comprise each compound.

   d. Readers look for compound words that can be illustrated humorously. When they have compiled at least ten such illustrations, they place them in a booklet.

3. *Contractions*

   a. Readers are given a one-paragraph story calling for many contractions. They must fill in the blanks with the missing contractions. Some students may prefer developing their own stories and exchanging these with partners.

   b. Student voices are tape-recorded during committee work, whole class discussion, or a learning game, without the knowledge of the participants. Later, as the tape is played, the children must listen for contractions and note them on their workpapers. Finally they must write what words were combined for each contraction.

   c. Students are asked to search through a browsing book (which they have checked out of the library media center) and write down numerous different contractions. They may also copy the sentences in which the contractions appear. (The teacher may wish to limit the list to common contractions, excluding colloquial expressions such as *ya'all*, for greater clarity.)

4. *Syllabication and Accent*

   a. Students are assigned (or choose) a page from their science or social studies text and are then handed a worksheet with four columns. They must record all one-syllable words in the first column, all two-syllable words in the second column, and so on. Each word, however, can only be recorded once.

   b. Readers are each given a sheet of paper ruled into large squares, totaling either nine or sixteen. They draw an object in each square and write its name by syllables under the picture.

   c. Readers are given a list of multisyllabic words taken from a current unit in math, health, or science. The words appear in a column on the left side of the paper. Next to each word is a blank line on which the readers must write the number of syllables appearing in that word.

   d. Readers are given a worksheet on which appear sentences using pairs of *homographs* (words with the same spelling but different meanings and sometimes different pronunciations) such as *léad/leád, próduce/prodúce, content/cóntent*. By examining the context, each reader must determine the correct pronunciation and place the accent mark in the proper place. Dictionaries may be used.

   e. Intermediate-grade readers are each asked to write a silly paragraph using two-syllable homographs. As each student reads his or her paragraph aloud to the group, he or she must use the wrong pronunciation for each homograph. The listeners, however, must place the accent mark correctly on the homographs as they write them down on a worksheet.

Using Phonic Analysis

Used in elementary reading instruction for more than 175 years, this word-recognition technique involves the association of phonemes and graphemes in unlocking the pronunciation of unfamiliar words while reading. The goal of phonics is to teach children the alphabetic principle of systematic relationships between sounds and letters, which operates consistently to help young readers unlock unknown words independently.

Boys and girls who have difficulty discriminating among phonemes (inadequate auditory discrimination) or letter forms (inadequate visual discrimination) may encounter problems in learning phonics. They must be able to perceive and distinguish among the more than forty sounds of spoken English and among the varied sequences of those sounds. This ability may often be affected by speech impediments, dialect variations, and differences in native language backgrounds. Children must also be capable of visually perceiving and distinguishing the twenty-six letters of the English alphabet and the sequences of those letters. Readers who are visually deficient may have difficulty distinguishing letters with similar features (such as *m* and *n*), uppercase and lowercase forms of the same letter, and various versions of script and print.

Another area of readiness for phonics instruction is knowledge of letter names, which has been the subject of much disagreement. Harris and Sipay concluded that there is no evidence that teaching letter names is harmful, and they added that letter-name knowledge can serve useful purposes.[28] It is important, however, that children understand the distinction between letter names and the sounds that letters represent.

The two major approaches to phonics instruction, are *analytic* (or implicit or inductive) and *synthetic* (or explicit or deductive). The analytic involves teaching some sight words, as discussed earlier in this section, and then teaching the sounds of the letters within those words. It is used during the basal reader approach because it avoids the distortion that can occur when consonants are pronounced (whether blended or in isolation). Children can visually examine a polysyllabic word that has been divided into syllables, sound the portion of the word within each syllable, and then blend the syllables together to unite the complete word. Two critical problems associated with the analytic approach are the stress it places on phonemic segmentation, or the ability to identify separate speech sounds in spoken words, and the emphasis it puts on previous knowledge of sounds associated with the separate letters.

The synthetic method is concerned with instructing girls and boys in the phonemes that are associated with individual letters, and it is generally accomplished by repeated drills on sound-grapheme relationships. Children blend the sounds of separate letters in a word to form the complete word, such as *cuh-a-tuh* to enunciate the word *cat*. Blending is the critical step, and research shows that primary teachers who spend more than average amounts of time on blending observe larger than average gains on first- and second-grade reading-achievement tests.[29] A possible problem that may arise in conjunction with the synthetic approach is that children and teachers alike have a hard time saying single speech sounds in isolation.

Although controversy has dominated the importance of phonic analysis for many decades, most authorities now agree with the following guidelines:

1. There is no dichotomy between phonics and meaning because the objective of all reading instruction is comprehension.
2. A child should discover phonics generalizations (or learn them inductively) rather than be presented with them as deductive rules.
3. Short, frequent sessions devoted to phonics are more worthwhile than long, infrequent ones.
4. Phonics instruction should proceed from the simple to the complex, with more time spent on generalizations with broad applicability that must be internalized.
5. Consonant sounds should be presented before introducing vowel sounds.

The Commission on Reading adds that phonics instruction should be kept simple, started early, completed by the end of the second grade (except in cases of diagnosed individual need), and draw from both the analytic and synthetic approaches.[30]

Before introducing any of the numerous important phonics generalizations to children, teachers should be completely familiar with the terminology listed in Table 10.1. Phonics principles or generalizations should be presented to boys and girls one at a time and inductively. They must be carefully chosen so that each is learned well. Although there is no agreement as to which or how many such principles should be introduced, Burns, Roe, and Ross consider the following generalizations to be useful in the majority of circumstances:[31]

1. When two like consonants are adjacent to each other, only one is sounded; for example, *lass*.
2. When the letters *c* and *g* are followed by *o, a,* or *u,* they generally have hard sounds: *c* has the sound of *k*, and *g* has its own special sound; for example, *cat, go, out, gut*. When the letters *c* and *g* are followed by *e, i,* or *y,* they generally have soft sounds: *c* has the sound of *s*, and *g* has the sound of *j*; for example, *city, gem, cyst, gym*.
3. The digraph *ch* usually has the sound heard in *church,* but it also sometimes sounds like *k* or *sh* as in *chord* or *chef*.
4. When the letters *ght* are adjacent in a word, the *gh* is not sounded; for example, *bought*.
5. When *kn* are the first two letters in a word, the *k* is not sounded; for example, *know*.
6. When *wr* are the first two letters in a word, the *w* is not sounded; for example, *wrong*.
7. When *ck* are the last two letters in a word, the sound of *k* is heard; for example, *brick*.
8. The sound of a vowel preceding *r* is neither long nor short; for example, *car, her*.
9. In the vowel combinations *oa, ee,* and *ay,* the first vowel is usually long, and the second is not sounded; for example, *coat, beet, ray*. This rule may also apply to other double vowel combinations.

Table 10.1
Definitions of Terms Commonly Used in Phonic Analysis

Term	Definition and or Examples
Vowels	Letters *a, e, i, o,* and *u.* Letters *y* (when in the middle or final position in a word or syllable) and *w* (when in the final position of a word or syllable).
Consonants	Letters other than *a, e, i, o,* and *u.* Letter *w* and *y* when in the initial position in a word or syllable.
Consonant Blend or Consonant Cluster	Two or three adjacent consonant sounds that are combined, although each retains its separate identity; for example, *pl*ay, *str*ike, a*sk*, *br*ake, *dr*ove, *sm*ell, *sw*ing, *tw*ig.
Consonant Digraph	Two adjacent consonant letters that are combined into a single speech sound; for example, *sh*ip, *ph*one, *th*is, *wh*at, ne*ck*, ri*ng*.
Vowel Digraph	Two adjacent vowel letters that are combined into a single speech sound; for example, d*ay*, *ea*ch, f*oo*t, r*oa*d, f*ai*r, m*ee*t.
Diphthong	Two vowel sounds combined, beginning with the first and gliding smoothly into the second; for example, *oi*l, t*oy*, *ou*t, pl*ow*.
Phonogram	Combination of letters within a word that functions as a pronounceable unit; for example, r*ake*, m*ine*, f*ight*, b*all*, p*ick*, t*ack*.

10. *Oi, oy,* and *ou* usually form diphthongs. Although the *ow* combination often represents the long *o* sound, it may also form a diphthong; for example, *now.*
11. When a word has only one vowel and that is at the end of the word, the vowel generally represents its long sound; for example, *me.*
12. When a word has only one vowel and that is not at the end of the word, the vowel generally represents its short sound; for example, *man.*
13. When there are two vowels in a word and one is a final *e,* the first vowel is usually long, and the final *e* is not sounded; for example, *kite.*
14. The letter combination *qu* often represents the sound of *kw,* although it sometimes stands for the sound of *k;* for example, *queen, quay,* respectively.
15. The letter *x* most frequently represents the sound of *ks* although it sometimes stands for the sound of *gz* or *z;* for example, *box, exact, xylophone,* respectively.

Teachers concerned about the utility of presenting phonics generalizations to children should be reassured by recent research that found there were statistically significant relationships between knowledge of and ability to use such generalizations and reading achievement.[32] The fourth graders in that Ohio school were not always able to state a particular phonics rule, but this inability did not seem to hinder the children's effort to analyze unfamiliar words. Boys and girls in the elementary school apparently need not consciously know or verbalize generalizations in order to apply them.

Although there are vast quantities of commercial materials available for developing phonic skills, the following is a sampling of teacher-developed activities that offer group or individualized practice:

1. *I Spy.* Each child in a small group takes a turn locating an object in the classroom which begins with a particular sound; for example, "I spy something that begins like *cheese.*" The player who names the correct object (*chair*) then has a turn. The teacher may direct the choice of a beginning or final sound that the class has been learning.

2. *Mail Order Catalog.* Boys and girls find in discarded mail-order catalogs pictures of objects that begin with certain consonant blends or consonant digraphs. They mount the pictures on separate sheets of paper and label each one correctly.

3. *Planning a Meal.* Children pretend to be meal-planners as each in turn names something to eat that begins with the letter *a.* When a child cannot add to the list of *a* foods, he or she begins naming foods starting with the letter *b.* This activity can be an ongoing one, taking place as children wait to be dismissed each day or as a culmination to a group reading session every day for one week.

4. *Snoopy Says.* Every player is given a small card with *Yes* written on one side and *No* on the other. The teacher makes a statement that helps review the players' knowledge of phonics generalizations. Should the statement be true, the players hold up the *Yes* side of their card, but should the statement be false, they hold up the *No* side. If a player displays an incorrect response, he or she is out of the activity until the next time it is played. The winner is the last player remaining in the game.

5. *Newspapers.* Copies of several newspapers are brought to class and distributed among the group members. Each child chooses an article and circles in it all the words that contain unsounded letters. She or he then exchanges articles with a partner. Partners mark through all the unsounded letters in the marked words. Finally articles are traded back and checked.

6. *Pictures.* A series of pictures of objects is given to each child. She or he must name each object shown and also tell whether the vowel in the noun is long (glided) or short (unglided). This activity can be done orally or with a worksheet.

7. *List of Words.* Each child is given a list of words. A younger child might be asked to underline all the words that have the same vowel sound as that appearing in the first word. An older child might be asked to check all the words in the list that have the same vowel sound.

8. *Table Display.* On the table where the group is seated, the teacher places numerous small objects whose names call attention to certain sound elements that have previously been introduced. The teacher pronounces a sound, such as the diphthong *oy.* One child selects an object that contains that sound, names the item (*toy*), holds it up for the group to see, and then replaces it on the table. Once the word has been pronounced, the teacher should either write the word on the chalkboard or hold up a flashcard that contains the word.

Comprehension

Comprehension is the process of reader interaction with the text. By using their existing knowledge (or *schemata*) to interpret the printed page, students can reach a personal construction of what the text material means to them. Reading comprehension therefore involves not only understanding the new information in the text itself but also altering whatever knowledge was used initially to figure out what that information meant.

Underlying this current process approach to comprehension are four assumptions:[33]

1. *What children already know affects what they will learn from reading.* The one principle that emerges clearly from recent research is that people must bring prior knowledge to bear when interpreting any event; lacking the crucial background information to make sense of what one reads, the best that any individual can do is merely reiterate or slightly paraphrase the author's words.[34] Such prior knowledge is termed schemata (plural for *schema*), which are frameworks for interrelating various elements of information about any one subject.

2. *Both concept-driven and data-driven processes are needed for comprehending the text.* The first calls for activating schemata and applying them in establishing expectations for reading as well as for completing any gaps in one's schemata with information gained by reading the text. This "top-down" strategy means that the reader's goals determine what is read. In contrast, a "bottom-up" approach, or data-driven process, occurs when the reader attends to the text and then searches for schemata in which to set the new information. He or she places initial expectations alongside the new ones suggested by the text.

3. *The deeper the student processes text, the more he or she will remember and understand it.* Deep processing depends on two strategies for understanding text—elaboration and use of the author's framework. The first is actually an embellishment of the text; the second requires the reader to identify the patterns by which the text is organized—narrative, or story-type, material differing substantially from expository or informational material.

4. *The context in which reading occurs influences what will be remembered.* Purpose and perspective affect reader judgment about the significance of upcoming elements of the text. Each activates particular schemata.

Briefly then, schemata are the conceptual structures, or categories, of knowledge (specific knowledge of topics or concepts, general world knowledge, and knowledge of rhetorical structures) formed in the reader's mind through experiences. The term *schema theory* is used to explain how the structures are formed and related to each other as the student acquires knowledge. Obviously the process of comprehension is easiest and most effective when the schemata of the reader match closely those of the author.

Besides schemata (termed by some as prior existing knowledge), there are other factors that affect the teaching of comprehension, according to recent research.[35] The first of these is *interest;* for example, gifted students will not always use their maximum reading comprehension power unless given challenging passages and individualized reading assignments of interest to them. Second and third factors are *cognition* (or the ability to think while reading) and *metacognition* (or the ability to monitor one's own cognition so as to select skills and strategies peculiar to the demands of the reading task). A fourth factor is *chunking,* or reading natural linguistic units that are generally phrases. Students reading materials that have been chunked for them do better than readers without chunked materials. A fifth factor is the *difficulty of the reading selection;* for example, poor readers in the upper grades can make inferences as well as their average reader peers if they are allowed to read material commensurate with their ability level. A sixth and final factor that plays a significant role in comprehension is the *use of pictures in the reading material.* When illustrations are directly related to the text, the overall comprehension of readers improves and positive attitudes toward reading develop, although pictures usually do slow the readers' speed.

Survey of the literature reveals numerous labeling systems for the levels of comprehension, although there is a trend away from the use of the term *levels.* This is because *levels* imply sequence, and although the first type (or *literal* understanding) is necessary for other types of comprehension, the learner should develop skill in all three types simultaneously. The system that seems to be most widely accepted categorizes the comprehension process as follows:

Types or Levels of Comprehension

1. *Literal, or text-explicit, comprehension.* Often described as "reading the lines," this type requires the reader to process information that was explicitly stated in the text. It covers understanding what the author specifically stated. For example, the reader may be called upon to recall or locate specifically stated main ideas, details, or sequences of events.
2. *Interpretive, or text-implicit comprehension.* Frequently described as "reading between the lines," this type demands that the reader process ideas based on what was read but not explicitly stated in the text. It covers understanding what the author meant, and the reader must call upon his or her intuition, personal experiences, and imagination as the foundation for making inferences. Children may be asked to predict oucomes or infer cause-and-effect relationships.
3. *Critical/Applied/Schema-implicit comprehension.* Often stated as "reading beyond the lines," this type requires the reader to evaluate, integrate, and apply information and ideas from the printed page to his or her own experiences and judgment. It calls for the student to think creatively or to develop original ideas based on the pages read. He or she interprets the text in terms of individual personal values and experiential background.

Questioning and Its Relevance to Comprehension

Question-and-answer sessions that accompany reading lessons (as well as lessons for reading content-area texts) are an integral part of classroom life. Furthermore, the kinds of questions that the teacher asks are important because they directly influence the sort of thinking that students do as they read. Following the six categories of the well-known Bloom's Taxonomy, the teacher could devise such sample questions as the following:

Knowledge—recalling information
    Where did . . .
    List the . . .
    What was . . .
    How many . . .
    Name the . . .

Comprehension—understanding meaning
    Give me an example of . . .
    Describe what . . .
    Tell me in your own words . . .
    Make a map of . . .
    What does it mean when . . .

Application—using learning in new situations
    If you had been there, would you . . .
    How would you solve this problem in your own life?
    What would happen to you if . . .
    Would you have done the same as . . .
    In the library, find information about . . .

Analysis—using ability to see parts and relationships
    What kind of person is . . .
    What is the main idea of the story?
    What message was the author trying to tell us?
    What part of the story was the most exciting? funny? sad?
    What events could not have happened in real life?

Synthesis—using parts of the information to create an original whole
    What would it be like to live . . .
    Pretend you are . . .
    Write (or tell) a different ending . . .
    What would have happened if . . .
    Design a . . .

Evaluation—making judgments based on criteria
    Could this story really have happened? Why or why not?
    Select the best . . . Why is it best?
    Which person in the story would you most like to meet? Why?
    Was . . . good or bad? Why?
    What do you think will happen to . . . Why do you think so?

If students are consistently asked only literal or recall kinds of questions, they will focus their attention on remembering details and not on analyzing or evaluating the information and storing it for future use. Instead, the information will often be remembered only until the questions have been asked (and answered) and then will be promptly forgotten. If, however, students are asked to read between or beyond the lines on the page, they will be forced to integrate new input with what they already know about the topic, and therefore much of it will more likely be retained.

Four general goals about the role of questions concern the likelihood that students will (1) focus attention on significant aspects of the text, (2) relate information from the text to the most appropriate set of background experiences, (3) develop a coherent framework for remembering or understanding the text material, or (4) practice cognitive skills that they will ultimately be able to use alone.[36] A consensus that represents an effort to balance these goals where they conflict and also to integrate them where they agree with one another is as follows:

1. The teacher begins the lesson with questions that focus student attention on appropriate background experiences or knowledge; for example, *Have you ever been to the zoo? What do you know about the zoo?* Should knowledge or experiential background not be available or developed, the teacher might attempt a longer question such as the following: *In our story today about South America, there is a family of jaguars. A jaguar is somewhat like a house cat, somewhat like a wolf, and somewhat like a sports car. Let's see whether we can figure out how a jaguar is like all of those.*

2. The teacher then allows students to use background knowledge, whenever possible, to predict what might happen in the story; for example, *If you were lost in the forest as the jaguar family is and needed food, how would you get it?*

3. The teacher sets up a purpose that lasts as long as possible throughout the story; for example, *What did the jaguar family try to do to solve its problem?*

4. During the guided reading (which occurs *during* the reading in the primary classroom and immediately *after* the reading in the intermediate grades), the teacher asks questions that tie together the significant elements in the "story map" (the outline on the chalkboard that is a causal chain of events); for example, *What was the first thing that Jenny tried to do to get rid of her tooth? What lesson did Jenny learn?*

5. Immediately following the reading, the teacher returns to the purpose-setting question(s), as suggested in item 3 above. Rewording or paraphrasing can occur; for example, *Can you tell me in order the three things the jaguar family did to find food?*

6. In discussing the story, the teacher uses this sequence for generating questions: (a) retells the story map at a fairly high level of generality, (b) takes students beyond the literal stage by asking them to compare this story to their own experiences or to another selection or by asking them to speculate

about the reactions of the characters when placed in a different situation, and finally (c) returns to the selection in an effort to appreciate the talent of the author. Activities useful for item (a) include dramatization, discussion, production of a time line of events, or the development of a flow chart of events. (The last can be done with children as early as third grade.) Questions appropriate for item (b) would include: *Do you think that the jaguar family acted prudently? Why or why not?* and *What would you have done if faced with a similar situation?* Questions illustrative of item (c) would include: *What is your favorite part of the selection? What made you choose that part?* and *How does the author tell you that the father jaguar feels proud?*[37]

There are three important elements of questioning: the teacher's question, the student's answer, and the teacher's response to the student's answer.[38] Student answers to teacher questions fall into three general categories: correct, partially correct, and incorrect. A correct response is one that is in line with the teacher question, although it may differ substantially from the particular answer the teacher had hoped to elicit. What matters, however, is that the teacher be open to many possible correct answers to a particular question and not have a preconceived statement of one "correct" response. He or she should give the student immediate feedback concerning a correct answer to a reading-comprehension question in order to reinforce learning. Should the student response be only partially correct, the teacher should recognize all of the correct aspects of the answer while simultaneously directing the student's thinking toward the correct response. Even when the child gives an incorrect answer that is irrelevant or incongruent to the teacher question, it is important that the teacher respond in an accepting manner and, at the same time, redirect the child's thinking by using clarification measures such as *Let's go back to the story to check that fact* or *Let me ask the question in a different way.* Briefly, then, teacher responses to student answers fall into three broad categories: acceptance, clarification, and rejection, with rejection being defined as a teacher response that could damage the child's self-image and his or her subsequent learning.

Incidentally, an important factor that is often overlooked in developing reading comprehension is *wait-time.* This has been defined as the amount of time between a teacher's asking a question about the passage read and calling upon a child to respond to that question. It is particularly significant in the area of higher types of comprehension because boys and girls must have adequate time in which to organize complete, original, and thoughtful answers. Research has shown that, even though both the quantity of the student response (i.e., the actual number of words used in the answer) and the quality of that response (i.e., level of thinking demonstrated) are affected by the amount of wait-time, teachers give students an average wait-time of only one second.[39] Furthermore, if the teachers respond too quickly following student answers, those answers are more often apt to be incomplete. Consequently, by increasing wait-time after a child's response, the teacher discovers that responses will probably be clearer and more elaborate, and at the same time, his or her own reply to the student will be more appropriate.

Directed comprehension instruction includes explaining the skills involved, providing practice in using those skills, assessing and (if necessary) reteaching the skills, and finally demonstrating how the skills can be applied. Teachers need to pose questions and then to show the students how those questions may be answered by modeling aloud the thinking process used to come up with the responses. This includes sharing with students what kinds of clues are found within the selection itself, as well as how previously known information can be intergrated.

By beginning lessons with questions that focus attention on what students already know about the topic, and by encouraging them to use that knowledge to make predictions, teachers are helping the children deal with the questions in a more familiar framework. It is not enough to assign students to read a story and then answer questions about it. Instead, each teacher should have students share their thinking processes by going back to the assigned story and inquiring, "How did you know? Which words gave you clues that led you to this answer?" Although children who give incorrect responses are often redirected through clarification measures, teachers generally overlook the value of questioning students who give correct responses. Such boys and girls not only reinforce the thinking process of the individual but model that process for their classmates. By sharing his or her own knowledge as a teacher and by drawing on the background and knowledge of students, the teacher can make the task of presenting comprehension skills more manageable.

Suggestions for comprehension instruction can be divided among those that occur before reading, during reading, and after reading.[40] *Before* the children begin their reading lesson, the teacher can first promote comprehension by (1) making certain the boys and girls are reading materials of an appropriate level of difficulty, with slower readers often needing to spend more time at a particular plateau than one basal series can accommodate and with advanced pupils doing most of their reading in content texts and other materials because they can read through their basals so quickly. Then the teacher can enhance comprehension by (2) making certain the children have appropriate background concepts by using the introductory activities outlined in the reading series in an effort to activate or build on prior knowledge, whether on the topic of laundromats, for instance, or life in the Amazon jungle. Finally, the teacher can promote comprehension by (3) making certain that the girls and boys understand that the purpose of reading is to get meaning and that what they already know can help them attain that purpose. Children must be made aware of what the teacher is doing and understand why she or he is doing it because they can gradually be taught to accept responsibility for comprehending.

During the reading lesson, the teacher can identify trouble spots (such as vocabulary or figurative language) and instruct boys and girls on how to solve those problem areas. (The questions that accompany each guided reading lesson in most basals may be helpful in this area.) However, the teacher's responsibility is not complete until each child assumes an equal share of the responsibility for comprehension. Students must be taught to monitor their reading, taught to identify problems (such as cohesion), and taught problem-solving strategies. Skilled readers can use the following general strategies: ignore and read on, suspend judgment, form a tentative hypothesis, reread the current sentence, reread the previous context, or go to an expert source.[41]

After the reading lesson, the teacher should focus the instruction on summarizing the entire text and on relating it to other information or to other books or stories. All pupils, and particularly the slower readers, need this kind of comprehension activity. Other activities include having children write their own stories and participate in oral discussions concerning the comparison of the most recently completed story to other stories or concerning the contrast of characters found in various assigned selections. One activity that does *not* belong in this segment of the reading lesson is asking a series of detailed, literal questions; boys and girls must not get the impression that reading is only an exercise in factual recall.

Sorting Out Comprehension Problems

Many so-called comprehension problems are not really failures to understand the author's message, state some educators.[42] Instead, the child who fails to respond properly to a comprehension assignment may actually be encountering other difficulties that masquerade as comprehension problems. Teachers should therefore consider the following questions before sending the child back for more directed practice in comprehension skills:

1. *Was the reader able to decode most of the words in the selection?* If the child seems generally confused about an entire selection, the teacher should ask him or her to choose a particularly difficult passage and read it aloud. Then, if the problem seems to involve decoding, the teacher should try to ensure that the pupil's next assignment involves material at a more acceptable level of decoding difficulty.
2. *Did the reader understand the specialized vocabulary of the selection?* When the code is too complex, decoding cannot occur. So the teacher must give careful attention to technical vocabulary and introduce such words prior to their appearing in a reading assignment. Students will then be able to recognize those words in print quickly and be alert to important points in the assignment before reading begins.
3. *Did the reader follow directions?* Teachers must be certain that children understand directions before starting a task and can do so by (a) having the directions rephrased by a student or aide or by (b) having the pupils do one sample question together as a written guide for children to follow.
4. *Did the reader's experiential background interfere with comprehension?* When the reader's background is substantially different from that of the author's or the teacher's, a "wrong" interpretation of a paragraph or passage is possible even though that interpretation is completely understandable in terms of the reader's own experience. Consequently the teacher should evaluate readers' backgrounds through informal discussion before making reading assignments and then either (a) change the assignment or (b) introduce the necessary background or concepts.

5. *Was the reader interested in the selection?* Comprehension is likely to be enhanced when students have questions that they are seeking to answer or when the teacher has introduced the assignment in such a way that their curiosity is piqued or their enthusiasm aroused.

6. *Was the reader able to express the answer correctly?* Teachers must be able to distinguish between a child's composition, spelling, or handwriting problems and his or her comprehension problems. One way to handle this situation is to ask for oral answers if written responses are not decipherable. Student dictation may help, too.

7. *Did the reader understand the question?* Sometimes misunderstandings arise from the form in which a question is asked, not from the student's lack of knowledge. When a student can repeat a question accurately but still does not understand it, the teacher should either (a) rephrase the question or (b) have another student explain what was asked.

8. *Could both the teacher's and the child's answers be right?* Or could the child's answer be right and the teacher's wrong? As mentioned earlier, teachers must be open to the possibility of several correct answers and must not restrict themselves to answers suggested in the manuals or to those based on personal interpretations of the author's message. Although a teacher can hardly accept every answer a child offers, he or she should examine each answer on its own merits.

Because the ultimate goal in reading is for each student to become a proficient reader without the teacher's aid, student development of questions must be gradually encouraged, together with students learning to read text material independently in order to answer those questions. Although teacher questioning is important and does promote comprehension, most authorities agree that it probably does not help readers learn to comprehend better on their own.

Developing Active Comprehension

Consequently, teachers must arrange to move children along in a plan that starts with teacher-generated questions and culminates with student-developed questions. One such plan of successive withdrawal, or so-called fading, involves three stages: *modeling behavior,* or demonstrating to children what good questioning techniques are; *phase-out, phase-in strategies,* wherein teachers take progressively less responsibility in formulating questions about the text material; and *active comprehension,* when children can ask their own questions about the text without external prompting.[43] Such comprehension has been attained once teacher input is minimal or has been totally eliminated.

Cooper has suggested the following four-step instructional strategy for showing students how to acquire active comprehension, or comprehension monitoring: (1) teach readers to *summarize* by asking themselves what they have read, (2) teach them to *clarify* by asking themselves whether they clearly understand the material, (3) teach readers to *question* by asking themselves what the teacher might demand during a discussion or on a test about the material just read; and (4) teach them to *predict* by asking themselves what might come next or later in the text.[44] This strategy should be used at least once every other week at the primary levels and at least once every week at the intermediate levels until proficiency has been attained. One research study found that students can attain active comprehension with this strategy after fifteen to twenty consecutive days of thirty-minute sessions each.[45]

Evaluation of Student Progress

Standardized reading achievement tests are norm-referenced and therefore let the teacher know how the students are doing in relation to a given sample population that has taken the same test earlier. Two tests that have been favorably reviewed are

a. *Gates-MacGinitie Reading Tests* (1978 Edition). (Riverside Publishing Company, Chicago, IL). There is one Basic R form (for grades 1.0–1.9) which runs 60–70 minutes in two sessions; and four Levels which each run 55 minutes in two sessions. The Levels A–D cover grades 1.5–1.9, 2, 3, and 4–6, respectively.

b. *Stanford Achievement Test: Reading Tests* (1982 Edition). (Psychological Corporation, Cleveland, OH). There are three Primary Levels, each running 95–110 minutes in two sessions; and two Intermediate Levels, each running 100 minutes in two sessions.[46]

Another type of reading test is criterion-referenced and can be used to compare students with a predetermined objective. In contrast to a norm-referenced test, a criterion-referenced test offers the teacher more specific data about any one student's strengths and weaknesses in the field of reading. Most basal series include skill tests that are criterion-referenced.

The teacher may also choose to develop his or her own criterion tests, following a format of objective multiple-choice testing recently developed by the California State Department of Education.[47] Because the Department believes that comprehension is the central goal of reading, the majority of reading questions are comprehension items with percentages ranging from 60 percent in the third grade to 80 percent in the sixth grade. Sample items from the instrument administered to third graders follow Reading Passages A and B.[48]

Passage A

The time is midnight. The full <u>moon</u> is <u>high</u> in the sky. Here and there a bonfire lights the beach. People are gathered around the fires, waiting. Suddenly, the beach is alive with thousands of <u>wiggling</u> fish as wave after wave carries them to shore. At once the people are splashing through the waves, snatching up the fish.

Does it sound like a wild story? It is not just a story. It is a grunion run, and it happens several times every year in southern California.

The grunion is a small, silvery fish that is between five and six inches long. The season for laying eggs is from the middle of February to early September. During those months, on the nights of the highest tide, the grunion swim to shore to lay their eggs in the sand. The next high tide uncovers the eggs. The baby grunion burst out like <u>popcorn</u> and ride the waves to sea.

Passage B

George <u>woke</u> up one bright Saturday morning feeling wonderful. He and Gloria were at last going to Disneyland.

After an hour's drive on the freeway, they were there!

The first thing they <u>saw</u> was Mickey Mouse leading his band to the railway station. Uncle John took a picture of the twins with Mickey Mouse.

"Let's go on the Matterhorn," <u>shouted</u> Gloria.

"<u>I'll</u> sit here and watch," said Uncle John.

They climbed into a <u>car</u>, and soon they were at the top of the mountain. Then down they rushed, <u>faster</u> and faster, in and out of tunnels, flying like the wind.

All of a sudden they came to a stop. They were glad to be safely on the ground again!

They had many more exciting rides and saw lots of wonderful things.

As they rode home, tired but happy, they thanked Uncle John for a thrilling treat.

Skill Area	Description of Skill Area	Illustrative Test Question
I. Word Identification A. Phonics 1. Vowels	The student will identify a word that rhymes with a word used and underlined in a passage or will identify a word that contains the same tested vowel sound as a word used and underlined in a test passage.	Mark the word that rhymes with *moon.* ○ tin ○ tune ○ tan ○ tone (See Passage A.)
2. Consonants	The student will identify a word that rhymes with a word used and underlined in a passage or will identify a word that contains the same tested consonant sound(s) as a word used and underlined in a passage.	Mark the word that has the same sound as the *c* in *car.* ○ chose ○ circle ○ color ○ chick (See Passage B.)
B. Structural analysis 1. Prefixes, suffixes, and roots	The student will identify (1) the way in which a suffix or prefix alters the meaning of a base word, (2) the root or base form of a tested regular verb (for example, *hurried → hurry*), and (3) the semantic association between an irregular past tense of a verb and its infinitive (for example, *taught → teach*).	In the word *faster,* the *er* makes the word mean ○ not as fast. ○ more fast. ○ just as fast. ○ less fast. (See Passage B.)

Skill Area	Description of Skill Area	Illustrative Test Question
2. Contractions and compound words	The student will identify the words that make up a contraction or compound word, both of which are used and underlined in a passage.	The two words in *popcorn* are ○ po + pcorn. ○ pop + corn. ○ popc + orn. ○ popco + rn. (See Passage A.) The word *I'll* means the same as ○ is all. ○ I will. ○ it will. ○ I fill. (See Passage B.)
II. Vocabulary A. Recognizing word meanings	The student will identify the definitions, synonyms, and antonyms of words that are used and underlined in a passage.	In this story, *shouted* means ○ watched. ○ climbed. ○ yelled. ○ pictured. (See Passage B.) The opposite of *high* is ○ small. ○ alive. ○ low. ○ tall. (See Passage A.)
B. Using context	The student will use the context of a passage to identify the meaning of a multiple-meaning word that is used and underlined in a passage.	In this story, *saw* means ○ a tool. ○ to cut wood. ○ a fun ride. ○ looked at. (See Passage B.)
III. Comprehension A. Literal 1. Details a. From a single sentence	The student will identify the verbatim answer to a question that is derived entirely from a single sentence within a passage.	Who took a picture? ○ Uncle John ○ George ○ Mickey Mouse ○ Gloria (See Passage B.)
b. From two or three sentences	The student will identify the verbatim answer to a question that is derived from putting together two or three sentences within a passage.	Where were the people waiting? ○ in a boat ○ near a house ○ under a tent ○ on the beach (See Passage A.)

Skill Area	Description of Skill Area	Illustrative Test Question
2. Pronoun references	The student will answer a question that involves identifying the antecedent of a pronoun.	Who saw Mickey Mouse? ○ the band ○ George and Gloria ○ the mountain men ○ Aunt Mary (See Passage B.)
3. Sequence	The student will answer a question that involves identifying the sequence of events, facts, or other elements in a passage.	Which of these does the story tell about last? ○ the bonfire ○ the baby grunion ○ laying eggs ○ the waiting people (See Passage A.)
B. Inferential/Interpretive 1. Main ideas	The student will identify the primary topic of a passage.	This story is mostly about ○ a ride in the car. ○ Uncle John. ○ a day at Disneyland. ○ the Matterhorn. (See Passage B.)
2. Cause and effect	The student will associate a cause with an effect.	Why were people waiting on the beach? ○ to ride the waves ○ to cook the popcorn ○ to see the moon ○ to snatch up the fish (See Passage A.)
3. Drawing conclusions a. About characters	The student will draw a conclusion about the feelings or attitudes of a character.	At the beginning of the story, Gloria probably felt ○ sad. ○ angry. ○ excited. ○ disappointed. (See Passage B.)
b. From details	The student will draw a conclusion from a detail in a story.	You can tell from the story that baby grunion probably ○ will die in very deep water. ○ need to be taught to swim. ○ will lay five or six eggs. ○ can stay alive in deep water. (See Passage A.)
c. From overall meaning	The student will draw a conclusion from the overall meaning of a story.	This story tells about ○ a day of fun and excitement. ○ a day of hard work. ○ a night of worry and fear. ○ a night of quiet rest. (See Passage B.)

1. Why does the basal reader approach continue to be the most popular way to teach reading in the United States?
2. How does the computer contribute to reading instruction?
3. What should be the role of the parent in the elementary school reading program?
4. Describe the type of reading or language program that a professionally staffed preschool might offer in an effort to meet parental demands.

1. Administer the checklist for beginning reading readiness to a five- or six-year-old child. Record your findings.
2. Visit a kindergarten and observe which kinds of reading readiness skills are presented in that kindergarten. Take note of the amount of time spent on those skills.
3. Try using the language-experience approach with an older nonreader or with an immigrant child who has only recently arrived in the United States and is LEP (limited-English proficient).
4. Choose a basal reader story at a grade level that interests you. Then for that story develop four literal comprehension questions, four interpretive comprehension questions, and four critical/applied/schema-implicit comprehension questions.
5. Conduct an individual reading conference with a child in the primary or intermediate grades shortly after the girl or boy has independently read a self-selected book.
6. Examine six series of contemporary basal readers (together with their teachers' manuals) and evaluate each in terms of its balance of ethnic groups, sexes, geographic settings, and literary genres. Which of the manuals would you feel most comfortable using?
7. Set up the learning center on reading shown in Figure 10.8.

Berrent, H. 1988. "Using Cloze Reading Comprehension," *Academic Therapy, 23,* 383–387.

Cairney, T. 1988. "The Purpose of Basals: What Children Think," *The Reading Teacher, 41,* 420–428.

Choate, J. and Rakes, T. 1989. *Reading: Directing and Correcting Special Needs.* Boston: Allyn and Bacon.

Eshelman, M. 1988. "Read to Eat: A Teaching Strategy," *Instructor, 97*(8), 34–37.

Five, C. 1988. "From Workshop to Workshop: Increasing Children's Involvement in the Reading Process," *The New Advocate, 1,* 103–113.

Klein, M. 1988. *Teaching Reading Comprehension and Vocabulary.* Englewood Cliffs, NJ: Prentice Hall.

Throne, J. 1988. "Becoming a Kindergarten of Readers," *Young Children, 43*(6), 10–16.

Tovey, D., Johnson, L., and Saporer, M. 1988. "Beginning Reading: A Natural Language Learning Process," *Childhood Education, 64,* 288–292.

Trachtenburg, P. and Ferraggia, A. 1989. "Big Books from Little Voices," *The Reading Teacher, 42,* 284–289.

Zakaluk, B., and Samuels, S. J., eds. 1988. *Readability: Its Past, Present, and Future.* Newark, DE: International Reading Association.

Figure 10.8. Language Arts Learning Center: Reading.

TYPE OF CENTER:	**Literature—Sequence Reinforcement**	TIME: Unlimited
GRADE LEVEL:	2-4	NUMBER OF STUDENTS: 3

INSTRUCTIONAL OBJECTIVE:

The child will be able to analyze and read the comic strips and put them in sequential order, using the pictures or words as a guide.

MATERIALS:

Ten 4-frame comic strips (each frame must be separated and pasted on a plain four-by-five-inch index card), duplicates of the entire comic strip in correct order for the answer strips (these should be pasted on three-by-nine-inch construction paper). Each comic strip and its duplicate should have the same number. This number should be written on the back of each index card that contains a frame from that strip, and also on the corresponding duplicate answer strip. The center should have an answer pocket and a covered box for the playing cards.

DIRECTIONS:

1. One student plays "dealer."
2. The dealer removes the playing cards from the box. He deals four cards to every player.
3. Use the rest of the cards for playing cards. Take the top card from the pile of playing cards and place it next to the pile. This is the discard pile—all cards are face up.
4. The first player chooses a card from either pile. After the card has been chosen, the player may keep it but must put one down in the discard pile.
5. The game continues until one player has four cards with the same number on the back. The player must then try to put the comic strip in the correct order. The player must do both to win the game.
6. Answers can be found on the answer sheets.

EVALUATION:

The children can check their own answers to see whether they have accomplished the task. The teacher will observe whether the children become more proficient at placing pictures in sequential order. This activity may also indicate the students' ability to visualize a sequence of ideas.

Chapter Notes

1. Commission on Reading, *Becoming a Nation of Readers* (Washington, D.C.: The National Institute of Education, 1984), p. 7.
2. J. B. Carroll, "The Nature of the Reading Process," in *Readings on Reading Instruction,* 3rd ed., A. J. Harris and E. R. Sipay, eds. (New York: Longman, 1984), pp. 31–32.
3. Commission on Reading, *Becoming a Nation of Readers,* pp. 9–18.
4. California State Department of Education, *Reading Framework for California Public Schools* (Sacramento: Author, 1980), p. 3.
5. P. B. Mosenthal, "Research Views: Relating Taxonomies of Reading Methods to Taxonomies of Reading Goals," *The Reading Teacher,* 1987, *40,* pp. 812–813.
6. P. Burns, B. Roe, and E. Ross, *Teaching Reading in Today's Elementary Schools,* 4th ed. (Boston: Houghton Mifflin, 1988), pp. 22–29.
7. D. Hammill and G. McNutt, "Language Abilities and Reading: A Review of the Literature on Their Relationship," *Elementary School Journal,* 1980, *80,* p. 273.
8. D. Lapp and J. Flood, *Teaching Reading to Every Child,* 2nd ed. (New York: Macmillan, 1983), p. 79.
9. J. Mitchell, Jr., ed., *The Ninth Mental Measurements Yearbook,* Volume I (Lincoln: University of Nebraska Press, 1985) pp. 421 and 968.
10. P. Weaver, *Research within Reach* (Washington, D.C.: National Institute of Education, 1978), p. 44.
11. Commission on Reading, *Becoming a Nation of Readers,* p. 29.
12. J. K. Black and M. Puckett, *Developmentally Appropriate Kindergarten Reading Programs: A Position Statement* (Denton, Texas: Texas Association for the Education of Young Children, 1985).
13. Clark County (NV) School District, *Reading and the Kindergarten Child* (Las Vegas, Nevada: Author, n.d.), pp. 1–12.
14. Commission on Reading, *Becoming a Nation of Readers,* pp. 29–30.
15. W. Otto, R. Rude, and D. Spiegel, *How to Teach Reading* (Reading, Massachusetts: Addison-Wesley, 1979), pp. 243–247.
16. R. V. Allen, *Language Experiences in Communication* (Boston: Houghton Mifflin, 1976), pp. 51–53.
17. L. Harris and C. Smith, *Reading Instruction: Diagnostic Teaching in the Classroom,* 3rd ed. (New York: Holt, 1980), pp. 363–364.
18. L. Searfoss and J. Readence, *Helping Children Learn to Read* (Englewood Cliffs, New Jersey: Prentice-Hall, 1985), p. 125.
19. California State Department of Education, *English Language Arts Framework* (Sacramento: Author, 1987), pp. 6–9.
20. L. Henke, "Beyond Basal Reading: A District's Commitment to Change," *The New Advocate,* 1988, *1*(1), pp. 42–51.
21. K. Goodman, "Reading: A Psycholinguistic Guessing Game," in *Readings,* A. J. Harris and E. R. Sipay, eds., pp. 45–52.
22. P. Groff, "The Significance of Word Length," *Visible Language,* 1983, *17,* pp. 396–398.
23. D. Schubert and T. Torgerson, *Improving the Reading Program,* 5th ed. (Dubuque, Iowa: Brown, 1981), pp. 249–252.
24. M. Ceprano, "A Review of Selected Research on Methods of Teaching Sight Words," *The Reading Teacher,* 1981, *35,* pp. 314–322.

25. F. Duffelmeyer, "The Effect of Context on Ascertaining Word Meaning," *Reading World,* 1984, *24*(1), pp. 103–107; J. Kendall and J. Hood, "Investigating the Relationship Between Comprehension and Word Recognition: Oral Reading Analysis of Children with Comprehension or Word Recognition Disabilities," *Journal of Reading Behavior,* 1979, *11,* pp. 41–48; and W. Nagy, P. Herman, and R. Anderson, "Learning Words from Context," *Reading Research Quarterly,* 1985, *20,* pp. 233–253.

26. Schubert and Torgerson, *Improving the Reading Program,* pp. 255–256.

27. A. J. Harris and E. R. Sipay, *How to Increase Reading Ability,* 7th ed. (New York: Longman, 1980), pp. 390–391.

28. A. J. Harris and E. R. Sipay, *How to Increase Reading Ability,* 8th ed. (New York: Longman, 1985), p. 393.

29. B. Rosenshine and R. Stevens, "Classroom Instruction in Reading," In *Handbook of Reading Research,* P. D. Pearson, ed. (New York: Longman, 1984), pp. 745–798.

30. Commission on Reading, *Becoming a Nation of Readers,* pp. 42–43.

31. Burns, Roe, and Ross, *Teaching Reading,* pp. 123–124.

32. B. R. Rosso and R. Emans, "Children's Use of Phonic Generalizations," *The Reading Teacher,* 1981, *34,* pp. 653–657.

33. J. McNeil, *Reading Comprehension,* 2nd ed. (Glenview, Illinois: Scott, Foresman, 1987), pp. 2–5.

34. A. Bussin and E. Chittenden, "Research Currents: What the Reading Tests Neglect," *Language Arts,* 1987, *64,* pp. 302–308.

35. K. C. Stevens, "The Effect of Interest on the Reading Comprehension of Gifted Readers," *Reading Horizons,* 1980, *21*(1), pp. 12–15; P. Babbs and A. Moe, "Metacognition: A Key for Independent Learning from Text," *The Reading Teacher,* 1983, *36,* pp. 422–426; W. Brozo, R. Schmelzer, and H. Spires, "The Beneficial Effect of Chunking on Good Readers' Comprehension of Expository Prose," *Journal of Reading,* 1983, *26,* pp. 442–445; K. C. Stevens, "Chunking Material As an Aid to Reading Comprehension," *Journal of Reading,* 1981, *25,* pp. 126–129; D. R. Rice, R. Doan, and S. Brown, "The Effects of Pictures on Reading Comprehension Speed, and Interest of Second Grade Students," *Reading Improvement,* 1981, *18,* pp. 308–312; and G. Malicky and D. Schienbein, "Inferencing Behavior of Good and Poor Readers," *Reading Improvement,* 1981, *18,* pp. 335–338.

36. P. D. Pearson, "Asking Questions About Stories," in *Readings,* A. J. Harris and E. R. Sipay, eds., p. 274.

37. *Ibid.,* pp. 281–282.

38. R. M. Wilson et al. *Programmed Reading for Teachers* (Columbus, Ohio: Merrill, 1980), pp. 138–141.

39. M. Rowe, *Teaching Science as Continuous Inquiry* (New York: McGraw-Hill, 1973), pp. 243–293.

40. C. R. Wilson, "Teaching Reading Comprehension by Connecting the Known to the New," *The Reading Teacher,* 1983, *36,* pp. 385–389.

41. A. Collins and E. Smith, *Teaching the Process of Reading Comprehension,* Technical Report #182 (Urbana, Illinois: University of Illinois, Center for the Study of Reading, 1980).

42. D. Spiegel, "Ten Ways to Sort Out Reading Comprehension Problems," in *Readings,* A. J. Harris and E. R. Sipay, eds., pp. 298–302.

43. H. Singer, "Active Comprehension: From Answering to Asking Questions," *The Reading Teacher*, 1978, *31*, pp. 901–908.

44. J. D. Cooper, *Improving Reading Comprehension* (Boston: Houghton Mifflin, 1986), pp. 259–261.

45. A. S. Palinscar and A. L. Brown, *A Means to a Meaningful End: Recommendations for the Instruction of Poor Comprehenders* (Urbana, Illinois: University of Illinois, Center for the Study of Reading, 1984).

46. J. Mitchell, Jr., ed., *The Ninth Mental Measurements Yearbook*, Volumes I and II (Lincoln: University of Nebraska Press, 1985), pp. 593 and 1454.

47. California Assessment Program, *Survey of Basic Skills, Grade 3: Rationale and Content* (Sacramento: California State Department of Education, 1980); and California Assessment Program, *Survey of Basic Skills, Grade 6: Rationale and Content* (Sacramento: California State Department of Education, 1982).

48. California Assessment Program, *Survey of Basic Skills, Grade 3*, pp. 7–12.

Reading and Vocabulary Development 11

Major Chapter Goals

After studying Chapter 11, the reader will be able to

1. Explain the factors that influence vocabulary growth in children.
2. List guidelines for a curriculum in vocabulary development for the elementary school.
3. Describe the three major approaches for teaching English vocabulary.

Discover As You Read This Chapter Whether*

1. Students' reading comprehension levels correlate only slightly with students' demonstrated vocabulary knowledge.
2. Vocabulary improvement demands periodic and repeated use of the new words by the teacher and the students.
3. Elementary school children have three general vocabularies.
4. The first vocabulary to develop is the speaking vocabulary.
5. The vocabulary to grow most rapidly during the elementary school years is the reading vocabulary.
6. Pronunciation is the object of vocabulary instruction.
7. Direct instruction in vocabulary is relatively unimportant in the teaching of content areas.
8. Internal context clues concern mastery of both affixes and roots.
9. Learning to use a thesaurus is a skill for students beyond the elementary school.
10. Students' names provide an interesting springboard for an etymology project in the elementary grades.

*Answers to these true-or-false statements may be found in Appendix 5.

School success depends heavily upon the size and utility of the child's stock of words. Due to the verbal nature of most classroom activities, a knowledge of words and the ability to use those words competently are essential to academic success.

Fortunately, there is strong agreement among teachers that vocabulary instruction is a critical part of the elementary curriculum. One recent survey of 228 first- through fifth-grade teachers from seven areas of the country showed overwhelming support for teaching vocabulary words *before* students read a basal selection, as commonly occurs during the directed reading activity, with figures ranging from 100 percent (of first-grade teachers) to 88 percent (of fifth-grade teachers).[1] Furthermore, 99 percent of these teachers confirmed that they also teach vocabulary as part of content-area lessons.

As necessary as direct vocabulary instruction is for all students, it is especially important for poor readers. One study of fourth graders found that although high-ability readers encountered only one unknown word out of one hundred words in a typical passage, low-ability readers encountered one unknown word out of every ten words in their assigned readings.[2]

Whenever students have difficulty understanding individual word meanings within connected paragraphs, reading comprehension suffers—this according to more than fifty years of research that supports the high correlation between students' demonstrated vocabulary knowledge levels and their reading comprehension levels.[3] Three hypotheses, or positions, have been offered to explain that strong relationship: the *general aptitude position,* the *general knowledge position,* and the *instrumentalist position.* The first two suggest that vocabulary and reading comprehension are both related to a common third factor, either intelligence or world knowledge. The general aptitude position particularly attributes vocabulary development to inborn traits that are relatively unaffected by instruction. And the general knowledge position suggests that persons who score highly on vocabulary tests do so because of their conceptual knowledge; understanding a single word implies knowing many related words because each new word learned is added to the individuals' store of concepts.

The third hypothesis is the instrumentalist position, which implies that knowledge of word meanings directly permits one to comprehend text. Of the three positions, the instrumentalist believes most strongly that vocabulary instruction promptly improves comprehension.

Types of Vocabularies

Each child has four general and related vocabularies with which the elementary teacher must work. Two of them—the listening and reading vocabularies—are receptive and emphasize understanding and decoding. Speaking and writing vocabularies, on the other hand, are expressive and can be viewed as encoding in its broadest definition. All four vocabularies overlap and develop continuously into adulthood, although at different rates. Of course, it is initially the listening and speaking vocabularies that contribute to reading and writing skills.

The *listening, or hearing, vocabulary* refers to all the words that children recognize and understand when they hear them in an oral context. It is the first vocabulary to develop during the language acquisition stage and is also the one that continues to grow most rapidly during the elementary school years. It remains substantially larger than a student's visual vocabulary until the age of ten, at which time the size difference diminishes.

The teacher must realize that the listening child may comprehend one meaning of a word or one shade of meaning and yet be wholly ignorant of the other denotations. In addition, the teacher must recognize that the size of a primary child's listening vocabulary ordinarily will not affect the reading progress experienced by the pupil until the third grade.

The *speaking vocabulary* includes all the words that children use in everyday speech. It forms the basis for the development of the reading and writing vocabularies, and it is at the oral/aural level that vocabulary development generally takes place in the classroom. The recommendation has been made that pupils should possess sizable speaking vocabularies in a language before they begin reading lessons in that language, whether it be their first or second tongue.

The *reading vocabulary* consists of all the words that children recognize and understand in print or in writing. When boys and girls enter school, their reading vocabularies are generally limited to their names and the few words they have learned to recognize from billboards, television, and food container labels. It is during reading instruction that children build their word banks. By the time they reach reading maturity in the upper grades, their reading vocabularies overtake and surpass their oral/aural vocabularies. The more students read, the more their reading vocabularies grow.

Reported to lag perpetually behind the other three vocabularies is the *writing vocabulary*. It is the last to develop and includes only the words that children can use in written compositions. It is closely tied to spelling instruction. Pupils' writing vocabularies reportedly overlap more than 90 percent with their speaking vocabularies. Moreover, writing vocabularies are generally nonexistent when children begin school.

Planned instruction in any one area of vocabulary tends to result in improvement in all four areas. They are interrelated and uniformly based on conceptual development.

Growth in Word Meaning

As boys and girls acquire experiences and learn to regard the environment in various ways, their ability to attach meaning to words changes and grows. Four ways in which this growth develops have been identified.

First, *children are able to see and label an increasing number of critical properties of events, objects, persons, and actions*. Young boys or girls are solely concerned with the physical attributes of size, color, and texture. More experienced children, however, can describe an object or condition in terms of other physical attributes as well. Similarly there is growth in the connotative meanings that boys or girls attach to a person or an object. Initially they may have only been able to experience anger or happiness but later they experience many other reactions as well to events or people. As their experience broadens they are able to identify more functional attributes and more aesthetic qualities of objects and actions.

Second, *children acquire a more precise label for any critical property as they begin to differentiate shades of meaning.* Young girls or boys experience everything so simply that they only need words for either end of the meaning spectrum: *rough/smooth, happy/sad, round/square.* More experienced children differentiate the extremes of meaning and try to qualify their words. Still later, pupils acquire standard labels or create their own metaphors for clear meaning.

Third, *children's words become more generalized words;* a single word may be applied to more objects, in more contexts, from more physical points of view, and in more time frames. Pencils for example, are no longer just yellow or wooden. Instead, they can be purple or green, dull or sharp, thin or oversized. They may be used in school or at home, in the car or at the library media center. They may be mechanical pencils, colored pencils, or cased pencils.

Fourth, while they are differentiating and generalizing their experiences, *children are building a supply of expressions relating to any one element of meaning.* Young boys or girls have only one way to describe a certain color. More experienced pupils retain their original expressions but simultaneously collect new expressions. They thereby become better able to communicate personally and to understand the speech and writing of others.

Factors Influencing Vocabulary Growth

There are many specific factors that significantly affect the development of vocabulary in children. While some of them are beyond the domain of the teacher, others can be influenced by his or her planning.

The first factor is the controversial matter concerning the *socioeconomic status of the child's family.* One survey of word recognition among 210 primary children revealed that boys and girls from schools that served upper SES families did better than children from schools that served lower SES families.[4] Although the age at which significant differences first appear in vocabulary performance among boys and girls of varying socioeconomic groups has not been firmly set, some studies do indicate that these differences have been established by age three.

Nevertheless, a language-model in the home environment alone cannot assure a wide vocabulary for children who are not alert and able to learn. Because there is a high correlation between vocabulary and *intelligence,* what children gain from their environment is conditioned by their native capacities to learn. Retarded readers have a limited writing vocabulary and possess a listening vocabulary that is larger than their reading vocabulary. Bright children, on the other hand, remember their experiences with greater clarity. They can abstract and generalize words and terms that are beyond those of students with limited mental ability.

The *age or grade level* of the child is an important factor too. The older the child, the more words he or she knows. Eighth graders commonly recognize four to six times as many words as first graders. Even second graders outperform first graders, according to two separate vocabulary surveys.[5] Children in grade two recognized 90 percent of the 306 words presented; children in grade one, 64 percent.

The factor of *motivation* is always crucial. Dale and O'Rourke believe that motivated individuals can increase their working vocabularies by 10 percent.[6] Such an increase will result, in part, from bringing into sharper focus those words, those parts of words, and those expressions whose meanings are presently fuzzy. The teacher can help motivate students into moving some of their words and word phrases out of a so-called twilight zone into their working vocabularies.

Such *instruction and guidance in the use of words* is vital. Besides teachers, children's parents, grandparents, and other interested adults—at home and in the community—can and should take the time to explain unfamiliar vocabulary to boys and girls. Conversing with the mail carrier, for instance, can help children enrich and refine their use of words.

Furthermore, girls and boys must also have *repeated opportunities to practice each new word* so that it may be assimilated into individual word banks. A recent review of eight vocabulary studies which were completed between 1963 and 1982 and mostly with pupils in grades four through six, has shown that, although all of the programs did increase children's word knowledge, very few of them reported any corresponding improvement in reading comprehension.[7] Those programs that did prove beneficial demanded large amounts of practice with the instructed words. Length and breadth of training in the use of the words helped promote automacity of lexical access and, thereby, comprehension. Active attempts by the children to use the new words and even to make decisions about their use also had positive effects on performance of reading comprehension tasks.

The *continued and regular listening to storybooks* is also a critical factor. Vocabulary appears to be learned best by young children in a context of emotional and intellectual meaning. Pupils, especially those who are slow academically, find it difficult to deal with words in isolation. Reading aloud to boys and girls, however, has resulted in increasing their knowledge of words as well as the quality of their vocabularies.

Another contributing factor covers the *personal interests* that the child has developed. Boys and girls engrossed in sports or science readily acquire the specialized vocabulary that their avocation demands. Interest centers in the classroom (which are properly planned and frequently changed) can stimulate word study too. A current area of interest both at school and at home is the microcomputer for which children would be likely to acquire some of the vocabulary associated with commercial educational software as shown in Figure 11.1.

Sex differences have also been noted in all types of vocabularies. Girls develop larger speaking vocabularies prior to school entrance and they soon exceed elementary school boys in reading vocabularies. These differences, however, level off as the students enter adolescence.

Figure 11.1.
Vocabulary for the
Computer Age.

Essential Words for Computer-Assisted Instruction
in the Elementary Grades, Based on a Sample of 35 Programs

activity	description	lesson	ready
adjust	different	letter	regular
again	directions	level	remove
another	disk	list	repeat
answer	diskette	load	*return
any	display	*loading	[rewind]
*arrow	document	match	rules
audio	down	memory	save
bar	drive	*menu	score
before	edit	[module]	screen
begin	effects	monitor	select
bold	end	move	selection
button	*enter	*name	*sound
[cartridge]	erase	need	*spacebar
[cassette]	*escape or < esc >	no	speed
catalog	exit	*number	start
change	find	off	team
choice	finished	on	text
*choose	follow	options	then
colors	format	paddle	try
column	*game	password	turn
compete	good	picture	*type
complete	help	play	up
command	hit	player	use
computer	hold	*please	video
*continue	incorrect	point	wait
control or < cntrl >	incorrectly	practice	want
copy	indicate	*press	which
correct	insert	print	win
correctly	instructions	problems	word
cursor	joystick	*program	work
delete	*key	quit	yes
demonstration	keyboard	rate	your

*Words present in at least 10 of the 35 programs
[ ]Additions—not in any of the 35 programs

Source: L. Dreyer, K. Futtersak, and A. Boehm, ''Sight Words for the Computer Age: An
Essential Work List'', *The Reading Teacher*, 1985, *39*, p. 14. Reprinted with permission of
L. G. Dreyer and the International Reading Association.

Television viewing is yet another factor. It offers simultaneous visual-auditory presentation of vocabulary. It promotes concept building and offers experience with standard English, allowing many pupils to increase both their speaking and reading vocabularies. However, the teacher must stress *selective television viewing* if he or she wishes to insure that the medium will make a useful contribution to the vocabulary growth of the children.

The *social organizations* to which boys and girls belong make a difference in their vocabularies. If they regularly attend a synagogue or church, for example, they are more likely to be acquainted with Biblical terms than if they did not attend.

The final factor is *locale,* which is growing less significant under the influence of the mass media. Still, there are words dealing with coal mining or condominiums that are not commonplace to everyone in the nation.

Based on research studies and classroom experience, the following principles should permeate a curriculum promoting vocabulary growth among elementary school pupils.

Guidelines for a Curriculum in Vocabulary Development

Developing a vocabulary requires understanding of the meanings and concepts that underlie words. Concepts may be expanded both by differentiation and by generalization. Children learn to group lemons and limes under *fruit.* They also learn to separate *cats* into Angora, Manx, and Persian. Boys and girls with learning difficulties or bilingual backgrounds generally find it hard to recognize the various meanings of a single word such as *big.*

The vocabulary of the home and community greatly affects the school program in vocabulary development. Not only have children learned to listen and speak long before they enter kindergarten, but even after they have been enrolled in school, they continue to spend many hours listening and talking at home and in their neighborhoods. Consequently, if the type of vocabulary that the boys and girls hear and use outside of school is limited, it is little wonder that such a deficiency partly offsets the teacher's efforts to help them improve their stock of words. In this delicate area of home-school relations, it is critical to take care that children do not develop feelings of inadequacy about their families or communities due to matters of vocabulary.

Vocabulary development is closely related to general maturation and varied interaction with a stimulating out-of-school environment. Teachers generally cannot expect proper vocabulary growth in immature, impoverished, or retarded children. Although heredity sets the limits of possible development, the child with an IQ slightly below normal who is growing up in an out-of-school environment favorable to language development is likely to have a better vocabulary than the child with an IQ slightly above normal who is being reared in relatively sterile surroundings.

Motivation is the critical factor underlying any school environment that promotes word study. It is as important as any other aspect of vocabulary instruction, and no classroom teacher honestly attempting to teach vocabulary will overlook it.[8] Motivation for developing a personal vocabulary is related to the in-depth study of words, the list of words chosen to be mastered, the learner's involvement, and the care given to planning a curriculum program of word learning.

Children need direct instruction in vocabulary, and teachers of beginning readers must be especially certain that the labels and terms they use are fully comprehended by the pupils.[9] Because word boundaries are almost impossible to identify during oral language, it is better to have the children's own words shown in print during language-experience activities, for example. Such direct instruction of vocabulary is also important when teaching social studies, science, mathematics, and other content areas.

Researchers conducting a recent analysis of studies concluded that vocabulary instruction does have a strong and significant effect on the comprehension of passages containing taught words and also has a significant effect on comprehension of passages not necessarily containing taught words.[10] Elementary grades that were surveyed ranged from second through sixth.

Not only does planned vocabulary instruction yield greater gains than incidental or unorganized instruction, but *a variety of instructional methods appears to be more effective than any single method.* The three major groups of useful strategies for fostering vocabulary development may be labelled *learner's independent approach, learner's dependent approach,* and *teacher's direct instructional approach.* Each is described later in this chapter.

For beginning readers, word shape alone does not seem to be a useful word-recognition technique. Too many first-grade words have the same configuration. Fluent readers, however, as well as other students who are beyond the developmental level of beginning readers, do find and use helpful information in word configurations.[11]

In the lower grades, growth in the pupil's meaning vocabulary is obtained chiefly through oral methods. The words that boys and girls encounter in primary reading books are chosen partly from concepts that have meaning for those children. Therefore, it is in these grades that much emphasis must be placed on vocabulary improvement through oral communication. The issue is critical because the absolute scale of vocabulary development and the longitudinal studies of educational achievement indicate that approximately 50 percent of general achievement at grade twelve has been reached by the end of grade three.

Oral language allows for interaction and feedback and typically contains a smaller proportion of low-frequency, or difficult, words than written language. This makes it easier to learn those new words that do occur.

Vocabulary development must grow out of experiences that are real to the learner. A teacher cannot overlook the need for carefully structured experiences. For primary children especially, firsthand experiences are the best and often the only source of conceptual development. The teacher must recognize that pupils

Vocabulary development for all children grows best out of firsthand experiences that are real to the learner. (© Dianne Carter.)

at any level who lag behind their peers in vocabulary growth do not need additional written work. Instead they will profit from nonprint media and direct experiences.

Comprehension, an integral part of word knowledge, was once defined as relating new experiences to those already known. It is not surprising then that students with enriched backgrounds of experience bring more to the vocabulary they hear or read than do children with limited experiential backgrounds.

Such results are consistent with the current concept of reading embodied in schema theory and discussed in Chapter 10. Schema networks, or schemata, allow the readers to integrate what they know with new and additional information found in the text or basal reader. The more completely rooted in experience each schema is, the more substance it possesses. In the same way, word meanings rooted in experience result in more substantial schemata than word meanings lacking such an experiential base.

Children's work with words should be as active as the teacher can arrange because vocabulary improvement requires periodic use of the new words by the teacher and the students. There must be adequate opportunities to use the new vocabulary in order to classify and reinforce word meanings. Only when a child has made a word his or her own has that word been mastered. The process does take time, and rapid gains in vocabulary occur less frequently than in comprehension or rate of reading. Still, children can be encouraged to participate in physically active word games, they can discuss literal and figurative word meanings, and they can record words in their personal notebooks. Two other valuable learning strategies recently uncovered in fifth-grade classrooms in Illinois were (1) group exercises in categorizing new words and (2) short improvised dramatic activities about those words.[12] The superiority of the two approaches for both good and poor readers was demonstrated on multiple choice tests and on sentence tests of word usage, with results holding true for both immediate recall and long-term retention. (Additional instructional activities for vocabulary growth are outlined later in this chapter.)

The dictionary is a valuable tool for extending vocabularies. Although the proper use of the picture dictionary is introduced in grade one, some pupils never seem to grasp the importance of any dictionary or develop the habit of using one. The teacher should therefore informally evaluate the dictionary competencies of the class and periodically schedule group lessons in the use of the dictionary. Also the teacher should insist that each child have access to a dictionary appropriate to his or her reading and maturity levels.

Sometimes children who have acquired words in their reading vocabularies fail to use them in their speech. It may be that they do not know how to pronounce those words properly and need to be reminded of still another use of the dictionary.

Context has a facilitative effect on the learning of new words, although the role it plays in the recognition of any one single word will depend on the level of sophistication of the reader, the strength of the context, and the word itself.[13] Teaching words in isolation creates a transfer problem for children who have "learned" words separately, one at a time, or else in random order, but who later have difficulty recognizing these words in context. One recent study of fourth graders in a rural elementary school showed that, although both good readers and poor readers were significantly more accurate when reading connected text than they were when reading the identical words in random order, it was the poor readers who particularly benefited from the additional information contained in the contextual clues.[14]

Furthermore, contexts presented for the purpose of vocabulary development should be *pedagogical* contexts, or those particularly designed for teaching designated unfamiliar words.[15] The second kind of contexts are *natural* contexts, which cover four catagories (misdirective, nondirective, general, and directive) of which only the directive context is apt to lead the reader to the specific meaning for a word.

Finally, *beginning in about the third grade, the major determinant of vocabulary growth is the amount of free reading done individually,* according to Nagy and Anderson.[16] These researchers estimated that in the middle grades, the least able and least motivated children might read one hundred thousand words a year; average boys and girls, one million words; and the voracious readers, ten to fifty million words.

Basal reading programs strongly influence the content as well as the form of the vocabulary study that accompanies the reading lessons. Although the various series may introduce various words at different levels, their procedures for teaching those words remain fairly alike and sometimes divert vocabulary instruction from a stress on concept development and comprehension skills. Six of these procedures appear to be based on misconceptions about words generally and about the nature of vocabulary learning in particular:[17]

1. *All words are equally learnable.* Although individual words possess traits that demand variations in instruction, suggestions in the teachers' manuals tend to be the same, word for word, lesson to lesson, level to level. Nouns and verbs, for example, are easier to learn than prepositions or pronouns; and concrete words such as *leopard* are easier to learn than abstract ones such as *democracy*. Yet many manuals do not take such matters into consideration. What is needed therefore is a program including strategies that take into account the differences in word function and word difficulty.

2. *Pronunciation is the object of vocabulary instruction.* Emphasizing detailed phonic analysis at the expense of concept development makes vocabulary instruction a form of applied phonics with a corresponding loss in text comprehension. A good instructional program must involve constant monitoring of vocabulary understanding, particularly at the higher levels of the reading program where vocabulary selection is much less controlled.

3. *Words have only one meaning.* Words are often discussed in the manuals in relation to a single context, and that of course is the one concerned with that particular reading selection. Basals frequently overlook unusual uses of common words either during prereading vocabulary instruction or during the directed reading activity. A sound vocabulary program, however, allows teachers to elaborate on word meanings and to provide that information as a typical portion of the directed reading lesson. Critical to the comprehension of many literary forms is an awareness of the effects of word choice on meanings.

4. *Teaching a word insures that it has been learned.* Manuals that offer exactly one lesson for new vocabulary per assigned selection, little systematic review of word meanings, and few suggestions for the continued monitoring of vocabulary knowledge fail to accommodate the highly individual nature of word learning. Such accommodation can occur when teaching strategies making up basal lessons become more flexible. It should surely include generic lessons for presenting various word categories, function words, descriptive words, pronouns, abstract words, and overall reviews.

5. *Mentioning words is sufficient for learning.* During a typical basal vocabulary lesson, the teacher introduces a printed word, generally in sentence context. Next, the students read the word and try to explain its meaning or try to use it in their own sentences. Sometimes there is a review exercise before the vocabulary instruction ends. This one-time-only presentation of

Teaching English Vocabulary: Misconceptions

Intermediate students need vocabulary instruction carefully planned by their teacher as much as primary children do. (© James L. Shaffer.)

new words has been termed *mentioning* by some, and will not suffice as long as words are essentially labels for concepts that readers must acquire. A program based on vocabulary as an integral element of comprehension instruction will promote elaboration of concepts in sequential lessons.

6. *Older readers need little or no direct vocabulary instruction.* Any series that assumes older readers' complete independence places a substantial burden on those learners because the word recognition skills (discussed in Chapter 10) on which students rely are not always exact or efficient. Not only do primary *and* intermediate girls and boys need regular and planned practice in those skills, but it is up to the teacher to determine the individual's skill success in order to guarantee more dependable vocabulary growth. A good instructional program continues in the upper grades with an emphasis on in-depth development of key concept words, with opportunities to practice independent word-recognition skills, and always with the understanding of the differing needs of older students.

The foundations of vocabulary development are laid in the home during the pre-school years. The school builds upon those foundations. It introduces new words to children during each curricular activity. It also teaches them how to develop their word power independently both in and out of school.

The process of vocabulary building involves sensory perception of an object (or the attributes of an object) or perception of the relationships of objects with one another. As each new perception is added to the earlier ones, the composite is then associated with familiar words or with new words spoken or written by other people.

Teachers must recognize that the more pupils learn about a given vocabulary concept, the broader and deeper their understanding of that concept becomes. O'Rourke terms this the BVD strategy for enlarging children's word stock; that is, the broader (B) the knowledge of synonyms for the vocabulary (V) concept (of *old,* for example), the deeper (D) the knowledge of the basic concept.[18] Conversely, the deeper the children's understanding of the concept of *old,* the broader their knowledge of suitable synonyms.

There are many ways to help children acquire word knowledge and proficiency, including audio and visual experiences. However, which method of vocabulary instruction works best at a particular grade level or with a particular type of student has not yet been firmly established. Nevertheless, there are three broad headings of approaches for developing vocabulary growth in the classroom: the *teacher's direct instructional approach;* the *learner's independent approach;* and the *learner's dependent approach.* Whether any specific method falls into one category or another depends primarily on the amount of teacher or adult follow-up that is required once the child has acquired the technique.

One five-step strategy for teaching new words, especially sight words that have unusual or infrequent letter combinations, is as follows:

1. *Seeing the word.* The new word is first written on a flashcard, a wall chart, the chalkboard, or worksheet. It is then uttered in an oral context. Finally, with some nouns (e.g., *clock, squash*), three-dimensional objects (or realia) can be displayed and labelled in much the same way that this occurs in ESL (English as a second language) classrooms. With many other words (e.g., *astronomer, cloud*), flat pictures can be used to promote understanding of the new terms.
2. *Discussing the word.* After step one, the new word (e.g., *cavity*) is reviewed orally and tied to earlier or on-going experiences or interests of the boys and girls.
3. *Using the word.* Following steps one and two, the children relate orally or write a sentence that uses the new word. Sometimes they may offer synonyms or synonymous phrases. In either case, the teacher writes the sentence on the chalkboard in an effort to clear up promptly any misunderstandings (as in homographs such as *lead/lead, conduct/conduct*).

Teaching English Vocabulary: Methodology

Teacher's Direct Instructional Approach

4. *Defining the word.* After steps one, two, and three, the boys and girls tell in their own words what the new term means. They should not need to use a dictionary to define a common word such as *manufacture.*
5. *Writing the word.* Following steps one–four, girls and boys can practice writing the new word in their personal dictionaries. They can also write the word during some of the instructional activities outlined later in this chapter. It takes considerable repetition of practice and review in a variety of contexts to provide the necessary overlearning of an unfamiliar word to make it part of the children's vocabulary.[19]

All of the steps described above are involved in the Vocabulary Self-Collection Strategy (VSS) that can be implemented in the classroom, especially with intermediate students, with no additional costs or lengthy curriculum revisions.[20] Although teachers will wish to make adaptations to meet individual classroom needs, the Strategy essentially works like this:

> On Monday the teacher and every pupil each bring in two words that the owner feels the entire class should know. The words are *written* on the board (the teacher offering assistance with spelling if necessary) so that everyone can *see* them. Each owner *defines* his or her words and *tells* why they are important to learn.
>
> The class now prunes the list to a predetermined size by eliminating duplicates and familiar words and by keeping high-frequency or important words. Then the owner of each word still on the list *defines* it again, and the teacher and class *discuss* the words while the students *write* the words in their vocabulary journals together with the definitions.
>
> During the next few days the students *use* the words from the class list in *writing* stories, dialogues, or plays; in making or solving crossword puzzles; or in other activities.
>
> At the end of the week, the students may be tested on the class list. The following Monday, the cycle begins again.

The VSS emphasizes context because students must describe where they found their words and why those words are important; thus it is also a worthwhile approach for use in classes enrolling children learning English as a second language. It is also a technique that stresses daily encounters with the words under study, preferably on a five-day cycle.

One recent two-year study with fourth graders also called for daily (30-minute) lessons, with each set of words taught during a five-day cycle.[21] The researchers concluded that it was the frequency and richness of the pupil encounters with the new vocabulary that contributed to how well those words were learned. Each word was given between ten and fifteen exposures during the weekly cycle, and strategies included oral production, defining, sentence generation, learning games involving speed of response, and competition for points on a Word Wizard Chart awarded to children who had heard, seen, or used the new words outside of class. Results showed that after the first year of implementation, the instructed children made significantly greater gains on a standardized measure of reading comprehension and vocabulary than did the boys and girls who had not received the instruction.

As soon as the teacher has introduced a child to any one of the three major techniques or subheadings of this approach, the boy or girl may unlock the meaning of many unknown words by using knowledge of familiar words. The three techniques are *external context-clue methods* of word attack, *mastery of affixes,* and *mastery of roots.* The last two may also be grouped together as morphological, or *internal, context-clue methods.*

At least one research study has shown that due to the sheer volume of vocabulary that students will encounter in reading, any program of vocabulary instruction must include those methods that will increase children's ability to learn words on their own.[22] Consequently, any strategy of direct vocabulary instruction must be established with the complete understanding that it can cover only a small fraction of all the words the girls and boys need to know. Efforts to expand vocabularies of children by teaching them words one by one, ten by ten, or even hundred by hundred are obviously exercises in futility. Instead, vocabulary instruction should always include the valuable teaching of methods that will allow students to become independent word learners.

By using external context clues, a child can frequently figure out the meaning of a strange word without using the dictionary. Therefore, the teacher must demonstrate the various kinds of such context clues so that the child will be aware of their availability. The teacher can (1) construct several sentences to illustrate each kind of clue, (2) point out random context clues in paragraphs the pupil may be reading, or (3) present sentences that typify three or four kinds of clues and let the pupil explain which kind each sentence represents. Dale and O'Rourke have delineated the following kinds of external clues (together with illustrative sentences) that students can learn to recognize:

1. *Formal definition.* Expressing the meaning of a word in a direct statement. *Example:* A phoneme is one of a group of distinct sounds that compose the words of the English language.
2. *Definition by example.* Defining a word by example alone or by further clarifying a formal definition. *Example:* An example of a phoneme is the *f* in *fan* or the *n* in *fan.*
3. *Definition by description.* Listing the physical characteristics of the object representing the word. *Example:* An orange is a reddish-yellow, round, juicy fruit. (A definition by description often does not distinguish one word from others in its class. It does, however, distinguish classes.)
4. *Definition by comparison.* Stretching the meanings of words creatively, even to the extent of sometimes using similes or metaphors. *Example:* The map of Italy is shaped like a boot.
5. *Definition by contrast.* Telling the reader what the word is not. *Example:* A tomato is not a vegetable. (The effectiveness of this context clue depends heavily on the reader's experience.)
6. *Defining by synonym.* Providing a short, similar word that is closer to common usage than the original word. *Example:* Bondage is slavery.

7. *Defining by antonym.* Providing a short, opposite word often used to show the extreme of an object or idea. *Example:* She was willing, but he was loath to walk to the stadium.
8. *Definition by apposition.* Placing a clarifying word or phrase next to another noun or pronoun. *Example:* Jute, the plant, grows in India.
9. *Definition by origin.* Providing a setting in which the word was first used. *Example:* Samuel Maverick was a Texan whose cattle were unbranded wanderers.[23]

Most context clues demand some degree of inferential thinking. The reader should gradually learn to use the sense of the sentence or the surrounding sentences as an aid in identifying the probable meaning of a difficult word.

Teachers should be aware of the results of a recent study in the use of context clues for vocabulary growth.[24] It involved third and fifth graders in a midwestern semirural community school who worked for eight weeks with four methods of learning twelve new and difficult words each week. The context method proved significantly more effective than (1) using the dictionary, (2) categorizing the new word with other familiar words, or (3) associating known synonyms with the new word. It worked equally well for girls and for boys. Although good readers (not unexpectedly) did significantly better with the method than did poor readers, nevertheless the context technique was the most effective for both groups and for both third and fifth graders.

In this instance the context method introduced new words in several sentences, one of which was defining. Then after these sentences had been studied with the assistance of the teacher, the student was asked to apply the meaning of the new word in a written response concerning his or her personal experiences.

Incidentally, current language arts texts for the elementary school sometimes contain exercises to help pupils learn about context clues even as early as the primary levels; sample textbook exercises were shown in Chapter 10. Teachers' manuals or pupil workbooks for major basal reading series always include such exercises.

Using Internal Context Clues: Mastery of Affixes

Although most boys and girls accept the importance of context, some of them do not understand morphology or how words also derive meaning from their component parts. To introduce this valuable generalization, the teacher must start with a familiar word, break it into meaningful parts, and then transfer the meaning of these parts to new words. The teacher should move stepwise from known words (*triangle* or *good*) to unknown words (*tricolor* or *goodness*). Children will then be able to infer the meaning of a difficult word if (1) they know the meaning of the prefix or suffix used to form the word, and if (2) they realize that meanings of mastered prefixes and suffixes can be transferred from one word to another.

The value of such mastery can be quickly shown by an examination of Edward Thorndike's list of the 20,000 most common words in the English language. Five thousand words, or 25 percent of those listed, have prefixes. Of this group, 82 percent use one of these prefixes: *ab* (away from), *ad* (toward, to), *be* (overly, on all sides), *com, con, co* (together, with), *de* (downward, reversal, from), *dis* (apart from, not, opposite), *en* (in, into, to cover), *ex* (former, out of), *in* (not, into), *pre* (before), *pro* (for, before, in favor of), *re* (again, restore), *sub* (beneath, under), and *un* (not, the opposite of).

Common derivational suffixes that children should learn in an effort to develop their vocabularies independently include *able, ble, ible* (can be done, inclined to), *al, ial* (relating to), *fy* (make, form into), *ic* or *ical* (in the nature of), *ism* (system, state of), *ist* (person who), *less* (without), *let* (small), *ment* (concrete result, process, state of), *ness* (quality, condition of), *ory* (place where), and *ward* or *wards* (course, direction).

Inflections or inflectional suffixes that pupils can readily learn include verb tenses (*helps, helped, helping*); plurals (*dogs, plates, watches, babies*); possessives (*Wendy's, boys'*); and comparisons (*smaller, smallest*). Inflectional suffixes differ from derivational suffixes because they do not change the part of speech (or form class) to which a word belongs; derivational suffixes generally do.

The exact value of an understanding of inflections (or inflected endings) has not been finally established. On the one hand, a study in Illinois, Texas, and Ohio of fifty-four average students in Grade 4 and fifty-six poor readers in Grades 6 through 9—all reading at the fourth-grade level—showed that many students recognize one form of a word and not another.[25] Errors among the eighty-seven words tested could not be explained in terms of frequency of use of a particular word form, and the unpredictability of word recognition was not confined to poor readers. The researcher concluded that recognition vocabularies exist on a continuum, with some words being recognized immediately wherever and whenever they appear and with others never being recognized no matter how many times students are tested. In the broad area between these extremes are words that are sometimes recognized and sometimes not.

On the other hand, the relationship existing between children's reading abilities in grades one and two and children's abilities to apply inflections is closer than the relationship existing between reading ability and either auditory or visual perception.[26] Young children surveyed were able to change pseudowords (such as *wog*) to plurals, past and progressive verb tenses, possessives, and comparatives or superlatives with ease.

Incidentally, current language arts texts for the elementary school do contain exercises to help pupils learn about affixes. They generally introduce suffixes by level three and prefixes by level four, although some begin even earlier. Sample textbook exercises in suffixes are shown in Figure 11.2.

Figure 11.2. Exercises in Using Suffixes.

Using Word Parts: Suffixes

Focus

A **suffix** is a word part added at the end of a base word.

You have learned that you can change the meaning of a base word by adding a prefix at the beginning of the word. Another way to change the meaning of a base word is to add an ending. These endings are called **suffixes.** See how the base words *breath* and *help* are changed by adding the suffix *-less*.

Base Word		Suffix		New Word
breath	+	less	=	breathless
help	+	less	=	helpless

The suffix *-less* means "without." *Breathless* means "without breath." *Helpless* means "without help."

Here are four other common suffixes and their meanings.

-able
or
-ible

These suffixes have two meanings. They can mean "can be." For example, a *divisible* number can be divided. A *crushable* box can be crushed. The suffixes can also mean "having this feature." For example, a *comfortable* chair has the feature of comfort. A *sensible* question has the feature of good sense.

-er
or
-or

These suffixes mean "a person or thing that does something." For example, a *traveler* travels, and a *collector* collects. The suffix *-er* may also mean more." *Colder* means "more cold."

-ful

This suffix has two meanings. It can mean "full of." A *handful* of dirt means "a hand that is full of dirt." The suffix can also mean "having." A *beautiful* person has beauty.

-ous

This suffix also means "full of" or "having." A *vigorous* person is full of vigor or energy.

Be careful! Sometimes the spelling of the base word changes when a suffix is added. Notice how these words change.

beauty	sense	flip
beautiful	sensible	flipper

Exercises: Adding Suffixes to Base Words

A. Copy these words on a piece of paper. After each word, write the base word. Then write the suffix that was added.

Examples: dipper = dip + -er
ridiculous = ridicule + -ous

1. carrier
2. eventful
3. thoughtless
4. continuous
5. pitiful
6. famous
7. valuable
8. actor
9. lovable
10. fearless

B. Answer these questions.

1. If *pacify* means "to bring peace," what is a *pacifier?*
2. If *decipher* means "to change a code into plain language," what does *decipherable* mean?
3. If *worth* means "value," what does *worthless* mean?
4. If *glee* means "joy," what does *gleeful* mean?
5. If *advantage* means "benefit or favor," what does *advantageous* mean?

Source: Pgs. 12–13, *McDougal, Littell English, Silver Level.* Copyright © 1987 by McDougal, Littell & Company, Box 1667, Evanston, Illinois 60204.

Unlike affixes, which are bound morphemes, most roots are free morphemes. Still, mastery of roots or base words will also help children attack new words that may come up outside the classroom. With a knowledge of base words, children will be able to unlock dozens of words by transferring the meaning of a single root to other words.

During a beginning lesson, for instance, the students could be asked to underline the common element in the following words: *telephone, microphone, saxophone, earphone, phonics*. They could discuss the meaning of *phon* (sound) and then write other words they know that contain the same root. They might even make up new words.

Common roots the children can learn include *cap* (head), *cav* (hollow), *circ* (ring), *dent* (tooth), *form* (shape), *geo* (earth), *gram* (letter), *mari* (sea), *min* (small), *mov* (move), *scrib* or *script* (write), and *vis* (see). Some current language arts texts for the elementary school contain exercises to help boys and girls learn about the roots or bases of words. Samples of such exercises are found in Figure 11.3.

A dependent approach does not teach for transfer. Instead, the child studies one word at a time and learns it only under the close supervision of the teacher (or paraprofessional aide). Still the approach is organized, and any systematic strategy to vocabulary growth is preferable to incidental or unorganized learning. The two major techniques or subheadings of the dependent approach are *mastery of a word list* and *dictionary/thesaurus study*.

Weekly or monthly, the teacher assigns a specific number of whole words from lists suggested in children's texts or from word counts developed by educators or psychologists. Such lists vary in length, as is readily apparent from an examination of some basic word lists in use today, including those by Albert Harris and Milton Jacobson (1982, a Core List of 5,167 words), Edgar Dale and Joseph O'Rourke (1981, Living Word Vocabulary of more than 44,000 entries), Edward Fry (1980, 300 New Instant Words), William Durr (1973, 188 words most often used in primary library books), Robert Hillerich (1973, 240 Starter Words), John Carroll, Peter Davies, and Barry Richmond (1971, 86,740 different words for grades 3–9), Dale Johnson (1971, 306 Basic Vocabulary Words for Beginning Reading), and Henry Kučera and W. Nelson Francis (1967, 50,406 different words).

Older lists that still appear in the literature and are often used include those by Edgar Dale and Jeanne Chall (1948, 2,946 words used in the Dale-Chall Readability Formula), Henry Rinsland (1945, 25,632 different words), Edward Thorndike and Irving Lorge (1944, 30,000 words), and Edward Dolch (1936, 220 Basic Sight Vocabulary). Generally, the longer lists are for those teachers or students interested in writing vocabulary. The shorter lists are for those concerned with reading vocabulary.

Figure 11.3. Exercises in Using Base Words.

Using Word Parts: Base Words

Focus

A word part can be added to the beginning or end of a base word to form a new word.

Many words are made up of several parts. Often, there is a **base word,** or main word. One or more word parts may be added to the beginning or end of the base word. Sometimes, you can unlock the meaning of an unfamiliar word by studying the parts.

When a word part is added to a base word, a new word is formed. For example, the word part *dis-* is added to the beginning of the base word *agree* to form *disagree.* Adding the word part *-ment* to the end makes the word *agreement.*

What base word is in these three words?

thoughtless   rethought   unthoughtful

The base word is *thought.* The word part *-less* was added to make *thoughtless.* The word part *re-* was added to make *rethought.* Two word parts, *un-* and *-ful,* were added to make *unthoughtful.* What is the base word in each of these two sets of words?

preshrink   repay
shrinkable   payment
unshrinkable   prepayment

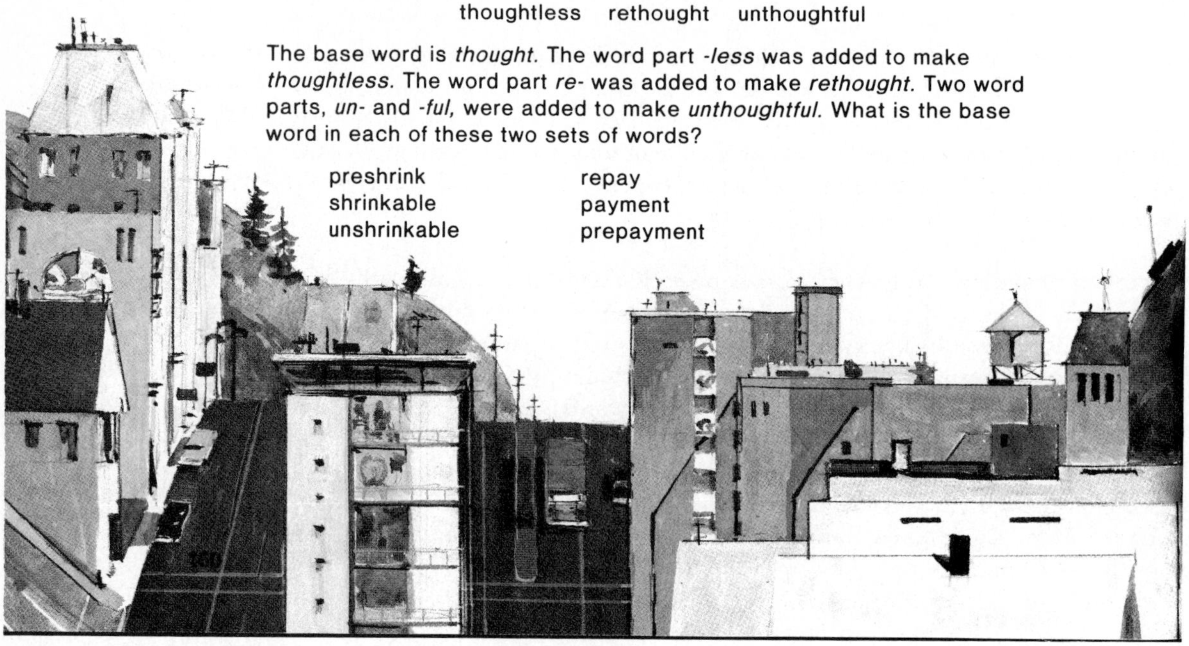

Source: Pgs. 150–151, *McDougal, Littell English, Gold Level.* Copyright © 1987 by McDougal, Littell & Company, Box 1667, Evanston, Illinois 60204.

Exercises: Building on Base Words

A. Copy each of the following words on a sheet of paper. Find and write the base word after each word.

1. senseless
2. mouthful
3. unreadable
4. preview
5. restatement
6. misfit
7. thunderous
8. incomplete
9. kicker
10. nonprofit

11. happiness
12. successful
13. unlucky
14. helper
15. redo
16. prewrite
17. inhuman
18. penniless
19. spoonful
20. colorless

B. Add a word part to the beginning or the end of each of the following base words. If you wish, add word parts to both places. Write the new words you have made on your paper. Tell what the new word means.

1. flaw
2. move
3. heat
4. speak
5. wonder

6. lock
7. worth
8. paint
9. spell
10. joy

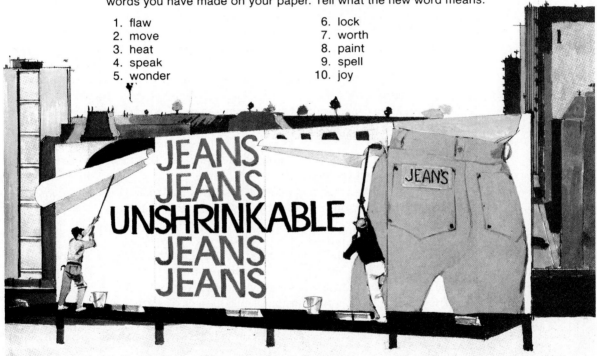

Mastery of such a basic word list readily meets demands for classroom accountability. The children may be quickly assessed by means of a short test on the number of words they have learned from all those assigned. Teachers may also choose to use lists of words introduced during science or social studies units.

Dictionary/ Thesaurus Study

Such study is sometimes linked with mastery of a word list. The teacher may ask the children to look up one or more words from their list in the dictionary so that they become familiar with the meaning of the assigned word or words.

At other times, a new word may appear in the current events lesson or math assignment. The children locate this word in their dictionaries, or sometimes in their thesauruses, at the teacher's suggestion. Later they may find that the new word reappears in a follow-up activity planned by the teacher.

Of course the dictionary is more than a book of word meanings, and proper use of the dictionary is an important skill. Locating one or two unrelated words in the dictionary, however, does not lead to substantial vocabulary growth. The children learn only those exact words that their teacher has assigned and that they must use in a written exercise or test. Further discussion about dictionary skills can be found in Chapter 12.

Unlike the dictionary, which arranges entries alphabetically and provides considerable information, including pronunciations and word meanings, a *thesaurus* arranges entries by topics and contains lists of synonyms and antonyms only. It begins with a meaning and presents context words that represent some part of that meaning.

Children can consult a thesaurus to find replacements for tired words such as *interesting, nice, happy, big,* and *little.* They can also use it to find synonyms for such multisyllabic words as *parsimonious, euphemistic, caricature,* and *serendipity.* Most important, however, is the use of the thesaurus during the preparation of written compositions.

A current and recommended thesaurus is *In Other Words: A Junior Thesaurus* (Scott, Foresman, 1987) by W. Greet and colleagues.

Teaching English Vocabulary: Etymology

When the current edition of *Webster's Collegiate Dictionary* was published by G. & C. Merriam Company, it was announced that 11,000 new words had been added in one decade alone. Interest was then expressed in the increasing number of sources for those words. Primary sources such as science and technology had remained productive, but new words had also arrived from almost every aspect of life, including health, food, government, politics, music, the economy, and varying lifestyles.

Etymology is the study of the origins of words, their relations to similar words in other languages (also known as cognates), and the way word meanings have changed over the years. Its significance is not restricted to college students and other adults, however. Young children also need to know that language is living and changing and that their own use of words contributes to the evolution of vocabulary. Dixon recommends that a good etymological dictionary be required in even the primary classroom and that any girl or boy who wishes to use it should be shown how to do so.[27] Possible adoptions include the following:

E. Pinkerton's *Word for Word: A Dictionary of English Cognates* (Gale, 1982)

R. Smith's *Dictionary of English Word Origins* (Littlefield, 1980)

E. Partridge's *Origins: A Short Etymological Dictionary of Modern English* (Macmillan, 1977)

E. Klein's *A Comprehensive Etymological Dictionary of the English Language* (Elsevier, 1971)

If an etymological dictionary is not available, children in the intermediate grades would enjoy learning the sources of favorite words and phrases in a recommended book such as Sarnoff's *Words: A Book About the Origins of Everyday Words and Phrases* (Scribner's, 1981), which has small humorous drawings.

Students' names provide a good springboard for an etymological project in the elementary grades. Each child can discover what his or her first name means and also in which country it originated. Pupils can consult the following:

G. Stewart's *American Given Names: Their Origin and History in the Context of the English Language* (Oxford, 1979)

L. Dunkling's *First Names First* (Universe Books, 1977)

F. Loughead's *Dictionary of Given Names with Origins and Meanings* (Arthur Clark Company, 1974)

Then additional vocabulary growth can be promoted by listing words from the dictionary that involve that student's first name. For instance, after *Ann* has been introduced as meaning *year,* and once its Latin root is understood, words such as *annual, annuity,* and *anniversary* can be discussed. Crist describes an activity in which a different child's name was honored each week and a class notebook developed with a separate page for each member of the class.[28] In some instances the matter of colloquialisms also arose so that *Bill* was linked to *fill the bill* and *foot the bill.* Family names also have interesting origins. Children may wish to examine Hazen's *Last, First, Middle and Nick: All About Names* (Prentice Hall, 1978) or Smith's *New Dictionary of American Family Names* (Harper, 1973). 1973).

Other topics that provoke the interest of boys and girls include words about people (e.g., *barber*), words about the animal world (e.g., *hippopotamus*), words about plants (e.g., *tangerine*), words about food and beverages (e.g., *ketchup* and *chocolate*), words about clothes (e.g., *pajamas*), and words about transportation (e.g., *bicycle*).

More advanced students may wish to determine how some places got their names (by reading Fletcher's *100 Keys: Names Across the Land,* Abingdon, 1973), how the days and months were named (by checking Asimov's *Words from the Myths,* Houghton, 1961), how slang expressions developed (by examining Carothers' and Lacey's *Slanguage,* Sterling, 1979), how brand names evolved (by consulting Arnold's *What's in a Name: Famous Brand Names,* Messner, 1979), and how some common everyday expressions or folk idioms originated (by using Terban's *In a Pickle and Other Funny Idioms,* Clarion, 1983).

Instructional Activities

Vocabulary building requires attention. Every day at least a few minutes should be taken for discussion of words used or needed for the communication of ideas. This is the only way that precise meanings can be learned. Teachers must understand that when a word is introduced too quickly or too casually, pupils often receive only a vague impression of its definition.

Some of the following instructional activities appeal especially to children with learning disabilities or to younger pupils. Others will interest gifted pupils at all levels or intermediate students. Finally, there are activities that are suggested for all elementary classes, primary and intermediate alike.

1. Listing things needed to (a) bake cookies, (b) build a tree house, (c) go camping, (d) set the table, or (e) go to school on a rainy day.
2. Giving more than one meaning for such words as *run, pipe, can, shell, ice, bark, sheet, park, slip, call, date, yarn, strike, spring, roll, light, fall, cut, check,* and *charge.*
3. Making interesting beginnings for these endings:
    ". . . slipped down the icy slope"
    ". . . struggled wildly"
    ". . . called for help"
    ". . . huddled in the cave"
4. Constructing definitions from handling such objects as a *locket,* a *darning needle,* an *abacus,* or an *avocado.*
5. Illustrating such mathematical and geographical terms as *plateau, diagonal, perpendicular,* and *plain.*
6. Constructing a simple crossword puzzle that uses a series of related words, for example, *airplane, pilot, fly, sky, hangar.*
7. Drawing a pear (pair) tree and adding pears. On each pear should be written a word and its homophone.
8. Describing scenes on picture postcards.
9. Making a sound-train by painting and lettering shoe boxes and then filling them with realia whose names begin or end with the letters shown.
10. Keeping a list of unfamiliar words that appear in newspaper headlines during one week.
11. Discovering colorful words in travel brochures or in newspaper travel advertisements.
12. Examining the *Reader's Digest* section entitled "It Pays to Increase Your Word Power."
13. Listing "moody" words that make readers and listeners feel angry or that keep them in suspense.

14. Collecting job words about computer technicians or anthropologists.
15. Reading juvenile magazines such as *Cobblestones, Cricket, National Geographic World, Odyssey, Owl, Penny Power, Ranger Rick's Nature Magazine, Scienceland, Inc.,* and *Stone Soup.*
16. Describing one food item (*pickles*) according to the five senses (*green, crunchy, sour, slippery, brined*).
17. Discovering how three acronyms (e.g., *radar*) have developed.
18. Collecting "loaded" words gleaned from speeches made by political candidates at election times.
19. Preparing menus based on a single food specialty such as desserts or sandwiches.
20. Writing or listing reduplications (*helter-skelter, dilly-dally, wishy-washy*).
21. Discussing environmental sounds.
22. Keeping word folders after study trips, such as "Visiting a Greenhouse" or "Going to the Planetarium."
23. Consulting Greet, Jenkins, and Schiller's *In Other Words: A Beginning Thesaurus* (Scott, Foresman, 1982) to locate five synonyms each for *break, go, jump, push, say,* and *send.*
24. Charting specialized words for such pastimes as tennis, bowling, fishing, or stamp collecting.
25. Promoting alliterative phrases (*ferocious flea, courteous crocodile*) that are humorous.
26. Making an illustrated dictionary that relates to a special project by incorporating magazine pictures or personal drawings.
27. Using an opaque projector to display pictures of people or animals that plainly describe adjectives such as *grim, impatient, excited,* or *amazed.*
28. Building with a classmate a semantic map by choosing a key word or topic that represents the main subject of a book or of a shared hobby or interest (e.g., *soccer, Star Wars, sharks, cooking*). After writing the key word in the center of a large sheet of paper, a diagram is prepared by brainstorming as many words as possible that are related to the key word and then listing them by categories around the sides of the sheet. Next, those word categories are identified and labelled. Finally, the map is shared with the class and the key word or topic, as well as the categories are discussed.
29. Drawing a favorite baked food such as chocolate cake and then writing all of the recipe ingredients of that food underneath the picture.
30. Adding up words instead of numbers (e.g., *high speed* plus *careless driving* equals *a highway accident*).
31. Creating a mysterious art gallery on a large bulletin board by posting several exciting and colored pictures (clipped from magazines) that have each been covered by sheets of numbered construction paper. A small rectangle is cut out of each numbered sheet so that one segment of each picture becomes visible. The caption above the gallery reads: "Can you solve the mystery of the hidden pictures?" Children can relate their guesses orally or on paper.

32. Writing words to reveal their meanings (e.g., *fat* would be drawn or written with plump thick letters, *f, a,* and *t* while *flag* could have a flag drawn in place of the *f*).
33. Rewriting familiar proverbs or creating new ones.
34. Writing some homophone riddles (e.g., Why is Sunday the strongest day of the *week?* Because the others are all *weak* days).
35. Illustrating humorously some compound words, as in Basil's *Breakfast in the Afternoon* (Morrow, 1979).
36. Collecting definitions of common soccer terms, much like James Gardner does in *Illustrated Soccer Dictionary for Young People* (Prentice, 1978).
37. Examining some of the specialized vocabulary found in Scout manuals.
38. Miming *outrage, delight, terror* and other emotional reactions.
39. Listing items (*nylon, vinyl*) composed wholly or partly of synthetics.
40. Playing a commercial word game such as Junior Scrabble or Password.
41. Charting words that first surfaced during the past decade (e.g., *radon*).
42. Developing fresh similes (*fragile as a new pencil point*) or collecting familiar ones (*nose like a cherry*).
43. Writing word puns after perusing Basil's *Nailheads and Potato Eyes* (Morrow, 1976).
44. Expressing one action word (*lag* or *leap*) graphically through one of the art media.
45. Listing some of the specialized vocabulary used by sportscasters or found on the sports pages of local papers.
46. Identifying some of the photographs found in the McMillans' *Puniddles* (Houghton, 1982).
47. Listening to newscasters to elicit five current terms of recent and local origin.
48. Creating cartoons for a series of antonyms, much like Richard Wilbur does in *Opposites* (Harcourt, 1973).
49. Drawing some amusing and confusing figures of speech such as *fork in the road* and *foot in his mouth.*
50. Listing some one-word palindromes (*nun, rotor, Otto*), words that can be read backwards and forwards with the same result.
51. Writing some intonation riddles (e.g., Why did the pilot take his pony on the airplane? Because he wanted to see a horse fly [*horsefly*]).
52. Drawing five UGH(!) terms such as *fish guts* and *a moldy cucumber.*
53. Collecting oxymorons (such as *jumbo shrimp* and *cruel kindness*), contradictory words or groups of words that are opposite in meaning although they are commonly used in our language.
54. Developing an alphabet of words originating from famous names (e.g., *pasteurization* from Louis Pasteur). The list might begin with *America* (Amerigo Vespucci), *Braille* printing (Louis Braille), *Celsius* thermometer (Anders Celsius), and *diesel* engine (Rudolph Diesel).

55. Perusing one of the following from the library table:
    C. Basil, *How Ships Play Cards: A Beginning Book of Homonyms* (Morrow, 1980)
    N. Bossom, *A Scale Full of Fish and Other Turnabouts* (Greenwillow, 1979)
    J. Hanson, *More Similes: Roar Like a Lion, as Loud as Thunder. . . .* (Lerner, 1979)
    A. Steckler, *One-Hundred-One More Words and How They Began* (Doubleday, 1981)
    J. Thayer, *Try Your Hand* (Morrow, 1980)
    A. Weiss, *What's That You Said? How Words Change* (Harcourt, 1980)

Learning Games in Vocabulary Development

As more and more commercial word games are being produced, teachers in increasing numbers are using vocabulary games in the classroom. They should therefore be aware of the results of a study recently conducted in a large urban school system concerning the use of games to increase sight vocabulary among black first-grade remedial readers.[29] Teachers introduced two new words each morning, Monday through Thursday, for six weeks. After ten minutes of introductory activity (using the chalkboard and flashcards), the children spent the next twenty minutes in one of three treatment groups: playing active games (such as Word Toss), playing passive games (such as Word Rummy), or completing vocabulary worksheets. Posttest results showed that games led to increased learning in children who had earlier mastered few words, with physically active games being the most effective treatment of the three groups. Young boys and girls apparently enjoy competition and are more interested in playing a game in order to learn words than in using pencil and paper exercises.

Regardless of their grade level or their academic achievement, however, elementary children do enjoy playing instructional games. Most of the noncommercial group games described in Figure 11.4 require little, if any, special preparation.

Figure 11.4. Fifteen Learning Games in Vocabulary Development.

1. The teacher writes a long word on the chalkboard (e.g., *hippopotamus*). **Break-Down**
2. At their desks, the players write as many smaller words as they can from any arrangement of the letters contained in the board word.
3. The winner is the player with the most words correctly written and is allowed to put a new word on the board for the class to use.
4. Suggestions: Seasonal words such as *pumpkin* or *valentine* are appropriate and interesting to break-down. Gifted classes enjoy sesquipedalian words (or long words) to break-down, such as *pneumonoultramicroscopicsilicovolcanoconiosis* with forty-five letters.

Figure 11.4. (cont.)

1. The teacher writes the name of a category (e.g., *sports*) on the board.
2. At their seats, the players write as many words as they can recall that fit that category (e.g., *boxing, tennis, baseball, soccer*).
3. One point is awarded for each word correctly listed. (The teacher may also award an extra point for each item correctly spelled.)
4. The winner is the player with the highest number of points. The winner may choose the next category (e.g., *trees*) of Classified Information.

Classified Information

1. The players are divided equally into teams. The teacher uses a timer.
2. The teacher calls out a simple word (e.g., *wash*), which is generally of one syllable. The first player on Team One must match the teacher's word with an advanced synonym or College Word (e.g., *launder*), which need not be longer than one syllable (e.g., *rinse*) but must definitely be more erudite.
3. If the first player on Team One fails to match the teacher's word before the timer buzzes, the first player on Team Two gets a chance to score.
4. The team with the most synonyms wins College Words and can label itself after its favorite (or local) college.
5. Examples include: *eat/dine, sweat/perspiration, pants/trousers, job/occupation*.

College Words

1. The teacher writes on the board a short sentence, using only the first letter of each word and a dash for the rest of the word, (e.g., *M— b— c—f— t— p—*).
2. At their seats, the players try to complete the sentence by writing in their versions of the letters needed to complete each word, (e.g., *Mother baked cookies for the party*).
3. The winners of Dash-Dillers are the players whose sentences are not only reasonable but comply with the board arrangement (even though the final sentences may not be ones the teacher had in mind).

Dash-Dillers

1. Each player receives a portion of a newspaper and then circles five published words that he or she can define but that he or she believes will be difficult or impossible for others to define.
2. The teacher chooses a player to read one of his or her words. Should one of the other players be able to give an acceptable definition, then that player in turn reads a word for the class to define.
3. The winners are all pupils who announced words for which only they could furnish a satisfactory definition.

Definition

Figure 11.4. (cont.)

Descripto	1. The teacher writes on the chalkboard a sentence containing two or three nouns but no adjectives (e.g., *Children are eating apples and oranges.*).
	2. The players rewrite the sentences, using one or more uncommon adjectives before each noun.
	3. The winners of Descripto are the players who chose unique but appropriate adjectives not selected by the rest of the class.
Fill-In	1. The teacher writes an incomplete sentence on the chalkboard (e.g., *Sam lives in a* _____).
	2. Each player copies the sentence and completes it with the most original word he or she knows.
	3. The winners are the players with suitable words which no one else has chosen. They may help to write the next incomplete sentence that requires a fill-in word.
Name-O	1. The teacher writes a pupil's name on the chalkboard vertically: J A M E S
	2. The players copy the name on their papers exactly as it appears on the board.
	3. They use each letter of the name as the first letter of a word to be completed on the paper.
	4. The winner is the first player who has used all the letters correctly. This player's name heads the next round of Name-O.
	5. Variation: The winner is the first player who has used all the letters correctly and formed a sentence out of the words.
Printers' Words	1. The teacher distributes a portion of a newspaper (advertisements and articles) to each player, who is then asked to circle with a crayon or colored pencil any three affixes.
	2. At a signal from their teacher, all children who have completed the task stand at their seats. Every player who can give the meaning of the printed words that he or she has circled is a winner.
	3. Variation: The game may be repeated for root words, depending upon the interest and maturity of the group.

Figure 11.4. (cont.)

1. The teacher, or a child chosen as "It," draws one card from the word box or one entry from a word notebook. 2. "It" then describes the word drawn; for example, "The word has two syllables; it begins with *Q* and means to shake or tremble. What's the riddle word? 3. The other players try to write the riddle word at their seats. 4. "It" now says the riddle word (*quiver*) and also writes it correctly on the board.	**Riddle Word**
1. The players are divided equally into teams. 2. The first player on each team writes any word he or she chooses on the chalkboard. The second player on the same team adds another word toward building a sentence, placing it either before or after the first player's word. Each child receives a turn. But if a player cannot add a suitable word, the player forfeits his or her turn, and the next team begins to build a sentence. 3. The team with the longest sentence after every player has had at least one turn wins Sentence Relay.	**Sentence Relay**
1. The teacher writes a short word on the chalkboard (e.g., *pin*). 2. The players, at their seats or at the board, then write as many words as they can by adding one or more letters before or after the chosen word (e.g., *spin, pint, spinning, pints*). 3. The winner of Stretcher is the player with the longest list of words correctly written when the round has been completed. 4. Suggestion: The teacher may wish to use a timer to stop a round after only thirty to forty seconds if the group of players is mature.	**Stretcher**
1. The teacher writes a key word on the chalkboard (e.g., *chair*). 2. The players, at their seats or at the board, then write a word starting with the first two letters of the chosen word (e.g., *charm*). 3. Within a time limit of one to three minutes, each player must compile a string of words, starting each word with the first two letters of the key word. 4. The winner is the player with the longest string of words correctly written when the round has been completed.	**String of Words**
1. The teacher writes a one-syllable word on the chalkboard (e.g., *bid*). 2. The players, at their seats or at the board, then write as many words as they can by substituting one or more vowels for the orignal vowel (e.g., *bad, booed, bead, bud*). 3. The winner of Substitute is the player with the longest list of words correctly written when the round has been completed. 4. Variation: Teams may be chosen and then provided with individual dictionaries.	**Substitute**

Figure 11.4. (cont.)

1. Two children compete, each in turn, either at the chalkboard or using a sheet   Tic-Tac-Toe
   of writing paper.
2. The object is to write correctly three words, in a line or diagonally, that contain
   a common element such as an affix, phonogram (graphemic base), or root
   word. For example, if the first player wrote words all in capital letters,
   and the second player wrote words in small letters, the Tic-Tac-Toe board
   might look like this after three turns:

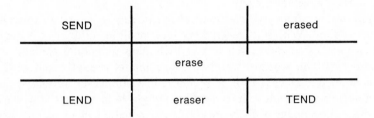

The first player could write in *MEND* (or any word containing the phonogram
end) in the first column and so win Tic-Tac-Toe with a completed vertical
line.
3. Variation: Teams of three to four members each may be chosen with the
   game played only at the chalkboard.

To assist in the planning of a program of vocabulary building, the teacher needs
measured insight into the progress made by individual pupils in their acquisition
of broad listening, speaking, reading, and writing vocabularies.

Evaluation of Student Progress

Numerous standardized reading and reading-readiness tests contain sections on vocabulary, as do various standardized achievement batteries, including
the *Comprehensive Tests of Basic Skills* (published by CTB/McGraw-Hill of
Monterey, CA), the *Metropolitan Achievement Tests* (published by the Psychological Corporation of Cleveland, OH), and the *SRA Achievement Series* (published by Science Research Associates of Chicago).

There is also a recently revised, norm-referenced instrument that has earned
positive reviews and is suitable for ages 2.5 to 40 years:[30]

Peabody Picture Vocabulary Test (1981, Revised). An individually administered
test in two forms, each with 175 items. The examinee is asked to indicate which
of four pictures presented on a carousel-mounted plate corresponds to the
stimulus word read aloud by the examiner. The responses to the bold outline
drawings may be either verbal or nonverbal. Although it is an untimed test,
administration time averages fifteen to twenty minutes. The test publisher is
American Guidance Services of Circle Pines, MN.

A teacher may also choose to devise his or her own tests. There are four major ways of testing vocabulary, according to Dale and O'Rourke: (1) *identification,* whereby pupils respond orally or in writing by identifying a word according to its use or definition; (2) *multiple-choice,* whereby the students choose the correct definition of the tested word from three or possibly four meanings; (3) *matching* (which is really another form of multiple-choice), whereby the tested words are presented in one column and the matching definitions are listed out of order in another column; and (4) *checking,* whereby pupils check the words they know or do not know, although they may also be required to define the words they have checked.[31]

Within these four groups, the teacher can employ a variety of techniques to test vocabulary. With middle-grade or intermediate children, it is hoped that the teacher will often choose self-tests, which allow individual students to make an inventory of their stock of words to determine its strengths and weaknesses. Words contained in an easy-to-hard sequence in a sample self-inventory checklist (relevant to a fourth-grade unit on nutrition) might each be marked with a simple ✓ (to indicate knowledge of the word) or ○ (to indicate lack of such knowledge):

_____	nutrition	_____	legumes
_____	diet	_____	calories
_____	muscle	_____	calcium
_____	vitamin	_____	cholesterol
_____	protein	_____	carbohydrate
_____	energy	_____	thiamine

The most important evaluation of vocabulary growth, however, is that which looks to the performance of the pupil in all the other areas of instruction. Proper measurement of word recognition and understanding is best seen in the light of evaluation of the student's progress in the total process of education.

Discussion Questions

1. Why is it necessary to see vocabulary development as conceptual development?
2. Which of the factors affecting vocabulary growth may be influenced by teacher planning?
3. When, if ever, should the teacher ask a student to look up the meaning of a word in the dictionary?
4. With what kinds of exceptional children would some of the independent methods for teaching vocabulary be especially successful?
5. How could a unit on word origins be made appealing to a heterogeneous group of intermediate pupils of varying abilities and backgrounds?

1. Design a learning game that could be used to teach vocabulary to kindergarten children.
2. Compare lists of new vocabulary to be introduced at the same reading level (e.g., Level 6) in three separate basal series from major publishers.
3. Discover how antonyms are presented in two current language arts series.
4. Compare the presentations on suffixes in various language texts for students at the intermediate levels. Are any of them appropriate for pupils with learning disabilities or for gifted boys and girls?
5. Develop an animal crossword puzzle appropriate either for upper primary or for intermediate children. Possible clues could include: the official bird of the United States, a baby cow, the king of beasts, and so forth.
6. Set up the learning center on vocabulary shown in Figure 11.5.

Figure 11.5. Language Arts Learning Center: Vocabulary.

TYPE OF CENTER: **Etymology**
GRADE LEVEL: 4-6

TIME: 30-40 minutes
NUMBER OF STUDENTS: 1-2

INSTRUCTIONAL OBJECTIVE: The pupil will recognize how rich our vocabulary is with words that we have borrowed from other languages.

MATERIALS: A dictionary, sheets of paper with the following sentence at the top: Worldly Sentence—The *gypsy girl* wearing a *scarlet belt*, an *indigo veil*, a *cotton blouse*, a *gingham skirt*, a *sprig* of *heather*, and a *fez*, and carrying a *tangerine*, a *boomerang*, a *ukulele*, and an *umbrella*, walked down the street with a *negro tycoon*, who lived in an *igloo* and traveled only by *canoe*, *sled*, or *dinghy* to a *bungalow* with a *dirty tile floor*, to make *telephone calls* and to *purchase* some *wine*, *vodka*, *brandy*, *cocoa*, *tomatoes*, *balsam ointment*, *tobacco*, *chop suey*, *yams*, and *goulash* for her *clan*.

Figure 11.5. (cont.)

Additional Materials

Folders for finished papers and key sheet, picture of girl (try to use some of the colors and items mentioned as well as the action).

DIRECTIONS:

1. Read the sentence below the picture.
2. Using the dictionary, look up the origin of the underlined words. Use the guide in the front of the dictionary for the meaning of abbreviations.
3. Write your answers on the paper provided in the *worksheets* folder.
4. Make sure to write your name on your paper.
5. Compare your origins to those on the key sheet. Are yours right? Can you identify anything in the picture with the words you have just looked up?
6. Place your paper in the *finished papers* folder.
7. Return the key sheet to its folder.

KEY

gypsy—Egyptian	ukelele—Hawaiian	call—Anglo-Saxon
girl—Anglo-Saxon	umbrella—Italian	purchase—French
scarlet—Persian	street—Latin	wine—Latin
belt—Latin	negro—Spanish	vodka—Russian
indigo—India	tycoon—Japanese	brandy—Dutch
veil—Latin	igloo—Eskimo	cocoa—Nahuatl
cotton—Arabic	canoe—Arawak	tomatoes—Nahuatl
blouse—French	sled—Flemish	balsam—Greek
gingham—Malayan	dinghy—Bengali	ointment—Latin
skirt—Scandinavian	bungalow—Hindi	tobacco—Arawak
heather—Scottish	dirty—Scandinavian	chop-suey—Chinese
fez—Turkish	tile—Latin	yams—Portuguese
tangerine—French	floor—Anglo-Saxon	goulash—Hungarian
boomerang—Australian	telephone—Greek	clan—Irish

EVALUATION:

Self-checking: The students will compare their findings to correct derivations provided on the key sheet.

Source: From PATHWAYS TO IMAGINATION by Angela S. Reeke and James L. Laffey, © 1979 by Scott, Foresman and Company. Reprinted by permission.

Recent Related Readings

Blachowicz, C. 1987. "Vocabulary Instruction: What Goes On in the Classroom?" *The Reading Teacher, 41*, pp. 132–137.

Cunningham, P. 1987. "Are Your Vocabulary Words Lunules or Lupulens?" *Journal of Reading, 30*, pp. 344–49.

Dixon, R. 1987. "Strategies for Vocabulary Instruction," *Teaching Exceptional Children, 19*, pp. 61–63.

Herman, P. and Dole, J. 1988. "Theory and Practice in Vocabulary Learning and Instruction," *Elementary School Journal, 89*. pp. 43–54.

Hillerich, R. 1987. "Developing Vocabulary," *Teaching Pre–K–8, 17*, pp. 25–26.

Marzano, R. and J., 1988. *A Cluster Approach to Elementary Vocabulary Instruction.* Newark, DE: International Reading Association.

Miller, G. and Gildea, P. 1987. "How Children Learn Words," *Scientific American, 257*(3), pp. 94–99.

Nagy, W. 1988. *Teaching Vocabulary to Improve Reading Comprehension.* Urbana, IL: National Council of Teachers of English.

Shipley, J. 1987. *The Origins of English Words.* Baltimore: John Hopkins University Press.

Urdang, L. 1988. *The Whole Ball of Wax and Other Colloquial Phrases: What They Mean and How They Started.* New York: Putnam.

Chapter Notes

1. D. Johnson, K. Levin, and S. Pittelman, *A Field Assessment of Vocabulary Instruction in the Elementary School Classroom,* Progress Report 84-3 (Madison: Wisconsin Center for Education Research, University of Wisconsin, 1984).

2. L. Gambrell, R. Wilson, and W. Gantt, "Classroom Observations of Task-Attending Behaviors of Good and Poor Readers," *Journal of Educational Research,* 1981, *74,* pp. 400–404.

3. S. Stahl and M. Fairbanks, "The Effects of Vocabulary Instruction: A Model-Based Meta-Analysis," *Review of Educational Research,* 1986, *56,* pp. 72–110.

4. D. D. Johnson and T. C. Barrett, "Johnson's Basic Vocabulary for Beginning Reading and Current Basal Readers: Are They Compatible?" *Journal of Reading Behavior,* 1972, *4,* pp. 1–11. Also see W. Loban, "Research Currents: The Somewhat Stingy Story of Research into Children's Language," *Language Arts,* 1986, *63,* pp. 608–616.

5. Johnson and Barrett, "Johnson's Basic Vocabulary"; and D. D. Johnson and E. Majer, "Johnson's Basic Vocabulary: Words for Grades 1 and 2," *Elementary School Journal,* 1976, *77,* pp. 74–82.

6. E. Dale and J. O'Rourke, *Techniques of Teaching Vocabulary* (Addison, Illinois: Field Educational Enterprises, 1971), p. 8.

7. K. Mezynski, "Issues Concerning the Acquisition of Knowledge: Effects of Vocabulary Training on Reading Comprehension," *Review of Educational Research,* 1983, *53,* pp. 253–279.

8. W. Nagy and R. Anderson, "How Many Words Are There in Printed School English?" *Reading Research Quarterly,* 1984, *19,* p. 325.

9. T. C. Standal, "How Children Recognize Words in Print," In *Research in the Language Arts,* V. Froese and S. Straw, eds. (Baltimore: University Park Press, 1981), p. 251.

10. Stahl and Fairbanks, "The Effects of Vocabulary Instruction," p. 100.

11. K. Rayner and E. Hagelberg, "Word Recognition Cues for Beginning and Skilled Readers," *Journal of Experimental Psychology,* 1975, *20,* pp. 444–455.

12. M. Jiganti and M. Tindall, "An Interactive Approach to Teaching Vocabulary," *The Reading Teacher,* 1986, *39,* pp. 444–448.

13. Standal, "How Children Recognize Words," p. 252.

14. R. Allington and A. McGill-Franzen, "Word Identification Errors in Isolation and in Context: Apples vs. Oranges," *The Reading Teacher,* 1980, *33,* pp. 795–800.

15. I. Beck, M. McKeown, and E. McCaslin, "Vocabulary Development: All Contexts Are Not Created Equal," *Elementary School Journal,* 1983, *83,* p. 181.

16. Nagy and Anderson, "How Many Words," pp. 327–328.

17. N. Sorenson, "Basal Reading Vocabulary Instruction: A Critique and Suggestions," *The Reading Teacher,* 1985, *39,* pp. 80–85.

18. J. O'Rourke, *Toward a Science of Vocabulary Development* (The Hague: Mouton, 1974), pp. 83–86.

19. D. D. Johnson and P. D. Pearson, *Teaching Reading Vocabulary,* 2d ed. (New York: Holt, 1984), pp. 101–102.

20. M. R. Haggard, "The Vocabulary Self-Collection Strategy: An Active Approach to Word Learning," *Journal of Reading,* 1982, *26,* pp. 203–207.

21. I. Beck and M. McKeown, "Learning Words Well: A Program to Enhance Vocabulary and Comprehension," *The Reading Teacher,* 1983, *36,* pp. 622–625.

22. Nagy and Anderson, "How Many Words," pp. 325–328.

23. Dale and O'Rourke, *Techniques,* pp. 28–34.

24. J. P. Gipe, "Use of a Relevant Context Helps Kids Learn New Word Meanings," *The Reading Teacher,* 1980, *33,* pp. 398–402; and J. P. Gipe, "Investigating Techniques for Teaching Word Meanings," *Reading Research Quarterly,* 1978–79, *14,* pp. 624–644.

25. R. Hillerich, "Recognition Vocabularies: A Research-Based Caution," *Elementary School Journal,* 1981, *81,* pp. 313–317.

26. M. Brittain, "Inflectional Performance and Early Reading Achievement," *Reading Research Quarterly,* 1970, *6,* pp. 34–50.

27. G. Dixon, "Investigating Words in the Primary Grades," *Language Arts,* 1977, *54,* p. 419.

28. B. Crist, "Tim's Time: Vocabulary Activities from Names," *The Reading Teacher,* 1980, *34,* pp. 309–312.

29. D. Dickerson, "A Study of Use of Games to Reinforce Sight Vocabulary," *The Reading Teacher,* 1982, *36,* pp. 46–49.

30. J. Mitchell, Jr., ed., *The Ninth Mental Measurements Yearbook,* Volume II (Lincoln: University of Nebraska Press, 1985), p. 1123.

31. Dale and O'Rourke, *Techniques,* pp. 20–26.

Reading and Study Skills

12

Major Chapter Goals

After studying Chapter 12, the reader will be able to

1. Understand the important role of study skills in the reading program.
2. Describe some of the study techniques that are available to students in the intermediate grades.
3. Distinguish among the four major groups of study skills that elementary teachers or media specialists can present.

Discover As You Read This Chapter Whether*

1. Many children do poorly in school because they have never been taught study skills.
2. The SQ3R study method can be introduced successfully to students in the primary grades.
3. Presenting book utilization skills to children should be delayed until junior high school.
4. Teachers and media specialists should introduce boys and girls to the Dewey Decimal Classification System rather than the Library of Congress Classification System.
5. Elementary readers usually request library materials by title.
6. Picture dictionaries can help nonnative speakers learn English as a second language.
7. Publishers of most of the good general encyclopedias follow the continuous-revision policy.
8. Teachers should introduce the topic outline before the sentence outline.
9. Summarizing is part of the reading program from the first grade onward.
10. A special type of scanning is called skimming.

*Answers to these true-or-false statements may be found in Appendix 5.

Reading in the content areas demands the acquisition of study skills so that the learner can obtain, organize, and present information. And although that acquisition process may not seem especially exciting, the skills themselves are critical if the reader is going to be able to do anything with what he or she has decoded and comprehended. Study skills enable the children to find and interpret information from numerous sources and to synthesize it into the resolution of a question or the solution of a problem. In other words, study skills are valuable *tools,* and many students do poorly in school because they have never learned to use them.

When teachers or media specialists can instill in each reader a sense of excitement about the problem-solving process, they simplify the whole procedure of teaching study skills. Students soon begin to realize the value of acquiring those skills, so they can indeed "learn to learn independently."

Study skills must be taught either by the media specialist or by the elementary classroom teacher. Because there remains an insufficient number of media specialists for the elementary school centers, primarily due to budgeting problems, the only apparent solution to the problem of teaching study skills involves two aspects. First, the classroom teacher must acquire and maintain mastery of elementary study skills. (However, at least one survey of teachers in Illinois, Virginia, and Wisconsin showed such mastery to be only in the 51–60-percent bracket on a test intended for use with students completing elementary or junior high schools.)[1] And second, in schools that maintain strong media facilities and staff, children can attain the needed skills from a teacher-specialist team, whereas boys and girls in schools without media specialists can learn study skills from their classroom teacher.

Although there has been comparatively little research on study skills over the years, one recent survey in Arizona of administrators, classroom teachers, counselors, education college faculty, and elementary student teachers drew the following conclusions: (1) Teachers are interested in presenting study skills, think it is important to teach them, and yet feel unprepared to do so; (2) the skills should be introduced in elementary school and gradually increased in complexity; and (3) study skills should be integrated into the content areas because teaching them in isolation is both unproductive and artificial.[2]

Besides the skills themselves, children should also learn how to study or should become familiar with one or more study techniques. Armbruster and Anderson believe that any one of those techniques can be beneficial, provided it helps students process information appropriately.[3] Students must know (1) about ability, background knowledge, and motivation in studying; (2) why, when, and how to use particular study techniques; (3) how to determine the actual assignment and how to match the study skill to that assignment; and (4) how to identify the properties of texts (e.g., headings) and how to use those properties when studying. They claim that studying is not a general process but varies from subject to subject, and that teachers have a responsibility to teach study skills rather than mistakenly assuming that every child already knows them.

Besides acquiring study techniques, girls and boys also need to learn the following:

Book utilization skills
Library and locational skills
Organizational skills
Reading flexibility skills

There are several study techniques that teachers can introduce to elementary students in the intermediate grades, techniques that will eventually be used as self-directed strategies by the children themselves.

Study Techniques

Developed during World War II by Francis Robinson to help military personnel understand and recall what they had read, the SQ3R study method consists of five steps:

SQ3R Study Method

1. *Survey.* Children quickly read the table of contents, the introductory and concluding (or summarizing) paragraphs, and the headings and marginal notes; then inspect any visual aids such as maps, graphs, or illustrations. The purpose is to obtain an overview of the author's intent and of the format of the section, article, or chapter. Sometimes unfamiliar vocabulary poses a problem for some students and should therefore be defined promptly.

2. *Question.* Children change each heading and subheading into a question before that section is read. The purpose is to focus reader attention, to offer a means for self-checking comprehension, and to provide a goal for reading. This step requires the most explanation from the teacher.
3. *Read.* Children read in order to answer the questions just formulated. The objective is to notice how the paragraphs are organized (in order to help readers recall the answers they uncover). Students should also be warned not to overlook any important information not included in the questions already developed and should be cautioned to make brief notes during this purposeful reading time.
4. *Recite.* This step is considered by many to be the most critical of the five. Children give the answers to each of the questions formulated earlier and do so without looking back at the material. Recitation may be done subvocally or in some more permanent written form such as note-taking or informal outlining. The primary purpose is a self-check to determine how well the material has been understood and recalled, and the check is readily accomplished by the student's expressing the author's language in his or her own words. A secondary purpose is to help memorize the information.
5. *Review.* Children reread to correct or verify the answers given during the recitation just made. The purpose is to recall the main points of the selection, article, or chapter and to understand the relationships among the various points. This involves spending considerable time in order to go over the material promptly (both after reading and at varying intervals later on) to ascertain how well the material is still understood.

One research study of fifth graders who were taught a modified SQ3R method for thirty to forty minutes daily for four days showed that the students scored higher than the control groups on the short-answer test (of a social studies passage) that involved factual information.[4] There was no significant difference, however, among the groups in their retellings of the passage. Still, learning the separate steps of the SQ3R method proved valuable to students on subsequent occasions when children did not feel the need to add all the steps into one continuous act.

EXPLORE Study Technique

Developed by Deborah Evans and Eunice Askow especially for students in the elementary grades, the EXPLORE study technique involves four steps:[5]

1. *Examine.* Children survey, or examine, the assigned reading. They read chapter headings, subheadings, marginal notes, graphic aids, and all introductory and final paragraphs. Even italicized or special print is noted.
2. *Plan.* Children write questions that they considered during the overview, or examination, of the various headings and graphic aids. These questions are prepared on notebook paper, not by groups but by individual students.
3. *Absorb.* Children read the assignment and write key words as answers to questions prepared during the planning step. Children keep their question lists handy and are ready to absorb the information in the article or chapter at hand.

4. *Evidence/Express.* Children complete answers to questions posed during the planning step. Logical and adequate answers are expected for every question appearing on the notebook page. That question-and-answer sheet later becomes the review sheet for recalling the content reading and for self-checking the information covered.

Developed recently by George and Evelyn Spache, the PSRT method involves four steps:

PSRT Study Method

1. *Preview.* Children read the title, headings, introductory or summary paragraphs, and the opening and final sentences of paragraphs.
2. *Summarize.* Children make a rough outline of the main ideas identified during previewing. An alternative strategy is underlining those ideas during the previewing step.
3. *Read.* Children read the chapter or article and either complete the outline made during the previous stage or underline the facts that support the main ideas.
4. *Test.* Children develop questions just as a teacher would, or they complete a self-check. In either case, glancing at the text or student outline will verify the answers.

Termed a relatively idealistic plan for studying a textbook, the authors warn that PSRT must be presented and practiced numerous times under teacher guidance before students will adopt it or modify it to meet their needs.[6]

Developed by R. Schmelzer, C. Smith, and W. Browning, the PREP system has been endorsed by Searfoss and Readence as a system simple enough for use at the elementary school level.[7] It involves four steps and works well with factual selections from the basal reader:

PREP Study System

1. *Preview.* Children preview the selection, thereby getting a road map for reading, which is accompanied by oral discussion. All visual aids are examined. Students then read the title and the first and last paragraphs, using headings and subheadings to determine major concepts.
2. *Read.* Children read the selection. For older students, it is possible to introduce note-taking as a means of recording and retaining information. One form that intermediate readers can use is a summary sheet made up of two columns: A narrow left column, or recall column, which has very general headings or subheadings; and a wider right column on which the actual notes are made. Notes taken on the summary sheet can be studied later by covering either side and reciting; a cover card can be moved up and down the summary for self-check. Beginning readers would of course omit all note-taking procedures.
3. *Examine.* Children construct questions about the selection, either during or after the reading. They will generally require some assistance in formulating questions.

4. *Prompt.* Children utilize various techniques to help them remember what they have read. One such device is recitation, first as a group activity and later as an individual one. Topics for recitation include the headings and subheadings found in summary-sheet notes or taken from the selection directly. Students can be shown how to quiz themselves at convenient intervals during the reading.

It should be noted that with beginning readers, only the first two steps (Preview and Read) should be used. Then as children develop their reading skills, the third and fourth steps can be added.

Book Utilization Skills

Textbooks are the fundamental tools in the learning process. Obviously then, students must become familiar with the many features that texts contain, features often overlooked by the majority of children in the elementary grades. All content-area specialists, such as science resource teachers for example, share the responsibility with the classroom teachers of helping students use textbooks effectively and efficiently.

First Skill: Understanding the Parts of a Book

Children must gradually gain an understanding of the parts of a book, the publication of books, and the technical vocabulary that relates to books. Early in the second grade, the students learn about the parts of a book, beginning with the spine ("you have a spine, too, that runs down your back"); they discover that books are always kept on the shelf with the spines facing out. A few weeks later, the children become acquainted with the title page when the media specialist brings in several stacks of books with appealing titles, shows them the title pages of several books, and then asks each child to select one book and attempt to locate the title page. By the end of the third grade the students have been introduced to three items in the physical makeup of books (front and back covers, spine, and text or body of book) and two printed parts of the book (title page and table of contents).

Older children become familiar with the parts of a book that precede and follow the main text: frontispiece; title page; copyright page; dedication; table of contents; list of maps, plates, or illustrations; foreword; preface; acknowledgments; introduction; appendix; glossary; bibliography; index; and end papers. They may be introduced to the signature (or printed sheet containing a section of a book) and may also participate in a demonstration of the making of a signature by folding, numbering, and cutting large sheets of newsprint. Sixth graders may be taken through the steps involved in the physical production of a book, from the original idea to the finished volume; they may attend demonstrations on book mending; or they may tour a local print shop.

All students should become aware of the importance of graphic media and know how to read or interpret charts, diagrams, tables, and other aids. Some textbooks even contain marginal notes, which will serve children as guides to reading.

Activities that will enhance student learning of this skill are varied. Students in all grades will enjoy, for example, a presentation by an author, printer, publisher, illustrator, or binder who can describe his or her contribution to the evolution of a book. Children can make original title pages for book reports, draw book jackets of favorite books to be displayed in the library media center, or create a book individually or in cooperation with their peers. They can occasionally demonstrate the proper handling of books when new sets are distributed for classroom assignments. Sometimes they may be allowed to take apart a discarded volume in order to demonstrate the construction of a book.

Because of the nature of reference tools in the content areas, the one part of the book that should demand special attention is the index. Children must necessarily acquire the ability to locate and use indexes. They will enjoy comparing the tables of contents to the indexes in several books, but it should be pointed out to them that whereas the table of contents gives the broad areas of a book's coverage, the index offers a more detailed listing of the contents of that book. A teacher-specialist in Clear Lake, California, for example, has one of the fifth graders draw from a hat a slip of paper containing an easily located subject such as "the moon," "Abraham Lincoln," or "bluebirds." The child then locates a book that has that subject listed in its table of contents. Presuming that the fifth grader has drawn a slip with the word "bluebirds" written on it, the discussion can soon revolve about an opaque projection of the following initial index entry:

Second Skill: Using an Index

> BLUEBIRDS, 32–48; description, 32–33;
> food, 35, 38–40; migration, 46–48;
> nests, 34, 36–37.

The teacher-specialist reminds the children that when they use the table of contents, they are looking for a broad area of information such as a general chapter on bluebirds. Then the teacher asks the girls and boys, "If we wish to learn more about bluebird nests in particular, how can we locate this specific information and locate it readily?" A few pupils may suggest skimming through the entire chapter, but gradually the class begins to realize that using an index will make the task much easier.

In an attempt to help elementary teachers present the index skill, an analysis was made of more than one hundred actual index entries in several curriculum subjects at three grade levels of representative textbooks and elementary encyclopedias. Components of index entries included the following: main topic, page numbers, comma, period, semicolon, hyphen, colon, synonymous subtopic, related but not synonymous subtopic, *see, see also, illus., map, diag., pict.,* and pronunciation (both phonetic and with diacritical marks). The analysis concluded that the larger the number of components, the more difficult was the entry. In other words, the criterion of complexity was the number of components. Consequently, boys and girls must be given experiences that will enable them to develop insight into the composite nature of the index skill.

x

Library and Locational Skills

Instruction in the use of materials in the school media center and in the classroom library should be functional and preferably related directly to assignments in social studies, science, health, and other curricular areas. It can, however, also occur indirectly through separate units that parallel curricular units. A fourth-grade class, for example, is studying the weather, so the media specialist may plan a unit on myths and legends that have evolved as people over the centuries attempted to explain climatic and seasonal changes. In this way the specialist or teacher-specialist can use classroom science to motivate students to learn more about two areas included under the genre of traditional literature.

The instructional program in library and locational skills should incorporate the interests, needs, and developmental tasks of children, including activities within the students' understanding and ability. There are six major skills.

First Skill: Understanding the Classification of Books

Because the minimal book collection in schools with 500 or fewer pupils (according to recent guidelines established by the American Association for School Librarians) contains 9,000 to 12,000 volumes, any child looking for a book needs a knowledge of the basic arrangement of books and of the Dewey Decimal System for the classification of books. Lessons that relate to call numbers and the proper placement of books on the shelf should begin by stressing the importance of careful arrangement of volumes and by reviewing the division of books into fiction and nonfiction groupings. Then the lessons could proceed as follows.

Fiction and Call Numbers

While showing flash cards with enlarged call numbers (covering both fiction and nonfiction), the teacher-specialist establishes the difference between the two categories of numbers. He or she emphasizes that a fiction call number is the initial letter or letters of an author's surname (and sometimes in large libraries, the entire surname), and then sends several children to get fiction books from the shelves. The children discuss the selections and justify the call numbers appearing on the book spines.

Next, the teacher tells how fiction is arranged, explaining why shelf labels are a quick way of locating the right call number, and how the library media center "landmarks" (corners, windows, pictures, and doors) will save the readers' time in finding the proper shelf label. Finally, the teacher drills on locating fiction via call numbers by showing certain flash cards and calling on the pupils to walk to the shelves and point out the books bearing the desired call numbers.

Nonfiction and Call Numbers

The teacher-specialist randomly arranges on the chalk tray some flash cards with enlarged nonfiction call numbers, and asks the class to suggest a way to place the cards in numerical order. The children will usually respond correctly, although the teacher must be careful not to omit a card with a 000 number in the tray. Another more time-consuming way of introducing the arrangement of nonfiction is by working from the numbers on the shelf labels: children are carefully dispatched to each of the nonfiction shelves—except individual biography—and, one by one, they read the numbers off the shelf labels.

Table 12.1
Dewey Decimal Classification Numbers in Use in Elementary Schools

028	Reading	551	Weather	914.3	Germany
030	Encyclopedias	560	Prehistoric life	914.4	France
070	Journalism	570	Life sciences	914.5	Italy
150	Psychology	574	Biology	914.6	Spain
220	Bible	580	Plants, trees	914.7	Russia
260	Christian church	595	Insects, worms	914.8	Sweden, Norway
292	Greek and Roman Myths	598	Birds	915	Asia
300	Social science	599	Mammals	915.1	China
320	Political science	600	Technology	915.2	Japan
332	Banking, trade, money	608	Inventions	915.3	Arabian countries
333	Conservation	614	Health, safety	915.4	India
340	Law	620	Engineering	915.5	Iran
341	United Nations	621	Radio, television	915.6	Middle East
352	Police	625	Highways, roads, bridges	915.9	Southeast Asia
355	Armed forces	629.1	Aviation	916	Africa
380	Transportation,	629.2	Automobiles, trucks	917	North America
	communication, commerce	630	Farming, gardening	917.1	Canada
383	Postal service, stamps	636	Domestic animals	917.2	Mexico, Central America
385	Railroads, trains	640	Food, clothing	917.3	United States
387	Waterways, ships	700	Fine arts	917.98	Alaska
391	Costume	740	Drawing	918	South America
392	Families, homes	770	Photography	919	Oceania
394	Holidays	778	Motion pictures	919.8	Polar regions
395	Etiquette	780	Music	920	Collective biography
398	Fairy tales, folklore	790	Recreation	921	Individual biography
400	Language	800	Literature	929.9	Flags
423	Dictionaries	811	Poetry	930	Ancient history
425	Grammar	812	Plays	940	European history
500	Pure Sciences	900	History	970.1	Indians of North America
510	Mathematics	910	Geography	973	United States history
520	Astronomy	912	Atlases	978	The West
530	Physics, electricity	914	Europe	E	Easy (everybody) book
540	Chemistry	914.1	Scotland, Ireland	F	Fiction
550	Geology, rocks	914.2	England		

To establish "landmarks" in the nonfiction section of the library media center, the teacher hands out flash cards representing the major classifications to each of ten children and asks the pupils to place their cards on the top shelf of the proper section. In this way the class can easily see, for example, that the 500s are under the clock or that the 800s are by the door.

Next, the teacher distributes copies of the abbreviated Dewey Decimal Classification System appropriate for elementary school library media centers, as in Table 12.1. The teacher explains that most libraries in the United States use the Dewey System to determine which number to use on each book. Then he or she selects a few examples from the handout sheet and has various pupils verify these numbers on the shelves. Finally, the teacher refers back to the flash cards

Table 12.2
Library of Congress Classification System

	Classes A to Z		
A	General works	L	Education
B	Philosophy, psychology, and religion	M	Music
		N	Fine arts
C–D	History: general, European, African, Asiatic	P	Language and literature
		Q	Science and mathematics
E–F	History: United States and American	R	Medicine
		S	Agriculture
G	Geography, anthropology, etc.	T	Engineering, technology, etc.
H	Social sciences (general), economics, sociology, etc.	U	Military science
		V	Naval science
J	Political science	Z	Bibliography and library science
K	Law		

and reminds the children that nonfiction numbers are composed of a first line, which indicates the subject of a book according to the Dewey System, and a second line, which—like the fiction call numbers—indicates the initial letter or letters of an author's surname. (In those few elementary schools that use the Library of Congress Classification System, as shown in Table 12.2, the teacher-specialist should use the same teaching strategies to introduce that system.)

Other Activities

The children may play a relay game when locating and returning books to the shelves, or they may straighten shelves of books that have been scrambled. They may arrange themselves in alphabetical order as if they were fiction books on the shelf, or they may rearrange oversized sample book spines made of felt board. They will enjoy completing a floor plan of the library media center on which they designate the locations of various classifications of books. Some girls and boys may wish to read and report on pertinent topics such as the Library of Congress or the life of Melvil Dewey. Others will be interested in visiting their local public library to compare its book locations and arrangements with those used in the school center.

Second Skill: Using the Card Catalog

Because the card catalog is a distinctive and important tool, children must understand it as a complete index to all the materials in the library media center. Sample catalog cards are shown in Figures 12.1 through 12.8.

More than one lesson may be needed to acquaint students with this skill. The first could relate to the cabinet itself and to the use of labels on the drawers (and could include a poster-sized chart of the front of the card catalog showing the labels on each drawer, if the group of children is too large to sit directly in front of the cabinet). The teacher-specialist explains that it is through the card catalog that students learn to find independently the materials they want and that, although catalogs are sometimes in book form, they are more generally in

HORSES—FICTION

HEN   Henry, Marguerite.
       One Man's Horse. Illustrated by
    Wesley Dennis. Rand, McNally, ©1977
       103 p. illus.

      1. Horses—Fiction   1. Title

HEN   Henry, Marguerite.
       One Man's Horse. Illustrated by
    Wesley Dennis. Rand, McNally, ©1977
       103 p. illus.

      1. Horses—Fiction   1. Title

One Man's Horse

HEN   Henry, Marguerite.
       One Man's Horse. Illustrated by
    Wesley Dennis. Rand McNally, ©1977
       103 p. illus.

Figure 12.4. Sample Catalog Subject Card: Nonfiction.

> POETRY
>
> 821   Stevenson, Robert Louis.
> STE   A Child's Garden of Verses. Illustrated by Ruth Sanderson. Platt and Munk, © 1977
>
> 18 p. illus.
>
> 1. Poetry   1. Title

Figure 12.5. Sample Catalog Author Card: Nonfiction.

> 821   Stevenson, Robert Louis.
> STE   A Child's Garden of Verses. Illustrated by Ruth Sanderson. Platt and Munk, ©1977
>
> 18 p. illus.
>
> 1. Poetry   1. Title

Figure 12.6. Sample Catalog Title Card: Nonfiction.

> A Child's Garden of Verses
>
> 821   Stevenson, Robert Louis.
> STE   A Child's Garden of Verses. Illustrated by Ruth Sanderson. Platt and Munk, ©1977.
>
> 18 p. illus.

Figure 12.7. Sample Catalog Audiovisual Card: Author.

821   Stevenson, Robert Louis
STE   A Child's Garden of Verses; read by Judith An-
         derson. (AA).

         Phonotape Cassette
         CAEDMON CDL 51077.

1. Poetry   1. Title

Figure 12.8. Sample Catalog Cross-Reference Card.

Dinosaurs

see

Animals, Extinct

card form in order to be kept up-to-date easily. Then the teacher calls the group's attention to the guide letters on the catalog drawers, which are a means of finding the right drawer, and demonstrates how guide cards save the reader's time. Because elementary school children almost invariably begin to inquire for materials by subject rather than author or title, the teacher now shows them a poster-sized catalog subject card and discusses what questions the card is intended to answer. Finally, as the class studies the labels on the catalog drawers, the teacher lists some subjects or topics that require either a choice between two drawers containing the same letter or finding a letter not shown on the labels.

A second lesson begins with a review of the poster-sized catalog subject card, proceeds to a display of poster-sized cards showing the author and title cards for the same book as the subject card, and culminates in a discussion with

This student is using an important study skill as he demonstrates his understanding of the card catalog. (© James L. Shaffer.)

the pupils of the information contained on the three cards. The teacher-specialist then uses the opaque projector to show sample author cards, title cards, and subject cards taken from the catalog in the school library and points out the publisher's name and the copyright date. He or she explains how to find titles of other books written by a favorite author and how to compare dates of books on one subject when recency of publication is an important factor. Finally, each student is provided with a set of questions based on the cards in one catalog drawer in the library. Because there are not enough drawers to provide one for each pupil in an average-sized class, plans are made for some of the children to read while the others work on the catalog lesson. As boys and girls complete the catalog assignment, they become readers, viewers, or listeners, and the drawers that they have been using are given to other members of the class.

A third lesson, especially appropriate for sixth graders, would begin with a brief review of author, title, and subject cards, and then proceed to an introduction of cross-reference cards. These "see" and "see also" cards refer the reader from one subject to another.

During other activities that lead to skill acquisition, students may alphabetize sets of discarded catalog cards, demonstrate various ways that a single book may be located in the catalog, or practice locating books on the shelves by referring to the card catalog. They may make simplified author, title, and subject cards by using the title pages of ten nonfiction books, or they may use prepared slips with which to practice locating book titles in the catalog. They may develop a notebook on the use of the card catalog or find answers to specific questions by using the catalog. The children may make guide cards for some of the drawers, or they may interpret the bibliographic data on a few catalog cards. Some may wish to explain how to use the catalog to classmates who have been unable to attend school on the days when the teacher-specialist initiated the study of the card catalog. Others may enjoy demonstrating the use of the catalog to the group through an improvised skit or dialogue. Older boys and girls will be interested in keeping a record of their recreational reading in the form of catalog cards, complete with guide cards, or they may use the catalog to compile lists of books on unusual subjects or by favorite authors. Some may wish to complete exercises concerned with the use of the card catalog; such exercises are found in current language arts series, as shown in Figure 12.9.

Incidentally, catalog cards for audiovisual materials are filed like any other cards—up to the parentheses that enclose the type of medium. The elements, arrangement, and style of the catalog cards for nonprinted materials are essentially the same as for printed matter. The library media center that uses Dewey numbers for books would use these for audiovisual materials as well. Color-coding of catalog cards for such materials or the use of symbols or abbreviations in place of fully spelled-out media designations is no longer recommended because such techniques emphasize form over content and confuse the catalog users.

Third Skill: Using Dictionaries

Primary and intermediate students alike must possess the ability to use dictionaries to discover information about words. They will enjoy examining various dictionaries that have been set up on the library table and that range from a picture dictionary to an unabridged volume. They may compile a list of the kinds of information that can be found about most words in the dictionary or define terms that relate to dictionary usage. They may engage in contests to see how long it takes to locate a particular word in order to prove the usefulness of guide words.

In the primary grades, the children should have an opportunity to become familiar with the picture dictionary. This is a suitable readiness device that generally presents words in most of the following ways: picture and caption, simple explanation of the word, the word used in a sentence, the word used in a quotation, and the word and its antonym used in a phrase.

Although the picture dictionary is less a reference book than an enrichment source (because no dictionary that most primary children can read themselves will be comprehensive enough to function as a real dictionary), picture dictionaries can be used in the classroom, library media center, and home in a variety

Figure 12.9.
Exercises Using the
Card Catalog.

Exercises: Using the Card Catalog

A. Here are two sample cards. Answer all of these questions about each of them.

1. What is the title of the book?
2. Who is the author of the book?
3. What is the call number of the book?
4. Is this an author card, a title card, or a subject card?
5. Under what letter of the alphabet would the card be filed?

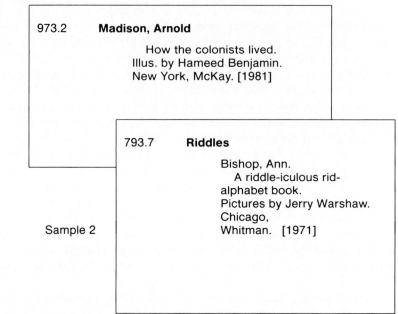

Sample 1

973.2   **Madison, Arnold**

How the colonists lived.
Illus. by Hameed Benjamin.
New York, McKay. [1981]

793.7   **Riddles**

Bishop, Ann.
A riddle-iculous rid-
alphabet book.
Pictures by Jerry Warshaw.
Chicago,
Whitman.   [1971]

Sample 2

B. Choose three of these subjects. Use the card catalog to find one book on each subject. List the title, author, and call number of each book.

1. Birds	4. Black history	7. Curie, Marie
2. Weather	5. Thanksgiving	8. Photography
3. Cookery	6. Dinosaurs	9. Gymnastics

Source: Pg. 225, *McDougal, Littell English, Aqua Level.* Copyright © 1987 by McDougal, Littell & Company, Box 1667, Evanston, Illinois 60204.

of ways. They can teach the order of the alphabet, encourage independence in learning words, and teach the users to discover meanings and to develop an interest in words through browsing. Through the picture dictionary, the children can recognize various forms of the same letter (uppercase and lowercase, cursive, and printed) and identify various words that begin with the same letter. They can also learn to spell. Should they come from a foreign language background, the picture dictionary will also help them learn English as a second language.

Among the current and better picture dictionaries are the following:

American Heritage Picture Dictionary (gr. K–1), Houghton Mifflin, 1986.
Cat in the Hat Beginner Book Dictionary (gr. 2–3), Random House, 1984.
Macmillan Very First Dictionary: A Magic World of Words (gr. ps–2), Macmillan, 1983.
My First Dictionary (gr. 1–3), Houghton Mifflin, 1980.

The students' readiness for instruction in dictionary skills should include recognizing each letter and learning its name, becoming familiar with the location of the letters in relation to each other, learning the consecutive arrangements of letters in the alphabet, and making alphabetical arrangements of words starting with a limited group of various letters.

Middle-grade children should be told about the aids contained in the dictionary for the location of words (the thumb index by letters and the guide words on each page) and the information provided by the dictionary on spelling, abbreviations and other arbitrary signs, pronunciations, definitions, proper geographical names, synonyms, antonyms, English usage, foreign words and phrases, parts of speech, quotations, and word derivation.

Although each major area of the dictionary has specific skills that should be presented in the elementary grades, some of the skills are more important than others and should therefore be taught first. A majority of dictionary authorities have graded five areas as indispensable. Should a pupil then master all of these prior to leaving the sixth grade, the teacher can be confident that the child is well prepared in the following areas of dictionary matter:

1. **Pronunciation**
   Knowing the pronunciation key being used
   Knowing that correct pronunciation is regional
   Knowing that pronunciations are usage reports
2. **Location**
   Knowing location of pronunciation keys
   Knowing alphabetical order
   Knowing how to locate idioms
3. **Meaning Selection**
   Selecting the meaning to fit the context
   Understanding status or usage labels
   Interpreting status or usage labels
   Knowing how the parts of speech are abbreviated
   Knowing each definition is numbered under different parts of speech
4. **Spelling**
   Knowing there are alternate spellings to some words
   Knowing that the basis of spelling is custom and usage
   Knowing how to locate plural spellings
   Knowing that the dictionary gives the principal point of view
   Knowing that the dictionary shows capitalization
   Knowing homographs
   Knowing that the dictionary shows syllabication of words

5. **History and Structure of the Dictionary**

Knowing that the dictionary is a guide, not a rule book

Among the current and better dictionaries useful for the elementary grades are the following:

American Heritage Student's Dictionary (gr. 6–9), Houghton Mifflin, 1986.
Macmillan Dictionary for Children (gr. 1–6), Macmillan, 1982.
Macmillan Dictionary for Students (gr. 6–11), Macmillan, 1984.
Random House School Dictionary (gr. 6–10), Random House, 1983.
Thorndike-Barnhart Beginning Dictionary (gr. 3–5), Scott, Foresman, 1988.
Thorndike-Barnhart Intermediate Dictionary (gr. 5–8), Scott, Foresman, 1988.
Webster's Elementary Dictionary (gr. 1–6), G. & C. Merriam, 1980.

Elementary school children should be allowed to peruse at least one unabridged dictionary so they may realize there is one volume to which they can refer for quick answers to a variety of questions.

Incidentally, students and teachers alike should be aware that the name "Webster" in the dictionary field can now be used by any publisher. Although it once distinguished the dictionaries published only by the reputable G. & C. Merriam Company, it no longer has any bearing on the worth of a dictionary. Publishing houses of every quality are now permitted to label their dictionaries as

"Webster's". It therefore becomes even more important for educators to consider the following areas when evaluating a dictionary: purpose and scope; authority; vocabulary treatment; encyclopedic features; graphics; physical format; and price.

Selected activities which teachers may wish to plan with and for their classes Activities generally demand that each pupil have a copy of an appropriate dictionary. Less advantaged districts, however, sometimes distribute dictionaries on a one-to-three or one-to-four basis (meaning one dictionary per three or four pupils). Therefore, the sample activities briefly described here may be conducted either as whole-class or group assignments.

1. Drill: What letter comes right before *L*?
   What is the second guide word on page 172?
   On what page can you find a picture of a prehistoric animal?
   How many nouns can you find on page 212? (A small letter *n* will be printed after the word or at the end of the definitions.)
   How many pictures of birds can you find under the *K* section of the dictionary?
   Can you find the pictures of three musical instruments? Then list the name of the instrument and the number of the page on which you found its picture.
2. Examine the quarters of the dictionary and list which letters are located in each quarter.
3. Look up the following words and write "yes" after the hyphenated words and "no" after those that are not hyphenated: *baseball, workman, takeoff, overcoat,* and *tonguetied.*
4. Find a homophone for each of the following: *way, ewe, be, our, cent,* and *seen.*
5. Decide which of the two spellings of the following pairs of words is the correct one: *aqueduct/aqueduct, business/busness, calendar/calander,* and *certainly/sertainly.*
6. Substitute synonyms for five words in the following sentence: *The lad with the pallid and morose countenance peered into the murky bayou.*
7. Paraphrase sentences to accommodate general meanings of specific words that are underlined (e.g., Jeff looked puzzled. Jeff looked as if he didn't understand.)
8. On a timed basis, practice opening the dictionary at a given letter, without thumbing through the pages.
9. Answer yes-no questions involving words that are not in the present vocabulary of the members (e.g., Can Lisa and Sandy play a *duet* at the piano recital?)
10. Find several meanings for such common words as *safe, husband,* or *signal.*
11. Determine the meaning of one prefix (e.g., *sub*) and then find "sub" words to fill the blanks in a list such as the following:
    A boat that travels under water   sub _____
    An underground electric railway   sub _____

12. Supply one root word and then list other members of the same family (e.g., *kind*).
13. Determine roots of words used in modern advertising (e.g., *Aqua Velva*).
14. Change phonetic spellings of certain words to the regular spellings (e.g., *fikst* to *fixed*).
15. Make up a list of words in which
    ph or *gh* sound like *f*
    ch or *ck* sound like hard *c*
    c, x, and *s* sound like *sh*
16. List the plurals of words such as *alumnus, basis, index, stratus*, and *bacillus*.
17. Look up English words that have been adapted or borrowed from other languages, such as *ski, coffee, kimono, sonata*, and *waltz*. Then identify the language in which the word first appeared.
18. Tell whether each of the following is found in the air, on land, or in the water: *sturgeon, tripod, coracle*, and *obelisk*.
19. Write the words for which the following abbreviations stand: *PO, RFD, pp., dept., riv., a.m., ans.*, and *inc.*
20. Write the phrase or sentence from your dictionary that shows the correct use of the following words: *urge, noble, mellow, rummage*, and *commerce*.
21. Write the abbreviation for the word class of each of the following words: *whereas, hereby, gratis, forever, martial*, and *confident*.
22. Copy from your dictionary the following words, properly divided into syllables: *dirigible, final, nicety*, and *miraculous*.
23. List the guide words connected with each of ten words introduced during the current social studies unit.
24. Extract root forms of five words in the weekly spelling lesson (e.g., *unpaved/pave*).
25. Indicate the syllable with the primary stress in a list of ten familiar two-syllable words (e.g., *cár toon*).

Fourth Skill: Using Encylopedias

Before children are abruptly plunged into certain kinds of supplementary assignments, they must attain the ability to use encyclopedias to discover information about broad topics. Because many students and a few teachers speak of the encyclopedia as though there were only one and as if it were entitled The Encyclopedia, it is better from the first to have both children and teachers refer to encyclopedias by their individual names.

A two-part demonstration is generally effective in teaching discrimination among sets. During the first portion, which emphasizes the number of various encyclopedias available, the students are given a week to look at various sets found in public libraries and homes and then return to class to draw up a composite list of titles. During the second portion, the children become aware of the differences among encyclopedias and the need to comprehend the arrangement and content of each set, for they must examine several identical topics in three or more sets. An opaque projector can be used during the second part of the demonstration in order to save class time. Publishers of juvenile encyclopedias also sometimes supply printed aids for teaching the use of their particular sets.

Among the multivolume encyclopedias for children ages nine through eighteen is the *World Book Encyclopedia* (22 vols.), which is rated by Kister as the best general encyclopedia currently available.[8] Its chief challenger is the *Merit Students Encyclopedia* (20 vols.). Among the multivolume sets for children ages seven through fourteen is *The New Book of Knowledge* (21 vols.). All three of these sets use the continuous-revision policy (presently followed by most of the good general encyclopedias, according to the American Library Association), which means that instead of publishing thoroughly revised editions at spaced intervals, the editorial staffs make changes with each annual printing to update some portions of each volume.

Even though students often learn at home about general encyclopedias, which are alphabetically arranged and which discuss numerous subjects, they need to be introduced at school to special subject encyclopedias. These bring together related materials under broad topics in a nonalphabetical arrangement. One example is *The New Book of Popular Science* (6 vols.).

Encyclopedias are not difficult to use, particularly for students already familiar with the card catalog. The principal instructional problems lie in the various methods of indexing (including the use of the cross-reference) and in the various spine markings. To help the children acquire facility in the use of encyclopedias, the teacher-specialist should discuss finding words alphabetically, understanding volume letters or words, using an index or an index volume, and using guide words and cross-references. The teacher should be certain that students understand the definition of an encyclopedia, as well as the difference between an encyclopedia and a dictionary. Moreover, the teacher should explain the importance of reading for facts and then rewriting or retelling those facts honestly in the reader's own words. He or she should also alert older children to the significance of the date of publication and to the use of the encyclopedia for validating material in textbooks and newspapers.

A good exercise for use in beginning research work is to have the class locate pictures in an encyclopedia by using the index to look for illustrations, which are listed in italics. Pencils and paper are not needed because each pupil is asked to locate a picture of a particular person, place, animal, or item. (For example, a child who picks up the last-designated volume in most general sets must find a picture of a zebra.) Even though the completed task can be evaluated at a glance, the teacher must be sure to assign an interesting list of illustrations that are readily located under the proper headings. Other exercises can be found in some language arts series, as shown in Figure 12.10.

Competence in using the encyclopedia is cumulative and involves alphabetizing, searching, reading, and acquiring and organizing information. These skills are also necessary for using the *yearbooks,* which are annual supplements to most encyclopedias. They give new, factual information on the highlights of

Figure 12.10.
Exercises Using an
Encyclopedia.

The Encyclopedia Article

Each encyclopedia entry includes a written article on the topic. If the topic is long, the article will be divided into parts. These parts are usually indicated by subheads in boldface type. By examining the subheads, you can tell at a glance what is covered in the article.

In addition to the written text, an article may contain photographs, charts, or other illustrations. An entry may also include cross-references, which refer the reader to related articles in the encyclopedia. Some encyclopedias also list additional references at the end of an article.

Exercises: Using an Encyclopedia

A. Here are five topics. Choose an encyclopedia. Write its name on your paper. For each subject, write the key word that you would look up in the encyclopedia. Find the article on that topic. Write the letter or number of the volume and the page number of the article.

1. The talents of Benjamin Franklin
2. Beverly Sills's career in the opera
3. Where active volcanoes can be found
4. The description of a Neanderthal man
5. The economy of Thailand

B. Choose one of the following topics and look it up in the index of an encyclopedia. List all articles on that topic. Give the titles of the articles, their volumes, and their pages.

1. Mummies
2. Hercules
3. Soccer
4. Fashion
5. Dentistry

C. Look up one of the following topics in an encyclopedia. List the cross-references that appear at the end of that article.

1. Computers
2. Extrasensory perception
3. Reptiles
4. Astronomy

Source: Pg. 408, *McDougal, Littell English, Gold Level.* Copyright © 1987 by McDougal, Littell & Company, Box 1667, Evanston, Illinois 60204.

the year and update some of the material already in the encyclopedia set. Most yearbooks, however, are not a good buy because they are only indirectly related to the encyclopedia, are usually expensive, and are often never used.[9]

Teachers concerned as to whether or not the computer will replace the encyclopedia will be interested to learn that there is already at least one *Electronic Encyclopedia* (available from Grolier) which has been on-line for several years. Electronic and print encyclopedias differ not only in physical format and appearance but in terms of organization and accessibility of material, in price, in size, and in the critical ability to keep current. Finally, in 1986 the New York-based CEL Communications, Inc. began marketing its *Video Encyclopedia of the 20th Century,* a set of 75 hour-long cassettes packaged into individual volumes accompanied by an index and four reference books. The set is already in use in the public school systems of New York, Atlanta, and Detroit.

The ability to use almanacs, atlases, gazetteers, handbooks, and other special reference sources to discover geographical, historical, biographical, and statistical information becomes an increasing preoccupation of school children from the time that they are first introduced to these editions until they gradually develop or improve their techniques for independent study. By using late issues of the *World Almanac and Book of Facts* or the *Information Please Almanac,* pupils may participate in a "scavenger hunt" by finding answers to such prepared questions as "Who was the first black American to play professional baseball?" and "Which motion picture won the Acadamy Award last year?" In some areas of the country, there are published state almanacs that boys and girls can also peruse.

The students themselves may write questions whose answers are found in such references as an atlas ("Which states border Texas?"); a gazetteer ("Where is the Isle of Man?"); the *Fifth Book of Junior Authors and Illustrators* ("As an adolescent, which musical instrument did Myra Cohn Livingston play professionally?"); *Who's Who in America* ("From which service academy did former President Jimmy Carter graduate?"); or a handbook such as Bartlett's *Familiar Quotations* ("Who said, 'The only thing we have to fear is fear itself'?").

The boys and girls can produce a chart or table comparing various atlases or statistical reference books available in the library. They can define specialized words pertaining to gazetteers. The class may also enjoy locating in an atlas the places mentioned on the front page of the daily newspaper.

Incidentally, for the sake of those teacher-specialists who fear that many of the children in the middle- and upper-elementary grades have not developed sufficient reading skills to be effective users of such tools as *Current Biography, Contemporary Authors,* the *Guinness Book of World Records,* or the *Atlas of American History,* it must be mentioned that the introduction of these tools should best be left to the discretion of the media specialist or teacher-specialist. Some classes can work successfully with these resources and should be properly encouraged to do so. In other classes, the introduction of these materials must be postponed until junior high school.

Learning how to view and listen to nonbook media and developing the art of perception that evaluation and appreciation of the nonbook media demand—these are two abilities that students must acquire in much the same way that they master the word-recognition skills and developmental aspects of reading. Such instruction includes guidance in aiding children to turn naturally to media other than print as forms of communication. It also involves teaching them to realize when nonbook media complement printed materials and when they have no relevance to the assignment.

Although instruction in using many of these resources is handled on an individualized basis, in one or more classroom lessons the teacher-specialist can demonstrate how to find and read quickly the table of contents (of a magazine) or the index (of a newspaper) and how to evaluate readily the pictures, physical format, and contents of the magazine or paper. The teacher may discuss the kinds of readers to whom the magazine or newspaper would appeal and the types of services that it can render for those readers. The children can bring to class a

Fifth Skill: Using Specialized Reference Books

Sixth Skill: Using and Evaluating Nonbook Media

copy of one of the local papers and summarize at least three of its front-page stories into one statement each. They can examine some of the more popular juvenile magazines and become acquainted with the *Children's Magazine Guide* which indexes nearly fifty children's periodicals by subject.

Advanced students may also be introduced to the *Reader's Guide to Periodical Literature,* in which nearly 200 periodicals are indexed by author and subject. Once the pupils have noted the list of periodicals included and the abbreviations used for each, they should be encouraged to consult the *Readers' Guide* routinely before completing assigned reports.

The teacher-specialist should also acquaint children with vertical-file materials. These are miscellaneous items that are not individually catalogued because of poor physical durability, varied sizes, and short subject treatment. Examples include pamphlets, leaflets, clippings, and unmounted pictures printed on lightweight paper. Such materials often brighten displays in the classroom and hall, and they meet the informational needs of both beginning and older readers.

Library and Locational Skills: Learning Games

To reinforce presentations on various library and locational skills, and to help children feel comfortable using media center facilities and the classroom library, the teacher-specialist may occasionally schedule a learning game appropriate for children of middle and intermediate grades. Directions for some of these games are outlined in Figure 12.11.

Figure 12.11. Nine Learning Games in Library and Locational Skills.

Big Stack (for the media center only)

1. The class is divided evenly into teams or pairs, each of which receives a "big stack" of book cards that must be returned to the proper volumes on the shelves.
2. All the players walk about the media center busily until the teacher-specialist calls time.
3. They then return to their seats and listen as the specialist checks the scores: one point added for correct pocketing and one point subtracted for each error.
4. The team or pair with the highest score wins the game.

Hidden Titles (for the media center only)

1. The class is divided evenly into teams. Each team receives a different paragraph or story prepared by the teacher-specialist and based primarily on titles of books available in the media center; for example.

> It was nine days to Christmas when Mei Li asked Madeline, "May I bring a friend, Cinderella, on our trip?" "Yes," said Madeline. "There's always room for one more." The girls then sailed for the little island on a boat that had to stop once to make way for ducklings. When the girls arrived, Mei Li said, "When the rooster crows, we will look for a tree to decorate for Christmas." So they each said a prayer for a child and went to sleep. Cinderella dreamed of the animals and of the Bible; Mei Li dreamed of white snow, bright snow, and Madeline dreamed of Baboushka and the Three Kings. . . .

Figure 12.11. (cont.)

2. The first player on each team goes to the card catalog in order to underline correctly one of the "hidden titles" appearing on the hand out sheet. When the player has finished checking, he or she hands the sheet to the second player.
3. When all the team players have finished checking, the last one gives the sheet to a class committee, appointed by the teacher-specialist.
4. The team that has located the greatest number of Hidden Titles properly within a designated time wins the game.

Hot Shelf (for the media center only)

1. The student chosen to be "It" selects one card from a pile of cards of names of authors whose fiction books are in the center.
2. "It" must try to locate the shelf on which those books have been placed. The class is permitted to call out "Hot," "Warm," or "Cold" as "It" approaches or misses the crucial "hot shelf."
3. When "It" has finally placed the author card on the proper Hot Shelf, he or she chooses another boy or girl to become "It."
4. Should "It" fail to locate the correct Hot Shelf within a reasonable period of time, the teacher-specialist selects another child to be "It."

Library Cart (for either the classroom or the media center)

1. The class is evenly divided into teams. Each team has one captain and several players who are "books."
2. Each captain is given a sheet, listing as many call numbers as there are "books" on the team. The captain assigns one call number to each "book."
3. At a signal from the teacher-specialist, each captain tries to assemble his or her "books" in correct order for the "library shelving cart."
4. The first Library Cart to be arranged correctly wins the game.

Lost in Space (for the classroom only)

1. The class is divided evenly into teams whose players sit in rows.
2. The first player on each team is given a pencil and a large sheet of blank paper. At a given signal, this player must properly position on the future map any area of the school media center (e.g., the vertical files) that he or she wishes.
3. The player then quickly passes on the map to the second player, who must label a different area on the map before forwarding it to the third player.
4. The team that first completes its map correctly with no duplications has proven that it will never be "lost in space" at the media center and therefore wins the game.

Match Box (for either the classroom or the media center)

1. The class is divided into two equal groups.
2. Each member of the first group receives a sealed slip containing a Dewey Decimal Classification System number. Each member of the second group receives a sealed slip containing the name of a subject corresponding to one of the classification numbers held by members of the first group.
3. At a signal from the teacher-specialist, all the slips are opened. The members scatter about the room, trying to match numbers and subjects. The first "match box" wins the game.

Figure 12.11. (cont.)

Misspell (for either the classroom or the media center)	1. The class or group is evenly divided into teams whose members are seated in rows. 2. On the first desk (or table) in each row are placed a copy of the class dictionary, a pencil, an empty red box, and a blue box filled with slips. Each slip contains three spellings of a single word, of which only one is correct, that appears in the class dictionary. 3. At a signal from the teacher-specialist, the first player on each team draws one slip from the blue box, checks the spellings in the dictionary, circles the correct spelling, and drops the slip in the red box. The first player then moves to the end of the row, all the other team members move up one desk, and the game continues. 4. The winning team has proved that it cannot "misspell" when it has been able to empty its blue box of slips first, and when its red-box entries have been approved by a class committee or the teacher-specialist.
Order Please (for the classroom only)	1. The class is evenly divided into teams. 2. On the chalkboard in front of each team is written or placed a list of authors' names that are not in alphabetical order. Each team receives a different list, and that list always contains one more name than there are players on that team. 3. At a signal from the teacher-specialist, the first player on each team walks to the board and marks with the numeral 1 the author's name that should appear in the initial position on that list. The first player then returns to his or her seat, and the second player goes to the board to indicate the second name in alphabetical order with the numeral 2. 4. The first team to mark all of its authors' names properly wins the Order Please game.
Shelf Fever (for the media center only)	1. The class or group is divided into two teams. 2. The first player on each team chooses one card from a large box of cards with book titles on them. The player then uses the card catalog to find the call number of the title on the card. Last, he or she removes the book from the shelf and hands it to the second player on the team. 3. The second player promptly returns the book to the shelf. Then he or she touches the shoulder of the third player, who chooses a card and follows the actions of the first player. 4. The game continues until every odd-numbered player has removed his or her chosen book and every even-numbered player has reshelved a book. 5. The team that performs best within a designated period of time is the winner of Shelf Fever.

As children prepare reports in content areas, they need to organize the facts and ideas they encounter in their reading of periodicals, encyclopedias, specialized reference books, and general texts. Sometimes teachers at the elementary level overlook the importance of presenting the three organizational skills of *outlining, note taking,* and *summarizing* because they mistakenly believe that such skills are more appropriately presented to students at the junior high level.

Organizing factual material that has been collected and assimilated requires a high level of classification ability. Although the purpose of an outline is the more significant point for students to learn, some attention should still be paid to promoting an understanding of the structure of an outline. Such a form generally reflects a hierarchy of ideas or a sequence of events much like the following example:

I. A *main topic* demands a roman numerial.

    A. A *subtopic* requires indentation and a capital letter.
        1. A *detail* needs indentation and an arabic numeral.
            a. A *subdetail* must have indentation and a lowercase letter.
            b. Another subdetail.
        2. Another detail on the same subtopic needs indentation and an arabic numeral too.

    B. Another subtopic requires indentation and a capital letter too.

II. Another main topic demands another roman numeral.

    A. Subtopic
        1. Detail
            a. Subdetail
            b. Subdetail
        2. Detail
        3. Detail

    B. Subtopic
        1. Detail
        2. Detail

    C. Subtopic
        1. Detail
        2. Detail

Two types of outlines important for students to understand and develop are the *sentence outline* (in which each point is a complete sentence) and the *topic outline* (which is composed solely of key words and phrases). Teachers should present the sentence outline first, because the task of selecting key words and phrases is a difficult one for most boys and girls.

Although students need to begin learning to outline in the intermediate grades, the prerequisite skill to outlining is identification of main ideas and supporting information, which should be taught at all grade levels. Then the boys

Organizational Skills

First Skill: Outlining

and girls can be told that the first step in forming the skeleton, framework, or outline is to extract the main ideas or topics from the material they have heard or read and then to list those topics with roman numerals in sequential order. Next they list subtopics beside capital letters, which are placed below the main topics they support. Details subordinate to the subtopics are indented still further and preceded by arabic numerals. The next level of subordination covers sub-details and is indicated by lowercase letters, although most elementary students do not need to prepare outlines that go beyond the level of arabic numerals.

A five-stage program to teach outlining has been developed by Harris and Sipay.[10] The first stage covers two or three sessions during which a complete outline of the material is displayed, the formal format is discussed, and all questions are answered. During the second stage, outlines are assigned on which the complete skeleton is shown but only a part of the outline itself is provided. Some of these incomplete outlines contain only the subtopics with details, and the main topics have to be inserted; other incomplete outlines contain only the main topics and demand that the subtopics with details be filled in. After reading the accompanying text, the students complete the outlines and discuss their work. During the third stage, only the structure of the outline is provided; and then during the fourth stage, only some of the main topics are given. Finally, during the fifth stage, the children produce a complete outline without teacher help.

It is recommended that the use of a formal outline be taught before teaching children how to prepare informal outlines, which of course do not contain the various numerals and letters.

Second Skill: Note Taking

Once students understand outlining, it is easier for teachers to present the note-taking process in which children actually learn to make meaningful notes in their own words about information from a textbook or speaker. They can be helped to develop some group standards for note taking:

1. Read or listen first before writing down the information in your own words.
2. Write down only the important facts, rechecking for accuracy whenever possible.
3. Use underlining to indicate emphatic ideas.
4. Never record every word, except for laws, rules, and direct quotations.

In early grades, note taking is generally a group subject culminating in an experience chart. In the middle and upper grades, however, children can be encouraged to keep individual notes (sometimes written on file cards) during a field trip or as they listen to a resource speaker, watch a film, or work in cooperative learning groups. Older boys and girls should also understand how to use other media for note taking in the modern school, such as transferring pictures, graphs, or diagrams to transparencies for sharing with the class. Some current language arts series include exercises in note taking, as shown in Figure 12.12.

Taking Notes

Figure 12.12.
Exercises in Taking
Notes.

Focus

Taking notes helps you collect, organize, and remember information.

Sometimes you read to collect information about a subject. For example, before you write a report, you need to gather facts. Taking notes makes collecting facts easier.

You can take notes on three-by-five-inch note cards. At the top of each card, write the title and author of the book in which you found the information. If the book is an encyclopedia, write the name of the encyclopedia and the article. Then write a fact about your subject in your own words. Use as few words as you can. Write each fact on a new card.

Note Card 1

Title

Hungry Sharks

by John E. Waters **Author**

Fact

A shark can smell blood from a wounded fish.

Note Card 2

Encyclopedia

World Book Encyclopedia

"Sharks" **Article**

Fact

Sharks have a good sense of smell.

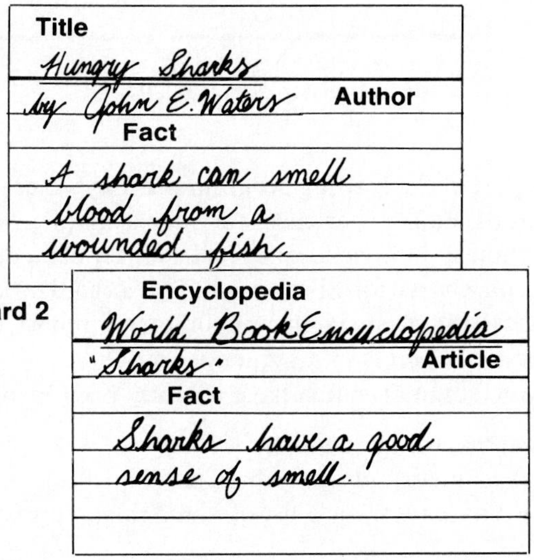

Look carefully at the sample note cards. Note card 1 shows a fact taken from a book. Note card 2 shows a fact from an encyclopedia. On both cards, the fact is written in the student's own words.

Guides for Taking Notes
1. Write the name of the book and the author, or write the name of the encyclopedia and the article.
2. Write the fact in your own words.
3. Write each new fact on a separate card.

Figure 12.12. (cont.) | **Exercises: Taking Notes**

A. You have found this paragraph on queen bees. It is in *The True Book of Honeybees* by John Lewellen. Read it slowly and carefully. Find the facts about the queen bee's stinger. Make two note cards. Write one fact on each. Make the cards look like sample note card 1.

> The queen bee is larger than the other bees. Her tongue is shorter. She will not gather nectar, so she does not need a long tongue. Even her stinger is different. Her stinger has only the tiniest barbs. She can use it over and over. However, she will never use it except on another queen bee.

B. Choose an American President. Look up his last name in an encyclopedia. Skim the article to find the state he was born in and the first year he was President. Write each fact on a note card. Make each one look like sample note card 2.

Source: Pgs. 292–293, *McDougal, Littell English, Aqua Level.* Copyright © 1987 by McDougal, Littell & Company, Box 1667, Evanston, Illinois 60204.

Third Skill: Summarizing

Summarizing occurs as part of the reading program in today's elementary school from the first grade onward. Each experience story, for example, is a small summary; and during unit studies, the conclusions reached after class discussions are frequently summarized on charts for all to read. This organizational skill demands the ability to choose the most significant points in a report, article, story, or incident and to relate those points in a sequential order.

Six rules essential to summarization have recently been identified:[11]

1. Delete trivial or unnecessary information.
2. Delete material that is important but redundant.
3. Substitute a superordinate term for a list of items (e.g., *pets* for *dogs, goldfish, canaries*).
4. Substitute a superordinate term for the components of an action (e.g., *"Scott went to Chicago"* for *"Scott left the apartment. He got on a bus that went to the airport. Finally he boarded the plane for Chicago"*).
5. Select a topic sentence.
6. Invent a topic sentence if one is not given.

Children can use the two deletion rules (1 and 2) at an early age but fifth (and even seventh) graders have difficulty with the generalization and integration rules (3 and 4) and with the topic sentence rule (5). The invention rule (6) is the last to develop.[12]

A positive effect on reading comprehension has been reported among fifth graders who were taught to understand and use the rules of summarization.[13]

Reading flexibility has been defined as adjusting one's rate of reading to one's purpose for reading, to one's prior knowledge, and to the nature of the reading matter.[14] It therefore becomes one aspect of monitoring one's reading comprehension, and is a concern during silent reading only. Children in the intermediate grades should be introduced to two skills: skimming and scanning.

Skimming is a quick type of superficial reading that is completed in an effort to get the overall gist of the material. Boys and girls generally read at about twice their normal rate, selectively eliminating nearly one-half of the material because they are in a hurry and therefore willing to accept lowered comprehension. They may read only the topic sentence and then let their eyes drift down through the paragraph, picking up a date or a name. Their intention is to get the main idea from each paragraph with only a few specific facts.

Skimming

Instances when skimming is useful include sampling a few pages to determine whether the material is worth reading, looking through reading matter to judge whether it contains the kind of information the reader is researching, and previewing a text chapter before settling down to serious study in an effort to get a general idea of its scope. In this kind of skimming, the student must have a particular purpose in mind.

One study of fourth and sixth graders showed that only one-half of the fourth graders and two-thirds of the sixth graders could describe "how to skim."[15] However, children at both grade levels could skim after having been carefully instructed how to do so, which indicates the importance of teacher aid in the acquisition of this skill.

One special type of skimming is called *scanning* and involves rapid reading to locate answers to very specific questions concerned with such matters as names, dates, or telephone numbers:

Scanning

Which state produces the most corn?
What are the leading industries of Chicago?
Who was Roald Amundsen?
When did Robert Perry reach the North Pole?
When was the first television broadcast?
What is the telephone number of this school?
What is the telephone number of the local Girl Scout Council?

For practice in skimming, schools can make use of such reading materials as the daily newspapers, local telephone directories, and textbooks in content areas. The teacher can prepare a list of questions based on the reading matter to be scanned. The list is then presented to the children before they read the selection assigned. They are encouraged to work quickly and to write down their answers. Later there can be discussion of the correct answers together with oral reading of the appropriate sentences or telephone-page guide names.

Two common occasions that call for scanning are the need to use a dictionary and the need to use an index or television schedule. Children quickly identify with such practical needs and sense the obvious importance of scanning.

Evaluation of Student Progress

There are both informal teacher-developed tests and formal standardized tests for evaluating study skills among elementary school students. Both types are printed and must be read by the children.

Sample items (with correct answers circled) from an achievement test on library and locational skills might be devised by the teacher-specialist for intermediate-grade children as follows:

1. There are three main types of catalog cards. Two of them are known as the author and subject cards, and the third is
   a. the book card
   (b.) the title card
   c. the date-due card
   d. the circulation card
2. A list of subjects arranged in alphabetical order at the back of the book is called
   a. a table of contents
   b. a title page
   c. a glossary
   (d.) an index
3. To find out how many informational resources your media center has about Texas, you would use
   a. a magazine about new books
   b. the Dewey Decimal System of Classification
   (c.) the card catalog
   d. the encyclopedia
4. When you are looking for books on the shelves, the call number is found
   (a.) on the spine of the book
   b. on the pocket
   c. on the title page
   d. on the table of contents
5. When looking up information about a person in the card catalog or encyclopedia, you would look up the person alphabetically by his or her
   a. first name
   (b.) last name
   c. middle name
   d. initials
6. Cards in the card catalog that have "see" and "see also" on them are called
   a. author cards
   b. guide cards
   (c.) cross-reference cards
   d. subject cards

There are also standardized study-skills tests included within such test batteries as the *California Achievement Test* (CTB/McGraw-Hill, Monterey, CA). However, no separate test per se is presently published in the United States for use with elementary school children.[16]

1. If everyone agrees that study skills are critical, why are they so often overlooked in the planning of reading programs?
2. At which grade level should instruction in study skills begin, or should it be postponed until a particular reading level has been attained?
3. Is having a well-staffed media center in the elementary school as important as having one in every secondary school? How can elementary teachers persuade communities to fund more such centers?
4. Rate the groups of study skills in order of importance. In which of the groups can instruction begin in the primary grades, even though reading in the content areas is generally considered to be more a part of the intermediate curriculum?
5. Should an elementary school media center be open year-round? Should it be open on Saturday mornings during the regular school term?

1. Plan a library corner for a third-grade classroom.
2. Examine basal readers from one series for the second-, fourth-, and sixth-grade levels. How much material is devoted to content-area reading? Which study skills could therefore be introduced or reinforced?
3. Using discarded shoe boxes for file drawers, make a card catalog. Be sure to label each "drawer" carefully.
4. Ask three elementary school media specialists which teaching strategies and materials each has found to be particularly useful in presenting study skills to girls and boys.
5. Practice using the SQ3R technique with an intermediate-grade student. Then determine which of the steps proved to be most difficult for him or her and which proved the easiest.
6. Prepare a bulletin board on the Dewey Decimal System that might be used in the fifth grade.
7. Visit the children's room of your local public library and decide how you as a classroom teacher could best utilize its resources.
8. Set up the learning center on one of the library and locational skills shown in Figure 12.13.

Bragstad, B. J., and Stumpf, S. M. 1987. *A Guidebook for Teaching Study Skills and Motivation,* 2nd ed. Newton, MA: Allyn and Bacon.

Daniels, L., and Pollard, R. 1987. *The Library Experience: Sharing the Responsibility.* Amherst, NY: Cambridge Stratford.

" 'Exemplary Elementary Schools' and Their Library Media Centers: A Research Report," 1987, *School Library Media Quarterly, 15,* pp. 147–153.

Kaplan, D. 1987. "The House That Books Built," *Instructor, 96*(8) pp. 36–37, 39.

McDonald, F. 1988. *The Emerging School Library Media Program.* Englewood, CO: Libraries Unlimited.

Prostano, E., and Prostano, J., 1987. *School Library Media Center,* 4th ed. Englewood, CO: Libraries Unlimited.

Figure 12.13.
Language Arts
Learning Center:
Locational Skill

Type of Center: **Dictionary—Locational Skill**
Grade Level: 3–6

Time: 25–30 minutes

Number of Students: 1

Instructional Objective: Given a listening tape, the students should be able to find telephone numbers in an alphabetical list.

Materials: Cassette player and teacher-prepared tape with information requested; headphones; phone book with teacher-prepared list of names, addresses, and telephone numbers; plastic-covered cards for answers; grease pencil; teacher-made scoring key; and yarn with a plug (tack) at the other end.

Directions:
1. Find your name and plug yourself in. Put on the headphones.
2. You are a telephone operator. People will call to ask you for a telephone number.
3. Look for the number in the telephone book.
4. Write the number on a card, listing each call as received in order: 1, 2, 3, etc. Also list the same information on the operator's log.
5. Put the card in a pocket in the computer, or set it aside to check later.
6. To start, press "PLAY" on the recorder.
7. After a call, press "STOP" until you find the number.

Suggested Ideas: Questions for the tape could include the following:

Figure 12.13.   (cont.)

1. Operator, could you give me the number for Nancy Smith? She lives on State Street.
2. Operator! I just broke my arm. What is the number for the hospital?
3. Operator, Operator, there's a lion in my backyard! What's the number for the zoo, so they can come and get him?
4. Hello, Operator. Can you tell me the number for Bob Smith, please? He lives on Market Street.
5. I'm having a party tonight and I don't have enough ice cream. Could you please tell me the number for the Embassy Dairy?
6. Operator? Could you please tell me the number for Tom's store?
7. I can't find the number for the Keister School anywhere! Can you tell me what it is, please?
8. Operator, what is the number for the rescue squad? My kitty is stuck in a tree and I can't get her down.
9. Operator, what is the number for the newspaper? I have some important news for them!
10. Operator, I want to report a fire! Please give me the number for the nearest fire company.

Evaluation: The numbers the student located will be checked against the teacher-made key:

OPERATOR'S LOG

Name _____

Date _____

	THIS CALL IS TO	THE NUMBER IS	I FOUND THE NUMBER ON PAGE
1.			
2.			
3.			
4.			
5.			
6.			
7.			

Source: From PATHWAYS TO IMAGINATION by Angela S. Reeke and James L. Laffey, Copyright © 1979 by Scott, Foresman and Company. Reprinted with permission.

"The School Space That's Everybody's Place," 1986, *Instructor, 95*(8), pp. 72–75.

Toor, R., and Weisburg, H. 1986. *Ships and Potato Chips: Curricular Library Instruction.* Berkeley Heights, NJ: Library Learning Resources.

Vandergrift, K., and Hannigan, J. 1986. "Elementary School Library Media Centers as Essential Components in the Schooling Process." *School Library Media Quarterly, 14,* pp. 171–173.

Woolls, B. 1988. *Managing School Library Media Programs.* Englewood, CO: Libraries Unlimited.

Chapter Notes

1. E. Askov, K. Kamm, and R. Klumb, "Study Skill Mastery Among Elementary School Teachers," *The Reading Teacher,* 1977, *30,* pp. 485–488.
2. L. Rickman, "Arizona Educators Assess the Teaching of Study Skills," *Clearing House,* 1981, *54,* pp. 363–365.
3. B. Armbruster and T. Anderson, "Research Synthesis on Study Skills," *Educational Leadership,* 1981, *39,* pp. 154–156.
4. A. Adams, D. Carnine, and R. Gersten, "Instructional Strategies for Studying Content Area Texts in the Intermediate Grades," *Reading Research Quarterly,* 1982, *18,* pp. 27–55.
5. D. Evans and E. Askov, "Teaching Study Skills in the Content Areas," in *Language Arts Instruction and the Beginning Teacher,* C. Personke and D. Johnson, eds. (Englewood Cliffs, New Jersey: Prentice Hall, 1987), pp. 130–131.
6. G. Spache and E. Spache, *Reading in the Elementary School,* 5th ed. (Boston: Allyn and Bacon, 1986), p. 375.
7. L. Searfoss and J. Readence, *Helping Children Learn to Read,* 2d ed. (Englewood Cliffs, New Jersey: Prentice Hall, 1989), pp. 311–313.
8. K. Kister, *Best Encyclopedias: A Guide to General and Specialized Encyclopedias* (Phoenix, Arizona: Oryx Press, 1986).
9. *Ibid.,* p. 8.
10. A. J. Harris and E. R. Sipay, *How to Increase Reading Ability,* 8th ed. (New York: Longman, 1985), p. 521.
11. A. Brown, J. Campione, and J. Day, "Learning to Learn: On Training Students to Learn from Texts," *Educational Researcher,* 1981, *10,* pp. 14–21.
12. A. Brown and J. Day, *Macrorules for Summarizing Text: The Development of Expertise,* Technical Report #270 (Champaign, Illinois: Center for the Study of Reading, University of Illinois, 1983).
13. J. McNeil and L. Donant, "Summarizing Strategy for Improving Reading Comprehension," in *New Inquiries in Reading: Research and Instruction,* J. Niles and L. Harris, eds. (Rochester, New York: National Reading Conference, 1982), pp. 215–219.
14. Harris and Sipay, *How to Increase Reading Ability,* p. 539.
15. A. Kobasigawa, C. Ransom, and C. Holland, "Children's Knowledge About Skimming," *Alberta Journal of Educational Research,* 1980, *26,* pp. 169–182.
16. J. Mitchell, Jr., ed., *The Ninth Mental Measurements Yearbook* (Lincoln: University of Nebraska Press, 1985), p. 242.

Reading and Children's Literature 13

Major Chapter Goals

After studying Chapter 13, the reader will be able to

1. Understand the relationships among literature, the basal reading program, and elementary education.
2. Distinguish among the literary elements of good fiction and among the genres in a well-balanced literature program.
3. Outline some of the ways that classroom teachers can use bibliotherapy.
4. Describe ten instructional activities in literature that are motivational and ten that are interpretive.

Discover As You Read This Chapter Whether*

1. A good literature program for children provides a balance among the various genres of literature.
2. Picture books without words are now available from reputable publishers.
3. Elementary school children are too immature to exhibit strong sex differences in reading choices.
4. The volume of literature for children published annually has not increased much over the past twenty-five years.
5. Most teachers are well-informed about current juvenile books.
6. An important criterion for all children's books is the format.
7. No book of poetry has ever won the Newbery Medal Award.
8. Teachers inexperienced in choral speaking sessions wisely begin with unison arrangements.
9. Most of the poetry written for children is narrative poetry.
10. There has been increasing attention paid recently to testing in the field of children's literature.

*Answers to these true-or-false statements may be found in Appendix 5.

The major objective of reading programs in the elementary school is to develop readers who are not only able to read but who do read and will continue to do so throughout their lives.[1] To attain this aim, programs must offer children many opportunities to read literature. Skills instruction must unfailingly be presented in a context that motivates students to read and enjoy good books.

Although the basal reading series continue to be the core of the vast majority of elementary reading programs, none of them was ever intended to be a complete, self-contained approach. Teachers must always supplement the basals with other printed resources, including literary works, so that students can use the skills they have acquired and thereby maintain proficiency in reading. Both enjoyment and appreciation of good literature grow as children read widely among the various types of books presently available to them.

Literature and Elementary Education

Today more than ever, literature plays a critical role in elementary education. Even though children's first exposure to literature is Mother Goose and other traditional rhymes and stories, girls and boys should gradually experience every form of literature in a comprehensive school program that is sequentially plotted throughout the elementary grades. Such a program not only strengthens the developmental reading curriculum but contributes in a significant way to the attainment of several other objectives of elementary education:

- The school aims to meet the needs of individual students—and literature is widely diversified.
- The school aims to provide a learning program that will utilize the natural interests of its pupils—and literature in its many forms appeals to all age groups.
- The school aims to provide socially satisfying experiences for its children and to develop in its students a wider social understanding—and good stories and pleasing verse are enjoyed more when they are shared with others.
- The school aims to give each child self-insight—and books introduced in childhood can sometimes bring about a profound change in one's outlook on life.
- The school aims to give each student a knowledge and appreciation of his or her cultural heritage—and literature is the means whereby much of that heritage is preserved and perpetuated.
- The school aims to stimulate and foster creative expression—and book experiences are an exciting springboard to art, drama, and other expressionistic activities.

A properly-structured literature program provides a balance among the various genres relevant to this segment of the language arts—*genre* referring to the content (what is said and how it is said) and representing one of the systems for categorizing books. In this way children have at least minimal encounters with each genre of literature at every age level, and their teachers are constantly aware of the need to explore the many and diverse offerings included within each genre. A balance is readily attained between traditional literature and contemporary fiction, between poetry and prose, and between realism and fantasy. Such a balanced offering actively strengthens and expands the children's skill in language and composition as well as in literature. It could be charted, as shown in Table 13.1.

Finally, there are those who believe so firmly in the relevance of literature for today's child that they insist all reading programs should be literature-based. As discussed in Chapter 10, such programs still remain the exception rather than the rule. And one recent survey of children's literature instruction in the state of Ohio has shown that such instruction would have to be redesigned because effective literature-based reading programs

1. Contain a read-aloud component.
2. Provide extensive opportunities for the individualized reading of fiction.
3. Provide for the in-depth, or critical, study of books read in common.
4. Are interdisciplinary; that is, they encourage the reading of literature across all areas of the curriculum.
5. Promote among children a wide variety of responses to literature.[2]

Presently at least, children's literature courses are content-centered and therefore do not prepare preservice teachers to meet the elementary classroom demands associated with literature-based reading instruction, according to the Ohio survey.

Skeptics in this highly technological society often ask why students should be required to waste their time reading poetry or fabricated stories when so much practical knowledge is available. To that query Clifton Fadiman supposedly retorted that literature is one of those essential subjects that, once learned, helps students master all the rest. Indeed, the value of teaching literature *is* multifaceted:[3]

Value, Functions, and Current Trends

1. It promotes aesthetic and intellectual growth in several distinct ways; for example, it entertains; enchants; motivates reading; leads to improved reading skills; develops listening, speaking, and writing skills; and expands vocabulary.
2. It develops a sense of citizenship and fosters an awareness of society.
3. It builds a sense of rootedness, refines student feelings, and develops mature personalities.
4. It promotes ethical responsibility and shows the reader what good and evil look like.

The school literature program should be structured to attain certain objectives because literature itself performs particular functions. It provides both pleasure and understanding. It shows human motives for what they are, inviting the readers or hearers to identify with or react to fictional characters. Literature provides a form for experience, placing relevant episodes into coherent sequence,

Table 13.1
Planning Guide for a Literature Program in the Elementary School: By Genre (Recommended Sample Selections from *Adventuring with Books* [NCTE, 1985])

Genre: Poetry

Age Level: 4–7	*The Cozy Book* (Viking, 1982)
Age Level: 6–9	*Secrets of a Small Brother* (Macmillan, 1984)
Age Level: 7–10	*It's Snowing! It's Snowing!* (Greenwillow, 1984)
Age Level: 8–12	*Sky Songs* (Holiday, 1984)

Genre: Traditional Literature

Age Level: 4–7	*The Tortoise and the Hare* (Holiday, 1984)
Age Level: 6–9	*Rip Van Winkle* (Doubleday, 1984)
Age Level: 7–10	*And Me, Coyote!* (Macmillan, 1982)
Age Level: 8–12	*The Valiant Chatti-Maker* (Viking, 1983)

Genre: Modern Fantasy

Age Level: 4–7	*Chipper's Choices* (Coward, 1981)
Age Level: 6–9	*The Turkey Girl* (Macmillan, 1983)
Age Level: 7–10	*The Old Banjo* (Macmillan, 1983)
Age Level: 8–12	*Ralph S. Mouse* (Morrow, 1982)

Genre: Historical Fiction

Age Level: 4–7	*Tin Lizzie and Little Nell* (Bodley Head, 1982)
Age Level: 6–9	*A Royal Gift* (Coward, 1982)
Age Level: 7–10	*Charlie's House* (Crowell, 1983)
Age Level: 8–12	*A Gift for Mama* (Viking, 1981)

Genre: Contemporary Realistic Fiction

Age Level: 4–7	*Buffy and Albert* (Greenwillow, 1982)
Age Level: 6–9	*In My Treehouse* (Lothrop, 1983)
Age Level: 7–10	*Amelia Bedelia and the Baby* (Greenwillow, 1981)
Age Level: 8–12	*Tough-Luck Karen* (Morrow, 1982)

Genre: Informational Books

Age Level: 4–7	*Department Store* (Crowell, 1984)
Age Level: 6–9	*My Friend Leslie* (Lothrop, 1983)
Age Level: 7–10	*Burrowing Birds* (Lothrop, 1981)
Age Level: 8–12	*Nicole Visits an Amish Farm* (Walker, 1982)

Genre: Biography

Age Level: 4–7	*The Story of William Penn* (Prentice, 1964)
Age Level: 6–9	*Albert Einstein* (Barron's, 1982)
Age Level: 7–10	*Our Golda: The Story of Golda Meir* (Viking, 1984)
Age Level: 8–12	*The Great Alexander the Great* (Viking, 1983)

SOURCE: *Adventuring with Books* (Urbana, IL: National Council of Teachers of English, 1985).
The primary criteria for the book selections listed in the guide were literary and artistic quality, but attention was also paid to characteristics of books that might influence their appeal for children.

Children are eager to learn about innumerable subjects and literature can satisfy their curiosities. (© James L. Shaffer.)

thereby showing life's unity or meaning. Literature reveals life's fragmentation as well, sorting the world out into segments that can be identified and examined. It helps focus on essentials, permitting readers and hearers to experience with varied intensity but with new understanding the parts of life they have known. Literature reveals how both institutions of society and nature itself affect human life. Finally, literature leads or entices readers and hearers into meeting a writer-creator whose medium (words) they know, whose subject (human nature) they live with, and whose vision (life's meaning) they hope to understand.[4]

Children are eager to know about innumerable subjects, and literature can satisfy their curiosities. Boys and girls exhibit and share

An inward-looking *curiosity about themselves,* and a book such as Cole's *How You Were Born* (Morrow, 1984) responds to this concern.

A *curiosity about the natural world,* and Gans' *When Birds Change Their Feathers* (Crowell, 1980) helps them appreciate their environment.

A *curiosity about people and places,* and writers such as Margaret Ronan, Jean Fritz, and Ronald Syme help young readers discover facts about various American states, historical Americans, and famed explorers, respectively.

A *curiosity about machines and how they work,* which is satisfied by writers such as Gail Gibbons and Harvey Weiss.

A *curiosity about facts and proofs of facts,* and so a popular book is the *Guinness Book of World Records,* revised annually by the Sterling Publishing Company.

A *curiosity about the ideals by which men live,* which leads children to ponder Black's *The First Book of Ethics* (Watts, 1975).

A *curiosity about the social world and how to get along in society,* which is satisfied by books such as Parrish's *Mind Your Manners* (Greenwillow, 1979) and Naylor's *Getting Along with Your Friends* (Abingdon, 1980).

A practical and energetic *curiosity about creative experiences,* and writers such as Ed Emberley and Robyn Supraner help children have fun with arts and crafts.

A *curiosity about the world of make-believe,* and books about science fiction written by John Christopher or Monica Hughes are welcomed.

A *curiosity about the unknown world,* which is satisfied by books about unexplained phenomena by an author like Daniel Cohen.[5]

Two contemporary trends in children's books of special interest to primary teachers are the *pop-up or movable books* and the *wordless picture books.* The first actually surfaced about one hundred years ago, but the art work in many of the current books is so outstanding that there are those who predict the 1980s may well have been the start of the second Golden Age of movable books for children. Notable modern pop-ups include Pienkowski's *Dinnertime* (Price, 1981), de Paola's *Giorgio's Village* (Putnam, 1982), Carle's *The Honeybee and the Robber* (Philomel, 1981), Crowther's *The Most Amazing Hide-and-Seek Counting Book* (Viking, 1981), Goodall's *Lavinia's Cottage* (McElderry Books, 1983) and *Paddy Finds a Job* (McElderry Books, 1981). The fragile nature of pop-up books limits the life of the volume, but the books are particularly suited for very small groups or for individual children.

Almost unknown as recently as 1970, wordless picture books now appear regularly from reputable publishers. They are useful for reading-readiness activities, and they stimulate both language development and written composition. Because their interpretation depends solely on the illustrations, it is crucial that the immediate action of each picture as well as the cumulative sequence of action in all the pictures be distinctly portrayed and easily understood by children of the age group for whom the books are intended.[6] Therefore, two major criteria apply when evaluating wordless picture books: the quality of the illustrations and the quality of the story. Other criteria apply to the story line, which should be distinct if there is a narrative, and to the informational sequence whose development should be clear. A wordless book encourages girls and boys to embellish its story and to discuss the possible intent of the author and artist. Each promotes children's creativity and encourages language skills.

Although the majority of this type of picture are fantasy and most of the main characters are animals, there are also informational books, realistic stories, and subtle books with pictures that do not tell stories. Animal fantasy is shown in Goodall's *Paddy Pork—Odd Jobs* (McElderry Books, 1983) and child fantasy is the core of Heller's *Lily at the Table* (Macmillan, 1979). Informational wordless books include Crews' *Truck* (Greenwillow, 1980), and realistic stories without words include Ormerod's *Sunshine* (Lothrop, 1981). Finally, there are wordless books that provoke no narrative, such as Hoban's *Is It Rough? Is It Smooth? Is It Shiny?* (Greenwillow, 1984) and her *Take Another Look* (Greenwillow, 1981).

Wordless books have varying degrees of detail. Examples of exceptionally detailed books are Spier's *Noah's Ark* (Doubleday, 1977) and Anno's *Anno's Journey* (Philomel, 1978). Both are more appropriate for sharing with one or two children at a time, rather than with a group.

Children's Literary Interests or Preferences

Since the beginning of the century, several hundred studies of children's literary *interests* (actual reading behaviors) or reading *preferences* (expressed attitudes) have been completed. Although interest studies pinpoint what the population actually has read or does read, and though preference studies concern hypothetical situations, the terms are often used interchangeably by researchers[7] and therefore will be by this writer.

Although reading preference is highly variable and children can be expected to display different preferences by grade (maturation) or by community, boys and girls exhibit the most stable difference in terms of specific likes and dislikes for males and females.[8] Results from a recent study of 1,127 intermediate-grade children are consistent with previous findings about identifying strong sex differences in reading choices. Generally, boys have stronger preferences for the themes of history, geography, sports, science, fantasy, and travel. Girls have stronger preferences for animals, child and family, poetry, biography, romance, and mystery. Both, however, have similar preferences for adventure, humor, and nature study. Other studies regarding children's literary preferences have revealed that

1. Children's interest patterns change with age.
2. Sex-related preferences are now apparent at a younger age than they were before, possibly because of conformity to cultural expectations.
3. Social and environmental influences also affect children's book choices.
4. Peer recommendations are particularly important to fifth and sixth graders.
5. Gifted children prefer mysteries, fiction, science fiction, and fantasy.
6. Students of average ability prefer mysteries, comedy or humor, realistic fiction, and adventure.
7. Boys in grades three through five are interested in adventure, in tall tales, in sports, in science, and in historical nonfiction.
8. Girls in grades three through five are interested in animals, in fairy tales, in modern fantasy, and in children of the United States (as well as in children of other lands).
9. Children prefer to watch television rather than read.
10. Fiction rates high, especially humorous fiction.
11. The overwhelming majority of both primary- and intermediate-level children is initially attracted to a book by its subject matter.
12. Children's reading tastes have largely crystallized by the fifth grade.

Thousands of boys and girls across the United States were surveyed during the past decade for their reading interests.[9] Out of 1,060 book nominations, the top fifty titles included thirty-one realistic (contemporary) fiction books, eleven books of modern fantasy (of which two—*Charlotte's Web* and *Charlie and the Chocolate Factory*—were in the top ten), three picture-story books, two books of historical fiction, two poetry books, and one book of traditional literature. The author clearly dominating the selections was Judy Blume, whose name appeared ten times in the Top 50 Titles Chosen by Children.

Finally, a current and important indicator of children's reading interests is the "Children's Choices" project co-sponsored by the Children's Book Council and the International Reading Association. For this project, multiple copies of some 500 new books are distributed each year to sample classrooms across the country, and students designate their favorites. The resulting list of "Children's Choices" is then published in that year's October issue of *The Reading Teacher*. When a recent analysis was made of a sample of the choices, it was found that pupils will read about almost any topic if other factors are positive; in other words, topic alone does not determine the children's choice.[10] Children favor fast-paced books but also like explicit, vivid description. They like to be told exactly how settings look, and they want a detailed description of the actions. Young readers like an explicit theme, usually with a clearly stated lesson derived from a favorable outcome. In most of the preferred books, there are warm relationships as well.

Sources and Criteria for Selecting Well-Written Books

Until about 1960, the volume of literature for children was relatively small, averaging less than 1,000 juvenile titles published annually. Then came federal funding for the support of library materials, and by 1980 the average annual output was 2,500 new titles. Today the publication and distribution of juvenile books constitutes a business of nearly half a billion dollars, and it is still growing. In fact, a Gallup survey published in the February 26, 1988, issue of *Publishers Weekly* indicated that the sales of children's books represented 7 percent of all books published in the United States in 1987, up 2 percent from 1986. Purchases were predominantly (70 percent) fiction, and more than half of all children's books bought were hardbacks. That particular issue also marked the introduction of a national list of bestselling children's books.

Since 1918, when Macmillan established the first separate children's department in a publishing house in the United States (and probably the world), the children's book market has become a twentieth-century phenomenon. More than 200 publishing houses are presently engaged in printing juvenile books in both hardcover and paperback editions.

Despite this deluge, discriminating selection of a fine book for a specific class or student cannot yet be computerized. It still requires a knowledge of the interests, reading ability, and maturity level of that class or child, coupled with a knowledge of the best books to meet those interests and abilities.

The classroom teacher who has personally enjoyed some of the finest children's books can speak convincingly when introducing those books to the boys and girls. Children need to know a little of what each book is about, and a brief preview—or sales pitch—concerning a particular volume helps them gain this information. These days children can receive satisfaction from a variety of readily accessible media, including television, videos and films, and so the satisfaction a well-written book can bring must be explored in every classroom. This demands a personal knowledge by the teacher of many books in order to convey some of the excitement, wonder, and beauty of the printed page to young listeners and readers.

Yet according to a five-state investigation, many teachers need to update their information in the field of children's literature.[11] A total of 773 preservice and inservice teachers in California, Georgia, Maine, Nebraska, and Texas were asked to name their three favorite books *from childhood,* the three best children's books *now,* and the three most popular children's books *now.* On the best books list, out of 440 titles, the teachers chose only seven titles published since 1970 and also selected 39 percent of the titles from their list of childhood favorites. On the popular books list, out of 308 titles, the teachers selected only four titles (plus "Star Wars") published since 1970 and also picked 45 percent of the titles from their compilation of childhood favorites. Even more distressing was the 65 percent overlap of titles on both the best and the most popular lists! The researchers concluded that, because teachers' opinions regarding best and most popular books influence the selection of what teachers will recommend and read to their classes, it is important that teachers expand their own experiences with literature so that they may in turn introduce some of the more current high-quality books to children.

To learn more about new books and recent editions of older books, elementary school teachers can consult such periodicals as *Booklist* (published twice monthly but only once in July and August), *The Hornbook Magazine* and *The Five Owls* (each issued bimonthly), *Childhood Education* (published five times a year), *Bulletin of the Center for Children's Books* (published eleven times a year), and *Language Arts* (issued eight times a year); or teachers can examine book-review sections in national newspapers such as *The New York Times* and *The Christian Science Monitor,* which regularly compile material about new children's books. There are also numerous published bibliographies (available in many public libraries), including the following:

> *Adventuring with Books* (NCTE, 1985)
> *Best Books for Children* (Bowker, 1985)
> *The Black Experience in Children's Books* (New York Public Library, 1984)
> *The Bookfinder* (American Guidance Service, 1985)
> *Books for the Gifted Child* (Bowker, 1980)
> *Children's Books Too Good to Miss* (University Press Books, 1980)
> *Children's Catalog* (Wilson, 1986) and its annual supplements
> *The Elementary School Library Collection* (Bro-Dart, 1984)
> *Let's Read Together* (American Library Association, 1981)

Picture Books for Gifted Programs (Scarecrow, 1981)

Picture Books for Children (American Library Association, 1981)

Reading for Young People Series: The Great Plains (American Library Association, 1985); Other titles in the series include *The Northwest* (1981), *The Upper Midwest* (1981), *The Rocky Mountains* (1980), *The Southeast* (1980), and *The Middle Atlantic* (1980)

Shadow and Substance: Afro-American Experience in Contemporary Children's Fiction (NCTE, 1982)

Use of such book-selection aids will help keep classroom teachers informed of titles worthy of being termed children's literature. They can also keep in mind the many award-winning books, especially the Caldecott Medal and Newbery Medal winners (together with their Honor Books) listed in Appendix 2. Finally, they can request free catalogs from publishers specializing in children's books, such as Scholastic, Viking, Greenwillow, and Atheneum.

With the ever-increasing number of juvenile books from which to choose, classroom teachers must be aware of certain criteria to help them identify a quality book for children. The first criterion concerning all children's books is *format* (or the physical appearance of a volume), which is another system for categorizing books (besides genre). Technological improvements in printing and picture reproduction are making possible attractive books for young readers. Although no book should ever be selected on the basis of format alone, matters of illustration, typography, binding, spacing, and paper quality cannot be ignored when books are chosen for classroom use. Such books must represent the combined efforts of the best editors, illustrators, book designers, printers, and authors.

The importance of format was recently confirmed in a study of 145 third and sixth graders in New York State who represented all reading ability groups and who were interviewed individually.[12] Most third graders and all sixth graders in the low and middle reading groups considered format very important to book selection. Preferred by the total sample were books of larger page size, large type size, and the sans serif (without small finishing strokes at the top and bottom of letters) type style. In the area of illustrations, children were not as concerned with eye appeal as they were with a desire to avoid confusion when reading. Consequently they preferred illustrations placed at the bottom or top of the page.

Other criteria (besides format) for fiction and nonfiction are discussed in the following sections.

Fiction: Literary Elements

Although the pupils' reading will not be limited to stories, they will remain the first and enduring favorite of the boys and girls. Good stories possess six strong elements.

Plot

Children are most interested in the action or plot of the story. In a well-written book, the action is plausible and credible; it develops naturally from the behavior and decisions of the characters, and it does not depend on coincidence or contrivance. A story must have a beginning, a middle, and an ending. Children prefer an orderly sequence of events and generally lack the maturity to understand flashbacks. A well-plotted book is de Paola's *The Clown of God* (Harcourt, 1978).

The setting is the time and place of the action. It may be in the past, the present, or the future. The story may take place in a specific locale, or the setting may be deliberately vague to convey the feeling of all large cities or rural communities. It should, however, be clear, believable, and in the case of historical fiction, authentic.

Both the time and the place should affect the action, the characters, and the theme. Younger readers can quickly grasp the setting of Skorpen's *Old Arthur* (Harper, 1972), and older readers can understand the setting of Paterson's *Bridge to Terabithia* (Crowell, 1977).

A good book needs a worthy theme that provides a dimension of the story beyond the action of the plot. It may be the acceptance of self or others, the overcoming of fear or prejudice, or simply the process of growing up. The theme of a book reveals the author's purpose in writing the story.

In a well-written book the theme avoids moralizing and yet effectively evolves from the events in the story and unifies them. Such a book is White's *Charlotte's Web* (Harper, 1952), which has sold more than 1.5 million copies.

The style of writing in a book is the manner in which the author has selected and arranged words in presenting the story. A quality book possesses a style that respects children as intelligent individuals with rights and interests of their own. Children resent a style that is patronizing, that is overly sentimental, or that contains too much description or material for contemplation. Some students prefer books not written in the first person.

Primary-grade children like to listen to Goble's *The Girl Who Loved Wild Horses* (Bradbury, 1978). Intermediate-grade pupils appreciate the contemporary dialogue in many of the books by E. L. Konigsburg and Paula Fox.

The personalities (animal or human) portrayed in children's books must be convincing and lifelike, must display realistic strengths and weaknesses, and must be consistent in their portrayal. Though not every character in a well-constructed story will change, there is frequent personality development as happenings occur and problems are solved. Also, characters should speak and behave in accordance with their culture, age, and educational experience.

Books with sound characterizations for primary children include Lindgren's *Pippi Longstocking* (Viking, 1950) and Caudill's *Did You Carry the Flag Today, Charley?* (Holt, 1966). Two for intermediate-grade pupils are the Cleavers' *Me Too* (Lippincott, 1973) and Greene's *A Girl Called Al* (Viking, 1969).

A single incident may often be described differently by each individual witnessing or experiencing it. Consequently, point of view refers to the teller of the story and his or her values, feelings, or background. Contemporary fiction for middle-grade children is often told from a first-person point of view (i.e., the viewpoint of a child), whether he or she is the main character or only a bystander. Sometimes an author may choose to offer a variety of viewpoints by letting the

Setting

Theme

Style

Characterization

Point of View

actions of the characters speak for each of them. Other times an author may restrict the viewpoint, with the only change coming from the evolving attitude of one narrator. Points of view must be consistent to encourage readers to believe the characters, the narrator, and the ensuing action. The popular Ramona stories by Beverly Cleary are good examples of stories told from the viewpoint of a bright seven- or eight-year-old.

Nonfiction: Informational Books

Because trade books are today being used more and more to supplement texts and other curricular resources, teachers must be familiar with the varied criteria used to evaluate informational books. The first of these is *author qualification,* covering competence in the chosen field, ability to communicate knowledge to children, and responsibility to distinguish among opinions, theories, and facts. The second criterion is *accuracy and currency* because children cannot be supplied with facts that are out of date or superficial or that rely on anthropomorphism; in many informational books the copyright date is critical. A third criterion is *imaginative and accurate illustrations,* which help children comprehend technical principles and terms. A fourth criterion is the *scope and organization* of the text, with logical sequencing and both a simplification and a limitation of material. A fifth criterion is *elimination of stereotyping and the presentation of differing views on controversial subjects. Self-containment* is the sixth criterion so that children need not consult other books in an effort to understand the material presented because the enthusiasm or interest that boys and girls have for a particular subject may be quite brief. The seventh and final criterion is *style,* which should be lively and should employ vocabulary geared to the reading ability of the children.

Younger students are enthused about Gibbons's *Fire! Fire!* (Crowell, 1984) and Branley's *Rain and Hail* (Crowell, 1983). Older girls and boys enjoy Roth's *First Class! The Postal System in Action* (Pantheon, 1983) and Kyte's *In Charge: A Complete Handbook for Kids with Working Parents* (Knopf, 1983). All ages like to read Horwitz's *Doll Hospital* (Pantheon, 1983) and Lerner's *A Biblical Garden* (Morrow, 1982).

Nonfiction: Biography

If biography is a branch of literature, then it demands a worthy subject, a theme that provides dramatic unity, a pleasing style, and an organizational pattern particularly suited to the content. Most biographies for children are *fictionalized biography,* which can allow the author more freedom to dramatize certain events and to personalize the subject even though the book is grounded in thorough research. The author may invent dialogue, but the conversations are usually based on actual facts taken from journals and diaries of the period. This type of biography makes use of the narrative approach. Recommended examples are Kyle's *Girl with a Pen: Charlotte Brontë* (Holt, 1964) and Felton's *Mumbet: The Story of Elizabeth Freeman* (Dodd, 1970).

The second kind of juvenile biography is *biographical fiction,* which consists entirely of imagined conversation and reconstructed action. It takes a historical character and uses him or her as the core of a story that is only semihistorical. Outstanding examples include Fritz's *Where Do You Think You're Going, Christopher Columbus?* (Putnam, 1980) and Latham's *Carry On, Mr. Bowditch* (Houghton, 1955).

Children may also become interested in biographical series such as the Sports Hero Series (Putnam), the American Hero Series (Putnam), the Young Crowell Biographies, the Harper and Row Breakthrough Books, and the Houghton Mifflin North Star series. In all well-written biographies, the young readers enjoy a style that is vigorous and a narrative that is fast moving. The research material never detracts from the absorbing account of the life of the subject.

It was not until 1982—exactly sixty years after the Award had first been bestowed—that a book of poetry finally received the Newbery Medal Award. The winner was Willard's *A Visit to William Blake's Inn: Poems for Innocent and Experienced Travelers*. It also became a Caldecott Medal Honor Book for its splendid illustrations—an unusual dual honor.

Poetry: Literary Work in Metrical Form

Perhaps the reason it took so long for American critics to recognize an outstanding book of poetry is that there is truly no one definition of poetry that has been universally accepted. Although there are those who vow that poetry is simply a feeling, others contend that poetry is words performed, and so they compare the work of a poet to the composition of a musician. Still others believe that poetry, especially that for children, is writing that transcends literal meaning.

Should teachers need to defend their inclusion of poetry in the daily curriculum, they can list several reasons for sharing poetry with their students.[13] First, poetry provides pure enjoyment. Second, it gives children knowledge about concepts in the world around them: numbers, size, time, and color. Third, poetry encourages boys and girls to appreciate language and expand vocabularies because word choices play such an important role in poetic expression. Fourth, poetry helps children identify with situations and people. Fifth, it expresses moods familiar to girls and boys and helps them understand and accept their feelings. Sixth and finally, poetry provides children with insights into themselves and others, developing sensitivity to universal feelings and needs.

Unfortunately, as worthy as these reasons may be, a recent survey of objectives for poetry instruction (as found in sixth-grade manuals for the eight most widely used basal reading series) reveals only a superficial view of what student experiences with poetry should be.[14] The manuals stress cognitive rather than affective responses to poetry, they emphasize form rather than content, they encourage children to regard poetry as an isolated form of literature, and they discourage active participation of students in poetry lessons. Briefly, the manuals ignore the pedagogical procedures recommended by experts for poetry instruction, which run as follows:

1. Poetry should be presented in a meaningful context.
2. Poetry should be orally interpreted by the teacher.

3. Poetry instruction should encourage active participation.
4. Poetry instruction should be an exploration of thoughts, feelings, and ideas.
5. Poetry appreciation should be extended by providing opportunities to share the poetic experience in meaningful and interesting ways.

Because children are entitled to hear satisfying poetry as well as splendid prose, their teacher must plan creative lessons and should always test a chosen poem for students with these questions:[15]

1. *Does it sing?* Some poems have as much melody as music; the rhythm and the arrangement of the lines suggest the mood of the poem. There is movement as well. De La Mare's *Peacock Pie* (Faber, 1980) is filled with poems with pronounced melody and movement. Children are helped to understand the rhythm in poetry as they complete exercises in some of the current language arts series, as shown in Figure 13.1.
2. *Is the diction distinguished?* The words and phrases must be carefully selected and rich in sensory and associated meanings. Both connotative and descriptive words are interwoven in Updike's *A Child's Calendar* (Knopf, 1965).

Figure 13.1.
Exercises in Understanding Poetic Rhythm.

Feeling the Rhythm of a Poem

Listen for the rhythm, or strong beats, in a poem. The rhythm and meaning of a poem work together.

Many poems have a strong, regular beat. This pattern of strong beats is called **rhythm.** When you read poems aloud, listen for the rhythm. You can tap out the beats as you read or listen. Think about what the poet is saying. Let the rhythm and the meaning work together.

Listen while your teacher reads this poem. The poet has arranged the beats in a pattern. Notice how he captured the rhythm of a swing.

The Swing

How do you like to go up in a swing,
　Up in the air so blue?
Oh, I do think it the pleasantest thing
　Ever a child can do!

Up in the air and over the wall,
　Till I can see so wide,
Rivers and trees and cattle and all
　Over the countryside—

Till I look down on the garden green,
　Down on the roof so brown—
Up in the air I go flying again,
　Up in the air and down!

—ROBERT LOUIS STEVENSON

Figure 13.1.   (cont.)

Read the first stanza aloud. The strong beats have been marked for you.
Tap out those beats as you read. Do you feel the motion of the swing?

> Hów do you líke to go úp in a swíng,
>   Úp in the aír so blúe?
> Óh, I do thínk it the pléasantest thíng
>   Ever a chíld can dó!

Exercises: Feeling the Rhythm of a Poem

A. Here's another poem with a strong rhythm. Listen while your teacher reads it
aloud. Then see the directions below

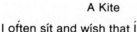

A Kite

I often sít and wísh that Í
Could be a kite up in the sky,
And ride upon the breeze and go
Whichever way I chanced to blow.

There are four strong beats in each line. Did you hear them? Copy the
poem. Put a mark (') above each word that has a strong beat. The first line is
marked for you.

B. Choose a poem with a strong rhythm. Practice reading the poem aloud
several times. Then read it to the class.

Source: Pgs. 210–211, *McDougal, Littell English, Brown Level.* Copyright © 1987 by
McDougal, Littell & Company, Box 1667, Evanston, Illinois 60204.

3. *Does the subject matter of the poem invest the strange or the daily experiences of life with new importance and richer meaning?* Poems should appeal to the intellect as well as to the emotions. Long or short, poems need a well-defined theme, such as those found in Ciardi's *Fast and Slow: Poems for Advanced Children of Beginning Parents* (Houghton, 1974).

In selecting a poem for children, the teacher must consider their background and age level, their needs, their previous experience with poetry, and the modern setting in which they live. The teacher should begin where the children are. For preschool and kindergarten pupils, the rhymes in Hague's *Mother Goose* (Holt, 1984) represent a strong and pleasant beginning. If primary children have not heard much poetry, the teacher can start with some of the traditional rhymes for games and tongue-twisters found in Lee's *Alligator Pie* (Houghton, 1975) as well as more modern poems such as those in Silverstein's *Where the Sidewalk Ends* (Harper, 1974). Older boys and girls who have not yet been introduced to poetry may be reached through books of narrative or humorous poems, such as the Benéts' *A Book of Americans* (Holt, 1952) and Bodecker's *Let's Marry Said the Cherry and Other Nonsense Poems* (Atheneum, 1974). The teacher can use country or folk music as a prelude to poetry with pupils in all grades. With older students, the teacher may wish to develop an introductory unit centered about a poet to whom pupils can relate, such as Jack Prelutsky.

The poetry presented should have relevance for today's child. It should be appropriate in theme and mood to the maturity of the group. It should not be didactic or filled with archaic vocabulary. Neither should it be coy, nostalgic, or sarcastic. Finally, it should generally be true poetry and not always merely verse.

The teaching of poetry can follow no set pattern. Unless the teacher enjoys poetry, the students will not respond enthusiastically. The teacher's personal choice of poetry guides girls and boys in building their own individual yardsticks. Therefore, the teacher's personal definition of poetry will determine how far he or she will carry the children into the realm of poetry.

Forms of Poetry for Children

One of the literary understandings to develop in elementary school literature is knowledge of types of poetry. These understandings grow gradually, so the wise teacher will provide balance in the selection of poetic forms as children exhibit readiness for them. There are two major forms in the English language for boys and girls.

Most of the poetry written for children is *lyric poetry*. It is usually short and emotional, often descriptive or personal, with no prescribed length or structure except that it should be melodic and could be set to music. Many of the poems of Robert Louis Stevenson, Christina Rossetti, Eleanor Farjeon, Elizabeth Coatsworth, Sara Teasdale, Walter de la Mare, Eve Merriam, and Henry Behn have this singing quality and can therefore be termed lyrical.

One of the best ways to capture pupil interest in poems is to present a variety of *narrative poetry*. Each of these so-called story poems relates a particular episode or event or tells a long tale. Seven- and eight-year-olds enjoy the long narrative verses of the many books by Dr. Seuss. Older children respond to Long-fellow's *Paul Revere's Ride* (Windmill, 1973) and Thayer's *Casey at the Bat* (Putnam, 1978). An outstanding classical narrative poem is Browning's *The Pied Piper of Hamelin* (Warne, 1971), which has wide appeal. Narrative poems may appear as lyrics, sonnets, or free verse.

A special type of narrative poem that has been adapted for singing and that contains repetition, rhythm, and a refrain is the *ballad*. With the current popularity of folk singing there has been renewed interest in the ballad form. There are both literary ballads with recognized authors and popular ballads with no known authors. Children in the middle grades will enjoy popular ballads such as "The Raggle Taggle Gypsies," "Get Up and Bar the Door," and "Bonny Barbara Allan." Literary ballads appropriate for use with children are included in Causley's *Salt-Sea Verse* (Puffin, 1981) and Kemp's *Ducks and Dragons: Poems for Children* (Puffin, 1983).

Children enjoy *limericks*, a nonsense form of five-lined narrative verse. The first and second lines rhyme, as do the third and fourth lines, but the fifth line generally ends in a surprising or humorous statement. Contrary to popular belief, Edward Lear did not originate the limerick. He did, however, do much to popularize it, and students listen attentively to many of the limericks in his *A Book of Bosh* (Penguin, 1982). Middle-grade children also find enjoyable Bodecker's *A Person from Britain Whose Head Was the Shape of a Mitten and Other Limericks* (Dent, 1980).

Although many poems are written in *bound verse* with requirements of rhyme and meter, children who have the opportunity to hear *free verse* are relieved to discover that all poetry does not rhyme. Free verse sounds much like other poetry when read aloud, but often looks different on the printed page. Sandburg's "Fog" and Hughes's "April Rain Song" are popular examples of the effective use of free verse, which depends on cadence or rhythm for its poetic form. A book of free verse for older children is Jones's *The Trees Stand Shining* (Dial, 1971).

Finally, some children enjoy hearing—and others enjoy writing—a Japanese verse form of three lines called *haiku*. Containing a total of only seventeen syllables, the first and third lines of the haiku have five syllables each, and the middle line has seven. Nearly every haiku may be divided into two parts: first a simple description that refers to a season; and second, a statement of feeling or mood. The teacher may wish to share with the class two volumes of haiku translated by Harry Behn and entitled *Cricket Songs: Japanese Haiku* (Harcourt, 1964) and *More Cricket Songs* (Harcourt, 1971). An American who writes haiku is Ann Atwood in her *Fly with the Wind, Flow with the Water* (Scribner, 1979).

Another old Japanese poetic form is *tanka*. Identical to haiku for its initial three lines, it adds two more lines of seven syllables each for a total of thirty-one syllables. Elementary children may wish to hear or read some of this kind of Japanese poetry as compiled by Virginia Baron in her *The Seasons of Time: Tanka Poetry of Ancient Japan* (Dial, 1968).

Children's Preferences

Because adults are unable to predict accurately which poems children will like, it is important to examine children's preferences directly. Two national samplings, using the same schools but in different years, found that elementary children prefer limericks and narrative poems and dislike free verse and haiku.[16] Children in both the primary and intermediate grades enjoy poems that have elements of nonsense, humor, familiar experiences, animals, holidays, people, and imaginative story lines. They all dislike poems relying on metaphor, simile, or personification but like rhymed poems and those with sound effects (alliteration and onomatopoeia). Boys and girls in grades one to three enjoy poems about fantastic and strange events, but those in grades four to six prefer more realistic content. A second area of distinction is that younger children prefer traditional poetry, but the older pupils like modern poems. There were no overall sex differences.

What may be even more significant is the conclusion reached in a national survey of 1,401 elementary students in urban, suburban, and rural schools with varied socioeconomic backgrounds: *two out of three pupils like poetry.*[17] Urban students like poetry more than either the suburban or the rural pupils. Incidentally, the poets mentioned most by children are Shel Silverstein, Jack Prelutsky, and Judith Viorst, according to a national survey of seventy-five school and public librarians.[18]

Research has also suggested that children do not like to talk about poetry; their negative feelings are based primarily on the insistence upon "correct" interpretation.[19] Frustration with critical analysis appears to be a major hurdle.

Boys and girls in most of the elementary grades find nothing peculiar, boring, or silly about poetry because so many of the experiences of the children and their language are related to poetic experiences and language. Elements that are shared by both young students and poets, such as love of concrete imagery, use of accentuated rhythm, and indulgence in playfulness, work positively for the interest that children have for poetry—at least through grade four. Fifth and sixth graders, whose teacher possesses a realistic concept of poetry and couples pupils and poems as subtly as pupils and prose, will also continue their initial enthusiasm for poetry. However, interest in poetry does begin to wane as students mature.

Boys and girls in the primary grades enjoy a wide variety of verse and poetry. They respond readily to nonsense and humor; ballads and narrative poetry; poems about animals, automobiles, and trains; and poetry that deals with daily activities. A sampling of the kinds of poetry and verse that they enjoy includes the following:

> Brown's "Jonathan Bing"
> Farjeon's "Cat"
> Field's "The Duel"
> Hoberman's "A Bookworm of Curious Breed"
> Lear's "The Owl and the Pussy-Cat"
> Lindsay's "The Little Turtle"
> Merriam's "The Motor-Boat Song"
> Nash's "The Tale of Custard the Dragon"

Prelutsky's "The Lurpp is on the Loose"
Richards's "Eletelephony"
Starbird's "Eat-It-All Elaine"
Viorst's "Mother Doesn't Want a Dog"

Children in the intermediate grades like poems that are related to their interests and experiences, poems that are humorous, and poems with strength of rhythm and rhyme. They will accept narrative verse that has action and excitement, such as Noyes' *The Highwayman* (Lothrop, 1983), and may be exposed to some serious poems such as the Benets' "Nancy Hanks." They also enjoy popular ballads that are not too difficult to read, including the traditional ones found in Plotz' *As I Walked Out One Evening* (Greenwillow, 1976).

Teachers concerned with helping children become familiar with poetry about minority groups will be interested in sharing one or more of the following books:

Adoff's *My Black Me: A Beginning Book About Black Poetry* (Dutton, 1974)
Amon's *The Earth Is Sore: Native Americans on Nature* (Atheneum, 1981)
Bierhorst's *The Sacred Path* (Morrow, 1983)
Jordan and Bush's *The Voice of the Children* (Holt, 1970)

Lastly, the teacher should be aware of the results of national polls of approximately 10,000 children in classrooms across the country for top selections among recently published poetry books. The finalists appearing in the "Children's Choices" for 1986 and 1987 were Babette Cole's *The Slimy Book* (Random), *Tomie de Paola's Mother Goose* (Putnam), Lee Bennett Hopkins's *Best Friends* (Harper), and Eve Merriam's *Blackberry Ink* (Morrow).[20]

Modern Poetry for Children

Children should hear poems—and poems were written to be read aloud—published earlier in this century as well as those printed for them in the eighteenth and nineteenth centuries. And teachers can readily locate such poems in the fine anthologies compiled by May Hill Arbuthnot and Shelton Root, Jr., (1968); Edward Blishen (1963); Joanna Cole (1984); Lilian Moore and Judith Thurman (1974); Iona and Peter Opie (1973); Jack Prelutsky (1983); and Louis Untermeyer (1978).

However, elementary children are also entitled to listen to poetry and verse written more recently and published by individual poets. The recommended publications listed here are divided among those appealing to all ages, to younger children, and to intermediate students.[21]

For all ages:

Adoff's *Today We Are Brother and Sister* (Lothrop, 1981)
Behn's *Crickets and Bullfrogs and Whispers of Thunder* (Harcourt, 1984)
Bodecker's *Snowman Sniffles and Other Verse* (McElderry Books, 1983)
Prelutsky's *The Baby Uggs Are Hatching* (Greenwillow, 1982)
Prelutsky's *The Sheriff of Rottenshot* (Greenwillow, 1982)
Prince's *The Secret World of Teddy Bears* (Harmony, 1983)

For ages four through nine:

>Fisher's *Rabbits, Rabbits* (Harper, 1983)
>Hoberman's *Yellow Butter, Purple Jelly, Red Jam, Black Bread* (Viking, 1981)
>Kumin's *The Microscope* (Harper, 1984)
>Livingston's *A Circle of Seasons* (Holiday, 1982)
>Prelutsky's *What I Did Last Summer* (Greenwillow, 1984)
>Zolotow's *Some Things Go Together* (Crowell, 1983)

For ages eight through twelve:

>Adoff's *All the Colors of the Race* (Lothrop, 1982)
>Baylor's *Desert Voices* (Scribner's, 1981)
>Cendrars's *Shadow* (Scribner's, 1982)
>Esbensen's *Cold Stars and Fireflies* (Crowell, 1984)
>Moore's *Something New Begins* (Atheneum, 1982)
>Viorst's *If I Were in Charge of the World and Other Worries* (Atheneum, 1983)

Finally, teachers should realize that since 1977 when the National Council of Teachers of English established the first and only award for children's poetry—the NCTE Excellence in Children's Poetry Award—the following American poets have received this prestigious honor and therefore deserve to have their writings brought to the special attention of elementary school children: Arnold Adoff, John Ciardi, Aileen Fisher, Karla Kuskin, Myra Cohn Livingston, David McCord, Eve Merriam, and Lilian Moore.

Bibliotherapy— or Books That Help Children Cope

As children grow and develop, they encounter a multitude of problems stemming from sibling relationships, family mobility, hospital confinement, parental separation, physical handicaps, or other sources. Some of their concerns arise chiefly within themselves; others evolve from outside events or conditions that affect the boys and girls: Jim and his divorced mother live alone; Jennifer is fat and friendless; Kim Chu is the first Asian in the school; and seven-year-old Chris has already lived in nine different states.

To help these children attain some degree of understanding of their personal difficulties, there are books that can be used to enable the reader or listener to accept problems in a wholesome manner. Books for precisely such mental hygiene make up *bibliotherapy* and provide a source of insight and relief from the varied pressures that young readers face during the ups and downs of normal development. Bibliotherapy may help boys and girls relieve conscious problems in a controlled manner and gain information about the psychology and physiology of human behavior. What it cannot do, however, is provide therapy through literature for those who have emotional or mental illnesses and are in need of clinical treatment.

Once defined as a process of dynamic interaction between literature and the personality of the reader (which may be utilized for personality assessment, adjustment and growth), bibliotherapy may generally be used by the teacher in two ways. With *therapeutic* bibliotherapy the teacher may attempt to solve children's actual problems by presenting similar experiences vicariously through books. By recognizing their problems and possible solutions in literature, the children presumably gain new insight and are then able to take a step toward resolving their personal difficulties. On the other hand, the teacher who employs *preventive* bibliotherapy believes that students will be better able to make satisfactory adjustments to some trying situations in the future, provided they have met similar problems in the stories they presently read or hear. In a sense, preventive bibliotherapy is analogous to an inoculation to prevent a contagious disease. It contributes to understanding and compassion as it offers children attitudes and standards of behavior that will help them adjust to some or most of the personal difficulties they will encounter.

Books designed to help change social and emotional behavior among nonclinical cases should still exemplify good literature. Their content must be worthwhile, and their style must be respectful to children. Racial, religious, or nationality groups must each be pictured with accuracy and dignity. In short, any book selected for bibliotherapy should be a book that today's boys and girls want to read.

Choosing and Using Books to Help Pupils Cope

The teacher may choose to use a particular book either with a large-group guidance session, with a small-group session, or in an individual conference. The large session is especially suited for preventive bibliotherapy in which each member can benefit from exposure to the book. The small-group session, much like a group reading lesson, is appropriate for therapeutic bibliotherapy in which several children all have a common problem. Individual conferences may incorporate preventive bibliotherapy when the teacher has been made aware of a forthcoming change in a child's life; for example, that seven-year-old Rhonda will be leaving California for upstate New York before the end of the term. An unforeseen occasion may also demand therapeutic bibliotherapy; for example, when Mike's grandfather suddenly dies. In preparation for either the personal conference or the group session, the teacher is advised to maintain a supply of index cards, each containing the title and subject matter of a recommended book available in the school library media center.

After either the individual conference or the group guidance sessions, the teacher must assign follow-up activities. Younger children can be challenged through such projective devices as drawing, painting, puppetry, or dramatic play. Older students, however, often wish to retell what happened in the story itself and explore the results of certain behaviors or feelings before reaching a generalization about the consequences of particular conditions or traumas. With both age groups, follow-up activities are important, for without them no significant amount of behavioral change can occur.

Selected Books Useful in Bibliotherapy

Of the books included in the following list, those marked with an *E* are picture books or easy books, planned especially for the primary grades; juvenile books marked with a *J* are intended for intermediate-grade children. In either case the teacher will wish to examine each book personally to determine its appropriateness and utility for the individual child's or group's needs.[22]

1. Exceptionality: Adjustment to Handicaps
   Cerebral Palsy
   - (J) Gould's *Golden Daffodils* (Addison-Wesley, 1982)
   - (E) Mack's *Tracy* (Raintree, 1976)
   Epilepsy
   - (J) Hermes's *What If They Knew?* (Harper, 1980)
   - (J) Young's *What Difference Does It Make, Danny?* (Deutsch, 1980)
   Hearing Impairment
   - (E) Arthur's *My Sister's Silent World* (Children's, 1979)
   - (E) Litchfield's *Words In Our Hands* (Whitman, 1980)
   Mental Retardation
   - (E) Clifton's *My Friend Jacob* (Dutton, 1980)
   - (E) Wright's *My Sister Is Different* (Raintree, 1981)
   Multiple Handicaps
   - (J) Greenfield and Revis's *Alesia* (Philomel, 1981)
   - (J) Robinet's *Ride the Red Cycle* (Houghton, 1980)
   Paraplegia
   - (J) Miner's *New Beginning: An Athlete Is Paralyzed* (Crestwood House, 1982)
   - (J) Redpath's *Jim Boen: A Man of Opposites* (Creative Education, 1980)
   Speech Problems
   - (J) Kelley's *The Trouble with Explosives* (Bradbury, 1976)
   - (E) Stanek's *Growl When You Say R* (Whitman, 1979)
   Visual Impairment
   - (E) Brown's *Arthur's Eyes* (Little, Brown, 1979)
   - (J) Leggett and Andrews's *The Rose-Colored Glasses: Melanie Adjusts to Poor Vision* (Human Sciences, 1979)
2. Family Relationships
   Adopted Child
   - (E) Goldon's *The Boy Who Wanted a Family* (Harper, 1980)
   - (J) Krementz's *How It Feels to Be Adopted* (Knopf, 1982)
   Extended Family
   - (E) Tax's *Families* (Atlantic, 1981)
   - (J) Wolkoff's *Happily Ever After . . . Almost* (Bradbury, 1982)
   Grandparents
   - (E) Goldman's *Grandpa and Me Together* (Whitman, 1980)
   - (E) MacLachlan's *Through Grandpa's Eyes* (Harper, 1979)

New Baby
>	(E) Galbraith's *Katie Did!* (Atheneum, 1982)
>	(E) Relf's *That New Baby!* (Golden, 1980)

Siblings
>	(E) Grant's *Will I Ever Be Older?* (Raintree, 1981)
>	(E) LeRoy's *Billy's Shoes* (McGraw-Hill, 1981)

Stepfathers
>	(J) Berger's *Stepchild* (Messner, 1980)
>	(E) Keats's *Louie's Search* (Four Winds, 1980)

Stepmothers
>	(E) Vigna's *She's Not My Real Mother* (Whitman, 1980)
>	(J) Wright's *My New Mom and Me* (Raintree, 1981)

3. Personal Traits

Courage
>	(J) Calhoun's *The Night the Monster Came* (Morrow, 1982)
>	(J) Crofford's *A Matter of Pride* (Carolrhoda Books, 1981)

Determination
>	(E) Bottner's *Dumb Old Casey Is a Fat Tree* (Harper, 1979)
>	(E) Chaffin's *We Be Warm till Springtime Comes* (Macmillan, 1980)

Honesty/Dishonesty
>	(E) Blue's *Wishful Lying* (Human Sciences, 1980)
>	(J) Hughes' *Honestly, Myron* (Atheneum, 1982)

Loneliness
>	(E) Skurznski's *Martin By Himself* (Houghton, 1979)
>	(E) Teibl's *Davey Come Home* (Harper, 1979)

Obesity
>	(E) Philips's *Don't Call Me Fatso* (Raintree, 1980)
>	(J) Smith's *Jelly Belly* (Delacorte, 1981)

Patience/Impatience
>	(E) Corey's *Everybody Takes Turns* (Whitman, 1980)
>	(J) Rounds' *Blind Outlaw* (Holiday House, 1980)

Perseverance
>	(E) Simon's *Nobody's Perfect, Not Even My Mother* (Whitman, 1981)
>	(E) Watanabe's *Get Set! Go!* (Philomel, 1981)

Resourcefulness
>	(J) Naylor's *Eddie, Incorporated* (Atheneum, 1980)
>	(J) Phelan's *The Week Mom Unplugged the TV's* (Four Winds, 1979)

Shyness
>	(J) Oppenheimer's *Working On It* (Harcourt, 1980)
>	(E) Sharmat's *Say Hello, Vanessa* (Holiday House, 1979)

4. Adjustment to Change in Environment or in Personal Circumstances

Camp Experiences
>	(J) Danziger's *There's A Bat in Bunk Five* (Delacorte, 1982)
>	(J) O'Connor's *Yours Till Niagara Falls, Abby* (Hastings, 1979)

Death of a Grandparent
    (E) Brandenberg's *The Two of Them* (Greenwillow, 1979)
    (E) Bunting's *The Happy Funeral* (Harper, 1982)
Death of a Parent
    (J) Jones's *Holding Together* (Bradbury Press, 1981)
    (J) Wallace-Brodeur's *The Kenton Year* (Atheneum, 1980)
Death of a Pet
    (J) Fairless's *Hambone* (Tundra Books, 1980)
    (E/J) Graeber's *Mustard* (Macmillan, 1982)
Divorce of Parents
    (J) Hogan's *Will Dad Ever Move Back Home?* (Raintree, 1980)
    (E) Paris's *Mom Is Single* (Children's Press, 1980)
Going to the Hospital
    (E/J) Ciliotta and Livingston's *Why Am I Going to the Hospital?* (Lyle Stuart, 1981)
    (E/J) Marino's *Eric Needs Stitches* (Addison-Wesley, 1979)
New Home
    (J) Blume's *Superfudge* (Dutton, 1980)
    (J) Galbraith's *Come Spring* (Atheneum, 1979)
New School
    (E) Hamilton-Merritt's *My First Day of School* (Messner, 1982)
    (E) Delton's *The New Girl at School* (Dutton, 1979)
Working Mother
    (E) Power's *I Wish Laura's Mommy Was My Mommy* (Lippincott, 1979)
    (E) Schick's *Home Alone* (Dial Press, 1980)

Minority Americans in Modern Children's Literature

Learning to accept and respect the diverse cultures in our pluralistic society—another phase of bibliotherapy—involves more than recognition of differences in family custom, diet, and language pattern, according to the Committee on Reading Ladders for Human Relations of the National Council of Teachers of English. Literature that goes beyond a mere acknowledgment of difference to an appreciation of the richness of cultural distinctions leads to sensitivity and feelings of empathy. It also allows the reader or listener to span the barriers of race, color, and religion that keep people apart.

Literature can explore and extend three major understandings critical to life in a multicultural society:

1. It can show how all of us are connected to each other through our needs, our emotions, and our desires. Such an understanding of our common humanity is an awesome weapon against any forces poised to divide us from one another.
2. It can help us appreciate, understand, and even celebrate the differences that make each cultural group special and that enrich the larger society.
3. It can promote an understanding of the effects of social issues and forces on the lives of average individuals. Issues such as racism and poverty in this

country and in other countries must be faced if our major problems are to be resolved. Through books children can understand the potentially devastating effects of negative forces on everyday lives.[23]

During the middle and late 1970s, books about minority groups became more plentiful and projected more positive and authentic images. During the 1980s however, the picture changed, and fewer books were published about minority Americans. The following are sample recommended selections for each of six minority groups (titles preceded by [E] designate easy books particularly appropriate for younger children, and titles preceded by [J] mark books more appropriate for intermediate students):[24]

1. *Afro-Americans*
   - (J) Campbell's *A Girl Called Bob and a Horse Called Yoki* (Dial, 1982)
   - (J) Clifton's *The Lucky Stone* (Delacorte, 1979)
   - (J) Hamilton's *Willie Bea and the Time the Martians Landed* (Greenwillow, 1983)
   - (J) Irwin's *I Be Somebody* (McElderry Books, 1984)

2. *American Jews*
   - (J) Brooks's *Make Me a Hero* (Dutton, 1980)
   - (J) Chaikin's *Finders Weepers* (Harper, 1980)
   - (J) Herman's *What Happened to Heather Hopkowitz?* (Dutton, 1981)
   - (J) Hurwitz's *The Rabbi's Girls* (Morrow, 1982)

3. *Asian Americans*
   - (J) Lord's *In the Year of the Boar and Jackie Robinson* (Harper, 1984)
   - (E) McCunn's *Pie-Biter* (Design Enterprises, 1983)
   - (J) Uchida's *A Jar of Dreams* (McElderry Books, 1981)
   - (J) Yep's *Sea Glass* (Harper, 1979)

4. *Mexican Americans*
   - (J) Lampman's *Go Up the Road* (Atheneum, 1972)
   - (J) Newton's *Famous Mexican Americans* (Dodd, 1972)
   - (J) Smith's *Josie's Handful of Quietness* (Abingdon, 1975)
   - (E) Tester's *We Laughed a Lot, My First Day of School* (Children's Press, 1979)

5. *Native Americans*
   - (E) Leech and Spencer's *Bright Fawn and Me* (Crowell, 1979)
   - (J) Miner's *Navajo Victory: Being a Native American* (Crestwood, 1982)
   - (E/J) Thayer and Emanuel's *Climbing Sun: The Story of a Hopi Indian Boy* (Dodd, 1980)
   - (J) Wisler's *Buffalo Moon* (Lodestar Books, 1984)

6. *Puerto Rican Americans*
   - (J) Gonzalez's *Gaucho* (Knopf, 1977)
   - (J) Mohr's *Felita* (Dial, 1979)
   - (J) Mohr's *In Nueva York* (Dial, 1977)
   - (J) Mohr's *Nilda* (Harper, 1973)

Instructional Activities

Literature can be shared in a variety of meaningful ways in which children enjoy taking part and which grow naturally from the love of books. Such learning experiences furnish an avenue through which children can relate their personal feelings and develop their creative potential. These experiences also provide exposure to new media and new ways of thinking about books while they simultaneously build appreciations and develop standards in literature.

The activities that teachers can plan with or for their students should meet varying ability levels. Some are primarily *motivational* activities, and others are especially *interpretive* experiences, but the division between the two groups is not always clear-cut. Often an interpretive or culminating activity for one pupil will serve as a motivating literary experience for another child. The teacher serves as the primary force, bringing literature into the classroom to motivate children's reading; he or she also guides and assists the readers when they wish to share their books with one another. Aware that each book that is read need not be followed by some kind of report or interpretive exercise, the teacher is not disturbed when some children (notably the higher achievers) prefer to continue reading rather than participate in creative expression.

More than fifty selected motivational and interpretive activities that have been used successfully in elementary classrooms are described as follows:

Motivational Experiences

Story Telling

The most appropriate way developmentally for children first to be exposed to narrative literature is through the medium of the storyteller—and not through movies, television, records, or even books. Once introduced to story telling, boys and girls can begin to understand the oral tradition of literature and may even be stimulated to tell their own stories, especially after completing exercises from some language arts series, as shown in Figure 13.2.

The heart of any story-telling experience is the tale itself. Consequently, the teacher-storyteller should develop a familiarity with various kinds of story collections by spending some time reading in the children's room of the public library. When the teacher has located a promising tale, he or she should consider the following: Is the story one that personally excites me? Is it a story that I wish to share with others? Is it a story that *I* can tell? Is it a tale that lends itself to telling (or should it be read aloud instead)? Is it a tale that will appeal to the age group of the listeners? Is the length of the tale correct for the attention span of the audience for which it is intended?

Story telling is not difficult, and child audiences are generally highly appreciative. Busy teachers must therefore discount the notably tough requirements from the traditional writers on story telling, which call for exceptional efforts at memorization, overlearning of stories, and considerable speech work.

Instead, once the teacher-storyteller has chosen a tale and prepared adequately, he or she must only establish an effective setting for the narration before proceeding with the performance. Successful story telling does demand an informal and relaxed atmosphere in which every child can see and hear the teller

Speaking and Listening

Figure 13.2.
Exercises in Story
Telling.

Telling a Story

Everyone enjoys listening to stories. Did you ever notice how some people are very good at telling stories? They make the story funny or exciting when they tell it.

You can become a good storyteller too. Choose a story you like. Get to know the story well. You need to know the beginning, middle, and end of your story. When you know all the parts of your story, you can build suspense up to the climax, or most exciting part. Then you can end your story well.

When you tell a story, remember these guides.

Guides for Telling a Story

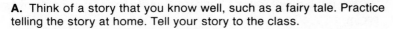

1. Look directly at your listeners.
2. Speak clearly.
3. Let your voice and body help you show what is happening in the story.
4. Lead your listeners toward the climax.
5. Know the last sentence of your story.
6. Pause when your story is finished.

Exercises: Narrating a Story

A. Think of a story that you know well, such as a fairy tale. Practice telling the story at home. Tell your story to the class.

B. Make up your own ghost story. Plan and practice your story. Tell your story to the class.

Source: Pg. 130, *McDougal, Littell English, Aqua Level.* Copyright © 1987 by McDougal, Littell & Company, Box 1667, Evanston, Illinois 60204.

without strain. It also demands that the modern teacher-storyteller perform with as much dramatization as possible—including gestures, body movements, facial expressions, and voice changes—for the child audience is truly television-minded.

When the story is over, there is often no follow-up planned by the teacher, for the simple responses of the children are adequate. Trite remarks such as "Wasn't that a nice story?" add nothing to the story hour; however, questions prompting insight into cultural similarities or into social values may seem in order after certain kinds of tales.

By setting an example as a storyteller, the teacher may inspire students to try story telling themselves. Some may wish to tell stories to their classmates; others will enjoy entertaining younger children. Students and teacher alike will find many good tales for the storyteller in collections from the *Best Books for Children* (Bowker, 1985) such as the following:

Crouch's *The Whole World Storybook* (Merrimack, 1983)
Dewey's *Pecos Bill* (Greenwillow, 1983)

Fisher's *The Olympians: Great Gods and Goddesses of Ancient Greece* (Holiday, 1984)

Gifford's *Warriors, Gods and Spirits from Central and South American Mythology* (Schocken, 1983)

Grimm Brothers' *Favorite Tales from Grimm* (Four Winds, 1982)

Hadleys' *Legends of the Sun and Moon* (Cambridge, 1983)

Kellogg's *Paul Bunyan: A Tall Tale* (Morrow, 1984)

Leach's *Whistle in the Graveyard: Folktales to Chill Your Bones* (Penguin, 1982)

Lurie's *Clever Gretchen, and Other Forgotten Folk Tales* (Harper, 1980)

Manning-Sanders's *A Book of Spooks and Spectres* (Dutton, 1980)

Story Reading

Although many stories may be either told or read aloud to the children, there are two broad categories of stories that can never be told effectively and must always be read. The first covers picture books because their illustrations are an integral part of the plot, as shown in Kent's *The Caterpillar and the Polliwog* (Prentice, 1982). The second includes stories whose charm lies in their language, due to either (a) the marked use of dialect, as exemplified in Gammell's *Git Along, Old Scudder* (Lothrop, 1983); or (b) the strong individualistic style of the author, as in Kipling's *Just So Stories* (Rand, 1982).

For reading aloud to boys and girls, teachers should look for materials that they know and genuinely like and that they believe the students are not apt to read themselves. Some of the older Newbery Medal Books, for example, are considered dull by the standards of today's children—until the teacher reads them aloud to the group.

This type of listening is an important and pleasurable experience for the children from all socioeconomic levels. For younger students, it is also a precursor to success in learning to read, for such children often score significant increases in vocabulary, word knowledge, and reading comprehension (in contrast to children denied the opportunity to hear good stories). With intermediate boys and girls, listening to stories helps them significantly to understand or draw inferences from selections of good literature.

One recent study of reading aloud to second and fifth graders found that the more exposure children have to literature, the more they initiate reading on their own, want experiences with books, write stories on their own, establish reading practices, and feel they have learned from books read aloud.[25] However, the classroom setting plays an important role in the interest that children show and in the gains they make during stories read aloud. The teachers described in the study as working in informal settings believed that books read aloud were integral to their program, and not surprisingly, their students also recalled more books and believed they had learned from books read aloud. On the other hand, teachers in more formal settings regarded the time for oral reading as set apart from the curriculum; one-third of their fifth graders no longer liked having books read aloud, and the other two-thirds believed they had gained little from the experience of having books read aloud.

Nevertheless, most older students still like to hear their teacher read to the class from Giff's *The Winter Worm Business* (Yearling Books, 1983) or Lowry's *The One Hundredth Thing About Caroline* (Houghton, 1983). Primary children enjoy hearing Hoban's *The Flight of Bembel Rudzuk* (Philomel, 1982) or Blume's *The Pain and the Great One* (Bradbury, 1984). Some elementary boys and girls prefer reading aloud themselves to younger children in the school whenever teachers can arrange such visits.

Incidentally, teacher-readers should be interested in the results of a study of behaviors that contribute most substantially to the quality of oral reading, especially in primary children.[26] In the order of influences, these behaviors are child involvement in the story reading; the amount of eye contact between reader and audience; the amount of expression injected into the reading; the voice quality of the reader; the pointing to words or pictures by the reader; the reader's familiarity with the story; the selection of an appropriate book; the proper seating of boys and girls so that all can see; and finally, the highlighting of words and language by the reader.

The teacher may plan a listening period for playing some of the fine commercial cassettes or records of dramatizations or readings of such children's stories as Andersen's *The Emperor's New Clothes* (Little, 1984) or Carroll's *Alice's Adventures in Wonderland and Through the Looking Glass* (Macmillan, 1963).

Listening to Records and Cassette Tapes

Poets such as John Ciardi have also read from their own works for children, and such presentations have been carefully recorded for classroom use. Some school districts carry a collection of such materials. Others prefer that their teachers borrow the records or audio cassettes from the public library.

Attending Children's Theater Productions

The teacher may occasionally see an announcement in the daily paper concerning the production of a children's theater group that will be presented locally. Classroom discussions of the book on which the production will be based may then be planned. Paul Galdone's *The Elves and the Shoemaker* (Clarion, 1984) is one of the tales frequently dramatized by professional or college groups for child audiences.

Often the admission prices for such productions are substantially reduced for young pupils. In some districts, school buses are used to transport the children to the theater, particularly on Saturdays.

Watching Telecasts

The teacher should check the listings in the weekly television guides in order to suggest or assign the pupils to watch a suitable production of a story such as Byars' *The Winged Colt of Casa Mia* (Viking, 1973), which is done with taste and fidelity.

Watching Filmstrips

The class may sometimes wish to watch one of the many acclaimed sound filmstrips of such children's stories as Grifalconi's *The Village of Round and Square Houses* (Little, 1986). On other days, the boys and girls in the primary grades enjoy seeing nonverbal filmstrips made from such wordless books as de Paola's *Pancakes for Breakfast* (Harcourt, 1978). Many recommended filmstrips are listed in Appendix 1.

Reading in a Basal Series

Pupil texts of basal reader series often include adaptations, abridgements, or even exact reproductions of chapters from such books as Cleary's *Ramona Quimby, Age 8* (Morrow, 1981) or Burch's *Christmas with Ida Early* (Viking, 1983). Children are more eager to read the complete story or separate book after they have enjoyed discussing an introductory selection. Often they will also wish to read other books by the same author, especially those about the same character.

Attending Book Fairs

During the annual Public Schools Week or National Children's Book Week, some schools schedule book fairs at which all the grades are invited to display their creative reactions to certain children's books. The fairs are generally held in the school library media center and may involve commercial exhibits and films.

In other schools, the teachers prefer to plan book fairs within their own classrooms, holding these on a bimonthly basis and encouraging children to participate in the planning. Parents are often invited to the fairs so they may have the opportunity to discover more about the school reading and literature program and to learn how they may assist the classroom library.

Making Bulletin Board Displays

Bulletin boards can announce new books or book events, display unusual book illustrations, and encourage imaginative writing in the classroom. Some boards point up authors such as Katherine Paterson or Roald Dahl. Others stress categories such as sports stories or tall tales. An interesting addition is a pegboard that holds books and other three-dimensional objects.

Studying Assigned Units

Background for in-depth understanding of many units in social studies and a few units in science or health can be furnished through broader use of selected books. A primary unit on transportation, for example, benefits from such books as Gibbons's *New Road!* (Harper, 1983) and Nichols's *Big Paul's School Bus* (Prentice, 1981). An intermediate unit on the expansion of the American West encourages reading of Chambers's *California Gold Rush: Search for Treasure* (Troll, 1984) and Freedman's *Children of the Wild West* (Clarion, 1983).

Keeping an Author's Birthday Calendar

The primary teacher can post a large monthly birthday calendar and mark it with pictures of authors whose prose or poetry the class has enjoyed hearing and reading. In the intermediate grades, the calendar can include a list of the author's books as well. Such calendars are more stimulating to young readers if pupils' names are also listed, especially when a class member was born on the same day of the year as a favorite writer-illustrator such as Maurice Sendak (June 10).

Playing Charades and Other Games	Some children, singly or in small groups, can act out the names of books while their friends try to identify the correct titles. Others will enjoy matching book-jacket pictures with their corresponding titles. Still other pupils can take turns unscrambling the names of authors or story characters out of jumbled letters fastened to a magnetic board.
Working in the School Media Center or Classroom Library	Boys and girls can help with the charging out and returning of books. They can prepare magazines and books for circulation. They can repair torn pages, make catalog cards, and shelve books. They can set up attractive displays and exhibits. All of these activities involving the handling of books and magazines stimulate interest in the contents of the materials.
Writing Goodbye Book Briefs	Children can copy their favorite literary passages on slips of paper and place the signed slips into a large envelope that hangs by the classroom door. Then, as the boys and girls are lined up for dismissal near that door—and a few minutes remain before the bell—a child can be chosen to reach into the envelope and draw out one of the selections. The pupil who copied the passage is pleased to hear his or her choice read aloud. In the meantime, classmates become acquainted with still another good book, such as Naylor's *The Solomon System* (Atheneum, 1983).
Examining Free or Inexpensive Materials from Publishers	Publishers of children's books often supply free or inexpensive bookmarks, maps, illustrations suitable for framing, buttons, brochures, photographs, and other display materials, sometimes in quantity lots. Such offers are described in *The Calendar,* issued quarterly by the Children's Book Council, 67 Irving Place, New York 10003, and are directed to all its members. The Council invites teachers to join its ranks at a onetime charge of twenty-five dollars.
Planning an Author's Afternoon	An Author's Afternoon is an exciting event during which children hear an author discuss his or her life and books. The Children's Book Council offers speakers' lists of authors and illustrators who are willing to speak to various groups—sometimes for fees and sometimes for the payment of transportation costs alone. The lists are compiled by states and available for the price of a large, self-addressed, stamped envelope. Publishing houses, local libraries, and educational organizations can also help the children in arranging an Author's Afternoon.
Attending Story-Telling Workshops	In schools with media centers and professional media specialists, a series of story-telling workshops may be held under the supervision of the specialist. Interested pupils from the middle and intermediate grades are invited to attend in order to learn how to tell folktales and other stories to kindergarten and primary children.

In schools without library media centers, the children's librarian from the nearest public library may schedule the workshops, which help introduce good stories and good story-telling techniques to older boys and girls.

Although some schools prefer to hold the workshops during National Children's Book Week, nearly any time during the academic year that is convenient for the librarian is appropriate for the children. |

Primary classes that visit the harbor during a study trip return to school with a special desire to read Gibbons's *Boat Book* (Holiday House, 1983). Classes in districts whose budgets do not allow for many trips away from the school building may be privileged to hear resource speakers from the community, who visit schools to make presentations to the students and thereby elicit interest in books such as Branley's *Feast or Famine? The Energy Future* (Harper, 1980).

Using Community Resources

School newspapers and magazines often have a column for book reviews, and children throughout the building can be encouraged to write reviews of new and old favorites in order to inform their friends of books they have enjoyed. Older pupils may even review books for readers outside the immediate school or community. In one elementary school in Austin, Texas, for example, the book editor of the local newspaper came to discuss book reviewing with the more advanced members of the sixth grade. She provided a number of new books for them to review, and subsequently all their reviews were published in the book section of the Sunday edition. Later, reviewing new books for the paper became a regular activity at the school.

Reviewing Books for Publication

Children can dress up as their favorite book characters and tell about themselves and their experiences. Sometimes they may even be invited to parade through a neighboring classroom and introduce briefly the characters they are representing.

Meeting Book Characters in Person

Pupils who like to read realistic stories of the here and now, such as Lowry's *Anastasia's Chosen Career* (Houghton, 1987), find it easy to borrow appropriate costumes for the book characters they want to be in the parade.

Some girls and boys become interested in literature through membership in a book club that caters to their age bracket. Sponsors of book clubs for elementary school children include the following:

Joining a Book Club

Dell Publishing Company, One Dag Hammarskjold Plaza, 245 E. 47th Street, New York: Trumpet Club (grades four to six).
Field Publications, 245 Long Hill Road, Middletown, CT:
  (1) I Can Read Book Club (ages four to eight). Hardcover selections from Harper & Row's *I Can Read* Series.
  (2) Paperback Book Clubs. Quality paperbacks from major publishers.
    (a) Buddy Books Paperback Book Club (kindergarten and grade one)
    (b) Goodtime Books Paperback Book Club (grades two and three)
    (c) Discovering Books Paperback Book Club (grades four to six)
  (3) Weekly Reader Children's Book Clubs (ages four to eleven). Hardcover selections from all children's book publishers. Three age groups: primary (4–7), intermediate (7–9), and senior (9–11).
Grolier Enterprises, Sherman Turnpike, Danbury, CT.: Beginning Readers' Program (ages three to six) and Disney's Wonderful World of Reading.
Junior Literary Guild, 245 Park Avenue, New York (ages three to fourteen). Hardcover selections. Seven age groups.

Parents Magazine's Read Aloud Book Club, division of Gruner & Jahr USA, 685 Third Avenue, New York (ages two to seven). Original hardcover picture books from Parents Magazine Press.

Scholastic, 730 Broadway, New York. Paperback reprints and originals:

(1) See-Saw Book Club (kindergarten and grade one)
(2) Lucky Book Club (grades two and three)
(3) Arrow Book Club (grades four to six)

Watching Films

A class that can observe on the screen the famed doughnuts episode from McCloskey's *Homer Price* (Viking, 1943) is generally anxious to read the entire story. Watching a full-length film of a book such as O'Brien's *Mrs. Frisby and the Rats of Nimh* (Atheneum, 1971) will also lead children to examine the published story.

Reading and Writing Newspaper Headlines

A provocative headline such as "Brave Dentist Threatened by Patient" might be tacked on the bulletin board, and primary children might be encouraged to guess which book is represented. The answer of course is Steig's *Doctor De Soto* (Farrar, 1982). Older students can develop their own headlines to entice their classmates to read more literature.

Interpretive Activities

Using Story Dramatization

Children who have heard or read Cauley's *Jack and the Beanstalk* (Putnam, 1983) are quickly prompted into participating in story dramatization. Any properties that are needed can be readily improvised by the players.

Singing

The class may be interested in singing some of the poems written by Robert Louis Stevenson that have been set to music. Several series of elementary music books carry songs based on his poems from *A Child's Garden of Verses* (Rand, 1981). Another favorite poem that has been set to music is the lengthy *The Night Before Christmas* (Holiday, 1980) written by Clement Moore.

Making Puppets and Holding Puppet Shows

Children of every grade level can construct puppets of their favorite book characters, using a variety of materials ranging from paper bags to soda straws. Some groups may even prefer to hold puppet shows based on such stories as de Regniers' *Beauty and the Beast* (Bradbury, 1978) or Zemach's *The Little Red Hen* (Farrar, 1983).

Filing Instant Replays

In an attempt to avoid overstructured book reporting, children can be encouraged to dictate or write on index cards their brief accounts of the most exciting or critical incident in a book they have read, such as Wright's *The Dollhouse Murders* (Holiday, 1983). The cards are placed in a small box on the library table and shared by both teacher and class.

When children have read a satisfying book such as Maruki's *Hiroshima No Pika* (Lothrop, 1982) or McHugh's *Karen's Sister* (Greenwillow, 1983), they can prepare a mosaic report. They sketch on a sheet of white paper a character or scene from the story. Next they paste small pieces of colored tissue paper on the sketch, using a brush dipped in liquid starch. Then they fold black construction paper and cut it to make a frame for the mosaic. Finally, they tape the mosaic to a window. When the light shines through the mosaic, the sketch assumes the appearance of stained glass.

Making Mosaics

Boys and girls can design their own book jackets and display them next to the original ones issued by the publishers. Inside the jacket may be written or dictated a synopsis of a book such as Clymer's *The Horse in the Attic* (Bradbury, 1983). A biographical sketch of the author can be substituted for the synopsis if adequate reference books are available and if the boy or girl is skilled in using them.

Designing Book Jackets

In schools where overhead projectors are readily available, pupils can make transparencies of drawings of selected characters or scenes from books that they have enjoyed reading. Once the drawings are completed, the book (like Peck's *Soup's Goat*, Knopf, 1984) can be read aloud, wholly or in part, as the transparencies are projected on the screen.

Making Transparencies

Boys and girls, individually or in groups, can prepare a collage depicting a favorite scene from a book such as Speare's *The Sign of the Beaver* (Houghton, 1983). On a background of a large piece of brown wrapping paper or burlap is attached an assortment of materials to represent the characters and objects. The finished collage may later be displayed if its producers approve.

Making Collages

Maps can be made of individual states, countries, continents, or the entire world. On them are sketched or marked the birthplaces of authors such as Donald Crews; the settings of favorite books such as Voigt's *Homecoming* (Atheneum, 1983); or the travels of a character such as Fanny in Cohen's *Gooseberries to Oranges* (Lothrop, 1982). Where fictitious places are key points in books, the class members may create original maps, as for Baum's *Wizard of Oz* (Holt, 1982). Although some children may prefer to make small individual desk maps, others will wish to work together on a huge wall map.

Drawing Maps

With the aid of room mothers, the teacher can arrange an unusual Halloween or end-of-the-semester party. Each pupil, at home or during an earlier school art period, makes a paper hat to help depict a well-known story character and then wears the hat to the Mad Hatter's Party.

Attending a Mad Hatter's Party

When a group or the entire class has completed a book such as Winter's *Hush Little Baby* (Pantheon, 1984), the boys and girls may like to create a rhythmical interpretation of the story. Their teacher may either compose music for the dance

Creating Rhythms and Dances

or use a recorded accompaniment. More than one series of basic movements may be possible, and the audience can then select the dance interpretation that it prefers.

Making Roll Movies

Scenes from a well-liked story such as the Grimms' *Little Red Cap* (Morrow, 1983) can be painted or crayoned on a long sheet of shelf paper. Then the sheet is rolled up on two dowels inserted through the holes in the back of a puppet stage. As the movie rolls slowly along, a pupil reads the matching excerpt from the book.

Painting Murals

Brightly colored murals involving tempera paint, construction paper, and colored chalk may develop from the reading of a single book such as Taylor's *The Trouble with Tuck* (Doubleday, 1981). They may also represent the composite of many books on a single unit such as "The Zoo."

Making Posters

Posters of every size and sort can be created by readers who wish to inform others of an exciting book such as McDermott's *Daughter of Earth* (Delacorte, 1984). When they are three-dimensional, posters add special interest to book exhibits.

Participating in Panel Discussions

Children enjoy panel discussions during which they informally explore a popular or current topic. One group of intermediate-grade students that had read biographies of Maria Mitchell, Margaret Mead, Jane Goodall, Susan La Flesche, Marie Curie, and Elizabeth Blackwell centered its panel discussion on the theme of Women in Science.

Creating Finger Plays

Both nursery rhymes (as in Wildsmith's *Mother Goose,* Oxford, 1982) and counting poems (as Rosenburg's *One, Two, Buckle My Shoe,* Simon, 1981) lend themselves to adaptation for finger plays. Kindergarten and first-grade children enjoy creating rhymes for such activities.

Using Flannel or Felt Characters

Children can cut out of remnant pieces of flannel or felt the characters described in a book such as Friedman's *How My Parents Learned to Eat* (Houghton, 1984) that the group has enjoyed. Sometimes the pupils will wish to decorate the pieces or to back tiny lightweight realia with flannel. Finally, they are ready to share their book adventure by means of a cloth board.

Producing Shadow Boxes

Large shallow boxes can be quickly converted into shadow boxes when the box fronts have been removed; the remaining frames are then painted and hung on the wall. In them the children can display three-dimensional objects that are essential to the plot of a favorite story such as Hicks's *Alvin's Swap Shop* (Holt, 1976). The boxes can also be prepared to represent the settings for a story such as de Paola's *Strega Nona's Magic Lessons* (Harcourt, 1982).

Making Dioramas

Children can build dioramas of several scenes from a book such as Davies's *Miracle on 34th Street* (Harcourt, 1984). Similar to shadow boxes in construction, dioramas can be made simply from cartons or more elaborately from wood and heavy cardboard. When the teacher helps the boys and girls see the relationships between the available materials and the mood or scene to be depicted, children find more creative ways of making dioramas realistic and attractive.

Dioramas with some sort of movement added are box theaters. They can be adapted to finger puppets and used for a children's favorite such as Fox's *One-Eyed Cat* (Bradbury, 1984) when the pupils or teacher wish to depict a scene or story without too much preparation. Larger box theaters can be used with hand puppets.

Constructing Box Theaters

A child who has read a story such as Smith's *Blue Denim Blues* (Atheneum, 1982) may want to show classmates how some of the characters in the story looked. Should the teacher have a stock of small inexpensive dolls available from a variety store as well as a supply of colorful remnants donated by room mothers, the child may easily sew the clothes to dress the book characters. At other times, children enjoy making paper clothes for a sturdy paper doll character.

Dressing Character Dolls

Primary pupils especially enjoy preparing a rebus review of a book such as the Boyds' *I Met a Polar Bear* (Lothrop, 1983). In place of certain portions of a sentence or paragraph, old magazine pictures are substituted. Such clippings can cover significant persons, places, objects, or actions. Some exceptional children in the upper grades enjoy writing rebus reviews too.

Preparing Rebus Reviews

Some young readers, particularly those with speech handicaps, enjoy sharing with their peers scenes from a book such as Perez and Robison's *Your Turn, Doctor* (Dial, 1982). The pantomimes they present are short, lasting five minutes or less.

Presenting Pantomime Skits

Beginning readers can cut pictures from magazines to prepare a report of a story such as Cazet's *The Duck with Squeaky Feet* (Bradbury, 1980). Each picture is properly mounted and accompanied by an appropriate caption.

Preparing Picture Reports

Pupils may occasionally prepare book reports to communicate their feelings about books in purposeful, written fashion. Whereas some children are ready to begin such reports in the middle primary years, others are not ready until the intermediate grades. There are, however, five levels of book-report writing adaptable to children's written language maturity.

Preparing Written Reports for a Reason

- Level One—The pupils record on a four-by-six-inch card the title and author, the number of pages read, and a one-sentence opinion of the book. They later arrange their cards in chronological order of books completed.
- Level Two—The students use a five-by-eight-inch index card to record the title and author, and to write one sentence on each of the following: the general idea of the book, the part liked best, the reasons for recommending or not recommending the book, and the place where a copy of the volume was located.

- Level Three—The pupils use the same form as at Level Two, but they expand to a short paragraph each of the following points: the general idea of the book, the part liked best, and the reasons for recommending or not recommending the book. In place of one of the aforementioned points students may substitute a discussion of the plot or an analysis of the characterization. In this case, however, they abandon the index card for writing paper.
- Level Four—The pupils respond at length about the title and author, the type of story, its main idea or subject, its outstanding qualities or features, and their general comments or opinion. They write or use a typewriter.
- Level Five—The students follow the assignment for Level Four, but they also complete one or more of the following activities: a biography of the author, a discussion of the effect of the book on the reader, a different ending for the story, a commentary on the characterizations, or a comparison of books by the same author or on the same subject. They write on notebook paper or type the report.

Performing in Shadow Plays

Almost any story or poem lends itself to a shadow play, which may be done in pantomime or with voices and movement. Scenes for such a play can be made by cutting simple shapes from wrapping paper or newspaper and pinning them to a sheet. Then a bright light is placed behind that sheet and the students stand between the sheet and the light. Even shy children enjoy performing in a shadow play by acting out roles from a favorite such as Marshall's *George and Martha Back in Town* (Houghton, 1984).

Modeling Clay

Children can use clay to model their favorite characters or scenes. Later, after the clay has been fired, painted, and glazed, the models are displayed before a backing made of a folded piece of cardboard on which the pupils can write the words best describing their representations. The text may be copied from a book such as Van Allsburg's *Jumanji* (Houghton, 1981) or created by the children.

Cooking and Eating

Pupils from six to ten can make pancakes after the group has read or heard Lobel's *The Pancake* (Greenwillow, 1978). The younger children especially will each like to make a "happy day pancake" by first forming the eyes and smile with batter, then letting it bake a while before adding the rest of the batter, and finally flipping the pancake over to see its "happy face."

Drawing Cartoons

Intermediate boys and girls familiar with newspaper and magazine cartoons can draw their own cartoons to depict important situations, problems, and events from a favorite book such as Clymer's *My Mother Is the Smartest Woman in the World* (Atheneum, 1982).

Several children who have heard or read the same story, such as Evslin's *Hercules* (Morrow, 1984), may wish to turn it into a ballad that may later be presented either with or without a musical accompaniment. One pupil in the group begins and then points to another child to continue the ballad until all have had an opportunity to participate.

Although the framework of the three-dimensional design is made of wire or wood, the pendants or suspended objects on the mobile are made from a wide collection of materials that the pupils can bring from home. The class may prefer to restrict the pendants to represent the characters or events from a single story (such as Collier's *Planet Out of the Past* [Macmillan, 1983]) or to confine them to the stories of a single author (as Virginia Hamilton).

Sometimes it is the teacher that supplies the materials for the mobile-making project. First the students make a list of important quotations, incidents, words, or characters from a book recently heard or read. Then they are given some index cards, glue, thread, and scissors. The cards are cut into different shapes; for example, squares for quotations. The students copy each item on their list on a different card. Finally, they hang the card shapes one below the other in proper vertical sequence.

When they use a Super 8 camera with a built-in viewfinder, children can be taught quickly how to take movies. The teacher can borrow a camera from a staff member or from one of the room parents. If the school lacks indoor lighting equipment, the pupils can paint scenery on large sheets of heavy cardboard and film all scenes outdoors. The major expenses incurred in this activity lie in the cost of film and film development.

Many of the folktales that the teacher reads aloud or tells to the class—such as Cauley's *The Goose and the Golden Coins* (Harcourt, 1981)—are suitable for an elementary class project in filmmaking.

Choral speaking is sometimes called "choral reading," "verse choirs," or "choric speaking." All of these terms refer to a similar technique of group recitation or reading of poetry (or poetic prose) without music but under the direction of a leader.

Suitable for any group of elementary school children (even those with speech handicaps), choral speaking is also appropriate for any class size. It produces positive personal, social, psychological, cognitive, affective, and language values.[27] It is a beneficial experience because it synchronizes three linguistic skills: listening, reading, and speaking. It improves the everyday speech of children, builds positive group attitudes, and offers an acceptable outlet for emotional expression. It promotes desirable personality traits and offers a socializing activity for both the shy and the forward. Lastly, it develops imagination and heightens the appreciation of poetry.

Creating Ballads

Constructing Mobiles

Making Films

Choral Speaking: A Unique Interpretive Activity

To make effective use of choral speaking, however, teachers must first understand the rhythm and the tempo of the poetry as well as the color and quality of the children's voices. Then, with that background in mind, they must be able to choose wisely among the five types of arrangements that are possible.

The Refrain Arrangement

Easiest for beginners are poems with a refrain or chorus. The teacher or pupil leader recites most of the narrative, and the class responds with the words that constitute the refrain or the repeated line(s). Typical examples of poems with refrains include the following:

> Hoberman's "Whale"
> Lindsay's "The Mysterious Cat"
> Prelutsky's "The Yak"
> Stevenson's "The Wind"

and (by Unknown)

Little Brown Rabbit

Leader:	Little brown rabbit went hoppity-hop,
Group:	Hoppity-hop, hoppity-hop!
Leader:	Into a garden without any stop,
Group:	Hoppity-hop, hoppity-hop!
Leader:	He ate for his supper a fresh carrot top,
Group:	Hoppity-hop, hoppity-hop!
Leader:	Then home went the rabbit without any stop,
Group:	Hoppity-hop, hoppity-hop!

The Antiphonal or Dialogue Arrangement

Poems demanding alternate speaking between two groups require an antiphonal or dialogue arrangement. High voices may be balanced against low voices or boys' voices may be contrasted with girls' voices. This arrangement may simply be a question-and-answer session. Poems that provide dialogue between two people can also be used for this form of choral speaking. Typical examples include the following:

> Fyle's "Witch, Witch"
> Meigs's "The Pirate Don Durk of Dowdee"
> Rossetti's "Who Has Seen the Wind?"
> Starbird's "The Spelling Test"

and (by Unknown):

To London Town

Group A:	Which is the way to London Town
	To see the king in his golden crown?
Group B:	One foot up and one foot down,
	That's the way to London Town.

Group A:	Which is the way to London Town
	To see the queen in her silken gown?
Group B:	Left! Right! Left! Right! Up and down,
	Soon you'll be in London Town!

This arrangement differs from the antiphonal variety only in that it engages not two, but three or more individual children or choirs. The line-a-child or line-a-choir arrangement is always popular with pupils because it possesses variety and offers the challenge of picking up lines quickly in exact tempo. Students must come in on cue, of course, so early effort with this kind of choral speaking should find the students standing in the order in which they present their lines. Teachers who wish to use it with younger children, however, will find it helpful to choose poems that have lines or couplets that end with semicolons, periods, or even commas, so that the poet's thoughts are not broken up after the assignment of parts. Typical examples include the following:

The Line-a-Child or Line-a-Choir Arrangement

Coleridge's "The Months of the Year"
Field's "The Duel"
McCord's "At the Garden Gate"
Snyder's "Poem to Mud"

and (by Unknown), for five children or five groups of children that begin and end their reading together:

Five Little Squirrels

All:	Five little squirrels sat in a tree.
Group A:	The first one said, "What do I see?"
Group B:	The second one said, "A man with a gun."
Group C:	The third one said, "We'd better run."
Group D:	The fourth one said, "Let's hide in the shade."
Group E:	The fifth one said, "I'm not afraid."
All:	Then bang went the gun, and how they did run.

The cumulative arrangement differs from the line-a-choir arrangement in that the addition of each group to the presentation is permanent, not temporary, in order to attain a crescendo effect. It is one of the more difficult forms of choral speaking because it involves the use of voice quality to achieve interpretation. The addition of voices is not simply to gain greater volume but also to build toward a more significant climax. An entire class can readily take part. Typical examples of poems for cumulative arrangement include the following:

The Cumulative Arrangement

Ciardi's "Mummy Slept Late and Daddy Fixed Breakfast"
Lear's "The Owl and the Pussycat"
Lobel's "The Rose in My Garden"
Silverstein's "Smart"

and (by Mother Goose):

The House That Jack Built

Group A: This is the house that Jack built.

Groups A–B: This is the malt
That lay in the house that Jack built.

Groups A–C: This is the rat,
That ate the malt
That lay in the house that Jack built.

Groups A–D: This is the cat,
That killed the rat,
That ate the malt
That lay in the house that Jack built.

Groups A–E: This is the dog,
That worried the cat,
That killed the rat,
That ate the malt
That lay in the house that Jack built.

Groups A–F: This is the cow with the crumpled horn,
That tossed the dog,
That worried the cat,
That killed the rat,
That ate the malt
That lay in the house that Jack built.

Groups A–G: This is the maiden all forlorn,
That milked the cow with the crumpled horn,
That tossed the dog,
That worried the cat,
That killed the rat,
That ate the malt
That lay in the house that Jack built.

Groups A–H: This is the man all tattered and torn,
That kissed the maiden all forlorn,
That milked the cow with the crumpled horn,
That tossed the dog,
That worried the cat,
That killed the rat,
That ate the malt
That lay in the house that Jack built.

Groups A–I: This is the priest all shaven and shorn,
That married the man all tattered and torn,
That kissed the maiden all forlorn,
That milked the cow with the crumpled horn,
That tossed the dog,
That worried the cat,
That killed the rat,
That ate the malt
That lay in the house that Jack built.

Groups A–J: This is the cock that crowed in the morn,
That waked the priest all shaven and shorn,
That married the man all tattered and torn,
That kissed the maiden all forlorn,
That milked the cow with the crumpled horn,
That tossed the dog,
That worried the cat,
That killed the rat,
That ate the malt
That lay in the house that Jack built.

Groups A–K: This is the farmer sowing his corn,
That kept the cock that crowed in the morn,
That waked the priest all shaven and shorn,
That married the man all tattered and torn,
That kissed the maiden all forlorn,
That milked the cow with the crumpled horn,
That tossed the dog,
That worried the cat,
That killed the rat,
That ate the malt
That lay in the house that Jack built.

Even more difficult than the cumulative variety is the unison type of choral speaking. An entire class or group reads or recites every line together. Only an experienced teacher-leader can skillfully direct a large number of voices speaking simultaneously.

The Unison Arrangement

Unison reading is unfortunately where most teachers begin choral speaking, although it is the hardest of all the popular arrangements and often elicits the singsong monotony that results when inexperienced children read together. However, when the class—and the teacher—have developed considerable background in choral speaking, unison arrangements become dramatically effective. Obviously they are better suited to intermediate-grade children. Young children will enjoy saying nursery rhymes and other simple verse together, but they should not be given a heavy dose of unison experience because of the problems of coordinating timing and inflection. Typical examples of poems for unison recital include the following:

Falls's "September"
Morrison's "On the Skateboard"
Livingston's "O Sliver of Liver"
Thurman's "Campfire"

and (by Unknown):

Weather

Whether the weather be fine,
Or whether the weather be not,
Whether the weather be cold,
Or whether the weather be hot,
We'll weather the weather,
Whatever the weather,
Whether we like it or not.

Guided Sessions

The teachers who experience little difficulty in commencing choral speaking are the ones who enjoy poetry themselves and share it often with their classes. These are the same men and women who write poems on charts and display them about the room, and who encourage students to create their own poetry. Such class saturation of all kinds of possible selections for verse choirs is a natural beginning because the children acquire an ear for rhythm, a sense of mood, and a desire to say enjoyable poems with their teacher. It can also be a successful beginning if the sessions are short, simple, and well directed. The director or teacher must set the example for the choral speaking periods insofar as phrasing, tempo, diction, and emphasis are concerned. He or she must help the students understand that with verse choirs, every word must be readily understood by the listeners. To make direction easier, the teacher groups the children in a standing position where all can see.

The first poems presented should be those that the class memorized earlier. Later the group's repertoire can be increased by duplicating and distributing copies of other longer poems that the girls and boys have enjoyed.

After everyone is familiar with the content of the material and has had several pleasing experiences with choral speaking, the children should be encouraged to suggest a variety of interpretations and executions. Sound effects may be introduced on occasion.

Two techniques for helping groups improve their choral efforts are (1) the use of tape recordings so that all may share in the evaluation, and (2) the appointment of a small group within the class to divorce itself from the chorus and act as a critical audience of listeners.

Finally, the teacher must learn the progressive phases through which a choral speaking moves so that he or she can place the whole experience in proper perspective. The first phase is an understanding of rhythm and tempo, and its purpose is to encourage each child to sense that rhythm and tempo. The second phase is an understanding of the color and quality of the voices, which demands that the teacher also comprehend the meaning of such specialized terms as *inflection* (the rise and fall within a phrase), *pitch level* (the change between one phrase and another), *emphasis* (pointing up of the most important word) and *intensity* (loudness and softness of the voices). And the third phase that the teacher must understand is the arrangement or orchestration of choral speaking in order to help convey the meaning of a poem.

Literature for choral speaking should have a story or theme that is both dramatic and simple so as to be understood promptly by an audience that hears it for the first time. It should possess a marked rhythm and express a universal sentiment. Prose suitable for group reading includes—for older children—portions of Rachel Carson's *The Sea Around Us* (Oxford, 1958) and selections from Scott O'Dell's *Island of the Blue Dolphins* (Houghton, 1960). For younger readers there are the texts from Beatrix Potter's *The Tale of Peter Rabbit and Other Stories* (Knopf, 1982), as well as some portions of Robert McCloskey's *Time of Wonder* (Viking, 1957).

Appropriate Selections

Whether the selection is prose or poetry, it must not only meet the teacher's criteria for literature and fulfill a specific objective in the day's planning but also win the pupils' interest and involvement as well. Children prefer selections that contain humor, repetition, surprise, action—and brevity.

Anthologies and literature textbooks are crowded with poems and pieces of poetic prose that can readily be done by a choral group. In selecting material for choric interpretation, the classroom teacher should consider (1) the appropriateness of the subject matter as well as its treatment, (2) the richness of the rhythmic elements and tone color or sound values, and (3) the author's overall method of organization so that a vocal group can be utilized impressively.

Besides the danger of mediocre material, choral speaking has several other possible pitfalls of which the teacher must be aware. One of these that occurs when children speak together is the mounting volume of their voices. Therefore, the teacher must listen continually to the tone quality of the individuals in the choir, marking the time firmly, and keeping the voices warm and light. Another pitfall is the children's tendency to singsong their lines. Consequently, the teacher must focus the attention of the class on the meaning, the story, or the idea of the selection, and not on the delivery. Still another pitfall is the lapse into cuteness or overdramatics, which makes the children believe that it is they and not their efforts that are being put on exhibition.

Pitfalls

The teacher must also be certain that the class develops and maintains unity in the following areas of choral speaking: articulation, pitch, inflection, and thought or feeling. Good diction and articulation must be accomplished first, and individuals who speak at various rates of speed must learn to enunciate each word clearly at the exact time in group work. Pitch will become more uniform as children develop better understanding of poetry and as they become accustomed to the voices of those around them. Due to a tendency to end sentences on an upward inflection, unity in the modulation of the voice is difficult to accomplish. Speakers must first hear themselves to correct any bad habits. Finally, all participants must have the same understanding of any poems and possess a depth of feeling and a sensitivity to words.

Evaluation

Classroom teachers can briefly rate the results of their choral speaking sessions if they ask themselves the following:

- Has there been an improvement in the speech and voice quality of the children?
- Do the students have a greater enjoyment of poetry because they have spoken it together, and are they genuinely eager for more and better poetry?
- Are the students developing growing powers of interpretation so that they speak their selections with understanding and vitality?
- Has the anonymity of choir work helped individual children?
- Are some of the boys or girls able to take over the leadership of the choir, showing a real feeling for the possibilities of the work?
- Are the children completely simple, natural, and sincere in their work?

A majority of positive answers would indicate that the teacher is doing sound and careful work.

Evaluation of Student Progress

Although there has recently been increasing attention paid to the testing of writing and reading, no comparable growth of interest has occurred in the testing of literature.[28] This is unfortunate because such testing affects curriculum generally and also helps teachers and test makers refine their understanding of the entire field of literature and the way that it is presented to girls and boys.

It is well recognized that work with literature must be evaluated on both a short-term and a long-term basis. The first is related to objectives for a particular literary experience. Because each individual lesson plan has specific goals, just as it does in other areas of the curriculum, teachers can readily observe whether the children have accomplished one of the following sample tasks:

- Dramatizing three stanzas of a poem
- Stating two ways in which three books were alike and two ways in which they differed
- Interpreting five idioms
- Joining in the refrains as certain tales are read aloud
- Preparing an art project that reflects feelings about a story read earlier this week
- Tape-recording each committee's favorite selection by a popular poet

Long-term evaluation is more general and occurs at the end of the school year. It looks at children's behavior in relation to literature:

- Does the class look forward to the literature period?
- Does the class enter into the motivational or interpretive activities with enthusiasm?
- Is its attention span prolonged during those activities?
- Is there a high degree of group interaction?
- Does the class wish to share its literary findings with other classes or with parents?

Information regarding each child's growth toward the objectives of the literature program can be secured by noting the following:

- Does the student read widely in various genres?
- Does the student like to share his or her pleasure in reading?
- Does the student express in composition form some of the ideas he or she has gained from books read or discussed?
- Does the student's speaking vocabulary include new words from the books he or she has read or discussed?
- Does the student's writing vocabulary include new words from the books he or she has read or discussed?
- Has the student read books related to personal interests?
- Has the student's reading helped with personal problems?
- Does the student use a variety of art media to illustrate situations from a book he or she has read or discussed?
- Do the student's comments indicate the building of a personal philosophy that appears to be influenced by the books he or she has read or discussed?
- Does the student visit the public library regularly?

Long-term evaluation demands teachers recall that the basic goal of a literature program in the elementary school is to "educate" children's imaginations.[29] This means helping boys and girls understand and enjoy the language of literature, discover the interrelatedness of literary works, and respond to literature in imaginative ways.

Discussion Questions

1. How can literature contribute to the achievement of some of the objectives of elementary education? Document your answer with specific book titles if possible.
2. What are some of the means by which busy classroom teachers can readily keep up with at least a small percentage of the hundreds of new children's books published each year? Could this responsibility be handled more efficiently by grade levels or on a district-wide basis?
3. When and how should a teacher employ bibliotherapy in the classroom?
4. Which motivational experiences in literature would you use comfortably with a class of slow achievers?

5. Why is it often difficult to secure the participation of high achievers in exercises and activities involving the books they read? How can a teacher promote at least minimal creative expression among such readers?
6. Should children's progress in literature be evaluated? If so, how can it be done fairly and effectively?

Suggested Projects
1. Begin collecting pictures of illustrators and authors of children's books.
2. Design and construct a hanging book mobile to interest children in reading biographies and informational books.
3. Make an annotated file of at least twenty book titles (arranged by genre) that you would include in a balanced literature program for the elementary grade of your choice.

Figure 13.3. Language Arts Learning Center: Literature.

| TYPE OF CENTER: | **Poetry Appreciation** | TIME: Varies |
| GRADE LEVEL: | K-3 | NUMBER OF STUDENTS: 1 (or a small group) |

INSTRUCTIONAL OBJECTIVE:	The children will listen to several poems on tape. They will draw a picture of one that has meaning for them.
MATERIALS:	Manila paper, crayons or paints, a tape recorder, and a cassette of recorded poems.
DIRECTIONS:	

1. Press down the green button (the "on" button is colored green).
2. Listen to the poems.
3. Press the red button (the "off" button is colored red).
4. Pick the one you liked best.
5. Draw a picture of what you heard, saw, or felt.
6. Put your picture on the left side of the table.

| SUGGESTED IDEAS: | The poems could be read into three separate tapes, and children could select one. |
| EVALUATION: | The teacher will be able to determine how interested the students are in poetry by observing the number that use the center and whether the students understand the poems by the pictures drawn. The teacher may also discuss the pictures and the meaning of the poetry with the children individually or as a group. The pictures could be displayed on a bulletin board near the center. |

From PATHWAYS TO IMAGINATION by Angela S. Reeke and James L. Laffey, © 1979 by Scott, Foresman & Company. Reprinted by permission.

4. Select ten poems suitable for choral speaking. Then plan how you would use at least two of them, utilizing appropriate arrangements.
5. Compile a list of classroom activities for National Children's Book Week celebrated in November.
6. Read, and later tell, a story suitable for a kindergarten class, using the flannelboard if you like. Finally, record that story on a cassette tape.
7. Set up the learning center on literature shown in Figure 13.3.

Recent Related Readings

Andrews, J. 1988. "Poetry: Tool of the Classroom Magician," *Young Children, 43*(4), pp. 17–25.

Cullinan, B. 1989. *Literature and the Child,* 2nd ed. New York: Harcourt.

Denman, G. 1988. *When You've Made It Your Own: Teaching Poetry to Young People.* Portsmouth, NH: Heinemann.

Freeman, E., and Levstik, L. 1988. "Recreating the Past: Historical Fiction in the Social Studies Curriculum," *Elementary School Journal, 88,* pp. 329–337.

Galda, L. 1988. "Readers, Texts, and Contexts: A Response-Based View of Literature in the Curriculum," *The New Advocate, 1,* pp. 92–102.

Harmon, J., and Lettow, L. 1988. "Emerging Authors and Illustrators in the 80's: Noteworthy Contributions to Children's Literature," *Childhood Education, 64,* pp. 152–156.

Livingston, M. 1988. "Children's Literature Today: Prospects and Perils," *The New Advocate, 1,* pp. 18–28.

Shumaker, M., and Shumaker, R. 1988. "3,000 Paper Cranes: Children's Literature for Remedial Readers," *The Reading Teacher, 41,* pp. 544–549.

Stewig, J. 1988. *Children and Literature,* 2nd ed. Boston: Houghton Mifflin.

Trousdale, A. 1989. "Let the Children Tell Us: The Meanings of Fairy Tales for Children," *The New Advocate, 2,* pp. 37–48.

Chapter Notes

1. I. Aaron, "Enriching the Basal Reading Program with Literature," in *Children's Literature in the Reading Program,* B. Cullinan, ed. (Newark, Delaware: International Reading Association, 1987), p. 126.
2. J. Zaharias, "Implications of State-Wide Survey of Children's Literature Instruction," *The Bulletin,* 1986, *12*(1), pp. 10–13.
3. California State Department of Education, *Handbook for Planning an Effective Literature Program* (Sacramento: Author, 1987), pp. 6–10.
4. R. Lukens, *A Critical Handbook of Children's Literature,* 3rd ed. (Glenview, Illinois: Scott, Foresman, 1986), pp. 3–8.
5. R. E. Toothaker, "Curiosities of Children That Literature Can Satisfy," *Childhood Education,* 1976, *52,* pp. 262–267.
6. Z. Sutherland and M. Arbuthnot, *Children and Books,* 7th ed. (Glenview, Illinois: Scott, Foresman, 1986), p. 103.
7. K. Spangler, "Reading Interests vs. Reading Preferences: Using the Research," *The Reading Teacher,* 1983, *36,* pp. 876–878.
8. E. G. Summers and A. Lukasevich, "Reading Preferences of Intermediate Grade Children in Relation to Sex, Community, and Maturation (Grade Level)," *Reading Research Quarterly,* 1983, *18,* pp. 347–360.
9. B. Elleman, "Chosen by Children," *Booklist,* 1982, *79*(7), pp. 508–509.

10. S. Sebesta and W. Calder, "A Canon of Children's Literature," Unpublished paper delivered at the World Congress of the International Reading Association, 1986, London.

11. K. H. Wendelin, R. A. Zinck, and S. M. Carter, "Teachers' Memories and Opinions of Children's Books: A Research Update," *Language Arts*, 1981, *58*, pp. 416–424.

12. M. J. Weiss, "Children's Preferences for Format Factors in Books," *The Reading Teacher*, 1982, *35*, pp. 400–406.

13. J. Le Pere, "For Every Occasion: Poetry in the Reading Program," Paper presented at the Eighth Southwest Regional Conference, International Reading Association, 1980, Albuquerque, New Mexico.

14. S. Shapiro, "An Analysis of Poetry Teaching Procedures in Sixth Grade Basal Manuals," *Reading Research Quarterly*, 1985, *20*, pp. 268–381.

15. Sutherland and Arbuthnot, *Children and Books*, p. 276.

16. C. A. Fisher and M. Natarella, "Young Children's Preferences in Poetry: A National Survey of First, Second, and Third Graders," *Research in the Teaching of English*, 1982, *16*, pp. 339–354; and A. C. Terry, *Children's Poetry Preferences: A National Survey of Upper Elementary Grades* (Urbana, Illinois: National Council of Teachers of English, 1974).

17. M. Roush, "Is the Role of Literature Different in Urban, Suburban, and Rural Classrooms throughout the Nation?" *Elementary English*, 1973, *50*, pp. 745–747.

18. B. Eleeman, "Poetry from Two Sides," *The Bulletin*, 1987, *13*(2), p. 10.

19. A. McClure, "Crystal Moments: Sharing Fine Poetry with Children," *The Bulletin*, 1987, *13*(2), p. 3.

20. *Children's Choices for 1986* and *Children's Choices for 1987* (Newark, Delaware: International Reading Association).

21. All titles in this section appear in *Adventuring with Books* (National Council of Teachers of English, 1985).

22. Most of the titles listed appear in S. Dreyer's *The Bookfinder: When Kids Need Books* (Circle Pines, Minnesota: American Guidance Service, 1985).

23. R. Bishop, "Extending Multicultural Understanding Through Children's Books," in *Children's Literature in the Reading Program*, B. Cullinan, ed. (Newark, Delaware: International Reading Association, 1987), pp. 60–61.

24. All titles in this section appear in *Adventuring with Books* (National Council of Teachers of English, 1985) or in *The Bookfinder: When Kids Need Books* (American Guidance Service, 1985).

25. M. Reed, "Children's and Teachers' Recall and Reactions to Read Aloud Books," *Dissertation Abstracts, International*, 1981, 4280-A.

26. L. Lamme, *Reading Aloud to Children: A Comparative Study of Teachers and Aides*. Unpublished research report, 1977.

27. J. W. Stewig, "Choral Speaking: Who Has the Time? Why Take the Time?" *Childhood Education*, 1981, *57*, p. 25.

28. A. Purves, "ERIC/RCS Report: Testing in Literature," *Language Arts*, 1986, *63*, p. 320.

29. J. Glazer, *Literature for Young Children*, 2nd ed. (Columbus, Ohio: Merrill, 1986), p. 69.

Part E   Language Arts for Every Child

Chapter
14 Teaching Linguistically
Different Children

Teaching Linguistically Different Children 14

Major Chapter Goals

After studying Chapter 14, the reader will be able to

1. Distinguish among the three groups of children presently described as limited English proficient.
2. Understand the stages in the acquisition of English language skills by nonnatives.
3. Explain the guidelines for teaching standard English to nonstandard-English speakers.

Discover As You Read This Chapter Whether*

1. Limited-English-proficient students currently include only those who are learning English as a second language.
2. Some bilingual students are predominantly English speakers.
3. More than 10 percent of all Americans come from non-English-speaking homes.
4. At any given time the limited-English-proficient students are at a higher level in external language skills than they are in the corresponding internal language skills.
5. Highly motivated learners of English as a second language are those students who are most eager to identify with English speakers.
6. Beginning ESL learners often go through a silent period that may last for several weeks or months.
7. Dialect properly refers to incorrect or corrupted speech.
8. There are three dialect regions in the United States.
9. Upon entering school, children must abandon any nonstandard dialect they have learned at home.
10. Children's literature may be used to teach standard English to young students.

*Answers to these true-or-false statements may be found in Appendix 5.

The term *linguistically different children* describes elementary school students who do not speak standard English but who speak another language or dialect. Saville-Troike considers three linguistically different groups as LEP, or Limited-English-Proficient:

1. Those who acquire a language other than English in early childhood and then learn the English language as a second language upon starting school.
2. Those who have apparently been placed in a "subtractive" bilingual situation in which they are exposed to both an ancestral language and English in early childhood but seem not to have developed fluency in either language by the time they start school.
3. Those for whom English is the native and only language but who acquire a nonstandard variety that differs markedly from the kind used in written texts and by teachers.[1]

Children in the first group acquire language as part of the native culture in the home and community. They are likely to be fairly recent arrivals in the United States, and yet, for a number of reasons, they prove to be least at risk academically in this setting. The native language of these students is a primary medium for transmitting other aspects of their culture so that if the children remain in contact with their native culture, their first language proficiency will expand to include new role relationships in which they participate, new concepts which they develop, and new domains in which they function. By the time these children start their formal education at the age of five or six, they have already learned the rules of behavior considered proper for their role in community life. They have internalized many of the basic beliefs and values of the families into which they were born, the community of which they are a part, and the environment in which they live. In other words, they have learned how to learn.

When students in this first group learn English as a second language in regions where it is the language of the dominant culture, English must eventually be able to serve many of the same functions for them as it does for native speakers; it can be a medium of instruction and allow participation in expanding role relationships and social domains. Consequently, second-language speakers must be able to function according to the rules of the English-dominant American culture at least part of the time. The process for children acquiring a second culture is *acculturation,* or the addition of a second set of behavior rules that may either replace the first set, modify it, or coexist beside it. One possible result is *anomie,* the rejection of both sets of behavior rules, which of course has serious negative educational and psychological consequences.

Children in the second group are considered "bilingual" but actually have not developed fluency in either their first or second language. Research has shown that (1) from 25 percent to more than 50 percent of these students are no more proficient in their first language than they are in English, and that (2) English, rather than the first language, is their predominant language form. In Houston, Texas, for example, more than one-third of the district's 34,000 "bilingual" students have been found to be predominantly English-speaking.

One study in Illinois of 311 children who had come from other countries (and entered the English-dominant areas at ages ranging from three to twelve) showed that age of entry into the English-dominant setting is a major factor in determining whether the experience will be one of "additive bilingualism" or "subtractive bilingualism."[2] Children who first learned English between ages three and five shifted in dominance rapidly and became English-dominant within two years—even when their parents spoke only the native language at home. However, children who first encountered English between the ages of six and seven shifted more slowly; and those who did not encounter English until age eight or later shifted more slowly at first but then tended to level off after the second year. Only these older students seemed to be successful in maintaining a balance between the two tongues. A critical factor concerning bilingualism is the setting in which it occurs; in settings where bilingualism is not valued by family and community or in which English is dominant and the other language is not valued, children are much more likely to lose or fail to develop fully their native language skills.

Children in the third group who acquire only nonstandard English (NSE) encounter cultural and language development that is in essentially the same relationship as that for students in the first group. English is part of the native culture being learned in early childhood, and words and sentences are first given meaning only because they are embedded in the context of interaction. That interaction covers not only what is immediately perceived by the child's senses but also includes his or her interpretation of the acts taking place, the emotional tone, the relationship of the participants, and other crucial aspects of the setting. The process of interaction covers linguistic, social, and cultural development. What must not be forgotten is that the meaning of language forms and the norms for their interpretation rest on the social and cultural experiences of that particular community and home environment because children who speak the same language will not necessarily have the same culture. Girls and boys learning English in Alaska, for example, are not always learning the culture of the dominant English-speaking society and its schools. Similar linguistic forms may develop in various settings, but it is the cultural differences that entail the distinctions in the ways that those forms are used and the differences in the meanings that are based on experience.

Children in this third category generally do less well academically in U.S. schools than do students in the first category who may enroll with no English whatsoever. For this group of children, the label LEP reflects differences between the variety of English they have acquired in their homes and communities and the variety needed and demanded by the schools. Surveys conducted by state departments of education in Texas, New York, and Illinois as well as by the U.S. Commission on Civil Rights in California, New Mexico, Arizona, and Colorado show that it is the speakers of nonstandard English—not of other languages— that attain the lowest academic achievement of all (monolingual English *and* bilingual) students. It is suspected that a differing language of instruction is only one dimension of traditional cultural discontinuity between home and school.

This Asian student is part of the fastest growing ethnic minority group in the United States, and her elementary school must provide learning situations to help her become a participating member of the classroom and total community. (© James L. Shaffer.)

Teaching and Learning English as a Second Language

According to the recent United States Census, 11 percent of all Americans come from non-English-speaking homes.[3] They live in all fifty states, and they comprise over 25 percent of the population in Hawaii and New Mexico and between 16 and 25 percent of the population of Arizona, California, Connecticut, Louisiana, Massachusetts, New Jersey, New York, North Dakota, Rhode Island, and Texas. Briefly, the non-English minority constitutes 10 percent or more of the total population in twenty-three states scattered all over the country, with the fastest growing ethnic minority group being the Asians. Of these millions of non-English speakers, an estimated eight million are children enrolled in United States schools.

The elementary school program must therefore provide a structured learning situation that will help all of its students become participating members of the classroom and the total community. An ESL, or English as a Second Language, program incorporates four general goals for learning English as a second language. First, students must be able to carry on and understand a conversation with a native English speaker on topics of interest to persons of their peer group. Second, students must be able to read materials in English with comprehension, ease, and enjoyment, consistent with their level of oral proficiency. Third, students must be able to write correctly (and in time creatively) in English consistent with their level of oral proficiency. And finally, students must recognize the differences between their own culture and that of their English-speaking peers, as expressed through the various arts.

Guidelines for Instruction

Because teachers are ultimately accountable for all formal instruction that occurs in their classrooms, their skill in working with LEP students who have little or no knowledge of English will be related to their understanding of the types of conditions that help establish a strong language-learning environment. Guidelines for assisting this LEP group in the elementary school are as follows:

1. Orient the student to the school setting and to the classroom. Take him or her on a school tour, pointing out the principal's office, the media center, the bathroom, and other important sites. It may also be helpful to draw maps of the school and classroom.
2. Teach the student survival vocabulary, including phrases, courtesy words, and greetings.
3. Attempt to find an older student (or an adult from the community) who speaks both English and the child's native language to serve as a temporary aide for helping the child adjust to the American classroom.
4. Ask the child's classmates to serve as "buddies" by helping the newcomer on the playground, in the cafeteria, and during other school activities involving language.
5. Encourage the child to speak only when he or she is ready, and be patient during the "silent period," which may last for several weeks or even months.
6. Accept the accent of the newcomer in order to promote communication. Phonological changes will occur later, during interaction with native English speakers.
7. Use resources already in the classroom or in the school. Manipulatives and readiness materials of many kinds usually found in kindergarten and first-grade rooms can be adapted for use in upper primary and intermediate grades as well.
8. Develop questions that require multiple-word answers and for which there is no one single correct response. This will prevent rote replies that are often meaningless during ordinary conversation or written communication.
9. Talk with the child in normal tones and on a variety of topics. She or he must be given many opportunities to converse in the classroom. It is important not to correct mistakes (until the child is secure or asks for such assistance) but to use modeling of acceptable responses instead.
10. Smile genuinely to show the newcomer that you are pleased that she or he is enrolled in your class and that you want to help *every* child learn.

Second-Language-Learning Model

The model in Table 14.1 is patterned after the well-known Bloom's Taxonomy and represents the cognitive aspects of second-language learning described at six levels. Each level builds on the skills and concepts acquired at previous levels, and the line of dots between levels three and four represents a threshold level of proficiency. Levels 1–3 cover survival language skills, and levels 4–6 concern more

Table 14.1
Second Language Learning Model

Cognitive Domain Taxonomy	Linguistic Process	Internal Language Skills	External Language Skills
1 Knowledge	Recalling	Discrimination of and response to sounds, words, and unanalyzed chunks in listening. Identification of labels, letters, phrases in reading.	Production of single words and formulas; imitation of models. Handwriting, spelling, writing of known elements from dictation.
2 Comprehension	Recombining	Recognition of and response to new combinations of known words and phrases in listening and oral reading. Internal translation to and from L_1.	Emergence of interlanguage/ telegraphic speech; code-switching and L_1 transfer. Writing from guidelines and recombination dictation.
		———Social Interaction———	
3 Application	Communicating	Understanding meaning of what is listened to in informal situations. Emergence of silent reading for basic comprehension.	Communication of meaning, feelings, and intentions in social and highly contextualized situations. Emergence of expository and creative writing.
4 Analysis	Informing	Acquisition of factual information from listening and reading in decontextualized situations.	Application of factual information acquired to formal, academic speaking and writing activities.
5 Synthesis	Generalizing	Use of information acquired through reading and listening to find relationships, make inferences, draw conclusions.	Explanation of relationships, inferences, and conclusions through formal speech and writing.
6 Evaluation	Judging	Evaluation of accuracy, value, and applicability of ideas acquired through reading and listening.	Expression of judgments through speech and writing. Use of rhetorical conventions.

Source: Reprinted from Anna Uhl Chamot, "Toward a Functional ESL Curriculum in the Elementary School," TESOL QUARTERLY, 1983, 17, p. 462, fig. 1. Used with permission of publisher and Anna Uhl Chamot.

academic language used for instructional purposes. Teachers must realize that, at any given time, the children are at a higher level in receptive skills (internal language skills) than they are in the corresponding productive or external language skills.

The language proficiency of levels 1–3 is the language of social communication, or *context-embedded,* communicative proficiency, which is crucial to a child's adjustment to a new culture and language.[4] It allows him or her to interact socially and affectively with others. Recent Canadian research has shown that most young children attain native-speaker ability in this type of language proficiency within two years of exposure to an English-speaking environment.[5] This may be due in part to the fact that the social context includes a variety of paralinguistic aids to comprehension (e.g., gestures, intonation, objects).

Levels 4–6 cover *context-reduced,* or academic, communicative proficiency, which is used in content subjects and on achievement tests. It is related to cognition and to the more formal language used to refer to concepts. Because it exists primarily in books (and oral lectures), children can understand the words and phrases only when they comprehend the concepts expressed. Most boys and girls need five to seven years to reach a context-reduced level in English comparable to that of native-speaking peers. This gap may be shortened if more academic language skills are taught within the ESL curriculum.

Strategies and Second-Language Learning

Recently 450 children's conversations that occurred in classroom or play activities across the United States were recorded from such diverse native-language groups as Italian, Spanish, Haitian, Chinese, Portuguese, and Japanese.[6] The conversations were then analyzed for strategies that are used often by children learning English as a second language, regardless of their first language. Such strategies allow children to exploit available information to improve their own competence in the second language and also allow boys and girls to communicate in social situations. They can be divided into two major groups: cognitive-developmental and social-affective.

Cognitive-Developmental Strategies

The three strategies in this group are described chronologically as bridging, chunking, and creating. In *bridging,* children tie English words to concepts they already understand in their first language. Pictures, objects, and actions are important. The children go from perception to understanding to labeling, and they depend heavily on the skills of the teacher to present words in meaningful contexts. The vocabulary must be organized into units and gradually expanded. All senses must be utilized in teaching vocabulary through such unit presentations as A Trip to the Zoo, Building a House, Buying New Shoes, or Going to the Restaurant. Learning games and activities, along with various word cards, are all helpful.

The second strategy, *chunking,* occurs when girls and boys imitate chunks of the second language. Such chunks consist of phrases or units of more than one word that are memorized as wholes rather than as segments. They serve as a transition from labeling to sentence fluency and are best remembered when they have a special meaning for the child or can be directly related to experience. They are not learned in isolation but must be practiced in social interactions where they make sense. As girls and boys receive language input from their environment, they selectively imitate those chunks, or phrases, that have meaning for them; then they proceed to use those chunks holistically again and again. Teachers are cautioned, however, not to plan drill or habit-formation lessons divorced from gamelike situations. Such sterile drills have little transfer value and cannot be ultimately integrated into sentence patterns promoting communicative fluency. Incidentally, among the first chunks of language mastered by second-language pupils are social greetings.

During *creating,* the final cognitive-developmental strategy, children are able to combine the words (acquired during bridging) and the phrases (learned during chunking) to express their ideas creatively. When girls and boys first begin to learn English as a second language, they do so without any comprehension of its underlying structure. Gradually, however, their syntactic development in English begins as they break down chunks and analyze them into component parts in order to build many new sentences.[7] Teachers must accept the fact that boys and girls acquire both their first and their second languages by learning how to carry on a conversation.[8] Classroom curricula must encourage children to become involved in as many highly specific language interactions as possible, with channeled conversations ranking as one of the best media for the development of the creative use of the second language. For that end, the following has been stressed:

1. The perception of patterns should be emphasized, not the intensity of the practice.
2. The teacher should respond to what the children are saying rather than to the grammatical structures they use to say it.
3. The teacher should plan lessons involving language patterns in gamelike settings and verbal play with partial repetitions of sentences and appropriate expansions of pupil sentences.
4. Above all, language should be integrated in all subject-matter teaching, not restricted to a twenty-minute segment in the day. Only thus can the ESL students become creators.[9]

Social-Affective Strategies

There are nine strategies that children use naturally.[10] The first of these is a *receptive-expressive strategy,* which can be labeled *listening in and sounding out.* It involves listening comprehension and expressive fluency and is based on numerous research findings indicating that the development of listening skills must precede, not accompany, the development of speaking skills. Some of these studies have been done by James Asher, utilizing the Total Physical Response approach, which requires that beginning students not respond verbally to commands in the second language but instead respond with appropriate physical actions.[11] It appears that delayed oral practice during the early stages of second-language learning can effectively develop both listening and speaking skills, provided there is a substantial period of active listening practice together with numerous physical responses.

Listening comprehension, or "listening in," can be developed through the expressive arts, employing listening posts with headsets and using pictures and objects. The second, or "sounding out," portion of this first strategy occurs when children engage in sound play as they chant in sing-song rhythms or make repetitive vocalizations. Both are important phases that allow children eventually to make associations from the sounds of words to the meanings of words, thereby promoting social interactions.

Follow the phrase, or the *pattern-practice strategy,* is the second social-affective strategy, and it is primarily concerned with the learning of the syntax of the second language. Word patterns are practiced and eventually varied by changing one or more words. Teachers, however, must provide many opportunities for the children to creatively experiment with the language already acquired, regardless of how limited it may be, so that pattern practice does not become mechanical and meaningless. When phrases are tied to a topic (e.g., Foods I Like) and practiced in gamelike situations, teachers can utilize all four types of pattern drills (chain, question-answer, repetition, and substitution) effectively. Later, children are able to transfer meaningful patterns to new social contexts.

Socializing, the third and *formal-informal-style social-relations strategy* in this group, represents a process by which girls and boys acquire social expressions holistically as chunks. They hear the expressions during various communication contexts (e.g., structured sports activities, games, cooperative learning group discussions), imitate them, and finally apply them to other appropriate social settings. Because language learned during interaction is always modified by the immediate situation, socializing must be considered an accommodating strategy. Essential to the development of a second language are the following social relations components: having social interaction, establishing and maintaining relationships or friendships by using social formulas, acquiring formal and information language styles, receiving feedback from teachers and peers, and possessing social skills that further language learning. Teachers must use both controlled exercises and decontrolled activities in order to help boys and girls acquire language naturally.

When children use gestural (involving sensory-motor actions), visual, or interpersonal cues for linguistic problem solving, they are pursuing an *inference-guessing strategy* labeled *cueing.* They are anxious to derive meaning from verbal input and rely on more proficient language speakers to give them cues. Because their desire to communicate is strong, they actively seek to interpret cues to better decode the meaning of language and eventually participate fully in the speech arena. Major functions of the teacher's cueing are to promote dialogue and demonstrate meaning. Advantages of cueing the second-language learner in classroom situations include the following: students are prompted to infer meanings and respond correctly; they are encouraged to participate actively (not passively); student attention is carefully directed; and boys and girls are given corrective feedback and compelled to understand exactly structures and vocabulary that may often go unnoticed.

An *imitative-repetitive strategy* known as *peer prompting* enables children to acquire the second language through modeling and feedback. Boys and girls learn from each other and are able to acquire language from both patterned and spontaneous encounters that demand verbal exchanges. Peer pairs can consist of one dominant or proficient English-speaking child who serves as a model and one child with only limited expressive ability in the language. Often the LEP pupil acquires a friend along with increased English vocabulary and grammatical structures during play interactions or even during subject-matter activities. The peer model uses repetition in an effort to encourage the LEP child to imitate correct speech. This kind of buddy system is a flexible approach demanding only the interaction of two children who become involved in language on personal, emotional, and academic levels.

The sixth social-affective strategy encourages switching to the language the listener knows best so that he or she can convey cultural meaning to others, and it is termed *wearing two hats*. It is a *bilingual-bicultural strategy* and is most successful with children who have internalized the following aspects of both languages: a sense of personal identity with each language; social situational meanings upon which effective communication is based and code-switching is employed; cultural beliefs, attitudes, and values; emotional and psychological factors because language enforces and reinforces behavior; and linguistic flexibility, which is an enriching dimension. Because language and culture cannot be separated, the strategy of *wearing two hats* is best developed in a multidimensional setting of bilingual-bicultural education.

When second-language learning occurs through a *role-playing strategy,* it can be termed *copycatting.* It involves dramatic dialogues in the classroom, both as free, imaginative role-play and as structured role-play activities. Boys and girls imitate language and also learn to use their hands, faces, and bodies to portray emotions. They become able to integrate English expression into a complete system of communication and conversational competency. They develop empathy and problem-solving skills because role-playing concentrates language around student attitudes, interests, concerns, and feelings. Further opportunities for practicing the second language evolve creatively.

The eighth social-affective strategy bridges motivational, social, and cognitive predispositions into several styles of second-language learning and is termed *putting it together.* Children learn language by various routes, processes, or styles, of which three have been labeled *beading, braiding,* and *orchestrating.* The first frames language in terms of semantics or word meanings and strings words one after another, focusing attention on content rather than form. The second frames language around syntax or language patterns and chunks words together into phrases so that attention is paid to form and the sequence of words. Orchestrating is occupied with phonology or the sounds of the language, placing initial emphasis on listening comprehension and concentrating on sounds first as syllables, then as words, and then as sentences.

As teachers begin to recognize the beaders, braiders, and orchestrators within any one classroom, they must plan group lessons accordingly. Beaders require highly structured lessons that do not contain too many concepts at once. Braiders prefer social interaction and function best in a fairly open-ended environment. Because orchestrators stress auditory input, they enjoy songs and other rhythmic poems or chants and are continually imitating the teacher's language behavior. Since the goal of the ESL program is to permit boys and girls to learn

English in the style that is most suitable to them, the teacher must be familiar with the major learning styles in order to define the learners and gain new insight into instructional planning.

The final and ninth affective strategy, known as *choosing the way,* describes children's three motivational styles in acquiring a second language. When boys and girls lack the desire to identify with English speakers, they also lack the motivation to learn the English language. Conversely, those who have a strong desire to identify with English speakers also possess a strong motivation to acquire the language. Because the primary model of the second language and culture is the teacher, it is important that the teacher's relationship with the students be a strong, positive, and sensitive one.

In their effort to resolve a psychosocial identity crisis, minority children can adopt any one of three *motivational styles* that reflect the owner's preferred way of participating in second-language acquisition. The first is called *crystalizing* and includes boys and girls who initially reject the second language because they want to maintain their identity with their first language culture. They crystalize their native language identity and refuse to participate in any interaction that would lead to learning the new language and culture. They also refuse to speak English until they are able to do so perfectly. As passive second-language learners, they are highly dependent on structured classroom activities and communicate with the teacher in English only when prodded to do so. Basically they are shy children who are cautious learners, stressing the receptive, not expressive, understanding of the English language. Only as a final step do they express themselves socially in the second language.

On the other hand, children who use the *crossing over* motivational style choose to identify with the second culture rather than their first culture, even to the extent of giving up speaking in their first language in the classroom. They interact with English speakers and capitalize on every opportunity to practice the new language both in and out of school. They admire English speakers and are anxious to identify with them, believing that immersion in the second language is the quickest method for developing proficiency. They are active language learners, flexible, impulsive, and independent.

The third motivational style, *crisscrossing,* applies to children who identify equally with both cultures and readily adapt languages to the situations that occur. They switch back and forth between languages and cultures, adopting a bicultural identity. They are versatile, spontaneous, and adaptable, adjusting communication patterns comfortably. They are able to socialize between groups of English speakers and native-language speakers.

Although no one motivational style is better than another, the teacher must comprehend how children differ in their approaches to learning English as a second language. Because the teacher represents the role model of the second language and the second culture, the more the boys and girls can identify positively with their teacher and their English-speaking classmates, the more easily they will adjust to the English language and culture. The teacher must make every effort

Figure 14.1. Cardona Oral Language Index: States in the Acquisition of English.*

Acquisition of Syntax	Acquisition of Semantic Structures
Stage 1	
1. Yes/no answers	1. Sentences with 1 part: agent or object or locative (attribute + noun = 1 part)
2. Positive statements	
3. Subject pronouns: *he, she*, etc.	
4. Present habitual verb tense	2. Sentences with 2 parts agent + action or + object or + locative action + object or + locative
5. Possessive pronouns; *my, your*, etc.	
Stage 2	
1. Simple plurals of nouns	1. Substitution of pronouns for nouns
2. Affirmative sentences	2. Fragmentary grammar
3. Subject and object pronouns (all)	3. Beginning regularization of sentence order
4. Possessives: *'s*	4. Sentence with 3+ parts: agent + *to* action/infinitive/ + object, or action + agent + object or locative, or agent + object + action or locative
5. Negation	
6. Possessive pronouns: *mine*, etc.	
Stage 3	
1. Present progressive tense	1. Regularized sentence order
2. Conjunctions: *and, but, or, because, so, as*, etc.	2. Conjoining with *and*, using deletions
	3. Addition of modifiers: agent + (modifier) action + object or locative

to match instructional strategies with children's motivational styles: indirect methods for Crystalizers, integration of English into the total school program for Crossovers, and additive bilingualism for Crisscrossers. Through individualization in ESL instruction, teachers can employ learning centers or other classroom arrangements that allow students to learn English easily and confidently.

Stages in the Acquisition of English Language Skills

It has been recognized for some time that English language skills of nonnatives develop in much the same sequential and definite way as do those of native speakers. These stages, described in the Cardona Oral Language Index, are shown in Figure 14.1. This Index has been used well by teachers of English-Spanish bilingual children in the Pacific Northwest to assess the stage of productive English language skill of each nonnative student as well as to evaluate the language demands of first-grade basals used for beginning English reading.[12]

Prior to Stage 1, a child may well exhibit a "silent period" until he or she becomes comfortable with the English-speaking environment. During the first stage, most commonly heard are one- and two-word utterances (usually consisting of nouns, verbs, or a combination of the two) that cover a multitude of

Acquisition of Syntax	Acquisition of Semantic Structures	Figure 14.1. (cont.)

Stage 4

1. Questions: *who? what? which? where?*
2. Irregular plurals of nouns
3. Simple future tense: *going to.*
4. Prepositions

1. Sentence with 4 parts:
   agent + action + 2 other parts, selected from
   additional agent, agent modifier, action modifier,
   1–2 objects, object modifier, locative

Initial reading readiness

Stage 5

1. Future tense: *will*
2. Questions: *when? how?*
3. Conjunctions: *either, nor, neither, that, since,* etc.

1. Sentence with 5+ parts
   agent + action + 3 other parts, additional agent, agent in additional action,
   1–2 objects, object modifier, locative

Stage 6

1. Regular past tense verbs
2. Question: *why?*
3. Contractions: *isn't,* etc.
4. Modal verbs: *can, must,* etc., and *do*

1. Permutations in word order
2. Substitution of phrases and sentence parts

Stage 7

1. Verb tense: irregular past
2. Past tense questions
3. Auxiliary verbs: *has, is*
4. Passive voice

Stage 8

1. Verbs: conditional
2. Summary of verb forms
3. Verb tense: the imperfect
4. Conjunctions: *though, if, therefore,* etc.
5. Verb mood: subjunctive

*Adapted from Cardona, 1980Source: Reprinted from Phillip C. Gonzales ''Beginning English Reading for ESL Students,'' READING TEACHER, November 1981. Reprinted with permission of Phillip C. Gonzales and the International Reading Association.

situations and that allow the speaker to appear to comprehend what is going on at any given time. Sample utterances would include "yes," "no," and "my turn." Egocentric speech also occurs.

During Stages 2 and 3, there is frequent mixing of English and native language. The concern appears to be communication by any means possible. Children use more readily recognized language and sentence structure.

During each of the subsequent stages boys and girls incorporate additional sentence parts (such as modifiers or objects) into the basic sentence utterances.

Each such addition indicates an increase in the acquisition of complex language; for example, the use of prepositional phrases during Stage 4 and the use of conjunctions during Stage 5.

By the conclusion of Stage 5, the children have a language that is related to initial reading readiness. They are then capable of making judgments concerned with correctness of form and may even ask for adult approval regarding such "correctness." They understand several hundred words and have refined both their lexical knowledge and their use through actual language practice in numerous situations.

During the final Stages—6, 7, and 8—boys and girls begin to experiment with changes in the order of parts of sentences and also start to substitute phrases and clauses for the main portions of sentences. They can use language well for purposes of problem solving or hypothesis testing.

Using the Oral Language Index

The teacher can determine the language proficiency of any nonnative child by tape-recording samples of spontaneous, informal speech that occur during non-threatening situations between student and teacher evaluator. During this initial use of the Cardona Index, language samples are first examined for grammatical forms and their location in the Index; for example, "Why does it rain?" relates to Stage 6 and "why" questions. Then the same samples are examined for types of grammatical structures by identifying and counting major sentence parts. Also at this point, they are inspected to see whether the samples follow the common English order: subject, action, object or locative.

Such analysis of a child's conversational language easily reveals the boy's or girl's command and use of various syntax structures and forms. It helps the teacher locate reading materials with syntax at (or not too far above) the level of the student's listening and speaking abilities. Obviously this is significant during the beginning stages of English reading.

Consequently, a second use of the Oral Language Index occurs during an examination of the linguistic demands made by various first-grade basals. If too great a discrepancy exists between the language used in a particular text and the actual language proficiency of the young reader, the teacher must plan special lessons stressing language structures and grammatical forms found in that chosen text. If, however, a better match occurs between the language used by the beginning reader and that printed in the book, the teacher may then plan more lessons in comprehension and word-attack skills.

A third and final use of the Oral Language Index takes place when the teacher initially examines the text for linguistic structures that have proven difficult for many ESL speakers and then proceeds to plan lessons around those structures and forms in an effort to aid comprehension and promote reading enjoyment. It has been suggested that, in this instance, direct and concrete hands-on experiences might be best, especially if teachers use language that is both appropriate to the situation and readily understood by the ESL students.[13] Role-playing and the employment of visuals are both effective. Another suggestion

Activities planned for individualized instruction or small-group sessions, whether indoors or outdoors, promote language learning in a setting where the language is a vehicle of true communication. (© Dianne Carter.)

calls upon the teacher to simplify the language found in the basal to structures already familiar to the nonnative pupil; for example, writing several simple sentences on the chalkboard based on one lengthy compound sentence.

Briefly, then, an efficient ESL teacher about to introduce reading to the class will first assess the language proficiency of the children, then evaluate the structures found in the assigned books, and finally plan lessons so that the LEP pupils will comprehend the language used in the reading books.

Instructional Activities

Activity-centered classrooms promote language learning in a setting in which the language is not an object of study but a vehicle of real communication.[14] Repetition occurs often and naturally as the learners interact with the teacher and with their peers in real situations. The newly discovered English language becomes a tool for cognitive growth, thereby promoting the learning of additional vocabulary and structures.

Other advantages of such classrooms include a nonthreatening atmosphere that allows physical movement during the lessons and support for self-concept development in areas such as problem solving and decision making. The interaction with their classmates gives children immediate feedback on their language performance or product at an impersonal level directed at the information presented. The motivation to communicate is strong, and students assume some degree of responsibility for their own progress.

Activities may be divided into in-school and out-of-school categories, the former including (1) events that commonly take place during the school year, such as science fairs; (2) academic themes, including an art unit on colors; and (3) development of personal skills through various projects such as cooking.[15] Out-of-school activities involve field trips and the celebrations of regional festivities.

Specific classroom activities planned for individualized instruction have been outlined by Rodrigues and White and are described in this section according to their levels of difficulty.[16] Each can of course be readily adapted to small-group or even large-group sessions.

Beginning-Level activities include the following:

Rhyming. The purpose is to give the child a chance to recall as many English words as possible which rhyme with words the teacher uses (e.g., *map, run, say, ant, wing*). The teacher says one of the words, and the student offers as many rhyming words as possible. Or the teacher says three words that are alike but of which only two rhyme, and the child must choose the word that does not rhyme. Sometimes the teacher begins a couplet with a line that ends with a word to be rhymed, and the pupil must respond accordingly with the next line. (This is strictly a listening and speaking exercise).

Acting Out Emotions. The teacher prepares flash cards containing English words stating emotions (e.g., *afraid, happy, sad, angry, excited*). The teacher displays one flash card at a time to the student and acts out the emotion. Then the pupil holds each card and acts out the appropriate emotion. Later, three flash cards are shown simultaneously to the student, and he or she must point to and pronounce the word for the one emotion the teacher is acting out.

Vocabulary Around the House. The teacher collects pictures of rooms in various houses and shows them one at a time to the student. The child must name all the objects that he or she can identify in the pictures and must also relate how each is used. The teacher then reviews the pictures and names any objects the student has missed, asking the boy or girl to repeat the names of the objects originally omitted. Later, the student may draw a map of the objects in his or her own bedroom, living room, or kitchen.

Beginning- to Intermediate-Level activities include:

Using a Telephone. The teacher reviews with the student the following terms: *ring* or *ringing, telephone, dial tone, busy signal, information, area code, operator, receiver, telephone number.* If the boy or girl is unfamiliar with any of the terms, the teacher should draw a picture or demonstrate by using sounds and gestures. Finally, the teacher and the pupil role-play the following situations:
_____ The teacher calls the student to give a message.
_____ The student calls and gets a busy signal.

_____ The student dials the operator for assistance in reporting a fire.

_____ The student places a local call at a pay telephone.

_____ The student calls the teacher to give a message.

Asking Directions in a New Town. The teacher supplies a map of the local city (or any other city) and reviews with the student the following key terms: *left, right, street, avenue, sign, stop, straight, turn, traffic light.* Common expressions of courtesy are also reviewed. The teacher and the student take turns pretending to be a newcomer in town and a police officer or other information provider. The map may be used to answer such model questions as *Where is the _____ ? How do I get to the _____ ?* First responses must be brief, but later ones may become more complex.

Giving Dictation to the Teacher. The purpose is to give the child a chance to discuss in English a topic mutually agreed upon by teacher and student. The child dictates to the teacher-secretary who spells and punctuates all sentences properly but is careful to write down exactly what has been said. Later, the two go over the composition, and the student is encouraged to correct or improve the language. Possible topics for dictation include favorite television shows, hobbies, and ways that the child's native land differs from that of the teacher.

Taking Dictation from the Teacher. The teacher selects a book that is apt to interest the student and meet his or her ability level. As the teacher slowly reads aloud short selections from the book, the student must write down the passages. A second reading aloud by the teacher of the same selections is done at a normal rate of speed so that the boy or girl may check the dictation. A third reading is done by the student who reads alone from the handwritten copy. The fourth and final reading is done by teacher and student working together from the student copy and noting any mistakes. Incidentally, during all the readings, the punctuation marks are read aloud also (e.g., Hello comma how are you question mark).

Intermediate-Level activities include:

Visiting a Library. The purpose is to give the child a chance to visit the library media center to learn how to locate and check out a book. Upon arrival at the center, the teacher introduces the child to the following terms: *librarian, library, card catalog, check-out desk, stacks, media center, reference section, library card.* The teacher also introduces the following model questions: (a) How do I find a book about _____ ? (b) Where is the card catalog? (c) When is this book due? The visit culminates with the student locating and checking out a book selected earlier by the teacher because it would especially interest that child.

Table Manners. The teacher places in front of the boy or girl all of the following items: tablespoon, teaspoon, knife, dinner fork, salad fork, cup and saucer, dinner plate, bread plate, salt shaker. The teacher picks up one item at a time, names it, and asks the student to repeat the name.

Then the teacher demonstrates how Americans eat at the table and discusses with the student such matters as the proper way to hold a fork, the polite way to ask for salt or butter or any other food on the table, and the correct way to cut a piece of meat and eat it. The teacher and student should practice their table manners as often as it seems necessary.

Teaching and Learning English as a Standard Dialect

Some people mistakenly assume that *dialect* refers to corrupted, inadequate, or incorrect speech. Actually the term implies no value judgment. It refers merely to a habitual variety of usage or to a distinct variation in how a language is spoken. Dialects are fully formed systems. Every language has dialects, and its native speakers use several dialects to meet the many needs of daily life.

Speakers of a particular dialect form a *speech community* that reflects the members' life styles or professional, national, family, or ethnic backgrounds. Certain common features mark the speech of the members, however these features may be defined.

Regional Dialect

One of the principal types of dialect is *regional,* or geographical, dialect used by speakers living in the same area. In the United States no single regional dialect is the accepted standard for the country. Instead, each area has its own standard that represents the dialect of its educated residents. The four major dialect areas in the United States today are shown in Figure 14.2. Note that the western United States does not fall as neatly into dialect boundaries as does the eastern region.

Regional dialects differ from each other in phonological, vocabulary, and syntactic or grammatical features. An example of the first difference is the "intrusive *r*" that appears in *Washington* and *wash* among residents of Indiana and Missouri. Vocabulary variety may be proved by the many synonyms for the word *relatives,* including *folks, people, kinfolk, folkses, homefolks,* and *kinnery.* Finally, a grammatical difference is the preference for *he don't* rather than *he doesn't* among residents in North Carolina. Americans are generally said to be puzzled by pronunciation differences, delighted by vocabulary differences, and repelled by grammatical differences.

On the whole, however, the speakers of American English have an advantage over those who speak the dialects of languages in most other countries where social and geographic mobility has been more limited for long periods of time. In the United States no functional block in communication normally intrudes among native speakers.

Social Dialect

Residents of the same geographical region do not all sound alike. The variations in their speech include differences in sounds, words, expressions, and sentence patterns. Such differences within a single regional speech community often correlate with social variables of occupation, isolation, education, and the resulting social status in the community. Speech variants used by one socially identifiable

Figure 14.2. Major Dialect Areas of the United States.

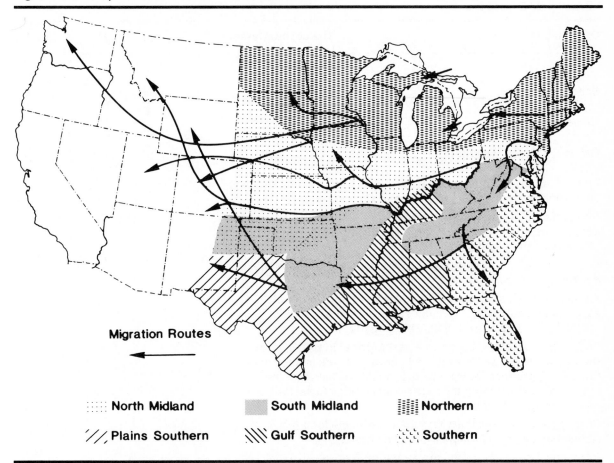

Migration Routes

<table>
</table>

:::: North Midland	▓ South Midland	▓ Northern
/// Plains Southern	\\\ Gulf Southern	∴ Southern

group of speakers comprise the second major type of dialect known as a *sociolect,*
or social dialect. Studies by sociologists and linguists—or *sociolinguists*—have
increasingly focused on this kind of dialect since the 1960s.

Sociolects are generally divided into two broad classes: standard and nonstandard dialects. Standard English (SE) is used by authors of books and news-
paper/magazine articles, by television commentators and reporters, by persons
who are generally well-educated members of occupations ranking at the middle-
to high-socioeconomic levels, and in schools. Other dialects are collectively labeled nonstandard English (NSE) and are used by persons with limited education
and mobility who interact with others of a similar background. These individuals
use nonstandard speech patterns in about 20–30 percent of their conversation.

Figure 14.3. Oral Language Rating Form for Use with Children Who Speak a Nonstandard English Dialect.

Oral Language Rating	Dialect Interference	5 Never	4 Almost Never	3 Sometimes	2 Usually	1 Almost Always

School _____ Date _____

Name _____

Grade _____ Teacher _____

Pronunciation: Distinguishes between *then* and *den; they* and *day; both* and *boat; thin* and *tin;* and *thin* and *sin.* ____ ____ ____ ____ ____

Comparison: Uses the correct form of comparison such as *bigger, biggest; more beautiful,* and *most beautiful* rather than *more bigger; beautifuller* and *beautifullest.* ____ ____ ____ ____ ____

Double Negative: Uses negative expressions, such as *don't have any* rather than *don't have none.* ____ ____ ____ ____ ____

Plurals: Distinguishes between regular and irregular plurals (i.e., says *feet* and not *foots*). Pronounces the *s*-ending of regular plurals correctly (i.e., boot*s* /s/, horse*s* /iz/, dog*s* /z/). ____ ____ ____ ____ ____

Past Tense: Uses the appropriate past forms of irregular verbs rather than participle forms (uses appropriate *I ate* instead of *I et*). Uses the appropriate past forms of irregular verbs rather than inappropriate forms with the regular *-ed* ending of past form (i.e., *I drank* instead of *I drinked* my milk). ____ ____ ____ ____ ____

Past Participles: Uses the appropriate participle form (i.e., *cut* rather than *cuted,* or *brought* rather than *brung*). ____ ____ ____ ____ ____

Pronouns: Uses appropriate pronoun form. ____ ____ ____ ____ ____

Uses of Do: Uses appropriate forms of *DO* in questions, in answers, and in negative statements. ____ ____ ____ ____ ____

Uses of Be: Uses, rather than omits, appropriate forms of *BE.* ____ ____ ____ ____ ____

Uses of Have: Uses, rather than omits, appropriate forms of *HAVE.* ____ ____ ____ ____ ____

Subject-Verb Agreement: Uses correct verb form when he or she is used as subject. Verb form has appropriate ending sound (i.e., *he takes* /s/, *he watches* /iz/, *he wears* /z/, rather than uninflected or simple forms (i.e., *he take, he watch, he wear*). ____ ____ ____ ____ ____

Source: *Michigan Oral Language Series* (New York: American Council on the Teaching of Foreign Languages, 1969).

Children also reflect a nonstandard or standard social dialect in their speech. Although this dialect is hardly the result of occupation or formal educational background, it is the social dialect used by the children's parents, neighbors, and friends. If boys and girls mature in a language-learning environment filled with standard dialect speakers, they are likely to speak a standard dialect. Similarly, if children are surrounded by nonstandard dialect speakers, they will typically speak a nonstandard dialect. An oral language rating form which teachers can use with pupils who speak a nonstandard English dialect is found in Figure 14.3.

Upon entering school however, children who speak a nonstandard dialect are no longer limited to speaking that one dialect for the rest of their lives. In school they learn a second and alternative dialect—the standard dialect—and gradually become able to *style-shift* from one dialect to the other depending upon the topic-setting and the number and identity of the participants. They retain the right to use their own first and nonstandard dialect in speech and writing. Furthermore, they gain an equal right to acquire a second and standard dialect for the same communicative purposes.

Guidelines for Instruction

Eight areas of language arts instruction needed for NSE students have been identified and rank as follows in order of importance: (1) understanding spoken SE, (2) reading books written in SE, (3) communicating effectively through talk, (4) communicating effectively through writing, (5) using SE forms in writing, (6) spelling words correctly, (7) using SE forms in talk, and (8) using SE pronunciation.[17]

Because the matter of teaching standard English as a second dialect is a critical problem in many parts of the country, particularly in urban areas, the teacher must respect the language of the NSE speakers and be sensitive to their needs. What these children know should be valued in the classroom and utilized. Furthermore, the teacher must also learn about the features of NSE in order to comprehend the frustrations and problem areas that NSE students encounter when learning to become literate in standard English. If the teacher will also demonstrate a confidence that the students can handle two or more dialects, the NSE speakers will learn more readily.

To teach standard English, some schools adapt techniques from ESL instruction, pointing up differences between SE and NSE expressions. Other schools prefer to use children's literature as a model because accompanying activities such as creative drama, story telling, and discussion promote oral communication using standard patterns.

One program for kindergarten or primary children combines features of both approaches and comprises three steps.[18] *The first step introduces the new pattern of expression* from among eight major contrasts between SE and NSE: plurals, possessives, person-number agreement, past tense, present participle, negative, verb "to be" in present tense, and verb "to be" in past tense. Once the standard-nonstandard contrast has been selected, the teacher also chooses an appropriate book from Table 14.2 to use in introducing the new pattern to the group.

Table 14.2
Pattern Books to Teach the Standard/Nonstandard English Contrasts.

SE/NSE Contrast	Sample Book	Book's Pattern	Step 2 and 3 Sample Activities	Other Books

Plural	*The Very Hungry Caterpillar*	The very hungry caterpillar eats through:
		   1 apple
		   2 pear*s*
		   3 plum*s*, etc.
			Have children draw pictures of more foods for the caterpillar to eat. Use a hole punch to make holes in the foods. Record children's dictation to accompany the pictures.	*Goodnight Moon*
				Millions of Cats

Possessive	*Ask Mr. Bear*	Danny asks Mr. Bear and other animals, "Can you give me something for my mother's birthday?"	Have children make labels using possessives for their desks, pencils, and other belongings. Then have them read the labels aloud.	*Whose Nose Is This?*

Person-Number Agreement	*The Judge*	Each prisoner describes the horrible thing in more detail:
		   It growl*s*, it groan*s*
		   It chew*s* up stones
		   It spread*s* its wings
		   And doe*s* bad things
			Have children use collage materials to construct their own horrible things. Then record children's descriptions of their horrible things.	*Over in the Meadow*
				The Green Grass Grows All Around
				Seven Little Monsters
				The Maestro Plays
				When It Rains . . . It Rains

Past Tense	*I Know an Old Lady Who Swallowed a Fly*	This is a cumulative tale about an old lady who swallows a fly and a series of other animals to catch the fly.	Have the children make a set of finger puppets to use in retelling the story.	*Elephant in a Well* *Too Much Noise* *Goodnight, Owl* *Where the Wild Things Are* *The Haunted House* *Roll Over!* *The Enormous Turnip*
Present Participle	*Chicken Licken*	Chicken Licken warns everyone that "The sky is falling!"	Have the children act out the story.	*Someone Is Eating the Sun* *The Chick and the Duckling* *Crocodile and Hen* *Henny Penny* *The Fat Cat* *Brown Bear, Brown Bear, What Do You See?*

Table 14.2

SE/NSE Contrast	Sample Book	Book's Pattern	Step 2 and 3 Sample Activities	Other Books
Negative	*A Flower Pot Is Not a Hat*	This pattern is repeated on each page: A _____ is not a _____ .	Have children compose new sentences and record them on a chart or in individual booklets. Have children draw pictures to illustrate the sentences.	*It Looked Like Spilt Milk* *Never Hit a Porcupine* *Have You Seen My Cat?* *One Monday Morning* *The Grouchy Ladybug* *Crocodile and Hen*
Verb "to be" (Present tense)	*Where in the World Is Henry?*	Two children use questions and answers to look for Henry: Where is the bed? The bed is in the bedroom.	Have children compose new questions and answers following the same pattern. Record them on sentence strips for children to match.	*A Ghost Story* *King of the Mountain* *The Judge* *The House That Jack Built*
Verb "to be" (Past tense)	*10 Bears in My Bed*	A little boy tries to get 10 bears out of his bed. Each page begins: There were (number) in his bed and the little one said, "Roll over!"	Tape record the story leaving space on the tape for children to repeat the sentence pattern.	*There Was an Old Woman* *The Very Hungry Caterpillar* *What Good Luck! What Bad Luck!*

Source: From Gail E. Tompkins and Lea M. McGee, "Launching Nonstandard Speakers into Standard English," LANGUAGE ARTS. Copyright © 1983 by the National Council of Teachers of English. Reprinted with permission.

The teacher reads the predictable book to the children and gestures for them to repeat the pattern as soon as it has been established. For instance, in Eric Carle's counting book entitled *The Very Hungry Caterpillar* (Crowell, 1971), the pattern concerns plurals and so after "one apple," the girls and boys learn to say "two pear*s*," "three plum*s*," and so forth. Thus they are introduced to the SE plural form. The teacher then continues with the second and third steps (described next) with sample activities, using the same book.

The second step provides practice with the new standard English pattern. Although the children will first say the pattern in their own dialects, the teacher must continue to encourage them to use the SE form until they become comfortable with it. They can use that form during such practice activities as puppetry, story dramatization, or the production of tape recordings.

The third step is crucial and demands manipulating the new pattern. Children need to internalize the new SE form and can do so through inventing new content for that form. They may compose new episodes or additional verses for the story they have just heard.

When the teacher has proceeded through the three steps using one piece of children's literature, he or she should repeat the procedure using two or more other books that exemplify the same standard-nonstandard distinction. The children must become comfortable with that standard form before another SE pattern is introduced to them.

Learning Games for Limited-English-Proficient Students

The games described in Figure 14.4 are a viable and enjoyable method of attaining a variety of educational objectives.[19] They can *reinforce* newly acquired information, *review* material presented days or even weeks ago, *relax students* after grueling oral or written exercises, *raise attentiveness, aid retention, reward students, reduce inhibition* among shy or linguistically weak pupils, and allow the teacher to *rapidly rectify students' errors.* Although they provide motivation for learning, these games do not entail excessive preparation. The pictures, flash cards, or objects or materials that some of the games require are the kinds of resources routinely found in elementary classrooms.

Student responses should be in the form of complete sentences.

Figure 14.4. Fourteen Learning Games for Limited-English-Proficient Students.

Auction	1. Objects are placed on the "auction" table in front of the room, with one item secretly tagged by the teacher, who is the first "auctioneer." All the players come to the auction with an equal amount of play money.
	2. The auctioneer describes each item on the table as it comes up for auction, and each interested player is allowed to shout a bid only when he or she has been recognized by the auctioneer.
	3. A fixed number of bids should be agreed upon in advance, and the player winning the bid then walks up to the auctioneer to collect his or her purchase.
	4. The player purchasing the secret item becomes the next auctioneer.
	5. Suggestions: (a) The auctioneer should be garrulous. (b) Objects for sale may be brought from home or constructed in the classroom. (c) The player with the most purchases may be designated as the "big spender."
Baseball	1. The teacher selects one umpire, one scorekeeper, and two teams; then provides large picture cards or sentence cards.
	2. After each team has chosen its own catcher and pitcher, the pitcher of Team A flashes a card to the catcher of Team A and to the first batter of Team B, both of whom are standing at home plate.
	3. If the catcher answers first and correctly by identifying the picture or reading the card, there is a strike against the batter. If the catcher and batter answer simultaneously, the umpire calls it a foul ball. If the batter answers first and correctly, he or she advances to first base and the next player on Team B comes to bat. When the batter has three strikes, he or she is out and the next player on Team B is up.

Figure 14.4. (cont.)

	4. Players advance one base at a time, runs are scored, three outs constitute a change of teams' position, and the team with the greater number of runs in the designated time wins Baseball. 5. Suggestion: For simpler scoring among younger children, one strike constitutes an out.
Book Bag Relay	1. Each row receives an empty book bag, school bag, or bike bag that is placed on the desk or table of the first player. 2. Each player in turn takes the bag and puts into it one school article that he or she can identify properly (e.g., "This is my spelling book.") 3. Though each player in one row must insert a different item from his or her table or desk and must identify it properly (for duplication of items within one row is not permitted), a player may insert more than one of any specified item (e.g., three pencils, two pens) into the book bag. 4. The first row to have the greatest number of items correctly identified within a specified time wins Book Bag Relay.
Buried Treasure	1. "Buried treasure" (objects or pictures) is placed into a large box in front of the room, and teams are chosen. 2. One player at a time from each team walks to the box and draws out a buried treasure. If the player can identify or describe the treasure correctly, his or her team retains it. If the player fails, he or she must return the treasure to the box. 3. Each team continues to choose and identify items until one of its players misses. The team with the most treasures when time is called wins Buried Treasure.
Eraser Relay	1. Each row, consisting of the same number of players, receives an eraser that is placed on the desk or table of the first player. 2. The teacher asks the first player of the first row a question (e.g., "What day is this?"). If the player can answer it successfully, he or she passes the eraser down the row to the next player. If any player in the row fails to answer, he or she retains the eraser. The teacher then proceeds with the second row of players, questioning each briefly until one player is unable to respond or responds incorrectly. 3. The row that first passes its eraser down to its last player wins Eraser Relay. 4. Variation: For less advanced classes, the teacher reads some questions aloud and each player in turn responds "Yes" or "No" followed by a short sentence to indicate reasonable comprehension.

Figure 14.4. (cont.)

---

1. The teacher is "It" first. While the teacher turns his or her back to the class, the players pass a small rubber ball quickly around the circle or up and down the rows as if it were a "hot potato."
2. As each player receives the ball, he or she must say, "I have the ball" before passing it on.
3. Each time "It" turns around and calls, "Stop," the player holding the hot potato must come up and stand in front of the room. Then the game continues until each player has passed the ball at least once.
4. "It" must then issue simple penalties (e.g., "Count from 20 to 30," "Draw a cat on the board," or "Give the names of three vegetables") to all players who are standing in front of the room.
5. Suggestion: A baseball, tennis ball, or football may be used to stimulate interest during various seasons of the year.

Hot Potato

---

1. The teacher must provide an assortment of paper masks or a collection of paper hats.
2. All the players close their eyes, and the teacher quietly taps one player to be "It." "It" dons one of the masks or hats to assume a different identity.
3. "It" now hides under the teacher's desk or behind a screen. When "It" begins to "knock, knock" on the floor, the other players open their eyes and demand, "Who is there?"
4. "It" answers, "Guess if you can," and begins to describe his or her new identity (e.g., fire fighter, cowboy).
5. The first player to identify "It" correctly becomes "It" for the next round.
6. Suggestions: (a) Players may construct simple masks or hats during an art period. (b) Whenever possible, masks of famous national heroes of the United States or the native lands of the ESL players may be used with older children.

Knock, Knock

---

1. The teacher selects a timekeeper, and space is cleared for "It" to perform.
2. The player chosen as "It" mimes an action, and the other players, either individually or chorally, offer guesses as to what "It" is doing (e.g., "You are drinking water" or "You are washing your hands").
3. The first player to identify the action correctly becomes "It" for the next round. When there has been a choral response, "It" selects his or her own successor.
4. The player chosen as "It" who can puzzle the class the longest with a pantomime wins Look at Me.
5. Suggestions: This game is especially appropriate when the children have been overactive.

Look at Me

Figure 14.4. (cont.)

Red Ball	1. The teacher chooses a player to be "It" and allows "It" to hide the "red ball" somewhere in the room while the other players close their eyes. 2. Once the red ball has been hidden, all eyes are opened and each player is allowed one guess as to the location of the ball; for example, "The ball is by the door." 3. If a player's identifying statement is correct, he or she is permitted to look for the red ball in that place. 4. The first player to find the ball is "It" during the next round. 5. Suggestion: Instead of using the relatively large red playground ball, the teacher may prefer to paint a golf ball red or substitute a red tennis ball because a small ball is easier to hide.
Robber, Robber	1. The teacher places large pictures on the chalk tray, and chooses one player to be "It." 2. While the other players close their eyes, "It" removes one of the pictures and places it facedown on the teacher's desk. 3. All eyes are opened, and the class shouts, "Robber, Robber, what do you have?" 4. Then, each player is allowed one chance to identify correctly the missing picture, using a complete sentence, and the first player to do so successfully becomes "It" for the next round. 5. Variations: (a) "It" is permitted to rearrange the pictures each time; (b) Instead of using pictures, the teacher places objects on a table where everyone can see them, and "It" must remove one of the objects.
Show Me	1. Large pictures are placed on the chalk tray in front of the room or on the bulletin board. Two teams are chosen, and a scorekeeper is selected. 2. The first player on Team A asks the first player on Team B, "Show me a duck," and the first player on Team B must walk up and point to the correct picture and identify it (e.g., "This is a duck"). Then the second player on Team B asks the second player on Team A, "Show me. . . ." 3. The scorekeeper allows one point for each command that is properly issued, and one point for each correct identification. The team with the greater number of points wins the Show Me game. 4. Variation: The game may be called Draw Me if sufficient chalkboard space is available and the students are talented.
Super Chair	1. The players sit in a semicircle, with the teacher seated at one end on a "super chair" (high stool). A timekeeper stands nearby. 2. While holding up picture or sentence cards, one at a time, the teacher calls on a player in the semicircle to identify the item(s) shown (using a complete

Figure 14.4. (cont.)

sentence) or to read the card. If the player succeeds, all the players remain in their own seats. If the player fails, he or she moves to the end of the line and the other players move up clockwise.

3. The teacher is soon replaced by the player who formerly sat at his or her right but who now has succeeded to the Super Chair and must continue the game.

4. The player who remains longest in the Super Chair is declared the winner.

	Three Chances

1. After one player leaves the room, the teacher selects another player to be "It" and describes "It" softly to the class (e.g., "He has brown hair, blue eyes, and wears a red shirt").

2. The outsider now returns to the room and must guess which player is "It" by asking three questions (e.g., "Is it a boy?"; "Is he tall?"; "Is he wearing a sweater?"). The class answers chorally "Yes" or "No."

3. Then, the outsider has Three Chances to identify "It." If the outsider is successful, he or she may select the next player to leave the room. Should the outsider fail, the player who has been "It" becomes the next outsider.

4. Suggestion: In the primary grades, the outsider is told, before beginning his or her questioning, the row or part of the room in which "It" is seated.

	Triple Play

1. Three teams are chosen, a scorekeeper is selected, and everyone stands.

2. The teacher holds a stack of large pictures or large sentence cards that can be readily seen about halfway across the room. The first players on all three teams try simultaneously to identify the picture (using a complete sentence) or to read the card the teacher flashes to them.

3. The first player to succeed scores one point for his or her team and the game continues with the next trio of players. In case of a tied score in identification or reading during the "triple play," the teacher puts the cards back into the pile, and the next trio steps up.

4. The team with the most points after a specified period of time wins Triple Play.

5. Suggestion: If the class is small or if the game is played for a long time, a Most Valuable Player can be chosen.

Elementary teachers who are responsible for classroom ESL programs may use self-evaluation sheets and a typical checklist is found in Figure 14.5. To rate student progress, however, they may choose to use either commercial evaluation or noncommercial procedures.

Evaluation of Teachers and Students in the Programs

Commercial Instruments

Teachers should be familiar with some nationally distributed commercial instruments often used in ESL programs, especially in English/Spanish bilingual programs.[20] The first is the *Spanish/English Reading and Vocabulary Screening,* or SERVS, published by CTB/McGraw Hill of Monterey, California. It is a language-screening test that determines the student's dominant language for taking an achievement test. It is a pretest useful in determining whether the Hispanic child should be tested with the Spanish or the English version of the *Comprehensive Tests of Basic Skills.* There are three forms (for grades one through two, grade three, and grades four through eight), each of which takes about thirty minutes to administer.

The second and third instruments are the *Bilingual Syntax Measure* (for grades kindergarten through third grade) and the *Bilingual Syntax Measure II* (for grades three through twelve), published by the Psychological Corporation of Cleveland, Ohio, for assessing proficiency of syntax in Spanish or English. After a test administration of ten to fifteen minutes, it can be determined whether the child is stronger in English, is stronger in his or her primary language, or is comparably skilled in both. The format consists of a story and colorful cartoonlike pictures. The scorer can assign the child to one of six proficiency levels.

Use of the fourth and final instrument is not limited to Spanish/English speakers because it can assess the oral ability of any nonnative English speaker; it is entitled the *Second Language Oral Test of English* (published by Alemany Press, Hayward, California). Its twenty subtests provide the examiner with estimates of a student's ability to provide standard English grammatical structures. It takes fifteen minutes to administer to children or adults, either individually or in groups.

Noncommercial Evaluation Procedures

Procedures designed to reveal students' overall language proficiency and ability to use language in real communication contexts include observations, oral interviews, cloze tests, and dictation.[21] Regular periodic *observations* provide the teacher with an informal ongoing evaluation process, as well as with help in planning appropriate classroom activities. Another informal measure of student progress is *oral interviews,* which allow the teacher to become better acquainted with students and student needs and which also stimulate a sampling of the language ability of students. Interviews may be taped and can follow the format shown in Figure 14.6.

A typical example of a *cloze test* consists of a paragraph of some 250 words at a level appropriate to that of the student. Although the first and last sentences are left untouched, all other sentences have every fifth word deleted from the passage. The student must use contextual and grammatical clues to fill in the

Figure 14.5. Teacher's Self-Evaluation Checklist in the ESL Program.

Self-Evaluation of Teacher	Yes	No
1. Do I demonstrate adequate planning and sequencing?	___	___
2. Do I use material that is relevant to the students' world and at an appropriate level for the students?	___	___
3. Is the aim of my lesson clear to the students; for example, is the target structure or activity clearly delineated and reflected in my preparation?	___	___
4. Do I have a clear understanding of the structure so that I will not be "surprised" by irregular items?	___	___
5. Are my directions clear and to the point?	___	___
6. Do I keep rules, diagrams, and explanations to a minimum?	___	___
7. Are my handouts well prepared and legible and NOT poor duplications characterized by light print or minute type that students, already struggling in a second language, must struggle to read?	___	___
8. Do I speak naturally and at normal speed?	___	___
9. Do I maintain an appropriate pace to keep the class alert and interested?	___	___
10. Do I have good rapport with my class, respecting the students' time as well as exhibiting sensitivity to the students as children and offering positive reinforcement?	___	___
11. Do I listen to my students and am I aware of student errors, limiting correction to what is necessary and relevant?	___	___
12. Do I promote student self-editing?	___	___
13. Do I utilize peer correction?	___	___
14. Do I respect students' abilities to use their own grey matter to come up with new items, and do I invite them to use their own powers of analogy or analysis to make "educated guesses"?	___	___
15. Do I promote student participation and activity?	___	___
16. Am I aware of the ratio of student and teacher talk, keeping teacher talk to a minimum rather than dominating the class?	___	___
17. Do my students have an opportunity to communicate with each other in real language activities so that the emphasis is not on pattern practice?	___	___
18. Is my class arranged for successful communication between students and for easy accessibility to the teacher?	___	___
19. Can my students do something linguistically new after the class?	___	___
20. Would I, as a student, enjoy my own class?	___	___

Source: GUIDELINES OF THE NEW YORK STATE TEACHERS OF ENGLISH TO SPEAKERS OF OTHER LANGUAGES AND THE BILINGUAL EDUCATION ASSOCIATION (n.d.).

Student Name: _____ Age _____ Grade _____ Date _____

Figure 14.6.
Checklist for Interview
Findings.

Speaking and Listening

Accent

Grammar
    One word
    Two words
    Complete sentence
    Word order in sentence
    Complex sentences
    Use of idioms or figurative language
    Knowledge of deep structure of questions

Vocabulary

Fluency

Comprehension
    Understood main idea of questions
    Understood details of questions
    Answered inference questions

Reading

Vocabulary

Rate of reading

Comprehension
    Understood main idea of note
    Understood details in note
    Understood inference in note

Writing

Vocabulary

Grammar
    One word
    Two words
    Complete sentence
    Word order in sentence
    Complex sentences
    Use of idioms or figurative language

Comments: (interests, desires, needs)

Source: R. Rodrigues and R. White, MAINSTREAMING THE NON-ENGLISH SPEAKING
STUDENT (ERIC Clearinghouse on Reading and Communication Skills, 1981), p. 45.

blanks with possible words. Particularly useful for beginning ESL students is a cloze test that permits the use of several word choices for each blank. Incidentally, the results of the cloze test correlate highly with results of listening comprehension tests.

Dictation tests require several readings by the teacher. First, the students merely listen. Second, they try to write down what they hear. Third, they attempt to correct mistakes and fill in any blanks they still have. Finally, they reread what they have written, making further corrections and additions. These tests evaluate general language ability and can also be used to diagnose specific language problems.

Discussion Questions

1. What is your reaction to the possible introduction of an amendment to the U.S Constitution declaring the English language the official language of the country?
2. Do you feel that the activity-centered classroom constitutes a better approach to learning English as a second language? Why or why not?
3. Would you rather teach NSE or ESL students? Defend your answer.
4. Why must schools be more concerned with social dialects than with regional dialects?

Suggested Projects

1. Determine the non-English minority in your state and in your local school district.
2. Tape the conversations of five children learning English as a second language. Then analyze the results to see which of the twelve strategies the girls and boys are using to attain fluency and understanding.
3. Prepare a unit about the culture of the country or territory—such as Vietnam or Puerto Rico—from which some of the local ESL students have emigrated.
4. Develop a series of lesson plans that can be used equally well with NSE or ESL learners.
5. Administer the Oral Language Rating Form to a child who speaks a nonstandard English dialect. Review the results with your peers.
6. Examine some of the pattern books used to teach contrasts in standard and nonstandard English.

Recent Related Readings

August, D. 1987. "Effects of Peer Tutoring on the Second Language Acquisition of Mexican American Children in Elementary School," *TESOL Quarterly, 21,* pp. 717–736.

Commins, N. 1989. "Language and Affect: Bilingual Students at Home and at School," *Language Arts, 66,* pp. 29–43.

Enright, D. and McCloskey, M. 1988. *Integrating English: Developing English Language and Literacy in the Multilingual Classroom.* Reading, MA: Addison-Wesley.

Grant, C. 1988. "The Persistent Significance of Race in Schooling," *Elementary School Journal, 88,* pp. 561–569.

Hudelson, S. 1987. "The Role of Native Language Literacy in the Education of Language Minority Children," *Language Arts, 64,* pp. 827–841.

Hudelson, S. 1988. *Teaching ESL Writing in the Elementary School.* Old Tappan, NJ: Prentice-Hall Regents.

Johnson, D. 1988. "ESL Children as Teachers: A Social View of Second Language Use," *Language Arts, 65,* pp. 154–163.

Johnson, S., and Johnson, V. 1988. *Motivating Minority Students: Strategies That Work.* Springfield, IL: Thomas.

Kuhlman, N. 1988. "Evaluating Writing of Bilingual Students," *Writing Teacher, 2*(3), pp. 35–40.

Perez, G., and Vela, I. 1987. *Let's Learn English: Second Language Activities for the Primary Grades.* Glenview, IL: Scott, Foresman.

Chapter Notes

1. M. Saville-Troike, "Language and Cultural Development of LEP Students in Early Childhood Years," *Elementary ESOL Education News,* 1988, *10*(3), p. 1.

2. *Ibid.,* p. 2.

3. N. Conklin and M. Lourie, *A Host of Tongues* (New York: Macmillan/Free Press, 1983), p. 3.

4. J. Cummins, "The Construct of Language Proficiency in Bilingual Education," in *Current Issues in Bilingual Education,* J. Alatis, ed. (Washington, D.C.: Georgetown University Press, 1980), pp. 81–103.

5. J. Cummins, *Tests, Achievement, and Bilingual Students* (Rosslyn, Virginia: National Clearinghouse for Bilingual Education, 1982).

6. L. Ventriglia, *Conversations of Miguel and Maria: How Children Learn a Second Language* (Reading, Massachusetts: Addison-Wesley, 1982), pp. 3–27.

7. L. Fillmore, *The Second Time Around: Cognitive and Social Strategies in Second Language Acquisition.* Unpublished doctoral dissertation, Stanford University, 1976.

8. E. Hatch, ed., *Second Language Acquisition: A Book of Readings* (Rowley, Massachusetts: Newbury House, 1978).

9. Ventriglia, *Conversations,* p. 26.

10. *Ibid.,* pp. 31–161.

11. J. Asher, *Learning Another Language Through Action: The Complete Teacher's Guidebook,* 3rd ed. (Los Gatos, California: Sky Oaks Productions, 1986).

12. P. Gonzales, "Beginning English Reading for ESL Students," *The Reading Teacher,* 1981, *34,* p. 155.

13. *Ibid.,* p. 160.

14. F. Stevens, "Activities to Promote Learning and Communication in the Second Language Classroom," *TESOL Quarterly,* 1983, *17,* p. 269.

15. *Ibid.,* pp. 262–267.

16. R. Rodrigues and R. White, *Mainstreaming the Non-English Speaking Student* (Urbana, Illinois: ERIC Clearinghouse on Reading and Communication Skills, and the National Council of Teachers of English, 1981), pp. 18–27.

17. W. Labov, *The Social Stratification of English in New York City* (Washington, D.C.: Center for Applied Linguistics, 1966).

18. G. Tompkins and L. McGee, "Launching Nonstandard Speakers into Standard English," *Language Arts,* 1983, *60,* pp. 463–469.

19. J. Steinberg, "Laugh and Learn," *TESL Reporter,* 1983, *16,* p. 54.

20. J. Mitchell, Jr., ed., *The Ninth Mental Measurements Yearbook,* Volume II (Lincoln: University of Nebraska Press, 1985).

21. Rodrigues and White, *Mainstreaming,* pp. 41–43.

One Hundred Award-Winning Media Resources for Elementary School Language Arts

NOTE: In this list, the proper names that appear in parentheses after the titles are those of the authors. All films, videos, and filmstrips are in color. *Every resource listed has received one or more awards in national or international competitions.* A complete list of producers can be found at the end of this Appendix.

Level	Producer	Medium	Title	Other Information
I	Barr	film or video	*The Accident* (C. Carrick)	22 min.
P	Weston	film or video	*The Amazing Bone* (W. Steig)	11 min., animated
P	Live Oak	filmstrip	*Beady Bear* (D. Freeman)	w/cassette and guide
P	Weston	film or video	*The Bear & the Fly* (P. Winter)	5 min., animated
PI	Weston	filmstrip	*Beauty and the Beast* (W. Hutton)	52 frames, 12 min.
PI	Churchill	film or video	*Beep, Beep*	12 min., animated
PI	Barr	film or video	*Cabbages and Kings* (Grimm Bros.)	17½ min.
P	Live Oak	filmstrip	*Christmas in Noisy Village* (A. Lindgren)	w/cassette and guide
P	Weston	film or video	*Corduroy* (D. Freeman)	16 min.
PI	Churchill	film or video	*Creole*	7½ min.
P	Churchill	film or video	*Curious George* (M. & H. Rey)	14 min., animated
P	Churchill	film or video	*Curious George Goes to the Hospital* (M. & H. Rey)	15 min., animated
P	Weston	film or video	*Curious George Rides a Bike* (M. & H. Rey)	10 min., iconographic, captioned film available
PI	Barr	film or video	*Dictionary: The Adventure of Words*	16 min.
P	Weston	film or video	*Doctor De Soto* (W. Steig)	10 min., animated
PI	Churchill	film or video	*Dogs*	15 min.
PI	Barr	film or video	*Friends*	20 min.
PI	Churchill	film or video	*Friends*	16 min.
P	Churchill	film or video	*Frog and Toad Are Friends* (A. Lobel)	17½ min.
P	Britannica	filmstrips	*Fun for Storytelling Hours: Facts and Fancy*	set of 6, w/cassettes and guide
I	Churchill	film or video	*The Giving Tree* (S. Silverstein)	10 min., captioned film also available
PI	Weston	recording	*Hans Christian Andersen in Central Park*	1 LP
P	Weston	film or video	*Happy Birthday Moon* (F. Asch)	7 min., animated
PI	Pyramid	film or video	*The Happy Prince* (O. Wilde)	25 min.
PI	Churchill	film or video	*Hopscotch* (Revised)	12 min.
PI	Churchill	film or video	*How the Kiwi Lost His Wings*	12 min.
PI	Churchill	film or video	*Hug Me*	5 min.

Level	Producer	Medium	Title	Other Information
PI	Churchill	film or video	*The Hundred Penny Box* (S. Mathis)	18 min.
PI	Churchill	film or video	*I'm Not Oscar's Friend Any More* (M. Sharmat)	7 min.
PI	Churchill	film or video	*The Incredible Book Escape*	45 min., animated, set of 4 films
P	Weston	film or video	*In the Night Kitchen* (M. Sendak)	6 min., animated
P	Live Oak	filmstrip	*Ira Sleeps Over* (B. Waber)	w/cassette and guide
PI	Film Fair	film or video	*Isabella and the Magic Brush*	13¾ min., captioned film also available
PI	Barr	film or video	*It's Me, Claudia* (A. Newman)	19½ min.
PI	Weston	recording	*Jack Tales: More Than a Beanstalk*	set of 2 LPs
PI	Churchill	film or video	*A Kite Story*	25 min.
I	Pyramid	film or video	*The Legend of John Henry*	11 min.
PI	Pyramid	film or video	*The Legend of Paul Bunyan*	13 min.
I	Pyramid	film or video	*The Legend of Sleepy Hollow* (W. Irving)	13 min.
I	Barr	film or video	*Library Report*	24½ min.
I	Barr	film or video	*Library World*	16 min.
PI	Pyramid	film or video	*The Little Mermaid* (H. Andersen)	25 min.
PI	Barr	film or video	*Manners: The Magic Words*	16 min.
PI	Churchill	film or video	*Martha Ann and the Mother Store* (N. & B. Charnley)	7 min.
PI	Live Oak	filmstrip	*Merry Ever After* (J. Lasker)	w/ cassette and guide
PI	Britannica	filmstrips	*Monsters and Other Friendly Creatures*	set of 5, w/cassettes and guide
P	Weston	film or video	*The Most Wonderful Egg in the World* (H. Heine)	6 min., animated
PI	Churchill	film or video	*The Mouse and the Motorcycle* (B. Cleary)	41 min.
P	Britannica	filmstrips	*My Family and Me*	set of 4, w/cassettes and guide
PI	Barr	film or video	*My Grandson Lew* (C. Zolotow)	13 min.
P	Britannica	filmstrips	*Myself and Me*	set of 5, w/cassettes and guides
P	Britannica	filmstrips	*My Senses and Me*	set of 4, w/cassettes and guide
P	Weston	film or video	*The Mysterious Tadpole* (S. Kellogg)	9 min., animated
P	Weston	filmstrip	*The Napping House* (A. Wood)	w/cassette
I	Churchill	film	*Nate the Great Goes Undercover*	10 min.
I	Barr	film or video	*The Nutcracker* (E. Hoffman)	26 min.
PI	Pyramid	film or video	*Oh Brother, My Brother*	14 min.
P	Live Oak	filmstrip	*Ox-Cart Man* (D. Hall)	w/cassette and guide
P	Churchill	film or video	*Paper Wings*	13 min., no narration
PI	Film Fair	film or video	*Petronella*	13¼ min., captioned film also available
P	Live Oak	filmstrip	*A Pocket for Corduroy* (D. Freeman)	w/cassette and guide
P	Live Oak	filmstrip	*Private Zoo* (G. McHargue)	w/cassette and guide
PI	Barr	film or video	*The Promise*	17 min., captioned film also available
PI	Pyramid	film or video	*Rainbow War*	20 min.
PI	Churchill	film or video	*Rainshower* (Revised)	14½ min., no narration
I	Barr	film or video	*Reading Is . . .*	25 min.
I	Barr	film or video	*The Reference Section*	22 min.

Level	Producer	Medium	Title	Other Information
PI	Churchill	film or video	*The Reluctant Dragon* (K. Grahame)	12 min.
PI	Churchill	film or video	*Roundabout*	19 min.
PI	Pyramid	film or video	*The Selfish Giant* (O. Wilde)	27 min.
PI	Churchill	film or video	*Seven With One Blow*	10 min.
PI	Britannica	filmstrips	*Show Me A Poem*	set of 6, w/cassettes and guide
P	Weston	film or video	*The Silver Cow* (S. Cooper)	13 min., iconographic
PI	Churchill	film or video	*The Silver Pony*	7 min.
P	Weston	film or video	*The Snowman* (R. Briggs)	26 min., animated, no narration
PI	Weston	recording	*Songspinner: Folktales & Fables Sung and Told*	1 LP
PI	Pyramid	film or video	*The Sorcerer's Apprentice*	26 min., animated
PI	Film Fair	film or video	*Sound of Sunshine—Sound of Rain* (F. Heide)	14½ min., animated
PI	Barr	film or video	*A Special Trade* (S. Wittman)	17 min.
I	Barr	film or video	*Spring—Six Interpretations*	13 min.
P	Live Oak	filmstrip	*Squawk to the Moon, Little Goose* (E. Preston)	w/cassette and guide
I	Churchill	film or video	*Story of a Book* (2nd ed.)	16 min.
P	Live Oak	filmstrip	*The Story of Ferdinand* (M. Leaf)	w/cassette and guide
I	Film Fair	film or video	*Strange Occurrence at Elm View Library*	17½ min.
PI	Film Fair	film or video	*A Tale of Till*	11¼ min.
P	Britannica	filmstrips	*That's Delightful*	set of 4, w/cassettes
PI	Barr	film or video	*Through Grandpa's Eyes* (P. MacLachlan)	20 min.
PI	Churchill	film or video	*Tom Thumb*	9½ min.
P	Churchill	film or video	*The Tree* (2nd ed.)	11 min.
PI	Barr	film or video	*Urashima Taro*	11½ min., animated
PI	Churchill	film or video	*Waffles*	11 min.
I	Barr	film or video	*Watch Out For My Plant*	13½ min.
P	Barr	film or video	*What Mary Jo Wanted* (J. Udry)	14½ min., captioned
P	Weston	film or video	*Why Mosquitoes Buzz in People's Ears* (V. Aardema)	10 min., animated
P	Live Oak	filmstrip	*Will's Quill* (D. Freeman)	w/cassette and guide
P	Weston	film or video	*The Wizard*	8 min., animated
PI	Churchill	film or video	*Wonders in a Country Stream* (2nd ed.)	12½ min.
P	Britannica	filmstrips	*Words To Work With: Part I*	set of 4, w/cassettes
I	Barr	film or video	*Writing Says It All*	24 min.
I	Churchill	film or video	*Writing Well: Paragraphs*	15½ min.

PRODUCERS: Barr Films, 12801 Schabarum, P.O. Box 7878, Irwindale, CA 91706

Encyclopedia Britannica Educational Corp., 425 N. Michigan, Chicago, IL 60611

Churchill Films, 12210 Nebraska, Los Angeles, CA 90025

Film Fair Communications, 10900 Ventura Blvd., P.O. Box 1728, Studio City, CA 91604

Live Oak Media, P.O. Box 34, Andramdale, NY 12503

Pyramid Film & Video, Box 1048, Santa Monica, CA 90406

Weston Woods, Weston, CT 06883

The Caldecott Medal is named in honor of Randolph Caldecott (1846–1886), an English illustrator of children's books. The Medal is presented annually by a committee of the Children's Service Division of the American Library Association to "the artist of the most distinguished American picture book for children." The book must be an original work by a citizen or resident of the United States.

Caldecott Medal Books

1989 Award: *Song and Dance Man*. Illustrated by Stephen Gammell. Written by Karen Ackerman. Knopf.

Honor books: *Goldilocks and the Three Bears*. Illustrated and retold by James Marshall. Dial.
The Boy of the Three-Year Nap. Illustrated by Allen Say. Retold by Dianne Snyder. Houghton.
Mirandy and Brother Wind. Illustrated by Jerry Pinkney. Written by Patricia McKissack. Knopf.
Free Fall. Written and illustrated by David Wiesner. Lothrop.

1988 Award: *Owl Moon*. Illustrated by John Schoenherr. Written by Jane Yolen. Philomel.

Honor book: *Mufaro's Beautiful Daughters*. Illustrated and retold by John Steptoe. Lothrop.

1987 Award: *Hey, Al!* Illustrated by Richard Egielski. Written by Arthur Yorinks. Farrar.

Honor books: *The Village of Round and Square Houses*. Written and illustrated by Ann Grifalconi. Little, Brown.
Alphabetics. Written and illustrated by Suse MacDonald. Bradbury.
Rumpelstiltskin. Illustrated and retold by Paul O. Zelinsky. Dutton.

1986 Award: *The Polar Express*. Written and illustrated by Chris Van Allsburg. Houghton.

Honor books: *The Relatives Came.* Illustrated by Stephen Gammell. Written by Cynthia Rylant. Bradbury.
King Bidgood's in the Bathtub. Illustrated by Don Wood. Written by Audrey Wood. Harcourt.

1985 Award: *St. George and the Dragon.* Illustrated by Trina S. Hyman. Retold by Margaret Hodges. Little, Brown.

Honor books: *Hansel and Gretel.* Illustrated by Paul O. Zelinsky. Retold by Rika Lesser. Dodd.
Have You Seen My Duckling? Written and illustrated by Nancy Tafuri. Greenwillow.
The Story of Jumping Mouse. Written and illustrated by John Steptoe. Lothrop.

1984 Award: *The Glorious Flight Across the Channel with Lewis Bleriot.* Written and illustrated by Alice Provensen and Martin Provensen. Viking.

Honor books: *Ten, Nine, Eight.* Written and illustrated by Molly Bang. Greenwillow.
Little Red Riding Hood. Illustrated and retold by Trina S. Hyman. Holiday House.

1983 Award: *Shadow.* Illustrated by Marcia Brown. Written by Blaise Cendrars. Scribner.

Honor books: *A Chair for My Mother.* Written and illustrated by Vera Williams. Greenwillow.
When I Was Young in the Mountains. Illustrated by Diane Goode. Written by Cynthia Rylant. Dutton.

1982 Award: *Jumanji.* Written and illustrated by Chris Van Allsburg. Houghton.

Honor books: *On Market Street.* Illustrated by Anita Lobel. Written by Arnold Lobel. Greenwillow.
Outside Over There. Written and illustrated by Maurice Sendak. Harper.
A Visit to William Blake's Inn. Illustrated by Alice Provensen and Martin Provensen. Written by Nancy Willard. Harcourt.
Where the Buffaloes Begin. Illustrated by Stephen Gammell. Written by Olaf Baker. Warne.

1981 Award: *Fables.* Written and illustrated by Arnold Lobel. Harper.

Honor books:	*The Bremen-Town Musicians.* Illustrated and retold by Ilse Plume. Doubleday. *The Grey Lady and the Strawberry Snatcher.* Written and illustrated by Mollie Bang. Four Winds. *Mice Twice.* Written and illustrated by Joseph Low. Atheneum/McElderry. *Truck.* Written and illustrated by Donald Crews. Greenwillow.
1980 Award:	*Ox-Cart Man.* Illustrated by Barbara Cooney. Written by Donald Hall. Viking.
Honor books:	*Ben's Trumpet.* Written and illustrated by Rachel Isadora. Greenwillow. *The Garden of Abdul Gasazi.* Written and illustrated by Chris Van Allsburg. Houghton. *The Treasure.* Written and illustrated by Uri Shulevitz. Farrar.
1979 Award:	*The Girl Who Loved Wild Horses.* Written and illustrated by Paul Goble. Bradbury.
Honor books:	*Freight Train.* Written and illustrated by Donald Crews. Greenwillow. *The Way to Start a Day.* Illustrated by Paul Parnall. Written by Byrd Baylor. Scribner.
1978 Award:	*Noah's Ark: Story of the Flood.* Written and illustrated by Peter Spier. Doubleday.
Honor books:	*It Could Always Be Worse.* Illustrated and retold by Margot Zemach. Farrar. *Castle.* Written and illustrated by David Macaulay. Houghton.
1977 Award:	*Ashanti to Zulu: African Traditions.* Illustrated by Leo and Diane Dillon. Written by Margaret Musgrove. Dial.
Honor books:	*The Golem: A Jewish Legend.* Illustrated and retold by Beverly McDermott. Lippincott. *The Contest: An Armenian Folktale.* Adapted and illustrated by Nonny Hogrogian. Greenwillow. *Hawk, I'm Your Brother.* Illustrated by Peter Parnall. Written by Byrd Baylor. Scribner. *The Amazing Bone.* Written and illustrated by William Steig. Farrar. *Fish for Supper.* Written and illustrated by M. B. Goffstein. Dial.

1976 Award:	*Why Mosquitos Buzz in People's Ears*. Illustrated by Leo and Diane Dillon. Retold by Verna Aardema. Dial.
Honor books:	*The Desert Is Theirs*. Illustrated by Peter Parnall. Written by Byrd Baylor. Scribner. *Strega Nona*. Illustrated and retold by Tomie de Paola. Prentice.
1975 Award:	*Arrow to the Sun*. Adapted and illustrated by Gerald McDermott. Viking.
Honor book:	*Jambo Means Hello—Swahili Alphabet Book*. Illustrated by Tom Feelings. Written by Muriel Feelings. Dial.
1974 Award:	*Duffy and the Devil*. Illustrated by Margot Zemach. Retold by Harve Zemach. Farrar.
Honor books:	*Cathedral: The Story of Its Construction*. Written and illustrated by David Macaulay. Houghton. *Three Jovial Huntsmen*. Adapted and illustrated by Susan Jeffers. Bradbury.
1973 Award:	*The Funny Little Woman*. Illustrated by Blair Lent. Written by Arlene Mosel. Dutton.
Honor books:	*Anansi the Spider*. Adapted and illustrated by Gerald McDermott. Holt. *Hosie's Alphabet*. Illustrated by Leonard Baskin. Written by Hosea Tobias and Lisa Baskin. Viking. *Snow-White and the Seven Dwarfs*. Illustrated by Nancy Ekholm Burkert. Retold by Randall Jarrell. Farrar. *When Clay Sings*. Illustrated by Tom Bahti. Written by Byrd Baylor. Scribner.
1972 Award:	*One Fine Day*. Illustrated and retold by Nonny Hogrogian. Macmillan.
Honor books:	*If All the Seas Were One Sea*. Written and illustrated by Janina Domanska. Macmillan. *Moja Means One: Swahili Counting Book*. Illustrated by Tom Feelings. Written by Muriel Feelings. Dial. *Hildilid's Night*. Illustrated by Arnold Lobel. Written by Cheli Duran Ryan. Macmillan.
1971 Award:	*A Story—A Story: An African Tale*. Retold and illustrated by Gail E. Haley. Atheneum.

Honor books:	*The Angry Moon.* Illustrated by Blair Lent. Retold by William Sleator. Little, Brown. *Frog and Toad Are Friends.* Written and illustrated by Arnold Lobel. Harper. *In the Night Kitchen.* Written and illustrated by Maurice Sendak. Harper.
1970 Award:	*Sylvester and the Magic Pebble.* Written and illustrated by William Steig. Windmill.
Honor books:	*Goggles!* Written and illustrated by Ezra Jack Keats. Macmillan. *Alexander and the Wind-up Mouse.* Written and illustrated by Leo Lionni. Pantheon. *Pop Corn and Ma Goodness.* Illustrated by Robert Andrew Parke. Written by Edna Mitchell Preston. Viking. *Thy Friend, Obadiah.* Written and illustrated by Brinton Turkle. Viking. *The Judge: An Untrue Tale.* Illustrated by Margot Zemach. Written by Harve Zemach. Farrar.
1969 Award:	*The Fool of the World and the Flying Ship: A Russian Tale.* Illustrated by Uri Shulevitz. Retold by Arthur Ransome. Farrar.
Honor book:	*Why the Sun and the Moon Live in the Sky: An African Folk Tale.* Illustrated by Blair Lent. Retold by Elphinstone Dayrell. Houghton.
1968 Award:	*Drummer Hoff.* Illustrated by Ed Emberley. Adapted by Barbara Emberley. Prentice.
Honor books:	*Frederick.* Written and illustrated by Leo Lionni. Pantheon. *Seashore Story.* Written and illustrated by Taro Yashima. Viking. *The Emperor and the Kite.* Illustrated by Ed Young. Written by Jane Yolen. World.
1967 Award:	*Sam, Bangs and Moonshine.* Written and illustrated by Evaline Ness. Holt.
Honor book:	*One Wide River to Cross.* Illustrated by Ed Emberley. Adapted by Barbara Emberley. Prentice.
1966 Award:	*Always Room for One More.* Illustrated by Nonny Hogrogian. Written by Sorche NicLeodhas. Holt.

Honor books:	*Hide and Seek Fog.* Illustrated by Roger Duvoisin. Written by Alvin Tresselt. Lothrup. *Just Me.* Written and illustrated by Marie Hall Ets. Viking. *Tom Tit Tot.* Retold and illustrated by Evaline Ness. Scribner.
1965 Award:	*May I Bring a Friend?* Illustrated by Beni Montresor. Written by Beatrice Schenk de Regniers. Atheneum.
Honor books:	*Rain Makes Applesauce.* Illustrated by Marvin Bileck. Written by Julian Scheer. Holiday House. *The Wave.* Illustrated by Blair Lent. Written by Margaret Hodges. Houghton. *A Pocketful of Cricket.* Illustrated by Evaline Ness. Written by Rebecca Caudill. Holt.
1964 Award:	*Where the Wild Things Are.* Written and illustrated by Maurice Sendak. Harper.
Honor books:	*Swimmy.* Story and pictures by Leo Lionni. Pantheon. *All in the Morning Early.* Illustrated by Evaline Ness. Written by Sorche Nic Leodhas. Holt. *Mother Goose and Nursery Rhymes.* Illustrated by Philip Reed. Atheneum.
1963 Award:	*The Snowy Day.* Story and pictures by Ezra Jack Keats. Viking.
Honor books:	*The Sun is a Golden Earring.* Illustrated by Bernarda Bryson. Written by Natalia M. Belting. Holt. *Mr. Rabbit and the Lovely Present.* Illustrated by Maurice Sendak. Written by Charlotte Zolotow. Harper.
1962 Award:	*Once a Mouse.* Retold and illustrated by Marcia Brown. Scribner.
Honor books:	*The Fox Went Out on a Chilly Night.* Written and illustrated by Peter Spier. Doubleday. *Little Bear's Visit.* Illustrated by Maurice Sendak. Written by Else H. Minarik. Harper. *The Day We Saw the Sun Come Up.* Illustrated by Adrienne Adams. Written by Alice E. Goudey. Scribner.
1961 Award:	*Baboushka and the Three Kings.* Illustrated by Nicolas Sidjakow. Written by Ruth Robbins. Parnassus Press.

Honor book:	*Inch by Inch*. Written and illustrated by Leo Lionni. Astor-Honor.
1960 Award:	*Nine Days to Christmas*. Illustrated by Marie Hall Ets. Written by Marie Hall Ets and Aurora Labastida. Viking.
Honor books:	*Houses from the Sea*. Illustrated by Adrienne Adams. Written by Alice E. Goudey. Scribner. *The Moon Jumpers*. Illustrated by Maurice Sendak. Written by Janice May Udry. Harper.
1959 Award:	*Chanticleer and the Fox*. Adapted and illustrated by Barbara Cooney. Crowell.
Honor books:	*The House that Jack Built*. Written and illustrated by Antonio Frasconi. Harcourt. *What Do You Say, Dear?* Illustrated by Maurice Sendak. Written by Sesyle Joslin. W. R. Scott. *Umbrella*. Written and illustrated by Taro Yashima. Viking.
1958 Award:	*Time of Wonder*. Written and illustrated by Robert McCloskey. Viking.
Honor books:	*Fly High, Fly Low*. Written and illustrated by Don Freeman. Viking. *Anatole and the Cat*. Illustrated by Paul Galdone. Written by Eve Titus. McGraw.
1957 Award:	*A Tree is Nice*. Illustrated by Marc Simont. Written by Janice May Udry. Harper.
Honor books:	*Mr. Penny's Race Horse*. Written and illustrated by Marie Hall Ets. Viking. *1 Is One*. Written and illustrated by Tasha Tudor. Walck. *Anatole*. Illustrated by Paul Galdone. Written by Eve Titus. McGraw. *Gillespie and the Guards*. Illustrated by James Daugherty. Written by Benjamin Elkin. Viking. *Lion*. Written and illustrated by William Pène du Bois. Viking.
1956 Award:	*Frog Went A-Courtin'*. Illustrated by Feodor Rojankovsky. Retold by John Langstaff. Harcourt.

Honor books: *Play With Me.* Written and illustrated by Marie Hall Ets. Viking.
Crow Boy. Written and illustrated by Taro Yashima. Viking.

1955 Award: *Cinderella, or the Little Glass Slipper.* Illustrated and translated by Marcia Brown. Scribner.

Honor books: *Book of Nursery and Mother Goose Rhymes.* Illustrated by Marguerite de Angeli. Doubleday.
Wheel on the Chimney. Illustrated by Tibor Gergely. Written by Margaret Wise Brown. Lippincott.
The Thanksgiving Story. Illustrated by Helen Sewell. Written by Alice Dalgliesh. Scribner.

1954 Award: *Madeline's Rescue.* Written and illustrated by Ludwig Bemelmans. Viking.

Honor books: *Journey Cake, Ho!* Illustrated by Robert McCloskey. Written by Ruth Sawyer. Viking.
When Will the World Be Mine? Illustrated by Jean Charlot. Written by Miriam Schlein. W. R. Scott.
The Steadfast Tin Soldier. Illustrated by Marcia Brown. Story by Hans Christian Andersen, trans. by M. R. James. Scribner.
A Very Special House. Illustrated by Maurice Sendak. Written by Ruth Krauss. Harper.
Green Eyes. Written and illustrated by A. Birnbaum. Capitol.

1953 Award: *The Biggest Bear.* Written and illustrated by Lynd Ward. Houghton.

Honor books: *Puss in Boots.* Illustrated and translated from Charles Perrault by Marcia Brown. Scribner.
One Morning in Maine. Written and illustrated by Robert McCloskey. Viking.
Ape in a Cape: An Alphabet of Odd Animals. Written and illustrated by Fritz Eichenberg. Harcourt.
The Storm Book. Illustrated by Margaret Bloy Graham. Written by Charlotte Zolotow. Harper.
Five Little Monkeys. Written and illustrated by Juliet Kepes. Houghton.

1952 Award:	*Finders Keepers*. Illustrated by Nicolas, *pseud*. (Nicholas Mordvinoff). Written by Will, *pseud*. (William Lipkind). Harcourt.
Honor books:	*Mr. T. W. Anthony Woo*. Written and illustrated by Marie Hall Ets. Viking.
	Skipper John's Cook. Written and illustrated by Marcia Brown. Scribner.
	All Falling Down. Illustrated by Margaret Bloy Graham. Written by Gene Zion. Harper.
	Bear Party. Written and illustrated by William Pène du Bois. Viking.
	Feather Mountain. Written and illustrated by Elizabeth Olds. Houghton.
1951 Award:	*The Egg Tree*. Written and illustrated by Katherine Milhous. Scribner.
Honor books:	*Dick Whittington and His Cat*. Retold and illustrated by Marcia Brown. Scribner.
	The Two Reds. Illustrated by Nicholas, *pseud*. (Nicolas Mordvinoff). Written by Will, *pseud*. (William Lipkind). Harcourt.
	If I Ran the Zoo. Written and illustrated by Dr. Seuss. Random.
	The Most Wonderful Doll in the World. Illustrated by Helen Stone. Written by Phyllis McGinley. Lippincott.
	T-Bone, the Baby Sitter. Written and illustrated by Claire Turlay Newberry. Harper.
1950 Award:	*Song of the Swallows*. Written and illustrated by Leo Politi. Scribner.
Honor books:	*America's Ethan Allen*. Illustrated by Lynd Ward. Written by Stewart Holbrook. Houghton.
	The Wild Birthday Cake. Illustrated by Hildegard Woodward. Written by Lavinia R. Davis. Doubleday.
	The Happy Day. Illustrated by Marc Simont. Written by Ruth Krauss. Harper.
	Bartholomew and the Oobleck. Written and illustrated by Dr. Seuss. Random.
	Henry Fisherman. Written and illustrated by Marcia Brown, Scribner.

Newbery Medal Books

The Newbery Medal is named in honor of John Newbery (1713–1767), an English bookseller and publisher. The Medal is presented annually by a committee of the Children's Service Division of the American Library Association to "the author of the most distinguished contribution to American literature for children." The book must be an original work by a citizen or resident of the United States.

1989 Award: *Joyful Noise*. Paul Fleischman. Harper/Zolotow.

Honor books: *In the Beginning*. Virginia Hamilton. Harcourt.
Scorpions. Walter Dean Myers. Harper.

1988 Award: *Lincoln: A Photobiography*. Russell Freedman. Clarion/Houghton.

Honor books: *After the Rain*. Norma Fox Mazer. Morrow.
The Hatchet. Gary Paulsen. Bradbury.

1987 Award: *The Whipping Boy*. Sid Fleischman. Greenwillow.

Honor books: *A Fine White Dust*. Cynthia Rylant. Bradbury.
On My Honor. Marion Dane Bauer. Clarion/Houghton.
Volcano: The Eruption and Healing of Mount St. Helens. Patricia Lauber. Bradbury.

1986 Award: *Sarah, Plain and Tall*. Patricia MacLachlan. Harper.

Honor books: *Commodore Perry in the Land of the Shogun*. Rhoda Blumberg. Lothrop.
Dogsong. Gary Paulsen. Bradbury.

1985 Award: *The Hero and the Crown*. Robin McKinley. Greenwillow.

Honor books: *Like Jake and Me*. Mavis Jukes. Knopf.
The Moves Make the Man. Bruce Brooks. Harper.
One-Eyed Cat. Paula Fox. Bradbury.

1984 Award: *Dear Mr. Henshaw*. Beverly Cleary. Morrow.

Honor books: *A Solitary Blue*. Cynthia Voigt. Atheneum.
Sugaring Time. Kathryn Lasky. Macmillan.
The Wish Giver. Bill Brittain. Harper.
The Sign of the Beaver. Elizabeth G. Speare. Houghton.

1983 Award: *Dicey's Song*. Cynthia Voigt. Atheneum.

Honor books:	*The Blue Sword*. Robin McKinley. Greenwillow.
	Doctor De Soto. William Steig. Farrar.
	Graven Images. Paul Fleischman. Harper.
	Homesick: My Own Story. Jean Fritz. Putnam.
	Sweet Whispers, Brother Rush. Virginia Hamilton. Philomel.

1982 Award: *A Visit to William Blake's Inn*. Nancy Willard. Harcourt.

Honor books: *Ramona Quimby, Age 8*. Beverly Cleary. Morrow.
Upon the Head of a Goat: A Childhood in Hungary, 1939–1944. Aranka Siegel. Farrar.

1981 Award: *Jacob Have I Loved*. Katherine Paterson. Crowell.

Honor books: *The Fledgling*. Jane Langton. Harper.
A Ring of Endless Light. Madeleine L'Engle. Farrar.

1980 Award: *A Gathering of Days: A New England Girl's Journal, 1830–32*. Joan W. Blos. Scribner.

Honor book: *The Road from Home: The Story of an Armenian Girl*. David Kherdian. Greenwillow.

1979 Award: *The Westing Game*. Ellen Raskin. Dutton.

Honor book: *The Great Gilly Hopkins*. Katherine Paterson. Crowell.

1978 Award: *Bridge to Terabithia*. Katherine Paterson. Crowell.

Honor books: *Anpao: An American Indian Odyssey*. Jamake Highwater. Lippincott.
Ramona and Her Father. Beverly Cleary. Morrow.

1977 Award: *Roll of Thunder, Hear My Cry*. Mildred Taylor. Dial.

Honor books: *A String in the Harp*. Nancy Bond. Atheneum/McElderry.
Abel's Island. William Steig. Farrar.

1976 Award: *The Grey King*. Susan Cooper. Atheneum/McElderry.

Honor books: *The Hundred Penny Box*. Sharon Bell Mathis. Viking.
Dragonwings. Lawrence Yep. Harper.

1975 Award: *M. C. Higgins the Great*. Virginia Hamilton. Macmillan.

Honor books:	*My Brother Sam Is Dead.* James Lincoln Collier and Christopher Collier. Four Winds.
	Philip Hall Likes Me, I Reckon Maybe. Bette Greene. Dial.
	Figgs & Phantoms. Ellen Raskin. Dutton.
	The Perilous Gard. Elizabeth Marie Pope. Houghton.
1974 Award:	*The Slave Dancer.* Paula Fox. Bradbury.
Honor book:	*The Dark Is Rising.* Susan Cooper. Atheneum/McElderry.
1973 Award:	*Julie of the Wolves.* Jean George. Harper.
Honor books:	*Frog and Toad Together.* Arnold Lobel. Harper.
	The Upstairs Room. Johanna Reiss. Crowell.
	The Witches of Worm. Zilpha Keatley Snyder. Atheneum.
1972 Award:	*Mrs. Frisby and the Rats of NIMH.* Robert C. O'Brien. Atheneum.
Honor books:	*Incident at Hawk's Hill.* Allan W. Eckert. Little, Brown.
	The Planet of Junior Brown. Virginia Hamilton, Macmillan.
	The Tombs of Atuan. Ursula K. Le Guin. Atheneum.
	Annie and the Old One. Miska Miles. Little, Brown.
	The Headless Cupid. Zilpha Keatley Snyder. Atheneum.
1971 Award:	*The Summer of the Swans.* Betsy Byars. Viking.
Honor books:	*Kneeknock Rise.* Natalie Babbitt. Farrar.
	Enchantress from the Stars. Sylvia Louis Engdahl. Atheneum.
	Sing Down the Moon. Scott O'Dell. Houghton.
1970 Award:	*Sounder.* William Armstrong. Harper.
Honor books:	*Our Eddie.* Sulamith Ish-Kishor. Pantheon.
	The Many Ways of Seeing: An Introduction to the Pleasures of Art. Janet Gaylord Moore. World.
	Journey Outside. Mary Q. Steele. Viking.
1969 Award:	*The High King.* Lloyd Alexander. Holt.
Honor books:	*To Be a Slave.* Julius Lester. Dial.
	When Schlemiel Went to Warsaw and Other Stories. Isaac Bashevis Singer. Farrar.

1968 Award:	*From the Mixed-Up Files of Mrs. Basil E. Frankweiler.* E. L. Konigsburg. Atheneum.
Honor books:	*Jennifer, Hecate, Macbeth, William McKinley, and Me, Elizabeth.* E. L. Konigsburg. Atheneum. *The Black Pearl.* Scott O'Dell. Houghton. *The Fearsome Inn.* Isaac Bashevis Singer. Scribner. *The Egypt Game.* Zilpha Keatley Snyder. Atheneum.
1967 Award:	*Up a Road Slowly.* Irene Hunt. Follett.
Honor books:	*The King's Fifth.* Scott O'Dell. Houghton. *Zlateh the Goat and Other Stories.* Isaac Bashevis Singer. Harper. *The Jazz Man.* Mary Hays Weik. Atheneum.
1966 Award:	*I, Juan de Pareja.* Elizabeth Borton de Treviño. Farrar.
Honor books:	*The Black Cauldron.* Lloyd Alexander. Holt. *The Animal Family.* Randall Jarrell. Pantheon. *The Noonday Friends.* Mary Stolz. Harper.
1965 Award:	*Shadow of a Bull.* Maia Wojciechowska. Atheneum.
Honor book:	*Across Five Aprils.* Irene Hunt. Follett.
1964 Award:	*It's Like This, Cat.* Emily Neville. Harper.
Honor books:	*Rascal.* Sterling North. Dutton. *The Loner.* Ester Wier. McKay.
1963 Award:	*A Wrinkle in Time.* Madeleine L'Engle. Farrar, Straus.
Honor books:	*Thistle and Thyme.* Sorche NicLeodhas. Holt. *Men of Athens.* Olivia Coolidge. Houghton.
1962 Award:	*The Bronze Bow.* Elizabeth George Speare. Houghton.
Honor books:	*Frontier Living.* Edwin Tunis. World. *The Golden Goblet.* Elois Jarvis McGraw. Coward-McCann. *Belling the Tiger.* Mary Stolz. Harper.
1961 Award:	*Island of the Blue Dolphins.* Scott O'Dell. Houghton.

Honor books:	*America Moves Forward*. Gerald W. Johnson. Morrow. *Old Ramon*, Jack Schaeffer. Houghton Mifflin. *The Cricket in Times Square*. George Seldon. Farrar.
1960 Award:	*Onion John*. Joseph Krumgold. Crowell.
Honor books:	*My Side of the Mountain*. Jean George. Dutton. *America Is Born*. Gerald W. Johnson. Morrow. *The Gammage Cup*. Carol Kendall. Harcourt.
1959 Award:	*The Witch of Blackbird Pond*. Elizabeth George Speare. Houghton.
Honor books:	*The Family Under the Bridge*. Natalie S. Carlson. Harper. *Along Came a Dog*. Meindert DeJong. Harper. *Chucaro: Wild Pony of the Pampa*. Francis Kalnay. Harcourt. *The Perilous Road*. William O. Steele. Harcourt.
1958 Award:	*Rifles for Watie*. Harold Keith. Crowell.
Honor books:	*The Horsecatcher*. Mari Sandoz. Westminster. *Gone-Away Lake*. Elizabeth Enright. Harcourt. *The Great Wheel*. Robert Lawson. Viking. *Tom Paine, Freedom's Apostle*. Leo Gurko. Crowell.
1957 Award:	*Miracles on Maple Hill*. Virginia Sorensen. Harcourt.
Honor books:	*Old Yeller*. Fred Gipson. Harper. *The House of Sixty Fathers*. Meindert DeJong. Harper. *Mr. Justice Holmes*. Clara Ingram Judson. Follett. *The Corn Grows Ripe*. Dorothy Rhoads. Viking. *Black Fox of Lorne*. Marguerite de Angeli. Doubleday.
1956 Award:	*Carry On, Mr. Bowditch*. Jean Lee Latham. Houghton.
Honor books:	*The Secret River*. Marjorie Kinnan Rawlings. Scribner. *The Golden Name Day*. Jennie Lindquist. Harper. *Men, Microscopes, and Living Things*. Katherine Shippen, Viking.
1955 Award:	*The Wheel on the School*. Meindert DeJong. Harper.
Honor books:	*The Courage of Sarah Noble*. Alice Dalgliesh. Scribner. *Banner in the Sky*. James Ullman. Lippincott.

1954 Award: . . . *and now Miguel*. Joseph Krumgold. Crowell.

Honor books: *All Alone*. Claire Huchet Bishop. Viking.
               Shadrach. Meindert DeJong. Harper.
               Hurry Home, Candy. Meindert DeJong. Harper.
               Theodore Roosevelt, Fighting Patriot. Clara Ingram Judson.
               Follett.
               Magic Maize. Mary and Conrad Buff. Houghton.

1953 Award: *Secret of the Andes*. Ann Nolan Clark. Viking.

Honor books: *Charlotte's Web*. E. B. White. Harper.
               Moccasin Trail. Eloise McGraw. Coward-McCann.
               Red Sails to Capri. Ann Weil. Viking.
               The Bears on Hemlock Mountain. Alice Dalgliesh. Scribner.
               Birthdays of Freedom, Volume 1. Genevieve Foster. Scribner.

1952 Award: *Ginger Pye*. Eleanor Estes. Harcourt.

Honor books: *Americans Before Columbus*. Elizabeth Baity. Viking.
               Minn of the Mississippi. Holling C. Holling. Houghton.
               The Defender. Nicholas Kalashnikoff. Scribner.
               The Light at Tern Rock. Julia Sauer. Viking.
               The Apple and the Arrow. Mary and Conrad Buff. Houghton

1951 Award: *Amos Fortune, Free Man*. Elizabeth Yates. Aladdin.

Honor books: *Better Known as Johnny Appleseed*. Mabel Leigh Hunt. Lip-
               pincott.
               Gandhi, Fighter Without a Sword. Jeanette Eaton. Morrow.
               Abraham Lincoln, Friend of the People. Clara Ingram Judson.
               Follett.
               The Story of Appleby Capple. Anne Parrish. Harper.

1950 Award: *The Door in the Wall*. Marguerite de Angeli. Doubleday.

Honor books: *Tree of Freedom*. Rebecca Caudill. Viking.
               The Blue Cat of Castle Town. Catherine Coblentz. Longmans.
               Kildee House. Rutherford Montgomery. Doubleday.
               George Washington. Genevieve Foster. Scribner.
               Song of the Pines. Walter and Marion Havighurst. Winston.

Appendix 3

Language Arts Software Evaluation Form*

A. Is the program educationally valuable?
1. Is the content important to learning language?
2. Do the instructional techniques mesh with current trends in education?
3. Can the same work be done just as well with nonelectronic media?
4. Does the program involve actual experiences in reading or writing, or is all work isolated drill instruction?
5. Will the skills learned have value to students in your classroom?
6. Will this program serve as a useful supplement to your classroom language arts program?
7. Do the skills involved in the program fit into the scope and sequence chart that you use as a guide?
8. Is the program of use to students with special educational needs?
9. Does the program use correct standard English?
10. Are instructional objectives stated, and does the program fulfill those objectives?

B. Is the program easy to use (user-friendly)?
1. Is the level appropriate for students in your classroom?
2. Is there a wrap-around problem?
3. Are screen pages easy to read, with appropriate spacing between lines?
4. Is print size appropriate?
5. Is the student able to leave the program at any point?
6. Does the student control the rate of presentation?
7. Can the student return to previous screen pages?
8. Does the computer program accept abbreviations for frequent responses?
9. Is the dialogue style informal and conversational, addressing the student personally?
10. Is there a HELP command by which the student can return to the instructions?
11. Is the management system easy to use, yet safe from student penetration?
12. Does the program allow input mistakes to be corrected?
13. Is the program bug-free?

*Source: Ernest Balajthy, MICROCOMPUTERS IN READING & LANGUAGE ARTS, © 1986, pp. 44–46. Reprinted by permission of Prentice-Hall, Inc., Englewood Cliffs, New Jersey.

C. Does the program make maximum use of the computer's capabilities?
    1. Are students motivated?
    2. Are attractive graphics and audio included?
    3. Does the program time student work?
    4. Is a score kept of student achievement? Are these scores recorded on disk for teacher monitoring?
    5. Does the program provide for individual differences in ability?
    6. Does the program branch in some way to suit the needs of individual students?
    7. Does the student control forward or backward movement through the program?
    8. Is immediate feedback given?
    9. Are explanations of incorrect answers provided?

D. Is the program user-proof?
    1. Does the program crash if an inappropriate key is pushed?
    2. Does the program inform the user when an inappropriate key is pushed?
    3. If the RETURN key is accidentally pushed before any input has been typed, will the program give the user a second chance?
    4. If the space bar is accidentally typed before or after an input, will the computer ignore it?
    5. If the reader cannot figure out the answer, will the program refuse to go on?
    6. Will the program refuse to accept input of inappropriate length and inform the user why it refuses?
    7. Is the program reasonably protected against sabotage?

E. Is documentation provided in printed hard copy?
    1. Are objectives listed?
    2. Is there a summary of the program's function?
    3. Are prerequisite skills listed?
    4. Is grade-level suitability given?
    5. Does the documentation include practical suggestions for use in the classroom?
    6. Are suggested supplemental or elaborative materials listed?
    7. Are student guides provided, written in a form understandable by your students?
    8. Are supplemental worksheets provided?
    9. Is the teacher's instruction guide clear and adequate?
   10. If the program is modifiable, are suggestions offered?

F. What assurance of program quality is there?
    1. Is the program publisher well-established with a good reputation?
    2. Is there a thirty-day return guarantee?
    3. Are sales representatives willing to come to demonstrate the program?

4. Are published reviews available?
5. Has the program been classroom-tested?
6. Has the program been recommended by teachers whose judgments you trust?

Strengths of the Program:

Weaknesses of the Program:

Your Professional and Personal Reaction:

Student Reactions:

Appendix 4
Judging One Series of Basal Readers*

Directions: Complete the checklist, using as many as possible of the sources listed below.

1. One set of basal readers with as many levels as possible.
2. Material provided by the publisher of the series you select to use, including:
   Scope and sequence-of-skills list
   Brochures depicting all series components
   Publisher's catalog with the price list
   Any other materials the publisher has prepared to explain the series
3. *One* Teacher's Manual, with corresponding children's texts for a level about grades three to five; or select the manual by taking a level midway between readiness (usually Level 1) and the highest levels. If the range of levels is 1–20, select a level between 9 and 13, since these are typical. You will use two parts of this manual. The first part of nearly every manual, regardless of level, usually contains a common core of information explaining the entire series. The second part of the manual usually contains directions for teaching the stories found in that level of the children's texts. Use the workbook that is often included with each children's text, too.

Sensing Organization and Content

	Yes	No	Notes
1. Is the series arranged by levels in a sequence? (For example: Level 1, 2, 3 . . . 14, 15; or A, B, C . . . J, K.)			
2. Are grade equivalents also given for levels? (For example: Level 6 = Grade 3.)			
3. Does the series appear to contain a balance and variety of literary forms and types of writing? Check the ones you find (✓).			

_____ Information, fact selection	_____ Suspense
_____ Fantasy	_____ Plays
_____ Fiction	_____ Biography/autobiography
_____ Legends, myths	_____ Historical fiction
_____ Poems	_____ Content-area selections from
_____ Humor	social studies, science, health

*Source: Lyndon W. Searfoss / John E. Readence, HELPING CHILDREN LEARN TO READ, © 1985, pp. 96–99. Reprinted by permission of Prentice-Hall, Inc., Englewood Cliffs, New Jersey.

	Yes	No	Notes
4. Are children's classics, as well as contemporary stories, presented?			
5. At each level, does the series appear to be organized in thematic units in which a variety of literature is found?			

Examining the Teacher's Manual

	Yes	No	Notes
Locate a section in a teacher's manual at the beginning of a unit or story. Now answer these questions: 6. Is a pattern clearly evident in the lesson plans?			
7. Are you able to follow the lesson plan or routine to teach a story?			
8. Do you think a beginning or inexperienced teacher could teach a story from the manual without much additional guidance?			
9. Are the pages easy to follow in terms of format and arrangement of lesson steps?			
10. Are pages from the children's texts reproduced in the manual?			
11. As you read the lesson plan, can you easily find the objectives?			
12. Are there suggestions at the end of each lesson for follow-up activities that involve *transfer* of skills? (For example: transfer to variety of print, including trade books, newspapers, magazines, content areas such as social studies, science, drama, art, music.)			
13. What are the *major* steps involved in teaching each story? (For example: "Introduction and Motivation," "Guided Reading," "Follow-up Discussion.")	List steps here:		

Determining Scope and Sequence of Skills	Yes	No	Notes
Use the scope-and-sequence information you find in the teacher's manual you are using to complete this activity. Or use a separate scope-and-sequence chart supplied by the publisher as a reference in answering these questions: 14. Does the series include instruction and practice in these skill areas? Comprehension skills Decoding (word-attack) skills Vocabulary skills Study skills			
15. As you read through the teacher's manual, does it appear that each lesson integrates instruction in comprehension, decoding, *and* vocabulary skills?			

16. What other *major* skill areas does the series include?   List areas here:

Judging the Format and Features			
17. Are the books appealing, inviting, and attractive?			
18. Do pictures and illustrations contribute to understanding or appreciating the stories?			
19. Is the paper of good quality, durable, and free from gloss in both the children's texts and the workbooks?			
20. Are the bindings durable on Children's texts? Teacher's manual? Workbook?			

Examining the Components of the Series	Yes	No	Notes
21. Is a testing program included?			
22. Is there a management system for keeping track of test scores and other indicators of children's progress? Does it include: Individual checklists or folders? Class-summary data sheets? Test-summary data sheets?			
23. Are extra or supplementary components available, either to give children additional practice or to use as teaching aids?			

Check which of the following are included: (✓)

_____ Initial placement tests _____ Sets of tradebooks
_____ Games _____ Word cards
_____ Records, tapes _____ Films, filmstrips
_____ Skills kits or boxes _____ Skill ditto masters
_____ Additional tests

List any others you find:

Adding Up the Cost

24. Use the publisher's catalog or price lists, or consult with local school district personnel who purchase basals to estimate the cost of the following:

Teacher's manual used for this activity $ _____
Children's text for same level $ _____
Children's workbook for same level $ _____

25. Now estimate the cost for one classroom of twenty-five children if each child receives one basal reader and one workbook. Levels within a classroom will vary, but costs are similar for levels in the range found in a single classroom (for example, Levels 13, 14, 15 usually are about equal in cost). Manuals would be extra, of course.

25 × _(per children's text)_ = $ _____
25 × _(per workbook)_ = $ _____
Total classroom cost = $ _____

26. If you have time, check the cost of the extra or supplementary components from item 23 and list them here:

Chapter 1

1. true 2. false 3. false 4. false 5. true 6. true 7. false 8. true 9. true 10. true

Chapter 2

1. false 2. true 3. true 4. false 5. true 6. false 7. true 8. true 9. false 10. false

Chapter 3

1. true 2. false 3. false 4. false 5. true 6. false 7. false 8. true 9. false 10. true

Chapter 4

1. false 2. false 3. true 4. true 5. true 6. true 7. false 8. false 9. true 10. true

Chapter 5

1. true 2. false 3. false 4. false 5. false 6. false 7. true 8. true 9. false 10. true

Chapter 6

1. false 2. true 3. false 4. true 5. false 6. false 7. true 8. true 9. false 10. false

Chapter 7

1. true 2. false 3. true 4. true 5. false 6. false 7. true 8. true 9. true 10. false

Chapter 8

1. false 2. false 3. true 4. true 5. true 6. false 7. false 8. true 9. false 10. true

Chapter 9

1. true 2. true 3. true 4. false 5. false 6. false 7. true 8. false 9. true 10. true

Chapter 10

1. true 2. true 3. false 4. true 5. false 6. false 7. true 8. false 9. false 10. true

Chapter 11

1. false 2. true 3. false 4. false 5. true 6. false 7. false 8. true 9. false 10. true

Chapter 12

1. true 2. false 3. false 4. true 5. false 6. true 7. true 8. false 9. true 10. true

Chapter 13

1. true 2. true 3. false 4. false 5. false 6. true 7. false 8. false 9. false 10. false

Chapter 14

1. false 2. true 3. true 4. false 5. true 6. true 7. false 8. true 9. false 10. true

Author Index

l

Lee, D., 21
Lemons, R., 48
Leverentz, F., 71
Lindfors, J., 21
Livingston, M., 483
Loughlin, C., 39
Lundsteen, S., 46

m

McCaslin, N., 127, 147
McDonald, F., 431
Manning, M., 246
Marzano, J., 396
Marzano, R., 396
Miller, G., 396
Monson, D., 39
Moore, S., 48
Morgan, N., 147

n

Nagy, W., 372, 397
Neville, D., 303
Newkirk, T., 202

o

Ogilvie, M., 114
O'Keefe, V., 117
Oken-Wright, P., 117
O'Rourke, J., 367, 375, 377, 381, 394

p

Paley, V., 71
Parry, J., 202
Perez, G., 521
Piaget, J., 13
Plaum, S., 21
Prokopiw, E., 303
Prostano, E., 431
Prostano, J., 431

q

Quinn, C., 278

r

Readence, J., 403
Robinson, F., 401
Rodrigues, R., 504
Roe, B., 343
Rogers, D., 21
Ross, E., 343

s

San Jose, C., 147
Saville-Troike, M., 490
Saxton, J., 127, 147
Scher, A., 147
Schmelzer, R., 403
Schwartz, J., 39
Schwartz, S., 117
Searfoss, L., 403
Searls, E., 303
Shaffer, R., 31
Shaftel, F., 131, 137
Shaftel, G., 131, 137
Shanahan, T., 202
Shapiro, J., 39
Shipley, J., 397
Shumaker, M., 483
Shumaker, R., 483
Sipay, E., 426
Skinner, B., 6
Smilansky, S., 130
Smith, C., 403
Smith, F., 21, 59, 159
Smith, K., 31
Smith, P., 59, 159, 246
Spache, E., 403
Spache, G., 403
Staab, C., 31
Staton, J., 202
Stewig, J., 278, 483
Sticht, T., 49
Stowitscheck, J., 246

Strong et al.

Strong, W., 303
Strother, D., 71
Szekeres, S., 21

t

Temple, C., 39, 202
Thompson, G., 49
Thompson, M., 117
Thorndike, E., 381
Throne, J., 358
Thurber, D., 221
Tinzmann, M., 49
Tompkins, G., 59
Toor, R., 431
Tough, J., 31
Tovez, D., 358
Trachtenburg, P., 358
Trousdale, A., 483

u

Urdang, L., 397

v

Vandergrift, K., 431
Van Riper, C., 109

w

Wells, G., 21
White, R., 504
Williams, B., 246
Willows, D., 303
Winn, D., 71
Within, D., 202
Woolls, B., 431

z

Zakaluk, B., 358
Zigler, E., 21

Subject Index

i

Improvisation (*See* Dramatization, Story)
Index, using an, 405
Individual differences, providing for, 15–19
Individualized approach
   in reading, 325–30
   in spelling, 260–64
Inflectional affixes (*See* Affixes, Suffixes)
Informational books for children, 446
Innatist theory of language acquisition, 7
Instructional activities (*See* Activities,
   Instructional)
Intellectual development (Piaget), 13–15
Intelligence and
   handwriting, 207
   school readiness, 74
   vocabulary, 366
   written composition, 154
Interaction puppetry, 95
Interpretation (*See* Dramatization, Story)
Interpretive comprehension in reading, 347
Interviewing, 87–88
Intonation, 26, 288
Introductions, making, 90
Invented spelling, 251–53
Italic handwriting, 224, 226, 227

k

Kernel sentences (*See* Kernels)
kernels, 289–90
Keyboarding, 227–29
Kindergarten, 56, 60, 253
   reading program in, 319–22

l

Language
   categorizing by function, 31
   categorizing by modes, 30
   nature of, 24–26
   structure of, 26–30
Language acquisition
   theories, 6–7
Language arts curriculum, English
   proposed outcomes, 24
Language arts software evaluation checklist,
   Appendix 3
Language development, 7–11
Language, English
   acquisition/development of, 6–11
   beginning activities in, 34–38
   dialects in United States, 506–12

functions of, 31
   modes of, 30
   nature of, 24–26
   structure of, 26–30
Language experience approach (LEA),
   324–25
Language functions, 31
Language modes (*See also* specific modes
   such as Listening, Reading, Speaking,
   and Written Composition)
   expressive, 30
   productive, 30
   receptive, 30
Language readiness activities, 34–38
Learnability theory of language acquisition, 7
Learning centers in language arts, 70, 116,
   146, 202, 245, 276, 301, 359, 395–96,
   432–33, 482
Learning-disabled children, 231–34
Learning games (*See* Games, Learning)
Left-handed children, 234
Legibility in handwriting (*See* Handwriting,
   Legibility in)
Lessons, creative
   in handwriting, 231
   in spelling, 262
Letter formation in handwriting, 238
Library and locational skills, 406–22
Library of Congress Classification System,
Limited-English-Proficient students (LEP),
   490–91
Listening
   appreciative, 55–56, 60
   attentive, 56–57, 60
   critical, 58–59, 60, 61
   evaluation of progress in, 65–68
   factors influencing, 50, 52–53
   hierarchy of skills in, 49–50, 51
   importance of, 46–47
   instructional activities in, 60
   learning games for, 62–65
Literal comprehension in reading, 347
Literary interests/preferences of children,
   441–42
Literature, children's
   as bibliotherapy, 454–58
   contemporary trends in, 440–41
   evaluation of student progress in, 480–81
   functions of, 437, 439
   genres, 438
   minority Americans in, 458–59
   poetry, 447–54
   sources for selecting, 443–44
   values of, 437

r

Readers theater, 93–94, 125
Readiness for
    handwriting, 209–12, 219–20
    reading, 313–18
    school, 74
Reading
    components of, 310
    comprehension, 346–54
    definition of, 310
    evaluation of student progress in, 354–57
    goals of, 311
    instructional strategies for, 322–30
    nature of, 310–11
    principles of teaching, 311–13
    readiness for, 313–18
Reading flexibility skills, 429
Reading readiness checklist, 314–18
Recordings, award winning titles, Appendix 3
Reference books, using, 421
Regional dialect, 506
Reporting, 76, 77, 78–79
Revision of written composition, 166
Role playing, 136–39
Roots (or Bases), 28, 338, 381, 382–83
Round table discussions, 83

s

Scales
    handwriting, 243, 244
    writing, 156–57
Scanning, 429
Schemata, 346, 371
Schema theory, 346
Semantics, 29–30
Sentence combination/manipulation, 157,
    284, 285, 293–95, 298
Sentence patterns, 29, 288
Sentence recognition, 297
"Sesame Street", 37, 319
Sex differences and
    literary interests/preferences, 441
    stuttering, 114
    vocabulary development, 367
    written composition, 155
Sharing time, 78–79
Show-and-tell, 79
Sight vocabulary, development of, 332–35
Size and proportion in handwriting, 238, 242
Skimming, 429
Slant in handwriting, 217, 220, 243
Social courtesies, developing, 88–92
Social dialect, 506–7

Sociodrama, 136–37
Sociolects, 507
Software evaluation checklist, language arts,
    Appendix 3
Spacing in handwriting, 215, 222, 243
Speaking (*See* Communicative Development;
    Communicative Remediation for
    Handicapped Children; and Speech
    Arts)
Speech Arts
    choral speaking, 473–80
    conversation and dialogue, 81–82
    debating, 84–85
    discussion, 82–84
    drama, creative, 122–45
    interviewing, 87–88
    parliamentary procedure, following,
        85–87
    puppetry, 93–99
    readers theater, participating in, 93, 94
    social courtesies, developing, 80–92
    storytelling, 420–62
    talks, giving, 76, 78–80
Speech correction (*See* Communicative
    Remediation for Handicapped Children)
Speech development (*See* Communicative
    Development)
Speech improvement (*See* Communicative
    Development)
Speed in handwriting (See Handwriting,
    Speed in)
Spelling
    early, 251–52
    evaluation of student progress in, 271–75
    individualized or group approaches in,
        260–64
    instructional activities in, 265–67
    intermediate, 255
    invented, 251–53
    learning games in, 267–71
    recommended teaching practices in,
        259–60
    sample lessons in, 262
    stages of development in, 252–54
    teaching guidelines for, 256–59
    written composition and, 170
Stammering (*See* Stuttering)
Standard English (*See* Dialect, Standard
    English)
Stimulus-response-reward theory of language
    acquisition, 6–7
Story dramatization (*See* Dramatization,
    Story)
Story listening, 36, 367
Story reading, 182, 462–63

Storytelling, 56, 460–62, 466
Stress, 26–27
Structural analysis, using, 348–51
Structural grammar, 287–89
Structure words, 288
Study techniques/methods
    Explore, 402–3
    Prep, 403–4
    PSRT, 403
    3Q3R, 401–2
Suffixes (*See* Affixes, Suffixes)
Summarizing, 428
Surface structure of language, 289
Syllables and syllabication, 339–40, 341
Syntax of English language, 11, 28–29
Synthetic phonic analysis, 342

t

Talks, giving, 76, 78–80
Taxonomy, Bloom's, 127, 348
Taxonomy of personal engagement (for
    drama), 127–28
Telephones, using, 90–92
Television
    educational, 37, 175
    viewing, 155–64
Tests, commercial
    Arizona Articulation Proficiency Scale,
        112
    Bilingual Syntax Measure, 517
    Bilingual Syntax Measure II, 517
    California Achievement Test, 430
    Circus Say and Tell, 109
    Comprehensive Tests of Basic Skills, 200,
        393, 517
    Compton Phonological Assessment, 112
    CTBS/S Readiness Test, 318
    *Fisher-Logemann Test of Articulation
        Competence*, 112
    Gates-MacGinitie Reading Tests, 354
    *Goldman and Fristoe's Test of
        Articulation*, 112
    Iowa Tests of Basic Skills, 273
    Language Facility Test, 109
    Metropolitan Achievement Tests, 273,
        393
    Metropolitan Readiness Test, 313
    Northwestern Syntax Screening Test, 20
    Peabody Picture Vocabulary Test, 393
    Second Language Oral Test of English,
        517
    Signals Listening Test, 66

*Spanish/English Reading and Vocabulary
    Screening*, 517
SRA Achievement Series, 393
*Stanford Achievement Test: Listening
    Comprehension Tests*, 66
*Stanford Achievement Test: Reading
    Test*, 354
Stanford Achievement Tests, 200–201
Test of Early Language Development, 20
Test of Language Development, 20
Test of Written Language, 201
Test of Written Spelling, 273
Theater, children's, 56, 122, 123–25, 464
Theater, readers (*See* Readers Theater)
Thesaurus, 384
Traditional Grammar, 286–87
Transformational grammar, 289–95
Transformations or transforms, 291–95
    double base, 291–293–295
    single base, 291, 292
T-unit, 154
Typewriting for children, 227–29

u

Usage, English, 299–300

v

Verb phrase, 290
Videos, using, 35 (*See also,* Films)
Vocabulary
    growth in, 365–66
    lists, 381, 384
    misconceptions about teaching, 373–74
    types of, 364–65
Vocabulary development, English
    evaluation of student progress in, 393–94
    factors influencing, 366–67, 369
    guidelines for curriculum in, 369–72
    instructional activities in, 386–89
    learning games for, 389–93
    methodology for, 375–84
Voice disturbances, 113

w

Wait-time, 350
Whole language approach, 34
Word attack skills (*See* Word Recognition
    Skills)